海軍

KAIGUN

Strategy, Tactics, and Technology in the
IMPERIAL JAPANESE NAVY, 1887–1941

David C. Evans • Mark R. Peattie

Naval Institute Press • Annapolis, Maryland

Naval Institute Press
291 Wood Road
Annapolis, MD 21402

This paperback edition has been brought to publication with the generous assistance of Marguerite and Gerry Lenfest.

This book has been brought to publication with the generous assistance of Edward S. and Joyce I. Miller.

First Naval Institute Press paperback edition published 2012.
ISBN 978-1-59114-244-7

The Library of Congress has catalogued the hardcover edition as follows:
Evans, David C.
Kaigun: strategy, tactics, and technology in the Imperial Japanese Navy, 1887–1941 /
David C. Evans and Mark R. Peattie.
p. cm.
Includes bibliographical references.
ISBN 0-87021-192-7 (alk. paper)
1. Japan. Kaigun—History. I. Peattie, Mark R., 1930–. II. Title
VA653.E93 1997
359'.00952—dc21

97-11455

♾ This paper meets the requirements of ANSI/NISO z39.48-1992 (Permanence of Paper).
Printed in the United States of America.

19 18 17 16 15 14 13 12   9 8 7 6 5 4 3 2 1
First printing

To
Admiral Inoue Shigeyoshi
(1889–1975),
professional, patriot, and realist,

and to
Dr. Frederick J. Milford,
*whose knowledge, advice, and encouragement have informed
and illuminated this work.*

Contents

Illustrations

FIGURES

MAPS

Tables

Acknowledgments

As authors, we are by training, experience, and reputation historians of modern Japan. Neither of us is a professional naval officer (though one of us once held a naval commission). Nor are we historians of technology or specialists in any technology that we discuss. Therefore, we owe a great debt to the counsel of true specialists. Without their comments, criticisms, suggestions, and assistance, this work would be a thinner, poorer, and less ambitious undertaking.

First and foremost we must pay tribute—no lesser phrase will suffice—to Dr. Frederick J. Milford, one of the two persons to whom we have dedicated this work. Fred Milford's credentials in the sciences, naval matters, and management are not just impressive, they are awesome: a doctorate from MIT; mastery of physics, engineering, and electronics; distinguished naval service; and research and management in the defense industry. His wisdom on various matters scientific and technological has kept us from grounding on the shoals that threaten the novice in these dangerous waters. For scholarship, hard work, and enthusiasm, Milford was our nonpareil of consultants.

Unstinting, too, of his time, attention, and expertise on matters naval and military has been H. P. Willmott, renowned historian of World War II. "Ned" Willmott read all our chapters, and his extensive critique, marked by wit, erudition, and insight, has demonstrated an extraordinary devotion to our project. If we did not always agree, he usually made us rethink our assumptions and our sentences. Comdr. Alan D. Zimm, USN, Ret., was similarly rigorous and ebullient in his criticism, informed by his familiarity with war-gaming and operational analysis of the Japanese and American navies.

Capt. Yoshida Akihiko, JMSDF, Ret., knows more about the details of the Imperial Japanese Navy than any other individual on either side of the Pacific. His pride in its accomplishments is matched only by his microscopic knowledge of its history and technology. If we erred in stating a measurement, a date, or a place name, Yoshida has been on us like a hawk, serving to remind us that "God and the devil are in the details."

Edward S. Miller, acclaimed chronicler and analyst of the American plans for a Pacific war, has also read all our pages and, for each chapter, has offered helpful comment and sage advice. So too has Jon Tetsuro Sumida, one of the most innovative of contemporary naval historians. While our own approach to "doing naval history" is, to an extent, different from Sumida's, we are quick to acknowledge the formidable challenge he has posed to the accepted concepts and assumptions of the field. Captain Wayne Hughes, USN, Ret., who has brought to his critique of our work a lifetime of thinking about naval tactics, both as a serving naval officer and as one of the faculty of the Naval Postgraduate School at Monterey, has read most of our chapters and has provided helpful comment, as has Professor Clark Reynolds, one of America's most eminent naval historians. Captain Linton Wells, II, USN, Ret., whose own excellent work in Japanese naval technology is being published by the Naval Institute Press, has taken time out from his heavy responsibilities both at sea and in the Pentagon to offer us advice on a number of our chapters. The doyen of American naval historians, William Braisted, has offered similar help for a number of the earlier chapters of our work. Mark Campbell, an informed young student of navies and naval technology, has been helpful not only through his comments and suggestions concerning portions of the manuscript, but also by the contribution of a number of the diagrams which illustrate our work. We are particularly grateful to Jonathan Parshall who, at the eleventh hour, stepped in to take our maps and many of our illustrations from sketches into publishable form. In the process, he drew on his own considerable knowledge of the Japanese navy to improve them substantially.

We are pleased that our work has proven relevant among those in government responsible for bringing an historical perspective to current issues of naval policy. At the Naval Doctrine Command Center in Norfolk, Virginia, Dr. James J. Tritten read our pages and offered helpful advice, as did Capt. James FitzSimonds, USN, of the Office of Net Assessment in the Office of the Secretary of Defense.

Others who have read our chapters and offered similar assistance have been Mr. John Lundstrom of the Milwaukee Public Museum; Professor John H. Maurer of the Naval War College; Professor Richard Samuels of MIT; Dr. Thomas Hone; Major Budd Jones, USAF; Professor Geoffrey Till, Royal Naval College at Greenwich; Dr. Louis Brown of the Carnegie Institution; Thomas Wildenberg; Royce Grubic; Hervé Coutau-Bégarie; Dr. Marc A. Epstein; Dr. Carlos P. Rivera; Capt. Wayne Thornton, USN; Professor Paul Varley at the University of Hawaii; and Professor Karl Friday at the University of Georgia. Noel Peattie, brother, poet and bibliophile, weekend sailor, and judge of literary prose, has gone over our manuscript with a jeweler's eye and has saved it from countless infelicities of style. We have been greatly aided in our writing by Patricia E. Boyd, our copy editor.

In Japan, we have been guided by the wise counsel of Chihaya Masataka and Nomura Minoru, both former officers of the Imperial Japanese Navy and two of the most authoritative commentators on its history. Rear Adm. Toyama Saburō, JMSDF, Ret., a student of IJN battle history and likewise an officer of the old service, offered valuable support. Professor Asada Sadao of Dōshisha University has guided us to his own distinguished work on Japanese navy factionalism and the interwar naval treaties. Shinohara Hiroshi has shared with us his knowledge of the Japanese navy in the early Meiji period, as has Professor Tanaka Hiromi of the Japanese Defense Academy for late Meiji. At the Kaigun Bunko in Tokyo, Todaka Kazushige has been of inestimable value in giving us advice and helping us obtain various materials, as has Rear Adm. Hirama Yōichi, JMSDF, Ret., at the Defense Academy. Itō Naokazu, curator at the Museum of Maritime Science, Tokyo, kindly provided the line drawings of warships, which are the work of his skilled pen.

Naturally, despite the invaluable assistance, commentary, and advice we have received from all those whom we have listed, we alone bear responsibility for any errors of fact or interpretation in this work.

For their facilitative assistance in the publication of this work we should also like to thank Edward S. Miller, who made a generous subvention to the Naval Institute Press on our behalf; the University of Richmond, which likewise made a subvention; the Fulbright program of the U.S. Department of Education; the Faculty Research Committee of the University of Richmond; the University of Massachusetts at Boston; the Edwin O. Reischauer Institute of Japanese Studies at Harvard University; the Department of History at the University of Hawaii; and the Hoover Institution of War, Revolution, and Peace at Stanford University.

We conclude our acknowledgments by expressing gratitude and sympathy to our long-suffering wives, Carolyn Evans and Alice Peattie, without whose patience, understanding, and sacrifice this work could not have been forged over the past twelve years. To them we owe a debt that can never be repaid on the printed page.

Introduction

Kaigun. The word means "navy" in Japanese. But to older Japanese, the English translation hardly encapsulates the enormous difference between the Nihon Teikoku Kaigun—the Imperial Japanese Navy—which opened the Pacific War in December 1941, and the small Japanese Maritime Self-Defense Force (JMSDF), which today plays a modest role in cooperating with the U.S. Navy to preserve the security of Japan's home waters.

To begin with, the old navy constituted a mighty fighting force. At the opening of the Pacific War, it comprised 10 battleships, including the first of the 2 greatest battleships ever built; 10 aircraft carriers; 38 cruisers, heavy and light; 112 destroyers; 65 submarines, and numerous auxiliary warships of lesser size. At the time, Japanese naval aviation was world-class: its fighter aircraft and medium bombers were among the world's finest, and among the major navies, its air crews unquestionably the best trained and most experienced. To have observed the Japanese battle line in column on maneuvers in the northern Pacific during the interwar years, to have watched the clouds of fighters and attack aircraft lift off the decks of six carriers in the early morning of 7 December, or to have viewed the vast bulk of the superbattleship *Yamato* anchored in Truk lagoon early in the Pacific War, must have been among the great spectacles in modern naval history. Never again will Japanese naval power be so visually impressive.

Moreover, unlike the present JMSDF, the prewar navy was a truly "imperial" force. It was imperial first in the sense of its links to the Japanese emperor, whose own exalted status in the Japanese historical tradition gave to the navy a public prestige and a mystical aura scarcely duplicated by any national fighting force in the world. It was imperial, also, in that it guarded an enormous empire. Although the empire's original boundaries were defined by the coastline of the Japanese home islands, by the end of World War I, the boundaries had expanded to include Taiwan, Korea, the southern half of Sakhalin, the Liaotung Peninsula, the widely scattered island territories in Micronesia, and numerous concessions along China's coasts and rivers. In the acquisition of this empire, the navy had been a critical element.

The Imperial Japanese Navy was also emblematic of the rise of Japan as a world power. In 1868, when Japan emerged from its feudal isolation to join the comity of nations, its influence in the world counted for nothing. In a few short years, by prodigious effort, it had created the sinews of political, economic, and military power. In less than thirty years it had become the leading nation in Asia; in less than forty it had become a world power; and in less than seventy-five years it had risen to confront the foremost industrial power in the world. In this meteoric rise, the Imperial Japanese Navy had played a major role. It had come into existence not long after the American Civil War and had thus begun its life about the same time as did the "New American Navy." The Imperial Japanese Navy, however, did not have the precursor of tradition, the naval infrastructure, or the industrial backing that the Americans did. Within forty years Japan had reached fifth place in the world's navies and, by 1920, was clearly in third place. In another twenty years it was prepared to challenge the U.S. Navy and, in the three and a half years of naval war that followed, the Japanese navy gave a good account of itself against the greatest naval force on the globe. This was a remarkable achievement.

More than anything else, therefore, the Imperial Japanese Navy was—or, more exactly, became—an agent for the projection of Japanese power abroad. Along with the Imperial Japanese Army, the navy was responsible for a surge of Japanese power beyond the confines of the limited formal empire acquired by 1922 and recognized by the imperial West and by the international community as a whole. Specifically, the navy also helped to create the subsequent expanding imperium in Asia. This expanding domain threatened to engulf China and the western colonial territories in Southeast Asia and ultimately brought Japan into collision with the West.

Yet for both Americans and Japanese, the overriding aspect of the Japanese navy is its ultimate defeat. Indeed, it was not just beaten by the U.S. Navy; it was annihilated. To Americans of an older generation, particularly those who fought against Japan's navy, that defeat has been a cause of considerable satisfaction and pride. To older Japanese, particularly those who served in their navy, it is a source of humiliation and regret. For those scholars on both sides of the Pacific who study the Japanese navy, its ultimate defeat is the ineluctable fact in the assessment of its capabilities, its combat performance, even its victories.[1]

In writing this work, therefore, we have tried to keep in mind both the incredible success of imperial Japan as a modern naval power and the ultimate and utter defeat of its navy at the hands of its most dangerous naval enemy. Our purpose has been to explain as far as possible the sources of both the navy's triumphs and its defeat. The perspectives we have chosen are those of strategy, tactics, and technology, or, more precisely, the evolving interrelationship of the three. Within that nexus we have sought to understand the overriding strategic issues confronting the navy, the synthesis of foreign and indigenous influences in the shaping of its tactics, and how the navy acquired its technology and material assets. We have, at various points, discussed aspects of the navy—intelligence, manning, logistics, naval fuels, to name the most prominent—that relate directly or indirectly to our three main concerns. Finally, as much as anything else, we have attempted to explain how the Japanese navy thought about naval war and how to prepare for it.

Obviously, our emphasis on these issues makes it clear that we have attempted something far short of a complete history of the Japanese navy. To write such a history would have required, inter alia, detailed research into the following areas: the navy's administrative structures; the economic foundations of Japanese naval power, including Japanese naval budgets and naval contracts; the navy's relationship to Japanese civil government and its involvement in domestic politics (in the 1930s, malign and occasionally even violent); Japanese naval education and training at all levels; the navy's role in shaping Japanese foreign policy; and its reluctant participation in early efforts at arms control.[2] These are important topics worthy of investigation, and some have been the subjects of excellent monographs. For our purposes, however, they lie beyond the horizons of our work.

An additional explanation needs to be made concerning the scope of this work: our limited treatment of Japanese naval aviation compared to our much more detailed coverage of the surface and subsurface forces in the navy. We had originally planned to devote four full chapters to the evolution of Japanese naval air power, but considerations of space obliged us to reduce it to one chapter. It is our expectation that our research on the navy's air arm will, in the near future, be published as a separate volume.

Finally, it is important to explain the chronological boundaries of this study. As a prologue and as background we have devoted an opening chapter to the pre-1887 origins of Japanese naval institutions. But we have selected 1887 as the beginning date for the establishment of the navy because it was in that year that the Japanese navy first began to order itself as a fleet, to study and adopt modern naval tactics, and to assume the characteristics of naval professionalism. Up to then, the navy was not much more than an odd-lot assemblage of warships whose commanders possessed no clear purpose or understanding of how to fight together. After that, with foreign counsel and admirable initiative, the Japanese navy began to take on the attributes of a modern naval force.

As to the terminus of our study, the reader might reasonably ask why we did not fully address the conduct of Japanese naval operations in the Pacific War. The reasons are threefold. First, and most important, such a task would have taken far longer than we and the Naval Institute Press thought desirable. (The research and writing of this book had already consumed more than a decade.) Second, while there is as yet no exhaustive history of the Japanese navy in World War II, there already exist several excellent studies of the subject. Two of these, *A Battle History of the Imperial Japanese Navy, 1941–1945,* by Paul Dull, and *The Japanese Navy in World War II,* edited by David C. Evans, have been published by the Naval Institute Press. Conversely, the evolution of the navy between the world wars remains almost terra incognita. Obviously, the experience, the doctrine, and the technologies developed by the Japanese navy during the decades prior to Pearl Harbor had much to do with how the navy conducted its operations in the Pacific War. In our final chapter, therefore, we have included a summary of these operations during the first two years of the war. Yet, because the fortunes of the Japanese navy turned so disastrously by the end of 1943 and, because it was thereafter forced to turn to desperate improvisations to maintain the struggle against the Allies, few strategies, tactics, and technologies devised in the interwar years had any relevance in the last year and a half of the war. For that reason, we have concluded our summary of the navy's operations at the end of 1943. In any event, comments on specific aspects of Japanese naval strategy, tactics, and technology relating to World War II run throughout the latter chapters of this work.

The writing of Japanese naval history poses many major and often frustrating problems for the foreign researcher. The complexity of the Japanese language is one too obvious to discuss in detail, except to say that it exists on various levels, from the more than occasional ambiguity of meaning on the printed page to the great difficulty in reading *sōsho,* or cursive script, in which so much of the navy's archival materials are written.

A more serious problem is that, compared to Western naval archives, the archival base for the study of modern Japanese naval history is relatively slender. Among the many reasons for the scarcity of material, the most critical is the wholesale destruction of files and documents by the Japanese military services and civilian government in the several days after the Japanese surrender that ended the Pacific War. It is regrettable, but inevitable, therefore, that numerous issues of major importance concerning the Japanese navy and its plans and operations in the China and

Pacific Wars will never be resolved, or will be understood incompletely because of the absence of adequate documentation.

Nevertheless, our incomplete understanding of prewar and wartime Japanese naval affairs is as much due to the norms of Japanese culture and society as to purposeful destruction. The use of naval biography is a case in point. Although we have endeavored to supply basic information on prominent naval officers in an appendix, we have been hampered in our study of the leaders of the navy in several ways. Traditionally, biography in Japan is set in the classical Chinese mold: a recitation of the virtues of the individual so as to teach a moral lesson, usually without critical analysis. Certainly, this is true of the "official" biographies of some naval figures whom we discuss in the earlier chapters. Often compiled by committee and usually blanched of most controversy and of argument that might reflect badly on the subject, such works are often useful for fact, but are of little use in critical analysis of the man or his place in Japanese naval history. Postwar autobiography by leading Japanese naval officers provides better fare, but offers little of the biting comment and incisive judgments that enliven the pages of most Western counterparts. Moreover, societal restraints and the traditions of the old navy have made most Japanese officers reluctant to criticize Japanese naval policy or their former commanders. At the time, decisions were usually made in committee. With a few notable exceptions, records of such deliberations were not kept, or if kept, they do not clearly reveal the ferment of argument and controversy.

Most important, there clearly are significant differences between the questions that interest Western historians of naval affairs and those that interest the Japanese charged with compiling the official histories of Japanese naval operations and naval technology. In researching and writing this history we have relied heavily, for example, on the naval volumes of the 102-volume *Senshi sōsho* (War History Series) issued by the War History Department of the Defense Research Institute, Japanese Self-Defense Agency (Bōeichō Bōeikenshūjo Senshibu, formerly Senshishitsu) from 1966 to 1980. Based largely on the significant portion of the navy's records (some 33,000 documents) that escaped destruction at the end of the Pacific War, these volumes constitute the most detailed, most comprehensive, and most authoritative record of the navy's plans, operations, organization, weaponry, strategy, and tactics from 1937 to 1945. As such they provide a great treasure of data and fact. Yet they often omit discussion of questions of primary interest to the Western historian. For example, how did the navy's leaders make decisions? What were the motivations and arguments behind such decisions and of those who opposed them? What were the relations between elements of the Japanese naval bureaucracy or between responsible officers that led to particular changes in naval policy? Who was the central innovator in the development of a particular technology? Why was one particular technology adopted and another dropped? Who argued hardest for the adoption of a particular tactical doctrine, and who argued against it and why? Often maddeningly silent on such matters are not only the *Senshi sōsho* volumes, but also the other foremost published sources on the Japanese navy that we have used—*Nihon kaigun kōkūshi* (History of Japanese naval aviation), *Shōwa zōsenshi* (History of shipbuilding in the Shōwa era), and *Nihon kaigun nenryō shi* (History of Japanese naval fuels).

These difficulties underscore the need for a complete history of the Imperial Japanese Navy. What we have attempted is a history of the navy as a fighting force in the decades before World War II, written largely on the basis of published sources and directed toward a Western audience. This last point is important. While we have mined Japanese sources heavily in researching and writing this volume, we have not assumed a knowledge of Japanese on the part of the reader, and therefore, where possible in our citations, we have also cited reliable English language works.

It is useful, at the outset, to make clear our use of certain terms throughout this book, while realizing that there exist legitimate alternative definitions of these same terms and that naval specialists and historians often strongly differ on the existing definitions of these same terms. For the purpose of discussing the Japanese navy, we offer the following definitions: *Technology* is the application of science and technical know-how to naval war in the areas of weaponry, construction, communications, and logistics (including transportation). It influences and is influenced by strategy and tactics, as well as being shaped by political and economic factors. *Strategy* is the coordination and direction of naval forces toward achieving a national objective, usually, but not necessarily, through combat. It is shaped by policy, geography, national culture, historical experience, existing force structures, and external threat. *Operations*, to us, means those naval activities that occur during combat, or when plans for combat are being rehearsed. *Tactics* we view as the planning, training and direction of naval forces to achieve victory in combat. Tactics influence and are influenced by strategy, as well as by technology. *Doctrine* we hold to be those principles, sanctioned by naval authority, that guide the planning and training for, and conduct of, war at sea, at either the strategic or tactical level. Doctrine, in turn, is influenced by existing strategy, tactics, and technology, as well as by geography, the culture of a military service or nation, and threats posed by a hypothetical or actual enemy.[3]

We also draw the reader's attention to our use of systems of spelling and measurement. In writing Japanese we have followed the Hepburn system of transliteration, and in writing Japanese personal names we have followed the Japanese word order, that is, family name first, given name second. For Chinese we have followed the Wade-Giles system. For place names we have generally used Webster's New Geographical Dictionary[4] as standard. For those places in China (mainland China and Taiwan) and in Korea that were once under Japanese colonial control we have listed the indigenous name and sometimes added the Japanese equivalent in parenthesis upon first mention of it. We have also used a few common Western or Japanese place names that had general acceptance before World War II, such as Port Arthur and the Pescadores Islands.

The problem of measurement is a complicated one in writing about the Japanese navy, since the navy itself was not always consistent. Up until about the beginning of the second decade of this century, the navy used the English system of measurement for dimensions of ordnance, length, distance, and weight. Thereafter, the navy generally switched over to the metric system. But it continued to use the English system for some ordnance—torpedoes, for example—occasionally for distance, and for ship displacements. Our recourse has been to use the operative system of measurement by the navy and to put in parenthesis the equivalent conversion into the other system. We have attempted to be consistent, but may have sometimes misconstrued the system of units that was operative.

Unless otherwise indicated, displacements are given in long tons (English tons of 2,240 pounds) and denoted simply as tons. For warships designed before the 1922 Washington Treaty there was no generally accepted standard for warship displacement. The quantity usually tabulated was the "normal" or "design" displacement. For ships of the Imperial Japanese Navy, this was the displacement of the ship fully equipped and ready for sea with a one-quarter supply of fuel, without reserve feedwater, one-half to two-thirds supply of stores, and one-half to three-quarters supply of ammunition. The Washington Treaty introduced "standard" displacement, which indicated the displacement of a ship fully loaded and ready for sea without fuel or reserve feedwater.[5] Wherever possible we use standard displacement. On those few occasions when we refer to merchant shipping, we use gross registry tons, except for tankers, for which we use deadweight tons.[6] We have attempted to be accurate, but displacements sometimes changed as ships were modified, and sources are often ambiguous and occasionally disagree. We have resolved such issues by using our best judgment.

For distances, we have followed the Japanese practice of measuring longer distances in nautical miles. We have defined range as the total distance that an engine-powered ship can sail or an aircraft can fly on a given supply of fuel, for a given speed. By "radius," we mean the distance that an aircraft can fly, perform its mission, and return to base with sufficient fuel to land safely.

海軍

1

CREATING
—— *a* ——
MODERN NAVY

1868–1894

Since the dawn of Japan's history the country's unique geography has shaped its paradoxical relationship to the seas that surround it. To begin with, Japan has been both an insular and a continental nation. Insularity was the dominant strategic feature of Japan during the ancient and medieval periods of its history. At the western end of the island chain, the hundred miles of the Korea Strait between Japan and Korea was, for most of Japan's history, a formidable barrier to aggression from the Asian continent; from ancient times until the nineteenth century the ferocious and abortive Mongol invasions in the thirteenth century were the only threats ever mounted against Japan from abroad. Moreover, until modern times, the absence of human civilization in Siberia negated any real threat from the north. Japan's emergence as a nation with continental connections was slower to develop. Yet, from the earliest centuries of this millennium, the Japanese were close enough to Asia to be aware of the grandeur of Chinese civilization across the East China Sea. It was to China that Japan dispatched a series of maritime missions that brought back the cultural and political institutions that were to transform Japan and to bring it into the great Sino-centric orbit. Projection of Japanese power onto the Asian continent was more hazardous, of course. Only twice in nine hundred years did Japan attempt to invade Asia—once in the seventh century and once in the sixteenth. Both interventions were directed against Korea, and both ended in disaster. Yet each intervention established a precedent for Japanese involvement in Asia.

There were other contradictory circumstances as well. Japan was fortunate that neither China nor Korea—its only real neighbor states—were major naval powers. Except for the Mongol invasions, neither nation could attempt an amphibious landing on Japanese soil. Thus, for most of its premodern existence Japan had little need for a maritime defense. In addition, neither China nor Korea encouraged maritime and commercial contact, and Japan was, in ancient times, economically self-sufficient. Japan had therefore little incentive, until the later medieval period, to reach out upon the seas—to develop an overseas trade or a merchant marine to undertake it. Further, Japan's geography and climate held ambiguous implications for the development of Japan as a maritime country. The Japanese coastline offers natural harbors and protected waters, the finest of which are those of the Inland Sea—unparalleled for a nation with maritime ambitions. Yet much of this coastline is so strewn with rocky hazards and so swept with winter storms and summer typhoons that significant coastwise trade has been discouraged for most of Japan's history.[1]

THE PREMODERN BACKGROUND

Without a maritime challenge to its security and without major overseas trade, the Japanese central government in ancient times gave little thought to sea power. In the succeeding medieval period, *suigun* (water forces), organized by rival clans in the internal factional struggles and the widespread privateering on the Inland Sea, constituted the only significant naval units in premodern Japanese history. Out of the incessant piratical warfare on the Inland Sea from the fourteenth through the sixteenth centuries, there arose certain secret schools of "water force" tactics, of which the Nojima and Mishima Schools became the most elaborate. The texts produced by these schools were supposedly a blend of native Japanese experience with the study of classical Chinese tactical principles (based largely on the writings of the great military philosopher Sun Tzu), as well as with Korean and, later, Portuguese techniques. Although centuries later, modern Japanese naval analysts asserted that these writings formed the basis of a uniquely Japanese naval doctrine suitable for adaptation to the age of steam, the encounters on which they were originally based were more piratical than naval. Certainly, the tactical principles set forth were as yet unconnected to any concept of sea power by the Japanese state. Nor were they carried out by any formally organized navy.[2]

Even the surge of Japanese overseas expansionism in the sixteenth century did little to contribute to the development of Japan as a truly maritime nation. The ferocious *wakō*—half pirates, half traders—stormed along the coasts of Korea

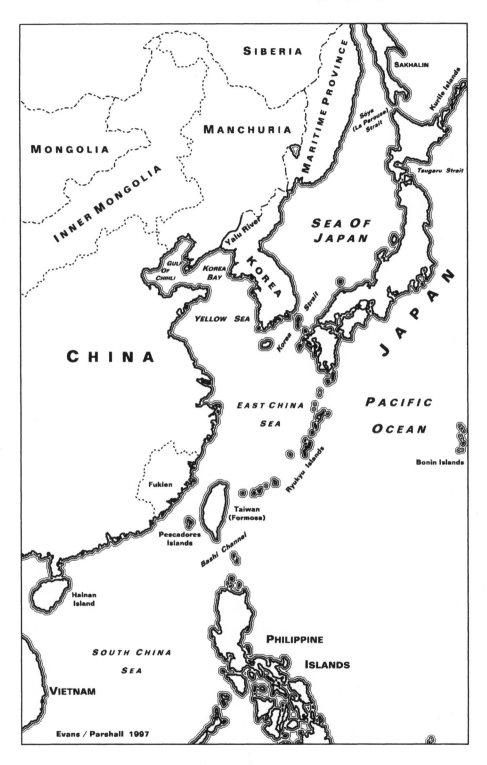

Map 1-1. Maritime East Asia

and China and even into the ports of Southeast Asia. Most of their fighting, how-ever, was inland, and their tactics are more relevant to land warfare than to sea warfare. Near the end of the sixteenth century, the supreme Japanese overlord, Toyotomi Hideyoshi, launched his invasion of Korea, but his assemblage of ships for those operations was more a convoy for his invading armies than a naval force. Without adequate training or equipment, the ships were scattered in com-bat by the superior armament, construction, and leadership of the Korean fleets.[3] Only Japan's Red Seal Ships, which carried on a nascent maritime trade between Japan, China, and the countries of Southeast Asia, made a positive contribution to the slender maritime traditions of premodern Japan. But with the advent of a policy of national isolation instituted by the Tokugawa shogunate early in the sev-enteenth century, even this tentative maritime initiative ceased.

The onset of the Tokugawa feudal period virtually eliminated Japanese over-seas navigation and curbed what military seafaring traditions the nation possessed. During the next two and a half centuries, the single most important contribution to Japan's future maritime development was the consolidation of an elite military class—the samurai—inculcated with the values of discipline, valor, and self-sac-rifice, assets vital to the creation of a modern naval officer corps.[4]

In other respects, the 250 years of isolation from all but minimal contact with the West worked to Japan's serious strategic and technological disadvantage. Strategically, Japan's prolonged isolation precluded its having oceanic and imper-ial power far from its own shores. During those same centuries, the sailing war-ships of Europe spread out across the oceans to lay claim to distant tropical coast-lines and subsequently established the trading stations, naval bases, and coastal ports that formed the links of burgeoning maritime empires. By the mid-nineteenth century, India and nearly all of Southeast Asia was under European control. Euro-pean commerce was flooding Chinese ports, and European vessels were advancing up China's great river systems. In the Pacific, European flags were beginning to rise over the numerous island territories scattered across that great ocean. Later in the century, when an awakened and revitalized Japan was sensitized to the potent rela-tionship between imperial and naval power, its sphere of action was necessarily restricted to nearby waters. The prospects of empire-building focused on near-at-hand territories on, or adjacent to, the Asian continent. These perceptions pro-foundly shaped the future strategic perspective of Japanese naval thought.

More immediately, Japan was obliged to learn the urgent lesson of the impor-tance of naval defense to national security. The arrival, in 1853, of the American flotilla under Comdr. Matthew Calbraith Perry shocked shogunal officials into recognizing the extreme vulnerability of Japan to maritime aggression after its long neglect of the sea. With only a collection of sail- and oar-powered coastal craft and a few vintage cannon scattered along the nation's coastline, and totally without naval personnel who understood the requirements of modern naval war, the Tokugawa shogunate was forced to accept Perry's demands for the end of Japan's long and stubborn isolation.

Now faced with the prospect of further Western encroachments on Japan's sovereignty, the entire nation, both the shogunate and some of the major domains (Satsuma in particular) became preoccupied with maritime defense. Hurried and belated efforts were made to acquire Western naval armament, technology, and training. In the latter half of the 1850s, with Dutch assistance, the shogunate opened a naval training center at Nagasaki, sent other samurai to Holland for further training, and acquired Japan's first steamship. In 1865, with French assistance, the shogunate constructed a navy yard at Yokosuka, where over the next decade, a few small ships were constructed according to Western design.[5] By the mid-1860s, mostly through purchase, the shogunate acquired an odd-lot collection of eight Western-style warships of the day. The ships were powered by sail or steam-assisted and were manned by personnel whose seamanship was only adequate for coastal sailing and whose combat training was nil. Satsuma, Hizen, and a few other semi-independent feudal domains had equally ramshackle collections of ships that comprised not navies in the modern sense but all-purpose maritime organizations whose functions were as much those of transport as of combat.

Satsuma possessed the largest and the most respectable domain navy, perhaps because the feudal lords of Shimazu, the ruling domain family, understood early the need for sea power. Soon after Perry's arrival Satsuma petitioned the shogunate for permission to build modern naval vessels capable of destroying foreign warships at sea. The domain set about acquiring Western ships and machinery, establishing a naval center at Kagoshima and sending students abroad for further training.[6] But even Satsuma's relative vulnerability to naval attack was apparent in 1863, when amidst the growing internal crisis of the country, a British naval squadron sailed into Kagoshima Bay and bombarded the port. Despite determined opposition from the Satsuma batteries, the British burned the city.

By the time the increasingly moribund Tokugawa feudal structure was overthrown in 1868 by a coalition of major feudal domains led by Satsuma and Choshu, a substantial portion of Japan's samurai leadership came to see naval forces as essential to Japan's future, even to the extent of giving naval forces priority over the creation of a strong army. But this conviction was not yet translated into effective naval power. In the naval clashes that ended the brief civil war following the "Restoration" of the Meiji emperor as symbol of a new imperial government, both forces (those allied with the defunct shogunate and those supporting the emperor) proved lackluster in combat. From a Western naval perspective, the

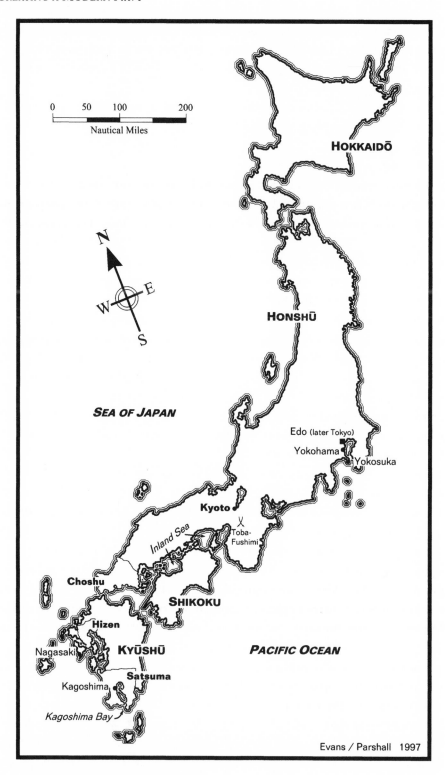

Map 1-2. Mid-nineteenth-century Japan

several engagements off northeastern Honshū and southern Hokkaidō that high-lighted the struggle added little to Japan's modern naval experience, since they were generally desperate melees between ships rather than gun battles between coordinated squadrons.

THE EARLY MEIJI NAVY
Purposes and Policies

In the early years of the Meiji era (1868–1912) the new imperial navy reflected both the problems and the opportunities of the new state it was supposed to defend. To begin with, the status of the navy was ambiguous. The leaders of the new regime were well aware that China was humiliated by European maritime strength. Based on Japan's own naval humiliations in the last years of the Tokugawa shogunate—the coming of Perry's Black Ships and the defeats inflicted on the Satsuma and Choshu domains by Western warships—the Meiji government, like the shogunate before it, initially viewed naval strength as paramount in the defense of the nation. This priority was manifest in official references to the two armed services: the references always placed the navy before the army. As part of this maritime emphasis, the fledgling government, in a burst of optimism in 1870, drew up a grandiose scheme that called for a two-hundred-ship navy, divided into ten fleets, and manned by twenty thousand trained men, all to be created over a twenty-year period. Completely beyond the nation's slender resources of the time, this plan was abandoned that same year.[7]

Despite the government's early concern with naval strength, the navy was, from the beginning, bound so bureaucratically close to its sister service that it could hardly be considered a separate identifiable force until 1872, when two independent service ministries were established. Indeed, for a number of reasons, the policy of naval preeminence, which had been implied in various official pronouncements, began to be reversed around the middle of the 1870s. To begin with, the fledgling government was suddenly faced with several serious domestic rebellions that posed a more immediate threat to Japan's national security than the somewhat diffuse Western maritime pressure. To put down such internal challenges, army forces were clearly more important than navy. In the Satsuma Rebellion of 1877, conscripts of the new army ran the dissident samurai to the ground at Kagoshima. The navy played only a supporting role of communication, supply, and blockade.

But even after the Japanese government consolidated its authority by forcefully suppressing the domestic rebellion, Japan's military weakness in relation to the industrial West induced the nation's leadership to make several assumptions about Japan's strategic situation in the 1870s. The first of these was that Japan's vital interests were restricted to the home islands: the existence and independence of the Japanese people, state, and homeland. Second, for that reason, Japan's security was bounded literally by the nation's shoreline. Given the enormous expense of assembling a modern navy, therefore, the only possible protective posture for Japan was a *shusei kokubō* (static defense) comprising coastal artillery, a standing army, and naval units that could act in a supportive role to drive an invading enemy from the coast. Third, because these first two assumptions meant a defense designed to repel an enemy from Japanese national territory, the chief responsibility for that mission rested upon Japan's ground forces. Hence, Japan's defense establishment should be *rikushu kaijū* (one in which the army comes first and the navy second). Specifically, this meant that the army should exercise overall command of Japan's national defense.[8]

These were arguments essentially made by army men largely from the dominant Choshu faction within the government. Choshu leaders were, as a whole, more politically skillful in directing national policy, in obtaining government funds, and in strengthening the position of the army than were the principal figures of the early Meiji navy. Navy leaders of the first generation were mainly holdovers from the shogunate who had little of the political acumen necessary to further the bureaucratic or budgetary interests of their service. Satsuma men within the navy were gathering their strength, but they were not yet politically effective and represented a small, new service of uncertain prospects. For all these reasons, the tide of government opinion began to turn in favor of giving the army pride of place and the lion's share of fiscal appropriations for the armed services. In 1878, with the establishment of an independent Army General Staff, the navy, which at this point had no independent staff organization, began to slip into a subordinate role, a position it occupied until the beginning of the 1890s.

While the navy was not subordinate to the army in a legal or organizational sense, in practice its lack of an independent staff (as distinct from the Navy Ministry) placed it in a position distinctly inferior to that of the army. From 1878 to 1886, the navy's command of forces, strategic planning, and administrative functions were all lodged within the Navy Ministry, following the British model. In 1886, a separate naval staff was created, but was placed within the Army General Staff until 1889, when it was once again made part of the Navy Ministry, leaving the Army General Staff as the only independent organization responsible for strategic planning.[9]

SHIPS, RECRUITMENT, AND TRAINING

Physically, the early Meiji navy was a ragtag collection of vessels thrown haphazardly together. Its nucleus was formed by the best units of the old shogunal navy, as well as ships contributed by those domains, particularly Satsuma, which rallied to the imperial cause: an armored ram (originally built for the American Confederate navy), a wooden gunboat, a wooden corvette, four paddle ships—all steam-assisted—and four old sailing vessels. Mostly purchased from various Western countries, these ships were indifferently armed and badly in need of repair and refitting. Collectively, they could hardly be called a fleet, since their differing speeds and conditions and the tactical inexperience of both their officers and their crews made maneuvering together an impossibility.

Even after the navy began to add its first steam-assisted warships, it remained, in the 1870s and 1880s, essentially a coast defense force. Its first effective commands were regional administrative districts termed *chinjufu,* each of which usually included a headquarters; docking, repair, and construction facilities; and coal and supply depots. In 1875, when the navy had few warships, its sixteen vessels were divided equally between only two of these commands: one in eastern Japan centered on the Yokohama Naval Station (moved to Yokosuka in 1884) and a western command at Nagasaki. From these two stations the ships of Japan's rudimentary naval force carried out their first training activities and coastal patrols.[10] In later years, as the navy grew in size and complexity, the coastal defense of Japan was divided between a greater number of *chinjufu.*

Professionally, the officers and crew of Japan's early navy were not of much better caliber than their amorphous collection of ships. At the outset, certainly, the leadership of the new navy was barely adequate. More than other branches of the new government, the Japanese army and navy reflected both the rural origins of leaders in the Restoration and the feudal class system in which for centuries the samurai had monopolized the military profession. Just as men of the former Choshu domain dominated the early Meiji army, men of Satsuma essentially controlled the new navy. The majority owed their positions not to maritime experience but to their class and domain status. Few understood the rapidly evolving technology or bureaucratic complexity of a modern navy. Indeed, some leaders of the early Meiji navy had never been to sea. Katsu Awa, navy minister from 1873 to 1878, was a survivor from the shogunal regime renowned for his diplomatic skills and learning. No one, however (except perhaps himself), pretended that he was a man of the sea. Nor were the rank and file who manned the ships much better prepared than their officers for naval life. Without a strong maritime tradition and, as yet, without a strong, modern sense of nationhood, Japan had no significant pool of men long familiar with the sea or experienced in disciplined national service.

These backward circumstances in men and material would have posed formidable obstacles to the modernization of Japan's maritime forces had it not been for fortunate position and timing. Because of the technological disadvantages of Japan's self-imposed isolation before it was forced to open its doors in the 1850s and 1860s, it was indeed impotent in the face of a superior Western naval challenge. Western preoccupation with China, and Japan's remoteness from the naval powers of the West, in the farthest corner of East Asia, may have bought Japan extra time.

In the long run, Japan's renewed contact with the Western world was of great advantage to the nation, for it came when Western industrialism was beginning to revolutionize transportation, communications, and the modes of production. Japan could thus take immediate advantage of Western technological developments without having to pass through the long scientific revolution that preceded the rise of industry in Europe. Nor were technological advances kept secret. Despite efforts to contain it, the technology spread rapidly from continent to continent with little or no restriction. Thus, the rapid and revolutionary changes in naval technology—the development of new materials for ship construction, improvements in both ordnance and armor, and the invention of new propulsion systems—were available to Japan as quickly as they were developed in Europe and America. Equally important, the Japanese navy, unlike the British navy, was not burdened with the dead weight of obsolete equipment, nor, except for a few survivors from the earliest Meiji years, was it stifled by leaders who held to obsolete ideas. Just as the Japanese navy made no investment in large numbers of wooden men-of-war that it might have been reluctant to abandon, its personnel generally were not committed to maritime traditions of the past.[11]

Fortunately for Japan, certain aggressive and influential officers in the early Meiji navy were quick to exploit this situation, recognizing that the midcentury revolution in naval technology made technical competence as important as the traditional skills of seamanship. It was this recognition, along with an awareness of the severely limited economic and material resources of the country, that induced Japan's early naval leadership to give initial priority to the education and training of officers and men rather than to the acquisition of additional naval units.[12]

One of the first steps to train a modern officer corps was the establishment of a naval academy not unlike those of Western maritime nations. Such a facility was established in 1869 on the waterfront at Tsukiji in Tokyo and moved in 1888 to Etajima on the Inland Sea, not far from Hiroshima. During an average course of four years, cadets at the Imperial Naval Academy were taught various subjects in naval science, such as seamanship, navigation, and gunnery, as well as general education subjects. The training program stressed physical fitness and toughness and placed great emphasis on the traditional Japanese military values of loyalty, courtesy, valor, and simplicity. Eventually, in the words of Arthur Marder, the naval academy turned out officers of "unquestioned professional competence, fanatical courage, and extraordinary *élan.*"[13]

Just as important as establishing a facility for training the navy's future officers was the creation of a system of officer recruitment based on merit rather than class or region. The merit system was a particularly important consideration in a service initially dominated by former samurai from Satsuma. Almost from the beginning, the new navy took steps to reform recruitment into the officer corps. In 1871, the government announced that naval academy applicants would be accepted from the public at large and that entry would be based upon competitive examinations. Although the academy encountered initial difficulties in attracting commoners, by the beginning of its third decade, officer candidates were accepted from all over the nation. Thus, while the "Satsuma faction" retained a strong influence in the top echelons of the navy throughout the Meiji period and indeed into the succeeding Taishō period (1912–26) the percentage of Satsuma officers in the navy as a whole became fairly low.[14]

While the beginnings of a professional officer corps were being established, similar steps were taken to train the sailors and petty officers who would man Japan's future navy. Unlike the army, the navy initially avoided using the universal conscription act of 1873, seeking instead to recruit volunteers rather than draftees into its ranks. Its obvious preference was for men who already knew something of the sea, particularly for the hardy sons of fishermen between the ages of eighteen and twenty-five. Later, as the navy grew, its enlisted personnel were drawn from both volunteers and conscripts. Of necessity, the initial training of navy enlisted personnel focused on inculcating an esprit de corps that fostered patriotism and loyalty, while renewing traditional Japanese military virtues of courage and obedience. Through example, through exhortation about the primacy of the imperial will, and through lectures that drew upon the nation's historical traditions, the officer instructors created among the enlisted ranks a standard of discipline, self-sacrifice, and devotion to duty that became the envy of all navies in the world. Japan's later victories at sea, one commentator has observed, came as much from the training and morale of the average Japanese seaman as from the effectiveness of the navy's ships or the caliber of its guns.[15]

THE BRITISH NAVY AS A MODEL

While the reinforcement of Japanese military traditions in their broadest sense was seen as fundamental to the fighting abilities of the officers and men, the new navy in its early years would clearly have to rely on a Western model. The model would apply both for the acquisition of modern naval science and for the imposition of uniform standards of procedure and operation upon what was until then a motley naval force. In its search for such a model, Britain was a logical choice because of its past and current dominance of the seas. There were also recent historical precedents for turning to the Royal Navy. Quick to learn from its defeat at British hands in 1863, Satsuma chose British procedures as the standard for its naval forces and acquired British support in its struggle against the shogunate. For its part, the shogunate briefly hosted a two-man British naval mission on the eve of the Meiji Restoration. In the early years of Meiji, as the new government decided to embark on a wider program of foreign naval instruction, it turned once more to Britain. In 1870, an imperial decree designated the British navy as the model for Japan's naval development. Three years later, at the request of the Japanese government, a thirty-four-man British naval mission, headed by Lt. Comdr. Archibald Douglas, arrived in Japan. Douglas directed instruction at the Naval Academy at Tsukiji for several years. Although he was apparently not at the cutting edge of the most recent naval technology, the mission, which remained until 1879, substantively advanced the development of the Japanese navy. Certainly, it firmly established British traditions within the Japanese navy from matters of seamanship to the style of its uniforms and the attitudes of its officers.[16]

By the end of the 1870s, however, the Japanese navy began to turn away from dependence on large foreign assistance missions, a trend impelled both by reasons of economy—the services of large numbers of foreigners were expensive—and national self-confidence. Also, young Japanese who trained abroad were beginning to return, bringing with them an expertise in Western technologies and institutions that made large, foreign, technical delegations unnecessary. Thus, the Douglas mission represented the last sizable foreign presence in the Japanese navy until the British provided assistance to the early efforts of Japanese naval aviation immediately after World War I. While the Japanese fully recognized the need to keep abreast of the latest developments in Western naval technologies, foreign naval advisers were now more selectively chosen, both in numbers and in nationality. With the rapid evolution of naval technologies and their impact upon the course of naval tactics, however, the counsel of these few foreign consultants profoundly influenced the tactical thinking of the early Japanese navy.

Certainly, not until the arrival of Lt. Comdr. L. P. Willan, RN, were the beginnings of modern naval thought stimulated in the Japanese navy. Hired to teach gunnery and navigation, Willan was appointed instructor at the naval academy in 1879 and concurrently was gunnery instructor aboard the screw corvette *Tsukuba*. At the academy, Willan provided instruction in contemporary naval tactics to a group of thirty-one naval cadets. Among these were Shimamura Hayao, Katō Tomosaburō, and Yoshimatsu Shigetarō, all of whom were destined, as instructors at the future Naval Staff College, to shape the evolution of modern tactics in the Imperial Japanese Navy. During Willan's six years as instructor at the academy, he wrote or edited several works on naval tactics that were translated into Japanese some years later. The works became, in the process, the earliest texts on modern tactics and fleet movements.[17]

More than any other foreign adviser, however, it was Capt. John Ingles, RN, who brought about a recognition within the Japanese navy of both the technical requirements and the tactical advances of modern naval professionalism. His arrival in Japan in 1887 coincided with the decision of Navy Minister Saigō Tsugumichi to establish a center for advanced training for the navy's most promising officers. The Higher Training School for Naval Officers (Kōtō Shikan Gakkō) opened its doors to the first select group of officers at Tsukiji in 1888, and its name was soon changed to the Naval Staff College (Kaigun Daigakkō). The institution became the foremost center in the navy for the development of tactical and strategic thought, a role essentially identical to that of naval war colleges in Western nations.

Captain Ingles was appointed both as an instructor at the original school and as an adviser in the general modernization of the Japanese navy. Shortly after assuming his responsibilities, he began a rigorous analysis of Japan's naval institutions. While satisfied with the good order and discipline he found at sea and ashore, he was understandably less impressed with the navy as a fighting force and with the tactical abilities of its officers. Ingles argued with Navy Minister Saigō that the development of a modern navy meant the gradual retirement of sail-equipped vessels and their replacement by steam-driven warships. Furthermore, advanced training of line officers should include a thorough grounding in the practical applications of modern science, particularly mathematics and physics, as well as training of engineering officers familiar with the technology of the age of steam. Ingles's recommendations were immediately adopted. The scientific bases of technology became both an entrance requirement to the staff college and the subjects of advanced training for students admitted to the college. Advanced engineering instruction was provided at a separate Naval Engineering School.[18]

During Ingles's tour of duty at the Naval Staff College from 1887 to 1893, he familiarized the Japanese with a wide range of technical information from the British navy, information supplemented by the training of selected junior officers in British naval schools. Although Ingles did a great deal to educate the Japanese navy technologically, his greatest contribution to the development of the Japanese navy as a fighting force was his series of lectures on modern naval tactics delivered to the second, third, and fourth classes of the Naval Staff College from September 1889 to September 1892. Covering a wide range of subjects—the organization, formations, movements, and tactics of modern steam fleets; blockades; and counter-battery fire against land fortresses—these lectures were eventually published in Japanese in 1894 as *Kaigun senjutsu kōgiroku* (A transcript of lectures on naval tactics).[19]

FROM SAIL TO STEAM
The Acquisition of Modern Warships

While the officers and men of the Meiji navy were being introduced to the fundamentals of modern seamanship, naval science, and tactics, the navy also undertook to acquire its first modern warships. As Japanese shipyards and expertise in naval construction were insufficiently advanced to build such vessels, the government placed its orders abroad and, not too surprisingly, with Britain. Launched in British yards at the end of the 1870s, the armored, steel-hulled frigate *Fusō* and the armored corvettes *Kongō* and *Hiei* were the first warships built abroad specifically for the Japanese navy. Designed by the distinguished naval constructor Sir Edward Reed, these were steam-driven, barque-rigged vessels of superior quality for their day. Because Japanese navigational and technological skills were still inadequate, the three ships, upon completion, were brought to Japan by British crews, with only a few Japanese aboard (one of whom on the *Hiei*, Tōgō Heihachirō, was the future victor of Tsushima). Once they arrived in Japan, the vessels provided vital experience to Japanese officers and men in handling steam warships. These construction projects also gave neophyte Japanese naval architects the chance to go to Britain to learn their trade and to observe firsthand the construction methods of contemporary warships and the options available in ordnance and protection. Among those young constructors selected for this training was the future father of Japanese naval architecture, Sasō Sachū.[20]

By the middle of the 1880s Japan began to phase out the use of sail on its vessels and to devote its resources to the construction of steam-driven warships. Although Japanese navy yards were not yet capable of building large warships from the keel up, the navy began to take the first steps toward creating a naval armaments industry. They established naval arsenals at Tsukiji in Tokyo and at Yokosuka, both taken over from the feudal government following the Restoration. In 1882, the navy decided to discontinue the construction of wooden warships, and in 1884, after importing the necessary machinery and temporarily hiring several skilled workers from Britain, the Yokosuka arsenal was ready to turn out a few iron warships of modest size. The Tsukiji arsenal was repairing ships and guns by 1874 and by 1882 began to produce small quantities of "Western steel" in Japan. The same period saw the establishment of small maritime construction enterprises, the forerunners of the great shipbuilding firms like Ishikawajima and Kawasaki, which prospered initially because of navy contracts for guns, torpedoes, machinery, and smaller warships. In the years immediately prior to the Sino-Japanese War of 1894–95, the firms went into accelerated production of these items, but for most of the Meiji period more of Japan's domestically built naval vessels were constructed in the navy yards and arsenals. The rapid growth of naval construction by private firms came only at the end of the period.[21]

By the 1880s Japanese constructors had sufficient expertise to negotiate contracts for warship construction. At mid-decade Sasō Sachū and another naval architect handled all the transactions for the construction in Britain of the second-class steel-decked cruisers *Naniwa* and *Takachiho*. These two warships, both 3,650 tons,[22] were capable of speeds up to 18 knots, and had 2- to 3-inch deck armor with a main armament of 10.2-inch Krupp guns, one each fore and aft, mounted in open barbettes. They were similar in design, but actually superior, to Britain's famed "Elswick" protected cruisers. Upon their arrival in Japan, Captain Ingles pronounced them the finest warships of their type anywhere in the world.[23]

While these British-built warships were of outstanding design, in the latter half of the 1880s, Japan briefly turned to France for its foreign naval construction. At the time, there seemed ample reason to do so. Japan had the natural desire of an emerging nation to maintain good relations with a range of naval powers by awarding contracts to various quarters. Japan, moreover, had maintained cordial relations with France since the days of the Tokugawa shogunate, and in the late 1860s and early 1870s, French naval constructors helped establish the principal Japanese navy yard at Yokosuka. Also, during the 1880s, largely because of the fine work of the distinguished naval architect, Emile Bertin, France temporarily stole a march on Britain in warship design. Finally, the 1880s marked the sudden strategic and tactical influence of the Jeune Ecole.[24] The unorthodox school of naval thought in France argued for a navy built of small, fast warships, particularly torpedo boats, which could prey on shipping. Such a force was considered more effective and far less costly than a fleet of lumbering capital ships. The ideas of the Jeune Ecole appeared to receive validation in East Asian waters when French torpedo boats summarily dispatched a Chinese cruiser during the Sino-French War of 1883–85.

The concepts of the Jeune Ecole, therefore, had obvious attraction to Japanese naval leaders, who were quick to seize on the torpedo boat as an ideal weapon for Japan's defense: it was inexpensive and easy to deploy among the Japanese islands and was seen by some navy men as admirably suited to the Japanese martial spirit.[25] Thus, the first naval expansion bill passed by the Diet, in 1882, called for the construction of a fleet of forty-eight vessels (later reduced to forty-six) to be built over an eight-year period. Of these ships, twenty-two were planned as torpedo boats to be assembled in foreign yards and broken down for shipment to Japan, where they would be reassembled. The remaining warships were mainly cruisers, for which Japan now looked to France.

The next logical step for the government was to invite the famed Emile Bertin to come to Japan on a two-year contract (later extended to three years) to guide an expansion of the navy as well as to supervise the placement and construction of naval arsenals.[26] In the Japanese navy, Bertin was best remembered for his design of the cruisers of the *Sankeikan* class, so called because the three warships of the class, the *Matsushima,* the *Hashidate,* and the *Itsukushima,* were each named after one of the three famous *sankei* (scenic spots) in Japan. These vessels, laid down in 1888, were all-steel, steam warships of slightly more than 4,000 tons' displacement, with a top speed of around 18 knots and a main armament of a single 12.6-inch Canet gun, mounted forward (on the *Matsushima,* mounted

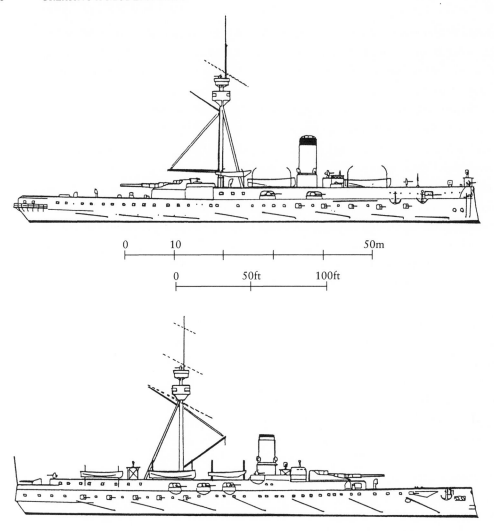

Fig. 1-1. *Sankeikan*-class cruisers: *Matsushima* (top) and *Hashidate* (bottom).

aft), supplemented by eleven 4.7-inch quick-firing guns located in barbettes on either side. This odd design was an attempt to match several heavy warships of German design acquired by the Chinese Peiyang ("Northern Seas") Fleet and to do so at minimum cost. As a recent study points out, however, on balance, these ships were not a success. Their design speed was never reached, their boilers proved unreliable, and too much (particularly armor protection) was sacrificed for its single great gun, one of the most powerful in the world at the time. Worst of all, the Canet gun itself not only proved slow and difficult to fire, but added to the poor sea-keeping qualities of the class. When the gun was trained to one side, moreover, its 65-ton weight caused the ship to heel, making it difficult to achieve the proper elevation. These deficiencies ultimately became glaring in combat.[27]

If the design of the class as a whole was deficient, however, the inclusion of so many smaller quick-firing guns was a master stroke. It was also exemplary of Japan's fortunate capacity to take advantage of the latest naval technology developed in the West, where the advent of quick-firing guns brought improvements in both gun mounts and breech mechanisms. The quick-firing guns could deliver ten shots in less than fifty seconds, as opposed to older guns firing the same number in five minutes. While the newer guns were not expected to penetrate the central armored belt of capital ships of the day, proponents of quick-firing guns anticipated that the cumulative effect of the explosive shells riddling the "soft" ends of an armored ship might inflict crippling damage. These speculations persuaded Lt. Yamanouchi Masuji, who later became the navy's foremost weapons specialist, to urge the immediate adoption of quick-firing guns. Thus, in 1888, after extensive test firings of the new ordnance, the Naval Weapons Committee ordered that 12-centimeter quick-firing guns be installed on the three *Sankeikan*-class cruisers under construction. The decision was fortuitous, for when fired in anger seven years later, the guns had a devastating effect.[28]

The *Sankeikan*-class cruisers represented the last major Japanese naval contract issued to French naval constructors. In 1892, the navy turned back to the British, purchasing the 4,150-ton *Yoshino,* built in Elswick. Her armament of twelve quick-firing guns was formidable for her size, and her 23-knot speed made her then the fastest cruiser in the world.[29]

In the 1880s, the navy also began to assemble its torpedo boat squadrons. Interestingly, the first step in doing so was to acquire a warship that in size and capabilities was a decade ahead of its time. Ordered from Britain, the *Kotaka,* which at 203 tons was the largest torpedo boat at the time of its launching in 1888, was the forerunner of the torpedo boat destroyers that appeared a decade later. Shipped in sections and assembled at Yokosuka, the *Kotaka* had a top speed of 19 knots and was armed with four 1-pounder quick-firing guns and four torpedo tubes, two at the bow and two at the stern.[30] She carried 14-inch Schwartz-kopf torpedoes with a range of 400 meters at 22–24 knots.[31] The Japanese navy did not follow up with orders for vessels of similar design. Most of the remaining torpedo boats ordered under the 1882 expansion plan were of French construction, far smaller in size, but several knots faster than the *Kotaka.* Nevertheless, a series of trials and exercises with the *Kotaka* in 1899 demonstrated that warships of this type would be useful in roles beyond that of coastal defense and would be capable of accompanying larger warships on the high seas.[32]

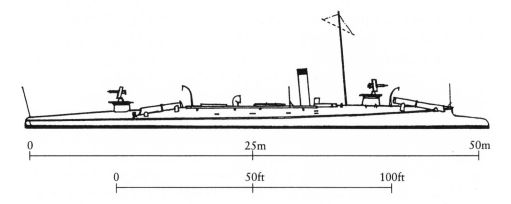

0   25m   50m

0   50ft   100ft

Fig. 1-2. The torpedo boat *Kotaka*.

Along with acquiring torpedo boat technology, the navy also made progress in torpedo training. In 1870, several naval officers being trained in Britain were ordered to begin the specialized study of the new self-propelled Whitehead torpedo then being developed by the British navy. Upon their return, they helped to establish the Torpedo Training Center at Yokosuka in 1886.[33]

By the early 1890s, therefore, the Japanese navy comprised a small but growing number of light, fast warships, essentially unarmored, but powerfully armed, some of which were rated the best of their type in any navy in the world. In building such a navy, the Japanese made a conscious decision to forgo the initial acquisitions toward a major battle fleet, in part because such a step was then beyond the government's resources. Another reason was Japanese caution in the face of the heated controversy in international naval circles regarding the primacy of the capital ship versus the lighter vessel armed with torpedoes or quick-firing guns. As a compromise, the Japanese navy adopted the idea of a few big guns supplemented by numerous medium-sized quick-firing guns as the formula for victory.[34]

MARITIME JAPAN
The Navy Acquires Support for Expansion

That such a fleet was assembled at all was the result of growing support for the navy within both the government and the general public. Furthermore, important institutional changes within the navy itself gave purpose and direction to this modernization effort. The 1880s saw a waxing public interest in maritime power, if not a sophisticated understanding of its requirements. In part, this interest stemmed from enthusiasm for the expansion of Japan's horizons that began with the clarification of Japanese authority over the nation's adjacent island territories: the Kurile Islands, the Ryukyu Islands, and the Bonin Islands. Essentially completed by the end of the 1870s, dominance over the territories literally turned Japan's attention overseas and stirred popular imagination toward the idea of acquiring territories farther out in the Pacific.[35] Such notions were provoked by a growing recognition of the relationship between imperial expansion and national power, a perspective encouraged by the worldwide surge of territorial acquisitiveness by the great powers in the last quarter of the nineteenth century. The sudden scramble by European nations for the remaining Pacific island territories quickly showed Japan its own inadequacy on the Pacific. The deficiency was compounded by disturbing evidence that at least some of Japan's few vessels were faulty in design or manned by inexperienced crews, and that the nation's maritime commerce was woefully dependent on foreign merchant shipping.[36] Around 1885, these concerns stimulated a propaganda campaign by naval spokesmen heralded by the slogan *kaikoku Nippon* (maritime Japan), which sought to magnify the Japanese presence in the west Pacific through increased naval strength and the construction of a modern merchant marine. The public enthusiasm resulting from this effort helped to contribute significant support within the government for the modernization and expansion of the navy.

In the promotion of public and governmental support for the navy in the mid-1880s, however, there was an even more immediate impetus. Japan perceived that China, beleaguered and tottering though its ruling dynasty might be, posed a formidable barrier to the tide of Japanese territorial ambitions in East Asia. By the mid-1880s, Japan's expanding interest in Korea and China's determination to check that interest led to a crisis in which Japan and China only narrowly avoided war through diplomatic compromise at the highest levels. But the agreement signed between Japan and China at Tientsin in 1885 merely postponed an inevitable confrontation, and the rest of the decade saw both countries preparing for it.

Geography dictated that the approaching conflict would be fought on both land and sea. To gain a foothold on the Asian mainland, Japan would need a major military force on the Korean peninsula and sufficient naval forces to protect that army and its communications with the home islands across the Korea Strait. For its part, China needed a navy that could intimidate Japan and thwart its expeditionary plans, if necessary. After naval humiliations at the hands of France earlier in the decade, China sought foreign assistance in creating such a navy. To that end, the strongest of its regional naval forces, the Peiyang Fleet, acquired two German-built battleships, the *Ting-yüan* and the *Chen-yüan*.

In armor and armament, these warships were far superior to any possessed by the Japanese, a fact brought home to the navy and the public when the Chinese ships called at Japanese ports early in 1891. The admiral of the Peiyang Fleet, Ting Ju-ch'ang, brought the two battleships and four other warships to Japan on a visit that was obviously more minatory than amicable. The demonstrations of the large guns of the Chinese battleships off Nagasaki and Yokohama apparently alarmed the public, but Capt. Tōgō Heihachirō, commander of the Yokohama naval base, who went aboard the *Ting-yüan* when it anchored at that port, made a mental note of the slovenly condition of the ship and the undisciplined appearance of its crew. The Japanese naval staff, however, was sufficiently worried to order one of its members, Lt. Saitō Makoto, to study the tactical and technological problems posed by the Chinese warships. His conclusion, that the navy required ships of similar armor and armament, induced the navy minister to seek eleven such warships, a request rejected by the cabinet for want of funds.

Since, in the 1880s, Japan lacked the resources, facilities, and inclination to acquire ships of a similar size, it contracted for Emile Bertin's *Sankeikan*-class cruisers. The ships, with their compromise arrangement of heavy guns and light armor, were planned as a counter to the Chinese battleships. The arrival in Yokohama of the first two new cruisers in late 1891 was marked by joyous special ceremonies and tremendous public enthusiasm. For the public, at least, the appearance of the *Matsushima* and the *Itsukushima* at Yokohama helped restore confidence in Japan's naval strength.[37]

YAMAMOTO GOMBEI AND PERSONNEL REFORM

During the 1880s, this groundswell of public support was matched by the increasing effectiveness of the navy in shaping its professional and institutional identity and in improving its bureaucratic position. These efforts began with the gradual acceleration of personnel reform. When the two service ministries were created in 1872, the Navy Ministry was largely a civilian organization in which few officers had a knowledge of the sea. For the next dozen years, the chain of command was loose. Communication between the ministry and its ships was poor because of inadequate organizational and professional understanding on both sides. This situation began to improve in 1884, when Rear Adm. Nire Kagenori left his post as fleet commander to head the naval staff section of the ministry, bringing with him a number of officers with considerable sea experience, including some Naval Academy graduates. The transition marked the first step toward the professionalization of the upper levels of the navy.

More than this, Saigō Tsugumichi, the new minister of the reorganized and bureaucratically strengthened Navy Ministry, proved to be of vital help in furthering the interests of the naval service. Navy minister in 1885–86, 1887–90, and 1893–98, Saigō himself had no professional naval background, but his position within the Satsuma faction and his respected reputation gave him formidable

Yamamoto Gombei in midcareer

influence within the government. Saigō's greatest contribution to the navy was his support and encouragement to those younger officers dedicated to its modernization. Of these, none was of more critical importance to the rise of Japan as a great naval power than Yamamoto Gombei (no relation to the World War II naval leader, Yamamoto Isoroku). His forty-year career was similar in many ways to that of "Jackie" Fisher, the great reformer of the British navy. With blowtorch energy, single-minded dedication, and considerable political skill, Yamamoto stripped the navy of its deadwood, battled the army for public attention and government support, and induced the Japanese Diet to provide funds for a major battle fleet. Along the way he amassed enormous power and influence, rising from ensign to navy minister, and eventually serving twice as prime minister of his country. It is no exaggeration to write that the navy of late Meiji Japan was in purpose, composition, and armament, the navy of Yamamoto Gombei.

Yamamoto was, first and foremost, a naval professional intent upon forcing the pace of change in the modernization of the Meiji navy, even at the risk of Satsuma dominance. He first made his mark as gunnery officer aboard the corvette *Asama* in the early 1880s. His work resulted in the designation of that warship as the navy's gunnery training vessel and the adoption of his treatise on gunnery as the official gunnery training manual for the fleet. After several sea commands and foreign travel in the mid-1880s Yamamoto's energetic professionalism caught the attention of Navy Minister Kabayama, who appointed him, at age forty, director of the ministry's secretariat, with primary responsibility for personnel matters. From this position and with the full backing of Saigō, he began to exercise great authority in the navy. Yamamoto's major objective was to sweep out from all echelons of the service those older and less professionally competent officers who continued to be a barrier to the rise of the younger generation trained at the academy and more capable of handling the technology of the newest warships. No step was more important in advancing the efficiency and professionalism in the Meiji navy than Yamamoto's personnel retrenchment of 1893. This reorganization challenged the Satsuma "old boy" system at the navy's upper echelons and enabled the rise of a cluster of young officers who shaped the strategic, tactical, and technological development of the Japanese navy from 1895 forward. It was only the first in a series of dramatic reforms.[38]

THE NAVY STRUGGLES FOR STRATEGIC STATUS

Parallel with his efforts to hone the professional edge of the navy's officer corps, Yamamoto fired the opening salvos against the navy's rival service for pride of place. In doing so, he opened up an interservice conflict that grew with increasing acrimony during the late nineteenth century and into the twentieth, with fatal consequences in World War II. The conflict's causes—professional hubris, jealousies that arose from old regional antagonisms, rivalry for public attention and budgetary support, as well as honest differences in strategic perspective—were multiple and became so intertwined that in tracing the history of the Imperial Japanese Navy, it is difficult for the historian to separate them.

When Yamamoto came to the Navy Ministry in 1891, the navy still occupied a distinctly secondary place, both functionally and organizationally. The navy was assigned the *kaibō* (maritime defense) of Japan, while the army had charge of *kokubō* (overall national defense). For this reason the chief of the Army General Staff was chief of staff for both services. The initially inferior position of the naval staff was also because the integration of the staffs brought together two very different staff models: for the navy, the British model, which stressed the subordination of staff to higher bureaucratic control; for the army, that of Prussia, which stressed the independence of the army and its direct links to the throne. It was not by coincidence, therefore, that the chief of the Army General Staff was a full general and a member of the imperial house, while initially, the naval chief of staff was only a rear admiral. Yamamoto, supported at all levels within the navy, was determined to overturn both this bureaucratic disparity and the strategic assumption behind it. His objective was to create an independent naval staff, and the focus of his effort was the formulation of the regulations that governed the combined Imperial General Headquarters (Dai Hon'ei, referred to hereafter as IGHQ) in time of war. The immediate argument with the army over the shaping of regulations was whether to adopt a unitary command—one general staff with responsibility over the conduct of both military and naval operations in wartime, as the army wished—or a dual command system of two separate staffs, with each staff responsible for its own operations, as the navy insisted upon. The controversy illuminated a basic strategic issue that plagued Japanese national defense for decades: whether decisive conflict in Japan's defense would be fought on land, giving the army primary responsibility for *rikushu ron* (Japanese security) or whether, because of geographic and economic considerations basic to Japan as an island nation, primacy should be given to a *kaishu ron* (maritime strategy).[39]

The army's argument was that a nation is essentially composed of territory, people, and government, and therefore the ultimate purpose of national defense was the protection of these three elements. Thus, even if the navy was annihilated and its trade cut off through the loss of command of the seas, as long as its land and people were secure under the protection of its military forces, no fatal damage could be done to the state. Navy men, of course, bridled at this strategic perspective and, since the early days of the Meiji period, repeatedly insisted that as an island nation, Japan's most vital interests included overseas communications and trade. Thus, in the navy's most moderate view, the nation's security depended upon an adequate development of both military and naval forces—*ryōyoku-ryōrin* (on "both wings and both wheels," in the words of a contemporary expression).[40]

In making his argument for a balance in strategic priorities, Yamamoto endeavored to establish a strategic basis for establishing a naval staff equivalent to and independent of the Army General Staff. Naturally, during the heated deliberations on the regulations for the IGHQ in wartime, the army, unwilling to see its authority diminished, adamantly insisted that there was no need for two general staffs in Japan's defense establishment. The Navy Ministry countered by arguing that the army simply did not have sufficient understanding of naval operations to oversee their conduct. Finally, in 1893, at the request of the Meiji emperor, a compromise was reached: an independent Navy General Staff (Kaigun Gunreibu) was established with the right of direct access to the emperor, but its chief of staff was responsible for the rather restricted role of coastal defense. The chief of the Army General

Staff retained overall responsibility for all Japanese military and naval operations in wartime. This arrangement continued to place the army in a superior command position, but its authority over naval affairs was weakened and made less explicit.[41]

Even by the time this temporary compromise was worked out, however, bureaucratic arrangements that reflected any sort of inferior organizational or strategic status for the navy were anathema to naval spokesmen and propagandists. Indeed, navy men like Yamamoto were no longer content with even interservice parity, but were ready to press for naval primacy in status, budgetary allocations, and strategic mission.

The impetus behind this new confidence of the navy in challenging the status quo on matters of national defense largely stemmed from their discovery of the heady doctrines of navalism—the idea that sea power, based on great battle fleets, was the key to national greatness. The doctrine seized the imagination of western governments through the writings of contemporary theorists like the Colomb brothers (John and Philip), Alfred Thayer Mahan, John Laughton, and others of the "Blue Water" school of naval thought.

In particular, the writings of Mahan arrested the attention of Japanese naval circles. While his ideas and writings were met with enthusiasm among naval circles the world over, they may have evoked the greatest response in Japan. According to Mahan himself, more of his works were translated into Japanese than any other language. Upon Saigō Tsugumichi's prompting, Mahan's *Influence of Sea Power upon History* was translated and published by the Suikōsha, the naval officers' professional association, in 1896. The Suikōsha had nearly two thousand members, including not only navy men, but also leading bureaucrats, editors, bankers, businessmen, and Diet members. Most importantly, that work was ultimately adopted as a text by the two service academies.[42]

Mahan's emphasis on the independence of naval operations and on the control of the sea lent the weight of expert foreign opinion to the navy's demand for primacy. Thanks to Japanese translations of Mahan, Japanese navy personnel could now call upon weighty and sophisticated theory, scholarly and rich in historical detail, to support their arguments. As discussed in a later chapter, the application of Mahanian principles to Japan's strategic situation was, in fact, ill-founded. But for Japanese navy leaders like Yamamoto, the principles provided the navy with an apparent rationale at the time. The rationale, based on a general (though not yet specifically Japanese) theory of sea power, argued not just for equal standing, but for the seniority of the navy. In the councils of government, on the floor of the Diet, and in the national press, the navy argued that it should be first and the army second *(kaishu-rikujū)*. From this eminence the navy would claim the larger part of government funding and public support that would enable Yamamoto to lay the foundations of a modern battle fleet.

In the short run, because no specialized Japanese theory of sea power yet existed, the navy settled for an unsatisfactory substitution. Not only were the two services to enter Japan's first modern war with an "army first" concept of strategic command, but the Navy Ministry was also initially thwarted in its request for a massive increase in capital ships with which to confront the Chinese navy.[43] Nevertheless, the navy began to assert itself as a professional elite and started to master the arguments of a sea power doctrine that would support its increasingly insistent claims for naval primacy.

As always, in the forefront of this interservice debate was Capt. Yamamoto Gombei, then serving as the chief of the Navy Ministry's secretariat. Yamamoto never ceased to argue that command of the sea was the prime prerequisite not only for the defense of Japan, but also for the expansion of Japan's interests on the Asian continent. In this, of course, he met with heated opposition from the army. On the eve of Japan's war with China, an interservice conference met to deliberate the strategic problems the nation would encounter in a campaign centered on Korea. At that meeting, Army Vice Chief of Staff General Kawakami Sōroku was expounding on why the war would be settled by decisive land combat on the Korean peninsula, when Yamamoto, the navy's representative at the talks, interrupted Kawakami to ask if the army had first-rate engineer units. Indeed, it did, Kawakami replied, but why on earth did Yamamoto want to know? "Because, General," came the retort, "if the army is to get to Korea without the Imperial Japanese Navy, those engineer units are going to have to build a very long bridge."[44]

AN EMPEROR-CENTERED NAVY
Organization of the Japanese Naval High Command and Subordinate Commands

The increasingly bitter interservice rivalry of Japan's imperial armed forces played out against an evolving institutional background that was unusual among naval and military organizations worldwide.[45] Theoretically supreme over all government agencies and institutions reigned the emperor, whose person and authority, according to the Meiji Constitution of 1889, was "sacred and inviolable," but whose practical involvement and responsibility in the workings of government was limited.

Functioning beneath the emperor were the civilian government, the armed services, and certain prestigious but generally passive advisory bodies. In theory, too, Japan was a parliamentary state, with a bicameral legislature—the Diet—and a cabinet headed by a prime minister. Yet, unlike parliamentary institutions in the West, the cabinet did not depend upon majority representation, but was largely the creature of the collective will of influential senior statesmen both within and outside the government. More important was that the two armed service ministers, while nominally selected by and responsible to the civilian prime minister, in reality looked to their respective services for direction, since they were usually active, not retired officers. They could, and sometimes did, veto any civilian cabinet by refusing to serve on it.

Eventually, real power increasingly resided not in the service ministries, which were generally responsible for matters of administration and logistics, but in the general staffs of both armed services. The staffs were charged with the preparation of war plans, collection of intelligence, and the direction of operations in the field or at sea. In performing these functions, the authority of the army and navy remained immune to any interference by the civilian government. The military maintained this virtual independence because the constitution gave the emperor supreme command over the army and the navy. Consequently, the chiefs of staff of these two services, acting in the name of the emperor, held the "right of supreme command." Thus, the two general staffs (the Navy General Staff after 1893) were answerable only to the emperor. Since the throne traditionally did not often interfere with the day-to-day workings of government, civilian or military, in practical terms the "right of supreme command" meant that except for their annual budgets, Japan's two armed forces were essentially accountable to no one. (Figure 1-3 shows the military institutions within the Japanese constitutional system.)

In these respects, the Japanese army and navy functioned much like those of Germany, on whose constitutional arrangements the Japanese armed services were based. But in its orientation toward the theoretical authority of the monarch, the organization of the Imperial Japanese Navy departed even from its German model. The various command, administrative, and advisory bodies common to all navies were not invariably marshaled under either the Navy General Staff or the Navy Ministry. Some came to exist as coequal commands or bureaucracies, each theoretically under the authority of the emperor.

Figure 1-4, showing the existing structure of the navy in 1903, demonstrates this unusual command structure in schematic form. First in prestige was the Navy General Staff itself, whose principal divisions eventually comprised war plans, mobilization, intelligence, and communications, and which directed the work of naval attachés abroad. In theory, all plans worked out by the Navy General Staff required imperial sanction; in practice, the emperor approved them automatically. Yet, for most of the navy's history, the authority of the chief of the Navy General Staff was somewhat limited compared with that of his opposite number in the army. In peacetime, direct command of the navy was held by the navy minister, whom the chief of staff was customarily obliged to consult before seeking authorization from the throne for operational plans. In wartime, of course, the chief of staff assumed direct control of all naval forces. For decades,

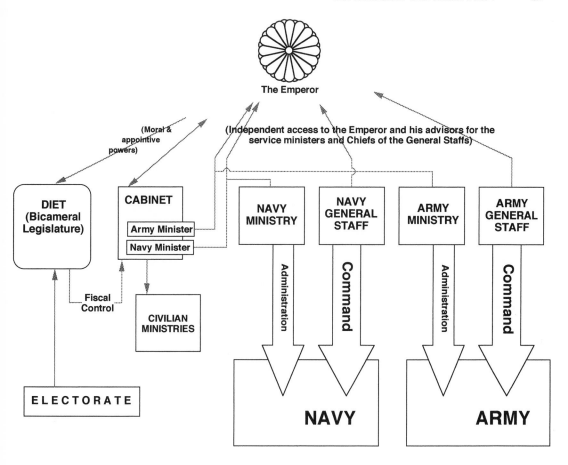

Fig. 1-3. Principal military institutions within the Japanese constitutional system.

this peacetime limitation was a sore point with the Navy General Staff, which in the mid-1930s forced a change, giving the chief of staff direct control over the navy in peacetime as in war.

The Navy Ministry itself was the largest organization within the high command, largely concerned with the administration of the navy: its finances, personnel, training, and logistics. Initially, the ministry comprised not only the secretariat, but also various bureaus—of which the Naval Affairs Bureau, responsible for the formulation of navy policy, was the most important—as well

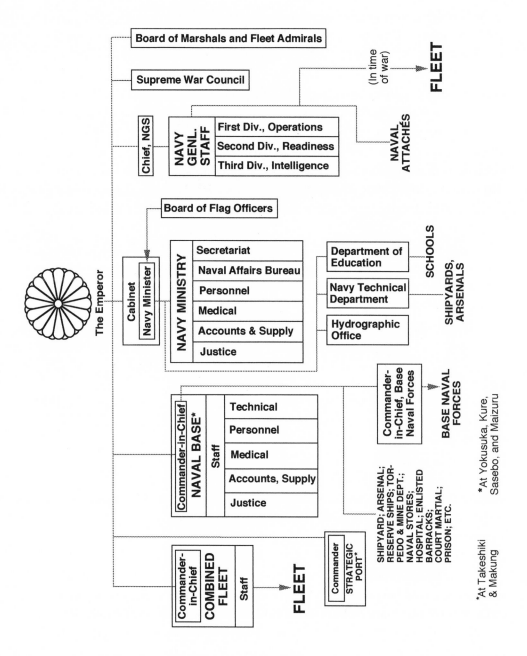

Fig. 1-4. Organization of the navy, 1903 (principal offices only).

as the Naval Academy and various specialized schools. In later decades, other powerful and independent bureaus and departments were added to the ministry. Though selected by the civilian prime minister to be a member of the cabinet, the navy minister was directly responsible to the emperor and was, for most of the navy's history, an officer on active service. Thus, in practice, he was greatly under the influence of the General Staff.

As described, most of the nation's actual naval forces initially consisted of small guard and coast defense vessels attached to shore stations. Formally organized fleets did not take shape until shortly before Japan's first war with China, that is, in the early 1890s. When they were established, however, their commanders also were directly appointed by the emperor. The commanders were thus, in theory, accountable to him.

Ashore there were several important base commands, each headed by a commander considered directly subordinate to the emperor. By the 1890s, the coastal defense of the home islands was divided between three *kaigunku* (naval districts), each centered on a *chinjufu* (naval base). The *chinjufu* was a primary port that served as headquarters of the naval district. It included navy yards, fuel and supply depots, naval barracks and guard and coast defense vessels. Each *chinjufu* possessed a dual character: administratively, during peacetime, it was under the direction of the Navy Ministry; operationally, during wartime, it took directions from the commanders of the fleets stationed within their districts, who in turn came under the authority of the Navy General Staff. Within naval districts there were also secondary shore-based commands—*gunkō* (naval ports)—which included harbor offices, repair shops, hospitals, and guard and defense vessels. On almost the same footing as *chinjufu* were *yōkō* (strategic ports). The *yōkō* were in effect scaled-down *chinjufu* in remote or overseas locations. The flag rank officers who commanded the *yōkō* no less than those who commanded the *chinjufu* did so by appointment from the emperor and therefore were theoretically also directly responsible to him.

Finally, several prestigious advisory bodies stood apart from the general navy structure and could hypothetically wield enormous influence in navy policy, especially in personnel matters. In practice, however, these groups did so only occasionally and then usually to attempt to resolve a policy or administrative crisis. The first was the Shōkan Kaigi, or Board of Flag Officers; it counseled the navy minister on coordinating ministry activities with those of the fleet and shore commands, and it also passed on personnel matters, particularly promotions. The second of these bodies was the Gensuifu, or Board of Marshals and Fleet Admirals. It was composed of senior generals and admirals who, by virtue of appointment to it, acquired the titles of marshal and fleet admiral (these being, therefore, not strictly

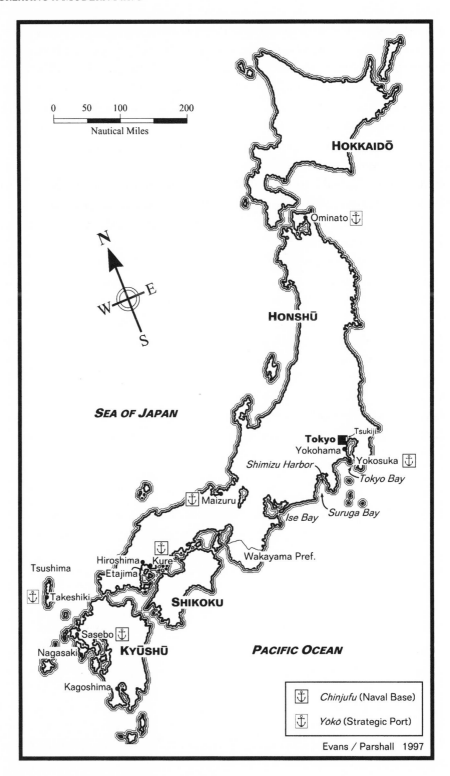

Map 1-3. Maritime map of Japan, 1887–1905

military ranks). The marshals and fleet admirals acted as the highest organ of military advisers to the emperor. The board met infrequently, and its influence was limited. The third body was the Gunji Sangiin, or Supreme War Council. Its members were the chief authorities and ranking officers of both services—the chiefs of staff, the ministers, and members of the Board of Marshals and Fleet Admirals. In addition to advising the emperor on technical military matters, the Gunji Sangiin was charged with coordinating the planning activities of the army and the navy. Given the ongoing history of antagonism between the two services in Japan, the Supreme War Council's primary function was not eminently successful, but as a distinguished sinecure for eminent officers, it offered and received prestige.

These arrangements help explain how, over time, the Japanese navy developed two administrative tendencies. First, in its status as an independent organ of the state, the navy was extremely reluctant to accept any compromise that appeared to infringe upon its authority. Second, the navy evolved into a series of bureaucratic satrapies, each jealous of its prerogatives and each less than devoted to the principle of intraservice harmony and coordination. When added to the tremendous bureaucratic energy spent competing with the army for status and preferment, these characteristics eventually caused serious damage to the efficiency and effectiveness of the Japanese navy. But the ominous consequences of these bureaucratic deformations lay decades in the future. In the mid-1880s, the navy concentrated its attention on mastering those tactical and technological skills necessary for its emergence as a modern fighting force.

2

FIRST SUCCESS

*The Evolution of Japanese Naval Tactics and the
Sino-Japanese War, 1894–1895*

The Japanese navy came into being during a period of rapid technological change and tactical confusion among the world's navies. By the latter half of the nineteenth century the dominance of steam over sail was clear enough, but the leapfrogging race between ordnance and armor had provoked kaleidoscopic changes in hull configuration, distribution of armor, and the placement of guns. Moreover, the successive emergence of a series of offensive naval weapons—the ram, the heavy rifled guns, the torpedo, and the light quick-firing gun—made it unclear which weapon might prove decisive in combat. At the Battle of Lissa in 1866, between the Austrian and Italian navies in the Adriatic Sea, the only major warship lost during the battle had been sunk by ramming. As a result, for the next thirty years, naval architects put ram bows on all the capital ships they designed. But, as there had been no major fleet engagement anywhere in the world since Lissa, it was impossible to know whether the ram was really the dominant naval weapon or whether (as it turned out) Lissa had briefly illuminated an aberration in naval technology.[1]

Parallel to the search for a decisive naval weapon was the question of warship design, a matter of critical importance not only to naval professionals, but also to civilian governments and parliaments that were expected to provide the funds for naval construction programs. Was a battle fleet of capital ships worth the enormous expenditures involved? Or, as the spokesmen of the Jeune Ecole had argued, did the destructive power of torpedoes and the relative inaccuracy of naval gunfire mean that it was cheaper and more effective to build a smaller fleet composed largely of swift torpedo-carrying craft?

Finally, there was the unresolved problem of the most effective tactical formation, a question that stemmed from the first two problems of weaponry and ship type. While the line ahead formation—the column—had proved to be the best tactical arrangement by the end of the age of sail, naval theorists pointed out that at the battle of Lissa, the victorious Austrian fleet fought in modified line abreast (wedge formation), a tactic that gave maximum advantage to the ram. Moreover, some proponents of line abreast warned that ships in column following the van would be vulnerable not only to ramming, but also to torpedoes. Thus a frontal attack on this formation might devastate it. Those who held to the superiority of the column pointed out the advantage of simplicity in having the commander in the lead ship and the accumulated power of its broadside. There was also another question. Since the increase in propulsive speeds and the emergence of quick-firing guns made prompt and precise deployment essential for battle, what should be the steaming formation prior to an actual engagement?

By the end of the century, articulate and influential Western commanders had begun to turn the controversy in favor of the line ahead formation. In the British navy, Capt. Reginald H. S. Bacon, one of Adm. John Fisher's "think tank" of younger officers in the Mediterranean Fleet, claimed to have proved the superiority of the line ahead in combination with superior speed in a series of tabletop war games. In these games, he asserted, he was never beaten when using the column.[2] In his memoirs a German admiral, Alfred von Tirpitz, later insisted that the German navy reached the same conclusion in 1894, based on the results of tactical maneuvers in Kiel Bay.[3] That the Japanese navy was working out similar tactical formations even earlier indicates the state of doctrinal flux in which all navies of the world operated during this period.

GENESIS OF JAPANESE NAVAL TACTICS, 1887–94

In the early 1880s, however, questions of fleet tactics had been of little concern to the Japanese navy. True, the navy's most modern vessels, the *Fusō*, *Kongō*, and *Hiei*, often patrolled the Japanese coast in formation and this effort occasionally led to discussions of various tactical difficulties, such as keeping station and entering or leaving harbor at night. Furthermore, at the Naval Academy, Lieutenant Willan, RN, had delivered some rudimentary lectures on fleet maneuvers for sail and steam ships. But since the navy then consisted of a few ships whose main functions were individual guard and training duty, to Japanese navy men, fleet maneuvers seemed to have more relevance for the distant squadrons of the British navy than for themselves.[4]

By the end of the decade, however, a number of developments promoted the evolution of fleet tactics within the Japanese navy. The first was an increase in the quantity as well as the quality of its ships. Initially, the navy's acquisition of warships was fairly slow,[5] but by 1882, there were enough first-line units to form the navy's first fleet. Shortly afterward, a basic regulation was established for the organization of fleets and fleet commands. In 1889, at the same time that this directive was succeeded by the navy's Fleet Regulations *(Kantai jōrei)* the navy formed the Standing Fleet (Jōbi Kantai), which became the navy's first-line warships, as opposed to its reserve units. In 1893, the navy organized a second force of first-line ships, the Western Seas Fleet (Saikai Kantai), and the next year, on the eve of the Sino-Japanese War, the Standing Fleet and the Western Seas Fleet were united to form the Combined Fleet (Rengō Kantai), a force of ten first-line warships.[6]

The numerical and organizational growth of the navy made it tactically imperative that ships of the fleet should be able to maneuver together in combat, a view that took on added urgency with the growing likelihood of eventual conflict with China. Inevitably, this perception began to generate real interest in the study and practice of tactical operations by the fleet. By the late 1880s, the navy had begun to acquire from several sources a greater understanding of current tactical theories and had begun to work out methods for sorting them out.

The year 1887 marks the initiation of that effort and therefore the beginning of Japanese naval doctrine. In January of that year, Shimamura Hayao, a young naval lieutenant on the staff of the Naval Division of the joint General Staff, had published *Kaigun senjutsu ippan* (An overview of naval tactics), which was essentially a compilation of contemporary views on naval tactics gleaned from the best British and American treatises, supplemented by his own commentary. As there was nothing in Japanese that explained the subject so comprehensively or in such detail, the work brought Shimamura instant acclaim within the navy and, for the first time, provoked real interest in fleet tactics.[7]

In his "Overview" Shimamura argued for the necessity of carrying out fleet exercises to develop a practical, sound tactical doctrine. He proposed that the best way to set up the exercises would be to form a study committee consisting of the commander of the Standing Fleet; individual ship captains; seconds in command; and gunnery, torpedo, and staff officers. The navy quickly seized on Shimamura's suggestion; thus was formed the "Committee to Investigate Tactics," which included officers from the Navy Division of the General Staff, the Navy Ministry, and the Naval Staff College. The locus for its study and experiment was Shimizu Harbor, a fleet anchorage on the western side of Suruga Bay between Shizuoka Prefecture and

Shimamura Hayao as a young officer

the Izu Peninsula southwest of Tokyo. The participants gathered in conference in June 1887 at the Seiken Temple in Okitsu, a little town just north of the harbor.[8]

At this point, Japan had largely a sailing navy, and a major obstacle to maneuvering ships together was the different ways that individual ships handled their rigging. The initial discussions of the conference thus concentrated on shipboard "preparations for battle" to standardize these evolutions. This having been settled, problems of fire, flood, defense against torpedo boats, and the capture of enemy ships were also studied in detail and practiced aboard those warships anchored in the harbor. Later, the conferees studied and debated methods for individual ship-to-ship engagements, problems of signaling with torpedo boats, and various offensive maneuvers.[9]

The first exercises mirrored the worldwide tactical confusion during the two decades following the Battle of Lissa. Assuming the ram to be an offensive weapon second only to the rifled gun, the navy undertook maneuvers in various formations to give maximum advantage to ramming tactics and simulated collisions caused by ramming. (To shield them from real damage the ships were fitted with bamboo aprons.) After reaching a tentative decision on a particular tactical method or evolution, the conference participants would always immediately try it out with the ships available in Shimizu Harbor. Thus, step-by-step, the participants began to shape the first tactical guidelines for the navy. In this sense, the Seiken Temple conferences and the Shimizu Harbor trials together comprise the cradle of Japanese naval tactics.[10]

As the harbor at Shimizu was too small for fleet exercises, these were first carried out at sea during the winter of 1887–88. With Lieutenant Shimamura aboard acting as umpire, the seven ships of the Standing Fleet undertook various experiments in tactical formation, signaling, and maneuver as the fleet carried out a patrol from Kyūshū to the Ryukyu Islands and back to Shikoku. In 1888, based on the lessons learned in these exercises, the Navy Division of the General Staff issued a detailed manual for future naval maneuvers, correcting some defects that had turned up in Shimamura's pioneering treatise. Four years later, the manual was once again revised into *Kaigun sentō kyōhan sōan* (Draft directives for naval engagements), which provided the basic tactical instructions for Japanese naval operations of the Sino-Japanese War and served as a model for the navy's famous *Kaisen yōmurei* (Battle Instructions) of later years.[11]

The date 1887 also marks an important contribution to the evolution of Japanese tactics from another source. In that year, Capt. John Ingles, RN, came to teach at the newly established Naval Staff College, where he remained as an influential instructor and adviser on naval matters for the next six years. In his lectures on tactics at the college, Ingles had taken up the hotly debated issue of the most effective offensive formation for naval combat in the age of steam. Ingles left no doubt that for tactical flexibility and simplicity, he favored the controversial *tanjūjin* (line ahead formation). With informed logic and lucidity, he examined in detail the various risks—particularly from torpedo and ramming attacks—that were supposedly inherent to the column. He explained how each could be overcome by three critical elements: superior speed, superior firepower, and superior gunnery.[12] Furthermore, in an era when visual signals—flags, lights, or semaphore—were the only system of communication available, the simplicity of the line ahead formation, particularly if the flagship was at the head of the column, made it the easiest for signaling and thus the most flexible. In the navy's subsequent fleet exercises, Ingles's tactical formula became a principal subject of experiment and debate. More importantly, his dicta on speed, firepower, and gunnery became the heart of Japanese tactical doctrine in later decades.

As faster and more heavily gunned steam warships like the cruiser *Yoshino* and the *Sankeikan*-class cruisers joined the fleet in the years prior to the Sino-Japanese War, the importance of fleet maneuvers became increasingly apparent.

But the question of the most effective battle formation remained unsettled until the very eve of that conflict. As the possibility of war with China loomed ever larger, Adm. Itō Yūkō had been ordered to station the ten warships of the newly formed Combined Fleet at Sasebo, Japan's westernmost base and that closest to enemy waters. In the months immediately before the hostilities, Itō put to sea from Sasebo every other day to further the navy's tactical training. These exercises caused concern in the naval community, particularly because of the inadequate training of many ship captains and crews in the signals necessary for complicated maneuvers. When the fleet remained in harbor, ship's launches were assembled and used in model maneuvers to determine which battle formation was most suitable. In the discussions and debates that surrounded these maneuvers, Rear Adm. Tsuboi Kōzō, commander of the Standing Fleet, and Lieutenant Shimamura, now an officer on its staff and trusted adviser to Admiral Itō, strongly urged that the line ahead be adopted as the standard offensive formation of the Japanese navy. Eventually, the Combined Fleet was divided into two divisions to carry out opposing tactics. In exercise after exercise it became clear that Ingles had been right: for flexibility, simplicity, and ease of signaling, the column was always the superior formation. By the outbreak of war this important tactical issue had been settled; the fleet would go into battle in line ahead, with the commander leading the line.[13]

During these years immediately before the war with China, the Japanese navy also took the first tentative steps toward employment of the torpedo as an offensive weapon. Although the navy had acquired a significant number of torpedo boats by the mid-1880s, there had been as yet no serious consideration of how they would be used in battle. This was partly because torpedo boats themselves were still unseaworthy, uncomfortable cockleshells that could scarcely be given a place on the high seas and partly because torpedoes, with their weak propulsive power, were still in their infancy. Given their slow speed, it was comparatively easy for a moving warship to evade them. Moreover, by their very nature, torpedoes could not, like naval gunfire, be rapidly adjusted as to range or angle. For these reasons, the navy contemplated torpedo attacks only on enemy warships lying at anchor. Because the effective range of the torpedoes used by the navy was no more than 400–600 meters,[14] presumably such close-in attacks during daylight hours would be suicidal. Thus was born the precedent of the torpedo as a Japanese weapon of night surface combat. The Japanese navy continued this strategy even after the capabilities of the torpedo and its delivery warship had vastly improved in subsequent decades.[15]

The navy acquired its first torpedoes in 1884. They were improved German versions of the original 14-inch Whitehead torpedo manufactured by Schwartzkopf. Called the type 84, after the year, it had a range of 400 meters at 22 knots and an explosive charge of 21 kilograms. The navy later bought an improved Schwartzkopf, the type 88. It was slightly faster (24 knots) and carried double the explosive charge. Its range is uncertain, but a torpedo exercise manual of 1894 has instructions for firing the "new type" at ranges of 600 meters.[16] Most torpedoes used in the war against China were of these two types, but some longer-range Whiteheads were purchased for the cruiser *Yoshino* in 1893. In 1897, the navy started producing its own torpedoes at its Tokyo arsenal based on Whitehead designs.[17]

THE JAPANESE NAVY ON THE EVE OF BATTLE

The two blazing victories that Japan achieved in the Sino-Japanese War of 1894–95 have blinded many historians to the generally cautious and even apprehensive view at the highest levels of the Japanese navy on the eve of hostilities. In retrospect, the navy seems to have been far less confident than the Japanese army about the outcome of a war with China. The naval strategist and historian Adm. Satō Tetsutarō wrote years later that on the eve of the war, few in the Japanese naval high command were complacent about facing the Chinese navy.[18] This perspective was largely due to the assessment by Japanese—and foreign—naval observers of China's apparent naval advantages over those of Japan.

There was, to begin with, the seeming quantitative as well as qualitative superiority of the Chinese navy, the four regional fleets of which not only comprised twice as many warships as that of Japan, but included the two German-built battleships, for which the Japanese had no counterparts, either in terms of armor or ordnance. In firepower, the Chinese navy had the advantage in weight of broadside, because of these two large warships. Moreover, the Chinese had aboard their leading ships a number of capable foreign advisers and technicians, whereas no foreigners now served with Japanese warships at sea. Additionally, as Japanese strategic objectives were centered on the Korean peninsula, the theater of combat would inevitably be along the western coast of Korea and in the waters of the Yellow Sea. Here the Chinese would have at hand two reasonably developed naval bases, Port Arthur (Lü-shun, Ryojun) on the Liaotung Peninsula and Weihaiwei on the Shantung Peninsula, while Japan would have none.

There was, in addition, the realization in the Japanese naval high command that the Combined Fleet was an irreplaceable force, foreign-built and purchased at great cost. To risk its destruction against a powerful enemy fleet was an awesome gamble, one which, in the navy's perspective, might well risk the fate of the nation itself.

Yet China's advantages were more apparent than real. Most of the Chinese warships were over-age and obsolescent. The greater armor and weight of single-salvo shell on the Chinese side were more than offset by the number of quick-firing guns on most first-line Japanese ships. These weapons gave the Combined Fleet

Table 2-1

RELATIVE STRENGTHS OF THE JAPANESE AND PEIYANG FLEETS
September 1894

IMPERIAL JAPANESE NAVY
- 4 capital ships (all old, 2 at Yalu)
- 1 armored cruiser
- 7 protected cruisers (plus *Izumi,* which was not ready)
- 12 unprotected cruisers (includes unprotected frigates and corvettes)
- 7 gunboats
- 26 torpedo boats

PEIYANG FLEET
- 2 capital ships
- 3 protected cruisers
- 5 unprotected cruisers
- 10 gunboats
- 5 (minimum) to 16 (maximum) torpedo boats

---

the edge in any sustained exchange of salvoes. The worst feature of both Chinese battleships, moreover, lay in their main armament. Each was armed with short-barreled guns in twin barbettes in echelon that could fire only in restricted arcs. The short barrels of the main armament meant that the shells had a low muzzle velocity and poor penetration, and their accuracy was poor at long ranges.[19] Finally, the Combined Fleet was far superior in terms of speed. The cruiser *Yoshino* was one of the fastest warships in the world, and the *Sankeikan*-class cruisers were faster than anything in the Chinese Peiyang Fleet.[20]

Tactically, too, Chinese naval units entered the war with only the crudest set of instructions: sister ships and ships assigned to designated pairs were to keep together, and all ships were to fight end-on, as far forward from the beam as possible, a tactic practically dictated by the obsolescent arrangement of Chinese naval ordnance. The only vague resemblance of a fleet tactic was that all ships were to follow the visible movements of the flagship, an arrangement made necessary because the signal book used by the Peiyang Fleet was written in English, a language with which few officers in the fleet had any familiarity.[21]

There was also the question of command. The Japanese Combined Fleet was a unified force; the Chinese navy was not. The latter was really four separate regional forces. The Peiyang Fleet, though the strongest of them, had to face the

Japanese alone. Nor were the foreign advisers and technicians, such as Philo McGiffin, formerly of the U.S. Navy, any substitute for experienced, decisive, and motivated indigenous officers, fired with patriotism and firmly supported by their government. Adm. Ting Ju-ch'ang, the commander of the Peiyang Fleet, though a man of courage and integrity, was a former cavalry officer with limited knowledge of the sea. From the outset he was hounded by his government with dire threats should he fail to defeat the enemy. In contrast, the command of the Japanese Combined Fleet was in the hands of officers who had considerably more sea experience, who appreciated the potential of the new technological and tactical developments of the past decade, and who had the confidence of their government. Admiral Itō, commander of the Combined Fleet, was the first full admiral to come up through the ranks as a sea officer. Though he leaned toward caution and lacked the full range of technical knowledge possessed by some of the navy's younger officers, he had been involved in the evolution of naval tactics since the Shimizu Harbor exercises and had the advice and counsel of a first-rate staff. Not the least of this staff was the navy's outstanding tactical innovator, Lieutenant Shimamura. Admiral Itō's second in command, Rear Admiral Tsuboi, had trained with the U.S. Navy early in his career and was an experienced sea officer. At Itō's back was Vice Adm. Kabayama Sukenori, the fiery, aggressive chief of the Navy General Staff who, despite his scant sea experience, was unrelenting in his desire to see the Combined Fleet close with the enemy.

Last of all, although China possessed bases near the likely theater of war, the generally passive strategy that it adopted shortly after the war broke out largely offset any advantage these bases might have provided. Instead of taking the war to Japan, the Peiyang Fleet, at the instructions of the Chinese imperial court, was confined to the northern half of the Yellow Sea and the Gulf of Chihli in order to defend the Chinese coast between Weihaiwei and the Yalu River. In addition to abandoning Korea to Japanese landings, this strategy foolishly relinquished at the outset any attempt to gain command of the sea and thus wasted China's most powerful naval asset, the Peiyang Fleet, by reducing it to convoy duty.[22]

Japan's strategy, though marked by caution, correctly assumed that command of the sea was critical to all that Japan hoped to achieve on land. It was imperative, moreover, that a decision at sea be reached quickly. An early victory would allow Japan to transport men and material to the Korean peninsula. Any prolongation of the war on land or sea would increase the risk of intervention by the European powers with interests in East Asia.

Reviewing the relative strengths of the two navies, Imperial General Headquarters (IGHQ, which was established at the outset of the war at Hiroshima to be closer to the naval base at Sasebo and military embarkation ports) drew up alternate military plans that would depend upon the course of the war at sea. The army's Fifth Division would land at Chemulpo (Inch' ŏn, Jinsen) on the western coast of Korea, both to press Chinese land forces northwest up the peninsula and to draw the Peiyang Fleet into the Yellow Sea, where it would be engaged in decisive battle. Depending upon the outcome of this naval engagement, Japan would make one of three military choices: If the Combined Fleet were to win decisively, the larger portion of the Japanese army would undertake immediate landings on the coast between Shan-hai-kuan and Tientsin in order to defeat the Chinese army and bring the war to a swift conclusion. If the naval engagement were a draw and neither side gained control of the sea, the army would concentrate on the occupation of Korea. Last, if the Combined Fleet were defeated and consequently lost command of the sea, the bulk of the army would remain in Japan and prepare to repel a Chinese invasion, while the Fifth Division in Korea would be ordered to hang on and fight a rearguard action.[23]

The naval high command believed that the decisive encounter at sea would be determined more by superior tactics than by superior quantity or quality of warships. Itō's tactical plans called for the Combined Fleet to enter battle in line ahead, with the fastest ships of the Standing Fleet—the cruisers *Yoshino*, *Takachiho*, *Akitsushima*, and *Naniwa* (all relatively new and plentifully armed with quick-firing guns)—organized into a "Flying Squadron" under Admiral Tsuboi in the lead. Approaching the enemy, the fleet, and particularly Tsuboi's squadron, would determine the weakest portion of the enemy's formation and launch an immediate and annihilating attack upon that portion, after which the fleet would turn its attention to the remainder of the enemy. Each ship captain was to refrain from firing until the range offered real prospects of success.[24]

BATTLE OF THE YALU
17 September 1894

These plans and arrangements were barely in place by the outset of the war. On 23 July 1894, as both nations began moving troops into Korea following disorders in Seoul, Itō slipped out of Sasebo with the Combined Fleet and entered Korean waters. This was one week before the formal declaration of war in either capital. Tsuboi's Flying Squadron, steaming up the western coast of Korea to intercept a Chinese convoy bringing troops to Seoul, stumbled into the convoy's small escort near P'ung Island, off Chemulpo, on 25 July, five days before war was declared. Tsuboi's detachment overwhelmed the weaker Chinese force, damaging an enemy cruiser, destroying a gunboat, capturing another, and sinking a loaded transport. This sequence of events—a naval attack preceding an actual declaration of war— became the pattern for the onset of each of the three major conflicts fought by modern Japan.

Emboldened by this minor victory, Itō took his force into the Yellow Sea to seek out the Peiyang Fleet. In brief demonstrations against the main Chinese bases, he bombarded both Weihaiwei and Port Arthur on 10 August. Finding only small ships in either harbor, the Combined Fleet returned to Korea to support further landings off the Chinese coast. The Chinese Court initially ordered Admiral Ting and the Peiyang Fleet to stay close to the Chinese coast while sending reinforcements to Korea by the circuitous land route. But the Japanese Fifth Division advanced northward from Seoul to P'yŏngyang so quickly that in mid-September the court was forced to reverse its policy and decided to rush troops to Korea by sea under Chinese naval escort.

Because there had been no decision at sea for or against Japan, IGHQ decided to send more army forces to Korea. Early in September, the Combined Fleet was directed to support further landings and otherwise support the army on Korea's western coast. As Japanese ground forces then moved north to attack P'yŏngyang, Itō and the Combined Fleet staff correctly guessed that the Chinese would attempt to reinforce their army in Korea by sea. At this juncture Admiral Kabayama, the impetuous chief of the Navy General Staff, was visiting the fleet on an inspection tour. Kabayama prodded Itō to seek out the enemy. On 14 September Itō took his force north to scour the Korean and Chinese coasts and to bring the Peiyang Fleet to battle. Sweeping northeast on 17 September, the Combined Fleet encountered Ting's force, which had just covered the debarkation of Chinese troops at Takushan, on the Manchurian coast some 60 miles east of the Yalu River. The ensuing naval combat, which took place off the Tayang River and Talu Island (map 2-1), was the first fleet encounter since the Battle of Lissa and only the second such engagement in the age of steam.[25]

Late in the morning, as the two opposing fleets of ten ships each approached one another, they assumed quite different formations. The Peiyang Fleet, intending to form a line abreast, through a confusion in signals and the differing speeds of its ships, came on in a ragged wedge formation, with the two battleships *Ting-yüan* and *Chen-yüan* at its apex and the weakest vessels at either end of its trailing flanks. The Combined Fleet approached in column with Tsuboi in the *Yoshino* leading the Flying Squadron, followed at an interval by the Main Squadron headed by Itō with his flag in the *Matsushima*. When the enemy was well in sight, Itō ordered, "Flying Squadron, attack enemy's right flank."[26]

The Chinese opened an uneven fire at 5,000 meters, a range far too great to do any damage, but the Japanese warships held their fire for another twenty minutes as they headed diagonally across the Chinese front at a speed twice that of the enemy. On signal from the commander, the Japanese squadrons divided. Increasing his speed from 8 to 14 knots, Tsuboi headed first toward the very center of the Chinese formation, a tactic that held the puzzled enemy in position. Then, turning slightly to

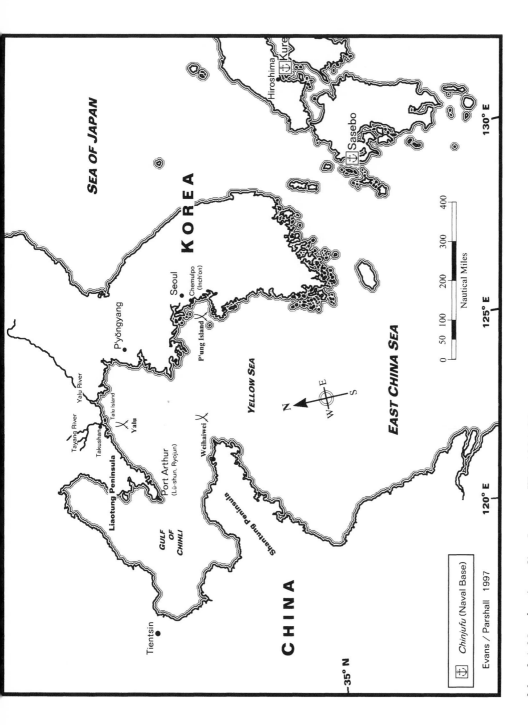

SEA OF JAPAN

Hiroshima

⚓ Kure

Sasebo ⚓

KOREA

Pyŏngyang

Seoul

Chemulpo
(Inch'on)

P'ung Island

Tayang River

Yalu River

Takushan

Talu Island

Yalu

Liaotung Peninsula

Port Arthur
(Lü-shun, Ryojun)

Weihaiwei

Shantung Peninsula

YELLOW SEA

EAST CHINA SEA

GULF
OF
CHIHLI

CHINA

Tientsin

35° N

120° E   125° E   130° E

N
W — E
S

0 50 100   200   300   400

Nautical Miles

⚓ | *Chinjufu* (Naval Base)

Evans / Parshall 1997

Map 2-1. Naval actions, Sino-Japanese War, 1894–95

port, he raced around the right flank of the Chinese formation to strike at the weakest units there. Holding fire until within effective range, the Japanese cruisers then used their quick-firing guns to shatter the two hapless sloops encountered. As Tsuboi's squadron then turned briefly northward to chase away feeble Chinese reinforcements emerging from the Yalu, Itō with the Main Squadron followed Tsuboi's initial course toward the Chinese left, but completed the turn all the way around to circle behind the Chinese rear. As Tsuboi's Flying Squadron once again turned south, the Peiyang Fleet was caught between two fires. Its slow speed and clumsy formation made it difficult for it to respond either by tactical maneuver or by gunfire. Itō's flagship, the *Matsushima*, opened with her starboard guns at 3,600 meters, though her single huge Canet gun failed to get off more than a few rounds. As the succeeding ships in the squadron neared the enemy, each opened fire in turn. The *Ting-yüan* and *Chen-yüan* in the center were naturally the focal point of the Japanese fire, but the armor of the two Chinese battleships resisted even the heaviest Japanese shells. The Japanese quick-firing guns, however, decimated the crews on their decks.

Tsuboi, meanwhile, had led his squadron back into the fray, sinking a Chinese cruiser that attempted to ram one of his cruisers. He then set off in hot pursuit of one of several ships on the Chinese left that, deserting their fleet, had fled toward the shallow waters to the north. Tsuboi successfully hunted down and destroyed a small Chinese cruiser, but so intent was he on doing so, that he inadvertently allowed the other demoralized Chinese vessels to escape.

By this time Itō was circling what remained of Ting's force at just beyond 2,000 meters. The two battleships and two cruisers poured in fire from his heavy guns and quick-firing guns that swept the decks of the Chinese ships and smashed their superstructures. But the Japanese also received some telling blows. The *Yoshino* was hit early in the afternoon, and the two weakest Japanese vessels, a gunboat and an armed steamer, were effectively put out of action. The *Hiei* also sustained serious injury. Owing to her inferior speed, her captain decided not to try to follow the Flying Squadron on its great sweep around the Chinese battle line, but instead to pass directly through the Chinese line. This maneuver made the *Hiei* an easy target, and she sustained a number of serious hits before she moved out of range. Yet the principal damage was to the *Matsushima*, which paid for her lack of armor when she was struck by two 12-inch shells that tore open the deck and ignited ready ammunition, causing nearly one hundred casualties and forcing Itō to transfer his flag to the *Hashidate*.

By sunset, Admiral Ting's force was near the point of total collapse: most of his fleet had fled or had been sunk and his two largest ships were nearly out of ammunition. Unaware of this last extremity, Itō had concluded that it would be impossible to sink the enemy battleships with the armament he had available. Moreover,

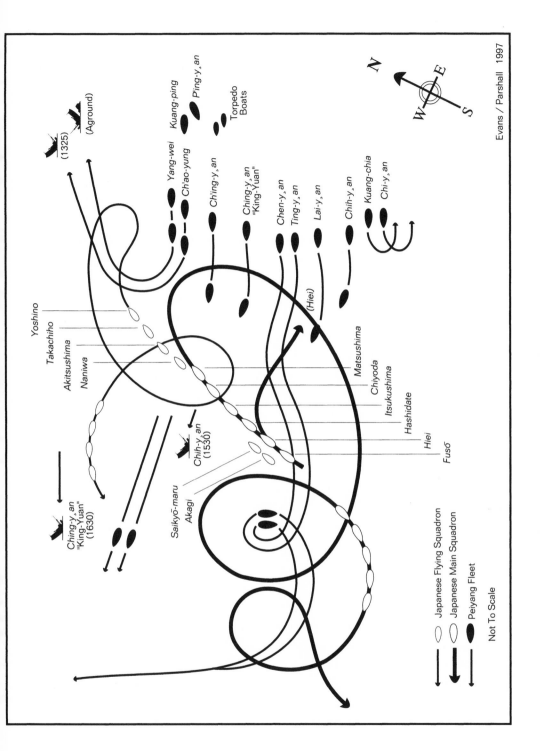

Fig. 2-1. The Battle of the Yalu. Because no track charts of the battle exist, this diagram is a schematic representation only, and is not to scale. (Based on drawings in the Japanese navy's official history of the war and on Shinohara, *Kaigun sōsetsu shi*, 388)

Evans / Parshall 1997

he feared a night attack by Chinese torpedo boats from Port Arthur. For these reasons, at 1730 Itō broke off the action and sent a signal to recall Tsuboi from pursuit of the fleeing Chinese cruisers.

Itō kept the battered remnants of the Peiyang Fleet in sight until dusk. Believing, as he later asserted, that the enemy would make for Weihaiwei, he set a course for that Chinese port. As later analysis now shows, it was illogical for him to have done so, since Port Arthur, to which Admiral Ting actually headed, was much nearer and had far superior docking and repair facilities. The historian John Perry, who has written the most detailed and comprehensive English-language account of the battle, believes that Itō chose this course because he did not really wish to continue battle. There were, Perry believes, several sound reasons for Itō's attitude: He had been unable to cripple, let alone sink, the Chinese battleships. By the damage the Chinese ships had inflicted on the *Matsushima,* the battleships obviously could sink anything the Japanese had afloat. Moreover, Perry noted, the Japanese ships and crews had been at sea for over two months and both needed a rest, and Itō, ever cautious, was wary of any further risk to the Combined Fleet.[27] Whatever the reasons, Itō's failure or inability to pursue and annihilate the enemy cost Japan a decisive victory, since the enemy's strongest warships, though battered, returned safely to base at Port Arthur, the nucleus of a fleet-in-being. Yet the Japanese had lost no ships, and only one of Itō's first-line vessels had received serious damage. Five ships of the Peiyang Fleet had gone down and the rest were in need of major repair.

Admiral Ting's respite was short-lived, however. At the end of October, the Japanese army, working closely with its sister service, made an unopposed landing on the eastern shore of the Liaotung Peninsula and moved rapidly toward Port Arthur, which fell on 21 November. A few days before, Ting had taken his ships across the Gulf of Chihli to Weihaiwei, where he was joined belatedly by warships from the other Chinese provincial fleets. There Itō blockaded him that winter, while Japanese army units made landings on the Shantung Peninsula. By early February 1895, the Japanese had captured the entire harbor shore, had removed the boom across the harbor's eastern entrance, and had captured the firing station for the mines outside the harbor. Now unimpeded, but operating in bitter cold, Japanese torpedo boats raced into Weihaiwei harbor in several close-in attacks during the nights of 3 and 4 February. The attacks, the first of their kind in East Asian waters, were pressed home so closely that the officer who led them, Lt. Comdr. Suzuki Kantarō, was nicknamed "the Demon." While the results were not spectacular (indeed, Suzuki's biography calls the second night attack a failure) they were unprecedented at the time: two hits on the battleship *Ting-yüan,* which was driven aground, and damage to a cruiser.[28] Ting ordered a breakout by the

Suzuki Kantarō

remainder of his force, but in the carnage that followed, only two ships escaped, the rest being captured or driven onto the rocks. Following his surrender, Admiral Ting committed suicide; two weeks later, China sued for peace.

Meanings and Portents

Because it was the first fleet encounter since Lissa, the Battle of the Yalu was scanned for its tactical lessons not only by the Japanese Navy General Staff, but by naval staffs around the globe. To a degree, these lessons were unclear, since the two fleet encounters in the age of steam seemed to cancel each other out: At Lissa, the victor had used the ram in a bows-on attack, line abreast, whereas the Yalu had been won by broadside naval gunfire delivered from line ahead. Moreover, the debate between the proponents of the big gun and advocates of armor remained unsettled by the encounter. Although the Canet guns of the *Sankeikan*-class cruisers had malfunctioned and thus the heaviest Japanese shells had not hit the *Ting-yüan* or the *Chen-yüan,* no other shells had penetrated their armor belts deeper than 4 inches.[29]

Yet some obvious conclusions could be drawn from the course and outcome of the battle. The first was that the line ahead was the formation that preserved the greatest flexibility and simplicity of movement, minimized tactical confusion, and maximized broadside fire. The case against the line abreast was not yet absolute, but certainly the wedge formation adopted purposely or accidentally by the Chinese could only have been effective in the hands of a commander whose ship captains had mastered fleet movements, which Ting's subordinates most obviously had not. Second, the one common denominator between Lissa and the Yalu appeared to be that the victor had fought in separated squadrons. This arrangement provided tactical flexibility and thus widened the options for maneuver during the chaos of battle.[30]

Of obvious importance in assessing the outcome was the Japanese superiority in speed.[31] Fast ships gave Tsuboi's Flying Squadron the perfect timing to cut across the enemy fleet's approaching path and to concentrate fire at the decisive moment on one of the weakest portions of the Chinese formation. Japan's superior speed also was critical in permitting Tsuboi to pursue successfully and destroy at least one of the fleeing enemy.[32]

Directly related to speed was the general homogeneity of a battle line. The Peiyang Fleet, a force composed of ships of quite different specifications, was woefully heterogeneous. The two or three slower and weaker vessels of the Combined Fleet paid a heavy price because of their inability to keep up or defend themselves.

Moreover, one of the principal factors in the Japanese victory was clearly its superiority in firepower, particularly an overwhelming advantage in quick-firing guns that proved to be devastating in the hands of well-trained and disciplined gun crews. This was not the same as a decisive advantage in gunnery, of course, since significant advances in fire control were still some years away. Thus, neither side achieved more than a fraction of hits out of the total number of rounds fired. Once longer-based range finders and director control were available, however, most naval tacticians would come to rely on the big gun rather than the smaller and shorter-range quick-firing gun, so clearly the winner at the Yalu.

The Japanese could draw specific tactical and technological conclusions from the encounter. Foremost, the tactical concepts propounded by Captain Ingles and Lieutenant Shimamura—use of the column, strict formation keeping, maintenance of narrow intervals, and concentration of gunfire—had been clearly validated in battle. The months and years of discussion and practice in working out those ideas had been rewarded by a victory that, if not annihilating, had certainly been decisive. Specifically, the formula of *shikikan sentō no tanjūjin* (line ahead with the commander in the lead), propounded by Ingles, urged by Shimamura, and carried out by Itō, became basic tactical doctrine in the Japanese navy from the Yalu up to World War II.[33]

Yet the results of the battle also made it clear that, in order to have a front-rank navy that could maintain command of the seas around it, Japan would have to acquire modern, heavily armed, and well-protected capital ships. Never again, Yamamoto Gombei demanded of the cabinet after the war, should the Japanese navy "go naked into battle, sword in hand against an enemy shielded by heavy armor." Armor would have to be combined with effective heavy ordnance in a design superior to that of any warship the navy then possessed. Certainly, Bertin's unstable *Sankeikan*-class cruisers with their single 12-inch Canet gun had proven a dismal disappointment in that regard. In almost four hours of battle, the Canet guns had fired a total of only thirteen rounds. Not only had the *Sankeikan* cruisers failed to play the decisive combat role expected of them, because of deficiencies in their ordnance, but the near destruction of the *Matsushima* had highlighted profound defects in their protection.[34]

On the other hand, the torpedo had proved to be at least a modest success. The deficiencies of these as yet primitive weapons had been overcome by the audacity and perseverance of the attackers. These "tactics" established a tradition of fearless close-in attacks by Japan's torpedo boats and later, by its destroyer forces, summed up in their slogan—*nikuhaku-hitchū* (press closely, strike home).[35]

As a whole, the Sino-Japanese War of 1894–95 shaped the thinking of the Japanese navy in important ways. To begin with, the course and outcome of the war strengthened the conviction of navy men that the navy had played the decisive role in the conflict. After all, they argued, it had been the navy's destruction of the Peiyang Fleet and the concomitant command of the sea that had permitted the army to land in perfect safety on the coasts of China in the last months of the war. Such proof appeared to strengthen the navy's ever-growing conviction that it was the more important of the two armed services. In the navy's view, wartime command arrangements at IGHQ had not reflected this reality. While the navy had worked effectively with the army in the conduct of joint operations on the Korean and Chinese coasts, the navy high command had chafed at having to take directions from the army-dominated IGHQ. After the war, Yamamoto Gombei, in particular, was determined to prevent this situation from occurring again in wartime. He seized the chance to do so when the "Regulations for Imperial General Headquarters in Wartime" came up for revision in 1899. In the ensuing heated interservice negotiations, he unsuccessfully attempted to argue for the independence of the Navy General Staff in war as in peace. Yamamoto was unrelenting in his determination to achieve complete autonomy for his service, however. In 1903, again using the crisis atmosphere of an impending war, he finally pressured the army into a reorganization of the IGHQ in wartime, which made the two general staffs totally independent of each other.[36] This independence, once established, opened the way for an equal, contentious, and unending tug-of-war between the two armed services for direction of the nation's grand strategy, for military spending, and for public enthusiasm and support. The struggle was played out in cabinet rooms, on the floor of the Diet, in lecture halls, and in the solemn treatises on national strategy and policy drafted by spokesmen and theorists on both sides.

The Sino-Japanese War also broadened the navy's strategic horizons. Heretofore the navy had lacked an overseas goal, being concerned only with the defense of the coastline of the home islands. But in the last months of the war, the navy had responded with alacrity to the opportunity to join in operations for the occupation of Taiwan (Formosa) and the Pescadores (P'eng-hu) Islands. With China's cession of these territories at the Treaty of Shimonoseki in 1895, Japan acquired a strategic dimension appropriate to the age of imperialism. Not only could the navy establish an important base at Makung (known to Japanese navy men as Bakō) in the Pescadores, but these new semitropical territories could now be considered as stepping stones for a *nanshin* (southward advance) of Japanese power, commerce, and influence into southern China, Southeast Asia, and the South Pacific. As articulated by its own spokesmen, the "southward advance" constituted a maritime alternative to the army's *hokushin* (northward advance) onto the Asian continent. Yet, because most of the region to which the advance was directed was already under the control or influence of Western powers, the *nanshin* concept at this period in the nation's history had only the most vaporous objectives. Indeed, it was far less a strategy than another argument with which to contend with the army for public attention and governmental appropriation.[37] It nevertheless became a navy dogma, unsupported by concrete planning, but eventually helping to shape the navy's thinking about the purpose and size of the fleet for which it argued.

Finally, the Sino-Japanese War provided the departure point for modern Japanese naval thought in the same way that American naval thought crystallized around the concerns of Mahan and the lessons of the Spanish-American War. Until that point, the navy's frame of reference had been entirely Western, and certainly, Western tactical ideas, now readily available in the numerous translations of Western naval commentaries, were still pervasive during the succeeding decade. Yet, a more purely Japanese naval doctrine also began to develop during the same period. The new doctrine was partly manifest in the almost incantatory use of certain catchphrases in official directives and regulations: *ka o motte, shū o sei-su* (using a few to conquer many), *kenteki hissen* (fight the enemy on sight), and others. The phrases were as much psychological in content as they were tactical.[38]

This semimystical approach to naval combat became a hallmark of much Japanese tactical thought from this period to the end of World War II. This is not to imply, of course, that Japanese naval thinking gave way to simple sloganeering. During the years 1894–1904, a body of thoroughly professional doctrine began to emerge, shaped by a nucleus of incisive, imaginative, and informed young officers who, working within the Naval Staff College, helped the navy prepare to do battle with its potential enemies at sea and with its service rival at home.

3

PREPARING
—for—
BATTLE

Japanese Naval Technology and Doctrine, 1895–1904

The jubilation in Japan following the Treaty of Shimonoseki, by which Japan gained and China lost Port Arthur and the Liaotung Peninsula, the island of Taiwan, and a sizable monetary indemnity, marked the apogee of Japanese optimism about its ability to realize its ambitions on the northeast Asian continent without interference. Russia, Germany, and France, alarmed by the sudden and single-handed success of Japan in altering the balance of power in northeast Asia, quickly demanded that Japan give up its most valuable prizes of the war: Port Arthur and the Liaotung Peninsula. Alone and unable to risk a war against the combination of Europe's most formidable land powers, Japan was forced to retrocede the port and the peninsula to China. Tokyo correctly guessed that Russia, long covetous of an ice-free port in northeast Asia, was the leading antagonist in this "Tripartite Intervention."[1] Within three years, all doubts on that score evaporated when Russia itself demanded and received from China a twenty-five-year lease on Port Arthur and the commercial port of Ta-lien (Dalny, Dairen).

At the same time, Russia began to assert pressure on Korea, traditionally regarded by Japan as a vital element in Japan's security and, since 1895, a special sphere of Japanese interest. Russian occupation of Port Arthur was an international humiliation for Japan; Russian occupation of Korea would be a strategic disaster. Should a Russian railway, connected with the Trans-Siberian Railway, be pushed down the Korean peninsula to supply an army of occupation and a Russian fleet be stationed on Korea's southern coast, Japan would find itself in extremis. A Russian fleet based at Chinhae on the southeast tip of Korea could coordinate with Russian naval forces in the Japan Sea, based at Vladivostok, or in the Yellow Sea, based at Port Arthur, and thus would make total the threat to Japan.

Japan was determined to prevent these ominous possibilities. Heeding the ancient Chinese admonition, *gashin shotan* (to "lie on kindling and lick gall"—to endure hardships for the sake of retribution), Japan set about with quiet but implacable determination to build such strategic strength that the nation's coasts would be secure and its interests on the continent would not again be thwarted. Two things were clear enough from the recent national humiliation. First, Japan would have to have sufficient military and naval power to challenge Russia for the hegemony of northeast Asia. Specifically, since control of the sea would be central to operations on the continent of Asia, Japan should have sufficient naval strength to defeat or bottle up whatever forces Russia might bring to northeast Asian waters. Second, it must seek the support of some Western power, so that in a future crisis, the nation would not again find itself alone in the international arena. In the nine years between the Sino-Japanese and Russo-Japanese Wars these two objectives were largely achieved with the help of Great Britain. British shipyards furnished the bulk of Japan's massive naval construction from 1895 to 1904, so that Japan went to war in 1905 with a largely British-built navy. Further, it was the Anglo-Japanese Alliance of 1902, largely naval in its implications, that assured Japan freedom of action without the interference of other maritime powers and encouraged the Japanese navy to think of dominating East Asian waters.

THE INCREASED PACE OF TECHNOLOGICAL DEVELOPMENT

Japan's decision to undertake a major naval augmentation program with British assistance was made within the context of a worldwide acceleration in naval technology that prolonged the uncertainties in naval tactics, naval training, and fleet organization in the last years of the nineteenth century.

There was, to begin with, the continued leap-frogging contest between armor and armament. In 1890, the American H. A. Harvey, improving on an earlier French discovery, had developed "nickel steel" armor plate that was approximately one and a half times as resistant as even the best iron armor. But Harvey armor plate was surpassed in 1894 when Krupp engineers added chromium and manganese to nickel steel. By following this with a special face-hardening forging process, the engineers had developed KC (Krupp cemented) armor, which possessed an extremely hard face and a tough and elastic obverse.[2]

These improvements in defensive armor inevitably spurred countervailing efforts in offensive armament. By the 1890s, advances in ordnance design and manufacture had led to the development of bigger, faster-loading, and longer-ranging guns. Among these advances were built-up gun construction pioneered by Armstrong Whitworth in Britain, improvements in hydraulic mechanisms for training and elevating the guns, and perfection of gun recoil and run-out arrangements. Similarly, radical developments in propellant charges led to the replacement of gunpowder by slow-burning "smokeless powders" that provided much greater muzzle velocity, reduced the weight of the charges, and improved visibility for more accurate gunfire. Single-base nitrocellulose propellants were first developed in France and quickly adapted by many other navies. The British developed the double-base propellant cordite, which consisted of nitroglycerine dissolved in nitrocellulose, with a small amount of petroleum jelly added. The invention of new fuses—percussion, time, and double-action—now made it possible to predetermine the timing for the detonation of naval shells.[3]

In the face of much harder armor plate, the shells themselves were improved to provide greater penetrating power. Armor-piercing (AP) shells were manufactured of chrome steel that went through a special heat treatment process to harden the point of the shell while the body retained its toughness. By the mid-1890s all navies were using APC (armor-piercing capped) shells. These were AP shells with a special cap of "soft steel" that took the initial impact and prestressed the target armor before the cap broke up and allowed the hardened tip of the main body of the shell to penetrate with maximum force.[4]

Although these developments had greatly increased the offensive power of the big gun battleship, at the end of the nineteenth century, the battleship's actual destructiveness was limited by the inadequate development of one kind of naval technology and actually threatened by progress in another. Great advances in naval ordnance, propellants, and shells had vastly increased the striking power of the naval big gun, but had widened the gap between its range—up to 10 miles at the end of the century—and its accuracy. The poor accuracy of the naval guns was largely because they were still sighted and fired on principles used by gunners well over a hundred years before and thus hit remarkably few targets. Not until mechanisms were devised for spotting shellfire, correcting ranges, plotting target course and speed, and coordinating the guns in a warship through a central system of fire control would this gap between firepower and accuracy be reduced.[5]

There was, moreover, increasing controversy over whether the big naval gun, or more precisely, its platform—the battleship—was still a viable weapon. The French Jeune Ecole viewed the battleship as an excessively expensive and exceedingly vulnerable warship type. Originally, the threat to the battleship had come from the smaller quick-firing gun, which by the 1890s came in calibers of up to 6 inches and fired up to ten 100-pound shells in less than fifty seconds, with the potential of annihilating enemy heavy gun crews operating unprotected in open barbettes. But the advent of far harder Harvey and KC steel armor plate and the covering of gun barbettes with armored hoods had thwarted this challenge.

Far more threatening was the rapid development of the self-propelled torpedo. Robert Whitehead's original invention of 1866 had been an underpowered and often erratically guided device, with a speed of not more than 6 knots. Through various improvements, by 1895 the torpedo had doubled in destructive power and had gained speeds of up to 30 knots at short ranges. Equally important, within a year or two, the incorporation of a gyroscope within the hull of the torpedo had given it directional stability and had reduced any deviation from course setting to less than one-half of a degree. The torpedo was now a fast and accurate (though not yet long-range) weapon to which unprotected hulls below the waterline were increasingly vulnerable.[6]

The destructive potential of the torpedo had necessitated a suitable warship to carry it. Thus, the torpedo boat had emerged in the 1870s. It was smaller, faster, and cheaper than any other warship afloat, and by the 1890s it appeared to threaten the existence of the slow-moving battleship, into which most maritime powers were pouring much of their naval budgets. Various defensive measures were summoned to the battleship's aid, including quick-firing guns and antitorpedo netting. But the former were hampered by the lack of any coordinating fire control, and the latter was effective only when a warship lay at anchor or was steaming slowly. The development of the torpedo boat coincided with the heyday of the tactical and strategic arguments of the French Jeune Ecole, for it was on the swift and inexpensive warship capable of dashing under the great guns and even the secondary batteries of the lumbering battleship that much of Jeune Ecole theory rested. Inevitably, the proliferation of torpedo boats in all the world's navies by the end of the century had led to an obsessive search for an effective counter weapons system. The British navy, which had the greatest investment in a battle fleet, had sought the development of another warship type that could chase torpedo boats at the same speed or better, but with guns that could sink its prey. But the first "torpedo catchers," built in 1887–89, were too slow or too frail for the job. They were succeeded in 1893 by the torpedo boat destroyer, a fast, seaworthy vessel capable of catching and destroying both torpedo boats and torpedo boat catchers. Unfortunately, these small warships were still cramped, thin-skinned and subject to great vibration. With the launching of HMS *Viper* in 1897, the true destroyer was born. The destroyer was a warship type of larger size, armed with guns *and* torpedoes, possessed of great speed, little vibration—due to its revolutionary steam turbine—and sufficiently economical in fuel consumption to serve as a genuine fleet escort, one capable of either attacking or defending heavy ships.[7]

Despite the development of weapons and weapons systems that seemed to challenge the supremacy of the battle line, the British navy was not deterred from its determination to maintain its lead in battleships over its two nearest rivals, France and Russia. With the navies of those two powers in mind, in 1895 Britain launched the *Majestic*, the first of a class whose unusually powerful main armament, well-arranged armor, 17.5-knot top speed, and 7,600-mile cruising radius (at 10-knot speed) gave these battleships unprecedented firepower, protection, range, and swiftness. Not only were the *Majestic*'s four hydraulically operated 12-inch guns a new type of compound construction, but their greater-than-usual barrel length for this caliber made them capable of firing shells with a muzzle velocity of over 2,300 feet per second. Theoretically, the shells could penetrate 18 inches of armor at 15,000 yards. The two barbettes into which these guns were fitted were equipped with central revolving hoists, and the guns themselves arranged to load at any angle of train, a novel feature at the time. The barbettes were covered with light armored hoods, an arrangement that eventually became standard for the main armament of all battleships. For antitorpedo boat defense, the *Majestic* carried twelve 6-inch quick-firing guns in armored casemates along the decks. The 9-inch Harvey nickel steel armor belt along the side was complemented by a 3-inch armored deck that protected the vital parts of the battleship.[8] In nearly every respect, the *Majestic* set a standard for offensive naval power for the next ten years.

The new developments in armor plate had also given a strong impetus to a lesser, yet major warship type—the cruiser. By 1880, the cruiser had evolved from a variety of fast vessels designed to prey on enemy commerce or to catch enemy raiders that attempted to destroy friendly shipping. Because of its tasks, the cruiser's need was for high speed and powerful armament, with little attention initially given to protective armor. In 1885, at its Elswick yard on the Tyne River, the firm of Armstrong furthered the development of this category of vessel by building a "protected cruiser" with high speed, powerful armament, and an armored deck that would provide at least some shielding for the ship's machinery, boilers, and magazines. While they were too light and not sufficiently seaworthy for the long-distance requirements of the British navy, the Elswick protected cruisers became extremely attractive for lesser navies like Japan, largely because of their apparent power and speed and the rapidity and relatively low cost with which the Elswick yards could deliver them. The French soon countered these warships with a somewhat heavier cruiser design that provided an armored belt along the sides of the ship, though the weight of the armor when the ship was fully loaded tended to drop the armor below the waterline, thus defeating its purpose. It was not until the introduction of the lighter but tougher Harvey and Krupp cemented armor plates that the first satisfactory armored cruisers were produced. In 1895, the Elswick yards built an armored cruiser that mounted much heavier armament, which was protected in individual casemates, and carried a steel belt varying from 5 to 7 inches along the side of the ship, as well as a protective deck at the lower edge of the belt. The protective deck was designed to stop any shells that might plunge through the unprotected sides of the ship above the armored belt. Like the earlier Elswick protected cruisers, the Elswick armored cruisers quickly became a model of cruiser design, widely sought by naval powers around the globe, including Japan.[9]

Thus, the end of the century saw the rapid development of naval technology, particularly guns, armor, torpedoes, and propulsion, and the concomitant development of battleships, cruisers, torpedo boats, and torpedo boat destroyers. Yet, without a decisive lead taken by any one technology, among all navies the fog of uncertainty continued as to the dominant weapon, the most effective fleet organization, and the most decisive system of tactics. For any government, the choice among these meant an enormous economic and strategic gamble. For Britain, the choices were narrowed by a century-long tradition of naval dominance and long-range strategic commitments. For a nation like Japan, newly embarking on the path to naval power, the selection of the right mix among these technological developments in building a modern navy was more difficult and required strong, decisive, and knowledgeable leadership.

YAMAMOTO GOMBEI AND THE "SIX-SIX FLEET"

As might be expected, it was Yamamoto Gombei who led the effort to commit the government to a naval buildup. The decade following the Sino-Japanese War witnessed both the dominance of Yamamoto in the navy and the emergence of Japan as a first-class naval power. Quick to exploit and manipulate public opinion, Yamamoto floated his plans for a massive naval expansion on the tide of popular enthusiasm for naval glory created by Japan's recent triumphs at sea. For the government, closer to reality, it was less a matter of glory than it was of survival. The Triple Intervention had underscored the extent of Japan's maritime weakness in relation to the West. Yamamoto, for one, was determined never to let this happen again. In 1895, while still chief of the Naval Affairs Bureau of the Navy Ministry, he drew up a proposal, to be submitted to the cabinet by Navy Minister Saigō, for a naval expansion program. Some expansion was to be funded by the indemnity paid by China as part of the settlement of the Sino-Japanese War.[10]

The centerpiece of this expansion was to be the acquisition of four new battleships in addition to the two battleships—the *Fuji* and *Yashima*—already being built in Britain under an earlier construction program. To supplement this battle fleet—Japan's first—the plan called for the construction of eight cruisers, four armored and four protected. The program also included the construction of twenty-three destroyers, sixty-three torpedo boats, and an expansion of Japanese shipyards and repair and training facilities. Approved by the cabinet in late 1895 and funded by the Diet in early 1896, Yamamoto's proposed program for a 260,000-ton navy was to be completed over a ten-year period, in two stages of construction. The first stage would begin in 1896 and be completed by 1902; the second would run from 1897 to 1905.[11]

As illuminated by Yamamoto's memorandum of explanation that he submitted with the original proposal to the cabinet, this naval construction plan was unprecedented in at least two ways. First and most obviously, it was by far the most ambitious naval building plan undertaken by the Japanese government. Whereas Japan had gone into the Sino-Japanese War with a makeshift force of warships, Japan would now have a true battle fleet. Second, while Russia was Japan's most likely enemy, Yamamoto chose to justify the navy's request by arguments that considered more scenarios than simply preparations for a war with Russia. Believing that Japan should have sufficient naval strength not only to deal with a single hypothetical enemy individually, but to confront any combined naval force that might be dispatched against Japan from overseas, Yamamoto included Britain and, to a lesser extent, France in his calculations. As he assumed that the conflict in their global interests made it highly unlikely that Britain and Russia would ever join together against Japan, Yamamoto considered it more likely that Russia or possibly Britain, in alliance with a lesser sea power like France or Germany, could dispatch a portion of its fleet against Japan. Calculating that four battleships would be the main battle force that either Britain or Russia could divert from their other oceanic commitments to use against Japan, and adding two more battleships that might be contributed to such a naval expedition by a lesser hostile power, Yamamoto came up with six as the magic number of battleships that Japan would have to have on hand.[12]

There remained the question of the size of battleships that Japan would need in order to face an enemy force with confidence. Here Yamamoto based his calculations on both geography and the world's foremost man-made strategic waterway, the Suez Canal. He noted that the depth of the canal (at that time) was only 27 feet and that the largest warships then being built—Britain's 15,000-ton *Majestic* class—had a mean draft of equal depth and therefore could not transit the canal. A battle fleet of such warships would have to pass around the Cape of Good Hope. Not only would this take time, but every European navy, with the exception of Britain's, would encounter considerable problems in coaling along the way. Moreover, establishing repair and docking facilities along the route and in East Asian waters for the largest warships would be an enormous expense for any nation.

Thus, for its minimum naval security Japan should have a force of six of the largest battleships supplemented by four armored cruisers of at least 7,000 tons.[13]

Today Yamamoto's reasoning conveys an air of unreality, including as it did the theoretical possibility of a war with Britain, with which Japan was then on the most cordial terms. Even his rationale for the number of enemy warships that might be sent against Japan seems based on rather hazy conjecture. Nevertheless, Yamamoto was clearly attempting to commit his government to a theoretical standard of naval power not unlike Britain's "two power standard" that had been reaffirmed in the British Naval Defense Act of 1889, and like that policy, his plan was based on capabilities, not intentions. Undoubtedly, underlying Yamamoto's attempt to establish such a standard was his desire to guarantee governmental support for a level of naval security that would be unaffected by the fickle nature of Japanese public opinion or by future political crises or cabinet changes. In making such an attempt, Yamamoto prefigured the thinking of Japan's foremost naval theorist Satō Tetsutarō (chapter 5) and set a precedent for material planning in the navy for the next two decades.[14]

The third distinctive feature of the 1896 naval expansion plan was its conscious projection of a quantum increase in the Japanese navy's qualitative strength relative to all other naval powers. Specifically, the four battleships to be built under the plan were to be more powerful in armament and armor than any other warships afloat, those of Britain explicitly included. Japan repeated this effort to gain a qualitative lead among the world's naval powers on several other occasions: when it constructed the *Kongō*-class battle cruisers on the eve of World War I, the *Nagato*-class battleships at the end of that war, and the *Yamato*-class superbattleships during the 1930s.[15]

Last, while battleship construction was the most dramatic feature of the expansion plan, Yamamoto was not simply recommending the building of a battle force. He was urging the assembling of a *balanced* fleet. Just as in the army the infantry was supported by the artillery, cavalry, and engineers, Yamamoto had argued, so battleships must be supplemented by lesser warships of various types. Specifically, this meant the inclusion of three classes of cruisers—armored, protected, and unprotected—that could seek out and pursue the enemy, along with a sufficient number of destroyers and torpedo boats capable of striking the enemy in his home ports.[16] (Here Yamamoto could only have been referring to the Russian Far Eastern Fleet.)

Given the kaleidoscopic changes in naval technology at the turn of the century, as well as the concurrent and rapidly shifting balance of naval strength among the maritime powers, it was inevitable that no sooner had the 1896 naval expansion plan been authorized than it had to be amended. The original program had called for the construction of four armored cruisers. Further consideration of Russian building plans led the navy to conclude that the six battleships authorized under the 1896 plan might not be sufficient after all, should the Russian navy decide to concentrate in East Asian waters. Yet budgetary limitations simply did not permit the construction of another battleship squadron. Since even a medium thickness of the new Harvey and KC armor plates could resist all but the largest AP shells, Japan could now acquire armored cruisers that could take a place in the battle line. Indeed, with the new armor and lighter but more powerful quick-firing guns, this new cruiser type was superior to many older battleships still afloat.[17] In the 1897 revisions to the ten-year expansion plan, therefore, provisions for the four protected cruisers were deleted and two additional armored cruisers were substituted in their place. Thus was born Yamamoto's "Six-Six Fleet"—six battleships and six armored cruisers—with which Japan jumped to become the fourth strongest naval power in the world in a single decade.

Japan's own industrial resources at the end of the century were by no means adequate for the construction of a main battle force of armored warships. Japan was still in the process of acquiring the industrial facilities—integrated steel plants, furnaces, and rolling equipment—necessary for the construction of heavy armor plate and the largest naval units. Thus, 90 percent of the 234,000 tons of naval construction contracted for under the ten-year beginning 1896–97 was to be foreign built and, when completed, would comprise 70 percent of the Japanese fleet. Of this tonnage, the overwhelming portion was built in British yards. British yards were used because most naval technological advances were developed, if not always initiated, by the British navy.

The first two of Japan's initial battleship force, the *Fuji* and *Yashima,* were already building in Britain and were not part of the 1896 expansion plan. Though they had been ordered prior to the Sino-Japanese War as a counter to China's two battleships, progress on their construction had been overtaken by that conflict. Even so, when they were completed and delivered to Japan in 1897, they constituted the largest and most powerful warships that Japan had to date possessed. An improvement on Britain's *Royal Sovereign* class, the *Fuji* and her sister, though lighter than the British original, had better speed (15.5 knots), more powerful 12-inch guns, and a higher rate of fire.[18]

It was the four new battleships, however—the *Shikishima, Hatsuse, Asahi,* and *Mikasa*—ordered from British yards under the 1896–97 plan and built in that order, that gave Japan a massive boost in its bid for naval power. Their basic design and specifications were similar to Britain's powerful *Majestic* class discussed earlier, yet each of the four, as it was completed, represented a greater improvement on the *Majestic* design. The improvements were because the greatly increased strength of the new KC armor made it possible to devise a different arrangement for protection that, in turn, led to a great saving in weight. At the same time, the Japanese navy had insisted on their complete compatibility with the two *Fuji*-class battleships in speed and gun calibers, so that all six ships could operate together as a single unit.[19]

Because of her remarkable specifications, the *Mikasa*, the last ship completed in this class, deserves particular attention. When completed at the Vickers yard in Barrow in 1902, the Mikasa was among the most powerful warships afloat. The ship possessed a main battery of four 12-inch cannon in two turrets, fore and aft, and fourteen 6-inch Elswick quick-firing guns. The main battery guns, worked by hydraulic or electric power (though they also could be worked by hand), could be loaded in any position at any elevation and could each fire three shells every two minutes. Her protection was just as formidable, since the strength of the KC armor plate permitted the thickness of the *Mikasa*'s main armor belt to be halved while maintaining a constant thickness over a much greater portion of her length to cover magazines and vital machinery. This rugged construction stood the *Mikasa* in good stead in the battles in which this famous ship was to take part.[20]

While British yards were working to complete Japan's main battle fleet, construction began on the Japanese cruiser force ordered under the 1897 revision of the ten-year expansion plan. The six armored cruisers called for under the plan were completed between 1899 and 1901: the *Asama, Tokiwa, Iwate, Izumo,*

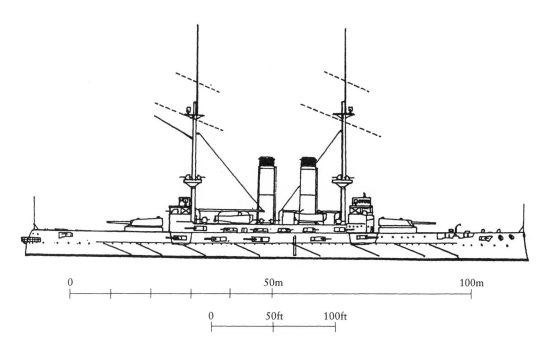

Fig. 3-1. The battleship *Mikasa*.

Azuma, and *Yakumo.* The first of these ships was ordered from Armstrong Vickers and built at the famous Elswick works, which had set a standard in cruiser construction for the past twenty years. The cruisers were fast, maneuverable warships armed completely with Elswick quick-firing guns (8- and 6-inch) and were amply protected above and below the waterline (with Harvey nickel steel for the *Azuma,* and KC steel for the *Izumo* and *Iwate).* The last two cruisers were built on the continent, the *Yakumo* at the Vulcan works in Stettin, and the *Azuma* at St. Nazaire. In order to insure ammunition compatibility, however, the Japanese stipulated that the two later vessels be armed with Elswick quick-firing guns.[21]

To supplement its six armored cruisers, the navy also acquired eight new protected cruisers in the decade before the war with Russia, 1894–1904. It is a mark of the progress of Japanese naval construction that five of these smaller warships were laid down in Japanese yards, built largely to Japanese designs (that were based on British concepts) and with Japanese materials, except for their armament of quick-firing guns, which were imported from Britain. Japanese naval constructors were learning their trade very well. Although the first of these cruisers, the *Suma,* was found to lack stability when completed, the Yokosuka and Kure navy yards were quick to make the necessary changes (greater freeboard and displacement) that improved the performance of the remaining ships based on the same general design.

Because of the relative success of Japanese torpedo boats in the final operations of the war with China and because the boats were regarded as potentially effective weapons against Russian ships in harbor, the 1896 Naval Expansion Plan also called for the creation of an even larger force of these vessels. Sixty-three of these small craft of various sizes were built on French, German, and Austrian designs and with materials provided by European yards, but they were largely assembled in Japan. Yet so rapid was the pace of technological change that the navy decided to cancel the orders for twenty-six of these boats and to substitute a lesser number of heavier torpedo boat destroyers. As Britain had pioneered this type, the Japanese navy ordered sixteen destroyers from British yards. In design and performance, they were almost identical to the superb "thirty-knotters" of the Royal Navy. By 1902, thirty-nine destroyers of similar design were being constructed at various Japanese yards.[22]

Notably even in its transitional stage, the Japanese armaments industry was beginning to turn out its own weapons, munitions, machinery, and explosives, as well as smaller warships. In 1896, the main naval arsenal had been moved from Tsukiji in Tokyo to Kure on the Inland Sea. The next year the Sasebo arsenal on Kyūshū's west coast was set up to undertake the completion, outfitting, and repair of warships. In the same year, with sufficiently large furnaces, presses, and steam hammers, the Kure arsenal was producing shell casings, mines, torpedoes, and gun barrels and mountings for large naval cannon, as well as quick-firing guns.[23]

Japanese specialists were also beginning to produce their own designs for machinery, munitions, weapons, and explosives. Much of these domestic advances in naval technology represented effort in research and development by the Japanese. Japanese engineers also developed their own designs for shipboard machinery and weaponry. Their Miyabara boiler, of simpler design and more reliable construction than foreign types, soon came into service. Working from basic foreign designs or information, the Japanese developed the Yamanouchi quick-firing cannon, the Oda mine, the Makimura torpedo, and the Kimura radio telegraph.[24]

In the area of naval explosives and ammunition, however, the navy made its greatest advances. By the late 1880s, the navy had acquired a new explosive for its shells that was far more powerful than any it had used before. Shimose powder was a Japanese variant of picric acid explosives, developed by the French.[25] The navy capitalized on the new explosive by maximizing two of its characteristics, the high pressure and the extreme heat of its blast. This was accomplished by designing a new type of shell to contain the charge. Whereas the trend of the world's navies had been toward thick-jacketed AP shells for use in battleship main ordnance, the Japanese began to produce new thin-skinned shells—known popularly in the navy as *furoshiki* shells, after the thin Japanese kerchief or wrapping cloth. The *furoshiki* shells allowed more weight to be allotted to the explosive charge (10 percent of the total weight of the shell as opposed to 2–3 percent for AP shells) and thus produced a far greater bursting effect. Finally, a research committee headed by Adm. Ijūin Gorō developed the Ijūin fuse, located at the base of the projectile, which caused the shell to explode upon impact, rather than after it had penetrated enemy armor. Apparently, the thinking behind the navy's adoption of this device was that it would maximize destruction of the unarmored but vital above-deck components of a warship and cause maximum casualties to its crew. This approach ran counter to contemporary naval tactics, which stressed the importance of inflicting internal damage by AP shells. In any event, the three technologies together—Shimose powder, the *furoshiki* shell, and the Ijūin fuse— proved awesomely destructive in the naval combat of the Russo-Japanese War.[26]

Domestic construction of warships developed somewhat more slowly, but by the beginning of the twentieth century, Japanese development of the largest armored warships was hindered only by the immaturity of the country's steel industry. With the help of British firms like Vickers, steel production in Japan soon doubled and private capital moved into the new industry to supplement governmental efforts. The total capacity of the nation's steel plants was still small, and until World War I made such imports impossible, most building materials for

Japanese naval shipyards were still imported from Europe. Nevertheless, in 1901, the first armor plate was manufactured in Japan, and the launching of the armored cruiser *Tsukuba* at the Kure Navy Yard at the outset of the Russo-Japanese War showed that Japan was approaching independence in naval armaments production.[27]

By 1902, the 1896–97 expansion plan was well under way. To Tokyo's dismay, however, renewed international tensions in Europe had generated a new round of naval competition among the Western maritime powers that threatened, by chain reaction, to erode Japan's new position of naval strength. Kaiser Wilhelm's naval aspirations were manifested in his nation's Fleet Law of 1900, designed to lay the foundations of a great navy. While directed principally to challenging British naval supremacy, the announcement of Germany's naval expansion also sent shock waves through Russian naval circles. That country, already in the midst of a major augmentation of its navy, now embarked upon a larger and accelerated program of naval construction that in turn was viewed by Japan as a threat to its security. Taking into account these new building programs, as well as those of the United States, France, and Italy, the Japanese naval leadership estimated that if nothing were done to match the foreign construction, Japan's naval position would slip from fourth to seventh by 1908. For this reason, the Japanese navy was obliged to submit a supplemental third stage to the original plan, now clearly justified by using Russia as the standard for Japan's required naval strength. Approved by the Diet in 1903, the supplemental plan called for the construction of three more battleships and three armored cruisers, though the numbers were eventually expanded to four and four. Work on these additional warships had just begun when relations between Japan and Russia rapidly worsened in the autumn of 1903. As a stopgap measure, the navy rushed to buy two powerful 7,600-ton armored cruisers, the *Kasuga* and *Nisshin*. The cruisers had just been completed in Italy and had originally been intended for Argentina.[28]

On the eve of the Russo-Japanese War, therefore, Japan had acquired truly formidable naval strength. Not only had Japan regained its position as the world's fourth largest naval power, it had built a well-balanced naval force of six battleships, eight armored cruisers, sixteen protected and unprotected cruisers, twenty destroyers, and fifty-eight torpedo boats.[29] In assembling this navy, Japan's naval leaders, particularly Yamamoto Gombei, had shown sound judgment in choosing among the world's trends in warship development, as well as correctly interpreting the lessons of the Sino-Japanese War. In his explanation of the 1896–97 expansion plan, Yamamoto had confirmed that the purpose of the plan was to gain command of the seas around Japan. He had argued that this could only be accomplished by a main battle force of armored warships. One commentator on Japanese naval history has noted that Japan, in thus opting for a Mahanian battle fleet, had demonstrated a better understanding of the purpose of a fleet than several other countries. China had used its fleet in 1894–95 largely as transport for its army. France at the time viewed the fleet only as a raiding force, and Russia (necessarily perhaps) thought of naval power principally in terms of dispersed naval commands that were local in orientation.[30]

Yamamoto had also clearly seen the value of the smaller auxiliary units in the Sino-Japanese War. Although the armored ships were vital in taking command of the sea, the smaller auxiliary units played an important part as well. These units carried out the relatively successful torpedo boat attacks on Chinese warships in harbor in the last days of the war. Finally, the superb design and fighting ability of the navy's individual warships, largely British built, were of critical importance. While the Japanese navy was superbly led and bravely manned in the coming conflict, no element was more important in Japan's victory at sea in 1904–5 than the quality of its warships.[31]

THE ANGLO-JAPANESE ALLIANCE

Despite this unprecedented increase in Japanese naval strength, the growth of the Russian navy posed serious problems. Japan could not contemplate the prospect of war with the world's third greatest naval power if the latter were to be allied with another maritime nation. The Tripartite Intervention of 1895 had taught Japan that a junction of hostile Western battle fleets in East Asian waters was a possibility. The surest means to reducing this risk seemed to be for Japan to initiate its own alliance with a European naval power. Britain, which had its own reasons for wishing to deter the expansion of Russian interests in Asia, seemed the perfect partner. Mutual interest, therefore, was at the core of the Anglo-Japanese Alliance of 1902. While the alliance did not commit either side to come to the aid of the other in case of hostilities with a single enemy, it did guarantee such support in the case of two or more antagonists. Japan gained not only the prestige of being linked to the world's foremost maritime nation, but also the freedom of action to plan hostilities against Russia without having to worry about the intervention of a second hostile power.[32]

The main import of the alliance, in any event, was political and strategic. While there is no evidence that the Japanese navy had pushed exceedingly hard for the arrangement, its leaders, like their opposite numbers in Britain, were the most enthusiastic advocates in the country in support of the treaty. The main framework of naval cooperation between the two countries was worked out in consultations at Yokosuka and London by representatives of the Japanese and British navies. Although the concrete details of combined wartime operations were lacking, provisions were drawn up not only for a concentration of allied fleets in East Asian waters, but also for the disposition of those fleets. The disposition included a system of maneuvering for a mixed force under British and Japanese commanders or an Anglo-Japanese fleet under a single commander, as well as for an exchange of intelligence and the provision of mutual facilities for docking and coaling.[33]

Ultimately, both sides were disappointed in their long-range and mutually incompatible expectations concerning the treaty. The Japanese had hoped that Britain would maintain a number of battleships and cruisers in East Asian waters equal with that of Russia; Britain resisted the idea of commitment to any particular force level. The British had hoped that increased Japanese naval strength in East Asia would allow the Royal Navy to withdraw most of its large ships to British home waters to help face down the rising naval challenge from Germany.[34]

But in the short run, the alliance proved very advantageous to Japan. Although the provisions of the treaty were never invoked during the Russo-Japanese War, Britain did lend Japan support and encouragement in various ways, including assistance in the purchase and transit of the armored cruisers *Nisshin* and *Kasuga* from Italy to Japan under the temporary command of two British officers.[35] Even more importantly, the alliance alleviated, at least temporarily, a critical problem of fuel for the navy.

JAPAN'S FIRST NAVAL FUEL CRISIS
Not Enough Coal

The birth of the modern Japanese navy had coincided with the age of steam and the use of coal as the main source of propulsive energy. Hence, the navy's fuel came from the plentiful lump coal in Japan. As early as 1872, the navy had set up a coal supply center in Kyūshū, and as the navy grew in size, its coaling requirements increased. By 1886, it was obliged to undertake a nationwide survey of the nation's coal resources. Nearly forty coal reserve sites were consequently identified and designated as such by the navy, their exploitation to be undertaken only in case of emergency. It was estimated that these new fields could produce about two-thirds of the navy's daily needs during wartime.[36]

But Japanese lump coal was low-quality bituminous. When burned it threw off prodigious clouds of black smoke that could be seen by the enemy and obscured signaling between friendly ships. Furthermore, the coal had a low heat value and hence was not really suitable for naval use. In briquette form, some bituminous coal was effective, but in the 1890s, the technology for coal briquette production did not yet exist in Japan. Thus, as Japan wrestled with the problem, it began to import good Cardiff coal from Britain, which soon supplied approximately one-fourth of the navy's annual energy needs. During the Sino-Japanese War, however, in order to reduce its dependence on overseas supplies, the navy used Japanese lump coal exclusively, though this reduced the power of Japanese warships. In the event, the loss of power was not critical in facing an inferior navy, but among the lessons of the war, the Japanese learned the importance of building adequate supplies of British coal while continuing efforts to make Japanese coal more efficient. By the eve of the Russo-Japanese War, the navy had managed to stockpile about 650,000 tons of coal, but little headway had been made on the technology of making briquettes from domestic coal. The prospect of going to war with a ranking naval power with inadequate domestic coal stocks on hand must have daunted Japan's naval leadership. At the last moment, however, thanks to the new treaty with Britain, the navy acquired an additional half million tons of superior British coal, a supply that enabled the navy to overcome a serious energy crisis as it entered hostilities with Russia.[37]

GETTING THE NAVY TO THINK
Akiyama Saneyuki at the Naval Staff College

While the navy was acquiring a battle fleet, it was also developing a sophisticated tactical understanding of how to use it. Indeed, it was the near decade between the Sino- and Russo-Japanese Wars that saw the maturation of modern Japanese tactical doctrine based as much upon the navy's combat experience and its own experimentation as it was on foreign example.

A flowering of naval thought took place, largely at the Naval Staff College, whose influence had been expanding since its founding in 1888. In its infancy, prior to the Sino-Japanese War, the institution did not play a great role in the genesis of Japanese naval tactics. The establishment of institutions of higher naval education was itself a recent world phenomenon: the U.S. Naval War College had only been established in 1884, and other nations had only recently followed suit.

In Japan, the emergence of the staff college as the generator of naval thought was due in large part to the initiative of one individual, Sakamoto Toshiatsu, a member of the Navy General Staff who had extensive training in France early in his career. In 1896, already renowned as the navy's "French scholar," Sakamoto was sent by the Navy General Staff to investigate the organization, courses, and teaching methods of the newly founded French Naval War College. Upon his return in 1897, he was made senior instructor at the college. Three years later he took charge at the college, first as acting president and then as president, 1902–4.[38]

During those years, Sakamoto undertook to change the fundamental character of the college through a series of reforms based not only on his personal observations in France, but also on a comprehensive institutional survey, under his direction, of advanced professional study in all the major navies of the world. His reforms broadened the sphere of recruitment to the college by eliminating prior sea duty as an entrance requirement, but he also restricted entrance to men who had good service records, were physically fit, and had passed an exacting intellectual

Sakamoto Toshiatsu as a rear admiral

screening process. He shifted the emphasis of the curriculum from technical and scientific study to the study of strategy and tactics and related fields. Central to Sakamoto's curricular reform was his division of instruction at the college into two principal course programs—a two-year "A" (or, in Japanese, *kō)* course for midcareer officers and a six-month "B" *(otsu)* course for junior officers—as well as an engineering course and an elective course (for continued professional training tailored to the individual interests of the officers selected). The "B" course was open to lieutenants and limited to instruction in the theory of gunnery, torpedo technology, and navigation, any of which might be followed by intensive practical training at one of the navy's various technical schools. Far more important from a professional and career standpoint was the "A" course, limited largely to officers approaching flag rank who had passed the "B" course as well as a rigorous selection process. Completion of the "A" course became a major step in a line officer's career, opening as it did the path to staff position and eventual flag rank.[39] This instructional structure remained in place with few changes in later years and came to play an important role in shaping not only the career paths in the navy, but the evolution of Japanese naval doctrine.[40]

Among the principal subjects taught in the "A" course during the decade or so when Sakamoto was connected with the college were general tactics and strategy, military and naval history, naval organization, warship design and construction, ordnance, naval engines, coastal fortifications, and international law.[41] But the most important contribution of the "A" course to the development of Japanese naval doctrine was its emphasis on *ōyō senjutsu* (applied tactics) that centered on practical problems, the solutions to which were sometimes sought from senior officers in the navy and sometimes from the students themselves.

Critical to this approach was Sakamoto's selection of the brightest, most experienced, and most articulate specialists in the navy to serve as instructors. Among these were officers like Lt. Comdr. Yamaya Tanin, a rising gunnery and torpedo specialist with fresh tactical insights, the aforementioned Capt. Shimamura Hayao, who had presided over the genesis of Japanese naval tactics at the Seiken Temple and Shimizu Harbor a decade before, and Lt. Comdr. Akiyama Saneyuki, one of the most brilliant tactical and strategic thinkers in the history of the Japanese navy.[42]

Yamaya Tanin, an officer of scholarly disposition, was one of the first of Sakamoto's "brain trust" at the college. While an instructor there (1899–1902) his chief contributions to its rapid improvement were his assiduous collecting of relevant naval information and his tactical innovations. It was largely to Yamaya that Sakamoto left the task of collecting information on higher naval education in the major Western navies, and Yamaya's comprehensive surveys on this subject enabled the Japanese Naval Staff College to stay abreast of the latest institutional and pedagogical developments at its American, British, French, and German counterparts. Yamaya was one of the first instructors at the college to experiment with new fleet tactics that went beyond Western precedents and were original Japanese contributions to the evolution of naval tactics worldwide.

Shimamura, mixing analyses of past combat with the insights of others, as well as with his own knowledge and experience, was one of the first instructors at the staff college to teach applied tactics. In developing instructional materials, he would often seek answers to certain tactical problems from Yamamoto, Itō, and other navy top brass. Such an inquiry by a mere captain would be inconceivable in later years. At other times he would pose tactical questions to the class and ask the students to prepare essay answers to solve them, a pedagogy already in use at the U.S. Naval War College.[43] It was in large part the essays prepared by "A" course students in response to the questions posed by instructors like Shimamura

Hayao that provided the Navy General Staff the basis for the earliest version (1901) of the *Kaisen yōmurei* (Battle Instructions), the ultimate formulation of officially sanctioned tactical thinking in the Japanese navy.[44]

Yet the most profound tactical influence at the staff college during these years, and indeed one of the greatest influences throughout the Imperial Japanese Navy for the rest of its history, was that of Akiyama Saneyuki, its most brilliant, most forceful, and most influential staff officer.[45] One of two illustrious brothers of the Meiji period (his elder brother went on to a distinguished career in the cavalry), Akiyama graduated from the academy in 1890. Though he missed an early opportunity for combat experience in Japan's war with China (his ship was on detached duty during the Battle of the Yalu), Akiyama would make his mark as a tactician, strategist, and planner. Like Mahan, he was less a professional fighting man than a naval intellectual devoted to the study of history and philosophy. He was more interested in the principles of war than in the fighting of it. This early interest, stimulated undoubtedly by the unresolved tactical and strategic questions of Japan's naval victories of 1894–95, led him to read voraciously in the naval treatises of the time and the great works of Western military literature, as well as the ancient Chinese classics of Sun Tzu and Wu Tzu.

In 1897, after torpedo training and a stint in the Intelligence Bureau of the Navy General Staff, Lieutenant Akiyama was sent for a two-year tour of duty in the United States, where he hoped to absorb the essentials of American naval doctrine and technology. But the doors of American naval education, which had once been open to Japanese naval officers, had swung shut. Unable to enroll in either Annapolis or the Naval War College at Newport, young Akiyama proved brilliantly resourceful. When he approached Alfred T. Mahan directly for advice on how to advance his professional education, the famed strategist gave him an expanded list of the most relevant and important works in Western naval history. Far more important, by writing directly to Assistant Secretary of the Navy Theodore Roosevelt, he obtained abstracts of the courses taught at the Naval War College (by pointing out that as the Japanese legation in Washington had past issues of the abstracts, it was hardly logical to treat them as classified information now). Then, in 1898, at the outset of the Spanish-American War and through the intercession of the Japanese legation in Washington, he sought and received permission to serve as a foreign observer aboard an American vessel during the blockade and destruction of the Spanish fleet at Santiago.[46]

Akiyama's observations while serving with American forces in the Caribbean were crucial to the professionalization of the Japanese navy. His comprehensive, detailed, and polished reports to the Navy General Staff in Tokyo on the Cuban campaign raised intelligence reporting in the Japanese navy to a real art. His efforts culminated in his famous Secret Intelligence Report 118 on Sampson's victory at Santiago, which for years remained a classic source of information on the U.S. Navy for Japanese naval planners. When he returned to shore, he passed along all sorts of intelligence about Sampson's fleet, as well as handbooks, technical manuals and articles, and a stream of books on American naval matters.[47]

Akiyama's return from America could not have been at a more fortuitous time for the Naval Staff College, since it came at the end of an unsuccessful search by the college for qualified foreign instructors in naval strategy and tactics. Originally, Sakamoto had thought that when the various new principles, terms, and schools of naval strategy and tactics were beginning to permeate professional discussions in all the world's navies, it would be well to hire foreign specialists with current expertise in all these subjects and who could sort them out for a Japanese naval audience. The idea of hiring British instructors had been set aside, since the Japanese navy had recently smuggled secret technological information out of Britain and the navy brass did not wish to risk the chance of this espionage being uncovered by any inquisitive British adviser. While French and German experts were a possibility, too few Japanese officers had a working knowledge of the relevant languages. This left only the Americans. Approval to hire Mahan himself was given by Yamamoto, but the prospect never materialized.[48] At this point, Sakamoto, now admiral and president of the staff college, turned to Akiyama, whom he had met in the United States and who had impressed him with his wide-ranging knowledge and his astutely analytical approach to naval study. In July 1902, Lt. Comdr. Akiyama was appointed instructor on tactics and strategy at the college, succeeding Yamaya Tanin. At thirty-four, Akiyama was only about a year older than the oldest of his students.[49] He taught until called away in November 1903 for service with the Combined Fleet. After the Russo-Japanese War, he served another tour of duty as instructor at the college from November 1905 to February 1908.[50]

Akiyama's arrival at the staff college marked the beginning of independent Japanese naval thought—influenced by Western naval thinking, certainly, but free to move out into its own channels. His first contribution was to organize and classify the diverse elements of contemporary tactics and strategy into a systematic study of naval warfare that had practical applicability in the advanced training of Japanese officers. At a time when navies around the globe were faced with the task of sorting out competing theories that related strategy, tactics, and technology, this was a task of great difficulty and great importance. Akiyama began by standardizing naval terms so that students at the college could, when they reached important positions within the fleet, communicate in a common professional language as they drafted battle plans or received operational orders. Written up in a widely distributed pamphlet, Akiyama's terms and explanations of them—*senryaku* (strategy), *senjutsu* (tactics), *sakusen* (operations), and such—were unexceptional and conformed largely to Western practice. Yet it was the first time that they had been clearly identified and their importance made clear to students of naval science in Japan.[51]

Several terms, however, were original in concept and for some time remained peculiar to the Japanese navy. The most important of these was *semmu,* often translated as "logistics." But where the latter term is taken to mean the science of providing and maintaining men, equipment, and supplies for military operations, Akiyama broadened it to mean, in effect, the "conduct of war"—the standard operating procedures for all tasks and evolutions short of combat, including such things as training, communications, the drafting of operational reports and battle orders, as well as what we now know as logistics. This third classification for the study of naval warfare initiated by Akiyama at the staff college—the other two being strategy and tactics—was unique to Japanese naval education at the time. Akiyama himself considered his contributions in this area to have been most important; after the Russo-Japanese War, he said, with an excess of modesty, "What I contributed to my country was not strategy or tactics but *logistics, semmu."* (He used the English word before the Japanese to make his meaning clear.) [52]

Influenced by the rigorous and meticulous planning that he had witnessed in the better American operations, Akiyama's approach to naval warfare relied on thoroughly planning operations rationally and scientifically. Central to this approach was a technique that had become common in the advanced military establishments of Europe: preparation of a "situation estimate" gauging the various elements of an approaching operation—weather, strengths of opposing forces, possible courses of action, and such. The analytical tool used by the Japanese Naval Staff College to prepare the estimate was the same as that used by the Americans at Newport: war-gaming.

War-gaming was the laboratory method for teaching strategy and tactics and for testing plans and doctrines. Exercises were worked out on large tables with ship models and markers to simulate real combat conditions, with rules of engagements and battle damage, and with umpires to judge the results.[53] At the staff college at Tsukiji, Akiyama instituted a similar method of tabletop war-gaming that became the standard practice for instruction and for working out naval problems in the Japanese classroom. To a limited extent, the technique had been used by Shimamura and Yamaya during their years as instructors at the college, but now Akiyama developed war-gaming to a high art. He began by dividing war-gaming into two activities. For the study of strategic problems, Akiyama developed *zujō senjutsu* (map exercises, or literally, map tactics) that used huge horizontal board maps of northeast Asian waters. Across them, student officers had to move fleets, consider the naval strengths and resources of a hypothetical enemy (usually Russia), and deal with the countless problems included in Akiyama's "conduct of war." For the decisive clash between fleets, the students would move to a separate game board marked off in squares for *heiki enshū* (tactical war-gaming). There the players practiced gun battles and torpedo attacks, first between individual ships, then between squadrons, and finally between fleets. They were watched closely by umpires who pronounced rules and announced losses. At the end of the game, instructors would give the students an extended critique. In this way, Akiyama led students to confront the hazards and opportunities of battle between fleets, between torpedo squadrons, and between forces of different strengths or speeds. They also learned the problems of cooperation with land bases, protection of transports, support of landings, and a myriad of other combat situations.[54]

War-gaming, however, was not only a technique for instructing future naval commanders and staff officers. It was a laboratory method for testing tactical and strategic concepts. On the great game boards of the staff college, many of Akiyama's ideas on tactical maneuvers, night attacks, fleet formations, principles of engagement, and use of supporting forces were worked out. Once perfected, many of these ideas became embedded in the Battle Instructions. Occasionally conducted in the presence of the emperor himself, the staff college war games, over the decades, provided the navy with the same sort of organized, practical application and analysis of naval theory being undertaken by American naval planners.[55]

Akiyama did more than import the newest and most relevant insights on naval doctrine from abroad. He also devised means to combine contemporary Western concepts with military classics from China and Japan. An avid student of Sun Tzu, he derived from the strategist of ancient times the general military principles concerning deception, concentration, "indirect attacks," and the like. More interesting still was his use of the insights of Japan's own maritime tradition. Introduced to the literature of medieval "water force" tactics by Lt. Comdr. Ogasawara Chōsei of the Navy General Staff, Akiyama became intensely interested in these classical texts that set forth certain tactical ideas that apparently prefigured modern formations (including the column), techniques (night attacks), and principles (including concentration of forces).[56] The Western historian might be skeptical about assigning the same degree of importance to these classical sources in the naval successes of the Russo-Japanese War as did Ogasawara and more recent Japanese commentators.[57] The medieval sources clearly influenced Akiyama, nevertheless, and it was Akiyama who provided much of the strategic and tactical planning by the Japanese navy in that war.[58]

But beyond the devices, maneuvers, and tactics that these ancient Japanese texts suggested, Akiyama found in them a concern with the intangible elements of combat—psychological, moral, spiritual—that he believed must be part of Japanese naval doctrine. Much of even the early writings of this Japanese naval officer was abstract and even mystical. Akiyama's approach was not unique, of course. His emphases, for example, on the importance of human will in combat and the importance of making the enemy yield rather than annihilating him bear similarities to certain ideas of Clausewitz. Yet surely few Western naval officers would have mixed into their professional lectures such frequent references to the influence of the intangibles in war. In later years, this abstract and psychological element became dominant in Akiyama's thought and foreshadowed a mystical quality in Japanese military thinking as a whole before and during the Pacific War. The mysticism was manifested most clearly in the assertions of inevitable victory over the United States through divine intervention.[59]

A last element in Akiyama's critical place in the formation of Japanese naval thought was the sense of authority that he brought to his lectures at the Naval Staff College. Until his arrival, there had been few instructors who had read widely in foreign naval doctrine and none who had witnessed modern naval combat outside the Sino-Japanese War. Now, with his store of personal observations on the conduct of modern naval warfare and with his command and instant recall of a wide range of naval information, Akiyama dramatically raised the level of professional inquiry and understanding at the college. Within a few years he was joined by other outstanding instructors, such as the torpedo tactician Suzuki Kantarō and the naval historian Satō Tetsutarō. Yet it was Akiyama who did more than anyone else in the history of the Naval Staff College to make it one of the finest centers of higher naval education in the world and to make the Japanese navy competitive with other navies in the development of tactical and strategic theory.[60]

THE EVOLUTION OF JAPANESE NAVAL TACTICS, 1895–1904

Within the context of this heightened professional competence as the new century opened, the tacticians at the Japanese Naval Staff College began to turn their attention to the major tactical problems of the day. They were influenced undoubtedly by what they knew of similar study and thought in Western navies, yet worked independently toward practical solutions. During these years, staff college tacticians reached the same conclusion as their counterparts in other navies, that the column or line ahead was the most advantageous formation for a decisive fleet engagement. First suggested in fleet exercises in the early nineties, then confirmed by the navy's victory at the Yalu, its continuing validity was demonstrated repeatedly in war games by Akiyama and other instructors at the college. Yet, for tacticians the world over, the line ahead formation posed serious problems. For example, it was unsuitable as a cruising formation in the age of the torpedo, since an extended line of warships was obviously more vulnerable to torpedo attack than a line abreast. Other problems presented themselves: How did a commander move from a cruising formation to a column? Where in the column should he place himself? Perhaps most difficult was the problem of how to overcome an enemy column of equal strength. In a battle fought on parallel courses victory would depend on which side had more guns or superior gunnery. But if one side could concentrate all the firepower of most of its ships against the enemy—an activity made possible by the advent in the latter half of the nineteenth century of long-range naval guns mounted in rotating turrets—while preventing him from doing the same, victory would be almost inevitable.

At the Japanese Naval Staff College Lt. Comdr. Yamaya Tanin first worked on these problems and first suggested a solution that would concentrate firepower against an enemy column in the shortest possible time while keeping him within range. Critical to Yamaya's thinking was the assumption that Japanese ships would be faster than their opponents. (The tactical effectiveness of superior speed had received dramatic confirmation in the Sino-Japanese War—and thenceforth became an article of faith in the Japanese navy.) Yamaya foresaw a Japanese column of warships heading toward an enemy column. When the two fleets had closed to 5,000 meters, the Japanese flagship would turn either to port or to starboard so that the Japanese column began to describe a circle as it moved forward. Yamaya guessed that the unsuspecting enemy would consider the movement odd, but would initiate no counter movement of his own. The Japanese ships would meanwhile continue on their circular course, so that within a minimum amount of time all the ships in the Japanese column could bring their guns to bear upon the head of the enemy column while only a few of the enemy's ships could concentrate against the circling Japanese. For this brief time, the Japanese fleet would have maximum opportunity to inflict major damage on the enemy (fig. 3-2). Should the enemy turn instead of holding to course, supposedly the Japanese van would immediately inscribe a circle in the opposite direction, to bring the enemy van under fire from all the ships in column for at least a period of time.[61] Yamaya's *en senjutsu* (circle tactics) appeared sufficiently promising that they were extensively tested in war games at the staff college in 1901.[62]

Those pondering the problem realized that the ideal position for achieving such a concentration would be to place one's column at right angles to the enemy's column, so that, in effect, it formed the top bar of the letter T. In the British navy, Admiral "Jackie" Fisher had employed this tactic during the maneuvers of the Mediterranean and Channel fleets in 1901. In his report to the admiralty in September of that year, Fisher wrote that "the lesson that has been emphasized is that the one all important, immediate imperative step is to form the Fleet *in one single line at right angles to the direction* in which the enemy is sighted. How far we can

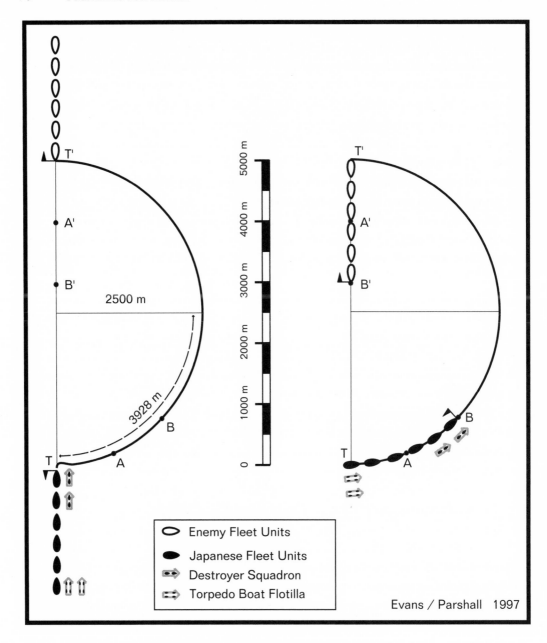

Fig. 3-2. Yamaya's circle tactics. (From a Japanese manual)

keep this a secret remains to be seen. If both sides practice this golden rule and employ the single line of Bearing then the Fleet with the superior speed must win, that is *Battleships of superior speed.*"[63] The Japanese could not have been far behind the British in their appreciation of the T disposition, because Capt. Shimamura Hayao gave a lecture that explained the tactic in detail at the Naval Staff College in 1902. He maintained that the tactic was already being practiced in fleet maneuvers.[64] At the Japanese Naval Staff College the T tactic was tested in war games played under Akiyama's direction. In them, Akiyama demonstrated that when two columns in line ahead were approaching a common point on converging courses, the column closest to that point would have the advantage because it could bring more guns to bear upon the other. The greater the angle of convergence (up to 90 degrees) between their courses, the greater the advantage to the closer fleet. The ideal situation would therefore be to place one's own column at right angles across the enemy's line, thus forming the letter T (fig. 3-3) .

In this classic position of "capping the T" a maximum number of one's own guns could bear upon the enemy, while he, by virtue of his position, was limited in the number of guns with which he could respond. (Experiments at the college showed that rarely would the T be capped perfectly; more often the victor would achieve a position more like the top bar of the Japanese katakana phonetic symbol *I*, in which the cross bar is at an angle). [65]

The tactic of capping the T, or as the Japanese called it, *tei sempo,* "the *tei* tactic" (after the Chinese character *tei),* soon became the tactical holy grail sought by naval commanders worldwide. But questions remained: how could one maneuver most rapidly to achieve this position, and in achieving it, what maneuver would best minimize the effects of changes in the enemy's range and course?

During the war-gaming sessions at the college, Akiyama noted that the T tactic often failed because of the enemy's ability to turn away: "The problem with the 'T' formation is that it is very difficult to maintain for any period. One way to maintain it is to carry out simultaneous turns of eight or sixteen points [45 and 90 degrees] in timely fashion."[66] Another solution of Akiyama's, called the *otsu* tactic because of its resemblance in shape to the Chinese character *otsu* (somewhat like an L in the Roman alphabet), was a deceptive maneuver designed to produce a converging attack. Using it, the Japanese fleet would approach the enemy in two separate formations. While the first engaged the enemy directly (attempting to cap the T), the second, approaching from an unexpected quarter, would position itself to catch the enemy in a crossfire. The two forces would each form one leg of an L, encircling the enemy and preventing him from escaping. Akiyama wrote, "The tactic for opposing a single enemy flag line is the *otsu* tactic, in which we subject the enemy to a scissoring attack . . . . Once we have succeeded in maneuvering in

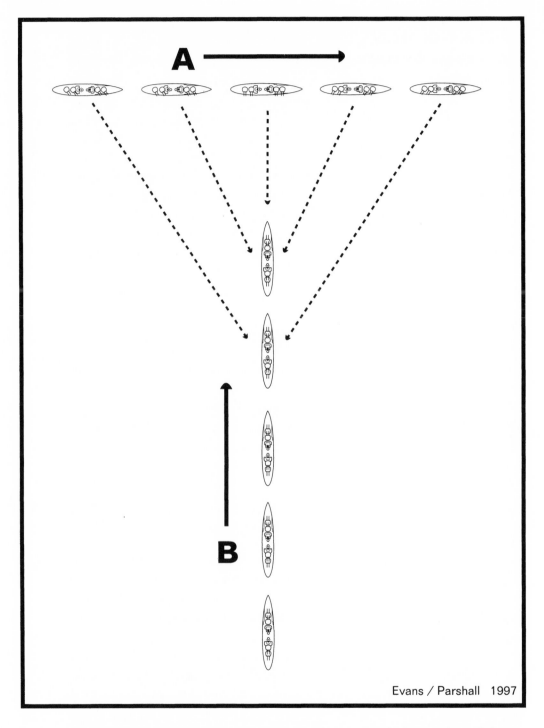

Fig. 3-3. Crossing the "T." Fleet A concentrates all its guns on the leading ships of Fleet B, which has difficulty replying because only its forward guns can be brought into action and the fire of its rearmost ships is obstructed by its leading ships. Not to scale.

this [L] formation against him, we can deal him a mortal blow."[67] This concentrated attack upon the enemy (fig. 3-4), tested on the war-gaming boards of the staff college and then practiced at sea, was incorporated into the navy's accepted battle tactics.[68]

THE JAPANESE NAVY AND THE DAWN OF FIRE CONTROL

During the decade preceding the Russo-Japanese War, naval powers had generally recognized that the potential of the relatively new rifled steel naval guns, especially at long range (greater than 2,000 meters), was not being exploited. But in order to do so, naval gunners needed to know accurately the range to the target and, with comparable accuracy, the internal ballistics (such as barrel wear and powder temperature) of the gun, the external ballistics (the motion of the projectile after it left the gun as affected by gravity, air resistance, wind, etc.), and the difference between the present or range finder range and the gun range at which the projectile was expected to hit the target. The difference between these ranges depends on the dead time (from the last range observation to the firing of the gun) plus the time of flight of the projectile and the courses and speeds (or the relative course and speed) of the firing and target ships.

None of this was well understood at the end of the nineteenth century, but around 1900 there appeared the first glimmerings of modern naval fire control—the entire process of directing a gun in such a way as to hit the target. Eventually, it came to be understood that the surface fire control problem essentially was divided into five major elements: target tracking and position prediction, interior ballistics, exterior ballistics, computation, and correction. Of these, only exterior ballistics and deck motion were reasonably well understood. Captain Percy Scott's invention of a continuous aim system in 1898 had partially solved the problem of deck motion in the employment of smaller guns. The most significant progress in target tracking in the years before the Russo-Japanese War was the development of optical single-observer range finders—most notably by the British firm of Barr and Stroud—and the adoption of telescopic sights to replace open sights. By the early 1900s, the majority of the major warships of the world's navies were equipped with both these important devices.[69]

By the time of the Russo-Japanese War, the Japanese navy had made significant progress in keeping up with the latest developments in fire control. Its principal warships were well supplied with Barr and Stroud range finders, some ships having as many as six of these important instruments.[70] Range tables (firing tables) for guns were supplied by the firm of Armstrong and provided at least rudimentary data for ranges at various elevations. The navy's gun sights were calibrated for the ballistics of the gun system and had been fitted with telescopes to

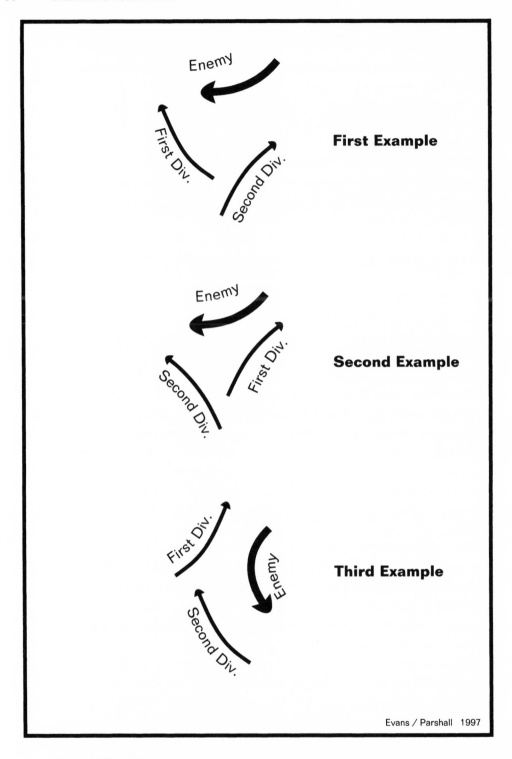

Fig. 3-4. The "L" tactic.
(Source: Battle Plan of 9 January 1904; see *NRKK*, 1:388)

improve their performance. The major deficiency in the navy was the incomplete understanding of the importance of the change of range associated with the relative motion of the firing ship and the target. As it turned out, the immature understanding of this aspect of the fire control problem was not crucial to the outcomes of the major naval engagements of the war. Most firing during the two main battles of the war was done while Russian and Japanese ships were on approximately the same courses and making approximately the same speed, so that target range and bearing changed relatively slowly. In any event, while Japanese naval fire control on the eve of the Russo-Japanese War apparently was somewhat behind that in Britain and the United States, it was on a par with, or even slightly ahead of, that of the Russian navy.[71]

THE COMBINED FLEET REORGANIZED

In the autumn of 1903, as Japan was in the last stages of its ultimately futile negotiations with Russia over political arrangements in northeast Asia, the navy began its organizational preparations, fleet exercises, and tactical training in anticipation of impending naval conflict. The first step was the reorganization of its main battle force. On 28 December the Standing Fleet was deactivated, and in its place, the Combined Fleet reactivated as the navy's main battle force. The Combined Fleet comprised two fleets of two battle divisions each: the First Fleet, composed of all six of Japan's battleships, plus four protected cruisers; and the Second Fleet, which included the navy's six armored cruisers, plus four lesser cruiser types. Separate from these two was the Third Fleet, made up of various lesser warship types and a collection of obsolescent vessels. This arrangement of the navy's main units—the heavily-gunned First Fleet and the somewhat lighter, faster ships of the Second Fleet—established a principle of combat organization in the Japanese navy that continued up to the Pacific War in 1941.[72]

To command the Combined Fleet Yamamoto Gombei picked Adm. Tōgō Heihachirō, then serving as commander of the naval base at Maizuru. At first glance it seemed an unlikely choice. Tōgō had made no dramatic impact in the navy and, because of recurrent illness in midcareer, had actually been considered more than once for retirement by the Navy Ministry. But Tōgō had seen extensive action in the naval combat of the wars of the Meiji Restoration, had trained in Britain (where he had come to revere Horatio Nelson), and had extensive service at sea, where he was recognized as a taciturn but competent officer.

Tight-lipped and imperturbable as Tōgō was, and enshrouded as he is now by legend and the great mantle of hero worship that his biographers have heaped upon him, it is still difficult to estimate his ability.[73] The apparent consensus before the war was that he was only an average officer. Common opinion held that

Tōgō Heihachirō at the time of the Russo-Japanese War

another admiral, like Hidaka Sōnojō or Shibayama Yahachi, known as *môshô* (fierce) and *yûshû* (bold) commanders, would lead the navy in the coming conflict. Yet Tōgō had a reputation as a "good luck admiral"; in combat, he had an unerring knack for making what turned out to be the right decision at the right time. When asked by the Emperor Meiji why Tōgō should be appointed commander of Japan's battle fleet, Yamamoto reportedly replied: "Because Tōgō is lucky."[74]

Tōgō was obviously more than just lucky. Yamamoto picked him apparently for his tactical skill, his composure, and his cool calculation in wartime, first demonstrated in the *Kowshing* incident years earlier. On 25 July 1894, as the first shots in the war with China had just been fired, Tōgō, in command of the cruiser *Naniwa* in the Yellow Sea, discovered the British merchantman *Kowshing* loaded with Chinese troops making for Chemulpo. He forced the vessel to heave to and sent officers aboard to investigate. During the several hours of negotiation that followed it became clear that the Chinese would not allow the British officers to surrender the vessel. Tōgō looked carefully into provisions of international law during the lull. Then, after recovering his officers from the *Kowshing,* he sank her with gunfire. Loud protests followed, especially from Britain, and Tōgō was summoned to Tokyo for conversations with Yamamoto. His actions were found to be justifiable under international law.[75]

In the intervening years, the officers in Tokyo, and in particular Yamamoto, became impressed with Tōgō's character, which combined caution with resolution. Typical in this regard was Tōgō's reply to a circular memo from Yamamoto to all fleet and base commanders in early 1903, seeking opinions on the timing and form of naval operations against Russia. Tōgō's response was one of the few that expressed optimism, but at the same time he recommended caution, urging that decisions to open hostilities be made on the basis of careful study of the respective naval strengths of Japan and Russia, rather than on national sentiment.[76]

With his flag in the battleship *Mikasa,* Tōgō also assumed direct command of a First Fleet that, with its six battleships, was the backbone of the Combined Fleet. The subordinate commanders of the Combined Fleet were largely battle-tested veterans. Rear Adm. Dewa Shigetō, who took command of the First Fleet's cruiser squadron, had been captain of Adm. Itō Yūkō's flagship at the Battle of the Yalu. To command the Second Fleet, the navy selected one of its most forceful figures, Vice Adm. Kamimura Hikonojō, a thorough fighting man whose combat experience in the battles of the Restoration and as a cruiser captain in the Sino-Japanese War rivaled Tōgō's own. Kamimura was bold, outspoken, and dogged, qualities he would sorely need during the misfortunes that attended his early command of the Second Fleet. His two squadron commanders, Rear Adm. Misu Sōtarō and Rear Adm. Uriu Sotokichi, were also officers with extensive sea experience.

The staff officers of the Combined Fleet were as well qualified as their commanders. As his chief of staff, Tōgō chose the navy's tactical pioneer, Capt. Shimamura Hayao, and as his senior staff officer, Capt. Arima Ryōkitsu. The senior staff officer had considerable knowledge of Russian naval strength, particularly concerning the Russian base at Port Arthur. As special staff officer with responsibility for operational planning, the obvious choice was Akiyama Saneyuki. This professional expertise was duplicated in each of the four divisions of the Combined Fleet, where most staff officers were top-ranking graduates of the Naval Staff College who had studied under Akiyama. Thoroughly conversant with Akiyama's tactical and strategic ideas and with his planning for specific naval operations, these staff officers were an indispensable link in the effective execution of those plans in wartime.[77]

In the autumn of 1903, with all its battleships and armored cruisers ready for service, the Combined Fleet began training in earnest at its main base at Sasebo. There the fleet constantly practiced weighing anchor as a fleet, running at high speed using carefully conserved Cardiff coal, firing at various ranges, embarking and debarking troops, and evacuating wounded from the shore. Particular attention was paid to torpedo tactics, coastal ambushes, and night attacks carried out by destroyers and torpedo boats.

Of great importance, too, was the perfection of communications within the fleet, since radio telegraph equipment had been installed in all ships larger than destroyers that year. This new communication system, whose rapid adoption by the navy symbolized the Japanese genius for adapting the latest foreign technology, was of vital importance in the Russo-Japanese War, which marked its first use in naval combat. In 1897, having observed firsthand the capabilities of radio telegraphy in the United States, Akiyama had sent a memo to the Navy Ministry urging that the navy push ahead as rapidly as possible to acquire the new technology. The ministry became actively interested, but found the cost of the Marconi wireless system, then operating with the British navy, to be prohibitively expensive. The Navy Ministry therefore turned to its own expertise, setting up a radio research committee, which eventually produced an acceptable system. In 1901, having attained radio transmissions of up to 70 miles, the navy formally adopted the radio telegraph. Two years later, it set up a laboratory and factory at Yokosuka to produce Type 36 (1903) radios, and in a race against time, these were installed in every major warship in the Combined Fleet by the time the war started.[78]

One of Tōgō's foremost concerns about communications before the outbreak of war against Russia was the laying of submarine cable from Japan to new fleet bases. Tsushima (already connected to the Japanese main islands) was the starting point for cables planned for Chinhae, the Hakkō anchorage off southwest Korea, and locations on the west coast of Korea. Tōgō wanted immediate and secure communications for the fleet and for this purpose depended largely on cable transmissions.[79]

TACTICAL PLANNING

Because of his reputation and his expertise, Akiyama Saneyuki, first as an instructor at the staff college and later as a staff officer with the Combined Fleet, was at the center of operational planning to defeat Russian naval forces in northeast Asian waters. Indeed, Shimamura Hayao, his immediate superior for the first half of the war, stated flatly: "There was not a single major operational plan of the war that was not drafted by Akiyama."[80] Shortly after his assignment as staff officer with the Combined Fleet Akiyama was given the responsibility of drafting the secret operational plan that would guide the fleet in the decisive battle with the Russians. His *Rengō kantai sensaku* (Combined Fleet battle plan) was completed on 9 January 1904 and distributed to all units of the fleet.[81] In the plan, under Tōgō's name, were set forth the responsibilities, the formations, and the movements for each unit of the Combined Fleet. The First and Second Divisions (the battle-ships and the armored cruisers), constituting the main force, would be responsible for the destruction of Russian battleships, armored cruisers, and protected cruisers; the Third and Fourth Divisions were to account for the smaller enemy cruisers and destroyers and to annihilate isolated or damaged warships. Finally, the destroyers and torpedo boats were to await the opportunity to attack the retreating Russian fleet.

The First and Second Divisions were to carry out the T and L tactics, for which detailed instructions and diagrams were provided. Akiyama's plan directed that "the First Division will choose the formation of the enemy that is easiest to attack, forming a line against it, a 'T,' . . . maneuvering so as to put as much pressure as possible on the enemy's lead ship; it will make efforts to maintain the T formation with respect to the enemy by carrying out simultaneous turns as appropriate."[82] Regarding the L tactic it specified, "The Second Division will pay attention to the enemy's movements with the aim of carrying out a cross-firing or scissoring attack on the enemy formation that is engaging the First Division. It will maneuver as appropriate, either following the First Division or taking an opposite course, so as to form the letter 'L' with the First Division . . . . Our two divisions will then carry out a fierce attack on the enemy with crossfire."[83] The plan also included tactical instructions for each division by its commander that essentially echoed the movements described above. Significantly, after the war, Tōgō himself affixed the following note to the text of the Battle Plan in the navy's secret and exhaustive history of the war: "The Battle Plan described for the Combined Fleet and each of its Divisions was the basis of all engagements in this war. From the Battle of the Yellow Sea to the great Tsushima Battle and other, smaller clashes in between, there was not a single action not based upon it."[84]

MATTERS OF STRATEGY
Planning the Opening Move

Japan's leaders tolerated the Russia's presence in Manchuria for a considerable time, but Russia's contravention of agreements to evacuate troops from Manchuria and its infiltration of Korea in 1902–3 were cause for alarm. In June 1903, an imperial conference concluded that "we must solve the Korean question . . . . We cannot concede to Russia even a part of Korean territory, no matter what the circumstances."[85] "Solving the Korean question" meant war, and Japan's initial strategy for that war was set forth in the army's "Operation Plan for War against Russia" of December 1903. The plan specified that the first campaign would be the Japanese capture of Korea. Once the army's position there had been consolidated, a second stage would begin, and further operations might be launched, "north of the Yalu." For the navy, protecting army expeditionary forces, rather than a fleet battle, would be the paramount concern at the outset. According to the Navy Staff (and probably reflecting Tōgō's opinion) the main enemy fleet at Port Arthur would avoid serious action. The Korean campaign would have to proceed "without depending on a decision at sea."[86] Yet once the first campaign was over, Japan would have to reckon with the Russian navy, including possibly the Baltic Fleet. It would be enough from that point onward, however, if Japan could demonstrate to Russia that the cost of retaking Korea was too high.[87]

The planners of the Japanese navy recognized from the first that the relative situations of Japan and Russia would make any conflict between them regional rather than global. Neither nation had worldwide command of the sea, neither had maritime colonial possessions scattered across the globe and vulnerable to enemy seizure, and neither conducted oceanic trade sufficiently important to make practical the strategy of high-seas commerce raiding. For all these reasons, as well as for the configurations of Japanese and Russian geography, the war would inevitably be restricted to northeast Asia, a fact that inherently worked to the disadvantage of the Russian navy in terms of geography and distance. To begin with, Russia's Far Eastern Fleet was separated from Russian naval headquarters and the other two Russian fleets (the Baltic and the Black Sea) by the earth's greatest land mass. This would make it impossible for Russia to bring its total naval strength against Japan at the outset of war.

Moreover, the Russian Far Eastern Fleet itself was divided between its squadron in the Yellow Sea, based at Port Arthur, and its squadron in the Japan Sea, based at Vladivostok. Between these two forces lay the Korean peninsula and the Korea Strait. A Japanese fleet based either in the Korea Strait or nearby on Kyūshū or at the western tip of Honshū would hold interior lines of communication and could move against either of the two Russian squadrons.

The first strategic problem facing the Japanese navy, therefore, was how to hold the Korea Strait in order to prevent the junction of the Port Arthur and Vladivostok squadrons. Three different war games centering on this problem took place at the Naval Staff College from 1900 to 1902. Early in 1903 grand maneuvers were held off the west coast of Kyūshū to test the navy's readiness to repel a Russian attempt to force the Korea Strait.[88] The second problem had even more ominous implications. By 1902, Russia had accelerated its naval construction program, and at the end of 1903 the number of battleships in its Far Eastern Fleet exceeded those of the entire Japanese navy. Should the Baltic Fleet, distant though it might be, somehow successfully transit half the globe and join forces with the Far Eastern Fleet, the prospect for a Japanese naval catastrophe might be very real.

Akiyama and other Japanese naval planners at the staff college who pondered the problem concluded that the inherently disadvantageous Russian naval position in northeast Asia would dictate an essentially passive Russian strategy. They believed that Russia would attempt to preserve its Far Eastern Fleet for as long as possible. When the opportunity presented itself the larger Russian Pacific Fleet at Port Arthur would probably sortie out to damage portions of the Japanese fleet or to prevent Japanese troop landings on the west coast of Korea. The smaller Vladivostok squadron might seek to lure portions of the Japanese fleet toward the defenses of that base, but neither squadron would attempt to bring the Japanese navy to a decisive encounter until reinforcements in the form of the Baltic Fleet arrived from European waters. Until then, the two squadrons in East Asian waters would comprise a "fleet in being" that would continue to constitute a potential threat to a Japanese expeditionary army on the Korean peninsula; to the security of the coasts, ports, and harbors of the Japanese home islands; and to the Japanese fleet itself. These dangers were spelled out in prophetic detail in a lecture on "The Russian Navy and Its Adjacent Seas" given at the staff college in 1902 by Lt. Comdr. Tanaka Kōtarō, who had just returned from a year in Russia, where he had studied Russian and carried out intelligence work.[89]

The naval leadership was concerned about the possibility of Russian armored cruisers from Vladivostok slipping through the Tsugaru Strait to threaten Tokyo, Osaka, and other ports along the Pacific coast. Nevertheless, the Japanese high command refused to consider a diversion of warships and, leaving the coastal defense of Japan largely to observation towers, land-based artillery, torpedo units, and naval garrisons, held fast to the strategic priority of opposing the principal Russian naval force in East Asia.[90] Just before the war began, Tōgō was asked about the threat to northern Japan from Vladivostok. He replied with characteristic nonchalance that there were "no particular countermeasures to be taken." He suggested dispatching torpedo boats from Yokosuka to the Tsugaru Strait, but said, "We should let the enemy do as he wishes at Otaru [a Hokkaidō port] for a while."[91]

From the outset of the planning process, navy staff officers recognized that the warships at Port Arthur posed the greatest threat, partly because Russia had chosen to base all the battleships of its Pacific Fleet there, and partly because the Port Arthur base was closer to the anticipated combat theaters in Korea and Manchuria. (The west coast of Korea was the more likely for Japanese landings since, as compared to the east coast, it had more and better harbors and more useful lateral roads.) Vladivostok, with its larger docking facilities and its two harbor channels admitting easy access, was in some ways superior. But because it was icebound part of the year and too remote (except for raids against Japanese coasts), it remained a subsidiary Russian base.[92]

During these years, Japanese naval intelligence services provided the navy with a wealth of information about the Russian Far Eastern Fleet in general and Port Arthur in particular. One reason for the high level of Japanese preparation against

Russia before the war was that Japanese intelligence concerning Russia was wide-ranging and accurate, while Russia was hampered by the lack of similar information on Japan.[93] In addition to the notorious exploits of Col. Akashi Motojirō of the Japanese army, the navy collected an enormous amount of information from various sources. Since 1894, the Intelligence Bureau of the Navy General Staff had been collecting information on the coastlines of East Asia. This data went into a classified and regularly updated publication on foreign ports, anchorages, islands, and facilities. Much of this information was provided by Japanese warships patrolling the coasts, some by Japanese merchant vessels going in and out of Vladivostok, and some by naval officers who made clandestine on-site observations along the coasts of Manchuria, the Liaotung Peninsula, and the Russian Maritime Province. Through the Japanese naval attachés in St. Petersburg (Yashiro Rokurō and Nomoto Tsunaaki), the General Staff intercepted a good deal of Russian maritime cable traffic. Japanese commercial companies abroad passed on information about Russian vessels in the East Indies and those transiting the Suez Canal. Much intelligence about Russian naval organization and naval bases was collected by naval officers sent to Russia for language training. Among the latter were Lt. Comdr. Tanaka Kōtarō, who gave the prescient lecture on Russian naval strategy; Lt. Comdr. Katō Kanji, future chief of staff; and Lt. Comdr. Hirose Takeo, who died a hero's death in an ill-fated Japanese attempt to block the entrance to Port Arthur.[94]

From this information, navy planners realized that Port Arthur had several serious defects as a naval base: it had no major docking facilities and thus was inadequate for repair of damaged warships; the channel from the inner to the outer roadstead was long, narrow, and too shallow to allow passage of large ships at low tide; the roadstead was not easily defended; and if the port were captured and surmounted by enemy artillery, the inner harbor was commanded by heights that could bring any warships in harbor under direct bombardment.[95]

Keeping in view the passive strategy of the Russian Far Eastern Fleet, the apparent weaknesses of its chief base at Port Arthur, and the possibility of the dispatch of Baltic Fleet to East Asian waters, Japanese navy planners debated their options for an effective opening move of the war. The Navy General Staff in Tokyo, despite its official estimate of Russian passivity, tended to favor a conclusive fleet action at the start. This view was represented by the staff's most active member, Vice Chief Ijūin Gorō, who foresaw a decisive fleet battle with the Russians despite Tōgō's objection that the Port Arthur fleet might not make itself available. For this eventuality Ijūin contemplated a direct attack on Port Arthur by the Japanese battle fleet. Consonant with this plan, the army, hoping to gain the benefits of early sea control, had even agreed that the navy should strike the first blow of the war. (There was considerable resentment in the army over being forced thus to follow the navy's lead).[96]

Comdr. Arima Ryōkitsu was the senior member of Tōgō's Combined Fleet staff. Backed by Akiyama, his immediate subordinate, Arima developed a novel approach to the opening attack on Port Arthur based on his personal knowledge of the harbor: sealing off the port with blockships. He had drawn up a detailed plan for sinking ships in the harbor mouth before a declaration of war, and in October 1903 the staff ordered him to begin preparations for the operation in utmost secrecy. By December, he had five blockships ready at Sasebo for a surprise assault on Port Arthur.[97]

Tōgō himself differed with Arima and the staff in Tokyo. For one thing, Tōgō was convinced that the Russians would be reclusive and stay bottled up in their harbors. For another, he believed that at the start of the war, complete control of the sea was not necessary and probably not possible; the navy's role in the combined operation of invasion should not be distracted by making Port Arthur a primary objective. Cover at some distance from the Russian naval forces at Port Arthur, along the southern and eastern Korean coasts, would be sufficient during the first phase of the war, when Korea was invaded and then secured. The Third Fleet, of course, would guard the Korea Strait against the Vladivostok Squadron.[98]

As war approached, the question of how the navy was to conduct its initial operations became urgent. Ijūin wrote Tōgō in mid-December 1903, asking for his opinions. The Navy General Staff believed the Russians would "avoid a decisive battle for the time being" but might "pick a time to unite the Vladivostok and Port Arthur Squadrons and with their great power challenge our fleet to a decisive battle."[99] Tōgō replied that a decisive battle was "what we hope for," and if it did not materialize, efforts would be made to bring it about. He expressed doubt, however, that the Russians at Port Arthur would be "so rash" as to attempt a showdown. He added, almost as an afterthought, that if the Japanese authorities had decided on war and the Russian fleet was at Ta-lien or the outer harbor of Port Arthur, it would be best to use destroyers to "carry out a surprise attack in place of a declaration of war." He also mentioned the "excellent stratagem" of blockships. But in Tōgō's opinion, this would mean sending the most capable officers and men to certain death, which for him was "insupportable."[100]

At the end of January, with war only a about a week away, Tōgō made his decision. He would send the destroyers to carry out a surprise night attack on Port Arthur. He did not contemplate a major clash of fleets; his intent, most likely, was a minor demonstration to hold off the Russians while the army made landings on the west coast of Korea.[101] He asked the navy staff for approval of his plan, saying that he would prefer not carry out the blockship operation at that time. The staff responded favorably. But soon after, Ijūin sent a telegram, sounding again his preference for a main fleet action. If the destroyers were prevented from attacking by the weather, would Tōgō consider using the main fleet to attack Port Arthur the

Table 3-1

RELATIVE STRENGTHS OF THE JAPANESE AND RUSSIAN FLEETS
1 January 1904

IMPERIAL JAPANESE NAVY
10 capital ships
    6 battleships less than 10 years old
    1 ex-Chinese, antiquated
    1 older ship rated coastal defense ship
    1 ex-Chinese coastal defense ship
 7 armored cruisers
    7 less than 10 years old; oldest, *Chiyoda,* was small and lightly armed
    2 building, completed January 1904
13 protected cruisers
    7 less than 10 years old
    6 older ships
    3 building, completed 1904
13 unprotected cruisers and similar vessels
    3 less than 10 years old
    3 over 20 years old
 6 gunboats (612–656 tons)
    4 *Maya* class, completed 1887–90
    1 additional, completed Aug. 1904
20 destroyers
    All less than 6 years old; 3 building, completed 1905
90 torpedo boats
    15 first class (115–203 tons); 1 ex-Chinese
    42 second class (79–110 tons)
    33 third class; one 16 tons (ex-Chinese); others 40–66 tons; 3 ex-Chinese
      (Of the 90 above, 58 were less than 5 years old.)
    3 first class building, completed 1904

THE RUSSIAN NAVY
33 capital ships
    12 battleships 10 years old (7 at P.A.)
    5 others under 10 years old
    8 coast defense ships
    8 barbette/turret ships
10 armored cruisers
    4 under 10 years old (3 at V., 1 at P.A.)
    3 additional laid down 1905
12 protected cruisers
    8 under 5 years old (5 at P.A., 1 at V.)
    5 additional building, 4 completed 1904–5
 9 sloops and protected cruisers (4 at P.A.)
    All over 20 years old and obsolescent

Table 3-1 (cont.)

THE RUSSIAN NAVY *(con't)*
   35 gunboats (8? at P.A.)
        4 armored (1,627–1,854 tons)
     10 unarmored (875–1,437 tons)
       2 minelayers (3,010 tons)
       9 torpedo gunboats (394–742 tons)
       9 smaller gunboats (321–455 tons)
       1 armed yacht (3285 tons)
   49 destroyers (25 at P.A.)
          All but 1 less than 6 years old
     11 additional building
   90 torpedo boats (11 at V.)
          Launched (completed) 1877–1902

Abbreviations: P.A. = Port Arthur; V. = Vladivostok. List shows all Russian navy ships operational on 1 January 1904, and all building on that date that were completed by 31 December 1905. Certain auxiliaries are not listed.

next morning? The answer was no. Tōgō replied that he would consider this last proposal "the last expedient from the point of view of strategy" because of the powerful guns at Port Arthur. A few days later, with the rupture of diplomatic relations with Russia imminent, the Navy General Staff in Tokyo sent orders to Tōgō that represented a compromise of sorts: Attack with destroyers, but accompany them with the full strength of the fleet to provide support.[102]

In this way, the destroyer attack was set. Though the decision was made on the spur of the moment, it had not been without preparation. Destroyer men had contemplated just such an attack for years. Beginning in 1900, at the instruction of the general staff, the navy had begun to work out torpedo tactics for use by its major fleet units against the big ships of the Russian Port Arthur squadron. During the first six months of 1902, the navy's newest destroyers had undertaken a series of torpedo exercises off the Korean coast that improved Japanese skills in attacking out of the sun, in approaching the target, and in minimizing bow waves, smoke and engine noise.[103] In undertaking such exercises, however, the navy began to move away from the *nikuhaku hitchū* spirit of close-in torpedo launches that had animated the attacks by Lt. Comdr. Suzuki Kantarō in the last weeks of the Sino-Japanese War.

In part, this change in tactical doctrine was due to an increase in the technical capabilities of the torpedoes themselves. As mentioned, the torpedo and its warship delivery system had been developed considerably in the near decade since the Sino-Japanese War, particularly in directional stability, though in speed and range, the torpedo was still in its infancy. Japanese torpedoes of the time, for example, had ranges of 600–800 meters at 26 or 27 knots, but to achieve a range of 2,500 meters the speed had to be reduced to 10–11 knots.[104] Yet it was the improved accuracy of the torpedo in hitting targets at further distances that led to proposals for firing torpedoes at greater ranges and slower speeds, an idea first suggested about 1900 in the Russian navy by its foremost torpedo expert, Stepan Makarov. Eventually adopted by the Japanese navy over the vigorous objections of torpedo specialists like Suzuki Kantarō, the new doctrine was a crippling limitation to the effectiveness of Japanese torpedo attacks in the coming naval war with Russia.[105]

ON THE EVE OF WAR
Some Contrasts

The outbreak of the Russo-Japanese War found the Japanese navy well situated and well prepared. It had the ability to concentrate its forces, and bases and repair facilities were nearby, thanks to the nation's geographic location and configuration. The design and construction of its individual warships were generally first-rate, and their speed, armor, and armament were homogeneous. The homogeneity deserves emphasis; insisting on uniformity was a Japanese stroke of genius, allowing as it did great ease and precision of maneuver. Japan had formed an alliance with the world's most formidable navy that, at the least, afforded Japan protection from the hostile interference of a third naval power. Naval leadership, both line and staff, understood that the purpose of a fleet was to secure command of the sea; it had conceived, tested, and practiced a set of operational plans to achieve this objective. A spirit of devotion, discipline, and self-sacrifice infused all ranks, from the commander of the Combined Fleet to the stokers in the engine rooms. This spirit was backed by similar qualities within the Japanese public at large.

The situation, qualities, and leadership of the Russian navy were in almost direct and adverse contrast to Japan's. But Russia had strengths that are sometimes ignored in hindsight. The cream of the Russian fleet had been sent to the East. The battleships, armored cruisers, and protected cruisers were all new ships, and the destroyers were all less than five years old. On a ship-to-ship basis, the Russian ships seem to have been slightly inferior, and proper maintenance was a continuing problem. These drawbacks, however, should not obscure the two critical advantages of the Russian navy in the coming struggle: It had numerical superiority over the Japanese navy (table 3-1) and could replace its losses. The Russian Far Eastern Fleet alone had more battleships than the Japanese Combined Fleet. More important was the existence of the Baltic Fleet, Russia's major force in home waters, though it was stationed halfway around the globe from Vladivostok. Furthermore, other warships were being built in Europe that could eventually reinforce the Russian fleet in East Asian waters. On the other hand, Japan had financed the purchase abroad of all the major warships it could afford, and its own naval construction industry was still too underdeveloped to add even one or two such ships to the fleet. Hence, while the Russian Far Eastern Fleet could be augmented eventually, Japan would have to fight with what it had on hand when the war opened (except for the armored cruisers *Nisshin* and *Kasuga,* which were on their way from Europe) and could expect no replacement of losses. In planning operations, therefore, the Japanese navy enjoyed no margin for error. This stark fact influenced how the navy prepared for the war,[106] how it planned to open it, and how it was to fight it.

4

Travail
—and——————
Triumph

The Japanese Navy and the Russo-Japanese War, 1904–1905

For the Japanese public as well as the Japanese army and navy, the exploits of Japan's armed forces in the Russo-Japanese War became the stuff of legend, moral precept, and tradition. In the navy, as in the army, publicists like Mizuno Hironori and Ogasawara Chōsei worked during and after the war to shape the national perception of its conduct by burnishing the tales of drama and heroism that would add luster to the reputation of their services. At the same time, the Navy General Staff produced an official history of the war for the general public that, though bland enough, presented nothing but triumphs. It also produced, however, a secret history, one that recorded the navy's failures as well as its successes in excruciating detail.[1] The document shows that the operations of the Combined Fleet were anything but a string of successes. The Japanese performed bravely and resolutely, but for much of the war struggled through a series of missteps that only fortune and Russian lassitude could turn into victory. At the end, however, the navy achieved a triumph of such completeness and glory as to cement Japan's naval tradition for the rest of its history. Although it provided powerful inspiration for the future, the triumph cast a baneful spell over the subsequent generation of naval leaders.

At the outset of hostilities, the Japanese government organized a *Dai hon'ei* (Imperial General Headquarters) to coordinate the overall conduct of the war. Like the IGHQ established during the Sino-Japanese War, it included representatives from both services, including the ministers and vice ministers, chiefs and vice chiefs of staff of the two armed services, along with one civilian representative, the foreign minister. Several aspects of its conduct of the naval war gradually became clear. The Navy General Staff exercised considerable independence, as exemplified by an early decision to open hostilities only with the navy's approval,[2] but at the same time it worked harmoniously with its army counterpart, perhaps to a degree never again to be equaled. Though in theory the staff was the supreme organ of naval command under the emperor, it brought its authority over the fleet to bear rather tentatively, particularly in the face of resistance from Admiral Tōgō, whose acumen was hugely appreciated. The IGHQ was in fact a consultative body, its decisions often arising from intensive staff work led by Vice Chief of Staff Ijūin Gorō, the real operational planner under Chief of Staff Itō Yōkō. One definite outsider strongly influenced its decisions, Navy Minister Yamamoto Gombei. Among other things, Yamamoto took part in the imperial conference that issued, on 5 February 1904, Navy Order Number One, the document that sent the navy to war.[3]

Under the emperor's name, Order Number One instructed the Combined and Third Fleets in their initial movements. The Combined Fleet was to proceed to the Yellow Sea to destroy Russian naval forces there and to direct the movements of the Korea Expeditionary Force, then in transit to Chemulpo on the Korean west coast, where it would make the first Japanese landings on the Asian continent. The Third Fleet was to occupy Chinhae Bay on the southern Korean coast, from which it was to maintain a watch over the Korea Strait.[4]

The Third Fleet's task came first, humble though it was. On 6 February, the day that Japan broke relations with Russia, Admiral Hosoya's Seventh Division occupied Pusan harbor; other units of the fleet took Chinhae Bay and Masan.

On the same day, Tōgō took the Combined Fleet to sea from its base at Sasebo. His rendezvous the next morning was just south of the Hakkō anchorage (formed by islands of the Naju group off southwest Korea). There he detached the Fourth Division under Admiral Uriu to cover troop landings from the Japanese army transports that it was to escort. On 8 February Uriu's division made short work of the Russian cruiser *Varyag* and gunboat *Koreets* at Chemulpo, forcing them to scuttle after a brief gun and torpedo battle. That night the troops quickly and uneventfully disembarked and began the march into Seoul. The invasion of Korea had begun.

Tōgō, meanwhile, steamed toward Port Arthur with the main force. We now know from the secret Navy General Staff history of the war that from the beginning,

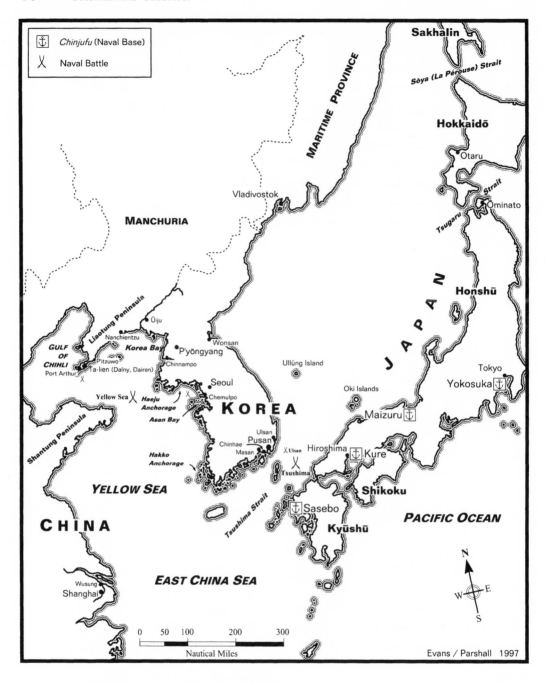

Map 4-1. Naval actions, Russo-Japanese War, 1904–5

Tōgō had never been keen on an attack on the port with all his fleet at the outset of the war. As mentioned, he had warned Vice Chief of Staff Ijōin of the dangers to his capital ships from the land batteries surrounding Port Arthur, and he therefore planned only a preventive attack on the Russian base by destroyers.[5] He saw clearly that his main task during the first phase of the war, despite the flamboyant injunction of Order Number One to "destroy" the enemy fleet, was to cover the movement of the army. He hedged on the Navy staff's orders to bring up the main fleet for the attack on Port Arthur by staging his advance so that his big ships lay between any Russian forces that might come from Port Arthur and the course of the Japanese troopships up the west coast of Korea. Once it became clear, however, that Russian battleships were not coming out to attack the Japanese, the assault at Port Arthur could go ahead as scheduled.

Tōgō planned to escort his destroyers to the vicinity of Round Island, some 45 miles east of Port Arthur. There the destroyers would part company from the main fleet, which would steam into the Yellow Sea for a distant circuit back to the vicinity of the attack the next morning. The destroyers, proceeding on their own, would make a slow and stealthy approach to the shore under cover of darkness. When they saw their chance, they would dash in to fire their torpedoes. The destroyer commanders received their final orders during the afternoon of 8 February. Their flotillas separated from the fleet for their attacks around 1800 and reached the outer harbor before midnight. They found the bulk of the Port Arthur squadron at anchor, unsuspecting and brilliantly illuminated. Racing in toward the enemy warships in a series of attacks just after midnight on 9 February, the destroyer flotillas damaged two battleships and a cruiser in what Corbett has called "the first great torpedo attack in naval history."[6]

Yet, given the multiplicity of important targets and the general absence of preparation by the enemy, the results were unimpressive. While the individual destroyer captains were brave enough in pressing home their attacks, of twenty torpedoes fired, only three found their mark. The poor results of these attacks may have been partly due to the long-range firing doctrine adopted by the navy before the war.[7] Another cause was certainly an absence of coordination. Two destroyers collided, but carried on with the attack anyway; others fell out of formation and got lost in the dark. With little semblance of formation, the destroyers had raced in to deliver their attacks singly or in pairs, whereas a coordinated assault might have accomplished a great deal more.

There were, of course, sufficient reasons for the failure to coordinate these initial attacks. The night, though clear, was bitterly cold. Also, night torpedo operations were notoriously difficult; enemy searchlights could blind the attackers and throw them out of formation, and fear of collision with their own vessels in the darkness could reduce the vigor of the attacks. Then, too, the captains and crews, in their first action, were understandably jumpy and subject to miscalculations and mistakes. They spoke frankly afterward of being "off balance" and "firing blind."[8]

More serious than any sins of the destroyer men, however, were lapses in overall design of the operation. No provision had been made for the destroyers to report their results to Tōgō in timely fashion, and the destroyers returned to their base on the Korean coast without a word to anyone. Although the destroyers might have overstated their successes and been of little help on that account, a cruiser could have met the destroyers at their first rendezvous point after the attack, Round Island, and sent the information to Tōgō by wireless.[9] As it was, Rear Admiral Dewa had to estimate the effectiveness of the attack when he reconnoitered the next morning with his Third Division. His eye, unfortunately, was not accurate. Also, Tōgō dispatched two divisions of destroyers—eight vessels—to attack the unlikely objective of Ta-lien, but they found no targets. Had the two divisions participated in the assault on Port Arthur, the attack might have been doubly destructive.[10]

By dawn, however, the Russian fleet was still in disorder. Admiral Dewa, approaching the port in midmorning, became convinced that the enemy was demoralized. He signaled Tōgō, who was coming up from the southeast, of the opportunity for a second attack. But not until noon did Tōgō's heavy ships stand in toward Port Arthur to open a slow fire on the ships in the roadstead. By then, the Russians had recovered from their surprise, and the Japanese had one of their own. The big Russian ships came out line abreast, firing at the Japanese, then turning to form a column on reverse course. The protected cruiser *Novik* charged directly at the Japanese column and discharged torpedoes. Soon the Russian shore batteries went into action. This fire drove the Japanese out to sea before they could inflict any real damage. Tōgō's withdrawal was due to his just concern for the safety of his big ships.[11] The question remains, however, why Tōgō sent them to the harbor mouth in the first place. That morning he had abruptly reversed himself, committing the main fleet to what was a diversion from the main task as he saw it, namely, covering the Korean invasion. His reason may have been the instructions of the Navy General Staff, which, during the opening days of the war, was insistent on seeking a quick decision. Committing himself hastily to an unplanned operation in which he had little faith, he came up with negligible results.

Whatever the reason, the naval historian Toyama Saburō has noted the critical importance of the failure at Port Arthur. If Tōgō was to press home the attack with his fleet, he should have done so as soon as possible after the destroyer raid.[12] He did not follow through until noontime the next day, which meant that instead of an attack that exploited the dismay and disorganization of the enemy in the wake of the Japanese destroyers, his strike was almost a second, separate operation. Taken together with the deficiencies of the night torpedo attacks, the ineffective daylight bombardment meant that the Russian Far Eastern Fleet would be left a dangerous "fleet in being." The continued presence of the fleet would now necessitate other seaborne means to try to neutralize it, as well as a land campaign against its harbor and base. "What might have been accomplished by the navy in a night, took almost a year at great cost in men and material," Toyama has argued.[13]

After the initial attack on Port Arthur, the Combined Fleet withdrew to the fleet anchorage on the Korean coast at Asan (and later Haeju). From his advance bases Tōgō continued to support troop movements as the Japanese army moved up the peninsula. To this end, he undertook a distant blockade of Port Arthur, keeping it constantly under surveillance with his cruisers and destroyers and occasionally filing past with his battleships to bombard it. The blockade was an exhausting task and anything but perfect. After the war Akiyama admitted that "gaps appeared" from time to time because, in his view, "a naval blockade, just like a surrounding operation on land, requires double the strength of your adversary; without it, the blockade cannot work. . . . Those being blockaded can lie at anchor and carry out preparations for action, waiting to catch the blockading force napping. . . . Those doing the blockading, on the other hand, must be on the picket line day and night for long periods. . . . Coal and water must be supplied to them, and one set of blockading ships must take the place of another from time to time."[14]

Akiyama explained that the Japanese navy, being approximately equal in strength to the Russian, was compelled, therefore, to use other tactics to neutralize the Port Arthur squadron.[15] The first was a continuation of the torpedo attacks by his light forces. Several times in the winter and spring of 1904, Japanese destroyers, with cruisers standing by for support, swept in to launch their torpedoes, but each time they were forced to withdraw before significant damage had been inflicted. Tōgō also ordered "indirect" bombardments of the port. On three occasions in the spring he took his battleships to the unfortified tip of the peninsula, where they opened fire overland with their 12-inch guns on the port and its warships. The range, 14,000 meters, was extreme for the time, and the ships had to be given a list to elevate the guns sufficiently to make it. The *Kasuga* and the *Nisshin*, two new cruisers acquired at the start of the war, took part in early May. They fired at even greater ranges, up to 18,000 meters. But observations of the fall of shot from Japanese ships offshore were always inadequate, and this mode of attack proved ineffective.

The third method of dealing with the Port Arthur squadron was to use blockships. It turned out to be a frustrating series of operations. The first blockship attempt occurred on the night of 23 February with five stone-laden vessels averaging about 2,000 tons and commanded by the main blockship advocate, Comdr. Arima Ryōkitsu. The ships were taken up to the harbor mouth under fierce enemy fire and sunk, but not sufficiently in place to seal the harbor. Virtually all hands, some seventy volunteers, were taken off safely by Japanese torpedo boats.

Arima led a second attempt on the night of 26 March with four ships. One vessel, the *Yoneyama-maru,* came very close to blocking the channel. This attempt, too, ultimately failed to choke the harbor, but it did produce a dramatic act of heroism that electrified the navy and the nation. Commanding the block-ship *Fukui Maru,* Lt. Comdr. Hirose Takeo, a specialist in Russian affairs and the Russian navy, took his ship to the harbor entrance in the face of heavy enemy fire and sank it, after which he and the ship's crew took to the ship's longboat to escape. Returning to rescue a missing man, Hirose was blown to pieces when a Russian shell struck the boat. In the hands of the navy's publicists, Hirose's act of heroism eventually became part of the mythology of not only the navy, but the Japanese people as a whole.[16]

Such deeds could not disguise the failure of the effort. At Tōgō's insistence, however, one more try was made with the blockships. He stunned the navy staff when he asked for no less than twelve ships for an all-out effort in early May. The staff tried to dissuade him, saying that there were no ships left. But he got them, and on the night of 3 May, the ships went in. This final operation had everything against it, starting with its crews, who were almost all inexperienced men from the Third Fleet anxious to get their chance for glory. Moreover, the Russians had perfected the harbor defenses with booms, mines, and improved gun positions. Finally, at the last minute the weather turned bad. The attempt was a disastrous failure. Few ships even got close to the harbor entrance. About half of the 158 volunteers were lost. The operation utterly failed to halt the free movement of Russian ships in and out of Port Arthur, and the Navy General Staff was obliged to call a halt to the fruitless operations.[17]

Frustrated in his attempts to close the Russian base, Tōgō had, in the midst of his blockship operations, turned to a more promising tactic: mining the waters outside the harbor.[18] The operation itself was less risky to the blockading fleet, though there was always the possibility of one's own warships accidentally colliding with mines sown earlier. Still, it was the one approach Tōgō had yet to try. During the stormy night of 12–13 April, a Japanese minelayer, accompanied by destroyers and torpedo boats, laid mines within the 3-mile limit off the port in waters usually traversed by Russian warships. The results were immediate and critical to the conduct of the war. Only the month before, Adm. Stepan Makarov, torpedo specialist and the most daring and innovative tactician in the Russian navy, had taken command of the Far Eastern Fleet and in so doing had dramatically raised its morale and efficiency. Now, on the morning following the minelaying, aboard his flagship, the *Petropavlovsk,* Makarov led a small force out of harbor to challenge the Japanese. Within a few miles of the harbor mouth his battleship struck a Japanese mine, broke in two, and went down with nearly all hands, including the admiral himself. With him went all prospects for a purposeful, aggressive strategy by the Port Arthur squadron. Upon the announcement in St. Petersburg that the Baltic Fleet would be sent to the East to reinforce the Far Eastern Fleet, Makarov's successor, Rear Adm. V. K. Witgeft, resumed the defensive, hoping to conserve his force until the arrival of the support from Europe.

Mine warfare is a two-edged sword, especially if the enemy retaliates by sowing his own mines. In May 1904, the Combined Fleet suffered two mine-caused disasters of its own. Early that month, Russian minelayers, taking advantage of the fog, laid mines in waters off the Liaotung Peninsula frequented by Japanese warships. On 15 May, the cruiser *Yoshino* struck a mine and capsized, and on the same day, steaming with a battle group near Port Arthur, the battleships *Hatsuse* and *Yashima* struck mines and went down. Within a single day, the Combined Fleet had lost a third of its battleship strength. As a result of these losses, Tōgō was even more cautious about risking his remaining capital ships. His reluctance would soon have serious consequences when he finally met the Port Arthur squadron in battle. In any event, the mine, though an unglamourous weapon, was one of the deadliest of the war, claiming eleven Japanese and seven Russian warships.[19]

Thus, from the start of the war in February and until the summer of 1904, the Combined Fleet had been thwarted in its effort to finish off the Port Arthur squadron. Frustration on the Japanese side was high; grumbling within the navy increased with each retirement of the fleet from the waters off Port Arthur. On the Russian side at Port Arthur, however, the prime fact of the war during this period was the unrelenting pressure applied by the Japanese navy. The efforts to neutralize the ships at Port Arthur had all failed. Yet, as a means of protecting the landings of Japanese troops in Korea and Manchuria, the efforts had succeeded, since each blockship operation had been undertaken in conjunction with a major army landing.[20] Tōgō undertook the final, last-ditch blockship attempt because he had to cover the landing of the Second Army on the Liaotung Peninsula within range of Port Arthur's torpedo boats and because he was convinced that Makarov would come out to challenge him. Makarov indeed planned to do so until his flagship, the *Petropavlovsk*, fell victim to a Japanese mine.

The success of Japan's land campaigns during the first phase of the war, during which Korea was taken, certainly rested in large part on the secure passage provided by the navy. Further, the unexpected rapidity of the army's progress up the Korean peninsula was facilitated by navy cover and support. Landing points were shifted northward several times to avoid arduous overland marches. The cardinal example is the debarkation of General Kuroki's two divisions at Chinnampo (Namp'o) in mid-March, when they had originally planned their advance from Chemulpo.[21] Tōgō's staff arranged meticulously for escorting forces all along the way, and Rear Admiral Hosoya of the Seventh Division provided fire support and transport services. By late April, Kuroki's First Army had completed its push to the Yalu River and was poised for an attack at the Russian strong point at Uiju.

The coordinated operations that began in early May effectively marked the end of the war's first stage (the capture of Korea) and the start of the second (the attack on Russian forces in Manchuria). Japan had taken its territorial objective and now could concentrate on destroying the enemy's armed forces. To varying degrees, General Kuroki's subsequent defeat of the Russians at Uiju and his crossing of the Yalu, General Oku's landing of the Second Army at P'itzuwo on the Liaotung Peninsula, and General Kawamura's Tenth Division's going ashore at Nanchientzu at the top of Korea Bay between Kuroki's and Oku's positions were all joint army-navy operations. Of utmost consequence for the naval war was the Second Army's landing, because it constituted the beginning a campaign to seize Port Arthur overland and destroy its fleet. By the end of May, the Second Army had moved down to seize the Port of Ta-lien and its valuable docks, wharves, and repair facilities. After a further month of ferocious combat, they had advanced to within a few miles of Port Arthur, but were halted by the formidable Russian defenses on the heights surrounding the port. Should these heights be captured and surmounted by heavy Japanese artillery, the position of the Port Arthur squadron would be untenable. Given this possibility, the situation called for an audacious decision by Russian naval authorities in St. Petersburg and bold action at Port Arthur by Admiral Witgeft, whose battleships now outnumbered Tōgō's, six to four. Yet instead of ordering an attack on Tōgō's blockading force to inflict as much damage as possible, the czar in early August ordered Witgeft to flee with his six battleships, four armored cruisers, and eight destroyers to Vladivostok. Witgeft was to avoid an encounter with Tōgō's fleet, if possible.

THE BATTLE OF THE YELLOW SEA
10 August 1904

Tōgō had long expected a sortie by Witgeft; indeed, he had already turned back a halfhearted sally by the Russian admiral in late June. But the breakout of the Port Arthur squadron on 10 August found Tōgō with his ships scattered off the Liaotung Peninsula and four of his armored cruisers with Kamimura and the Second Fleet. The latter had been reassigned to the Korea Strait to watch for the Vladivostok squadron. Warned of the enemy's departure from base by his scouts, Tōgō used his wireless to pull together his First Division of four battleships and two armored cruisers. With two other armored cruisers and all his destroyers and torpedo boats scrambling to catch up, the admiral steamed southwest to head off the advancing enemy. A little after noon, Tōgō discovered the Russian battleships and cruisers in line ahead with a cruiser and eight destroyers to port, advancing toward him. The two forces were roughly matched in heavy guns—sixteen 12-inch guns apiece—though the Japanese were superior in lesser calibers and quick-firers and had an enormous advantage in destroyers and torpedo boats.

Tōgō's objective was to place his battle line across the path of the Russian advance and thereby cap the enemy's T and destroy him, exactly in conformity to his battle plan drawn up at the start of the war. Yet, it is clear from the range—over 11,000 meters—at which Tōgō ordered his battle line to open fire that he was unwilling to purchase victory at the risk of serious losses to his own battle group. (His battle plan had cautioned, "Expect no more that one percent hits at ranges greater than 3,500 meters."[22]) Employing simultaneous turns to cross and recross Witgeft's column at ranges unlikely to be decisive, Tōgō attempted to "lure the enemy out to sea," where he might be destroyed.[23] But each time he was about to cap the Russian T, the enemy turned away. Had he pressed closer in he might have countered each Russian turn quite quickly. But when the Russians turned to port to pass behind his column at 1345, he unaccountably turned not to starboard, which would have kept him ahead of the Russians, but to port. He made a leisurely circle that eventually brought him onto a parallel course with the Russians but behind them (map 4-2). By the time he was around, their battleships were barely visible on the horizon. Witgeft had seized his opportunity and slipped past the Japanese line out of range; he headed full speed out across the Yellow Sea for the Korea Strait. Should he escape, all that would stand between him and Vladivostok would be Kamimura's four armored cruisers and some lesser units. "The plain truth," says Corbett, "is that he [Tōgō] had been outmaneuvered."[24]

Tōgō's blunder may have been simply what Corbett called it—the result of a moment of inattention or bad judgment. But it may also have been the result of an assumption that the Russians had come out finally to fight a pitched battle and not to flee. Such an assumption would help explain Tōgō's tentative opening maneuvers. He ordered the mistaken turn probably to take advantage of an apparent disordering in the Russian line right after its turn eastward at 1345. The range then was about 6,000 meters, and Japanese gunfire on the point of the Russian turn had begun to tell. Both the *Tsesarevich* and *Retvizan* were on fire, and the Russian cruisers were lagging behind on the unengaged side. It seemed to be a moment of critical Russian weakness. Tōgō planned to swing around behind the Russian formation and attack the cruisers, but when he got around, he found that the Russians had recovered from their difficulties and had started to run.

In order to recover the advantage of position, Tōgō moved south and then east with the hope of catching Witgeft somewhere north of the Shantung peninsula with the Japanese ships' superior speed. For two hours, their engines at flank speed, the two columns raced southeastward (map 4-3). In late afternoon Tōgō just managed

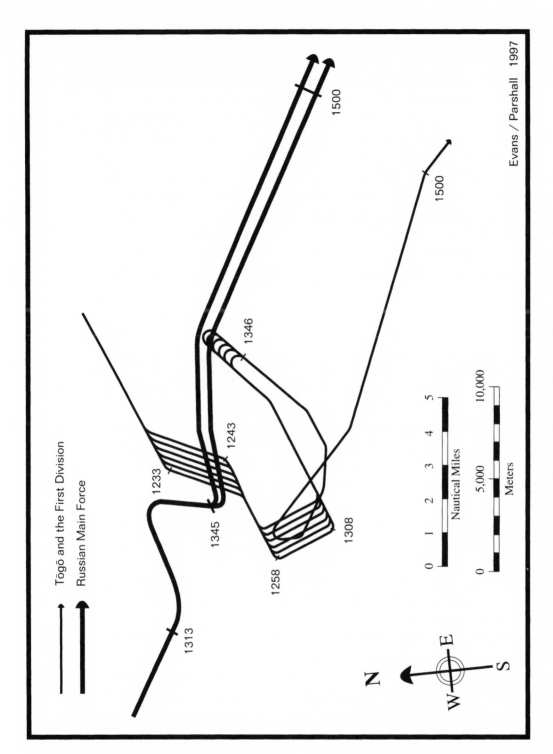

Map 4-2. First engagement of the Battle of the Yellow Sea (Adapted from *NRKK*, map appendix)

to overtake the rear ship of the Russian squadron and opened fire at 7,000 meters. The combat soon became general, during which time the *Mikasa* and her companions took a heavy pounding. Five of Tōgō's sixteen 12-inch guns were out of action by 1840 hours. At this critical juncture, however, the Russian squadron was overtaken by disaster. Two lucky Japanese shots struck the bridge and conning tower of the Russian flagship *Tsesarevich*, killing Witgeft and members of his staff, and jamming the helm so that the ship heeled violently to port. As if running amok, the *Tsesarevich* continued in a circle, threatening to run down the other Russian warships in line. With individual captains as yet uncomprehending, the Russian battle line quickly disintegrated into confusion as Tōgō's ships, in tight formation, circled in front of the Russians, closed to within 5,000 meters, and intensified their fire. Witgeft's second in command signaled the stricken mob of Russian warships to follow him back to Port Arthur, but the retreat was disorderly in the extreme. Some ships—the *Tsesarevich*, for example—made for neutral ports.

Had Tōgō continued to press home the attack with his main fleet units, he probably would have annihilated the disorganized Russian mass. However, since night was falling and he feared a torpedo attack from the oncoming Russian destroyers, Tōgō turned his heavy ships away and instead ordered his own destroyers and torpedo boats to strike at the retreating enemy.[25] During the night these small warships launched repeated attacks at the main force of the enemy now pulling hard for Port Arthur. Despite good weather conditions and determined efforts, none of the seventy-four Japanese torpedoes that were fired that night found its mark.[26]

By the morning of 11 August, the main body of the Port Arthur squadron was back in harbor. Of its original seven battleships, five remained; only two of the initial eight armored, protected cruisers and only twelve of the twenty-five destroyers were back in harbor. Like the German High Seas Fleet after Jutland, the Russian squadron, its morale crumbling, never again came out to do battle. To this extent, the August battle was a Japanese victory.

In another sense, the engagement was both a tactical and a strategic failure for Tōgō and the Combined Fleet. The equality of the two forces at the outset of the battle was largely superficial and numerical. In the design and construction of his ships, and in the training, discipline, and morale of his captains and crews, Tōgō had the unquestioned advantage over his opponent. Had he pushed to closer ranges, risking to the fortunes of battle the stout construction of his heavy ships, he would have most likely annihilated the Russian force. His failure—for the second time—to do so cost Japan time, matériel, and lives. A bloody campaign by the Japanese army against the last defenses at Port Arthur now followed. Moreover, the navy found itself facing the eventual arrival of the Baltic Fleet, which Russia decided to send as a desperate reinforcement to its beleaguered squadrons and

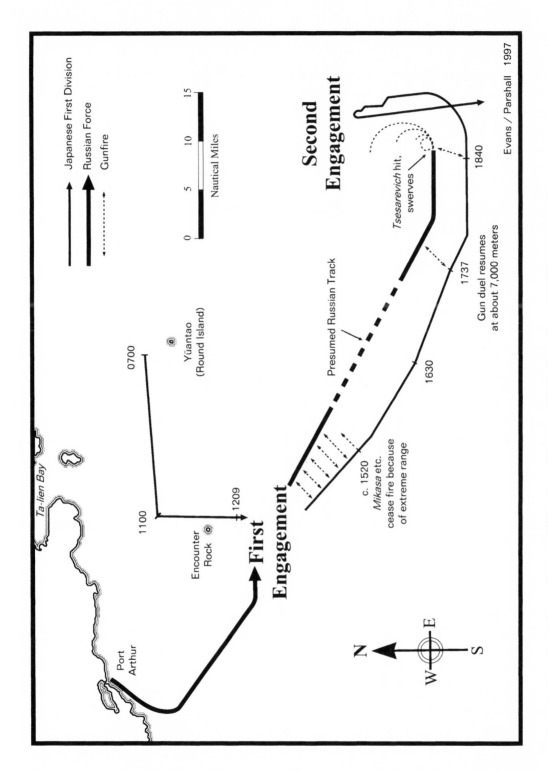

Map 4-3. Overview of the Battle of the Yellow Sea, 10 August 1904 (Adapted from *NRKK*, map appendix)

garrisons in the East in the wake of the Battle of the Yellow Sea. Had Tōgō immediately crushed the Port Arthur squadron, the Baltic Fleet might never have been sent, as there would have been little for it to reinforce. Given the consequences of Tōgō's judgment, his excessive caution on 10 August proved to be a serious, if short-lived, mistake. It was a mistake he would not repeat.

KAMIMURA'S TROUBLES WITH THE VLADIVOSTOK SQUADRON
February–August 1904

While Tōgō and the Combined Fleet had been occupied with attempts to destroy the Port Arthur squadron, the smaller Vladivostok force had begun to pose a serious threat to Japan's sea lanes and shipping in the Japan Sea. From the outset of the war, the Japanese navy had believed that the greatest threat posed by this smaller squadron was that it might attempt to force the Korea Strait and join up with the warships at Port Arthur. Consequently, the weakest of Japan's fleets, the Third, had initially been kept separate from the Combined Fleet and been stationed at Takeshiki on Tsushima in the Korea Strait.

From the first weeks of the war, it became apparent that the Vladivostok squadron was capable of playing a more threatening role than the Japanese navy had assumed and that in location and strength, the Third Fleet was an ineffective combat organization. Russian strategic plans called for the Vladivostok squadron to attack Japanese sea lanes and shipping in the Japan Sea and to threaten the Japanese western coast, causing the Japanese to divide their attention between the Yellow and Japan Seas.

In seven consecutive sorties over the first six months of the war, the Vladivostok squadron managed to accomplish all these objectives. After the second sortie by the squadron, which swept along the western coast of Honshū in late February 1904, IGHQ was sufficiently concerned about the threat to transfer the Third Fleet to Tōgō's command in the Yellow Sea. In the Third Fleet's place in the Korea Strait, IGHQ sent a powerful contingent of the Second Fleet under Adm. Kamimura Hikonojō to the Japan Sea. Twice in the winter and spring of 1904 Kamimura, with his armored cruisers, raided the waters off Vladivostok, hoping to catch the Russians out of their closely guarded base. Because of bad weather, however, he missed the Russian warships each time.

So far, the commanders of the Vladivostok squadron, showing greater boldness and skill than their counterparts at Port Arthur, had carried out operations in Japanese waters, but had escaped an encounter with any portion of the Japanese fleet. Far more important, they now exposed the vulnerability of Japan's ocean communications in what had been considered a Japanese backwater. The squadron's third sortie along the east coast of Korea in late April coincided with an opposing

Rear Adm. Kamimura Hikonojō

sweep of the northern Japan Sea by Kamimura who, with his formidable force of cruisers, hoped to run the Russians down. But the Russian warships slipped by Kamimura in the fog and, in their escape, came across a hapless Japanese troop transport at Wŏnsan, which they sank after a gallant but utterly futile resistance by the soldiers on board.

In June the Vladivostok squadron was back in the strait to strike at the Japanese sea route to the Yellow Sea and at the military transports, virtually unescorted, that passed along it. The results were immediate and dramatic: Two such ships were sunk, one loaded with over a thousand troops and howitzers for the Japanese siege train at Port Arthur. Again, the Russians evaded Kamimura and raced back to the safety of Vladivostok.

Public indignation over the raids, which had been growing ever since the start of the war and which was now whipped up by the press, found its focus in Kamimura. A mob stoned his house in Tokyo; politicians called for his court-martial;

and short swords arrived at his house with suggestions that he commit suicide to atone for his "incompetence" and "carelessness."[27]

In late July, the Russian squadron staged its most daring raid of all. Passing through the Tsugaru Strait between Honshū and Hokkaidō, the three enemy cruisers pushed down the Pacific coast with the object of catching Korea-bound transports coming out of Yokohama. In the process it sank or captured and then released a number of Western merchantmen and also sank several Japanese merchant ships before returning back through the Tsugaru Strait and home.[28] The Russian war against Japanese seaborne commerce, supplemented by cruiser actions in the Red Sea and the Atlantic, was by this time more than an irritant; it was a serious danger to a nation that depended on shipping. Trade with Japan in harbors on the American west coast was momentarily paralyzed. Insurance rates on vessels bound for Japan skyrocketed, and the three largest British shipping firms suspended service to Japan.[29]

In August 1904, however, luck ran out for the Vladivostok squadron. Learning of the breakout of Admiral Witgeft and the Port Arthur squadron, but not realizing that Witgeft was already dead and the Port Arthur squadron driven back to its beleaguered port, the three Vladivostok cruisers, the *Rossiya*, *Gromoboi*, and *Rurik*, made a seventh sortie on 12 August. The objective was to dash through the Korea Strait to link up with Witgeft. Early in the morning of 14 August the cruisers steamed toward Ulsan on the east coast of Korea. For once, Kamimura's four armored cruisers were in the right place to ambush them. A fierce three-hour gun duel ensued, with Kamimura between the Russian ships and their home base. The Russians fought gallantly. Admiral Iessen, their commander, doubled back repeatedly to succor the stricken *Rurik*. Kamimura generally held his distance, as Tōgō had at the Battle of the Yellow Sea, but he finally sank the *Rurik*. The other two Russian cruisers crawled back to their home base, both of them badly damaged. Without adequate repair facilities at Vladivostok, the squadron, now down to one effective warship, was finished as a fighting force, and like the Port Arthur squadron, it never again left its home port.

During its brief life, the Vladivostok squadron had attracted far more attention and concern from the Japanese than warranted by its accomplishments—the sinking of a few merchantmen (one, admittedly, with valuable military cargo). The drama of the relatively minor injuries it had inflicted and its immunity to the best efforts of a superior Japanese force to track it down had led to the public vilification of one of the most prominent of Japan's naval commanders, though it is clear that in the naval age before radar and search aircraft it was not easy to locate an enemy warship in the too-frequent mists of the Japan Sea.

The Vladivostok squadron played only a secondary part in the Russo-Japanese War. It nevertheless cast a long shadow. When Yamamoto Isoroku was proposing the attack on Pearl Harbor in 1941, he brought up the issue of allowing an enemy power to remain unchallenged near Japanese soil. He argued that the American fleet, if left undisturbed, could raid the home islands with incalculable consequences for public morale and public attitudes toward the Japanese navy. Further, hindsight shows that the exploits of the squadron pointed up a serious and long-range strategic problem for Japan: protection of its overseas shipping lanes. Limited for centuries to their own coastline, the Japanese had never given much thought to the defense of overseas communication and transportation routes. Where other naval powers like Britain and France, with vast overseas empires, had, perforce, become experienced in the problems of convoys and ocean escorts for commercial and military shipping in time of war, the Japanese navy, in its meteoric growth and concern with battle between fighting fleets, had ignored these questions.[30]

PREPARATIONS FOR THE FINAL BATTLE

It was left to the Japanese army to accomplish the final destruction of the Port Arthur squadron, since the mine-strewn waters around the port were far too dangerous for Tōgō to risk his capital ships in the attempt.[31] In the late fall of 1904, the army closed in upon the heights that surrounded the port. The battle for 203 Meter Hill brought fearful losses, making literal the stock phrase for a costly battle, *shizan kekka* (a mountain of bodies and a river of blood), and establishing the Japanese army's reputation for the massed suicide charge. Much of the impetus behind the army's attack, however, was naval. Tōgō and his staff, in particular Akiyama, had insisted on 203 Meter Hill as the main objective in the face of army opposition.[32] Once the hill was in their possession, the Japanese could bring every inch of the harbor under fire. One by one the Russian warships in the port were sunk or disabled. The last remaining battleship, the *Sevastopol,* steamed out of the harbor to shelter behind the torpedo net defenses. Repeated night torpedo attacks by the Japanese damaged but did not sink her, and she was scuttled in deep water the day that Port Arthur surrendered, 2 January 1905.

Halfway around the world, the Russians had belatedly organized the force with which they hoped to recover Russian prestige and power in East Asia. On 15 October 1904 the Baltic Fleet, under Admiral Rozhestvensky, had started on its epic eight-month voyage that would take it around Africa, through the Indian Ocean, through the Indies, and up the China coast toward Japan.

Meanwhile, no Russian warship of consequence remained in either the Japan Sea or the Yellow Sea, and Japanese intelligence reports clearly indicated that the Baltic Fleet would be months in arriving. The naval high command consequently concentrated on reconditioning Japan's naval strength and, in the process, turned aside army proposals for further joint operations on the Asian mainland.[33] Japanese warships that had been engaged in the near year-long campaign against the Russian Far Eastern Fleet were now sent to Japanese dockyards for complete overhaul and repair. The battleships and armored cruisers received particular attention, being given many minor improvements beyond their original design and construction. By February 1905, thanks to round-the-clock work by Japanese dockyards, the Combined Fleet was almost entirely reconditioned and materially ready for combat.

In December 1904, Tōgō had returned to Tokyo to consult with Chief of Staff Itō and Navy Minister Yamamoto in planning to meet Rozhestvensky's battle force. As a consequence, the navy took several steps to provide early warning of the progress of the Russian fleet once it reached East Asian waters. Patrols searching for possible clandestine enemy advance bases were sent to various coasts and ports in Southeast Asia, the watch in Japanese waters was extended as far north as the Sōya (La Pérouse) Strait between Hokkaidō and Sakhalin, a force of cruisers was stationed at the western end of the Tsugaru Strait, and a patrol of fast auxiliary ships was sent to patrol the western approaches to the Korea Strait. To facilitate the efforts of all these patrolling forces, each strait, as well as the Japan Sea, was divided into numbered squares. Each square represented 10 minutes of latitude and longitude, so that ships patrolling these waters needed only to communicate the number of the square to identify the location of an approaching enemy.

For the main base of the Combined Fleet Tōgō chose the broad waters of Chinhae Bay and the adjoining Kadŏk Channel (Douglas Inlet) on the southeastern coast of Korea. There, secure and isolated from most contact with the outside world, the Combined Fleet renewed its rigorous training in preparation for the impending battle. Sometimes singly, sometimes in small groups, sometimes as a fleet, the warships of the fleet went out to practice the communications, torpedo attacks, and maneuvers called for in the Battle Plan of 1903. Above all, the fleet practiced gunnery. Almost every day, weather permitting, at least one or two ships were out at target practice.[34] With the bitter experience of the incomplete victory at the Yellow Sea as an object lesson, the fleet, under Tōgō's direction, carried out continued practice in station keeping, steaming in columns, and especially maneuvering the battle divisions in concert. Readiness for rapid deployment was another vital element in Tōgō's preparations. In early April, he issued instructions that all ships of the fleet should be provisioned and ready to get under way within an hour and a half of receiving orders to do so.[35]

In the months that followed the move to Chinhae Bay, Tōgō and the staff of the Combined Fleet had ample time not only to recondition their ships and sharpen the combat skills of the officers and men, but to consider the lessons of the first eight months of the naval war and how these might apply to the final test of arms with the Russian navy. Since the Yellow Sea battle with the Port Arthur squadron was the only fleet engagement in the war thus far, this battle was the focus of the review. The Russian defeat the previous August had obviously been a matter of luck or, more exactly, of two lucky shells, and for the Japanese, it had obviously been a battle of lost opportunities caused by excessive caution and inadequate planning. Caution—the failure to narrow the range and reap the benefits of concentrated gunfire while capping the T—had allowed the Port Arthur warships to escape during the first phase of the engagement; inadequate planning had prevented Tōgō from exploiting the enemy's chaotic flight during the second phase. In rectifying the mistakes of 10 August, audacity by the fleet commander, material superiority of the fleet's weapons, and the superior combat skills of its officers and crew could do much to prevent a repetition of the first error; detailed planning for a battle prolonged in time and space would be the best means of eradicating the second.

Such planning, naturally, was entrusted to Akiyama Saneyuki, now senior staff officer with the fleet. Akiyama predicated his plans on the likelihood that the Russian enemy would head for Vladivostok. There was, however, considerable concern among members of the Navy General Staff that the Baltic Fleet might not head north, but instead seize a point somewhere off the China coast and operate from there against the Japanese. The Japanese base of Makung in the Pescadores was a likely target, offering not only facilities but advantages as a bargaining chip in peace negotiations to come. The very real possibility of Russian operations from the south was the main reason why Chinhae became the Japanese fleet base rather than a more northerly location such as the Oki Islands or Maizuru.[36]

The prospect of southerly Russian operations was particularly worrisome to Tōgō and the navy staff because of a larger concern than the mere deployment of forces. Such operations would probably prevent the sort of clear-cut naval decision that was imperative for Japan. The Russians were sufficiently strong in Manchuria to defeat, or at least exhaust, the Japanese forces there; anything less than a total reverse at sea would allow the Russians to hold on and hope for favorable peace terms. Japanese strength was ebbing rapidly. Consequently, from the early spring of 1905, talk on the navy staff about "annihilating" and "destroying" the Baltic Fleet was no longer mere rhetoric. Tōgō was repeatedly enjoined to win a complete victory.[37]

Whatever the navy staff believed that the Baltic Fleet would do, Akiyama and apparently his commander, Tōgō, went on the theory that Vladivostok was the goal. The Russians would have to run a Japanese gauntlet no matter which of the two most likely routes—the Korea Strait or the Tsugaru Strait—they would take to reach Vladivostok. For purposes of planning, Akiyama assumed that Rozhestvensky would take the Korea Strait, the closer of the two. To meet Rozhestvensky's attempt to force the strait, Akiyama planned an offensive-defense.

Strategically, he conceived a defense in depth; tactically, he planned for a series of phased blows to annihilate the enemy over a two-day period. Akiyama combined the strategy and tactics in a seven-stage plan of attrition that would employ both daylight assaults by the heavy units of the fleet and night attacks by destroyers and torpedo boats. The battle order for the first stage was designed to intercept the Russian fleet with destroyers and torpedo boats before it could slip through the strait under cover of darkness. Such operations would slow down the Russians' progress so that the main battle could take place in the strait during the day. The second stage called for the main forces of the fleet to launch a direct and over-whelming attack on the approaching Baltic Fleet as it attempted to transit the strait. The middle stages were to comprise further night attacks by destroyers and torpedo boats. The final set of battle orders envisioned mopping-up operations that would drive the remnants of the Russian force toward Vladivostok, whose harbor mouths would by then have been sown with Japanese mines.[38]

In addition to this phased strategic scheme, Akiyama was instrumental in drafting a plan for the main fleet encounter which used the basic outline of the Combined Fleet Battle Plan of 1903 (see chapter 3), but incorporated adjustments necessitated by the experiences of the first phase of the war. One adjustment concerned the T. Tōgō had remarked after the Yellow Sea battle, "I am afraid that the 'T' tactic lets the enemy get away."[39] His earlier instructions to his own division in the original document had been emphatic: "This Battle Plan takes the 'T' tactic as its foundation, as does the [Combined Fleet] Battle Plan."[40] The revision, dated 10 May 1904, stated merely that individual divisions of the Combined Fleet would make the T tactic their "standard."[41] In the revised plans the L tactic of "scissoring" the enemy with another division was upheld as before, but fighting on parallel courses was mentioned more prominently:

> The First Division, by putting pressure obliquely on the head of the enemy's second formation (whether the fast cruisers mentioned above or the main force), will seek to turn the enemy aside from his course, commence a battle on parallel courses, and subsequently continue the battle in this way. The Second Division will form an "L" with it insofar as circumstances allow and, by fiercely attacking the rear of the enemy force engaged with it, operate cooperatively with it in accordance with the principle of the "L" tactic.[42]

The T unquestionably remained an article of faith, but its practical applicability was coming under scrutiny, particularly in the eventuality that the enemy fleet did not want to defeat its opponent but only escape.

The duties of each division were much as before. The First Division would pin down Rozhestvensky's main force, while the Second, Third, and Fourth Divisions would attack the enemy's second-line warships from cruisers on down, exploiting such weak spots in the enemy's formation as might appear and using maximum fire power to destroy him. With the coming of darkness, destroyers and torpedo boats would undertake torpedo attacks that would begin as soon as possible after sundown and would be carried out repeatedly until dawn, when the main surface engagement would begin again.[43] A novel element in the revised plan, however, was the specification that the destroyers and torpedo boats should also carry out "linked mine attacks." The linked mine was in fact a new weapon just developed by Akiyama and others, and it was to be used in a surprise flotilla attack on the head of the enemy formation at the start of the main fleet battle.[44] Akiyama considered that such a tactic, along with a reversal of the policy of long-range torpedo firing, would finally vindicate the destroyer and torpedo boat forces whose performance had hitherto been so poor.[45]

On 17 April, Tōgō had issued to the fleet an instruction—drafted by Akiyama—that was the psychological and motivational counterpart to the technical stipulations of the battle plan. Emblematic of the state of mind of Tōgō's command, it called for the utmost vigilance against an enemy who should be neither feared nor despised and cautioned against the tendency for any hotly engaged force to overestimate the enemy's strength and progress in the battle. The instruction reminded the fleet that combat offense was the best defense and spoke confidently of Japanese superiority on gunnery, no matter what the odds. Finally, noting that "the Russian character is generally passive," it urged all fleet units to seize and hold the initiative.[46]

As Admiral Rozhestvensky, at the head of the Baltic Fleet, made his slow and weary way through the Indian Ocean and into the South China Sea by early May 1905, there remained for Tōgō and his staff the troubling question as to what the Russian force would do. If the enemy established a base off China and began to operate in the East China and Yellow Seas, the Combined Fleet might have to go south. If the Russians made for Vladivostok, the question was which of the three possible passages they would take. The Sōya Strait route, all the way around Hokkaidō, seemed unlikely, not only because of its fogs and difficult navigation, but also because it was far too long a route for ships and crews already near the end of their resources. The Tsugaru Strait was closer to Vladivostok than the other two passages, but its entrance was narrow and the current through it was strong. Russian ships entering it would be visible from either shore; they would take at least six hours to transit the strait; and once in it, the ships would have little room for maneuver. This left the Korea Strait, a passage that would take the Baltic Fleet directly in front of its enemy and make almost inevitable a major test of arms, as Rozhestvensky was undoubtedly aware. His only chance for avoiding battle was the hope that he might slip through the strait at night or undetected in the fogs that often covered them.

By his selection of a base on the Korea Strait, Tōgō had chosen the best strategic compromise. If Rozhestvensky chose to operate in the East China Sea, Tōgō was close by. If he approached the strait, the Combined Fleet lay waiting. If scouts reported that the enemy was passing up the Pacific coast, there would probably still be time to race across the Sea of Japan to meet him at the western end of the Tsugaru Strait, though destroyers and torpedo boats, in which the Japanese had superiority, might be left behind. Still, it was a gamble, and by late May, with no concrete intelligence on the whereabouts of the Baltic Fleet, the question of Rozhestvensky's intentions was critical. While still reasonably confident that the Russian commander would try to reach Vladivostok and do so by transiting the Korea Strait, Tōgō telegraphed the Navy General Staff on 24 May that he would wait at Chinhae a few days longer. Then if the enemy had not appeared, Tōgō would move north to the Tsugaru Strait.

To Tōgō's subordinate commanders and staff officers, including Akiyama and the new fleet chief of staff, Katō Tomosaburō, the absence of sightings off the Chinese coast and their own calculations concerning the enemy's last known course and speed indicated that Rozhestvensky was aiming for Vladivostok and probably already steaming around the Pacific side of the Japanese archipelago toward Hokkaidō.[47] Akiyama and the others were, it seems, prepared to act on this conviction, but Tōgō would not be pushed into a hasty decision to quit his base.[48] It was with enormous relief that fleet headquarters received word before dawn on 26 May that Russian transports and auxiliary cruisers were at Wusung (near Shanghai). This news confirmed that Rozhestvensky was heading up the China coast toward the Korea Strait. There was elation on Tōgō's staff. The Combined Fleet was in perfect position to meet the enemy.[49]

As the two fleets drew together, their relative strengths could finally be measured. Superficially, the two fleets were about evenly matched, with perhaps the slight edge to the Russians. Each side had four modern battleships. Rozhestvensky had seven other capital ships of older vintage, but Tōgō had eight modern armored cruisers to the Russian's one. While the Baltic Fleet thus had 41 10- and 12-inch guns compared to 17 for the Combined Fleet, Tōgō had superiority in secondary armament, so that he could bring to bear a total of 127 guns to the Russians' 92. To the extent that the weather would allow, Tōgō enjoyed an advantage because of his clear superiority in destroyers and torpedo craft. Tōgō also enjoyed a critical advantage in speed: 15 knots for all the Japanese capital ships, compared to the 10 to 11 knots imposed on the Russian fleet because of the obsolete warships in their battle line. Moreover, while Tōgō's force had fewer capital ships than did the enemy, the Combined Fleet's battleships and armored cruisers were some of the most formidable warships afloat in quality of design and sturdiness of construction. Finally, their uniformity in capability and performance made the Japanese ships a highly effective fighting unit. Rozhestvensky's fleet, on the other hand, was a melange of ships, many of which were top-heavy and ill designed.[50]

Other advantages also lay with the Japanese. The Combined Fleet was painted a uniform gray, which made its individual ships less distinct,[51] whereas the warships of the Baltic Fleet, with their black hulls and superstructures and their brilliantly painted yellow funnels, were highly visible. By this time the installation of wireless sets in destroyers had been completed. Virtually all ships of the Combined Fleet were not only so equipped, but also had officers and men trained in wireless operation.[52] The Russians, while adept at wireless, particularly jamming, were condemned to silence by Rozhestvensky, who believed that radio transmissions would reveal his whereabouts.[53] The high state of training among the officers and men of Tōgō's command was reinforced by their good spirits and sense of optimism, whereas the Russian men were exhausted and dispirited and had received little additional training on their long ocean voyage. Finally, in Tōgō, the Japanese had a commander who was determined upon the annihilation of his opponent and who had planned to achieve that objective. Rozhestvensky merely hoped that his fleet would survive and did little planning to realize that hope.[54]

THE BATTLE OF TSUSHIMA
27–28 May 1905

Early in the morning of 27 May, the *Shinano-maru,* one of Tōgō's fast auxiliary cruisers, sighted the Russian fleet in the western approaches to the Korea Strait (map 4-4). The cruiser flashed word of the enemy's location square and estimated course toward the eastern channel of the strait (the Tsushima Strait). Unfortunately, the *Shinano-maru* had judged her own location incorrectly, and shortly afterward the enemy force vanished into the mist. Other Japanese picket vessels steamed past the Russian formation without spotting it. The result was that contact was lost until shortly after 0600. Rozhestvensky thus entered the strait without being seen, costing Tōgō an early opportunity to reduce the Russian fleet by torpedo attacks.[55] It now became critical to prevent the Russians from slipping through the strait entirely.

A little after 0630 Tōgō, in the *Mikasa,* led the Combined Fleet out of Chinhae Bay and the Kadŏk Channel, steaming east and then southeast to do battle. In Tokyo, the Navy General Staff anxiously awaited information from Tōgō concerning the weather. Two situations in particular concerned the general staff: visibility and the condition of the sea. Dense fogs that often blanketed the strait might allow the Russians to slip through unseen, and a rough sea would keep torpedo boats in port and spoil plans for the surprise flotilla attack with linked mines. On the morning of the battle, Tōgō heralded the news of the enemy and the

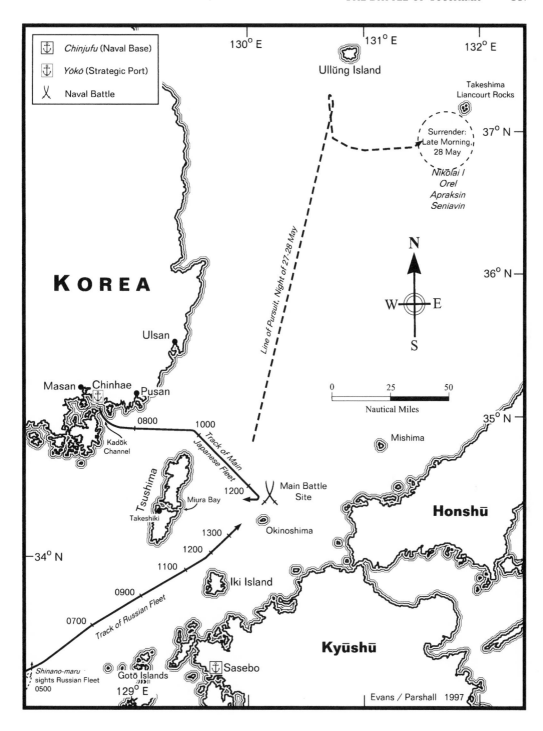

Map 4-4. General situation of the Battle of Tsushima, 27–28 May 1905

critical conditions of wind and weather. It was fitting to the drama of the hour that Tōgō's signal, largely drafted by Akiyama, concluded with an arresting phrase that to Japanese ears even now is highly poetic: *Honjitsu tenki seirō naredomo nami takashi* (Today the sky is bright but the waves are high). Despite the positive tone of the message, for the navy staff in Tokyo it carried the clear implication that the linked mine attack would have to be canceled. This was indeed the case; at 0850 Tōgō signaled the torpedo boats, "Because steaming is difficult, seek refuge in Miura Bay and await the opportunity to rejoin the fleet."[56]

Around noon, the Baltic Fleet was steaming through the middle of the eastern passage of the strait, trailed by the four cruisers of Admiral Dewa's Third Division, which had finally acquired contact. About this time, Tōgō and the main force in single column turned sharply west, looking for the enemy. He had learned from Admiral Kataoka, who was in the *Itsukushima* with the Fifth Division, that the Russians were proceeding northeastward in two main columns, the stronger one to starboard.[57] Tōgō had many other reports, but unfortunately they were not reliable; the enemy was closer and farther eastward than reported. At 1331, Tōgō turned roughly south-southwest, thinking he would be coming down on opposite lines to port of the Russians so that he could attack their weaker port formation. It was something of a surprise when at 1339 they suddenly appeared out of the haze at the limit of visibility, 8 to 9 miles away, steaming on a roughly opposite course slightly to starboard of him.

He immediately turned in column to northwest by north to gain room and time. After signaling for battle speed, 15 knots, at 1355 Tōgō unfurled his famous Nelsonian signal, the Z flag: *Kōkoku no kōhai kono issen ni ari; kakuin issō funrei doryoku seyo* (The fate of the empire rests upon this one battle; let every man do his utmost).[58] He then turned westward and held course for a few minutes. The two fleets were now about 6 miles (11,000 meters) apart, the Russians coming on at their battle speed of 10 knots. At 1402 Tōgō ordered a turn in succession to port, to southwest by south, "arraying as if to pass on opposite courses."[59] To have maintained this heading would have meant a choice for inconclusive combat, since the rapidly and continually changing range between his ships and the enemy's would have made the time of firing short and scoring hits difficult. Further, it would have repeated the error of the Battle of the Yellow Sea, allowing the enemy to get behind him and escape. Consequently, at 1407, Tōgō, determined to annihilate his opponent, gave the order by which the *Mikasa* turned fourteen points to port, each battleship and cruiser in column turning in succession in its wake to a course of east-northeast.

Few single movements in modern naval history have been as commented upon as this turn, which put Tōgō's force parallel to Rozhestvensky's fleet. Its origins and its timing, and even the risk involved, have been matters of intense scrutiny and debate in the ninety years since. The traditional view has been that Tōgō, the master tactician, turned boldly into danger—the Russian guns—at the last moment to press the enemy's van and cross the T, all according to plan.[60] Recent research yields another view of these critical minutes.[61] Tōgō was surprised by the unexpected appearance of the Russian fleet, which was not where reports had it. Mist obscured the Russian formations, which at the moment of the turn were moving back into a single line. Tōgō's plan of attacking the column to port while it masked the battleships to starboard was about to be nullified; Russian fire would be more intense. Clearly, there was consternation among the officers on *Mikasa*'s bridge, and some of them may have believed they were about to fight on opposite courses.[62] Yet there is little doubt that the maneuver was shrewd and aggressive. Tōgō was determined not to let the Russians get past him and planned to engage at close range. He could have brought his column most quickly onto a parallel course with Rozhestvensky by ordering a simultaneous turn by all ships, as the battle plan prescribed. But it would have left *Mikasa* as the last ship in the column, and Tōgō needed to retain a firm grip. Accordingly, he ordered the turn in succession to stay in the lead. The caution he had shown at the Yellow Sea was gone.

When the Russians saw the Japanese turning they were elated, thinking their moment had come. The Japanese ships, slowing in their turn, presented a fine target and were proceeding into extreme danger. At 1408 the lead Russian ship, the *Suvorov*, opened fire at 7,000 meters on the *Mikasa* and *Shikishima*, both of which had just completed the turn. The other Russian battleships soon joined in. Russian shells churned the sea at the spot where successive ships came out of the turn, yet it was the Japanese good fortune that no ship was seriously damaged.[63]

The turn was successful, and it was Tōgō's masterstroke. The Russians had not gotten past him, and he was moving into gun range with his entire battle line behind him. Steadying on their new course, his ships held their fire until the range closed to 6,400 meters. At 1410, the Japanese fired a 6-inch ranging shot and then at 1411 opened "normal" fire on the Russians.[64] At that moment the Russians were at a disadvantage because their maneuver to reform a single line had gone awry, some of the ships in the Second and Third Battle Divisions even stopping their engines to avoid collisions with ships ahead. Tōgō's speed was unchecked despite high winds and waves; he edged his line slightly to starboard to achieve what he considered the best range, about 5,500 meters, and steadied again.

The gun battle now began in earnest as the two fleets steamed in parallel. Fire on both sides became heavy. Shortly after 1418 Tōgō ordered "rapid" firing; his whole line concentrated on either the *Suvorov*, Rozhestvensky's flag, or the *Oslyabia*, the Second Battle Division leader. During the next quarter hour the enemy registered some heavy blows upon the Japanese column, hitting the *Mikasa* sixteen times[65] and causing the armored cruiser *Asama* to veer temporarily out of line. But Tōgō's fire on the enemy was much more destructive. As the powerful Japanese shells struck the battleships they scattered splinters that demolished superstructures and slaughtered crewmen on the decks. They produced intense heat that ignited everything flammable. "The paint," Rozhestvensky wrote much later, "burnt with a clear flame on the steel surfaces; boats, ropes, hammocks and woodwork caught fire; cartridges in the ready racks ignited; upper works and light guns were swept away; turrets jammed."[66] Under the awesome bombardment the Baltic Fleet began to lose formation and the Russian fire became erratic. Rozhestvensky held his course under increasingly accurate Japanese fire until about 1440, when he finally gave the order to turn four points to starboard, away from the Japanese. Tōgō soon adjusted his course, so that the two fleets were steaming on concentric arcs, with Tōgō using his superior speed to try to pull ahead on the outside. He kept the Russians under fire and, just as importantly, headed them away from Vladivostok and the chance to escape.

Though the contest lasted twenty-four hours longer, by 1450 on 27 May the Japanese had the upper hand. Mortally damaged, the *Oslyabia* had veered out of line and twenty minutes later capsized. At about the same time, the *Suvorov* went out of control, steaming around to port and back across her own course in a dark cloud of smoke, while Rozhestvensky, badly wounded, lay inside her. The Russian line was breaking apart. The *Aleksandr III* took over the *Suvorov*'s position in the lead, proceeding briefly eastward and then turning to port and charging Tōgō's line, which was gradually closing in on the stricken Russians. Tōgō responded to the *Aleksandr III*'s challenge with a simultaneous turn away at 1458 to avoid torpedoes and to stay ahead of his attackers, turning to a northwesterly course.

The battle then entered a phase of extreme confusion, which was in fact a lull in the action. Visibility was poor because the sea spray had been thickened by the smoke of shell bursts and fires. Russian ships circled in the gloom, trying to find their bearings. Japanese cruiser and destroyer formations attacked in the general melee. Admiral Kamimura and his Second Division parted from Tōgō at 1503 "to prevent the enemy from escaping southward." This maneuver was a mistake; Kamimura found nothing to the south and hurried north to rejoin Tōgō, but his action had broken the concentration of Japanese heavy guns.[67] For the next hour and a half, Tōgō and Kamimura steamed separate circles around the melee from east to north to south, coming back around to northerly courses at about 1730.

When they got clear of the confusion, after 1800, the Japanese found to their surprise that the Russian fleet had largely reformed and was running northward. A new phase of the battle began, with the Japanese chasing the Russians from behind as at the Yellow Sea (map 4-6). The *Borodino* led, followed by the *Orel*, and then Admiral Nebogatov's division, with the damaged *Aleksandr III* straggling

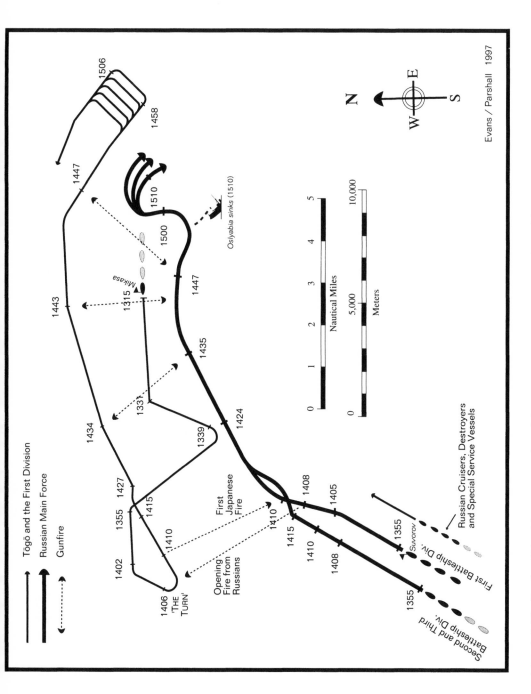

Map 4-5. The Battle of Tsushima, approach and decisive opening maneuvers (Adapted from *NRKK*, map appendix)

Tōgō and the First Division

Russian Main Force

Gunfire

1506
1458
1447
1510
1500
Oslyabia sinks (1510)
1443
Mikasa
1315
1447
1435
1331
1424
1434
1339
1355 1427
1415
1410
1402
First Japanese Fire
1406 'THE TURN'
Opening Fire from Russians
1410
1415
1408
1405
1410
1408
1355
Suvorov
1355
First Battleship Div.
Second and Third Battleship Div.
Russian Cruisers, Destroyers and Special Service Vessels

N E S W

Nautical Miles
0 1 2 3 4 5

Meters
0 5,000 10,000

Evans / Parshall 1997

behind. Cruisers and transports were also in company, following *Borodino*'s signal for course N 23° E. An intense gunnery action began between the Russians and Tōgō on roughly parallel courses. The Russians at first had the advantage, with the setting sun behind them. But Tōgō's superior speed closed the range. Both sides took punishment. At 1850 the *Aleksandr III* suddenly moved out of line, capsized, and sank. As daylight was failing and the action about to be broken off, the *Borodino* was hit and exploded. She sank at 1920. The remainder of the Russian fleet, disheartened, saw to the north "the black specks of the Japanese torpedo boats barring our passage," and turned away to port and south. The second major action was over, and although the battle was to continue until the afternoon of the next day, the issue was no longer in doubt.

Tōgō then gathered his heavy ships together, making for the next morning's rendezvous north of Ullung Island. As called for in the Akiyama plan, he turned the night battle over to his destroyers and torpedo boats. They launched a series of torpedo attacks on the enemy's ships that under the cover of darkness were plodding northward, making for Vladivostok. The Japanese attacks, though many and fierce, generally came to naught, and several Japanese craft collided.

The Fourth Destroyer Flotilla, however, scored notable successes. Its commander was Suzuki Kantarō, the fierce veteran of the torpedo attacks at Weihaiwei in 1895. In late afternoon Suzuki had found the flaming *Suvorov* and sent her quickly to the bottom with torpedoes. After dark, Suzuki searched the sea for targets without results until about 0230 on 28 May. He discovered the injured battleship *Navarin* and "without being detected by the enemy skillfully spread six segments of linked mines across her course."[68] An explosion followed; she sank soon after. Suzuki's destroyers discovered another target as they made away, the battleship *Sisoi Veliky,* and attacked her with torpedoes.[69] She sank the next morning. These two battleships, as it turned out, were the greater part of the harvest of the night's flotilla attacks.

Most of the surviving Russian ships still headed northward, but a few turned south to reach neutral ports where they were interned. On the morning of 28 May Nebogatov and the nucleus of the remaining Russian force—two battleships, two coastal armored ships, and a cruiser—were found and surrounded by Tōgō's battle fleet. Acknowledging his situation to be hopeless, Nebogatov signaled his capitulation. Akiyama was sent to the Russian flagship to escort the Russian admiral to the *Mikasa,* where Tōgō was waiting to accept his surrender. At midday, the destroyer *Bedovy,* carrying the wounded Rozhestvensky, was discovered by the Japanese and also surrendered. A few other isolated Russian ships scattered over the area were either sunk or scuttled when they refused to surrender, but by midday of 28 May, the battle was over.

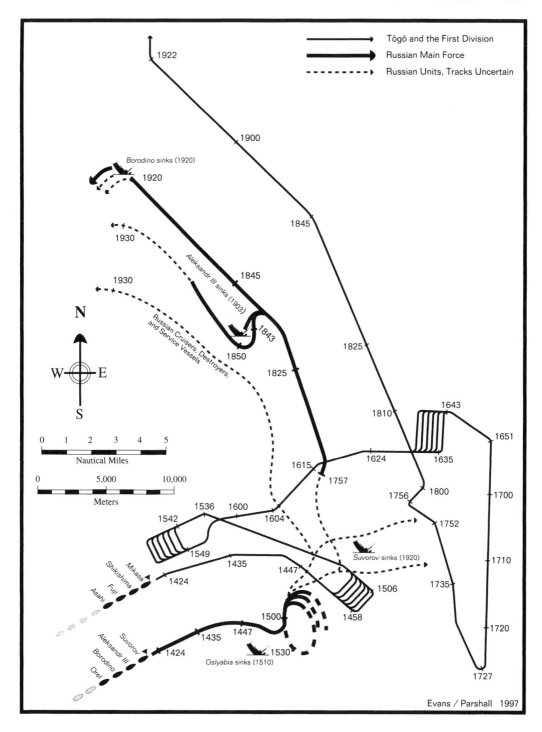

Map 4-6. The Battle of Tsushima, 27 May 1905, tracks of the battleship divisions (Adapted from *NRKK*, map appendix)

Tsushima was one of the few annihilating battles in naval history, and its scale is measured in the losses for each side. Of the thirty-eight warships and other vessels that Rozhestvensky tried to take through the Korea Strait, thirty-four had been sunk, scuttled, captured, or interned. The Russians had lost 4,830 dead and 5,917 captured, including two admirals. In contrast, the Japanese Combined Fleet had lost three torpedo boats sunk, three capital ships moderately damaged, eight destroyers and torpedo boats temporarily disabled, and 110 men killed.[70]

When peace came in October 1905, the fleet left Sasebo Naval Base and proceeded to Ise Bay. Tōgō and his commanders worshiped briefly at the grand shrine of Ise and then proceeded with their force up the coast to Tokyo Bay. On 23 October a great victory review was held at which the emperor announced, "We have personally inspected the triumphant navy and are pleased that it is in perfect order and its spirit is exceedingly high."[71] The Combined Fleet was finally disbanded in late December. Tōgō issued an instruction on this occasion, which began, "The war of twenty months' duration already belongs to the past and our Combined Fleet, having discharged its duty, is disbanded." He made a long plea for preparedness, ending with, "The gods refuse the crown of victory to those who rest content after a single triumph. They give it to those who exert themselves in peacetime training, who have therefore won before any fighting begins. As the men of old said, 'After a victory, tighten your helmet strings!'"[72]

THE BATTLE AND THE WAR IN RETROSPECT

It is frequently said that the qualitative disparity between the two sides at Tsushima in nearly every category of material and leadership was so great that the battle had really little meaning for the course of naval history and few real lessons to teach. "The truth of Tsushima was that the Russian Baltic Fleet was no more than an ill-assorted rabble with a commander who failed to command," one eminent British military historian has written.[73] While this is undoubtedly true, what resulted was not just a Japanese victory and a Russian defeat. The Tsushima battle was an annihilation with scarcely a parallel in the history of modern sea warfare, except perhaps the Battle of the Philippine Sea in World War II (which was primarily an aerial battle). At the time, as Corbett wrote, Tsushima was "the most decisive and complete naval victory in history."[74] The elements in the Japanese victory and its legacy for Japanese naval doctrine provide valuable lessons for naval establishments around the globe.

As previously discussed, the Combined Fleet entered battle with several advantages over the Russian fleet. Japanese gunnery at decisive ranges was a prime reason for the Japanese victory. This is confirmed by the superior rate and volume of Japanese fire, which fulfilled Tōgō's expectations. The Japanese made up for inferiority in large ordnance—only seventeen 12-inch guns to the Russians' forty-one—by skill in serving the guns. Nevertheless, the actual ratio of hits to shots fired by Tōgō's force was low, probably well below 10 percent.[75] Also, the Russians scored well on Japanese ships; in the two main periods of action, they made about forty hits with 12-inch projectiles, which is probably not grossly different from the number scored by Japanese gunners.

Japanese preponderance, then, was not so much due to the number of hits as to the relative damage per hit. Japanese ships were sturdy;[76] many ricochets were recorded; and Russian shells often were duds. On the other hand, Japanese shells that found their targets struck home with dreadful force because of their design and explosive power, as described in chapter 3. The Japanese favored high-capacity shells (HC),[77] which contained four times the explosive charge of armor-piercing shells (AP). When AP shells were used, they acted like HC because of their sensitive fuses, which caused them to burst at the instant of impact without penetrating to the vitals of the target. There is no recorded case of a Japanese shell penetrating even thin armor at Tsushima.[78] But both kinds of shell (which both contained Shimose explosive) caused numerous fires with their high-temperature gases. Their blast twisted Russian superstructures into grotesque shapes, and the shrapnel decimated crews on the decks.[79] Gunnery pundits of the period believed that to destroy heavy ships, AP shells were necessary; but at Tsushima the Japanese demonstrated that punishing fire on the decks severely damaged even heavily armored warships, and once disabled, they could be given the coup de grace by gunfire or torpedo.

Among the reasons for victory were Tōgō's advantages in speed and fleet homogeneity. Without his ability to bring his battleships forward quickly and smartly after his turn, in order to concentrate fire upon the lead ships in both Russian divisions, his qualitative superiority in ordnance and gunnery would have counted for much less. A further advantage was the high standard of ship handling shown by the Japanese fleet. Tōgō's division made five consecutive simultaneous turns in the course of sixty minutes. Simple as these maneuvers appear on track charts of the battle, they required extensive training to execute precisely. If his ships had not achieved the required precision and had they been out of place after the first turn, the fleet would indeed have been vulnerable to disaster. Yet Tōgō maneuvered at will, his warships maintaining a tight formation. The Russians, by contrast, having a lower level of fleet training and a disadvantageous collection of different ship types, had trouble executing the simplest maneuvers.

Finally, in terms of the advantage of leadership, there is no doubt that Tōgō's presence as commander was a prime element in the colossal Japanese success.

Careful, determined, and battle tested, Tōgō understood the nature of the battle he was to fight and the caliber of his enemy. His caution and imperturbability prevented early blunders. As long as he did not know the exact whereabouts of the approaching Baltic Fleet, for example, he would not be rushed into leaving Chinhae Bay, no matter how strongly he was urged to do so by his subordinates and staff. His order for the now-famous turn made clear his determination to fight a battle of decision from the outset of the encounter. His cool nerve in making this turn in front of the advancing Russian fleet was based as much as on his confidence in what his ships and ship captains could do effectively and what the enemy could not do, as on his willingness to take a risk.

The nonquantifiable element of the Japanese victory is the capacity of Tōgō and his staff to learn from the earlier mistakes of the war. No experience, in this sense, was more important than the Battle of the Yellow Sea and its examples of lost opportunities. The Japanese determination not to repeat the failures of that earlier engagement had as much to do as anything else with the enemy's annihilation.

Strategically, there seems very little for which Japanese planning for the battle can be faulted, even though Akiyama's seven-stage battle plan did not shape the beginning or the end of the battle. The Baltic Fleet entered the Korea Strait before Japanese destroyers and torpedo boats could launch their torpedo attacks as called for in the first stage of Akiyama's plan, and the remnant of the Baltic Fleet surrendered before the final stages of the plan could be executed. Yet these facts say less about the inadequacies of the plan than they do about the difficulty of locating ships in the darkness or mist before the age of aircraft and radar. The facts also show how the effective execution of the middle stages of the plan made its last phases unnecessary.

Tactically, Tōgō fought boldly and resourcefully from start to finish. Mastering the lessons of the Yellow Sea, he chose to fight at decisive ranges, to seize the initiative at the outset of the encounter, and, above all, to prevent the enemy from getting ahead of him. Tōgō's critical turn, made before a single Japanese gun had opened fire, was, of course, "the sovereign decision of the battle."[80] Naval historian Toyama Saburō has even said that of all the many causes of the Japanese victory at the Japan Sea, the most important was Tōgō's sixteen-point turn at the outset of the battle.[81] With it, Tōgō was able to dictate the nature of the struggle and to destroy the cohesion of the Russian fleet; without it Rozhestvensky's progress toward Vladivostok would have been much more difficult to impede.

Many accounts state that Tōgō won the battle because his turn allowed him to cross the T. Tōgō maneuvered *so as to cross* the T, and he sought to overwhelm the lead ship of the enemy. In these two respects the T tactic was important as the theoretical baseline of the battle. But the two main actions in which he achieved preponderance, lasting from 1408 to 1458 and 1800 to 1920, were really fought on parallel courses, as the maps show. When Tōgō sought to press the Russians during the first phase of the action, they edged away, keeping the ships in parallel. By the time Tōgō's First Division was in a position to cross, at about 1450, there was no more Russian line *to* cross; the Russians had been thrown into such confusion, and visibility was so limited, that the T could not be carried out. The later action was fought on slightly diverging courses but remained in essence a gun duel on parallel tracks.

Without the generally stable relative positions of ships steaming in parallel, it is unlikely that gunfire would have been the decisive weapon of the battle, because the technology of fire control of the age was still primitive. That is, Japanese gunners were only beginning to understand the problem of calculating the rate of change of range. They fired at range-finder range rather than gun range (i.e., they did not allow for the target's change of range during the flight of shell).[82] Russian fire control was, if anything, less developed than the Japanese. Both sides managed to score a significant number of hits in spite of their poor fire control systems because their relative positions were more or less fixed during the main phases of the battle. The Japanese preponderance was primarily due to the devastating topside damage inflicted by Japanese shells and to the relative impotence of Russian shells. Again, speed and homogeneity of ship design were important background factors that allowed the Japanese to bring their guns to bear effectively.

Japan's overall conduct of the naval war clearly followed the soundest of strategies against a numerically superior enemy, but Japan initially pursued it with inadequate tactics. Those in command of the navy, and particularly Tōgō, understood the purposes of a battle fleet. Control of the sea was a principle of particular importance in 1904–5, since Japanese land operations to secure Korea and southern Manchuria depended vitally upon the security of ocean communications with Japan. To obtain control, the Japanese high command followed sound principles in keeping the Combined Fleet together and seeking first to contain and then to destroy the largest enemy battle force in East Asia as quickly as possible. The tactical means initially adopted to achieve that objective—the attacks on the well-protected Port Arthur squadron—though often considered a failure, were nevertheless effective as holding actions. Devising a means to force the enemy to expose himself to being struck by the Combined Fleet in waters as unfavorable to him as possible, the Combined Fleet began the landward siege of Port Arthur. Yet once the Port Arthur squadron had been forced out of its base, Tōgō failed to dispatch it quickly at the Battle of the Yellow Sea because of faulty planning and an excess of caution. It was not until the confrontation with the Baltic Fleet ten months later that tactics were sufficiently matched with strategic ends to achieve overwhelming victory.[83]

For well over two decades after Tsushima, naval war colleges, naval staffs, and professional journals throughout the world contemplated and debated the naval lessons of the Russo-Japanese War. The lessons were quite contradictory, given that so many kinds of naval operations were conducted during the war with such different results. Almost every doctrinal school of thought could therefore draw inspiration from the war. Nevertheless, among the most cited lessons of the war was the primacy of long-range firing. Many analysts noted that the war had shown that opposing fleets could now come into action at greater distances than had been thought possible and certainly at ranges that exceeded normal practice firing. Whereas the Japanese at the Battle of the Yalu had opened the engagement at 3,900 meters and Dewey at Manila Bay at 4,500, Tōgō at the Yellow Sea had opened fire at over 11,000 meters and at Tsushima at 6,400. For this reason, others heralded the dominance of the big gun, arguing that only the 10- and 12-inch guns had caused appreciable damage at Tsushima and that, henceforward, only guns of the largest caliber had any place on capital ships. This, at any rate, was the view of "Jackie" Fisher and the British admiralty and the reasoning behind the launching of the all-big-gun *Dreadnought,* which burst upon an astonished world in 1906.[84] Still, there were others in the British navy who maintained that 6-inch guns had proved psychologically as well as materially damaging once the ranges had closed at Tsushima and that medium batteries would continue to be essential in the future.[85]

While some were debating questions of heavy armament, others argued the success or failure of other naval weapons like the torpedo and the mine and the relative value of lesser ship types like the destroyer and torpedo boat. Given its major place in the professional thinking as well as in the arsenals of the world's navies, the torpedo seemed the biggest disappointment. Suzuki Kantarō and the Fourth Destroyer Flotilla had scored some notable successes with torpedoes toward the end of the battle. Yet, for the naval war as a whole, only 2 percent of torpedoes fired against moving ships had found their mark, and even against anchored targets, the results were poor. A number of explanations have been advanced for the general ineffectiveness of Japanese assaults at Port Arthur, the Yellow Sea, and Tsushima. Of these, the most frequently cited has been the failure of Japanese torpedo tactics, particularly the doctrine of long-range torpedo firing. Other factors, however, all contributed to the poor results—poor weapons maintenance, the still primitive nature of torpedo technology and design, insufficient torpedo training, and inadequate tactical coordination between Japanese torpedo units.[86]

On the other hand, the indirect effect of torpedo attacks had probably been important: Tōgō's decision against sending his major units into action on the night of 10 August, when the enemy was routed, and Rozhestvensky's decision to pass through the Korea Strait at midday because of his apparent fear of night torpedo attacks, seemed cases in point. And, though destroyers and torpedo boats thus proved relatively ineffective in the their primary mission, they were apparently highly effective in secondary functions of patrolling, reconnaissance, blockading, protecting landing operations, and, by their repeated attacks, placing the crews of the larger Russian warships under great psychological pressure.

In the continuing debate over the relative performance of particular weapons during the war only the results of the lowly mine seemed unarguable. In this, the first war in which mines were used extensively by both sides, they sank three battleships (two of which were the only Japanese capital ship losses of the war), five cruisers, three destroyers, and seven other warships.[87]

THE WAR AND THE EVOLUTION OF JAPANESE NAVAL DOCTRINE

The impact of the Russo-Japanese War on world naval thinking has less historical significance than the legacies it provided to the evolution of Japanese naval doctrine. Four key ideas helped shape this doctrine: the concept of the decisive fleet engagement determined by big guns; the validity of a strategy of attrition against a numerically superior enemy; the preference for quality over quantity in naval weaponry; and the importance of nighttime torpedo tactics.

The first concept was based on the outcome of Tsushima. Experiences in this battle led Japanese leadership to believe that the only decisive encounter in modern naval war could be a surface engagement, a battle of annihilation fought during the daylight hours between main fleet forces. The outcome would be determined by capital ships armed with the largest cannon. This was a concept summarized in the Japanese phrase *taikan kyohōshugi*—the principle of big ships and big guns. It was, of course, a principle held by all major navies after 1905, but, as it had been Japanese warships and ordnance that had confirmed the principle, it is not surprising that it came to be indelibly etched into Japanese naval doctrine.

The second legacy of Tsushima was how to win a decisive fleet engagement against a foe having more big ships and big guns than one's own. (At this point, the navy's hypothetical enemy had changed from Russia to the United States.) The apparent remedy to this disparity was a campaign of attrition against an advancing enemy battle fleet like the campaign so effectively waged under Akiyama Saneyuki's seven-stage battle plan. That Tsushima had not exactly followed Akiyama's scheme did not dim its luster in the eyes of Japanese naval planners who pondered the question of the decisive fleet engagement. For the next three and a half decades they remained convinced that the basic strategy and tactics of attrition were the best means of equalizing Japanese and enemy strengths in capital ships and firepower prior to the decisive battle.[88]

The third conclusion that the Japanese navy drew from the Russo-Japanese War was the priority that must be given to superior quality in warship design and construction over superiority in numbers of warships. The rugged construction that enabled the *Mikasa* and her sisters to take a heavy pounding without appreciable reduction in their fighting power; their 18-knot speed; and the efficiency of their hydraulically operated main battery guns, each of which could pump out three shells every two minutes, had all been critical factors in the two fleet engagements of the war. Superiority in speed, armor, and gunfire remained cardinal principles in Japanese capital ship construction and was counted on to provide the Japanese navy with the winning edge in any battle-line-to-battle-line encounter between a Japanese fleet and an enemy fleet of equal strength. In this sense, the *Mikasa* and her sisters were the doctrinal progenitors of the superbattleships *Yamato* and *Musashi,* launched over three decades later.

Last, all these assumptions indirectly supported a resurgent emphasis on torpedo warfare in Japanese naval thinking after the Russo-Japanese War. On the surface, this seems odd because the torpedo had achieved so little during the war. Used by larger warships on three or four occasions, torpedoes had accomplished nothing. Employed at night by destroyers and torpedo craft six times during the conflict—four times against anchored vessels at Port Arthur and twice against moving warships in the two fleet engagements of the war—the only appreciable damage they inflicted was at Tsushima against the warships of an already routed enemy.

Yet the navy maintained its enthusiasm for torpedo warfare in part because of its search for ways to overcome enemy superiority in heavy ordnance. In an era of naval operations when radar did not yet exist, darkness tended to offset the predominance of the largest naval cannon. The Japanese navy held that night combat was thus an important remedy to numerical inferiority in capital ships and heavy firepower. Further, it was convinced that torpedo warfare, conducted by destroyers at ranges far shorter than those of naval gunfire, was the most promising means for night combat.[89]

There was another reason for continued interest in torpedo warfare. During the mid-Meiji period, the Japanese navy had seized upon the torpedo as an ideal naval weapon and had taken to torpedo warfare with surprising enthusiasm. At the time, not only had the torpedo been seen as the most suitable weapon for volunteer attack units of a small navy dealing with the warships of a large one, but the tactics it called for seemed to recall those of ancient Japanese warfare—the quick, close-in thrust of small groups of warriors against the heart of the enemy—and thus admirably suited to the Japanese martial spirit. This spirit remained very much part of the naval tradition in modern Japan and thus helped to insure the continued attraction of the torpedo as a prime weapon in the Japanese naval arsenal.[90]

For all these reasons, it seemed important to the Japanese navy not to abandon torpedo warfare, but to improve it. To do so, the navy undertook three efforts in the decade following the war. The first was to correct defects in the torpedoes themselves by increasing their size, speed, and range so that, following World War I,

Japanese torpedoes had grown from 35–45 to 61 centimeters in diameter, had attained speeds of 38 knots, and had ranges of 20,000 meters.[91] The second was to rethink the doctrine of long-range firing that had come to influence Japanese destroyer and torpedo boat units between 1900 and 1904 and to return to the *nikuhaku-hitchu* spirit of determined, close-in torpedo attacks. And third, recognizing that the capabilities of the torpedo system—the individual destroyer—was closely related to the success or failure of the organization of destroyer units, the Japanese gave constant and intensive study in the succeeding decades to the organization and reorganization of destroyer formations. In this, the Japanese navy was perhaps unique among the world's naval forces.[92]

Linked mines, though virtually unknown even inside the Japanese navy after their development during the Russo-Japanese War, provide further insight into ways that the Japanese hoped to overcome enemy superiority in heavy ordnance. As envisaged in the revised Battle Plan, linked mines would be laid in front of the enemy's main battle line by torpedo boats and destroyers. They were a means of eliminating a part of the enemy's battle force at the start of an engagement at minimal cost and risk to the fleet. Following the war they were developed as a top secret weapon, the *ichigō kirai* (type 1 mine), for use primarily by light cruisers. They were considered a decisive weapon, and the fleet was equipped with them until 1930, when the development of high-speed battleships and aircraft made them obsolete. The navy continued to uphold the David-versus-Goliath concept inherent in the linked mine, however, by developing the midget submarine as a replacement for the linked mine in the early 1930s. Midgets, like the linked mines, would be positioned across the path of the enemy's battle fleet and used to destroy several battleships at the outset of the decisive fleet encounter.[93]

As discussed, for Japanese naval thought, the most important legacy of the Russo-Japanese War in general and the Battle of Tsushima in particular, was the priority placed on the battleship as the means of destroying the enemy fleet. To be sure, the heavy-gun engagement was a concept shared by contemporary naval establishments elsewhere. But according to the eminent naval analyst Nomura Minoru, for the Imperial Japanese Navy, the battleship concept was a fatal legacy. As Nomura has pointed out, the eventual appearance of submarines and aircraft not only challenged the dominance of the capital ship and the big gun, but also became critical elements in attacks on and defense of sea lanes.[94] World War I, of course, offered excellent training and experience in the protection of ocean commerce, and while the primacy of battleships and surface engagements continued to constitute the mainstream of Anglo-American naval thinking, the participation of British and American navies in the war sensitized them to the newer aspects of naval warfare: submarine commerce raiding, antisubmarine warfare, and convoy protection. In these aspects, the Japanese navy was to have little experience during

World War I (aside from marginal participation by a few units in the Mediter-ranean) and thus little interest after the war. Instead, its attention was absorbed by the Battle of Jutland, the consummate surface battle that, for all the ambiguity of its victory at the time, seemed to confirm Japanese assumptions. The Japanese navy's neglect of the newer but less dramatic elements of naval warfare was a cru-cial element in Japan's defeat in World War II.

The most harmful legacy of the Tsushima battle itself was the conviction it instilled in Japan's naval leaders that one great battle at sea was the essence of naval war, and that such a battle would achieve command of the sea and even decide the outcome of war. Yet most naval wars, before Tsushima and since, were protracted and attritional, usually involving heavy losses even on the part of the victors. Behind the Japanese faith in "decisive battle" lay the assumption that the enemy would assemble his entire battle fleet and steam into a Japanese trap, an assumption that, if not entirely wrong-headed, was dangerous. The American Orange Plan did call for a trans-Pacific thrust of the U.S. battle fleet, and Ameri-can naval leaders, too, believed in a single great clash that would decide the issue of war. But Japanese leaders in the Russo-Japanese War had acquired at least an inkling of how difficult it was to bring the enemy to battle, and they should not have let this precious knowledge be lost. Almost invariably, the Russian fleet did not want to fight but to run, or to hide, and only the very particular circumstances at Tsushima delivered the Russian fleet into the hands of the Japanese. In the future, an enemy might not oblige Japanese plans by plowing across the ocean and, by falling into an ambush, suffer a crushing defeat in a great gun duel. Yet few Japanese strategists seem to have considered a different, less advantageous scenario. Faith in the decisive battle became dogma in the Japanese navy. In this way the confusion of tactical doctrine (for fighting battles) with strategic planning (for winning wars) began with Tsushima and fatally limited Japanese naval strat-egy.[95]

5

SATŌ TETSUTARŌ

The Contradictions of Japanese Naval Strategy, 1908–1911

In the space of a single decade, 1895–1905, Japan had fought and won two modern wars and in the process had risen from a struggling Asian nation to the front rank of world powers. The overwhelming victory over China had earned the respect of the Western world and had brought the first trappings of colonial empire. The much narrower defeat of elements of the Russian army, the world's largest, and the better portion of the Russian navy, the world's third largest, had not only left Japan the unchallenged maritime power in the West Pacific but had brought it valuable spoils: Port Arthur, the Liaotung Peninsula, and Russia's economic assets in South Manchuria. These strategic interests inevitably helped to pull the nation's attention, energies, and resources toward the Asian continent, a fact that complicated as well as intensified the effort by Japan's leadership to sort out the nation's strategic priorities.

In these two tests of strength, the Imperial Japanese Navy had played a formidable and, Japanese navy men argued, a critical part. In the process that service had advanced its fighting skills and its esprit de corps. Its tactics had moved from imitation and then mastery of Western doctrine to independent experimentation and innovation. It was at the Japanese Naval Staff College during this decade that a cluster of informed and imaginative instructors, Akiyama Saneyuki foremost among them, had worked out a series of tactical principles. Not only were the principles central to the victory of the Combined Fleet at Tsushima, but they influenced Japanese naval thought for decades to come.

But it proved easier to devise tactical maneuvers for the Combined Fleet in combat than to formulate a grand naval doctrine that explained the essential function of the Japanese navy and how it contributed to maintaining the vital interests of the Japanese empire. For the navy, the problem of grand strategy was more than a topic of theoretical discussion at the Naval Staff College. It was, in its origins, a matter of the now decades-old rivalry with its sister service. Having won organizational independence from the army just prior to the Russo-Japanese War, the navy now pressed for status beyond interservice parity, toward a position of seniority from which it could set the nation's strategic priorities and claim the lion's share of national prestige, public acclaim, and most important, the government's military budget. To gain such a position entailed more than naval victories, for the army had an equal share of triumph on land. It required the creation of a persuasive maritime strategy, an overarching argument that could justify the navy's budgetary demands for the greatly augmented battle fleet it sought.

As previously noted, the navy's effort to articulate such an argument had its beginnings in Yamamoto Gombei's bureaucratic battles with the Army Ministry during the 1890s. At the end of that decade, Yamamoto had pressed his case again, this time at the highest possible level. In October 1899, he had set forth his ideas on naval primacy in a memorial submitted directly to the throne. Laboring the point that it was far more effective for the preservation of Japan's security to maintain control over the surrounding seas than it was to try to defend the home islands themselves should control of these seas be lost, Yamamoto had argued that defense of the nation's home waters was best achieved by attacking the enemy as far from the nation's shores as possible. For this reason, he had insisted, the navy not only formed the nation's first line of defense, it also comprised its most critical component, and thus deserved senior status in relation to the army.[1]

Yamamoto's maneuver had not brought the Japanese navy the preeminent position he had sought for it, though it had provided a departure point for more detailed arguments on the purpose and function of the navy. The arguments could be sustained in those forums in which the navy sought support for its position: the council rooms of government, the floor of the Diet, and the pages of the national press. What was needed, Yamamoto realized, was a carefully elaborated statement of the preeminent importance of sea power, an argument backed by the weight of historical example, taken not just from Japan's own past, but also from the far greater experience of the traditional maritime powers of the West. The historical analyses of Mahan, John Laughton, and the Colomb brothers collectively provided a baseline or a general theory of sea power. Yet the arguments of the "Blue Water" school represented a Western discourse that obviously had little reference or application to the Japanese situation. Mahan, specifically, had provided an explanation for global sea power, using examples of British naval supremacy during the great age of sail. His explanation linked command of the seas with imperial expansion involving not only ocean commerce, but also the establishment of bases and trading stations in whatever seas were vital to the nation's communications and strategic interests. Yet the geographic and historical circumstances of the Japanese empire were quite different, since they confined that empire to the waters of East Asia. For these reasons, Navy Minister Yamamoto and Chief of Staff Itō Yūkō agreed that the navy did not need a universal theory of sea power applicable in all times and places. Instead the navy needed an explanation of sea power that might use Western historical examples, but that was directed to the Japanese situation, which was regional and thus particular.

While their objective was more the shaping of a public credo than the creation of a purpose for the navy, Itō and Yamamoto knew that such an explanation must come from within the navy itself. At the turn of the century there were two such officers in Tokyo who, by virtue of interest and intellect, could articulate the navalist argument Itō and Yamamoto had in mind: Lt. Comdr. Ogasawara Chōsei, serving in the Intelligence Bureau of the Navy General Staff, and Lt. Comdr. Satō Tetsutarō, a relatively obscure officer in the Naval Affairs Bureau of the Navy Ministry. As mentioned previously, Ogasawara was an important intelligence officer and official historian during the Russo-Japanese War. He had begun his career as a naval publicist when, in 1899, he was commissioned by Admiral Itō to write a popular history of the navy in order to incite public enthusiasm for the service. Yamamoto had a more select audience in mind when he picked Lieutenant Commander Satō to begin a serious study of naval strategy, one that would reach the most influential circles in Japan, particularly leading members of the Diet, the cabinet, and the upper levels of the bureaucracy, while at the same time being instructive to future generations of naval professionals.

SATŌ TETSUTARŌ AND THE IDEA OF OCEANIC DEFENSE

Satō Tetsutarō was a promising candidate for the job. To begin with, he had ample sea experience and had served with distinction at the Battle of the Yalu aboard the cruiser *Amagi*. More important, his early career was marked by an interest in naval history and strategy. Even before the Sino-Japanese War he had written a short treatise, *Kokubō shisetsu* (Personal opinions on national defense), based largely on his analysis of Japan's maritime operations against Korea in the sixteenth century. In it, Satō had set forth the same general argument that Yamamoto used in his debates with the army brass, namely, that an aggressive, distant, seaborne defense was much more likely to assure Japan's security than one that was static and land-oriented.[2]

After the Sino-Japanese War, while serving in the Naval Affairs Bureau and continuing his historical researches on the side, Satō had come to the attention of Yamamoto, who had called him in and instructed him to devote himself fully to the study of naval strategy and history, beginning with an initial period of research abroad. Convinced of the relevance of the British maritime experience to the Japanese case, given their similarity as island nations, Yamamoto in 1899 sent Satō off to Britain as one of a number of middle-echelon officers assigned there for research and training.

Satō (who, like most Naval Academy graduates, was reasonably facile in reading English) spent most of the next year and a half in London immersing himself in the classic works of Western naval history, some of which were unavailable in his own country. Then he traveled to the United States for six months of research.[3] Satō returned to Japan late in 1901, and the next year, he was appointed instructor at the staff college by Yamamoto. If Satō had been thinking of leisurely progress toward a magisterial study of his subject, Yamamoto had more urgent considerations in mind. Locked more intensely than ever in a struggle to obtain increased funding from the Diet for his fleet enlargement program, the navy minister ordered Satō to get started as quickly as possible on drafting a strategic manifesto for the navy that would garner support from influential members of the government and the Diet.

By the autumn of 1902, Satō had finished his treatise, *Teikoku kokubō ron* (On imperial defense), which was published by the Suikōsha, the influential professional association of navy line officers, and distributed through Navy Ministry channels after approval from the throne. As the opening shot in a now public campaign to secure a privileged position for the navy, the book was an elaboration of the navalist message already outlined here. It argued that since the defense of Japan was essentially an oceanic matter, the first strategic principle for the nation should be to defeat any approaching enemy at sea, far from Japan's own shores, and for these reasons, the need to strengthen the navy should take precedence over all other major obligations of the Japanese state. In the short run the blatantly partisan nature of Satō's argument worked against the navy's interest; the appearance of the work caused a storm of controversy rather than a wave of support for Yamamoto's fleet enlargement program. The circulation of the book in November 1902 to the Diet, the Privy Council, and the *genrō* (the ruling circle of elder statesmen) had caused a reaction not expected by Yamamoto. Old Marshal

Yamagata Aritomo, retired patriarch of the army, was so incensed at Satō's argument that he commissioned his aide-de-camp to draft a rebuttal. Far more serious, the numerous pro-army members of the Diet were sufficiently angered at Yamamoto's grandstand play that they actually cut his fleet enlargement plan.[4] Yet Satō's book served to air publicly the navy's position in its fundamental disagreement with the army over the proper strategic posture for Japan.

For the next four years Satō's assignments, mostly ship commands, took him out of the crossfire of debate, though his ideas continued to exacerbate relations between the two services. In 1906, Satō returned to the Naval Staff College, first to study in the elective course, then in 1907 to serve as an instructor. At the college in 1907, he delivered a series of lectures entitled *"Kaibō shi ron"* (On the History of Naval Defense), an extension of his earlier work, but now infused with historical example drawn largely from the Western maritime past. In 1908, Satō labored to put these lectures into manuscript form and that year, just before he left the college to take command of the cruiser *Sōya,* the Suikōsha published the massive work for which he became best known: *Teikoku kokubō shi ron (On the History of Imperial Defense)* based on his 1907 lectures.

Because of its length (nearly nine hundred pages), its relentlessly ponderous organization modeled on Rankean methodology in historical writing, its heavy doses of mystical rhetoric, and its cumbrous, formal style, Satō's *History* was not easy reading at the time, and the more than eighty years since have served to increase its opaqueness tenfold. Like Clausewitz's *On War,* it has been revered as a "classic," though it has been more often cited than read. Yet the book is the most extended and comprehensive essay ever formulated by a Japanese on the relationship of sea power to the Japanese situation. A survey of its arguments reveals not only the major dogmas held by the Japanese navy until the Pacific War, but their inherent contradictions.

The overarching theme of Satō's *History* is the preeminent importance of a navy in defending an island nation, or put more specifically, the advantage of an ocean-oriented aggressive (offensive) defense over a static land-oriented defense. Satō began with an elaboration of the simple proposition that both he and Yamamoto had at various times set forth: For an island nation like Japan, seaborne defense was the only defense. Theoretically, Satō noted, an enemy could be repulsed at any of three strategic lines or zones affecting an island nation's security: at sea, on the coast, or on the island itself. But as an island could only be invaded by sea, it stood to reason that control of the surrounding seas was all that mattered. "It is absolutely impossible for any country to land its armed force on our coast if it cannot take passage by sea," he noted. "[Even] should the great powers of the world combine against us and approach these narrow shores with several million men, if, on that occasion, they are not able to transport these forces to our shores, then we are unassailable. Hence, we have no reason to fear an enemy army; it is an enemy navy we have to worry about."[5]

But how to defend Japanese home waters against *superior* enemy sea power? In pondering the problem, Satō felt it necessary to refine his strategic analysis still further, dividing the ocean itself into three zones, as seen from the perspective of an island nation: the near seas (one's own ports, coasts, and territorial waters), the high seas, and the enemy's seas (his ports, coasts, and territorial waters). A nation that could gain victory in the enemy's seas would render control of the other two irrelevant. To strike an enemy a crippling blow in his home waters before he left them was thus the surest means to defend the nation.[6] Thus, while Satō spoke of the navy as Japan's first line of defense, the strategic stance he sought for it was essentially offensive.

There is, of course, an air of unreality to the concept of offensive defense as Satō suggested it in 1908. Directed against the United States, such a strategic posture would have been valid only in relation to the exposed American position in the Philippines. Pearl Harbor was not yet an important American fleet base,[7] and the Japanese navy at its current stage of development could not have seriously considered mounting an expedition against the American west coast. Such an operation would have required bringing with the fleet an immense train of auxiliary vessels across the breadth of the Pacific, with all the attendant difficulties involved in doing so.[8] In any case, by apparently arguing for a long-range preemptive strike against an enemy in his home waters, Satō was both confirming and prefiguring a central strategy of the Japanese navy. Such an operation had been undertaken by Tōgō in his attack on Port Arthur in 1904, and it was a strategy repeated by the navy in its 1941 strike at Pearl Harbor. It was, of course, an idea that lay fallow for many years. Over the decades following the Russo-Japanese War, the navy's planning for hostilities against the United States was (up until 1941, at least) essentially defensive, in that it involved waiting for the approach of the American fleet into the West Pacific.

A more serious problem undercut Satō's claim that Japan's only meaningful defense was oceanic defense. Prior to 1905, when Japan was literally an island empire comprising the home islands and Taiwan, the logic of Satō's argument might have been irrefutable. But by 1908, Japan had acquired continental interests as well, interests that inevitably required the commitment of significant land forces. To deal with this contradiction to his thesis, Satō made a twofold argument. First, he claimed that in the most recent war, the navy rather than the army had been the guarantor of Japan's security. To explain this assertion, he argued that had the expeditionary force in Manchuria been defeated, the loss of thousands of men would have been a national tragedy, but had the *navy* been defeated and Japan's coasts left open to invasion, the nation itself would have been at peril. Second, he dismissed claims by those in the army that Korea and Manchuria were vital links in Japan's security, and he uttered the heresy that there would be a number of advantages in abandoning them altogether. Using the historical example of England's futile efforts on the European continent during the Hundred Years' War, Satō contended that continental policies brought a nation few advantages and great risks, and he warned against adventures carried out for territorial gain that consumed the nation's resources and subverted true national defense. Above all, Satō concluded, Japan should not again field an army on the continent to defend the nation's interests (which, in his view, were more commercial than strategic). Rather, it should follow the example of modern Britain in seeking a continental ally, most probably China, to use as a buffer against Russia, the nation most likely to threaten what interests Japan had there.[9] Clearly, in making this argument against open-ended military commitment on the continent, Satō first sounded the navy's dissent to Japan's new strategic stance, a disagreement that provoked a fundamental rift in national policy over the next three decades.

If Satō rejected a continental strategy and land-based power for Japan, however, what then was a proper *maritime* strategy? This was a fundamental question to which Satō turned not only in his *History,* but also in later essays. The answers he provided clearly demonstrated a basic ambiguity in the arguments for Japanese navalism: whether Japan needed a navy to defend its existing interests, which were regional, or whether such a navy was a means to great power status and the projection of Japanese sea power on the high seas. This contradiction is evident in Satō's use of a central concept of Alfred Mahan's. Like Mahan, Satō continually referred to "command of the seas" *(seikaiken* in Japanese). But where Mahan used the term in a global context in connection with imperial expansion and the protection of distant trade routes, Satō usually employed it regionally, meaning the control of waters surrounding Japan and its possessions, largely in connection with the defense of these territories. Satō's use of the term within this narrower regional context tells us much about the essentially national perspective of Japanese naval thought. In studying world maritime history, Satō was not, like Mahan, interested in developing a universal theory of sea power. He instead sought justification for a particular navy, Japan's.[10] Whereas Mahan had used the study of British naval history to explain how sea power was linked to territorial expansion through a far-flung network of colonies and bases, Satō studied Western maritime history to understand how the Japanese navy might defend Japan from foreign aggression through a combination of offensive and defensive operations, a mobile fleet, and offshore bases.

Nevertheless, Satō seems to have fallen under the spell of Mahan's navalism in its most global sense—command of the seas as the projection of naval power abroad and thus the means to national greatness—though he could not explain how this would be accomplished. Although, like Mahan, he underscored the connection between naval strength, maritime trade, and world power, in 1908, the bulk of Japan's maritime trade was limited to East Asia, where Japan had colonial possessions and major commercial interests. This trade had been easily sheltered during the Sino-Japanese and Russo-Japanese Wars by Japan's modestly sized navy, and in the post-Russo-Japanese War decade, there seemed no imminent threat to Japan's limited transoceanic trade. Indeed, when Satō wrote of the protection of Japanese commerce he seemed again concerned only with the possible loss of Japan's territorial waters that could lead to a blockade of the home islands, rather than with the protection of distant Japanese trade routes. Like Mahan, too, Satō wrote of the expansive energy of maritime peoples. In his advocacy of *riku o sake, umi o susumu* (avoiding the continent and advancing on the seas), he seemed to suggest that Japan had a maritime destiny connected with imperial expansion. Like a number of his compatriots, at the time he urged a *nanshin* (southward advance) of Japan toward Southeast Asia, a concept that in later years became an article of faith with Japanese navy men. But he spoke in the most general terms, only to the prospects for Japanese trade and immigration in that part of the world.[11]

Satō's had to be vague about the navy's role in an expanding Japanese imperium because of two interrelated and inescapable facts during the decade between the Russo-Japanese War and the outbreak of World War I. First, Japan had nowhere to "advance upon the seas," certainly not in Southeast Asia, which (except for Siam) was entirely in the hands of Western colonial powers, as were the island territories of the western Pacific. Second, the one region in the world where there was yet room for the play of Japanese ambition and power between 1905 and 1914 was the northeast Asian continent—Korea, Manchuria, and China proper. But this was an area susceptible to military rather than naval pressure, the very region that Satō wished to abandon. If Japan were bent on expansion, it could hardly turn its back upon the Asian continent. Thus, a naval strategy predicated upon Satō's "advance upon the seas" was indeed no strategy at all.[12]

Satō's *On the History of Imperial Defense,* however flawed it may seem today, gained Satō wide attention within and outside the navy. In 1912, he published a condensation of his treatise, one-quarter the length of the massive original, in the hope of giving his ideas even greater circulation. The same year, he also wrote a slender volume for internal navy use, *Kokubō sakugi* (A proposal for national defense), which mixed some very generalized and mystical pronouncements on Japan's strategic situation with specific proposals for maintaining a certain level of naval defense, including his hypothetical standard for desirable force levels (see below).[13] In 1913, Satō was the principal author of a pamphlet closely modeled on this volume, *Kokubō mondai no kenkyū* (A study of the national defense problem). Published by the Navy Ministry, it reiterated many of his earlier views, but is most noteworthy for its references to the potential for Japanese trade and development in Southeast Asia and for its advocacy of maintaining a navy that was 70 percent of the strength of that of the United States (see below).[14]

In 1910, Satō returned to the staff college, becoming its senior instructor in 1911 and earning promotion to rear admiral in 1912. The years 1910–11 have been seen as a golden age of naval thought at the college, largely because they brought together three of the navy's most illustrious theorists—Satō, Akiyama Saneyuki, and Suzuki Kantarō—as instructors. Together, they developed a body of naval doctrine that influenced a whole generation of younger naval officers—Yamamoto Isoroku, Nagano Osami, and Yonai Mitsumasa among them—who passed through the college during these years and were destined to lead the navy during the Pacific War.

As a naval theorist, Satō has earned a mixed reputation among those who have studied Japanese naval history in the post–World War II era. The authors of the naval volumes of the huge history of military operations in the China and Pacific Wars issued by the Japanese Self-Defense Agency over the past twenty years assert that Satō, along with Akiyama, laid the bases for modern Japanese naval thought. Others are not so generous, contending that Satō's ideas were too imitative of the West, too generalized, and too ideological to form a persuasive naval doctrine.[15] A more realistic view is that Satō both confirmed and shaped the priorities of the Japanese navy. His stress on the idea of the *kantai kessen* (the single decisive fleet engagement) was shared by most of his colleagues, and the references in his *History* to the importance of firepower, based largely on his conclusions about the Battle of Tsushima, place him firmly in the "big ship, big gun" mainstream of contemporary Japanese naval theory. But more than anything else, Satō left the Japanese navy a powerful but baleful legacy of two interrelated concepts: his method of identifying a hypothetical enemy for the navy and his concept of a ratio for determining the minimum force levels to deal with that enemy.

A HYPOTHETICAL NAVAL STANDARD AND A 70 PERCENT NAVY

Satō assumed that the Japanese navy, particularly its battle fleet, should be shaped according to a hypothetical naval standard for its minimum forces. Of course, he was not the inventor of the concept of the "hypothetical enemy." Britain had been the first maritime power to adopt a theoretical yardstick for gauging its minimum requirements when in 1889 it had adopted the "two-power standard" asserting that Britain must maintain a fleet equal to the combined fleets of the next two largest naval powers. But his concept differed in two significant ways. First,

Britain adopted a standard to maintain global dominance, while Satō proposed that Japan adopt such a standard even though its strategic interests were limited to East Asia. More importantly, his concept linked the idea of a hypothetical standard to the notion of a "hypothetical enemy."

Naturally, Satō did not originate the concept of a hypothetical enemy, either. It was already an essential component of the naval race in Europe at the opening of the new century, sparked by the Anglo-German and other naval rivalries. Using the "hypothetical enemy" concept, a nation's military and naval establishments endeavored to identify the foreign power with which hostilities seemed most likely to occur, either because of obvious hostile intent or because of diametrically opposed national interests. What was different in Satō's use of the concept was his emphasis on the capabilities of other nations rather than on their intentions toward Japan. As early as 1902, in his *Teikoku kokubō ron,* Satō had argued that identifying a hypothetical enemy involved a perception about which state had the greatest *potential* to harm Japan, regardless of Japan's relations with that state. When he wrote his *History* (and for five years after that), Satō believed that Germany, because of its meddling in Chinese affairs and its obvious intent to build up its naval strength in East Asian waters, was the nation most likely to threaten Japanese interests. Yet, in Satō's view, the United States posed a far greater *potential* threat to the nation.[16] Thus, whereas relations between the Japanese and American governments were basically sound, Satō proposed to use the United States as the hypothetical standard against which the minimum force levels for the Japanese navy ought to be measured. Writing in 1913, Satō's own projections concerning American naval construction (wildly exaggerated, to be sure) estimated that by 1920 the United States would have sixty capital ships, including thirty-five of the dreadnought type.[17]

This enormous battle fleet and the vast industrial resources behind it made several things clear to Satō. To begin with, Japan could obviously never hope to match the United States warship for warship and that, for the foreseeable future, Japan would have to undertake a cautious foreign policy that worked to maintain friendly relations with the United States. Yet, Satō argued, the awesome disparity in naval strength did not mean that Japan could never challenge the United States at sea if the necessity arose. He based his confidence on two separate sets of assumptions. The first comprised the collective disadvantages of the American position. They included the need for the United States to divide its navy between the Atlantic and the Pacific Oceans, the problem of whether the Panama Canal, when completed, could handle the largest American warships, the vulnerability of the Philippines, the length of time that it would take for the American fleet to cross the Pacific, and the difficulty of coaling during a trans-Pacific crossing. His other set of assumptions revolved around the second great conceptual legacy that Satō left to the Japanese navy: a formula for the minimum force level that would enable Japan to succeed in any naval war with the United States. Specifically, it called for the Japanese navy to comprise at least 70 percent of the strength of that of the United States.[18]

The 70 percent ratio arose from research undertaken at the Naval Staff College, 1907–9, by Satō and by Akiyama Saneyuki on the force levels necessary for the Japanese navy to have a chance against an attacking American or German fleet.[19] Satō started with the widely held assumption of the day that it was necessary for an attacking fleet to hold a 50 percent superiority in firepower over a fleet defending its territorial waters. For that reason, Satō concluded, in order to repel an attacking fleet, a defending fleet had to possess 70 percent of the strength of an attacking fleet; anything less than this percentage—say, 60 percent of an attacking enemy's strength—would imperil the security of the defending nation.[20]

Thus was born the dogma of the 70 percent ratio, to which the Japanese navy clung for the next thirty years. As the central issue in a domestic campaign waged by the navy for funding to expand the fleet, the 70 percent ratio presented several advantages. It was so simple as to amount to almost a slogan; it sounded reasonable in that Japan sought to build only 70 percent of the strength possessed by the United States; and for some politicians, if not the admirals, it obscured the limits of Japan's own industrial base, which could probably not build a navy larger than 70 percent of the U.S. Navy, in any event. The same insistence on a 70 percent standard was later used for maintaining the fleet overseas during international negotiations on naval arms limitations.

Even as Satō was considering the United States as a hypothetical enemy and proposing naval forces to defend against them, a revolution in naval gunnery with far-reaching consequences was under way. The source of this revolution was the large-caliber trainable gun, which had evolved into the turret-mounted main battery characteristic of battleship ordnance. Improved fire control and longer ranges (discussed in detail in chapter 6) enabled many ships to concentrate on a single target. This ability to concentrate fire changed the dynamics of naval battle much to the advantage of the side with the larger number of ships. The effect was described in Comdr. Bradley Fiske's 1905 essay, "American Naval Policy."[21] Sometimes called the N^2 Law, it was given its algebraic form in 1914 by Frederick William Lanchester, a distinguished British engineer. Under this law, he demonstrated, the concentration of firepower made possible by modern gunnery conferred "an expanding, cumulative advantage" on the side with a preponderance of gun power, all other things being equal.[22] In the age of sail, a large fleet committed to battle would defeat a small one but would suffer the same losses as did the smaller fleet. But in the modern age of the battleship, the N^2 Law specified that not only would the force with more guns win, but its losses would be significantly less than those of its opponent. In the age of sail, a linear law of gunnery effectiveness held true; in the modern age, a square law. Thus, if a fleet of 10 sailing ships of the line met a fleet of 7 in a battle of annihilation, the larger would prevail but both sides would lose 7 ships. Under the N^2 Law, however, if a fleet of 10 modern battleships met 7 (of the same fighting efficiency and gun power per ship), the surviving ships of the large force would equal the square root of the difference between the square of the gun power of the two ships. That is, $\sqrt{(10^2 - 7^2)}$, or about 7, ships would remain in the larger fleet when the smaller had been completely destroyed. Ultimately, then, at a ratio of 10 American ships to 7 Japanese in a given battle, American firepower would clearly be superior, more than enough to encourage an American offensive against the Japanese fleet.

This reasoning, however, did not include several major factors that the Japanese saw working in their favor. The first was that certainly prior to 1913 and the completion of the Panama Canal and possibly even after its completion, it would be difficult for the United States to bring all of its fleet into the Pacific. If half the U.S. battle fleet were left in the Atlantic, the ratio of Japanese to American naval strength in the Pacific would be 7 to 5. Thus, the Fiske-Lanchester logic can be extended as follows: in dealing with the U.S. Pacific Fleet (with a strength of 5 units), the Japanese navy (7 units) would emerge victorious with the square root of $\sqrt{(49 - 25)}$, which equals roughly 5 units left over. Should the remaining 5 units of the U.S. Atlantic Fleet join battle, it would be an even match.

Two other offsetting considerations became fundamental in Japanese naval strategy for years to come: one was the prospect of building qualitatively superior capital ships that would cancel out American numerical advantage. The other, shaped after World War I, was the possibility of reducing the strength of a westward-moving U.S. battle fleet through attacks by light forces—submarines and aircraft, in particular—based in the former German Pacific islands acquired by Japan during the war.

BATTLE TACTICS AND FLEET ORGANIZATION

While Satō Tetsutarō was setting forth arguments for the augmentation of the fleet, his colleague at the Naval Staff College, Akiyama Saneyuki, was proposing a scheme for the fleet's tactical organization. This scheme followed what had, after Tsushima, become the tactical orthodoxy of the Japanese navy: daylight engagement by the battle fleet to force a decision, followed by night torpedo attacks by light forces to weaken the enemy should he still be undefeated at day's end. The *Kaisen yōmurei zokuhen* (Supplementary battle instructions), issued in

September 1912, called for a basic battle formation of line ahead with the commander in the van. Using this formation, the approved tactic was to cross the enemy's T, with the battle fleet's main batteries concentrating fire on selected enemy ships and the secondary batteries spreading their fire all along the enemy line. During the main engagement the heavy forces were to be supported by fast cruisers. The cruisers would prevent torpedo attacks by the enemy's supporting cruisers and destroyers and, when the opportunity presented itself, attack the enemy's main battle force. Should the engagement not bring about a decision by nightfall, the battle fleet would withdraw. (Except in unusual circumstances, night combat between main fleets was not authorized.) Light forces would launch torpedo attacks against the enemy, which would so weaken him that a decision could be attained when the two battle fleets resumed contact the next day.[23]

For Akiyama, the question of effective organization was all-important, given these general tactical principles. In a revision of his earlier *Basic Naval Tactics*, he argued that "when a nation builds a navy it must first plan the organization of its fleet and then build the ships to comprise it. Put another way, it is a mistake to set up an organization based on the ships available. First, devise the organization and then build the ships needed for it."[24] He readily appreciated that a fleet comprised more than just capital ships and that it also was an assemblage of lesser warship types, as well as of various sorts of fleet auxiliaries. Nevertheless, in his view, the organization of the battle force must determine the organization of the rest of the fleet. "Decide on the trunk—the main force," he insisted, "and the branches and leaves—the support and auxiliary forces—will take care of themselves."[25]

But how to structure the main battle force? For Akiyama, the determining principles were firepower and flexibility. And, based on what he perceived as a lesson of the Russo-Japanese War, these two principles were provided in optimum combination by a division (here Akiyama used the term *sentai*) of eight capital ships, a formation that could provide a formidable broadside, but also could be divided into halves or quarters. Experience had shown that it was possible to place two such divisions, but no more, under the effective direction of a single commander. Thus, the most powerful and maneuverable battle force imaginable, given the current state of naval technology, would be sixteen capital ships in two divisions maneuvering in concert.[26]

Following his own dictum, Akiyama then went on to prescribe the most effective organization of the rest of the fleet, beginning with a cruiser force that he proposed should comprise a maximum of two divisions for each division of capital ships. Exemplifying the current emphasis the Japanese navy placed on close-in night combat, an activity seen as the specialty of the destroyer, Akiyama also gave considerable attention to the organization of torpedo flotillas. He stressed the importance of small, flexible formations in order to minimize the sort of tactical confusion that characterized Japanese torpedo attacks in the late war with Russia. Last of all, Akiyama spelled out in detail the composition of a fleet of naval auxiliaries—depot ships, colliers, ammunition ships, repair vessels, and the like.[27] For Akiyama, this less glamorous side of naval force structure was an essential element of sea power, a view consistent with his concern for logistics. It was not, however, a priority that commended itself to the navy's high command. In a navy planning to wage a short, defensive-reactive war, his writings on naval supply gathered dust in later years. Japan's failure to develop an effective system of naval supply became a disastrous handicap in the Pacific War.[28]

In the years that followed, Akiyama's views on naval organization strongly influenced how the navy determined its minimum force levels. Indeed, until the end of World War I, his ideas, particularly those that centered on the navy's main force of capital ships, were followed very closely in drawing up the navy's expansion plans.[29]

THE IMPERIAL DEFENSE POLICY OF 1907 AND ITS CONTRADICTIONS

Even before the publication of Satō Tetsutarō's *History,* the army was preparing a counterattack on the navalist thought of Satō and his navy colleagues. It took the form not of a similarly massive and historically oriented study, but rather of a bureaucratic effort to provide Japan with a comprehensive and coordinated national strategy. The need for such an integrated strategy had become apparent in the years immediately following the Russo-Japanese War, as Japan's strategic interests had become more complicated and more vulnerable.

To most Japanese army men, Japan's recent territorial and economic acquisitions in Korea and Manchuria represented valuable assets in themselves, acquisitions that must be held at all costs; to others in the army they were stepping-stones for an ever-expanding advance upon the Asian continent.[30] In either case, army men believed that Japan's grip on its Asian foothold must be consolidated in the face of a resurgent threat from Russia, inevitably committed to a war of revenge against Japan. For these reasons, the army demanded that it be given precedence in drawing upon the nation's resources and that the government hold the line on further appropriations for the navy.

For its part, the navy had two concerns in the years immediately following the Russo-Japanese War. The first of these, voiced frequently and publicly by the navy during these years, was the declining position of Japanese naval strength in relation to that of the other leading naval powers. This predicament arose because of the furious naval arms race initially provoked by the Anglo-German naval rivalry at the outset of the new century. In 1901, Japan had a battle fleet of thirteen battleships and cruisers, larger than the U.S. Navy. But by 1907, Japan had fallen behind, with only twenty major warships to America's thirty-one. Moreover, the U.S. Navy was outdistancing other navies as well, moving ahead of the Germans in 1905 and ranking third in the world by 1907 (table 5-1). The relative decline in Japanese naval strength, which had occurred despite the destruction of the Russian fleet and the taking of prizes in 1904–5, represented, in the navy's view, a dangerous threat to its capacity to defend the nation's interests.

Table 5-1

STRENGTH OF THE WORLD'S NAVAL POWERS BY YEAR, 1900–1910

RANK ORDER BY TOTAL OF BATTLESHIPS, ARMORED CRUISERS, AND BATTLE CRUISERS

Year	1	2	3	4	5	6
1900	GB*	FR	RU	GE	U.S.	JP
1901	GB	FR	RU	GE	JP	U.S.
1902	GB	FR	RU	GE	JP	U.S.
1903	GB	FR	RU	GE	JP	U.S.
1904	GB	FR	RU	GE	U.S.	JP
1905	GB	FR	GE	U.S.	RU	JP
1906	GB	FR	GE	U.S.	JP	RU
1907	GB	FR	U.S.	GE	JP	RU
1908	GB	FR	U.S.	GE	JP	RU
1909	GB	FR	U.S.	GE	JP	RU
1910	GB	FR	U.S.	GE	JP	RU

STRENGTH BY TOTAL OF BATTLESHIPS, ARMORED CRUISERS, AND BATTLE CRUISERS

Year	Britain	France	Russia	Germany	U.S.	Japan
1900	39+11+0=50†	25+10+0=35	22+8+0=30	14+1+0=15	7+2+0=9	4+4+0=8
1901	41+12+0=53	25+9+0=34	22+8+0=30	15+1+0=16	9+2+0=11	6+7+0=13
1902	47+14+0=61	25+11+0=36	23+8+0=31	16+2+0=18	10+2+0=12	7+7+0=14
1903	49+19+0=68	25+12+0=37	23+9+0=32	18+2+0=20	11+2+0=13	7+7+0=14
1904	55+29+0=84	26+19+0=45	26+9+0=35	17+4+0=21	12+2+0=14	5+7+0=12
1905	58+29+0=87	26+20+0=46	14+4+0=18	19+4+0=23	13+6+0=19	5+9+0=14
1906	63+33+0=96	26+21+0=47	13+4+0=17	21+6+0=27	17+6+0=23	7+10+0=17
1907	62+35+0=97	27+21+0=48	10+4+0=14	22+6+0=28	22+9+0=31	8+11+1=20
1908	62+36+0=98	31+21+0=52	10+4+0=14	25+8+0=33	26+10+0=36	9+11+2=22
1909	62+37+0=99	29+23+0=52	10+4+0=14	26+8+0=34	26+11+0=37	11+12+2=25
1910	62+36+0=98	26+23+0=49	10+4+0=14	26+9+0=35	30+11+0=41	10+13+3=26

*Abbreviations: GB = Britain; FR = France; RU = Russia; GE = Germany; U.S. = United States; and JP = Japan).

† Figures represent, respectively, the numbers of battleships, armored cruisers, battle cruisers, and (after the equal sign) the total of all types.

The second problem had to do with the sudden and disturbing turn in relations with the United States after 1905. It had been provoked in part by the U.S. insistence on an open-door policy in China that had gradually developed into anti-Japanese pressure there, and in part by the American fears that Japan might use its newfound sea power to expand into the Pacific. But most of all, the soured relations had been caused by the spasm of racial hostility toward Japanese immigration on the American West Coast, 1905–7, which had set off angry denunciations in the Japanese press. While these antagonisms did not involve the two governments, both of which were intent on keeping their relations cordial, the tensions of 1905–7 had sensitized naval professionals on both sides of the Pacific to the possibility, however remote, of a future Japan–U.S. conflict.

All these elements—the changing situation on the northeast Asian continent, the spreading naval arms races among the great powers, and the shift in Japan–U.S. relations from cooperation to rivalry—seemed to point to the necessity to establish a coordinated national strategy for the Japanese armed services. The impetus to do so came from the army in 1906, when Lt. Col. Tanaka Giichi, a senior member of the Operations Section of the Army General Staff, drafted a memorandum that called for a basic national defense policy. It set forth Japan's strategic priorities as a great power, the establishment of a unified service command in wartime, the identification of a common hypothetical enemy for both services, and a decision upon a joint army-navy operational plan in the event of hostilities with that nation. The thrust of Tanaka's memorandum was to refute Satō Tetsutarō's insular, maritime, and commercial approach to national power, in favor of a forward, military position in Asia. Tanaka also reasserted the army's control over both the direction of grand strategy and wartime operations. Insisting that the army's aggressive, continent-oriented strategy must become that of the nation, Tanaka argued that "we must disengage ourselves from the restrictions of an island nation to become a state with continental interests."[31]

Marshal Yamagata Aritomo incorporated Tanaka's arguments in a memorial to the throne, calling for an overall national defense policy that would set forth an integrated strategy for Japan based on the primacy of army interests. Naturally, the navy raised vigorous objections. Tōgō, now chief of the Naval General Staff and backed by Yamamoto (who had retired the year before, but still wielded great influence), reaffirmed the navy's support for two independent command systems. He repudiated Yamagata's unification plan and insisted on the navy's right to designate its own hypothetical enemy.[32] Hammered out over the succeeding months in a series of negotiations between the two services, the *Teikoku kokubō hōshin* (Imperial defense policy), formally approved by the emperor in April 1907, was inevitably a compromise between the two fundamentally opposed approaches to a grand strategy for Japan.[33]

On the surface, it appeared that the army had reasserted its control over the determination of the nation's strategic priorities. Russia was formally identified as Japan's prime hypothetical enemy, and the army's forward position on the Asian continent became Japan's basic strategy. Yet the navy was allowed to designate the United States as its most likely opponent, in effect making that country equal in importance with Russia as the object of defense preparations. Moreover, the navy was able to reject Yamagata's hopes for a single command under army control. Further, in practical terms over the next decade, it was the navy, not the army, that received the largest share of public and budgetary support for its expansion.

Setting forth Japan's strategic priorities in broad terms, the 1907 policy statement provided two vital codicils that gave it teeth: *Kokubō shoyō heiryoku* (Military strength requirements for national defense), a statement on force levels necessary to support these priorities, and *Teikoku yōhei kōryō* (A general plan for the employment of the empire's forces), a general strategic plan for operations against the nation's hypothetical enemies. Together, they made up the Imperial Defense Policy, Japan's single most important grand strategic policy statement, which for the forty years of its existence was held to be the highest of all state secrets of the nation. It was revised three times after 1907, when the international situation seemed to require it: in 1918, after World War I and the shift in the international balance of power; in 1923, after the signing of the naval arms limitation treaty in Washington by Japan and the other maritime powers; and in 1936, after the abrogation of the naval limitation treaties.[34]

Henceforth, however, the plans subordinate to the Imperial Defense Policy were subject to more frequent review. The operational orders that were intended as a guide to both services for the execution of the defense policy were set forth in the *yōhei kōryō* (employment of forces) statement. The navy's specific operational responsibilities under the *yōhei kōryō* were spelled out in the *nendo sakusen keikaku* (annual operational plans), which were drawn up by 1 April each year by the Operations Section of the Navy General Staff. Once approved by the emperor, each operational plan remained in effect until 31 March of the following year. Although the general staff tended to base each plan on the previous year's plan, thus making it more vulnerable to compromise as well as perpetuating an inertia in the navy's operational thinking, the annual operational plans were obviously held in the tightest security.[35]

For all its importance, however, the Imperial Defense Policy was hardly an integrating document, since it failed to resolve the fundamental rift between the army and the navy over the nation's strategic priorities. The policy now formally perpetuated the interservice conflicts under the emperor's sanction: Thenceforth, the army prepared for war with one enemy, and the navy for war with another. Even allowing for the probable geographic conditions that would shape either of these two possible conflicts (military concentration for one, naval concentration for the other), the Imperial Defense Policy was a perilous stance for any nation, let alone a nation of limited resources like Japan.

THE IDEA OF AN "EIGHT-EIGHT FLEET"

For the Japanese navy in particular, the implications of the 1907 Imperial Defense Policy were ambiguous. On the one hand, the navy could get imperial sanction for its *taikan kyohōshugi* (big ships, big guns ideology). Specifically, the policy called for the construction of a battle fleet of eight modern (dreadnought) battleships of 20,000 tons each and eight modern armored cruisers of 18,000 tons each, to be complemented by the construction of several lesser warship types, including cruisers and destroyers.[36] This was the origin of the "eight-eight fleet" plan, which for the Japanese navy between 1907 and 1922, became as much an unquestioned article of faith as the 70 percent ratio.[37] Indeed, Satō argued that without the construction of an "eight-eight fleet," it would be impossible to maintain 70 percent of the naval strength of the United States, now designated as the navy's hypothetical enemy.[38]

Two factors influenced the Japanese navy's progress toward the assembly of a fleet of eight dreadnought battleships and armored cruisers (eventually termed battle cruisers). First, construction of warships lagged considerably behind the authorization for their construction. The laying down of a capital ship usually began six months to a year after the funds for its construction were authorized, and its completion, after being laid down, took another three years or so. Therefore, building programs by no means represented immediate naval strength. Consequently, when the eight-eight fleet program was suddenly abandoned in 1922, fewer than half the planned warships had actually joined the fleet.

Second, not every dreadnought originally launched as a unit intended for inclusion in an eight-eight fleet was counted as such a decade later. A critical element in the eight-eight fleet idea (stated in the force-level requirements of the 1907 Imperial Defense Policy) was an age limit applied to first-line battleships. Considering current world trends in the pace of naval construction and the development of naval technology, the navy concluded that the effective life of a capital ship over a twenty-five year period should be divided into three stages: when it was eight years old or less it could be considered a first-line warship; between nine and sixteen years it should be relegated to the second line; between sixteen and twenty-five years it would fall into a third-line status; and after twenty-five years it should be scrapped.[39] Thus, as the navy's relentless campaign for an eight-eight fleet stretched out over the years, some of the first dreadnoughts and cruisers constructed after the Russo-Japanese War reached obsolescence and had to be replaced in the navy's calculations for an eight-eight fleet.

Though the eight-eight fleet concept was at the heart of Japan's naval policy from 1907 to 1922, it was clearly ill-conceived from its very beginnings. First of all, there was in 1907 no clash of fundamental interests between Japan and the United States nor any indication that either the Japanese or the American government desired confrontation. Mirroring Satō Tetsutarō's concept of a hypothetical standard, the Imperial Defense Policy of 1907 promoted Japan's big-navy ideology in complete disregard of the realities of Japanese foreign policy. Far from providing a rationale for an eight-eight fleet by a detailed explanation of an American naval threat, the policy almost arbitrarily selected the United States as a likely opponent in order to justify the scale of naval strength it desired. More than Japan's most likely antagonist, the U.S. Navy became, in the words of British historian Ian Nish, the navy's "budgetary enemy."[40] Ironically, Japanese fleet expansion after the Russo-Japanese War really had its origins in European naval rivalry. The Anglo-German naval race had stimulated Theodore Roosevelt to build a navy second only to Britain's. The U.S. Navy's expansion in turn stimulated Japanese naval development.[41] Second, in 1907, the eight-eight program was far beyond the economic and material resources of the Japanese empire. Not only were there severe restraints on the naval budget brought on by the financial strains of the Russo-Japanese War, but there was little public enthusiasm for a massive naval buildup, now that Russia had been beaten.[42]

The eight-eight fleet concept was thus unattainable in the near future. Yet, in spite of the merciless strategic implications that eroded the logic of the eight-eight fleet plan, Satō kept up his big navy propaganda, and over the next thirteen years—despite various delays and obstacles—the Japanese navy pursued its realization with firm resolve.[43] It did so during a time when the battle fleets of all the world's great maritime powers were in the midst of yet another fundamental transformation, one in which the centralization of fire control produced an astounding leap in the range and accuracy of battleship main batteries and thus reinforced the Japanese navy's obsession with "big ships, big guns."

6

Toward
—an—
Eight-Eight Fleet

The Japanese Navy's Plans for Expansion, 1905–1922

There were two dramatic and immediately important developments in naval technology during the years that the Japanese navy was attempting to assemble an eight-eight fleet. The first was the advent of the 17,500-ton British *Dreadnought,* laid down in 1905 and completed in 1906. The second was the construction of three 17,250-ton British battle cruisers of the *Invincible* class, laid down in 1906 and completed in 1908. Though the conceptual origins of the *Dreadnought* are still a subject of intense research and reappraisal,[1] there is general agreement that the warship represented an unprecedented combination of firepower, protection, and speed. With her ten 12-inch guns, 11-inch KC armor for the turret barbettes and main deck, and 21-knot speed delivered by two sets of Parsons turbines driving four shafts, the *Dreadnought* revolutionized capital ship design and drastically altered the terms of the early twentieth-century naval race. The ship made obsolete all pre-dreadnought battleships, including Great Britain's (though for several years a number of nations, including Britain, continued building alternative designs).

Nevertheless, that nation, by stealing a march on every other naval power and through furious effort, maintained its lead in the construction of these awesome new warships. For the better part of two decades, the world's four great naval powers—Britain, Germany, the United States, and Japan—built dreadnought battleships at an increasing tempo. By the onset of World War I, these four nations were constructing 30,000-ton dreadnoughts capable of 28-knot speeds and armed with eight to twelve guns of 11 to 15 inches, which could throw armor-piercing (AP) shells twelve miles or more within a fairly tight pattern.[2] Though Germany dropped out of the dreadnought race toward the end of World War I in order to concentrate on submarine construction, Japan and the United States continued the building duel until 1922.

Recent scholarship has argued that the revolution in battleship design was in fact influenced by the design of the next largest warship type, the armored cruiser, as navies, beginning with the British, sought to combine the hitting power of the battleship with the speed of the cruiser.[3] The result was the dreadnought armored cruiser, known by 1912 as the battle cruiser. The 17,000-ton *Invincible*, laid down

Table 6-1

JAPANESE AND U.S. CAPITAL SHIP CONSTRUCTION, 1911–23

Year	IJN	USN
1911	2	2
1912	2	2
1913	1	0
1914	1	2
1915	3	0
1916	0	4
1917	2	1
1918	1	1
1919	0	1
1920	1	1
1921	1	2
1922	0	0
1923	0	1
Total	14	17

Capital ships are battleships, battle cruisers, and armored cruisers. Numbers show ships completed in each year for the Imperial Japanese Navy and ships commissioned in each year for the U.S. Navy.

in February 1906, just prior to the launching of the *Dreadnought,* was the first of this new type and was designed to lie in the line of battle. Battle cruisers were armed with ordnance as large as that of battleships and displaced at least as much as the latter in order to accommodate larger propulsion systems. To allow for the increase in weight of the more powerful machinery, however, the battle cruiser sacrificed most of the armored protection of the battleship.

In the near decade before World War I, the other principal categories of surface ships—cruisers and destroyers, in particular—benefited from the same developments in gunnery and propulsion that added to the efficiency of all warships. They did not, however, undergo the dramatic changes in size and offensive power demonstrated by capital ships between 1905 and 1914. The British navy undertook the principal initiative in cruiser development during this period. The British "C class" was a generation of smaller cruisers intended to work with destroyers. The cruisers' speed, maneuverability, 6-inch main armament, and new system of armoring made them ideal for close-range action and set a standard for cruiser design.[4] On their part, destroyers developed in size, speed, seaworthiness, and function, and were now employed together in large numbers, usually in flotillas. The size of these combat units, often up to twenty ships, and the speed of their individual components required a fast scout cruiser flagship to handle administrative business and to signal the flotilla. The "C-class" cruiser was developed to fill that role. By the eve of World War I, however, destroyers had so outpaced even these cruisers that the latter were replaced by flotilla leaders, larger destroyers designed to accommodate the flotilla commander and his staff. Most major navies looked upon the destroyer as the workhorse of the fleet, accompanying the fleet to sea in all weathers and serving in a variety of functions. Yet it was not until the emergence of the submarine as a devastating new weapon of commerce destruction in the last several years of World War I that the destroyer took on real importance in its antisubmarine role.[5]

Prior to World War I, the potential of the two naval weapons systems that dominated naval warfare by the middle of this century, the submarine and the shipborne aircraft, was still unrecognized. The submarine made great advances in size, range, and destructive capability by 1914 because of several significant improvements: the substitution of diesel for gasoline engines, the adoption of optically advanced periscopes, and the perfection of mechanisms for the subsurface firing of torpedoes. With few exceptions, however, the higher echelons in all the navies failed to foresee the devastating capabilities of the submarine as a commerce raider. Even Germany, which led in the development of the submarine as an offensive weapon, launched its first submersible only eight years before the onset of the war, though by 1913 German U-boats were capable of cruising 7,600 miles at 8 knots.[6]

Naval aviation still stood at the dawn of its evolution, though its early progress was remarkably rapid. Lighter-than-air craft (airships) began to be built about the turn of the century and assumed considerable importance in World War I; most navies, including the Japanese, experimented extensively with them. Manned, heavier-than-air flight was demonstrated as practical by the Wrights in 1903, but by 1911 naval aviation already offered two paths for development: the seaplane and the wheeled land-based aircraft.

Because it was waterborne, the seaplane (called a floatplane at first) seemed the logical type of aircraft for naval operations. At San Diego, in 1911, the American engineer Glenn Curtiss, who had pioneered the development of seaplanes, undertook the first flight from land to water and back again. As other seaplane records were set over the next ten years, a mother ship, the seaplane tender or carrier, was developed by the leading naval powers as a new warship category. Yet the limiting problem in the use of seaplanes for naval operations was their lengthy launch and recovery time. At launch and recovery, the mother ship had to stop and lower or retrieve her aircraft over the side.

The second approach to naval aviation was the employment of shore-based aircraft, but these were of too-limited range to operate with the fleet. As early as 1910, the U.S. Navy made an historic effort to solve this problem by launching shipborne aircraft. At Hampton Roads, Virginia, that year, an aircraft was flown off the temporary platform deck of an American cruiser. This was followed a few months later by the successful landing of an airplane on the makeshift deck of a cruiser in San Francisco Bay. Yet these attempts were flights by single aircraft off and on ships riding at anchor. Furthermore, naval professionals saw the role of seaplanes and shipborne aircraft as largely one of reconnaissance, not combat. It would take World War I to change these early limitations on naval aviation.[7]

The problem of surface fire control in naval gunnery was beginning to be understood in the major navies, but not yet sufficiently to exploit the potential range of rifled ordnance, which, by around 1912, could reach some 10,000 yards. The first part of the fire control problem—target tracking—had been partially solved, as discussed previously, by the adoption of optical range finders and telescopic sights. The two most pressing remaining problems were predicting the range and bearing at the time the projectile was expected to hit and finding a reliable way of correcting the aim on the basis of observation of the shell splashes. The first problem could be solved by maintaining an accurate geographic plot of the positions of the target and the firing ship. As long as both vessels maintained steady courses and constant speeds, the tracks were straight lines and easily extended to make predictions. This, however, was a slow and tedious procedure. Other approaches, some of which will be noted later, were developed, but the real solution to this part of the problem had to await the development of analog computers capable of simulating a two-ship engagement. The second problem, correcting the aim by observing shell splashes, was solved by salvo firing and spotting (see below).

By 1905, the composition of a typical main battery fire control system aboard a major warship showed how technology had advanced in solving these problems. Most often the control system consisted of several independent elements: a range finder, a sight to determine target bearing, a device for computing range and bearing rates (such as the Dumaresq, adopted by the Royal Navy in 1902), range tables that provided time of flight, and gun sights. Gun aim was adjusted by spotting—the observation of shell splashes and correcting for overs and unders.

In the succeeding years navies would come to understand that such a system was still far from perfect. It was slow and insufficiently integrated; it did not take into account all the significant factors involved in delivering concentrated fire accurately; and the solutions obtained were still not exact and might contain important residual errors. Navies recognized that further improvements were necessary along the following lines: centralization of the system to avoid duplication, the substitution of automatic for manual processes to speed the necessary functions of the system, and adequate communications between those doing the calculations and those setting the sights for the guns.

In the decade between the Russo-Japanese War and World War I, the Royal Navy and, to a somewhat lesser extent, the U.S. Navy led the way in dealing with these problems. Their efforts constituted a revolution in naval gunnery that saw the general consolidation of independent fire control functions into integrated fire control systems. The Royal Navy system, developed around 1912, had a "control top" responsible for ranging and spotting, a "director" responsible for collecting bearing data and estimating target course and speed, and a transmitting station below decks that performed the necessary plotting and calculations and disseminated the results to the director and thence to the guns. The aloft portions of the installation were eventually consolidated into a director control tower that provided range, bearing, level, and cross-level information to the fire control table. U.S. Navy fire control systems developed somewhat similarly, but unlike the Royal Navy, its semiautomatic director depended more on the judgment of plotting officers than on mechanical inputs.[8]

For the Japanese navy, the period 1905–14 was not one of great technological advance in fire control. Japanese instruments and techniques evolved parallel with those of the Royal Navy largely because both navies used essentially the same suppliers, particularly Vickers and Barr and Stroud. During World War I, however, the Japanese navy itself attempted to develop fire control instruments, including range clocks and range calculators, and this program laid the foundations of the navy's fire control systems in the years between the world wars.[9]

Beyond these improvements in gunnery, two other shifts in naval technology had a major impact on warship design and construction between 1905 and 1922. The first of these, a significant change in propulsion systems, had an important bearing on naval architecture, naval tactics, and naval strategy. In addition to seeking to improve reliability, navies of the late nineteenth and early twentieth centuries continually sought to improve two components of steam propulsion: speed and endurance.[10] For a given hull, speed depends on the horsepower available to drive the ship, and endurance depends on the quantity of fuel that is carried and the efficiency with which the engineering plant uses the fuel. The weight and space that can be devoted to the engineering plant of any ship are, of course, limited; warship designers have always faced critical tradeoffs that are dictated by the available propulsion technology. These technological constraints are complex, but are related to the steam pressure for saturated steam systems or, in a later period, the steam temperature and pressure (in superheated steam plants).[11] That is, at high pressures a greater weight of steam can be passed through an engine of a given size. Moreover, higher temperature yields both greater efficiency and more energy per unit weight. Improved efficiency also yields greater endurance, since a given quantity of fuel will produce more shaft horsepower per hour.

The use of steam for ship propulsion had begun with simple, single-expansion engines that made relatively inefficient use of the energy in the steam. The efficiency had been increased first by the introduction of compound (double-expansion) engines in the 1860s and then by triple-expansion engines in the 1880s, as well as increasing saturated steam pressure and temperature. Then, toward the end of the nineteenth century, turbines were tried for ship propulsion first in small vessels, and then increasingly in larger ships until the *Dreadnought* appeared not only as the first all-big-gun battleship, but also as the first turbine-powered one. From their beginnings, turbines had several advantages, including higher efficiency (since turbines made it possible to use superheated steam without increasing steam pressures and their attendant safety problems), lower center of gravity, and smaller weight and volume for a given horsepower.

But the revolution in ship propulsion did not begin with the introduction of the turbine alone. Engineering plans were improved with the development of supporting technologies: stronger materials that retained their strength at high temperatures, corrosion- and erosion-resistant metals for the turbine blades, precision manufacturing materials, and the like. Moreover, the use of turbines in warships remained controversial primarily because fuel economy was poor at cruising speeds. But cruising turbines and reduction gears or turboelectric drives solved the residual problems associated with turbines. More efficient, smoother running, smaller and lighter turbine plants became the standard for fighting ships. After 1918, almost all new U.S. Navy and Royal Navy ships were powered by geared turbines. By 1922, the transition was complete in all the major navies of the world.[12]

The second major shift in naval technology was the substitution of oil for coal as a naval fuel. This change not only influenced warship design, but had another, more important impact on the major navies of the world. As the thermal content of oil is twice that of coal, a given weight of fuel could now propel a ship twice as far and boilers could be more compact, saving space and weight. But other advantages accrued as well. Taking on oil required less time and labor than loading coal. Unlike coal, which had to be stored directly adjacent to the engine room and required enormous labor to be fed into an engine furnace, oil could be stored anywhere in a ship and pumped directly to the furnace. Moreover, since oil had almost the same density as water, the trim and draft of a ship did not need to change, since, as fuel was burned, tanks could be filled with seawater. Oil burned without forming an ash (coal formed an ash) so that furnaces did not become rapidly congested. Finally, the new fuel produced far less smoke; ships burning it would reveal themselves less quickly on the horizon.[13]

The first experimental oil firing took place in the Italian navy in the 1880s and was then tried by the British navy after 1900 in its high-speed destroyers. The disadvantage of using oil as a naval fuel was that, of all major sea powers, only the United States had large reserves of oil within its own territory. For this reason, the U.S. Navy had begun the shift from coal to oil in 1912 with the laying down of the battleship *Nevada*, the navy's first warship with oil-fired boilers. The British laid down the oil-burning *Queen Elizabeth* class in the same year. But for Britain, the prospect of a shift to oil posed a dilemma: the British Isles had unlimited supplies of the world's finest steam coal, while the only known petroleum deposits in the British empire were in Assam and Burma, halfway around the world. In 1912, the establishment of the Anglo-Persian Oil Company, which under admiralty control exploited the rich oil fields at the head of the Persian Gulf, provided an adequate supply of petroleum from a reasonably secure source. Three years later, the British navy decided to change from coal to oil firing for its future ships, though coal was still used in most British warships in World War I. The navies of other nations, not as fortunate in locating sources of oil within their national or imperial territories, decided either to continue to use coal, as Germany did, or to depend on foreign purchases and a relatively vulnerable tanker fleet, as Japan did. For a time before and after World War I, most navies, as an interim process on the way to complete conversion to oil, used a system of "mixed firing," which involved spraying oil on burning coal. But the increasing demand for power and speed in capital ships eventually led to the conversion to purely oil-burning engines in all navies, with wide-ranging strategic consequences.[14]

JAPANESE CONSTRUCTION OF CAPITAL SHIPS, 1905–16

The launching of the *Dreadnought* had caught the world's naval architects, including those in the Japanese navy, by surprise. Inevitably, then, some of Japan's capital ships being built during the Russo-Japanese War and completed some years after it, were obsolete from the day they were launched. This was certainly true of the *Kashima* and *Katori,* the last Japanese battleships built outside of Japan. Similar in design to Britain's *King Edward VII* class, they were extremely powerful warships for their day, but with their mixed armament, which included only four 12-inch guns, they were quickly surpassed by the *Dreadnought.* The battleships *Aki* and *Satsuma,* laid down in May 1905, could have been dreadnought "all-big-gun" battleships (indeed, at 19,000 tons, they were larger than the *Dreadnought),* since they were originally intended to carry twelve 12-inch guns. But, as Japan was in the midst of the Russo-Japanese War and the extra cost involved in this increased armament was considered too great, they remained pre-dreadnoughts. In the history of Japanese naval construction, the *Satsuma* and *Aki* are noteworthy for only one fact: they were the first capital ships built in Japan (at the Yokosuka and Kure navy yards, respectively). In design, however, they closely resembled the British pre-dreadnought *Lord Nelson* class, and the greater portion of the materials that went into the *Satsuma* was of foreign manufacture.[15]

Now that Japan could construct the largest warships in its own navy yards, all lesser types were also built domestically. In the latter half of the Russo-Japanese War, having found the armored cruiser a useful type, the navy had laid down two large armored cruisers, the *Tsukuba* and *Ikoma,* launched in 1905 and 1906, respectively, at its Kure yard. Armed with four 12-inch guns and protected with 7-inch KC armor (now produced in Japan) along the main belt and covering the turret barbettes, the ships were briefly the world's most powerful cruisers in service until the completion of the first true battle cruisers, the British *Invincible* class.

In August 1905, the navy yard at Yokosuka had laid down the *Kurama,* followed in 1907 at the Kure yard by a sister ship, the *Ibuki,* both designed as improved versions of the *Tsukuba.* Yet, in planning them, the navy, unaware of the latest British designs, had failed to recognize that the day of the armored cruiser was over, supplanted by the advent of the battle cruiser, with greater armament and speed. Delays caused by budgetary difficulties and a relaxed completion schedule meant that the *Kurama* did not join the fleet until 1911. By this time she and her sister had been completely outclassed by the British *Invincible,* the only significant feature of their construction being that the *Ibuki* was the first major Japanese warship to be equipped with turbines.[16]

It was not until January 1909 that the Kure Navy Yard laid down its first dreadnought battleship, the *Settsu,* followed four months later by her sister, the

Kawachi, at Yokosuka. Completed in 1912, these were the first battleships of independent Japanese design, though they resembled the German *Helgoland* class of dreadnoughts, and the guns and mountings were supplied by Armstrong Whitworth. With the fitting of turbines in these warships (Parsons in the *Settsu,* Curtis in the *Kawachi),* Japan became the third naval power to adopt turbine machinery for its capital ships. The 12-inch waterline belt of KC armor, their main battery of twelve 12-inch guns, and their unusually powerful secondary armament of ten 6-inch and eight 4.7-inch guns made these ships the theoretical equal of any warship then afloat. Yet the layout of the main battery—twin mountings in each turret, fore and aft, and in two turrets on each side—was a weaker arrangement than British dreadnoughts, since at any given angle of fire, at least four guns would inevitably be masked.[17] Further, the fore and aft turrets were of 50 caliber, the wing turrets of 45 caliber, violating the principle of homogeneity of main armament for dreadnoughts. Different calibers required different elevations to reach the same target. This limitation may support the recent contention that in the dreadnought's early years, naval architects and tacticians may not have been as aware of the dreadnought revolution as historians have been since.[18]

In any case, in 1910, the Japanese navy was impatient to implement a major naval expansion that would incorporate the advances in warship design occasioned by the British all-big-gun capital ships. Seeking to realize the eight-eight fleet plan in a single leap, the Navy General Staff asked the Navy Ministry to secure funding for eight battleships and eight armored (battle) cruisers. Given the economic strains of the nation after the Russo-Japanese War, however, even the ministry balked at such a mammoth program. They cut the staff request back to seven battleships and three armored cruisers. The cabinet then slashed the request still further to one battleship and four armored cruisers. This last request received funding from the Diet, which passed the bill of 1911 that authorized the design and construction of the world's most powerful warships to date: the four battle cruisers of the *Kongō* class, which collectively provided a quantum leap in Japanese naval strength and prestige.

In response to the British *Invincible,* Japanese naval constructors had turned their attention to the design of a battle cruiser that would surpass it. After intensive research and the drafting of some thirty plans, in 1909, the Japanese developed a design for an 18,725-ton battle cruiser, the *Kongō,* superior in specifications to the *Invincible,* only to discover that the British navy had just laid down a huge new battle cruiser, the 26,270-ton *Lion,* which would again outclass the best Japanese design. At this point, the navy decided to scrap its most recent plans for the design of the *Kongō* and to seek the help and technical assistance of the British to design and build it as a 27,000-ton improved version of the *Lion* class. In 1910, in order to give Japanese constructors experience in the latest British advances in design, weaponry, and shipbuilding technology, the Japanese navy placed an order with Vickers to have the *Kongō* built at the British firm's yard at Barrow. Designed by the distinguished British naval architect Sir George Thurston, the *Kongō* was laid down in January 1911, and she was launched May 1912. The other three ships of the class were built in Japan following the design and specifications of the *Kongō*.

In this class of Japanese battleships lies the entire panoply of the Japanese technology acquisition and development strategy: The *Kongō* was built abroad and was of entirely foreign design and manufacture; the *Hiei* was constructed at the navy's Yokosuka yard, using a large amount of imported material; the *Haruna* was built at Kobe by the Kawasaki Shipbuilding Company; and the *Kirishima* at the Mitsubishi Shipbuilding Company's yard at Nagasaki, the latter two using almost entirely Japanese materials.[19]

During the construction of the *Kongō*, the question of its main armament became a matter of intense discussion. The original plans had called for eight 12-inch guns, but according to secret information obtained from confidants in the British navy by the Japanese naval attaché in London, Capt. Katō Kanji, Royal Navy tests had demonstrated that somewhat larger guns had greater longevity and provided a smaller salvo spread, and the British were consequently planning to install 13.5-inch guns on their projected *Tiger* class of battle cruisers. Katō's superiors in Tokyo guessed that if the British went to a 13.5-inch gun, the United States would probably try to surpass them with 14-inch guns in their projected *Texas*-class battleships. Yet, since a 14-inch gun was a new caliber of ordnance, no one knew for sure whether the additional increase in caliber would be that much more effective. After close consultation with the British, the Japanese constructors decided to go to the expense of having the navy test-fire several 14-inchers. The results were highly satisfactory, and the *Kongō* was built with eight 14-inch guns. But the United States put *ten* 14-inchers on the *Texas* and *New York,* and in 1912, and the British laid down the first of the *Queen Elizabeth*-class battleships with 15-inch guns.[20]

Nevertheless, the *Kongō* was, when completed, the most formidable and most superbly designed capital ship in the world. Her eight 14-inch guns were divided between four turrets—two forward, a third amidships (but abaft the third funnel), and a fourth astern. At the time, this was a most innovative arrangement that allowed greatly increased traverse for the guns. The main battery was supplemented by a secondary armament of sixteen 6-inch guns (far more than the usual number, but considered necessary to repel most destroyer attacks) and, as the Japanese navy continued to have faith in the value of torpedoes fired by capital ships, the *Kongō* was armed with eight 21-inch submerged torpedo tubes, easily the heaviest torpedo armament of any capital ship then afloat. The turret barbettes had 9-inch VC (Vickers cemented) armor; their roofs had 3-inch VC armor. The ship's main belt was 8 inches up to the waterline and 6 inches above it; internal armor and subdivisions provided maximum protection against the shellfire and torpedoes of the day. Driven by four shafts powered

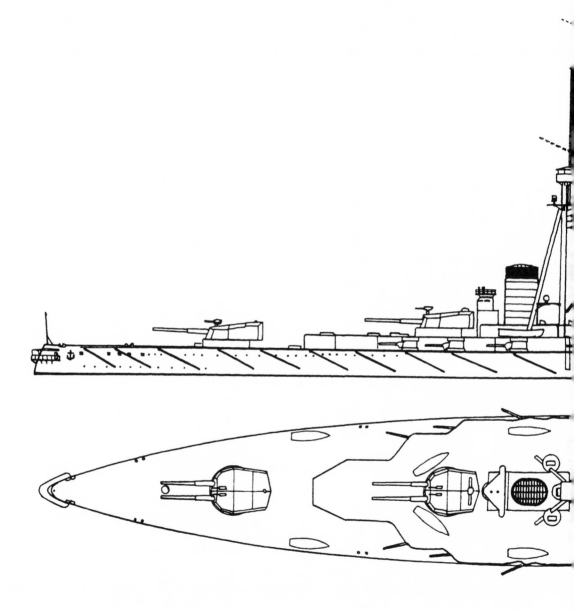

Fig. 6-1. The battle cruiser *Kongō*, 1914.

by Parsons turbines that took their steam from thirty-six mixed-firing Yarrow boilers, the *Kongō* achieved 27.5 knots during her trials. The other ships of the *Kongō* class were of almost identical design, but used Japanese weapons, machinery, and armor built to the British specifications, and were slightly superior to the *Kongō* in certain respects. The *Kongō*, the last Japanese capital ship

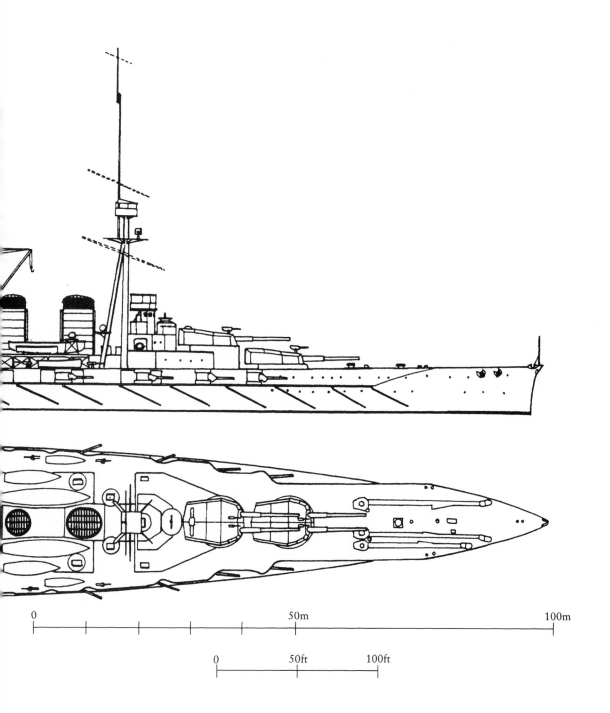

| 0 | | | | | 50m | | 100m |
| 0 | 50ft | 100ft | | | | | |

ordered from a foreign yard, was completed August 1913 and arrived at Yokosuka in November of that year. Her sisters being built in Japanese yards joined
her on active service over the next two years. Like the rest of the Japanese battle
fleet, none of these battleships saw combat during World War I, but they were so
greatly valued that in 1915, with only a narrow margin of superiority over Germany
in capital ships, Britain attempted to obtain a loan of all four ships of the class

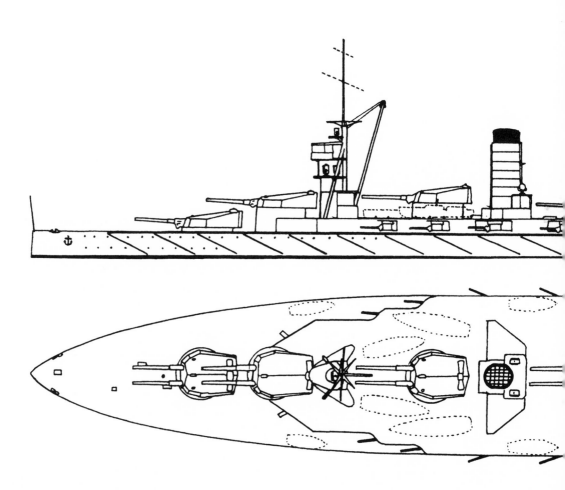

Fig. 6-2. The battleship *Fusō*.

to the Royal Navy.[21] Reclassified as battleships after their extensive reconstruction in the 1920s, the ships of the *Kongō* class would be in the thick of several naval engagements of World War II in the Pacific.

The same bill that had made possible the construction of the *Kongō*-class battle cruisers had authorized a new battleship, the *Fusō*, designed to work in conjunction with the *Kongō* class. Laid down at the navy's Kure yard in 1912 and

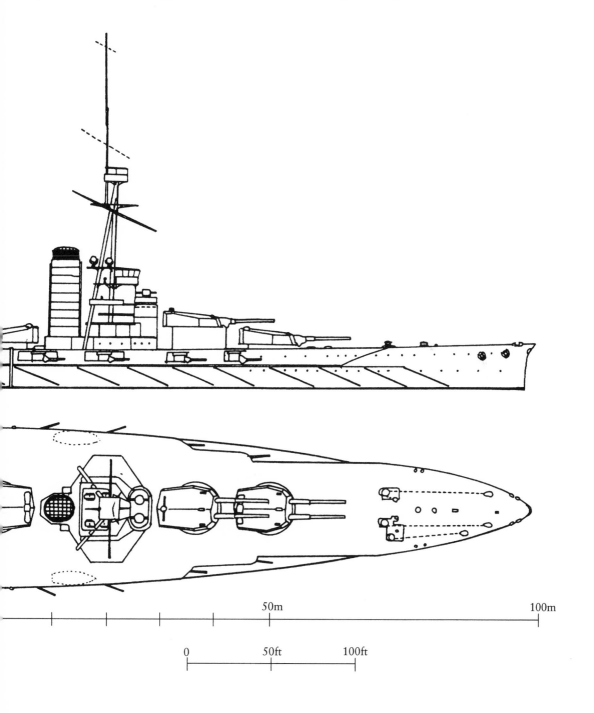

50m

100m

0   50ft   100ft

completed in 1915, the 29,330-ton *Fusō*, intended to rival the American battle-ships *Texas* and *New York*, was prime evidence that the Japanese navy had indeed entered the international naval race. Whereas the *Texas* had boasted ten 14-inch guns, the *Fusō* was built with twelve guns of this caliber, mounted in six in-line turrets (two forward, two alternating with the funnels amidships, and two aft), constituting the most powerful warship broadside in the world until the comple-tion of the *Nagato* class. The *Fusō* was 110 feet longer than the *New York,* and the Japanese battleship's four Brown-Curtis turbines produced 40 percent more horsepower than the *New York* and a 23-knot speed. When completed, she was the largest and most powerfully armed battleship in the world.[22]

In 1913, anxious to press forward with its expansion plans, the Navy Ministry submitted a request for three more battleships, which were funded by the Diet the same year. *Fusō*'s sister ship, the *Yamashiro,* was launched in 1915. The two other battleships, the 29,980-ton *Ise* and *Hyūga,* were planned as advanced versions of *Fusō* and were laid down in 1915 (*Ise* at the Kawasaki yard at Kobe and *Hyūga* at the Mitsubishi yard at Nagasaki). But, while being built, they incorporated so many improvements that upon their completion (in 1917 and 1918, respectively), the ships virtually constituted a separate class. The most important advance in the design of these battleships was a re-siting of the six main turrets, so that the two turrets amidships were positioned more closely together and thus provided improved angles of fire. Re-siting these turrets also allowed the repositioning of the twenty-four new Kampon boilers for greater efficiency.[23]

By World War I, Shimamura Hayao had taken over as chief of the Navy General Staff, and Katō Tomosaburō had become navy minister. Both men were now intent on accelerating the progress toward an eight-eight fleet. In 1915, emboldened by the prospect that the recovering Japanese economy could support a larger naval budget, Katō submitted a request to the cabinet for an expansion plan that would represent an interim stage on the way to the eight-eight fleet goal: an eight-four fleet. Count-ing warships already on hand—the battleship *Fusō* and the four battle cruisers, the *Kongō, Hiei, Haruna,* and *Kirishima*—and those that were under construction, the battleships *Yamashiro, Ise,* and *Hyūga*—the ministry asked for funds to complete four more battleships, which would give the navy an eight-four fleet. But in the wake of public distrust of the navy's insatiable demands that followed the Siemens arms procurement scandal,[24] the Diet rejected the navy's more grandiose plans. In 1916, however, the Diet did provide funds for the construction of one battleship, two battle cruisers, and other ships in several lesser categories.

Where the Japanese navy's own arguments and publicity failed to convince a skeptical Diet, an American naval expansion program had a dramatic and salutary effect. In 1916, the U.S. Congress passed a navy bill (never fully realized) that would add to the U.S. Navy 156 ships, including 10 battleships and 6 battle cruisers, an expansion that would increase the American naval superiority over Japan to 100 percent and would provide the United States with a gigantic new fleet of the most powerful battleships in the world.[25] The next year, the Japanese Diet, in response to this unprecedented American program, authorized the construction of some 63 warships, including 3 battleships, 10 cruisers, and several lesser categories of warships. Together, the 1916 and 1917 authorizations permitted the Japanese navy to attain its interim goal of an eight-six fleet. Finally, in 1918, the cabinet approved the construction of two more battle cruisers. Had they actually been launched, the eight-eight fleet would have been realized. But this was not to be.

WORLD WAR I AND THE JAPANESE NAVY

By the end of 1917, most of the major naval features of World War I had been demonstrated. In surface warfare, technology had outpaced command and, in the process, led to stalemate. This was nowhere more evident than in the North Sea, which had been the principal strategic arena of the naval war. Here the British and German navies had met in a series of inconclusive actions, culminating, in May 1916, in the Battle of Jutland, in which the British Grand Fleet, while enduring serious losses, had twice capped the T of the German High Seas Fleet, yet was unable to inflict decisive defeat upon its enemy. The greatest surface engagement in the history of naval history and the last daylight action between battleship columns, Jutland was endlessly discussed and debated over the next two decades by naval professionals around the globe. It influenced future naval construction and hardened the conventional naval wisdom that the rapid concentration of long-range, big-gun firepower would continue to be the decisive factor in naval combat. In reality, of course, Jutland had only demonstrated that the speed and maneuverability of the modern capital ship and—above all—the long reach of their big guns had outstripped the ability of opposing naval commanders to make timely decisions. This tactical dilemma had led to a drawn battle and had prolonged the strategic stalemate between the British and German surface fleets.[26]

Indeed, it was the surface stalemate following Jutland that led to the German decision to undertake unrestricted submarine warfare against Britain early in 1917, with results that soon threatened to cripple the British economy and that nation's capacity to continue the war. Added to the dramatic submarine sinkings of Allied warships by the end of the war—ten battleships, eighteen cruisers, and twenty destroyers—the titanic losses inflicted by U-boats on Allied merchant shipping made it clear that the submarine had at last emerged as a devastating naval weapon. Not until the adoption of the convoy system in 1917 and the development of counterweapons like the depth charge, did the tide of the naval war turn slowly yet decisively against the submarine.[27]

Although the impact of naval aviation in the war was far less dramatic and wide-ranging, the airplane had, nevertheless, occasionally demonstrated its potentially versatile role in naval operations. In 1913, even before the war, a Greek seaplane had been used in a reconnaissance sortie over a Turkish fleet in the Dardanelles. A British seaplane had made a practice drop of a standard naval torpedo in 1914, and the next year, British seaplanes had sunk a Turkish military transport in an aerial torpedo attack. In 1916, Austrian seaplanes sank a French submarine with bombs. Jutland itself was a naval battle that involved naval aviation, though in a small role, when an aircraft from a British seaplane tender attached to the Grand Fleet spotted the advancing German battle cruiser squadron and attempted to alert friendly forces about the enemy's position.[28]

Despite these "firsts," however, the limitations mentioned earlier—the time-consuming process of launching and retrieving seaplanes at sea and the difficulty of launching more than a single aircraft from the temporary platforms installed on regular warships—kept naval aviation from playing a significant scouting or striking role at sea. To operate land planes from ships under way at sea called for a new kind of warship with wide and permanent decks for the launch and retrieval of numerous aircraft. In so converting the battle cruiser *Furious* in 1917 to provide a permanent flight deck forward, the British navy produced the prototype of the modern aircraft carrier. In August of that year, the first landing on a moving carrier took place on the flight deck of the *Furious*. The next year, a landing flight deck was extended aft, though the warship's funnel and superstructure still separated it from the takeoff deck forward. In 1918, the first attack against a land target from an aircraft carrier was launched from this curious-looking warship.[29]

Of all these developments in naval warfare between 1914 and 1917, the Japanese navy had little direct knowledge, since its participation in the war was limited to three campaigns, all well away from the major maritime theaters in the North Sea and the North Atlantic, and all marginal to the outcome of the war. The first of these was a successful Anglo-Japanese siege of the German port and naval base at Tsingtao on the Shantung peninsula, September to November 1914. From the navy's perspective, the campaign was notable primarily for the use of Japanese seaplanes in reconnaissance and bombing operations over Tsingtao. Concurrently, the Japanese navy organized a battle group in August and another in September for dispatch to the central Pacific. Ostensibly, these forces had been formed in order to pursue the eastward-fleeing German East Asiatic Squadron; their real aim was the occupation of the German islands of Micronesia, a bloodless campaign completed by November 1914.[30] These two campaigns expanded the territorial limits of the Japanese empire and had important strategic consequences in the case of Micronesia, but did little to advance the navy's combat experience or understanding of the most recent developments in naval warfare.

The third campaign, which took place, unheralded, in the eastern Mediterranean did, however, offer the navy just such opportunities. In 1917, soon after Germany's declaration of an unrestricted U-boat campaign against Allied shipping, Japan acceded to a British request for a Japanese destroyer division to be sent to the Mediterranean, where some thirty-four enemy submarines, both German and Austrian, were causing havoc with Allied shipping. That March, the Japanese navy organized a special service squadron (one of two put at the service of her allies), consisting of a cruiser and two destroyer divisions, each composed of four of the navy's newest destroyers. Arriving at Malta in April at the height of the U-boat attacks, the small Japanese contingent under Rear Adm. Satō Kōzō was immediately put to work escorting Allied troopships between Marseilles, Taranto, and ports in Egypt. For the next year and a half, the squadron took part in some 348 escort missions, involving some 750 ships and covering over 240,000 nautical miles. The squadron quickly earned such an excellent reputation for smart shiphandling that the Royal Navy eventually turned over two of its destroyers to be manned by Japanese crews for the duration of the war. The Japanese contingent was even blooded during the Mediterranean campaign. One destroyer, *Sakaki,* was torpedoed and lost fifty-nine officers and men, including her skipper, but made it back to Malta and eventually rejoined the squadron.[31]

Despite the Japan force's inability to claim a U-boat sinking, Allied losses in the Mediterranean dropped sharply after the Japanese arrived on station. More importantly, from the perspective of Japanese naval history, the Japanese crews participating in this effort learned much in the way of antisubmarine tactics, technology, and weaponry. Yet, because of their small scale and their laborious, repetitive, and unglamourous nature, these operations in the Mediterranean were considered unremarkable by the naval staff in Tokyo. Thus, the important principles of the convoy system and the lessons of antisubmarine warfare, learned at the cost of much strenuous effort by a handful of Japanese officers and men on a distant station, were quickly forgotten. This oversight undoubtedly played some part in the disastrous failure of the Japanese navy to develop an effective counter to the ravages of American submarines in the Pacific War.[32]

What captured the attention of the Japanese navy brass were the great surface clashes in the North Sea, particularly Jutland.[33] Looking past the fact that the battle had ended in a tactical stalemate, the Japanese navy, like its counterparts in the West, remained convinced that the battle not only provided the tactical parameters for decisive naval combat in the future, but also dictated major changes in the design and construction of capital ships. Naval professionals counted many major changes in ship design and construction after the Battle of Jutland: Sixteen inches became the standard caliber for main batteries. Armor was concentrated and strengthened below the waterline, particularly around a warship's vital parts (the

Hiraga Yuzuru

engineering spaces and magazines), leaving the bow, stern, bridge superstructure, and secondary armament more lightly protected. A reinforced central pillar was substituted for the tripod arrangement of the foremast. Geared turbines were introduced, and engine rooms were compartmentalized to minimize the dangers of flooding and listing.[34]

The first Japanese battleships constructed under the 1916 and 1917 programs, the *Nagato* (laid down August 1917 at the navy's Kure yard) and the *Mutsu* (laid down in June 1918 at the navy's Yokosuka yard) incorporated a number of these features and represented another qualitative leap by the Japanese navy ahead of the capital ship designs of foreign navies. These ships had been planned for some time, and several months before Jutland, their general design had been drafted by Hiraga Yuzuru, destined to be the most famous, as well as the most controversial, Japanese naval architect.[35]

But within a few months, the information that had reached the Japanese navy about Jutland caused Hiraga to revise radically the displacement, armor, speed, and weight distribution of the ships he was building. He planned for ships of 32,720 tons with higher speeds and larger guns—16 inches—that would exceed the British *Queen Elizabeth* class in performance and set a world precedent. Because of their size, Hiraga decided that only eight of the huge guns were needed on each ship, instead of the twelve on previous ships, a decision that contributed to a great saving of weight and space on the *Mutsu* and *Nagato*. Reflecting the navy's gradual conversion to oil, their hulls contained fifteen oil-fired and six mixed-firing Kampon boilers that provided steam to Kampon turbines geared to four shafts (screws) capable of driving the ships at 26.5 knots, a speed that rivaled any battleship afloat. Only in protection—a 12-inch belt amidships and 12-inch armor covering the turret barbettes—could the *Nagato* and *Mutsu* be considered slightly inferior to foreign construction (specifically to the slower American *Pennsylvania, New Mexico,* and *Tennessee* classes of battleships, which traded speed for staying power).[36]

Two even larger battleships were planned under the 1917 authorization—the 38,500-ton *Kaga* and *Tosa*—but there was a three-year delay before these monsters were actually laid down. Designed by Hiraga, the *Kaga* and *Tosa* were planned to carry ten 16-inch guns, and their designs incorporated several distinctive features based on lessons apparently learned from British experience and battle damage incurred at Jutland. These included improved speed despite an increase in tonnage and the adoption of flush decks and inclined armor. But in 1919, scarcely had their blueprints been completed than Hiraga started work on the design of warships of even greater size, the two battle cruisers authorized under the 1917 bill.[37] Designated the *Amagi* and *Akagi*, at 40,000 tons, 30 knots, and mounting ten 16-inch guns, these vessels were intended to outclass the new British battle cruiser *Hood* and the projected American battle cruisers of the *Saratoga* class, but they were also delayed in their construction, their keels being laid in late December 1920.[38]

For the Japanese government, the last six months of World War I were less a time for great optimism than for a careful reassessment of the international situation and the nation's strategic position. Much was clear by June 1918. Germany was finished as a naval power in East Asia, and the chaos of revolution and civil war had ruptured Russian military power in the region as well. Yet Russia's separate peace with Germany that raised at least the theoretical possibility of an eastward offensive against Japan, and the rising tide of Chinese nationalism threatening Japanese interests in China, made the future uncertain in northeast Asia. Even more disturbing, Britain's determination to retain naval mastery and the apparent American determination to build a navy second to none threatened to set off a new and even greater naval arms race.

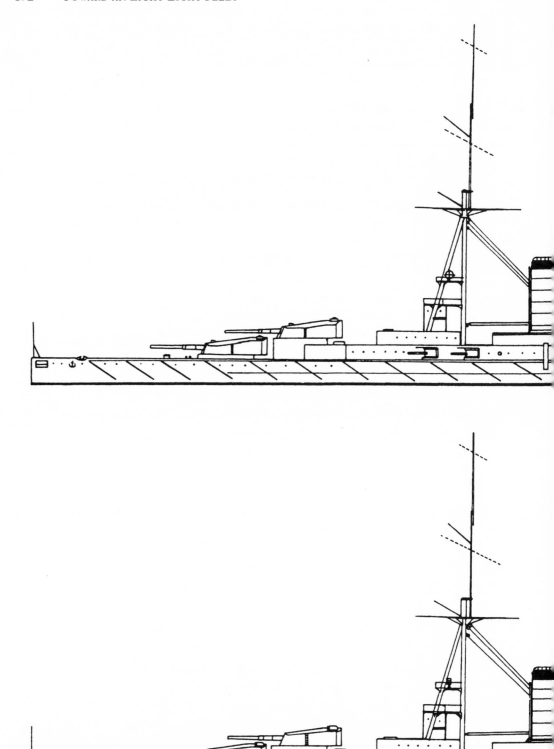

Fig. 6-3. The battleships *Nagato* (above, 1920) and *Mutsu* (below, 1921).

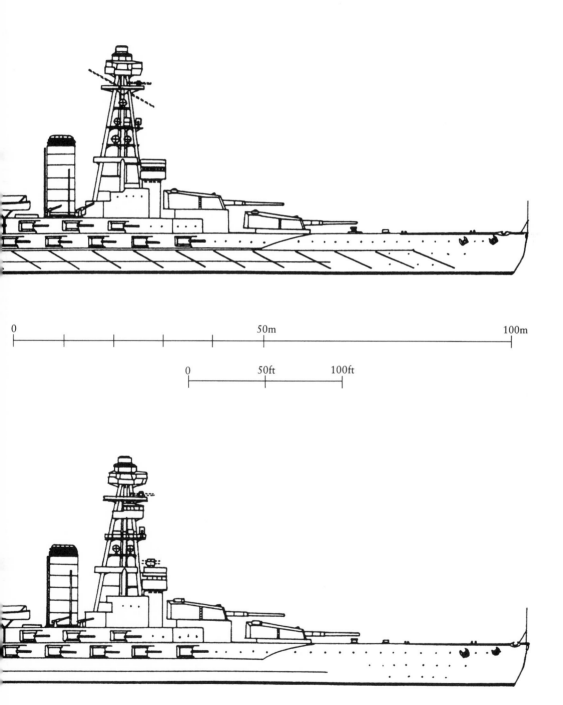

| 0 | | | | | 50m | | | | | 100m |

| 0 | 50ft | 100ft |

In view of these considerations, in June 1918, the Japanese government undertook the first revision of its Imperial Defense Policy. During the interservice discussions that preceded it, Navy Chief of Staff Shimamura and Navy Minister Katō had to accept the army's insistence that Russia be retained as the nation's chief hypothetical enemy, followed by the United States and China, in return for the army's grudging support for vastly increased naval construction. Japan had learned that the Wilson administration had placed before the U.S. Congress a navy bill that, if approved, would add ten new battleships to the ten already under construction under the 1916 bill and would thus provide the U.S. Navy with the world's greatest battle fleet. In response, the Japanese navy proposed to face down the American challenge by raising its sights to an eight-eight-eight fleet concept. The revision of force levels for the navy now called for the construction of *three* battle fleets of eight warships each—battleships and battle cruisers—according to a construction plan whereby three battleships or battle cruisers would be laid down each year and three of the same would be completed each year, so that in eight years Japan would have a battle fleet of twenty-four capital ships.[39]

But if the navy proposed, it was the Diet that disposed, in its capacity to approve or withhold funds for the construction of warships for such a mighty force. In 1918, many in the cabinet and the Diet recognized what the navy chose to ignore: Though the Japanese economy had grown remarkably during World War I, the navy's expenses had grown even faster. Indeed, the price tag of each new battleship and battle cruiser had increased so alarmingly that the Finance Ministry had warned that future naval budgets could spell the life or death of the Japanese economy. Thus, in 1918, the actual outlay by the Diet for naval expansion was for a considerably more modest naval augmentation: the construction of two additional battle cruisers also designed by Hiraga—the *Atago* and *Takao* (planned as sister ships of the *Amagi* and *Akagi*). When added to the navy's four newest battle cruisers (the *Kongō* and the *Hiei* becoming overage by 1923), the new cruisers would give the navy an eight-six fleet.

In 1919, President Wilson, now determined to achieve naval preeminence, not just parity with Britain, set before the American Congress a construction plan that called for ten battleships and six battle cruisers beyond those already authorized under the 1916 program. This American démarche was sufficient goad to the Japanese Diet, which in 1920 gave final approval for an augmentation plan that would at last make possible the long-sought goal of an eight-eight fleet. Under this program, all the units were planned to be completed by 1927. The navy planned four battle cruisers of 41,400 tons resembling the projected *Amagi* class, each armed with ten 16-inch guns, and four battleships of 47,500 tons resembling the *Kaga* class, each armed with unprecedented main battery of ten 18-inch guns.[40] The planning and construction of these superbattleships were overtaken by the

Japanese decision in 1922 to participate in the international agreement to limit capital ship construction hammered out at the Washington Conference. As it turned out, therefore, the eight-eight fleet concept was initiated but never realized, while the grander eight-eight-eight fleet remained only a heady vision.[41]

Yet, although the eight-eight plan was aborted, the designing of the largest of its projected units provided Japanese naval constructors with invaluable experience that was put to use twenty years later in the design and construction of the superbattleships *Yamato* and *Musashi*.

JAPANESE NAVAL CONSTRUCTION IN OTHER CATEGORIES

The plans of the Japanese navy between 1907 and 1920 to build an eight-eight fleet of capital ships was the central issue that drove Japanese naval policy during these years. But the navy also endeavored to catch up with foreign advances in naval technology across the board. The result was the construction of lesser warship categories, as well as developments in the Japanese submarine and naval air arms during these years. By 1918, the navy had clearly begun to modify its obsession with big ships and big guns: Its 1918 expansion program included significant representation of smaller warships and new weapons systems whose value had been demonstrated by Anglo-American naval forces during the world war.[42]

Jutland, for example, had demonstrated the importance of the cruiser, both as a fleet scout and supporter of destroyer attacks, roles that had been pioneered by the British navy. Prior to World War I, the Japanese navy had closely studied the British "C-class" cruisers and, from such research, developed a basic light cruiser

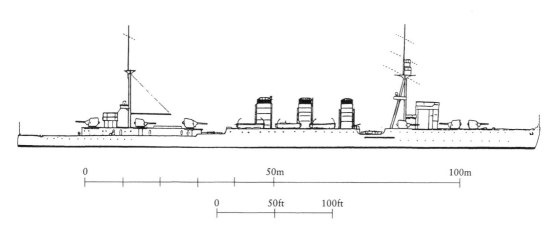

Fig. 6-4. The light cruiser *Tenryū*.

design, the first in the Japanese navy. The basic light cruiser design continued through the construction of sixteen ships until the mid-1920s, when the navy discontinued building light cruisers. The first two cruisers built under the 1916 expansion program and modeled on British "C" class cruisers were the 3,230-ton *Tatsuta* and *Tenryū,* both laid down in 1917 and completed in 1919. These were fast ships, driven by powerful British and American turbines, capable of 33 knots, which made them excellent flagships for destroyer flotillas. While lightly armed (a main battery of four 5.5-inch guns), they were the first Japanese warships to carry (two) triple torpedo tubes.[43]

In 1917, the Japanese navy reassessed its needs in the light cruiser category and decided in favor of somewhat larger, faster, and more powerful ships that could serve either as fleet scouts or destroyer flotilla leaders. The result was the construction of fourteen light cruisers between 1918 and 1925 that, though technically divided into three classes—the *Kuma* class (the *Kuma, Kiso, Kitakami, Ōi,* and *Tama),* the *Nagara* class (the *Nagara, Abukuma, Isuzu, Kinu, Natori,* and *Yura),* and the *Sendai* class *(Sendai, Jintsū,* and *Naka)*—nevertheless followed the basic *Tatsuta* design. All were a little over 5,000 tons (and the *Kuma* was nearly 6,000), were armed with seven 5.5-inch guns and eight torpedo tubes in four twin mounts, and were capable of 35 to 36 knots. Although many of these ships were twenty years old by the time of World War II, they served as workhorses in some of the fiercest campaigns in the Pacific.[44]

The layout of Japanese destroyers, from the Russo-Japanese War until World War I, had been based largely on British designs, though most of the units were built in Japanese yards, and of these a significant number were built by private firms. In 1911, in the interest of improving seakeeping qualities of its destroyers, the navy moved from 380-ton ships to 1,150 tonners. Yet, despite Japan's having several destroyers of excellent design, the onset of World War I found the Japanese with far too few of these warships for patrol and escort duty. Beginning in 1914, therefore, the navy undertook an emergency program of construction of ten destroyers of the *Kaba* class, ships of 665 tons. It was this class of destroyers that was sent to the Mediterranean in 1917 for escort and antisubmarine duty at the request of the British navy.

With the tightening control of information concerning warship design by the British during the war, the Japanese were forced back on their own designs and spent much of the rest of the war experimenting with various hull forms, and bridge, torpedo tube, and ordnance arrangements. The result was a new type of first-class destroyer, the *Minekaze* class, fifteen of which were built under the 1917 and 1918 expansion programs and nine more under the 1921 and 1922 programs. These were extremely fast vessels, driven by Parsons geared turbines and capable of 39 knots. Their designers had, moreover, made them capable of weathering the frequent heavy seas in East Asian waters by lengthening their hulls, retaining the turtle-back forecastle of the older destroyers, placing torpedo tubes directly behind the forecastle, and mounting the guns as high as possible to maximize their use in heavy weather. This class formed the backbone of the Japanese destroyer flotillas during the 1920s until replaced by the famous *Fubuki* class of the 1930s. Under the fleet expansion programs of 1918 and 1920, the Japanese also added more than thirty smaller second-class destroyers by 1921, but with the growing need for more powerful fleet destroyers, this type of warship was discontinued by the mid-1920s.[45]

Like most navies, the Japanese navy was slow to recognize the potential of the submarine. Various Japanese naval officers had been sent to the United States in 1897–1900 to inspect the American submarine *Holland,* and five of this type were subsequently ordered from the United States, while two others of the same design were built in Japan. None of these was ready for use in the Russo-Japanese War, though the first submarine flotilla had been formed while the first submersibles were under construction. The navy's interest in the submarine had increased following the Russo-Japanese War, in part because of the efforts of a few ardent submarine enthusiasts in the service and in part because the conflict with Russia had shown the possibilities for the employment of submarines both in blockading and in attacking blockading fleets. This interest had led to the acquisition of a dozen

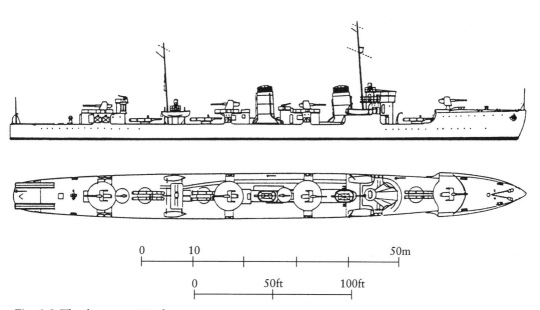

Fig. 6-5. The destroyer *Minekaze.*

or more additional submarines, mostly of foreign design, but assembled in Japan. Although two other submarine flotillas were organized prior to World War I and submarines were included in the naval maneuvers off Kyūshū, the weaknesses of these early craft, underpowered and of limited range, continued to make them little more than a dangerous curiosity to most navy men.[46] Indeed, the most publicized event in the development of Japanese submarines before World War I had been the accidental sinking of one of the boats in Hiroshima Bay in 1910.[47]

Inevitably, however, the stunning impact of German submarine warfare in World War I stimulated Japanese submarine development. Japanese naval observers in Europe learned much about German submarine strategy, tactics, and technology, which they passed back to navy staff headquarters in Tokyo.[48] German successes in the North Atlantic after the declaration of unrestricted submarine warfare were undoubtedly a key factor in the navy's decision to include the construction of eighteen oceangoing submarines in the 1917 naval expansion program. In addition, the transfer of nine German submarines to Japan as reparations at the end of the war accelerated the progress of Japanese submarine technology during the interwar period.[49]

The Navy Takes Wing
The Early Years of Japanese Naval Aviation

After an initial pairing with Japanese military aviation, Japanese naval aviation got its real start in 1912 with the creation of a Kaigun Kōkūjutsu Kenkyūkai (Commission on Naval Aeronautical Research), established under the authority of the Technical Department and charged with the furthering of aviation technology and training for the navy.[50] While the commission's initial focus of interest was in nonrigid airships, it quickly moved on to the development of winged and power aircraft.

The navy's venture into the use of lighter-than-air craft ultimately proved abortive and was merely an offshoot from the main direction of Japanese naval aviation. Toward the end of World War I, both the British and American navies devoted considerable effort to the development of semirigid airships, largely because of the effectiveness of German Zeppelins during the conflict. The Royal Navy had begun using airships in reconnaissance as early as 1917 and subsequently undertook serious research and training relating to such craft. The U.S. Navy, thanks to America's great supply of helium, which reduced the danger of explosions and made its airships somewhat safer, made even greater strides in this technology. In view of these advances, the Japanese navy began to investigate the utility of airships in its own tactical and strategic schemes. In 1918, it established an airship unit at its Yokosuka base (later moved to Kasumigaura) and began acquiring airship technology from abroad. The first airships acquired by the navy were nonrigid and motorless, essentially large balloons, which were tethered to warships and used for shell-spotting and torpedo-tracking. In 1921, the navy acquired several semirigid and self-propelled airships from Britain, France, and Italy. Following successful tests integrating these craft with fleet operations, the navy began to construct a number of its own airships of this type. After 1921, several rigid airships were attached to the Combined Fleet and regularly took part in the navy's annual maneuvers.[51]

During the 1920s, some officers on the Navy General Staff saw the rigid, self-propelled airship as a significant component of the navy's defensive strategy in the western Pacific. Because of its relatively great endurance, the airship offered the possibility of locating enemy fleet units far beyond the range of winged aircraft of the time. Armed with bombs to attack enemy ships and machine guns to defend itself, its advocates argued, the airship could provide the navy with a long-range strike capability. Yet doubts persisted. To begin with, all three major navies suffered serious accidents involving airships, the most spectacular being the crash of the American *Shenandoah* in 1925, which raised questions about the reliability of airship technology. Others on the Navy General Staff pointed to the liabilities of the airship: It was vulnerable to damage or worse in rough weather (witness the number of crashes in the British and American navies); it presented a large, soft target for enemy fighter aircraft; it was expensive to build; and its supposed military utility was a matter of speculation, not proof.

Ultimately, it was the emerging potential of winged aircraft that turned the Japanese navy away from further development of the airship. Given the expense of rigid airship construction and the continuing doubts about its utility and viability in combat, the winged airplane was a more promising agent for the navy's bid to enter the new dimension of the skies. Undoubtedly, too, the airship—large, slow, and ungainly—could hardly compete with the glamour of winged aircraft as the object of enthusiasm for aviation advocates in the navy. In 1931, for all these reasons, the navy abolished its airship unit and, over the next few years, phased out the airships attached to the fleet.[52]

In any event, the destiny of Japanese naval aviation was to be borne by wings and engines, not by lighter-than-air gases. It began with the decisions of the Commission on Naval Aeronautical Research to purchase foreign winged aircraft and to send junior officers abroad to learn how to fly and maintain them. In consequence, the navy purchased two seaplanes from the Glenn Curtiss factory in Hammondsport, New York, and two Maurice Farman seaplanes from France. To establish a cadre of naval aviators and technicians, the navy dispatched three officers to Hammondsport and two to France for training and instruction.[53] Upon their return to Japan at the end of 1912, two of the newly trained naval aviators made the first flights in Japanese naval air history at Oppama on Yokosuka Bay, one in a Curtiss seaplane, the other in a Maurice Farman.

Within a year, the navy had begun operational use of aircraft, and within two, Japanese naval aircraft had undertaken their first combat missions. In 1913, the navy converted the naval transport *Wakamiya Maru* into a seaplane carrier, the *Wakamiya,* capable of carrying two assembled and two disassembled seaplanes. As such, the *Wakamiya* participated in the naval maneuvers off Sasebo that year, and in 1914, the ship was sent to waters off Kiaochow Bay, where its seaplanes operated against the German naval base at Tsingtao. During these operations the Japanese aircraft made fifty reconnaissance and bombing sorties over the base while also undertaking search operations at sea.[54]

In 1916, the Commission on Naval Aeronautical Research was dissolved and the funds supporting it were set aside for the establishment of three *hikōtai* (naval air units) under the authority of the Naval Affairs Bureau of the Navy Ministry. The first unit was established at Yokosuka in April 1916. The lack of a concrete naval air policy in these early years, however, was demonstrated by the fact that the Yokosuka Air Group operated with the fleet only once a year when it was transported briefly to whatever training area the navy was then using for maneuvers. But Japanese naval aviation continued to make progress on a number of fronts. In 1917, officers at the Yokosuka Naval Arsenal designed and built the first Japanese seaplane, the Ro-Gō Kō-gata Reconnaissance Seaplane, which was much more useful at sea and much less dangerous than the Maurice Farman aircraft the navy had been using. The plane was eventually mass-produced and became the mainstay of the navy's air arm to the mid-1920s. By the end of the war, in increasing numbers, Japanese factories were beginning to turn out engines and fuselages based on foreign designs. A major increase in Japanese naval air strength was included in the 1918 naval expansion program that made possible a new air group and a naval air base at Sasebo. In 1918, the navy secured land around Lake Kasumigaura in Ibaraki Prefecture, northeast of Tokyo. The next year, a naval air base for both land and sea aircraft was started, and subsequently, naval air training was transferred there from Yokosuka. After the establishment of a naval air training unit at Kasumigaura, the base became the principal flight training center for the navy.[55]

While these initiatives were significant, by the end of the world war, aviation specialists in the navy concluded that it was the British navy that was making the greatest advances in naval aviation. Interest in the potential of carrier-borne air operations demonstrated by *Furious* led to the inclusion of an aircraft carrier in the eight-six fleet project of 1918. The 7,470-ton *Hōshō* was laid down in December 1919 in the Asano yard at Yokohama. *Hōshō* was the second warship after the British *Hermes* to be designed from the keel up as a carrier and the first to be completed as such. Meanwhile, in 1920 the navy sent a representative to Britain to observe air operations off the decks of *Furious*. Finally, in 1921, the Japanese government requested that the British naval air service dispatch to Japan a naval air mission to provide a professional edge to this newest arm of the Japanese navy. The Sempill Naval Air Mission of 1921–22 marks the true beginning of an effective Japanese naval air force and will be discussed in a later chapter.[56]

IMPROVING PROPULSION
Progress in Steam Engineering

Critical to maintaining technological parity with Western navies was the continued improvement of the navy's propulsion systems, particularly greater speed and endurance. For naval vessels, maximum speed is always a matter of great tactical importance, and for navies operating in the vast reaches of the Pacific, endurance is also vital. Ultimately, in designing its propulsion systems, the Japanese navy, like its Western counterparts, had to make important decisions that involved tradeoffs in the comparative performance of speed and endurance. Initially, however, it was simply a matter of catching up to Western standards in steam pressures.

The question of steam pressure was, of course, directly related to the structural design and materials used in the navy's boilers. To the end of the 1890s, the Japanese navy used return-type cylindrical boilers for its larger warships and locomotive-type boilers for its smaller vessels. Originally, these were of foreign manufacture, imported from abroad. But as Japanese domestic capabilities for boiler manufacture improved, these imports were produced in Japan under licensing arrangements. By later standards, the pressures these iron boilers produced were feeble—a little over 44 pounds per square inch. Then steel was introduced, and pressures increased progressively from 70 to 170 pounds per square inch. The battleships *Fuji* and *Yashima*, completed in 1897, had saturated steam plants running at 155 pounds per square inch. In the first years of the twentieth century, for use in its first-class cruisers and battleships, the navy began to adopt foreign-designed water-tube boilers, but given the Japanese pattern of technology transfer, it was not surprising that a Japanese-designed boiler plant of this type soon made its appearance. In 1895–96, Rear Adm. Miyabara Jirō presided over the design and development of a water-tube boiler of the large-tube type that took his name when it was adopted in 1903. The Miyabara boiler was cheap, simple to build, and held a large quantity of water, which it circulated efficiently; successive improvements eventually enabled it to produce pressures of 233 pounds per square inch.[57]

In these same years, the navy also developed small-tube water-tube boilers, patterned initially on foreign models. The first of these, designed by the Navy Technical Department in 1900 and adopted by the navy in 1902, was known as the Kampon boiler. First fitted and tested in the gunboat *Tatsuta*, it produced a steam pressure of 180 pounds per square inch, which drove two propeller shafts at 5,500 indicated horsepower. Installed in several destroyer classes before World War I, the boiler produced pressures of 180 to 274 pounds per square inch in the cruisers *Hirado, Chikuma,* and *Yahagi.* But the flat shape of the water drums of the boiler caused problems and led to the development of a new model, the Ro-Gō Kampon boiler, which used a cylindrical water drum configuration. The Ro-Gō was adopted in 1914 and remained the standard Japanese navy boiler throughout the Pacific War. By the mid-1920s, it was producing steam pressures of 274 pounds per square inch for Japanese battleships.[58]

This increasing pressure capability of the Japanese boilers stemmed from Japan's use of foreign (largely British) technology. A second factor was Japanese progress in metallurgy and engineering as domestic industry became more capable. It is another indication of the success of Japanese efforts to catch up with Western maritime and naval technology during these years that, by World War I, the navy had greatly narrowed the gap with Western navies in the competition to increase steam pressures and, consequently, in the race to attain power and speed.[59]

The Japanese navy was also alert to the advantages of the turbine over the reciprocating engine. In the first decade of the twentieth century, the navy experimented with foreign-designed and foreign-manufactured turbine systems in a number of warships then under construction. It was sufficiently satisfied with their performance to make a major effort to master turbine technology. But the adoption of turbine propulsion—smaller, lighter, vibration free, and more fuel efficient—was not without its problems. Like other navies, the Japanese confronted two problems: reconciling the high blade speed and attendant high shaft speed required for turbine efficiency with the lower shaft speed required for propeller efficiency, and operating turbine sets efficiently at lower power levels. During World War I, the first was solved, to an extent, by interposing reduction gears between turbines and propeller shafts (though the Japanese, like other navies, continued to have problems with reduction gears). The second problem was solved by means of cruising turbines. In the cruising configuration, the steam passed through the cruising turbines before being fed to the main turbine; in the high-speed/high-power configuration, the cruising turbine was bypassed.[60]

Using various gear and turbine configurations, the navy began to work out these solutions in the design and development of geared turbines. Consistent with its technological transfer strategy, it began by simply importing foreign turbines for installation in its warships and then moved to domestic production of foreign machinery by private firms under licensing arrangements. Mitsubishi installed Parsons turbines, and Kawasaki used Curtis-Brown equipment. At this point (around 1910), the Japanese navy was perhaps only a few years behind the other major naval powers in the construction of turbine systems.[61]

Then, during World War I, building on the knowledge thus acquired, the Navy Technical Department began the design and development of its own all-geared turbine, which soon became the standard turbine for the Japanese navy. The Gihon (later termed Kampon) turbine, a powerful machine entirely of Japanese design and manufacture, was installed first in the battleships *Nagato* and *Mutsu,* in which four sets of these turbines delivered a combined 80,000 shaft horsepower for a maximum speed of just under 27 knots.[62] The turbine was intended for the projected *Amagi*-class battle cruisers, of which only one, the *Akagi,* was completed (as a carrier). But the *Akagi*'s four shaft turbines delivered 131,000 shaft horsepower and 30 knots, a performance topped in the immediate post–World War I years only by the engineering plant of the British battleship *Hood.* Although the two American carriers built on battle cruiser hulls, the *Lexington* and *Saratoga,* had power plants that outstripped the *Akagi,* until 1941 and the launching of the *North Carolina*, no American battleship had a nominal shaft horsepower of 35,000, let alone the 80,000 of the *Nagato* class or the 45,000 of the *Ise* class.[63]

This comparison reveals the different strategic assumptions behind the design of the engineering plants for Japanese and American warships. Assuming that it would fight in the western Pacific and putting its emphasis on tactical speed, the Japanese navy installed relatively large engineering plants in its capital ships. The American navy, on the other hand, assuming that it would be fighting at the end of a trans-Pacific voyage, was willing to install smaller engineering plants that would leave more room for fuel—a tradeoff of speed for endurance.

Thus, since all three navies were working from different design specifications, it is difficult to say at the outset of the 1920s which was ahead in steam engineering. Nevertheless, as all three navies began to exploit the potential of superheated steam—the third element in the race for speed and power—the Japanese navy began to fall behind in this vital technological area.

THE NAVY AND OIL
The Beginning of a New Energy Problem

All the technological advances between 1905 and 1920 in which the Japanese navy had participated—the development of the fast battleship using oil-fired boilers, the emergence of the diesel-powered submarine, and the appearance of the gasoline-powered airplane—cumulatively presented the navy with a new and increasingly serious energy problem: the acquisition of sufficient petroleum for use as a naval fuel.

Actually, the use of oil-fired boilers had been considered by the navy as early as 1887. At that time, warships were barely out of the age of sail, and domestic coal, even if poor in quality, was readily available. For the rest of the century, therefore, there had been little incentive to advance research on oil fuel.[64] As previously noted, just prior to the Russo-Japanese War, the navy had begun importing good Cardiff coal from Britain while it strove to develop the technology for producing briquettes from domestic coal. When this technology was perfected, the navy was briefly self-sufficient in naval fuel, for the only time in its history. But, ironically, it was at this point that the advent of the *Dreadnought* and the demand for improved propulsion plants promoted the use of liquid fuels among the major navies of the world.

The Japanese navy itself had actually begun experimenting with petroleum between 1900 and 1904 and, in 1906, had made an official decision to adopt oil as a naval fuel and to install mixed-firing propulsion. In 1904, the old torpedo boat *Kotaka* had been experimentally refitted with propulsive machinery that was mostly oil-fired, but the first Japanese warship built with mixed coal and oil-fired burners had been the cruiser *Ikoma,* laid down in 1905. The *Kongō*-class battle cruisers and the *Fusō*- and *Ise*-class battleships had been constructed as principally coal-burning warships, though they were equipped to use oil in an emergency. The installation of the first completely oil-fired boilers in the destroyer *Urakaze* in 1915 marked a turning point for the navy. After that, the navy ordered no more warships whose boilers relied more than partially on coal. When the battleships *Nagato* and *Mutsu* were launched at the end of World War I, they were mainly equipped with oil-fired boilers.[65]

When the navy decided to adopt oil as a naval fuel, the nation's modest domestic petroleum resources were considered sufficient for the navy's needs. But as early as 1909, as naval demand became heavier and began to compete with growing industrial requirements for domestic oil, energy once more became a major problem for the navy. The navy was now forced to consider the question of this new fuel in its strategic calculations. To deal with the problem, the navy undertook several parallel courses of action over the next decade. The first of these was the stockpiling of oil reserves through the construction of heavy oil tanks at its four principal bases, the first at Yokosuka in 1909, followed by others at Kure and Sasebo. By the end of 1914, the navy had on hand a total of 24,500 tons of fuel.[66] But the Navy General Staff had already determined that in view of anticipated naval construction, the fleet would have to have at least 190,000 tons—six months' supply—on hand. With the outbreak of World War I, the fuel situation became even more critical. As the domestic production of petroleum apparently peaked in 1915, Japan had to obtain petroleum abroad. Thus, in 1916, the navy entered into a long-term purchasing agreement with the

Anglo-Saxon Petroleum Company for the purchase of oil from the fields at Tarakan, North Borneo, an arrangement that marked another departure in the navy's fuel policy and the beginning of the navy's interest in the strategic resources of Southeast Asia.[67] Two years later, the navy concluded a long-term contract with the Asahi Petroleum Company, the East Asian representative of a British firm, for the purchase of 150,000 tons of oil from Borneo (principally from Tarakan), and as the navy's needs increased, the contract was expanded to include oil from California.[68]

In 1920, the navy combined this import policy with a vigorous program of husbanding oil resources. The Navy General Staff declared that 360,000 tons of fuel oil should be set aside for use in the first year of any possible hostilities and another 260,000 tons reserved for use in a second year of combat.[69] In order to build up such reserves, the navy not only purchased some seven thousand oil storage tanks from the United States, but also encouraged the exploitation of new oil fields in Karafuto (the southern, Japanese half of Sakhalin). It entered into an agreement with the Soviet Union for the purchase of oil from northern Sakhalin and undertook experimentation in synthetic fuels, particularly liquefied coal and oil from shale. Finally, the navy moved to upgrade its fuel transport facilities. In the early years of its shift from coal to oil the navy had leased what tankers it needed from civilian shipping lines. But with the increase in demand it began constructing its own tankers in 1915, completing some fifteen of these vessels over the next decade.[70]

None of these steps rid the navy of its dependency on foreign oil, particularly that purchased through British or American firms, and the fact that one of these sources had been identified by the navy as a hypothetical enemy eventually had ominous strategic implications for the navy and the nation. But beyond these considerations lay the stark fact that Japanese demand on foreign oil kept increasing and there seemed to be nothing that Japan could do to lessen it.

THE NAVY AND THE DECLINE OF THE ANGLO-JAPANESE ALLIANCE

If the navy was becoming more dependent on foreign oil it was becoming less dependent on the special relationship with the British navy formalized by the Anglo-Japanese Alliance of 1902. The treaty, even though it did not come into full effect during the Russo-Japanese War, nevertheless had been advantageous to Japan during that conflict. In 1905, at the end of the war, the accord had been revised and renewed for ten more years, and its naval aspects had been the subject of naval discussions in London between Yamamoto Gombei and Admiral "Jackie" Fisher in 1907. But the naval talks of 1907 were far more restricted than those of five years before, largely because neither side attached the same degree of importance to the relationship. Despite its public posture about the navy's perilous decline relative to other naval powers, by 1907, the Japanese navy was becoming increasingly self-confident. For example, at the secret London naval talks, the Japanese delegation no longer sought a commitment of specific British force levels in East Asia. Instead, the delegation was content merely to inquire of the British what forces they planned to retain in East Asian waters and how those forces would be distributed.[71]

Nevertheless, the Japanese-British alliance had been renewed because it still served the interests of both signatories. On the one hand, it continued to facilitate Japanese access to British naval technology and to lessen the possibility of a Russian war of revenge against Japan. On the other hand, it allowed Britain to withdraw its naval strength from East Asian waters in order to concentrate British naval forces against Germany. Yet there were indications that Britain was growing wary of her partner and increasingly reluctant to share information on British naval advances in training and technology. The British admiralty, for example, reacted coolly to Japanese suggestions for the conduct of joint naval exercises.[72]

The original focus of the treaty, the Russian threat in East Asia, had greatly diminished after 1905, while the U.S. Navy had emerged as the Japanese navy's chief Pacific rival. The main point of tension in the treaty was the difference in attitude between Japan and Great Britain over the possibility of hostilities with the United States. Britain, which had no thought of an Anglo-American war, wished to make the United States an exception to the "third country" clause in the accord. Japan, which at least in theory contemplated the distinct possibility of a Japan-U.S. war, feared that in the event of such a conflict, a third country (presumably Russia, Germany, or France) might join America against Japan. In the event of an Asian war, Japan feared, the United States might join in an attack against her. Japan therefore wanted the alliance unchanged in this respect.[73] Ultimately, however, when the alliance was taken up for review in 1911, Japan, bowing to British insistence, was obliged to accept a clause providing, in effect, that neither Britain nor Japan was obliged to go to war with the United States under the terms of the treaty. The clause greatly diminished the value of the alliance in the eyes of the Japanese navy.[74]

For Japan and the Japanese navy in particular, the Anglo-Japanese accord served one last purpose in 1914. Eager to seize German colonial territories in China and the Pacific at the outset of World War I, Japan invoked the alliance to enter hostilities on the side of Great Britain, although, given the specific international situation and the actual terms of the treaty, Japan was under no real obligation to do so. The result was the swift Japanese occupation of both the German base at Tsingtao on the Shantung peninsula and the German islands in Micronesia, from the Marianas eastward to the Marshalls. The latter initiative appeared to improve substantially the Japanese strategic position in the event of a war with the United States. Though the alliance was a pretext blatantly exploited for the acquisition of these territories by Japan, by the end of the war the alliance itself was clearly in jeopardy. It was a matter of no importance to Great Britain and the object of outright hostility for most of Japan's wartime allies.

THE NAVY'S INITIAL PLANS FOR AN AMERICAN WAR, 1907

The apparent vagueness of Japanese naval thinking after the Russo-Japanese War about a possible conflict with its hypothetical American enemy has three causes. First, little of the historical record about the subject remains. Second, during these years, there was no national resolve to confront the United States over those issues that exacerbated relations between the two countries, a fact that made the navy's strategic planning concerning an American war more a justification for the navy's budgetary demands than a serious guideline for conflict with the United States. Third, the navy had neither the material strength to carry the war to America's shores nor the weapons systems and potential bases with which to offset a superior American battle fleet that might approach the Japanese home islands.

Because the navy lacked the material means to fight at great distance or for an extended period of time, it would have to fight a defensive war of quick decision. Moreover, the United States now possessed territories in the western Pacific and Southeast Asia that were both a strategic asset and a liability. The decisive naval encounter in any Japan-U.S. naval conflict, therefore, would probably be fought in the western Pacific between a Japanese home-based fleet and an American fleet moving westward to support, relieve, or reconquer the American positions in Guam and the Philippines. In doing so, the Americans would bring with them preponderant naval power. In the early years of the Japan-U.S. naval rivalry (1905–14), aircraft and submarines were still in their infancy, few destroyers were really seaworthy, and torpedo warfare was not yet fully effective. Consequently, the main arbiter of naval combat was still the capital ship, which the United States possessed in greater numbers than Japan. Even had the Japanese navy possessed large numbers of airplanes and submarines and shoals of light, torpedo-carrying vessels, all such craft of the day had limited range. Without advanced bases in the Pacific from which they could operate, they would have been restricted to a severely limited defensive role. These realities dictated a strategy that would exploit Japan's advantage of defensive position, a *yōgeki sakusen* (ambush strategy), in which the Japanese fleet would wait for the enemy to approach Japan's nearby seas and then deliver him a smashing blow, just as Tōgō had done at the end of the Russo-Japanese War.[75]

Although the absence of the necessary documentation makes it difficult to pinpoint the origins of the navy's strategic thinking concerning an American war, one can be reasonably sure that it began soon after the adoption of the Imperial

Defense Policy of 1907. The 1907 policy statement had, as an addendum, a general strategic plan directed against the nation's hypothetical enemies. Under the provisions of this plan each general staff of the two services drew up a *nendo sakusen keikaku* (annual operational plan) directed against the principal hypothetical enemies, which would remain in force from 1 April of one year to 31 March of the next. This annual plan would, in wartime, provide the basic directives for all strategy and operations, and in peacetime would be the basis for military and naval preparations, training, and intelligence planning. Attendant to each annual operational plan was the drawing up of detailed organizational plans for hostilities. The navy's plan was the *Nendo Teikoku Kaigun senji hensei* (Annual Imperial Navy plan for wartime organization). Actual orders for shifting from peacetime to wartime organization were contained in the *Suishi jumbi* (Preparatory fleet mobilization).[76] Each service still displayed continuing friction with the other service and obsessive concern with its own prestige: While the annual operational plans were supposedly the product of interservice consultation, in fact, the army and navy general staffs drew them up independently. Some historians have thus regarded them as only so much paper. Yet Nomura Minoru has argued that during the Pacific War, those operations that had the greatest success were those to which both services had given a great deal of thought over the years: the invasion of the Philippines (planning for which began in the late Meiji period), the occupation of Guam and the concomitant destruction of the U.S. Pacific Fleet (studied immediately after World War I), and the Hong Kong and Malaya operations (first planned in the mid-1930s). The exception, of course, was the attack on Pearl Harbor. Plans for it were drawn up immediately before the outbreak of the Pacific War.

There is no evidence to indicate that prior to 1906, the Japanese navy ever gave consideration to the remotest possibility of hostilities with the United States. Even the reference to a potential American conflict that appeared in the Imperial Defense Policy of 1907 merely stated in abstract terms that the principal objective was the destruction of American naval forces. While the sense of mutual hostility between Japan and the United States in the decade after the Russo-Japanese War was more episodic than deep-seated, the tensions of 1905–1907 (arising largely out of the demonstration of anti-Japanese racial feeling in California and the Japanese reaction to that feeling) had sensitized naval professionals on both sides of the Pacific to the possibility, however remote, of a future Japan-U.S. conflict. On the American side, this recognition was manifested in the drafting of the earliest versions of the "War Plan Orange" that for the next three decades, appearing in numerous revisions, was the basic strategic guide for American operations against Japan.[77]

While there are apparently no extant Japanese naval documents that describe in detail Japanese planning for a naval war with the United States during these years, a few sources indicate how the Japanese navy thought the war would be fought. A brief account exists, for example, of the Japanese naval maneuvers of 7–9 November 1908, east of Kyūshū, in which it was assumed that the enemy had occupied Amami Ōshima (strategically located between Kyūshū and Okinawa to the south) and that the decisive naval encounter would take place just east of that island.[78] Some time within the next several years, the navy began to include the Philippines in its strategic plans. At the opening of a war with the United States, the army and navy conducted joint operations against the Philippines, destroying American naval bases there and neutralizing American naval forces in Philippine waters. Light naval forces were distributed along a patrol line stretching from the Bonin Islands to the Izu Islands (map 6-1), acting as a trip wire for a massive counter blow against the advancing enemy main force by the Combined Fleet that would initially be concentrated near Amami Ōshima. A record of a map exercise conducted at the Naval Staff College in 1911 indicates that by that year, the navy had contemplated joint landing operations with the army at Luzon's Lingayen Gulf, the ejection of the U.S. Asiatic and Pacific fleets from Philippine waters, and the occupation of Manila—all prior to the arrival of the U.S. Atlantic Fleet. The exercise ended with a set-piece battle off Okinawa between the Combined Fleet and the U.S. Atlantic Fleet, but the outcome was inconclusive.[79]

By World War I, the naval staffs in both Tokyo and Washington centered their study of a Pacific war on two common assumptions: that Japan would conduct offensive operations against the Philippines at the outset of any such conflict,[80] and that the United States would move a battle fleet westward across the Pacific to come to the aid of the American garrisons and naval units there. For the Americans, the central dilemma was how to bring distance and time into a closer ratio in order to effect the rescue of their vulnerable position in the Philippines. Those who successively revised "War Plan Orange" wrestled with this nearly insoluble problem for the next quarter century.

For the Japanese, the issue was how to confront and defeat an American battle line superior in numbers and therefore in firepower. In drawing up its annual operations plans to deal with this problem, the Navy General Staff eventually concluded that the key to its solution lay in somehow reducing the strength of the enemy before the decisive engagement. Thus, the strategy against the westward-advancing American battle fleet would have to be conducted in two general phases. The first phase would be a series of preliminary attacks in the mid-Pacific by Japanese light forces that would gradually reduce the enemy until the American and Japanese battle fleets were numerically equal. Then, as the much-reduced American main force entered the waters of the western Pacific, the Japanese Combined Fleet, concentrated somewhere near Amami Ōshima, would sortie out to seek decisive battle (probably somewhere between the Ryukyu Islands and the

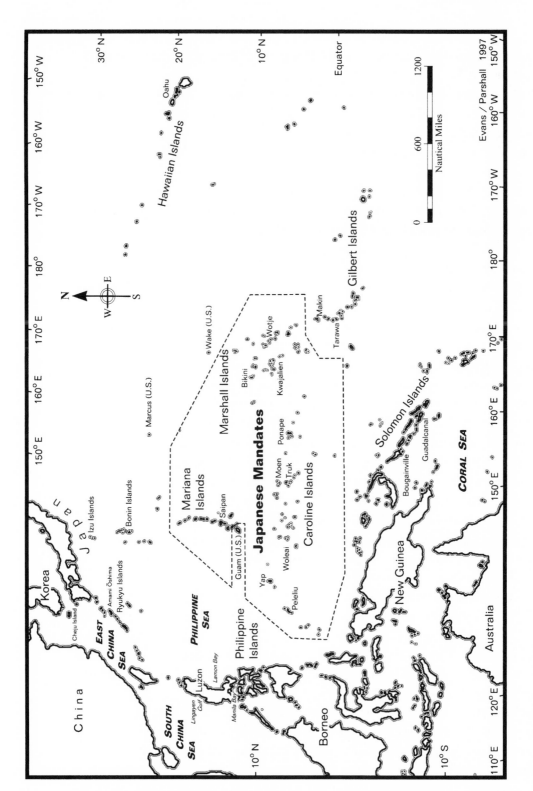

Map 6-1. Western Pacific, 1920s

northern tip of Luzon), counting on the heavier ordnance of its capital ships to win the day.[81]

None of this seems to have been worked out in any detail by World War I, in large part because of the operational limitations of all light forces, in particular destroyers, submarines, and aircraft, and because the nation possessed no advanced bases in the Pacific in which to position them.[82] These facts made it difficult for the Japanese navy to plan concretely for the attrition phase of its strategy against the American fleet. By the end of the war, however, two developments contributed greatly to future Japanese planning for a strategy of attrition. The first was the emergence of the submarine as a potentially effective weapon against surface warships, a development that would greatly enhance a strategy of attrition against a westward-moving American battle fleet. The other was the Japanese occupation of the German islands of Micronesia in 1914. In Japanese hands, the former German territories—the Marianas, the Carolines, and the Marshalls—would lie like a barrier across the western Pacific should the Japanese choose to base substantial naval forces there. Such a possibility would infinitely complicate the central strategic problem of the United States in any war with Japan. During World War I, Micronesia apparently figured little in Japanese strategy. After the war, Japan was obliged to agree to the withdrawal of all its naval forces from the islands and to pledge that it would not fortify them. Yet, by providing for the neutralization of potential American bases in the western Pacific while leaving most of the Micronesian islands in Japan's possession (albeit also neutralized militarily), this arrangement left Japan paramount in East Asian waters and made an American naval offensive across the Pacific a far more difficult and risk-laden venture. During the 1920s and 1930s, therefore, Micronesia clearly had an increasing importance in the navy's planning for a Pacific war, even though there is absolutely no evidence that Japan violated the letter of its pledge during at least the first decade of its League of Nations mandate over the area.[83]

COLLAPSE OF THE EIGHT-EIGHT FLEET PLAN
The Japanese Navy and the Washington Naval Treaty, 1922

In the several years that followed World War I, the naval construction programs of the three greatest naval powers threatened to set off a new, dangerous, and staggeringly expensive naval arms race. Of these programs, that of the United States appeared to make the most dramatic and potentially destabilizing bid for naval mastery. Because of the efforts of the Wilson administration, the United States already possessed sixteen modern capital ships. When finished, Wilson's 1916 expansion program would give that nation thirty-five such warships, and the completion of the projected 1919 program would provide a battle fleet of over fifty first-line battleships, quite overtaking Britain's fleet of forty-two battleships and battle cruisers. Even the vague and ambitious Japanese schemes for an eight-eight-eight fleet would be completely overshadowed by such a monster battle force. For these reasons, Britain was outraged and Japan alarmed, each concluding that it was the specific target of this vastly augmented plan for American naval expansion. The question of the motives behind Wilson's expansion plans lies outside the scope of this study; suffice it to say that by 1921 Wilson was out of office and his plans for naval supremacy were dropped. The succeeding Harding administration, recognizing that an arms race of such dimensions was in the interest of none of the contending powers, began to turn toward the idea of promoting an international agreement on naval arms limitation.

In the Japanese navy, the steady standard bearer for naval expansion for the past six years had been Navy Minister Katō Tomosaburō, a seasoned, dedicated, and careful naval bureaucrat. With Shimamura Hayao, chief of the Navy General Staff, Katō had worked tirelessly to obtain funding for an eight-eight fleet to meet the challenge of the wartime American naval expansion. On the eve of the new decade, however, Katō had come to believe that the threat of an unrestricted naval arms competition in the postwar era held ominous implications for all naval powers, but most particularly for Japan. To Katō, the recent conflict in Europe had set the shape of war for decades to come, one in which industrial and economic power determined the outcome of military conflict. With a far smaller industrial and economic base, Japan, in Katō's new perspective, was in no position to challenge the United States in a naval construction race. By 1921, the Japanese navy would have slightly more than half the total tonnage of its American rival. By 1925, when the American 1916 construction program was completed, Japan would have only 10 percent more tonnage than before, even if it made progress on its own eight-eight program. And by 1927, when the Japanese program was due for completion, Japan's naval strength would still be 200,000 tons under that of the United States and considerably below 70 percent of American naval strength. Given these merciless statistics, Katō thought that an escalating arms race with the United States would be a folly only exceeded by the greater folly of going to war with the United States at all. Viewing the battle fleet as a deterrent against American aggression rather than a force that would inevitably be used against the United States, Katō concluded that Japan's best interests lay in cooperating in an international effort to limit further capital ship construction by all naval powers.[84]

Katō Tomosaburō's growing acceptance of the concept of naval arms limitations was paralleled by similar thinking in British and American naval establishments. Still, he had been particularly prescient in anticipating the possibility of a postwar settlement of international naval arms issues. In 1919, he had appointed a special naval committee to ponder the question and to recommend policies. In

Katō Tomosaburō

its first report in 1920, the committee had urged that in the event of any international effort to reach a settlement on naval forces, the Japanese navy should insist on maintaining the two fundamental principles of its naval security: completion of an eight-eight fleet and retention of a tonnage ratio of 7 to 10 in relation to the United States. By 1921, the committee, like Katō himself, had come to perceive that the dangers of an unrestricted arms race might force the abandonment of the eight-eight program. But the committee held fast to the idea of a 70 percent ratio. Katō, who attached more importance to preventing the United States from fortifying its advanced bases in the Philippines and Guam, did not officially endorse the committee's report, though it had generally strengthened his position.[85]

In any event, Katō Tomosaburō's view of the need for cooperation with the Anglo-American naval powers in the pursuit of naval arms limitation was not the dominant view of the Japanese navy. Standing in direct opposition was a group of hard-lining young officers in the Navy General Staff and the Naval Staff College who were determined to maintain the unfettered expansion of the navy as a matter of both national security and national prestige. Their chief spokesmen were Vice Adm. Katō Kanji, president of the staff college, and Capt. Suetsugu Nobumasa, chief of the Operations Section of the Navy General Staff. It was Katō Kanji, a hot-headed and militantly nationalistic sea officer, who most clearly articulated a perspective on national defense utterly at variance with that of his senior, Katō Tomosaburō. Reading the implications of industrial war quite differently than the elder Katō, Katō Kanji argued heatedly that whereas the United States could afford to accept limitations on the size of its fleet, knowing that its huge industrial arsenal could easily build whatever warships it needed once a conflict began, Japan, with its smaller industrial resources, needed to maintain as large as fleet as possible. For the younger Katō and his supporters, the ultimate folly was not preparing as massively as possible for what they saw as an inevitable war with the United States.[86]

In the summer of 1921, the Harding administration issued its invitation to the international conference in Washington, D.C., on naval arms limitation and matters relating to East Asia. Because of his distinguished reputation in the Japanese bureaucracy, Katō Tomosaburō was appointed to head the Japanese delegation to the Washington conference while retaining his position as navy minister. In turn, because Katō Kanji represented a significant element in Japanese naval opinion, he was asked to join the delegation as the elder Katō's chief naval aide. This decision led to a near fatal split in Japan's representation at the conference.

The Washington naval conference, Secretary of State Hughes's surprise proposals for the stabilization of the existing strengths among the world's greatest navies, and the turmoil these provoked with the Japanese delegation have been well chronicled by other historians and will only be summarized here.[87] The United States had proposed a ten-year moratorium on capital ship construction and a schedule for the scrapping of specific warships in each of the five largest navies in order to reach stabilized limitations in total tonnage. After extensive negotiations, these limits turned out to be 525,00 tons each for the United States and Britain, 315,000 tons for Japan, and 175,000 tons each for Italy and France. In addition to this capital ship tonnage, Britain and the United States were allowed 135,000 tons for aircraft carrier construction, with 81,000 tons allotted to Japan, and 60,000 tons for Italy and France. No capital ship of any power was to exceed 35,000 tons (though an exception was eventually made for Britain's 41,000-ton battle cruiser *Hood*, then under construction). None could carry ordnance greater than 16 inches in bore, and no aircraft carrier could exceed 27,000 tons (though this limit was eventually raised to 33,000 tons, provided that the overall tonnage limitation for carriers was not exceeded). While no restriction was placed on the

Katō Kanji

amount of cruiser construction, no cruiser was permitted to exceed 10,000 tons or to carry any weapon greater than 8 inches in bore.[88]

The great sticking point for Japan, of course, was the inequity of naval tonnage allowed. The United States and Britain had argued that the greater limits reserved for them were justified on the grounds that the former had security interests in both the Atlantic and Pacific Oceans and the latter country required sufficient naval strength to protect an empire that circled the globe. Japan's security needs, they argued, were limited to the western Pacific. To the Japanese, the Hughes proposals threatened the sacrosanct twin pillars of Japanese naval policy, the eight-eight fleet and the 7 to 10 ratio in naval tonnage vis-à-vis the United States. Yet from the beginning of the conference, Katō Tomosaburō concluded that it was in the best interests of Japan to accept the proposals rather than face the prospect of an unrestricted naval arms race with the United States and possible economic collapse. In this he was so vehemently and continually attacked by the hard-liners in

Suetsugu Nobumasa

the Japanese delegation, led by his chief naval aide, Katō Kanji, that the delegation was brought almost to the point of rupture. Only by the elder Katō's consummate political skill and organizational leadership, ably assisted by his subordinates and allies in Tokyo, was the chief delegate able to gain the support of the high command for overriding and silencing Katō Kanji's opposition to the treaty.[89] Katō Tomosaburō's victory was Pyrrhic, however. In the years immediately following the conference, Katō Kanji exploited massive resentments among the "big navy" enthusiasts over the terms of the eventual treaty. The rift between the pro- and antitreaty factions within the navy flared anew in 1930 when the Washington naval powers met in London to consider renewal and revisions of the treaty.

On a few issues debated at Washington, the Japanese representatives were able to gain some concessions. One of these involved the battleship *Mutsu,* which, along with certain British and American battleships under construction, had been scheduled for scrapping under the original Hughes schedule. This was an extremely sore point with the navy, since not only was *Mutsu* one of the two greatest Japanese warships, but she had been built partly with funds raised by public subscription, largely donations from schoolchildren. Ultimately, the Japanese delegation argued successfully that *Mutsu* was already fully commissioned, had sailed one thousand miles under her own steam, and thus fell outside of the category of warships still under construction that were scheduled for scrapping.[90]

Far more important, Katō Tomosaburō and his colleagues won the approval of a nonfortification clause in the treaty providing that none of the Pacific powers would establish or strengthen any fortifications or naval bases in any of their island possessions, except that Singapore, Hawaii, and the Japanese home islands were to be exempt from this provision. The wording of the clause was brief and in retrospect fatally ambiguous, since it provided no definition of "fortification" or "bases." Undoubtedly, the framers of the treaty thought of these terms within a classical, pre-air-age context that centered on defensive works, coastal artillery, garrisons, dry docks, fuel dumps, and the like. In any event, the result was to prevent the United States and Britain from establishing secure bases anywhere in the western Pacific or Southeast Asia.

Nevertheless, in the new era of treaty limitations, the Japanese navy would face drastically altered circumstances. To begin with, if the navy was supreme in East Asia it was also alone, for the Washington accords had called for the end of the nation's essentially maritime alliance with Britain. Far more important, the eight-eight fleet, so long the navy's goal and so apparently within its grasp in 1921, was by 1922 a dead letter. As a result of the terms of the new five-power treaty, the battleship *Kaga* and the battle cruiser *Akagi*, well under construction, were completed as aircraft carriers; the keels of the battle cruisers *Atago* and *Takao* and those of the battleships *Kii* and *Owari* were scrapped; and the plans for the four remaining numbered, but as yet unnamed, battle cruisers were canceled. The battle force fell back to a six-four fleet of older capital ships (the four battle cruisers being reclassified as battleships after refitting in the 1920s), to be supported by three carriers. Potentially ranged against it was an American force of fifteen battleships and three carriers built or being built.

This disproportion in relative Japanese and American naval strengths served to underscore the bitter resentments of Katō Kanji and the navy's antitreaty faction that grew stronger after 1922. In order to further the new course of cooperation with the United States that he had set at Washington in 1922, Navy Minister Katō Tomosaburō had attempted to have it incorporated into the second revision of the Imperial Defense Policy drafted in 1922 and approved in 1923. But such were the nation's altered strategic circumstances and the influence of the younger Katō's insurgent group of "big navy" militants that, instead, the new document specifically identified the United States as the most likely hypothetical enemy for the army as well as the navy. Both services now regarded war with the United States as inevitable due to American economic expansion in China and anti-Japanese agitation on the American west coast. Nor was this all. By the summer of 1923, Katō Tomosaburō was dead of cancer, his passing hastened by overwork and exhaustion. While top posts on the Navy General Staff remained occupied until 1929 by officers who supported the treaty, with these developments, the influence of the antitreaty faction within the navy, especially within the Navy General Staff, rose dramatically.[91]

Still, for the time being, Japan had agreed to abide by the international agreements that restricted its naval status. It remained to be seen how well the navy maintained its effectiveness in the new "treaty era" of material limitations.

7

"USING A FEW
— to —
CONQUER MANY"

*The Japanese Navy from the Beginning of the Treaty Era
to the First London Naval Conference, 1923–1930*

For the remainder of the 1920s the terms of the Washington Treaty strengthened, not weakened, Japanese national security in its broadest sense.[1] The naval arms limitations saved the Japanese government a prodigious outlay of funds for the maintenance as well as the construction of capital ships during a decade of economic strain and uncertainty worsened by the massive expenses incurred in the reconstruction of Tokyo following the great earthquake there in 1923. Under these circumstances the completion of the eight-eight fleet plan would undoubtedly have been ruinous for the nation. As it turned out, the Japanese navy during these years had to carry out its development of lesser warship categories with selectivity and care.

Moreover, by providing for the neutralization of potential American bases in the western Pacific while leaving most of the Micronesian islands in Japan's possession (albeit also neutralized militarily), the treaty left Japan paramount in East Asian waters and made an American naval offensive across the Pacific a far more difficult and risk-laden venture. These advantages became all the more important when viewed against the greatly altered economic and strategic circumstances of Japan by the end of World War I. Prior to 1904, Japan had been an essentially self-sufficient agricultural nation with only limited overseas trade, restricted trade routes, and a modestly sized merchant fleet. In the Sino-Japanese and Russo-Japanese Wars the navy's responsibilities had been largely limited to the protection of supply lines for the army's expeditionary forces on the Asian mainland and patrol of trade routes across the East China Sea. By the end of World War I, Japan's increasing population and industrial growth had brought about its dependence on foodstuffs and raw materials from Southeast Asia as well as the northeast Asian continent. The growth had also stretched the nation's trade routes as far south as the oil wells of Borneo and had stimulated the development of the world's third largest merchant marine. That Japanese trade should have been granted a decade of security under the terms of the agreements on naval arms limitation must surely be counted a great benefit to Japan.

The naval treaty signed by the five powers in 1922 was but one of several compacts concluded in Washington that year. The others were regional in nature, reaffirming the principle of China's political and territorial integrity and of equality of economic opportunity in China for all the powers. To this extent, one of its principal objectives was to reduce the possibility of a collision of Japanese and American interests on the northeast Asian continent and so reduce the likelihood of armed conflict between the two nations. The subsequent peaceful pursuit of economic expansion in China without the risk of war was, for a time at least, a basic foreign policy of the Japanese government during the 1920s.

Given these advantages to Japan, it is easy to understand why the Japanese navy orthodoxy of the decade, fixed by the late Katō Tomosaburō, accepted the system of naval limitation as being, in balance, in the best interests of the nation, since it lessened the possibility of war and the need for a ruinous naval race to prepare for it. Even before the elder Katō's untimely death, however, this moderate orthodoxy was being eroded by the rising influence of an adamantly antitreaty group of officers found mainly in the Navy General Staff. As noted, the group centered around its vice chief, Vice Adm. Katō Kanji and, to a lesser extent, around the acting chief of the General Staff's Operation Section, Capt. Suetsugu Nobumasa. Ideologically and intransigently opposed to the treaty system as a tool of Western and specifically American interests, they fixated on the doctrine of "big ships, big guns" and on its corollary, the 70 percent ratio. Katō and the like-minded officers of his faction saw conflict with the United States as both inevitable and justified. Indeed, it was Katō and Suetsugu who in 1922 had taken the initiative within the navy to have the Imperial Defense Policy once again revised. Sweeping aside the possibilities of compromise with American economic interest in China, they had insisted upon a specific assertion in the revision that "the United States, by its limitless economic resources, by its pursuit of policies of economic aggression, and, in China in particular, by its provocation of anti-Japanese activities, threatens the Japanese position in China for which our nation has risked its destiny."[2]

The United States thus no longer served merely as the navy's "budgetary enemy," a convenient rationale for competing with the army for government funds, as it had in Satō Tetsutarō's day. The designation of the United States as Japan's chief "hypothetical enemy" in the revised Imperial Defense Policy of 1923 instead identified the bitter adversary with whom war was inevitable. Ironically, in the very years when the arrangements of the Washington Treaty seemed to have lessened the likelihood of a successful trans-Pacific naval offensive by either Japan or the United States, the conviction took hold in the Japanese navy that war with its American counterpart was unavoidable.[3]

Once again, the Imperial Defense Policy proved a source more of contention than of coordination between the two services. The navy gained a significant victory in the designation of the United States as the most likely hypothetical enemy, defense against whom should be the nation's highest priority. But the navy could not prevent wording in the policy's annual operational plan, inserted at the army's insistence, that considered the possibility of war against two or possibly even three enemies at once. A heated controversy thus erupted that a series of high-level negotiations failed to resolve, and not until 1933 did the two services agree on a one-enemy-at-a-time formula for operational planning.[4]

INTERCEPTION AND ATTRITION
Strategic Planning against an American Naval Offensive in the Pacific

Combined with the conviction about the inevitability of war with the United States was the reaffirmed belief that such a war with the United States would involve a westward offensive by the U.S. battle fleet, culminating in a decisive fleet engagement somewhere in the western Pacific. To a considerable extent, the Japanese navy had, by the outset of the 1920s, a good fix on the American strategic and tactical planning for a naval offensive against Japan. Perhaps this was due to some sort of clandestine access to American operational studies on problems involved in transoceanic campaigning.[5] More likely, the Japanese simply made commonsense deductions about the principal considerations that would shape an American naval expedition into Japanese waters. There were, for example, only four possible routes across the Pacific that an American naval force could take. The shortest course would be the northern route, by way of Pearl Harbor or the American west coast, up to Alaska and then along the Aleutians and down the Kuriles to Japan. This would be far too hazardous because of adverse weather, though it might be undertaken as a diversionary operation. There was a southern route, which could use American and possibly even British or French bases in the South Pacific for resupply and refueling. Being the most circuitous route, however, it was viewed as probably too time-consuming, particularly in view of the Japanese movement against the Philippines early in the war. Last, there were two central routes. One was directly across the Pacific from Hawaii to the Japanese defense line between the Bonin and Mariana Islands. This route would trigger a main fleet encounter along that line. The other was somewhat further south through the Gilberts, Marshalls, Truk, and Guam (the last-named presumably lost to Japan at the outset of the war). These Japanese-held islands would have to be seized and occupied but would provide better communications, refueling, and repair as the American fleet proceeded.[6]

Calculations as to which of these two central passages the U.S. battle fleet would take depended largely on the estimated pace of the American offensive. Some Japanese strategists believed that in view of the American temperament, the U.S. Navy would move to attack Japan directly across the more northern of the two routes. But ultimately, the orthodox estimate of American plans held that the United States would not assemble an offensive across the Pacific until it held a 50 percent superiority over Japan in capital ships and that, consonant with this caution, the American force would probably take the more southern of the central routes, seeking to establish bases as it proceeded.[7]

At the outset of the 1920s, the estimated ratio of American to Japanese capital ship construction capacity was three or four to one. Therefore, it was clearly in the interest of Japan for the conflict to be as brief as possible before the margin of superior American firepower became overwhelming. It was obviously impossible in the 1920s for the Japanese navy to bring about a short war by decisively beating the U.S. battle fleet off the American west coast or Hawaii. Hence, Japan's most realistic strategy, as it had been just before World War I, would be to move immediately to defeat the smaller U.S. Asiatic Fleet and to seize the Philippines and Guam at the outset of the war, in expectation that an aroused American public would demand an early dispatch of the battle fleet to recapture these territories.[8] But Japanese naval planners in Tokyo were also concerned that battle might be forced on the Japanese fleet before it was ready. Their considerable anxiety was that at some moment when the navy was unable to prevent it, the U.S. Asiatic Fleet, escaping discovery and destruction, would slip out and attack Japanese trade and communications routes in the seas north of Taiwan and toward the Tsushima Straits, prior to linking up with the main American battle group and forcing a decisive battle while the Japanese were still disorganized. For this reason, it was doubly important to smash the enemy's Asiatic Fleet and to seize his bases in the western Pacific at the outset of any Japan-U.S. war.[9]

At the opening of the era of naval limitations in 1923, therefore, Japanese plans against the United States generally resembled those drafted by the Navy General Staff prior to World War I, except that they were now far more detailed and gave a more prominent place to the newer elements in naval warfare, particularly cruisers, destroyers, submarines, and aircraft. The high command hoped to concentrate Japanese naval forces in East Asian waters at the outset of the war in order to move quickly against American bases and naval units in the western Pacific. The Japanese had in fact little reason to fear the Asiatic Fleet as a raiding force, given its puny size and the obsolescence of its ships. Nevertheless, the Japanese navy planned to dispatch submarines secretly to command all important ports, bays, and straits in the Philippines for the purposes of surveillance, reconnaissance, early warning, minelaying, and torpedo attack. Departing from advance bases at Amami Ōshima, Okinawa, and Makung in the Pescadores Islands, Japanese surface units, operating in conjunction with submarines and aircraft, were to locate and destroy the U.S. Asiatic Fleet at the earliest possible moment. As before, the navy was also to cooperate with the army in effecting landings at Lingayen Gulf and Lamon Bay in Luzon. The landings could be followed in succession by the occupation of Manila, the elimination of the enemy base at Cavite, control of the Bataan Peninsula, and an attack on Corregidor. At all events, these operations were to be completed before the anticipated westward departure of the U.S. battle fleet, which might or might not be accompanied by a train of transports and supply ships, depending upon the American strategic objective.[10]

The second stage of the navy's strategy was far more critical and far more difficult, dealing as it did with meeting and defeating the bulk of the American battleship force. As in the past, the navy's grand maneuvers of 1924 were predicated on *yōgeki sakusen* (interceptive operations) that entailed luring the enemy as close to Japanese waters as possible, to deliver him a concentrated blow by the full strength of the Japanese fleet. Specifically, the plans now called for the arrangement of two Japanese patrol lines that would alert the Japanese heavy forces to the imminent approach of the American battle force. The first of these, patrolled by oceangoing trawlers and submarines, ran south from northern Honshū to the Bonin Islands. (This idea of a picket line of small vessels was abandoned in the 1930s with the advent of long-range flying boats, but it was reactivated early in the Pacific War.) The second patrol line, more likely to be crossed by the enemy, stretched from the Bonins south to the Mariana Islands and was to be maintained by the cruisers and destroyers of the Japanese Third Fleet, supplemented by submarines, seaplanes, and various auxiliary units.[11] Once alerted, the Japanese main battle forces—the First and Second Fleets—were to descend upon the enemy to defeat him in a classic line-to-line gun battle, the anticipated location of which had now been moved eastward to the area between the Bonins and Marianas.[12] But the Japanese could win such a decisive engagement only if they were superior, or at least equal, to the U.S. battle fleet in firepower. After the Washington Treaty, the ongoing problem of how to contend with the numerically superior American force had become even more serious. Therefore, the navy, beginning with the annual operational plan based on the 1923 revision of the Imperial Defense Policy, gave increasing attention to its earlier concept of reducing the U.S. battle fleet through preliminary attacks by light forces as that fleet was still steaming through the mid-Pacific.[13]

In Japanese naval planning of the 1920s, this *zengen sakusen* (attrition strategy, or literally, "progressive reduction operations") became the essential preliminary to the decisive battle. Since no matter which of the two central routes was chosen by the U.S. battle fleet and since Hawaii was bound to be its point of departure, Japanese planning involved the early dispatch to Hawaii of submarines and seaplanes (carried aboard seaplane tenders) to keep watch on American naval movements. Once the course of the enemy was determined, Japanese naval forces would begin to concentrate, the lighter forces to the eastward for attrition operations, the main battle force farther west for the eventual big-gun engagement. Submarines, hastily dispatched to the Marshall, Caroline, and Mariana Islands, would launch attacks to whittle down the size of the enemy. At night, destroyers and light cruisers would deliver torpedo attacks against him. As the Japanese main battle force steamed eastward from Amami Ōshima or Okinawa, it was left to the overall Japanese commander to decide where and when to engage the enemy in the final showdown, a decision based on the results of the attrition operations, weather conditions, and a number of other variables. But in the 1920s, at least, it was assumed that the decisive fleet battle would take place during the day, probably in the first hours of daylight after a long night of attacks by light forces. (Such a battle was called *yokuchō kantai kessen,* literally, "decisive fleet battle the morning after.") This was in part because Japanese tacticians feared that night attacks by American cruisers and destroyers could play havoc with capital ships just as effectively as their Japanese enemy, and in part because, since 1912, the navy's Battle Instructions held that "cooperative action and unified control of large forces at night is difficult." Depending on the outcome of the night actions by light forces, therefore, the Japanese commander-in-chief would designate the assembly point for the following dawn, in order to coordinate the full strength of the Japanese fleets—battleships, battle cruisers, cruisers and destroyers—which would move in against a weakened and demoralized enemy. The battle cruisers would destroy the enemy screening forces, allowing the cruisers and torpedo squadrons of destroyers to get at the American battleships, while the latter were simultaneously bombarded at long range by the Japanese battle line.[14]

This, in outline, was the ideal outcome of the phased strategy against an American naval offensive, and it remained the basic Japanese tactical plan until 1941. But by the early 1920s, the Japanese naval high command also learned of an apparently new and seriously complicating factor: The U.S. battle fleet would not only steam westward with a superior number of big guns. It would do so in a disposition of warships that would be formidable in defense. This was the so-called ring formation, known officially in the 1924 U.S. Navy Instructions as "U.S. Fleet Cruising Disposition Number Two," designed for maximum protection to both the capital ships of the fleet and a large accompanying convoy. It was also drawn up for use in an overseas advance before Americans obtained control of the sea. The formation called for submarines, destroyers, and cruisers to surround the nucleus of the fleet—the battleship force as well as the fleet train and transports—protecting them from torpedo attacks by Japanese cruisers and destroyers by driving the latter off with their own torpedoes and gunfire. The fighting units of the battle fleet would be disposed in four concentric circles of 6, 11, 16, and 21 miles outward from the fleet center. Each circle would be divided into three sectors, numbered clockwise, and the screening forces would be assigned to fixed stations along each sector (fig. 7-1). Submarines would be positioned on the first or outermost circle to provide early warning and to take offensive action against suitable targets; destroyers on the second circle had a generally similar function; cruisers and destroyer divisions would be positioned on the third with a more defensive mission; and the battleship divisions would normally occupy the fourth ring, protecting the unarmed convoy. Within this innermost circle one battleship division would be stationed along the line of advance and one along each beam of the center. In this fashion, given sufficient warning of the approach of the Japanese fleet, at least two battleship divisions could be quickly combined, providing firepower superior to whatever capital ship strength Japan could muster. Developed as a concept about the same time as the organization of the battle fleet in 1920 and its stationing on the American west coast, the ring formation was purportedly modified and revised on the basis of study, maneuvers, and exercises over the next decade and a half. Nevertheless, its fundamental principle supposedly remained: protection of the U.S. fleet's main body—the battleships, along with the fleet train—from attacks by light enemy surface forces and, later, from enemy air units.[15]

"USING A FEW TO CONQUER MANY"
Japanese Efforts to Counter American Naval Superiority

This new American formation challenged the tactical planning and the technological innovation of the Japanese navy over the next decade and a half. The Japanese naval high command, the Navy General Staff in particular, viewed the formation within the context of a far greater problem. Under the naval limitations agreements that Japan had signed, the United States could not only bring many more capital ships into the Pacific—sixteen to Japan's ten during the 1920s—but also more ships in most other warship categories. For the entire "treaty era" of naval limitations (1923–36), the Japanese navy's strategic and tactical planning

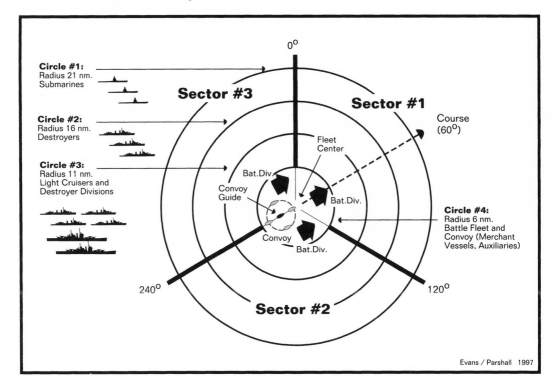

Circle #1:
Radius 21 nm.
Submarines

Circle #2:
Radius 16 nm.
Destroyers

Circle #3:
Radius 11 nm.
Light Cruisers and
Destroyer Divisions

Sector #3

Sector #1

0°

Course
(60°)

Fleet
Center

Bat.Div.

Convoy
Guide

Bat.Div.

Circle #4:
Radius 6 nm.
Battle Fleet and
Convoy (Merchant
Vessels, Auxiliaries)

Convoy

Bat.Div.

240°

120°

Sector #2

Evans / Parshall   1997

Fig. 7-1. U.S. Navy circle formation, 1924 (fleet cruising disposition no. 2). Screening forces were deployed on each of the four screening circles, each of which had seven to nine spaced stations per sector, where one or more warships would be located. This formation was designed "to permit a fleet to give maximum protection to a large convoy in an overseas advance" before control of the sea had been gained.
(Source: U.S. Navy, Chief of Naval Operations, *General Tactical Instructions. United States Navy. Fleet Tactical Publication Number 45,* Washington, D.C.: U.S. Government Printing Office, 1925)

and its warship and weapons development were directed to dealing with this stark issue. As in the past, the navy's solution was to emphasize better weapons and better planning that, it was hoped, would enable the Japanese navy to put its fewer numbers against the greater American enemy and emerge victorious. Indeed, all the measures of the Japanese navy that aimed to counter the quantitative superiority of the U.S. Fleet can be subsumed under the Japanese principle of *ka o motte shū o sei-su* (using a few to conquer many), which had been invoked in both the Sino- and Russo-Japanese Wars. These measures included the development of a

long-range subsurface offensive capability; the perfection of night combat techniques by torpedo squadrons; the achievement of superior design and construction in heavy cruisers; the devising of the tactic for "outranging" the enemy; the
development in the 1930s of a night combat force of fast battleships; the forging
of a superb naval air arm; and finally, the construction of the most powerful battleships ever to enter the ocean.[16]

These various initiatives were influenced by the general technological capacities and professional attitudes of the Japanese navy as it entered the treaty era. The
degree to which Japanese government facilities, in combination with the capabilities of private shipbuilding firms, had achieved technological sufficiency for the
navy was the most salient aspect of Japanese naval technology at the end of World
War I. This development was in striking contrast to the navy's situation on the eve
of the Russo-Japanese War. Whereas in 1904, Tōgō had taken a British-built fleet
to sea, nearly all warship types and weapons systems could now be constructed in
Japan solely with Japanese materials and labor and according to Japanese design.

Initiating the process of warship design and construction was the Navy General Staff. Once funds were appropriated by the Diet, the staff handed down the
specifications for warships it believed the navy required. These specifications were
passed on to the Navy Ministry, which in turn relayed them to the Navy Technical Department. The department, Kansei Hombu (literally, "Ship Administration
Headquarters," and sometimes shortened to Kampon) was the central agency
under the navy minister responsible for the design and construction of warships
(fig. 7-2). It was equivalent to the Bureau of Ships of the U.S. Navy. Its origins
went back to 1871, but it was first established in 1900. In the wake of the Siemens
scandal of 1914,[17] during World War I, the department and its functions were split
between two separate offices, but they were brought back together again when
the department was reestablished in 1920. Between the world wars, the department's functions came to include the maintenance, testing, research, design, and
planning of ships, weapons, and machinery. Two of the department's most important branches were Basic Design (located at various periods in the Third or Fourth
Section with offices at Ōfuna, in Kanagawa Prefecture), which was at the heart of
the navy's work on warship design, and the Naval Technical Research Center in
Tokyo (located first at Tsukiji and much later at Meguro), which conducted various experiments on materials, hull designs, electrical systems, and the like.
Excluding warships built at private yards, the actual construction of ships at the
navy's yards at Yokosuka, Kure, Sasebo, and Maizuru was ultimately the responsibility of the base commander at those places, though in practice it was the
responsibility of the yard's chief constructor.[18]

Construction at navy yards was supplemented by work undertaken at the
great private shipyards such as those at Yokohama, Kobe, and Nagasaki, owned

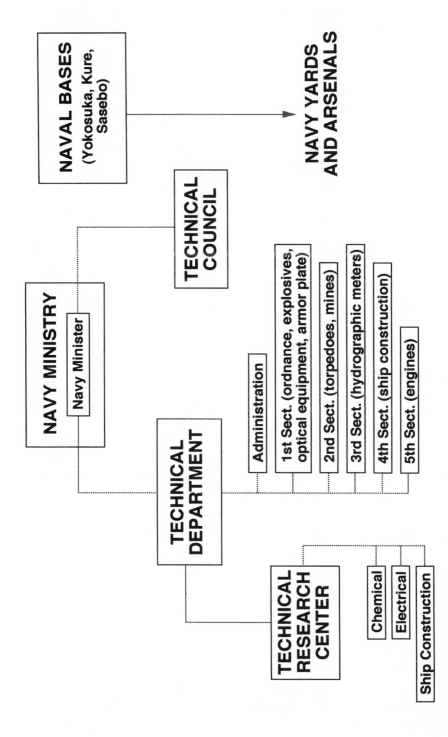

Fig. 7-2. Administration of technology in the Japanese navy, ca. 1925.

by the Mitsubishi Shipbuilding Company. Other important shipbuilding facilities were Ishikawajima Heavy Industries, Limited, at Tokyo, the Uraga Dockyard Company near Tokyo, the Kawasaki Shipyard Company at Kobe, the Fujinagata Dockyard at Osaka, and the Harima Dockyard at Hyōgo.

By the early 1920s, therefore, the skills available at both naval and private dockyards made Japan capable of turning out a range of warships that, in design, were equal or superior to those of any other navy in the world. Only in certain specialized fields such as submarine technology, aircraft design, and optics were Japanese technicians in the 1920s still dependent on foreign ideas and models. At the outset, the dominant influence was British, though during the 1920s, after the termination of the Anglo-Japanese Alliance and the cessation of special favors that had been extended to the Japanese over a range of technological fields, the navy turned largely to defeated Germany for expertise in optics and submarine design.[19]

Yet if Japanese naval technology was now generally autonomous in concept, material, and design, it was nevertheless subject to powerful restraints. In addition to the limitations in design and construction imposed by the Washington Treaty, there were domestic restrictions on the development of naval technology within Japan. One such restriction was the generally negative and frugal attitude of the Diet that, in the first half of the 1920s, at least, was filled with business-minded and somewhat liberal politicians averse to vast expenditures for military and naval purposes. Another restriction was a postwar economic slump that put the government in poor financial circumstances. Government budgets were strained even further by the great Tokyo earthquake and fire of 1923, which required extraordinary reconstruction costs. Together, these circumstances served as a serious check on Japanese naval construction in the 1920s. Again and again during the decade, naval construction programs drafted by the Navy General Staff were subjected to successive diminution and sometimes outright rejection by the Navy Ministry, the Finance Ministry, the Cabinet, and the Diet.

But this budgetary stringency combined with the limitations imposed by the Washington Treaty had two benefits for the navy: It obliged the navy to make choices and to think carefully about alternative technologies and strategies, and it reinforced the navy's drive for qualitative superiority. This produced a situation in which, as a former naval constructor remembered decades later, "the Chief Naval Constructors labored to produce vessels that would, type for type, be individually superior to those of the hypothetical enemy, even by a single gun or torpedo tube or by a single knot of speed."[20]

The Japanese naval leadership was astute enough to realize, of course, that the fighting edge of the navy rested on more than just the capabilities of its warships. It depended, too, upon the soundness of its tactics, the effectiveness of its bases, the efficiency of its organizational structure, the thoroughness of its training, the quality of the technical research of its various institutes and schools, and the professional training of its officers and men, both on shore and at sea. Thus, during the entire treaty period, the navy put a great deal of effort into "upgrading the contents" of all these elements *(naiyō jūjitsu)* as yet another contribution to the principle of qualitative superiority.

An example of this emphasis was the great store that the navy put on constant battle preparedness through a most rigorous program of naval maneuvers and exercises. The navy's training cycle ran from December of one year to November of the next. The cycle was based on the navy's operational plan for that year and on the training priorities handed down by the Navy General Staff. The navy minister tempered these with the results of the most recent tests of particular ships, weapons, and aircraft and notified the Combined Fleet of the most important training points. The Combined Fleet commander then added whatever other training items he thought necessary. The cycle began in January with basic crew training, during which time ships were repaired, refitted, and loaded with stores and ammunition. In February, individual fleet units proceeded to operations areas in home waters or off the China coast for cruises and exercises. In May they returned to their respective naval stations and ports for refit and replenishment, and the crews were sent on leave or rotated among various commands. In May or June, the various fleets moved to fleet operations areas, where general training and gunnery exercises were conducted under wartime conditions. In October, the Combined Fleet began large-scale maneuvers under simulated battle conditions. These could be either "grand maneuvers" ("special grand maneuvers" if the emperor was in attendance) or lesser maneuvers. Grand maneuvers were held once every three years and focused on a particular problem.[21]

Many of the navy's maneuvers, both lesser and grand, were held in the stormy waters off northern Japan to toughen the crews and sequester the fleet from foreign observation. To perfect the night combat capabilities of the navy, Katō Kanji, while commander in chief of the Combined Fleet, 1926–29, ordered the fleet to undertake high-speed, close-in night exercises "more heroic than under battle conditions."[22] Inevitably, such risky exercises resulted in some spectacular collisions, like that in the Japan Sea off Mihogaseki, in which one warship was sunk, three others severely damaged, and nearly 150 lives were lost. The Mihogaseki disaster took place off Shimane Prefecture on the night of 24 August 1927. Japanese destroyers were practicing attacks against an "enemy" main fleet. Because the cruisers supporting them "attracted enemy searchlights," they rapidly reversed course. Misjudging the position of the destroyer squadron in the darkness, the light cruiser *Jintsū* rammed and sank the destroyer *Warabi* with great loss of life, while the light cruiser *Naka* sliced off the stern of the destroyer *Ashi,* resulting in further fatalities. Both cruisers were badly damaged themselves. Far from daunted by the tragedy, Admiral Katō, while eulogizing the dead and wounded in a speech at the Suikōsha club in Maizuru, declared that such sacrifices in training were necessary to make up for the disadvantages forced on Japan by the Washington Treaty. He declared with great passion that the navy would continue with "more and more of the training of recent days, into which the navy has poured its life's blood" to provide "certain victory in the three versus five [i.e., the treaty proportion] struggle."[23]

Other accidents followed. Among the most serious was that off Cheju Island at the southern tip of Korea, on 24 June 1934, when two torpedo flotillas were practicing daylight attacks through smokescreens. In the smoke the destroyer *Inazuma* rammed and sank the destroyer *Miyuki*, with a number of fatalities.[24]

This determination to maintain and, if possible, to upgrade the navy's fighting capacity despite these hazards epitomizes its professional energy at all levels during this period. Japan's naval leadership in particular and its officer corps in general displayed serious weaknesses that have been catalogued by both Arthur Marder and Asada Sadao. Such shortcomings included the absence of independent and rational judgment in the average naval officer, his lack of assertiveness, the tendency of too many senior officers to delegate responsibilities to their staffs, the narrow strategic and tactical concerns that monopolized higher naval education at the Naval Staff College, a promotion system that emphasized seniority over capability, the overly rapid turnover in assignments that precluded continuity in naval policy, and, of course, the overweening pride of service that perpetuated the navy's continuing and destructive rivalry with the army.[25]

Assuredly, these were defects that contributed to the navy's part in Japan's heedless slide toward war with the Anglo-American naval powers in 1941 and, once in it, crippled the navy's conduct of the war. Yet during the treaty era, in training, technical innovation, and technical proficiency, the Japanese navy was probably equal to and in some cases superior to the other two major navies, because of the quality of its leadership. In these activities, certainly, the Japanese navy outstripped its British mentor during these years. Stephen Roskill, the chronicler of naval policies during the interwar period, writes of the war-weariness of the British navy in the 1920s. He discusses the tactical sterility of its leadership and the stereotyped and lethargic nature of its training. During the British training exercises, firing was directed at targets towed at a leisurely 6 knots and maneuvers were carried out with a view to minimize risk to life, limb, and professional reputation.[26]

There were, however, two serious blind spots in the Japanese navy's professional outlook during the interwar years. One was unique to Japan, and the other was shared with the leadership of the U.S. and British navies. Peculiar to Japan was the tendency of much of the navy's leadership to cast the solution of the navy's strategic and tactical problems in a spiritual and ideological light. Thus, the supposedly unique qualities of Japanese fighting spirit, willpower, and moral superiority were counted upon to make up for whatever quantitative inferiority limited its matériel. This perspective had its origins in the way that the modern Japanese military interpreted the values of the former samurai class and was first applied to Japanese naval thought in the later writings of Akiyama Saneyuki and Satō Tetsutarō. The emphasis on spirit and morale was given ever more vehement expression by a later generation of naval leadership beginning with the militant group centered on Katō Kanji and Suetsugu Nobumasa. Even though this emphasis directly contradicted the navy's relentless demands for material parity with the Anglo-American naval powers, it became a bedrock of faith in superior fighting qualities.[27]

The other distortion in Japanese naval thinking, shared with the Americans and British, was the continuing fixation on the decisive fleet encounter on the Jutland model, involving all types of warships but centering on the battleship as the ultimate arbiter of naval combat. For years, the collective strategy and tactics of Jutland, seen as confirming the validity of the navy's obsession with "big ships, big guns" since the late Meiji period, were subjects of constant and meticulous study at the Naval Staff College and the focus of periodic revisions of the Battle Instructions.[28] Ultimately, the instructions tended to discourage alternative strategies and weapons systems, for example, the submarine as a threat to commerce. In this oversight, however, the Japanese battleship-minded admirals were no different from their British and American counterparts during the treaty era. At the Royal Navy Staff College, at the Tactical School, and among the staffs of the various British fleet commands, Jutland was the focus of endless rumination in the 1920s, and historians have long argued that the battle fleet concept retained its powerful influence over British naval thought throughout the interwar years. In the U.S. Navy, too, the top brass was committed to the "fleet engagement" and the dominance of the battleship.[29]

JAPANESE SUBMARINE DEVELOPMENT, 1918–36

During World War I, the submarine, had proved itself technically and operationally as a formidable new element of sea power, particularly in its massive destruction of merchant shipping. By 1918, submarine technology, developed largely by Germany, was so advanced that during the two decades between the world wars, the major navies made few fundamental design changes other than strengthening hull structures for greater operational depth, perfecting escape and salvage equipment, and adopting hydraulic systems for more efficient control of valves, air vents, and rudders.[30]

At the end of World War I, the principal unanswered question about the sub-marine was the uses to which it would be put in the future. Was it an underwater extension of fleet power, to be used offensively in coordination with other fleet elements against enemy surface units or defensively to protect coasts and harbors? Or was it to be used as Germany had used it, as the ultimate commerce raider, capable of ravaging the enemy's supply lines and communications? So devastating had been the submarine in the latter role that Britain had made unavailing efforts at the Washington conference to have it outlawed as a weapon of war. But such fierce opposition had arisen from other conference participants that no restric-tions were placed on size, armament, or total tonnage for the submarines of any navy. Instead, an American-inspired compromise had imposed severe, though vaguely worded, restrictions on the use of submarines against merchant vessels.

Yet such hopeful (and ultimately impractical) injunctions apparently had less to do with the principles of submarine use and design during the treaty era than with the strategic problems and potential enemies that confronted each major navy. There was as well the particular outlook of their naval staffs and the prior-ities that those staffs assigned to individual warship categories and weapons sys-tems. In the 1920s, with their thinking dominated by the concept of the fleet engagement, the staffs of all three major navies conceived the submarine to be essentially an important element in fleet operations and, to a lesser extent, useful in coastal defense. Thus, the U.S. Navy developed two types of submersibles dur-ing these years, the "fleet submarine," large enough to accompany the battle fleet on its westward passage, and a small underwater vessels designed for the protec-tion of American coastal waters. As even the fleet submarines were not capable of operating independently over vast distances or for extended periods of time, they could not reach East Asian waters from bases in Hawaii or on the American west coast. Delayed in the 1920s by the U.S. Navy's decision to place priority on the development of naval aviation, the long-range American "patrol submarine," capable of striking at Japanese trade routes off East Asian coasts, did not appear until the late 1930s.[31]

The Japanese navy's development of the submarine as an element of the fleet was, again, a consequence of Japan's determination to make up for the numerical inferiority in capital ships. The Navy General Staff thought of the submarine gen-erally as a useful weapon in carrying out its attrition strategy against a westward-moving American fleet. But at the outset of the 1920s, Japanese submarines, in technology, organization, training, and esprit de corps, seemed ill-equipped to play an effective role in such operations. The submersibles that the navy had available at the time had insufficient range for much more than coastal defense. Thus, the Navy General Staff saw their employment primarily in defensive terms, in which attacks would be delivered on an enemy fleet once it had entered the western

Pacific, not in terms of strategic offensives carried out against American bases or operations against American warships in their own waters. Up to this time, moreover, there had been no real operational training for a submarine force because no such force existed: What passed for a submarine force was merely a collection of boats attached to the fleet. Finally, due to a series of various mishaps—accidental sinkings, explosions, and collisions—caused by primitive technology and inadequate training, morale among Japanese submarine crews was quite low.[32]

By mid-decade two developments changed this situation remarkably. A Sensui Gakkō (Submarine school) was established in September 1920 at Kure, but its initial facilities aboard the old protected cruiser *Itsukushima* were quite makeshift. In July 1924, the school moved to more permanent quarters just across the bay from Kure Navy Yard, and with the move, it began to provide thorough and rigorous training, offering both basic and specialized courses to submarine commanders, officers, and enlisted men.[33]

The second development was the appointment of Rear Adm. Suetsugu Nobumasa to take command of the navy's First Submarine Division. Although he had no submarine training himself, Suetsugu, who had studied German U-boat operations during his tour as naval observer in London during the war, believed that the submarine offered the best hope of shredding American capital ship superiority in the Pacific. With this conviction he set about giving the First Submarine Division the most rigorous and realistic training possible, ruthlessly sacking commanding officers, even veterans, who opposed his methods. By the time that he took command of both the First and Second Submarine Divisions for the grand naval maneuvers of 1924, he had begun to build real skills and esprit de corps among Japanese submariners in the same way that Karl Dönitz in Germany turned the Weddigen Flotilla into an elite U-boat force a decade later. During this period, too, Suetsugu began to devise those tactics by which Japanese submarines would spearhead the navy's attrition strategy against the American enemy.[34]

Gradually, Suetsugu and others worked out Japanese submarine doctrine in a number of areas—reconnaissance, port blockade, cooperation between submarines and aircraft, and the use of submarines in fleet operations, particularly in the decisive fleet encounter—aimed at transforming the submarine from a weapon of passive, short-range defense to one of long-range, active offense. In 1925, the navy assigned to submarine units the surveillance of American ports and harbors, and the following year Japanese submarines were given what was conceived as their most critical mission: the task of locating the enemy fleet upon its sortie from its principal advance base—presumably Pearl Harbor—attacking it, pursuing it, and keeping it under constant surveillance until the final fleet encounter.[35] These subsurface attacks were to take place at far greater range than any surface campaign of attrition against the advancing Americans and would not only inflict material damage on the enemy but injure his morale as well. This was the sort of long-range, offensive, and strategic use of the submarine that Suetsugu had advocated.

For this purpose the navy needed a submarine of greater speed and range than any in its possession at the end of World War I. Without expertise in designing such underwater vessels, the navy turned to foreign models. In 1921, it laid down at Kure a submarine based on the design of the large British "K-class" submersibles. Completed in 1924 as the *I-51,* at 1,390 standard tons, it was the largest submarine built in Japan to date and incorporated several novel features, including four diesel engines producing 5,200 horsepower. The boat could make 20 knots on the surface and 10 submerged. More remarkable was her range of 20,000 miles, making her the first of the Japanese navy's KD—*kaidai*—or large model submarines. But various problems, largely engine defects, halted further production of the KD 1 prototype.[36] Instead, the navy had turned to a much better source of foreign submarine technology—Germany—whose U-boats had almost brought Britain to its knees. Fortuitously, as part of the reparations that Germany was obliged to make to the Allies at the end of the war in 1918, Japan received seven German U-boats, five of which were of the latest German design. These vessels, thoroughly tested and studied by Japanese technicians, provided vital data from which to design new and formidable classes of submarines. To aid in the task of submarine design, the navy not only sent a number of its officers to Germany for consultation and study, but brought German naval constructors, technicians, and former U-boat commanders to Japan on contract. The navy also hired optical technicians from various European firms to aid in the design of range finders and periscopes.[37] The optical equipment used on Japanese submarines was at first imported and then based on foreign models, but by the 1930s, it was entirely designed and produced in Japan. By World War II, the Japanese had developed the high-quality bridge-mounted night vision binoculars with which their submarines were equipped.[38]

In 1922, exploiting much of this data and expertise, and based specifically on the German U-139 class of U-boat, the navy launched a KD 2 type submarine (laid down as number 51, but completed as *I-52)* of the same tonnage and machinery as the KD 1 *(I-51).* With reduced bunkerage the KD 2 had half the range, but a slightly faster surface speed. Though only one each was ever built of the KD 1 and KD 2 types, they were both used in a long series of trials to establish the role of the large submarine in the Japanese navy.

The KD 2 in particular was the prototype of the "fleet submarine" that was developed in successive variants between 1924 and 1939. It and later models were intended to operate in flotillas with the Japanese fleet. Despite their troublesome diesels and weak batteries, these vessels had markedly better speed and range for hull size than their American counterparts.[39]

Most Japanese diesel engines were imported from abroad in the 1920s, but following vigorous research and development, Japan began producing its own submarine propulsion systems by the 1930s. In 1931 the first Japanese diesel engine was produced, which was installed two years later in *I-68*. The engine was of the two-cycle, double-acting type, giving double the horsepower for engine weight when compared to the four-cycle, single-acting engines installed in U.S. submarines. But the Japanese engine was more difficult to maintain than the American.[40]

Because of the navy's strategy of "attrition and interception" against the U.S. battle fleet, its specifications for the fleet submarines called for a surface speed of 20 knots (though some fleet submarines made up to 23). Their armament was formidable, usually deck guns of 4.7 inches and six 21-inch torpedo tubes. Along with their excellent seakeeping and range, these advantages appeared to make such submersibles the ideal warships to realize Suetsugu's "interceptive" strategy.[41]

At the same time that the fleet submarine was being perfected, the navy also began to develop a new submersible. This was the J (for *junsen*) type, or "ocean-cruising submarine," called "cruiser submarine" in some Western sources. It was designed for independent operations into the distant reaches of the Pacific and Indian Oceans. It too was based on a German model. The navy bought plans for

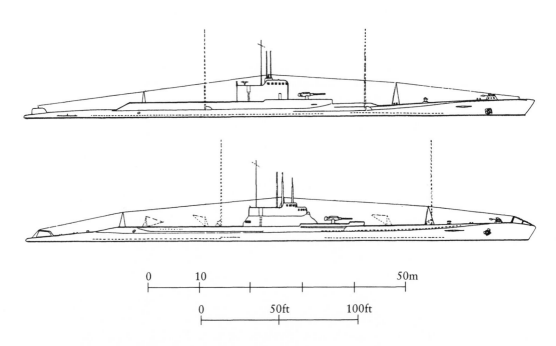

Fig. 7-3. KD 2 submarine (top) and KD 3 submarine (bottom).

the U-142, an advanced "U-cruiser" developed for raiding British commerce during World War I, from Krupp's Germaniawerft at Kiel. The construction of the first of these vessels began at the Kawasaki Yard at Kobe in 1923. A contingent of ten German technicians, working under a leading designer of World War I, Dr. Hans Techel, supervised the construction.[42] An American report stated, "During the first two years of their contracts, the [German] engineers . . . bore the brunt of the work in preparation of the working drawings of the submarines. As various submarines were completed, however, the Japanese staffs gradually took over the work, until finally a distinctly Japanese type of submarine was evolved."[43] These vessels became the *I-1* through *I-4*. Displacing 1,970 standard tons, they each had two screws powered by two MAN diesel engines and two electric motors. They had a relatively high surface speed of 18 knots. Double hulled, they could reach depths unprecedented for Japanese submarine. The *I-1* reached 260 feet on her trials. These were powerfully armed ships, possessing two 5.5-inch deck guns (which became standard on J submarines) and six torpedo tubes (four at the bow and two at the stern). But what was truly remarkable was their range and endurance. Their bunkerage allowed them to cruise for 24,000 miles without refueling; stocked with sufficient provisions they could, in theory, remain at sea for two months.[44]

The J submarines thus gave the Japanese navy an extraordinary reach. They could now undertake an effort never thought possible for Japanese surface warships: bringing the naval war to the American homeland. These vessels could reach the west coast of the United States and stay there for weeks. Potentially, they posed a threat to American commerce along that coast and to communications between the west coast and Hawaii. Yet while the navy built more than eight cruiser submarines between 1929 and 1938, it is clear that the Navy General Staff, fixed as it was on the idea of the decisive fleet battle, only occasionally gave thought to such a strategy.[45]

On the other hand, the Japanese navy failed to conceive of its submarines as commerce raiders perhaps because of a mistaken analysis of both commerce raiding in general and its use by the Japanese navy in particular to win the short-term war that it had traditionally envisioned. In general, this argument runs, commerce raiding is not a suitable strategy for winning a short war. Specifically, no nation has ever succeeded in bringing the United States, with its two vastly separated coasts, to its knees through commerce raiding. The Japanese navy was therefore understandably reluctant to squander valuable assets on an unlikely objective (that, in any event, could only be attained over the long term) when its real aim was to win a short war. Indeed, the possible extension of a maritime war with the United States would simply allow America's greater capacity in naval construction to take hold. Moreover, use of Japanese submarines in a commerce raiding role against the United States would actively undercut Japanese strategy, since the apparent decisive force that threatened Japan in the 1920s and 1930s was the U.S. battle fleet. If that fleet were defeated, supposedly, Japan would have a chance to win a war with the United States. The Japanese naval objective was to lure the American battle fleet westward. Attacks against American commerce and supply trains would have been certain to "de-lure" that fleet.[46]

This is a powerful argument and provides a justification for Japanese submarine strategy almost entirely overlooked by naval historians who have commented on the subject. However, this argument fails to include a number of considerations. First, it fails to consider how a Japanese submarine offensive against American supply lines in the Pacific would greatly complicate the tremendous problems of distance in any American attempt to recapture its advanced bases, presumably lost in the initial stages of the war. Second, it overlooks the possible psychological shock to American morale if a Japanese submarine campaign in the Pacific had been successful on the scale of the German U-boat offensive in the Atlantic in World War II. But most important, the argument ignores how Japanese neglect of the potential for commerce raiding against American targets by its own submarines led to a fatal blind spot in Japanese naval thinking. The Japanese could not envision the possible consequences of a concerted and massive underwater offensive by American submarines against Japanese commerce and supply lines.

In any event, innovations in Japanese submarine doctrine were directed toward fleet operations, not commerce raiding. A unique concept in Japanese submarine design and function was the interaction between submarines and aircraft, each extending the range of the other, a tactical innovation with which other navies experimented, but which the Japanese alone pursued extensively. The Japanese navy in the 1930s experimented with the use of submarines to extend the range of its seaplanes, particularly the large flying boats that the navy was developing during the decade, by having submarines refuel and rearm these aircraft at forward bases. Conversely, the navy also began to think of extending the range of its larger submarines by placing reconnaissance aircraft aboard them. This decision was largely based on the navy's expectations that its largest submarines, the J types, operate independently, relying on their own sources of intelligence. (Fleet submarines, usually more closely attached to Japanese surface units, could rely on their light cruiser flagships for information on the enemy.) In theory, coordination between submarines and reconnaissance aircraft was possible. But in the 1920s, tactical reconnaissance, specifically of distant enemy bases, was impossible for land-based aircraft, given their short range, and difficult for submarines, given their restricted level of vision. The apparent solution was to have one or more small floatplanes carried on board the larger submersibles in hangars built into the hull and launched to reconnoiter the enemy while the submarine was still over the horizon. The navy first experimented with aircraft operations from submarines as early as 1923, and in 1925 the first submarine-borne aircraft, a biplane with twin floats and folding wings for easy storage, was test flown from an *I*-class submarine. By 1933, many Japanese J submarines were fitted with catapults for launching specialized reconnaissance seaplanes and collapsible cranes to recover them. These submarines significantly influenced the navy's tactical and strategic concepts during the interwar period.[47]

By the mid-1920s, therefore, the availability of oceangoing submarines enabled the Japanese navy to work out a new set of tasks: the surveillance of an enemy fleet at its base, the pursuit and surveillance of that fleet after it left base, and finally, the ambush of the enemy prior to the decisive surface encounter between the two opposing battle fleets. Specific attention was devoted, of course, to the interception of the U.S. battle fleet on its sortie from Hawaii. The Navy General Staff envisioned that three or four fleet submarine squadrons were to take part. Some submarines were assigned to conduct close surveillance, and others were to wait at appropriate locations for the departure of the U.S. battle fleet. By 1930, the strategy called for six J-type submarines to be sent to Hawaii at the approach of hostilities, to keep the battle fleet under observation. The greater part of the Japanese submarine force—mostly fleet submarines—would be held in Micronesian waters for "picket duty" and ambush attacks along the anticipated course of the advancing Americans. Then, as the latter advanced toward waters predetermined as being the site of the decisive engagement, the bulk of the fleet submarines would race ahead to support the Japanese main body, while the smaller element would continue to track the course of the enemy. With a surface speed significantly faster than the anticipated cruising speed of the U.S. battle fleet (the latter about 12 knots), the fleet submarines were expected to keep up easily, even allowing time for taking up positions for subsurface firing positions.[48]

By 1930, Suetsugu's long-range interceptive strategy became an article of faith within the Navy General Staff and the Japanese submarine forces. Yet, surprisingly, it remained essentially untested for the remainder of the 1920s and for most of the following decade. While incorporating its general principles into various fleet exercises and maneuvers, untypically, and for reasons not clear, the Japanese navy did not subject its component elements to rigorous tactical practice and experimentation until the years immediately prior to the Pacific War. Then, too late, Japanese submarine commanders learned that much of the Suetsugu strategy was based on faulty assumptions.

JAPANESE DESTROYERS, NIGHT OPERATIONS, AND TORPEDO TACTICS

While the Japanese navy worked out a scheme for distant attrition of a westward-moving American fleet by submarine attacks, it had little expectation that such operations by themselves could bring about Japanese numerical superiority or even equality of firepower by the time of the decisive fleet encounter. Admiral Suetsugu himself, lecturing at the Naval Staff College in 1927, supposedly pointed out some of the risks that Japanese naval units might encounter in their attrition strategy, including the possibility that even as Japanese fleet submarines concentrated for an attack on the American fleet, the enemy might slip past them altogether. Hence, Suetsugu believed, a radically enhanced surface capability—largely that of torpedo units—would also be necessary to contend with the likely superiority of the enemy's firepower.[49]

Annihilating the main force of the enemy by the heavy guns of the fleet had been the basic tactical principle of the Japanese navy ever since the Sino-Japanese War. But the chief adjunct to this principle had been reliance on night operations by torpedo squadrons to create havoc and confusion among the enemy's formations before the final battle. As discussed, the Japanese navy placed a greater premium on night torpedo operations than any other navy of the time. By World War I, the main warship for such combat was the destroyer, on which the Japanese navy relied for the delivery of relentless torpedo attacks, even at the cost of heavy losses. But through its careful study of the successes and failures of night combat operations in World War I, particularly the employment of destroyers at the Battle of Jutland, the navy came to recognize that to be effective in night combat, destroyers had to be properly organized and skillfully deployed and that individual destroyers had to be capable of the highest performance. In 1914, following the British organization for destroyers, the Japanese navy grouped its four-ship *kuchikutai* (destroyer groups) into *suirai sentai* (torpedo flotillas) of sixteen destroyers each, each flotilla to be led by a light cruiser acting as a flagship.[50]

In the last years of World War I, the navy had made an effort to upgrade its destroyer designs, culminating in the fifteen fast destroyers of the *Minekaze* class. These ships ranked with the destroyers of other naval powers in performance, but soon after the war, the Navy General Staff requested a still more potent destroyer. It determined that the navy needed a destroyer with a maximum speed of 39 knots and a range of 4,000 miles at 14 knots (which would enable it to operate with the fast and powerful new cruisers then under design and construction). The destroyer would be capable of carrying a large number of the new 24-inch (61-centimeter) torpedoes that had just come into production.

The *Fubuki* class was a response to the navy's order. The twenty-four ships of this class, ordered under the 1923 construction program but built between 1926 and 1931, represented such an improvement over previous destroyers that they were officially known as the *tokugata* (special type), and as such they became the archetype for most Japanese destroyers that saw action in the Pacific War.[51] They were the most advanced and powerful destroyers of their day, presenting an out-standing example of the Japanese naval policy of aiming for a qualitative lead among the world's navies. With a 390-foot length and an officially listed dis-placement of 1,680 standard tons, they were huge for their time.[52] Because of their enclosed bridge, fire control spaces, and gun mounts, even in rough seas and bad weather their fighting qualities were outstanding. They were also powerfully pro-pelled, the geared turbines of its ships producing 50,000 horsepower, though their maximum speed, 35 knots, did not exceed that of previous Japanese destroyer classes, since their increased weight dissipated much of the extra power. More sig-nificant was their armament: six 5-inch guns, mounted in pairs in three gun hous-ings that were not only weatherproof, but also splinter proof and secure against poison gas. On the last fourteen ships of this class these guns could be elevated to 70 degrees, enabling them to be used against aircraft as well as surface targets. Ammunition was brought up on hoists directly from the magazines under each gun housing, permitting a far higher rate of fire than was possible on destroyers where ammunition had to be manhandled to each gun. These various arrange-ments for the main batteries, coming years before they were adopted for the destroyers of other navies, gave the *Fubuki* class firepower equal to that of many light cruisers.[53]

But it was the greatly increased torpedo armament that made ships of the *Fubuki* class the most powerful destroyers afloat, and it was this enhanced weapons system that caused their increased displacement. Each ship of the class carried eighteen 24-inch torpedoes, two each for the nine torpedo tubes housed in

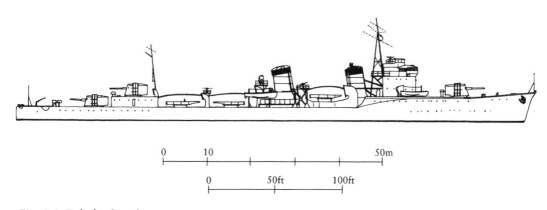

Fig. 7-4. *Fubuki*-class destroyer.

three triple mountings. This arrangement provided a larger torpedo salvo than was available on destroyers of other navies.[54]

All in all, these were warships ideally suited to the close-in night combat then being pursued by the navy. The *Fubuki* class took the naval world by surprise, since no other naval power had built large destroyers except for those few vessels in the "destroyer leader" (squadron leader) category, and none had constructed destroyers of the specifications and capabilities of the *Fubuki*. The official history of the navy's armament programs during these years has actually asserted that so great was the quantum jump in offensive firepower represented by the class, that in 1929 the navy decided to discontinue temporarily the construction of these vessels lest it provoke other powers into building their own destroyers of this model.[55]

By the 1930s, therefore, the Japanese destroyer, with its nine to twelve torpedo tubes, was an all-out attack vessel. In this sense, its function had become a good deal more specialized than destroyers in the British and United States navies. By circumstance and the organizational needs of Anglo-American navies during World War I, the destroyer had emerged from its original and exclusive torpedo-boat destroyer function to become a jack-of-all-trades. It engaged more in defensive operations—escort duty, scouting, screening for the battle fleet, conducting antisubmarine warfare operations—than in torpedo attacks against the enemy fleet. By contrast, in the Japanese navy, the original torpedo-boat function, linked particularly (but not exclusively) to night combat, remained the dominant role for destroyers. Specifically, the mission of the Japanese torpedo (destroyer) flotillas, usually positioned ahead of the van or abaft the rear on the engaged side of the fleet as in Western torpedo doctrine,[56] was to break through the enemy screen to attack the enemy's main formations, not merely to force the enemy to turn, but to sink, cripple, or throw into disorder as many of his capital ships as possible before the onset of the big-gun duel between the Japanese and American battle lines.

Throughout the 1920s, to achieve this objective, the navy refined its torpedo techniques through continual, relentless, and often hazardous exercises. As always, Japanese torpedo tacticians had to take into account the peculiarities of the torpedo. Its relatively slow speed and its detectable wake allowed the enemy to take evasive action. Nor was the torpedo a continuous-fire weapon: there was no means of rapidly correcting the fire of torpedoes, which either hit their targets the first time or missed them. The Japanese navy attempted to deal with these difficulties in two ways. The first of these was technological and involved an onboard system of torpedo fire control that combined the capabilities of a standard gyroscope (to determine the course of a torpedo after it was fired) and a method of computing both the probabilities of various course changes by a moving target and the probabilities of hitting that target at any given heading taken by the target. Using this system of fire control, torpedo officers on board Japanese destroyers (in theory at least) learned to direct torpedo fire easily and quickly under chang-ing conditions of enemy course and speed.[57]

The other means for dealing with the inherent difficulties of the torpedo as a weapon was to develop tactics that, if carried out with surprise, audacity, and pre-cision, would make it difficult for the enemy to avoid a torpedo attack. Japanese torpedo flotillas still followed the tradition of *nikuhaku hitchū* (close in, strike home), of course, but while this aggressive *spirit* remained as strong as ever, prac-tical considerations demonstrated that the standard range for aiming and firing torpedoes was 5,000 meters or less during day actions and 2,000 meters or less during night combat.[58] These ranges would remain in effect until the development of the long-range oxygen torpedo in the 1930s. Until then, Japanese tacticians were obliged to work out specific tactical methods to maximize the chances of success in a torpedo attack. One method was to attack the enemy suddenly on opposite courses, since this would give him little time to react and would afford the best chance for a close-in approach. Another technique was for Japanese tor-pedo flotillas to work their way to the enemy rear in an attempt to encircle a select number of targets that would then be subjected to successive torpedo assaults. The most promising tactic of all to neutralize the enemy's evasive maneuvers was to launch simultaneous attacks from different directions so that Japanese destroy-ers would lay down a mesh of intersecting torpedo tracks from which the enemy could not escape. Naturally, all these maneuvers were extremely hazardous, and the risks to one's own ships in the daytime, let alone at night, was an obvious rea-son for the navy's relentless practice in these operations.[59]

THE EMERGENCE OF THE "A"-CLASS CRUISER

The *Fubuki*-class destroyers provided the Japanese navy with a superb weapons system for the delivery of night torpedo attacks. Yet ever since World War I, Japanese tacticians had two concerns about the use of destroyers in this capacity. One was the problem of coordination and control, and the other was the possi-bility of heavy losses by destroyers before they came within attacking range of the enemy's capital ships. In both cases, the solution to these difficulties seemed to lie with the development of the cruiser, first as a destroyer squadron flagship and then as a heavier warship whose speed could yet match that of destroyers but whose firepower would allow it to blast a path through enemy defenses and make way for destroyer flotillas. As discussed, during and immediately following World War I, the navy developed the light cruiser as a warship type capable of acting either as a fleet scout or as a destroyer flotilla leader, and some sixteen warships of this category were constructed in the *Tatsuta, Kuma,* and *Sendai* classes. Starting from this early dual role as a fleet scout and torpedo flotilla flagship in the 1920s, the cruiser was developed by Japanese naval architects and technicians into a far more formidable fleet unit—the "A" class, or heavy cruiser—which became the core of the navy's night combat force.

The evolution of Japan's "A"-class cruisers is largely the story of the Navy General Staff's quest for an all-purpose warship, a substitute for the battleship whose further construction had been halted for the time being by the Washington Naval Treaty.[60] The result was that the Japanese led the way in cruiser design during the treaty era. In complying with the increasing demands of the Navy General Staff for combat performance, however, Japanese naval architects and constructors risked serious hazards of structure and stability in the design of these ships.

Japanese cruiser construction must be seen as part of a worldwide competition in cruisers in the 1920s, a rivalry that was probably inevitable. Although the Washington Treaty had placed quantitative limits on cruiser design—no displacement more than 10,000 tons and no guns greater than 8 inches in caliber— the treaty did not limit the aggregate tonnage in cruisers each nation could build. Since there was now a total ban on battleship construction, a naval race in cruisers—the next largest category of warship—was virtually inescapable, and navies would tend to build to the design limits permitted by the treaty. Thus was born the "treaty cruiser," favored particularly by the Japanese and U.S. navies.[61]

Clearly, Japanese cruiser design early in the decade did much to initiate the heavy cruiser race. From the earliest months of the postwar era the Japanese Navy General Staff was insistent on design specifications that would provide future Japanese cruisers with maximum speed and fighting power across a range of combat missions: distant scouting, protection of the battle fleet from torpedo attack, breaking into the defenses of the enemy battle fleet, defending Japanese sea routes, and attacking those of the enemy. As early as 1918, with these functions in mind, the navy had toyed briefly with the idea of building an 8,000-ton scout cruiser with 8-inch guns, but these plans had been halted by Japan's decision to participate in the Washington conference.[62]

Yet even before those deliberations had taken place, the Navy General Staff envisioned a cruiser that would combine heavy armament and high speed within a hull of modest proportions. In the postwar era, the imminent termination of the Anglo-Japanese Alliance meant that Japan could no longer count on British technology to achieve this feat of naval architecture. Fortunately, in Hiraga Yuzuru, who had designed Japan's last capital ships before the Washington conference and who was now head of the principal office for warship design, the Basic Design Section of the Navy Technical Department, the navy had a naval architect worthy of the challenge. While Hiraga's design, adopted by the navy in 1921, was unexceptional in armament, it was ingenious in its arrangements for hull structure and armor. To decrease the overall weight of the ship, Hiraga incorporated the armored elements (of high tensile and hardened chrome steel) into the internal structure of the hull rather than bolting it onto existing plates and beams as was the usual procedure. This not only reduced the weight of the hull but contributed greatly to its strength. Other novel features included a swan-neck bow curve to aid in the seaworthiness of the ship, the trunking of the two boiler exhausts into one funnel above the upper deck, and the provision of an enlarged bridge structure to centralize all command, communications, and fire control systems.[63]

The realization of this design, the 2,890-ton experimental cruiser, *Yūbari*,[64] was launched at Sasebo in 1922. The *Yūbari* was less important as an individual vessel than she was as the prototype for a series of Hiraga-designed cruisers with which Japan took the world lead in cruiser design, a lead that it did not relinquish until the Pacific War. Exploiting the experience gained from the *Yūbari*, Captain Hiraga and his assistant, Lt. Comdr. Fujimoto Kikuo, set about designing a larger and more powerful cruiser capable of surpassing both the American *Omaha* and the British *Hawkins*-class cruisers in speed and firepower. Laid down in 1922 before the Washington Treaty and intended to fulfill the dual functions of reconnaissance and protection for the battle fleet, the 7,000-ton *Furutaka* and *Kako* were the first of Japan's "A" class or *jūryō jun'yōkan* (heavy cruisers). Most features of *Yūbari* were incorporated into these two. They mounted six 8-inch (20 centimeters, actually 7.87 inches) guns in single mounts, three forward and three aft (replaced in 1936–39 by three twin 8-inch turrets, two forward and one aft). In keeping with the navy's renewed emphasis on night combat and torpedo attacks, the greatest offensive punch of the *Furutaka*-class vessels was provided by twelve 24-inch torpedo tubes. This unusually heavy torpedo armament and its specific distribution aboard these two cruisers had been insisted upon by the Navy General Staff over the vigorous objections of Hiraga, who believed that the staff's excessive demands for firepower involved serious risks to the stability and integrity of these ships.[65] The considerable top weight added by the twelve torpedoes and their tubes (plus another twelve torpedoes in reserve) would have made these ships dangerously unstable had not Hiraga already made every effort to keep the top weight down through his novel hull design and the use of lightweight materials. What concerned Hiraga more was that as the higher freeboard of the *Furutaka* class made it impossible to launch torpedoes at a correct angle to the water, the Navy General Staff had ordered fixed tubes to be fitted on the upper deck within the hull. From tests conducted on the hulk of the aborted battleship *Tosa*, Hiraga was convinced that these arrangements, which brought the torpedo warheads close to engine rooms and magazines, posed catastrophic risks to the ship in the event of fire or hits by enemy shells. Moreover, fixed rather than mobile torpedo mounts meant that the entire ship had to be turned broadside to the target to fire a torpedo salvo.[66] In any event, the Navy General Staff's adamant insistence on the priority of tactical armament over structural considerations in warship design plagued the performance of Japanese warships throughout the 1920s and led to a number of avoidable disasters in the 1930s.

In balance, however, the *Furutaka* class was a sufficient success to provoke the Americans into building their first postwar cruisers, the powerful 9,100-ton *Pensacola* class, to induce the British to begin work on their "County"-class cruisers and to encourage the Japanese navy to improve upon the basic *Furutaka* design. Japan's two succeeding 7,000-ton cruisers of the *Aoba* class (the *Aoba* and *Kinugasa),* laid down in 1924 and completed in 1927, were originally conceived as

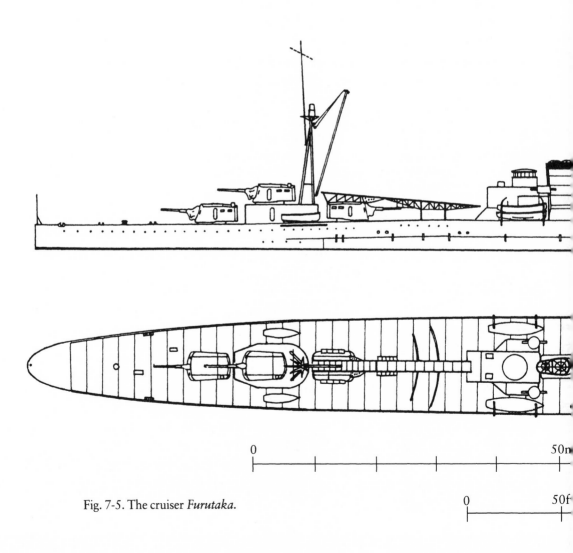

0   50m

0   50f

Fig. 7-5. The cruiser *Furutaka.*

being identical to the *Furutaka* class. Midway through their construction, however, again under the pressure of the Navy General Staff, the cruisers were
redesigned to mount six 20-centimeter (8-inch) guns on three twin turrets.[67] The
twin turret arrangement deserves special mention, because some navies by this
time had accepted the more efficient triple turret. For unknown reasons, the
Japanese navy made the twin its standard for cruisers in this era, and it is one of
their most visible characteristics.[68]

But even before the *Aoba* and *Kinugasa* were laid down, Hiraga Yuzuru had
set out to design a cruiser class that would not only reach the 10,000-ton limit, but

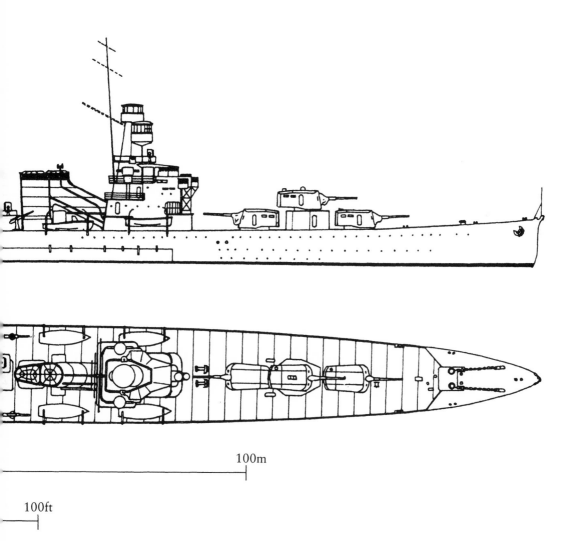

100m

100ft

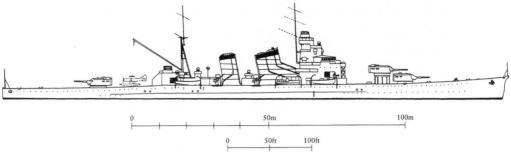

Fig. 7-6. The cruiser *Aoba*.

like *Fubuki* in the destroyer category, would be superior to every other warship of its type. The result of his efforts were the four heavy cruisers of the *Myōkō* class (the *Myōkō*, *Ashigara*, *Haguro*, and *Nachi*). While most of the novel structural features of Hiraga's earlier cruiser designs were incorporated into the planning of these ships, the *Myōkō* class collectively represented the first Japanese "treaty cruisers" in that their designs were initiated after the Washington Treaty and were planned to have displacements of 10,000 tons.

The construction of the *Myōkō* class again illustrates how the Navy General Staff attempted to impose its excessive demands for offensive power on warship design. The initial staff requirements for these four ships included armament of ten 8-inch guns in five twin turrets (three forward and two aft), eight torpedo tubes in fixed mounts below the upper deck aft, protection of vitals against direct hits by 15-centimeter shells, antitorpedo protection by bulges along machinery spaces, a maximum speed of over 35 knots, and a range of 10,000 miles at 14 knots. While Hiraga accepted most of these requirements (indeed, he convinced the staff to add a fifth turret aft), he balked at the plan to install fixed torpedo mounts below decks as dangerous and unnecessary. In 1925, during Hiraga's absence in Europe, torpedo specialists on the general staff prevailed upon Hiraga's successor, Commander Fujimoto, to install not just eight but twelve fixed torpedo mounts inside the ship above the engine room.[69] Yet by loading these ships to comply with the tactical requirements of the Navy General Staff, the ships were heavier than planned, or were permitted according to treaty limits, by about 1,000 tons of standard displacement. Consequently, their speed and power were bought at the price of seaworthiness, stability, and longitudinal strength. These disadvantages ultimately had to be corrected by partial reconstruction in the 1930s to reduce the additional weight.[70]

This excess weight has been the subject of discussion in some postwar literature on Japan's treaty cruisers, the assertion being that this violation of treaty limitations was deliberate. The issue is a complex one. On the one hand, it is hard to imagine that the Japanese navy would have knowingly accepted the acute disadvantages posed by this additional displacement. One disadvantage, the reduction of stability because of topside weight problems, plagued U.S. treaty cruisers as well, because when designing for an exact tonnage limit, it was difficult to build in any margin of growth. Increases invariably took place topside—in masts, antennas, improved weapons, sensors, and so forth. Also, Japanese designers and builders may have been less experienced and less skilled than their Anglo-American rivals in the difficult feat of achieving precisely the designed displacement. On the other hand, the Japanese navy's excesses in tonnage were extraordinary, even in an age when other navies went over agreed-upon limits. Its cruisers were thousands of tons rather than hundreds of tons over treaty specifications. Japanese ships were not designed from the outset to exceed treaty limits, but the Navy General Staff, by its insistence on incorporating extra weapons, knowingly mandated the growth of treaty cruisers far beyond treaty limits. This was particularly the case in the early 1930s, when it became apparent that Japan would renounce naval arms limitation.[71]

Yet these warships were superb additions to the fleet because their speed and firepower enabled them to enter or avoid battle as circumstances dictated. In an engagement with the advancing U.S. battle fleet they could maintain contact with the enemy battleships while keeping out of their range, trailing the enemy until dusk and decreasing visibility made it possible to send forward the torpedo flotillas. With a speed almost equal to that of destroyers (and greater than that of destroyers in heavy seas) they would be capable of leading these flotillas against the heavier warships of the enemy's support force.

By the end of the decade, heavy cruisers occupied a central place in the operational planning of the Japanese navy. For this reason, their place in the navy's operational organization should be briefly considered. During this period the basic fleet unit was the division *(sentai),* usually of four or more ships. Two or more divisions were formed during maneuvers (and in wartime) into the two main fleets, the *shuryoku kantai* (First, or "Main" Fleet), and the *yūgeki kantai* (Second, or "Mobile" Fleet). At mid-decade, the navy was well on the way to forming its first division of heavy cruisers, the four ships of the *Myōkō* class. Then, in 1925, the Navy General Staff decided to establish a second, more powerful cruiser division, to be composed of 10,000-ton cruisers armed with 8-inch guns, capable of more than 33 knots and having a range of 8,000 miles at 14 knots. Operating together, the ships would serve as an advance guard for the battle fleet, as an attack force to break into the elements supporting the enemy's battle fleet, or, individually, in a reconnaissance role. Given the speed and firepower projected for this division, the staff wanted its components to serve as fleet flagships in peacetime and as division flagships in wartime. Since Hiraga was on assignment in Europe, the design of these four cruisers of the *Takao* class (the *Takao, Atago, Chōkai,* and *Maya*) was made the responsibility of Fujimoto Kikuo, who followed the general plan of the *Myōkō*-class cruisers. There were, however, some substantial differences. The first concerned the main batteries. Their ability to elevate to a

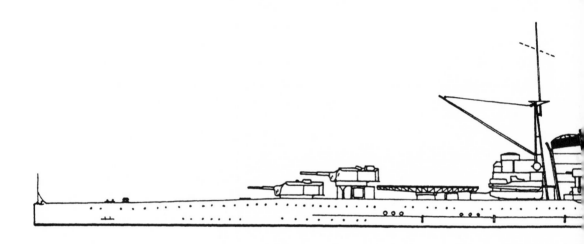

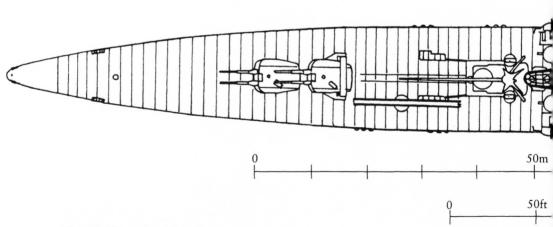

0   50m

0   50ft

Fig. 7-7. The cruiser *Myōkō.*

maximum of 70 degrees enabled them, in principle, to double as antiaircraft guns. Equally important was the arrangement of the eight 24-inch torpedo tubes. Having appreciated Hiraga's warnings against fixed mounts within the hull, Fujimoto took care to place the tubes in trainable twin mounts on sponsons located outside the hull, two on each side of the ship.[72]

The greatest change in these ships had to do with their anticipated function as fleet flagships. They were expected to serve as the combat command centers for a

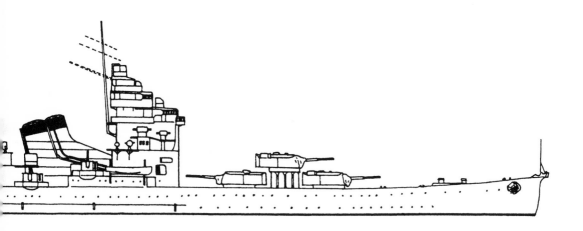

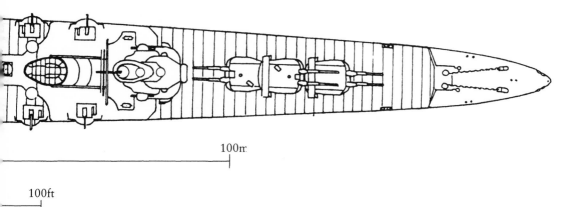

100m

100ft

fleet during both day and night battles involving long-range gunnery and torpedoes. The increasingly complex installations required to direct these engagements—all communications, command, navigation, and fire- and damage-control stations—were grouped together in an enormous bridge complex divided into ten different levels. This centralization of command installations was achieved at the cost of topside weight, a high resistance to the wind, and presenting a larger target for enemy fire.[73]

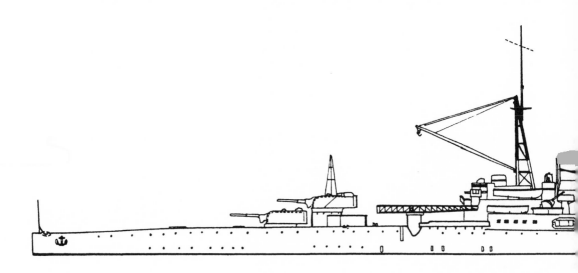

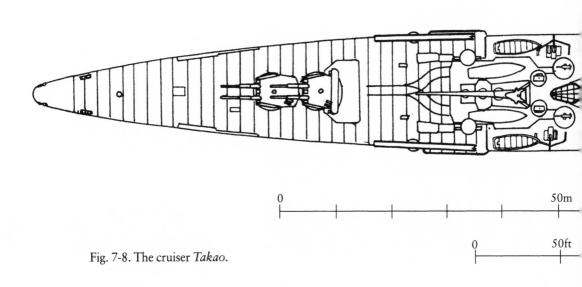

Fig. 7-8. The cruiser *Takao*.

THE LONDON TREATY
The Japanese Navy and the Eight-Inch Cruiser Question

Toward the end of the 1920s, the cruiser race touched off by Japanese construction had brought about an international dispute about further naval arms limitations. The Japanese and American navies, for different reasons, favored the heavy cruiser over light cruisers, since the former met their strategic and tactical needs

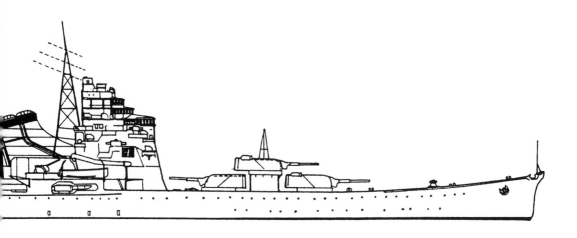

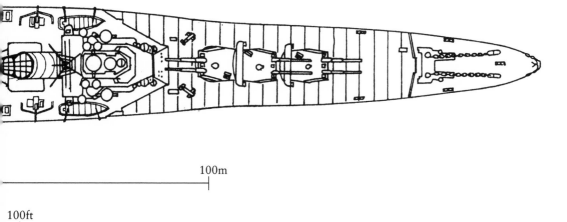

100m

100ft

for midocean combat. The Americans in particular opposed any reduction in limits for individual cruisers, destroyers, and submarines, but did seek restrictions in aggregate tonnage in those categories. The British navy, with its many overseas bases, global trade, and myriad obligations all dictating the need for many light cruisers, sought exactly the opposite. The British wanted a far higher figure on aggregate tonnage and the abolition, or at least severe reduction, of the specifications permitted in the cruiser category. The wrangling between Britain and the United States over this issue wrecked the Geneva naval limitations conference of 1927 and caused the controversy over unrestricted warship categories to be deferred until the fateful naval conference in London in 1930.[74]

At Geneva, the Japanese delegation had stood aside from the main confrontation, taking neither the American nor the British side and expressing willingness to discuss limits on both aggregate cruiser tonnage and cruiser size and firepower. The principal concern of the Japanese navy at both the Geneva and London naval conferences was that the aggregate tonnage for lesser warship categories not follow the 5 to 5 to 3 ratio in capital ships established at Washington.[75] Brandishing once again the Satō-Akiyama formula for Japanese naval security, the navy insisted that if Japan could not have parity with its two naval competitors, it must at the very least have 70 percent of the tonnage possessed by the British and Americans in these categories, particularly in heavy cruisers.[76]

In 1927, the Navy General Staff looked ahead to the London conference that was slated to take up these questions surrounding warship categories left unrestricted in tonnage by the Washington Treaty. The staff established a twenty-member committee headed by the vice chief of staff, Vice Adm. Nomura Kichisaburō, to review the navy's needs in light of Japan's strategic situation, the capabilities of its most likely opponents, and the past and anticipated limitations in naval armaments. The committee's report, submitted to the navy minister in September 1928, greatly influenced future Japanese naval planning, particularly in warship design and construction. The gist of its many recommendations was that the navy needed to reemphasize superior quality in both combat skill and naval armament as the principal means in overcoming inferior ratios and in fighting the decisive battle. To achieve the first of these objectives, the Nomura committee stressed the importance of perfecting the various capabilities of its "auxiliary"[77] warships: reconnaissance, patrol, pursuit, surprise attacks, submarine operations, and night attacks by cruisers and destroyers. In providing a schedule of warships needed in the future, the committee recommended important criteria to be followed when issuing specifications for individual warships: adequate protection and armament, improved accuracy and rate of fire for both shells and torpedoes, high speed for all warship categories, and hull strengths capable of dealing with all seas.[78] As will be discussed, neglect of the last criterion produced baleful results in the mid-1930s.

Such recommendations would count for little, however, if Japan agreed to further reductions in its naval strength at the forthcoming naval conference in London. Above all, the Navy General Staff was determined to preserve the 70 percent ratio in 8-inch-gunned heavy cruisers. The heavy cruiser had become critical to Japanese plans for the reduction of the U.S. battle fleet and the subsequent decisive encounter. The staff set great store by the superior weight of the 8-inch shell, over twice that of the 6-inch, and believed that the 8-inch gun provided a much longer range than the 6-inch gun, a range nearly comparable to that of the 14-inch gun. This was an important consideration for both daylight and night attacks on the American fleet.[79]

The nightmare of the Navy General Staff was that while Japan had stolen a lead on the United States in the construction of heavy cruisers in the 1920s, American building plans for the 1930s threatened to overtake both the Japanese and the British in this category. In particular, the 1929 "Fifteen-Cruiser Bill" would bring the American 10,000-ton cruiser force to twenty-three by 1935.[80] To spur the Japanese Navy Ministry, cabinet, and Diet into responding to this threat by the replacement of six of the navy's old 5,000-ton cruisers with five of 10,000 tons, in 1929 the Operations Division of the General Staff issued a lengthy statement on the importance of maintaining a 70 percent ratio in heavy cruisers. The declaration appeared to make the heavy cruiser—on the basis of its range, speed, and firepower—the arbiter of naval combat. Not only was the heavy cruiser more versatile than the submarine as a commerce raider, the staff argued, but the superior numbers of American heavy cruisers operating from a multitude of bases in the Pacific would cripple the Japanese navy's long-standing defense arrangements, particularly its interceptive strategy. The Pacific Ocean would thereby be turned into an American lake. Above all, the staff insisted, studies and maneuvers had demonstrated that the relative strength in heavy cruisers would be the key to the outcome of the decisive fleet encounter, and for this reason, a 70 percent ratio in heavy cruiser tonnage was the absolute minimum necessary for Japanese naval security.[81]

The hyperbole and illogic of this statement by the Navy General Staff is less important than the view it provides of Japanese naval thinking as Japan approached the discussions of the 1930 conference at London, called to complete the system of naval limitations. Having reluctantly agreed at Washington in 1922 to a capital ship ratio of less than 70 percent in return for the right to build an unlimited number of cruisers, destroyers, and submarines upon which it had subsequently based its plans for the reduction of the American fleet, the Japanese Navy General Staff was determined to maintain this ratio in these lesser categories. The details of the negotiations at London are beyond the scope of this book, but in brief, the treaty signed there completed the system of naval disarmament by establishing low aggregate tonnage levels in these categories and extending the ban on capital ship

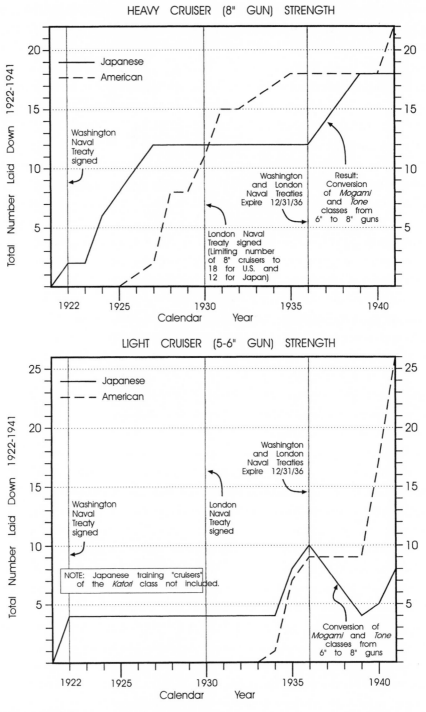

Mark A. Campbell

Fig. 7-9. IJN and USN heavy cruiser (8-inch gun) and light cruiser (5- to 6-inch gun) strengths, 1922–41.

construction through 1936.[82] For the Japanese navy, the arrangements dictated by the London Treaty were the cause of profound dismay. While the overall tonnage allowed to Japan (368,340 tons) amounted to 69.75 percent of the tonnage allowed to the Anglo-American naval powers, much of this was in categories of secondary importance to the Japanese. With considerable bitterness, the Japanese delegation was obliged to accept a ratio of 60.23 percent (108,400 tons) in 8-inch, 10,000-ton cruisers. Since Japan had already reached that limit by the time the treaty was signed, it meant that Japan could build no more heavy cruisers while the treaty was in force. The treaty allowed Japan to build up to 70 percent of the American light cruiser force (100,450 tons), but vessels in this class were limited to 6-inch guns. Though the navy had 132,495 tons in destroyers, the treaty allowed it only 105,500 tons (70.3 percent) in this category. Seeking to retain its submarine tonnage of 77,842, Japan was obliged to settle for parity in aggregate tonnage in this category: 52,700 tons. Only in light cruisers, a category the Navy General Staff had come to believe was too small to assure the success of the navy's attrition strategy, did the Japanese emerge with a modest gain, being allowed to build to an aggregate of 100,450 tons, or to a ratio of 70.15 percent.[83]

The real source of aggravation for the Japanese navy in the London Treaty was that the treaty resulted in not merely an inferior ratio in Japanese naval strength across the board, but an actual reduction in that strength vis-à-vis the other two naval powers. At Washington, the limitation ratios in capital ships essentially reflected the actual relative strengths of the three major naval powers as they then existed. At London, Japan was obliged to halt further construction of heavy cruisers—a category in which, during the past decade, it had labored with effort and skill to obtain a lead—while U.S. construction caught up in this category.[84] In total tonnage, however, Japan continued to enjoy an 80 percent ratio compared to the United States for several years after the London Treaty, since the latter made no effort until 1934 to build up to its treaty limits. Even after that, the United States did not catch up and surpass Japan until the end of the decade.

Nevertheless, the greatest rancor built up within the Japanese Navy General Staff, which, by 1934, caused the civilian government to reverse its fundamental policy of supporting the naval arms limitation system. Already, in the summer of 1930, the dominant faction on the staff, headed by Katō Kanji, the arch opponent of the treaty system and now chief of staff, made clear its determination to have Japan withdraw from the entire limitation system when the treaties expired at the end of 1936 and, even before that date, to prepare for the furious new naval race that would erupt once the treaty era ended.

8

"OUTRANGING" —the— ENEMY

The Japanese Navy from the First London Naval Conference to the End of the Treaty Era, 1930–1936

For all the Japanese navy's mounting frustration with the naval limitations system, in 1930 there were six years to go before Japan could leave that system, and until then the navy was obliged to deal with the new realities created by the London Treaty. Its response, undertaken with considerable skill and ingenuity, was to build to its allotted tonnage limits in each of the restricted warship categories and to strengthen those naval weapons and services not covered by the treaty.

The first material results of this effort were the post-London series of *hojū keikaku* (naval replenishment, or construction, plans), known unofficially as the *maru keikaku* (circle plans). The plans were, in fact, the culmination of a long process of negotiation between the Navy General Staff and the Finance Ministry that had begun in 1928 and had been interrupted by the London conference and treaty. They were now also the result of pressure on the government from the Japanese navy brass to provide additional funds to minimize the limitations on Japanese naval strength in return for acceptance of the arrangements of the London Treaty. Between 1930 and the outbreak of World War II there were four of these "circle plans," drawn up in 1931, 1934, 1937, and 1939.[1]

The "Circle One" plan of 1931, submitted by the Navy Ministry, approved by the cabinet in November 1930, and ratified by the Diet in 1931, allowed for the construction of thirty-nine new warships, of which the star acquisitions were the four cruisers of the *Mogami* class (the *Mogami, Mikuma, Kumano,* and *Suzuya)* laid down between 1931 and 1934 and completed between 1935 and 1937. These ships represented an effort by the Navy General Staff to place within a cruiser hull the maximum firepower allowed under the terms of the London Treaty. Faced with Japan's having reached its allotted quota in 8-inch gun cruisers, the Navy General Staff, still determined to make cruisers the centerpiece of its night combat tactics, decided to use its remaining cruiser allocation to build 6-inch gun cruisers capable of slugging it out with 8-inch heavy cruisers. To achieve this, Captain Fujimoto, who was given responsibility for their design, placed fifteen 6-inch guns in five triple turrets, three forward and two aft, and four triple torpedo mounts in the hull, two on each side. The staff's combat requirements, the same as those for the 10,000-ton "A"-class cruisers, called for armor capable of withstanding 8-inch shells and for gun turrets that could be rapidly converted to accommodate 8-inch ordnance. The displacement of these "B"-class cruisers, as they were designated, was significantly greater than the 8,400 tons called for in the staff's original specifications.[2] Fujimoto had tried to keep the weight down through the use of light alloys and electric welding wherever possible. When completed, the *Mogami* class was more heavily armored than any Japanese light cruiser heretofore and possessed greater firepower—including heavier antiaircraft armament—than any British or U.S. "light" cruiser. But at the same time, the Japanese Navy General Staff had once more insisted on a design that resulted in excessive top weight and thus dangerous instability. This defect was not the only problem: When the main batteries of the first two ships of the class—the *Mogami* and *Mikuma*—were test-fired they caused noticeable deformations in the hull because of faulty welding. All these flaws required extensive reconstruction of these ships over the next few years.[3]

In any event, just as the construction of the *Furutaka* had provoked a heavy cruiser race, the appearance of the *Mogami* class initiated what one commentator has called a "heavy light cruiser" competition.[4] To challenge these new Japanese B-class cruisers the Americans built the *Brooklyn*-class cruisers (10,000 tons and fifteen 6-inch guns) and the British constructed the *Southampton* class (10,000 tons and twelve 6-inch guns). But for most of the 1930s, the Japanese maintained their qualitative lead in cruiser design and construction. This advantage, like that in destroyers, had been purchased at the cost of producing ships so burdened with weapons, equipment, and installations incorporated into their designs at the insistence of Navy General Staff tacticians and theorists that the cruisers were dangerously unstable. It was thus inevitable that a disaster would overtake one of these top-heavy ships. Surprisingly, when it did so, the warship in question was one of the smaller units in the Japanese navy.

CALAMITY AT SEA
The Tomozuru *and Fourth Fleet Incidents, 1934–35*

Having been limited by the London Treaty to a lower aggregate tonnage in destroyers than it considered necessary for operational requirements, the navy decided to fill the gap with a new type of warship, a 600-ton *suiraitei* (torpedo boat) that could act as guard ship for Japanese ports and naval bases. The first

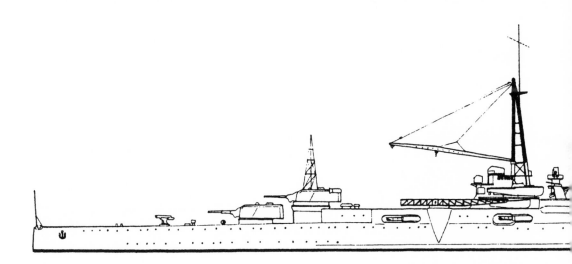

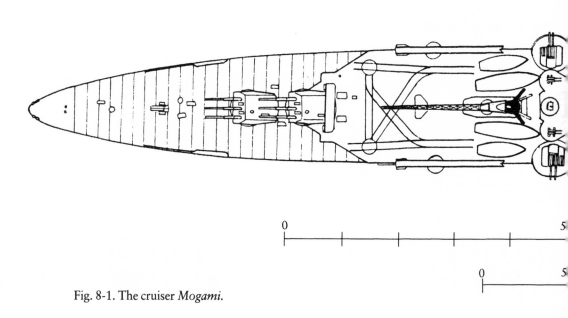

Fig. 8-1. The cruiser *Mogami.*

four of a projected class of twenty ships were laid down in 1931 and 1932 under the Circle One program and were completed between 1933 and 1934. The navy placed great hopes on these small vessels. Because of their small size, their aggregate tonnage was not limited by treaty and thus they could be built in considerable numbers. Mounting the heaviest possible armament—four 21-inch torpedo tubes and three 4.7-inch guns—on the smallest possible hull, the *Chidori* class was intended to take over the routine patrol and antisubmarine duties of larger

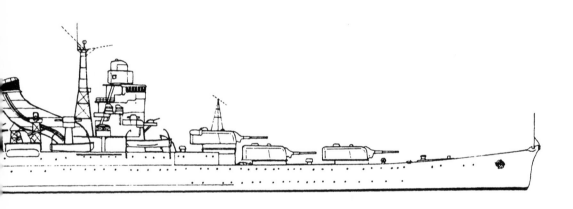

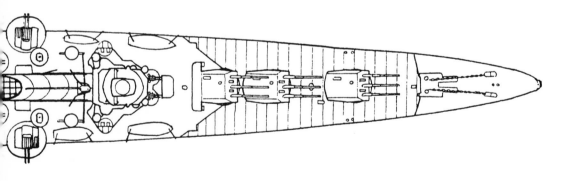

100m

100ft

destroyers. But, again, the demands of the Navy General Staff for offensive power resulted in a perilously top-heavy design. Tragedy struck when several of these small craft were engaged in maneuvers off Sasebo, March 1934, in a strong gale. Early in the morning of 12 March the *Tomozuru,* steaming at 14 knots, took a roll from which the ship never recovered. Found later that day drifting keel up, the *Tomozuru* was towed back to Sasebo, stern first, by the light cruiser *Tatsuta.* When the ship was righted in port it was discovered that only 13 of the original 6 officers and 107 crew were left alive. In the two subsequent official inquiries into the cause of the accident the fundamental instability of this class of torpedo boats became apparent, and measures were recommended to improve seaworthiness in those ships in the class that were still being built. The sixteen boats in the program that had not been laid down were canceled, and the idea that the four that were completed could replace even second-class destroyers was abandoned.[5]

The *Tomozuru* disaster sent shock waves through the Japanese navy. In particular, the Basic Design Section of the Technical Department and its chief, Rear Adm. Fujimoto Kikuo, came in for heavy criticism. Ironically, the second investigation board looking into the accident April through June 1934 was headed by Katō Kanji, former chief of the Navy General Staff, the institution whose continuing and adamant insistence on the overloading of Japanese warships with weapons and

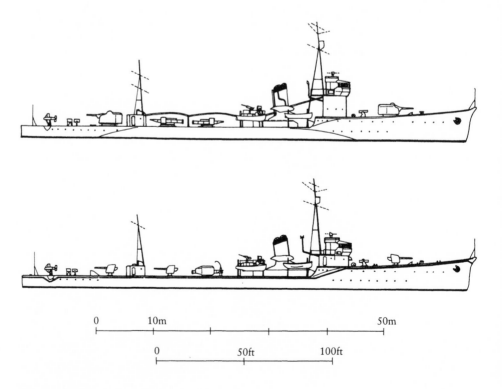

Fig. 8-2. The torpedo boat *Tomozuru.*

equipment had led to their faulty design. In any event, the blame fell on Fujimoto, the naval staff's willing executor, who was eventually sacked and replaced by Capt. Fukuda Keiji. A broken man, Fujimoto died the next year. Because of the criticism of Fujimoto's work, the design of many of the navy's ships was now suspect. A little more than a year after Japan's naval planners had begun to deal with this disturbing reality, a second calamity at sea occurred that confirmed these suspicions. In late September 1935, fifty-eight warships of the "Fourth Fleet," temporarily organized for the annual grand maneuvers of the Combined Fleet, were taking part in the final phase of the exercises. The maneuver area was in the northwest Pacific between northern Honshū and the Kurile Islands. Dawn of 21 September found the Fourth Fleet steaming eastward and then southward, about one hundred miles east of northern Honshū, when it was warned of a huge typhoon to the south, moving rapidly northward over a two-hundred-mile front. With insufficient time or room to avoid the storm, the ships of the Fourth Fleet attempted to ride it out. In the process the fleet took a terrific battering from the mountainous seas and winds of up to 79 knots. While the storm smashed the bridges of the carriers *Hōshō* and *Ryūjō* and weakened the amidships joints of the hulls of *Myōkō* and *Mogami*, the smaller ships suffered the most. The roll of the light cruiser *Kinu* reached 36 degrees, and some *Fubuki*-class destroyers took rolls of 75 degrees. Though miraculously none capsized, damage to some ships was appalling. The entire bow section of the destroyer *Yūgiri* broke off just before the bridge, as did that of the destroyer *Hatsuyuki*. The plates of *Oboro* and *Shirakumo* were severely buckled, and the hulls of other destroyers suffered loosened and ruptured joints. When the storm had passed, nearly all the ships of the Fourth Fleet had incurred damage, and fifty-four men had been killed or were missing.[6]

While a storm of this magnitude probably could have damaged any warship no matter how well constructed, the subsequent official inquiries into the travail of the Fourth Fleet revealed that both basic design and construction flaws had substantially contributed to the injuries that many of its ships had suffered. As already noted, a number of Japanese cruisers and destroyers designed during the treaty era carried a dangerous top weight. The storm of September 1935 had also revealed that the longitudinal strength of these ships, particularly the *Fubuki*-class destroyers, was far less than that expected, a nearly fatal flaw when these ships hogged and sagged as they rode out the great waves. Errors in welding had also caused the weakening of joints in both cruisers and destroyers.[7]

With the evidence of the *Tomozuru* and the Fourth Fleet disasters now manifest, the Japanese navy was obliged to delay by several years some of the construction projected under the Circle Two plan and to turn instead to a huge program of modification to correct a decade of faulty design due to the excessive demands of the Navy General Staff. To begin with, the navy's torpedo boats and destroyers were significantly redesigned and reconstructed. The design of the four vessels of the *Chidori* class that were completed or under construction was drastically modified by reducing the size and protection of the main batteries, reducing the number of torpedo mounts and torpedoes carried on deck, lowering the bridge one deck level, and adding a keel ballast. The eight torpedo boats of the succeeding Ōtori class, being built or completed, incorporated all the lessons learned from the capsizing of the *Tomozuru*. Six destroyers of the new *Hatsuharu* class and ten of the *Shiratsuyu* class (sometimes called the improved *Hatsuharu*, or *kai-Hatsuharu*, class) were extensively modified by a variety of correctives: redesigning the upper works for a more compact and efficient layout, repositioning the guns, removing one torpedo mount, adding extra ballast, and removing extra equipment from the deck.[8]

It was the navy's cruisers that caused the greatest concern, particularly the newest ones, those of the *Mogami* class. So severe was the problem of instability in the class that in the autumn of 1936 the *Mogami* and *Mikuma* were placed in reserve and sent for partial reconstruction to the Kure Navy Yard to improve their transverse stability. The enormous bridge on these ships was lowered, the deck heights were reduced, and extra bulges added to the hull. These modifications were incorporated into their sister ships, the *Kumano* and *Suzuya*, which were still under construction. The *Takao*-class cruisers were also temporarily placed in reserve in late 1935 for refitting at Yokosuka Navy Yard to improve their longitudinal strength (by addition of steel plates the length of their hulls on both sides) and to otherwise modify their structures. By these various modifications, a considerable number of Japanese warships, from torpedo boats to heavy cruisers, attained real stability, with only a slight drop in their potential abilities.[9]

In addition to necessitating the partial reconstruction of ships already in service, the lessons of the *Tomozuru* and Fourth Fleet "incidents" (as the Japanese referred to them) influenced the design of the two new *Tone*-class cruisers (the *Tone* and *Chikuma*), laid down in 1934 and 1935 under the Circle Two program and completed in 1938–39 for use as scout cruisers for the main fleet.[10] These ships were improved versions of the *Mogami* class, being far more stable (partly due to the addition of side armor and underwater bulges) and employing a radical arrangement for their main armament. The ships carried 20.32-centimeter (8-inch) guns in four turrets—all sited forward of the bridge, which left space aft, free from gun blast, for five reconnaissance aircraft and two catapults to launch them.[11] In terms of habitability, stability, seaworthiness, and speed, they were excellent ships. Nevertheless, by the time they were completed, they represented an obsolete tactical concept. Their sacrifice of considerable armament and balance of design for the purpose of carrying a larger than normal number of floatplanes made less sense in an era of increasing numbers and performance of carrier- and land-based aircraft.[12]

All in all, the mishaps of 1934 and 1935, as severe as they may have been, may have worked to the Japanese navy's advantage. Without them, the navy might not have recognized the weaknesses of the ships they had damaged in these mishaps. The accidents had occurred in a period of peace, when the navy had the time and the resources to correct the design and construction flaws revealed. Certainly, if one considers the combat performance of these particular cruisers and destroyers during the first two years of the Pacific War and their ability to absorb and deal out considerable punishment, the modification projects of the mid-1930s were clearly well worth the navy's effort.[13]

THE NAVY MODERNIZES
Refitting and Reconstruction of Existing Warships

It would be wrong, however, to view the modification of much of the Japanese fleet in the mid-1930s merely as a crash program to correct unusual deficiencies in design that had suddenly appeared as the result of a series of mishaps. Rather, it was part of a continuing effort at modernization that had been going on since World War I, not just by the Japanese navy, but by all navies. The shift from coal to oil, new boiler designs, the advent of the turbine engine, the development of new types of armor plate—hardened chrome, high tensile, and Ducol steels—improvement in aerial bombs, and the increase in the size and destructiveness of torpedoes all presented challenges and opportunities to which navies had to respond or face obsolescence.[14] While they could and did construct new classes of warships, it was cheaper, in a time of leaner naval budgets all around, to refit and reconstruct existing naval units to deal with or to take advantage of these developments. Then, after the Washington Treaty, reconstruction and retrofitting became essentially the only means to modernize a navy, and after the London Treaty the practice became more common.

During the treaty era, therefore, all the major units of the Japanese navy were rebuilt as part of a considered program of modernization. For example, many improvements made on the *Takao*-class cruisers in 1934–35 (replacement of the main guns and hoists, extension of radio facilities, improvement of crew's quarters, embarkation of new types of aircraft, and the like) had actually been ordered two years before as part of the effort to upgrade the navy's armaments. Beginning in the late 1920s and continuing through the end of the next decade, all the navy's capital ships went into the yard to increase the maximum elevation of the main batteries, to modernize bridge structures to incorporate the latest fire control systems, to install catapults and housing for floatplanes, to strengthen deck armor against plunging fire and aerial bombs, and to add antitorpedo protection below the waterline.[15]

Some new protective arrangements were already in place in the last Japanese battleships to be constructed before the onset of the treaty era, but had not been put to the test of combat. Some years before, the hulls of several obsolete or unfinished warships, in particular the battleship *Tosa,* had played a useful role in testing both offensive naval weaponry and defensive armament, and the lessons were incorporated into later naval construction. The *Tosa* and *Kaga,* under construction at the time of the Washington naval conference, were canceled under the terms of the subsequent treaty. Whereas the hull of the *Kaga* was later saved for conversion to a carrier, *Tosa*'s hull was taken over by the gunnery school in June 1924 for use as a target ship. As *Tosa* at launching had been projected as the most advanced capital ship in the Japanese navy, the tests carried out on her hull provided the navy with an unprecedented opportunity, short of combat, to try out weapons systems on the latest armor. By the time the *Tosa* sank in the Bungo Strait in February 1925, the Japanese navy had accumulated a wealth of important data not only for the refitting and reconstruction of existing warships, but also for the design of the superbattleships *Yamato* and *Musashi* a decade afterward.[16]

Other improvements in warship design were stimulated by the requirements of the Navy General Staff. A case in point was the formation of night combat formations in the mid-1930s. The subsequent need for fast and powerful units to accompany destroyers and cruisers in night actions led to the conversion of the battle cruisers of the *Kongō* class into fast battleships capable of 30 knots. The development of the oxygen torpedo eventually resulted in the redesign of some of the navy's light cruisers into torpedo cruisers.

THE PUSH FOR SPEED AND ENDURANCE
Further Advances in Steam Engineering

Some important improvements in warship performance were made possible by advances in propulsion technologies. As maritime nations of the world searched for speed and endurance in the late 1920s, they turned to ways to increase not only steam pressures, but also steam temperatures. For both merchantmen and warships the trend was toward "superheated" steam, since its advantages had been well established. Superheated steam saved fuel by making more efficient use of heat from fuel than did lower-temperature "saturated" steam, and since it contained no moisture, it decreased corrosion and erosion of turbine blades and thus improved both turbine operation and life. In 1930, the launching of the British destroyer *Acheron,* whose engineering plant used steam at 500 pounds per square inch and about 750°F, ushered in the use of high-pressure, high-temperature steam.[17]

In the Japanese navy, trials with superheated steam began with the Miyabara boilers of the turbine-driven pre–World War I battle cruiser *Ibuki* and had continued through the war and into the 1920s. But the navy had no fixed policy on the use of superheated versus saturated steam in these years; the decision to use either was left to the engineers who designed the steam plants for individual ship classes.

For that reason, as late as the design and construction of the *Myōkō*-class cruisers and the *Fubuki*-class destroyers in the mid-1920s, the navy was still using saturated steam at 284 pounds per square inch. But to keep up with developments in high-pressure, high-temperature steam in the American and British navies, the *Mogami*-class cruisers laid down in the 1920s and the *Hatsuharu*-class destroyers used superheated steam of 572°F at 312.4 pounds per square inch. In the mid-1930s, the *Chidori*- and *Ōtori*-class torpedo boats used superheated steam at 426 pounds per square inch and 662°F. Since these ships proved satisfactory, similar arrangements were made for the *Kagerō*-class destroyers and the *Shōkaku*-class carriers. After this, although considerably higher pressures and temperatures were eventually used in a few smaller warships, 426 pounds per square inch at 662°F became the standard pressures and temperatures in the Japanese navy.[18]

At the same time that high-pressure, high-temperature steam was being adopted by the Japanese navy, boiler power and efficiency were increased and total weight and volume of boiler per horsepower was decreased. Further, with the adoption of adequate seals for feed-water equipment, boiler feed lines were kept free of air and from machinery lubricants, thus greatly improving boiler water purity and facilitating the use of high-pressure, high-temperature steam. As a consequence of all these advances, the fuel consumption rates for many classes of Japanese warships dropped appreciably in the 1930s, as they did in most navies of the world.[19]

All these developments in steam engineering marked important technological improvements that contributed to the tactical flexibility and strategic reach of the Japanese navy, affecting as they did speed and endurance. The problem was that, beginning in the early 1930s, the American and British navies were developing engineering plants of even greater efficiency, power, and endurance. In the vast distances in the Pacific where the Japanese and U.S. navies would operate, endurance and fuel economy were matters of critical importance, particularly for the Japanese Combined Fleet, which lacked both a fleet train and easy access to sources of naval fuels.

The growing divergence in the relative efficiency of Japanese and American steam propulsion systems in the period between the world wars can best be demonstrated by comparing the performance of Japanese and American destroyers in the 1920s and 1930s, since as a warship category, the propulsive demands of destroyers are the highest. Their engineering plants need to be high powered, be reliable, provide economical cruising, have low weight and small volume, and be easy to maintain. Until about the time of the Washington Treaty, the steam plants of U.S. and Japanese destroyers were approximately equal, but when the U.S. Navy resumed building destroyers in the early 1930s, its steam propulsion plants were perceptibly better than contemporary Japanese plants. By the end of the decade, the gap had widened further, and by the eve of the Pacific War, American destroyer engineering plants were clearly superior in all respects. The American advantage almost certainly stemmed from the use of higher-pressure, higher-temperature steam and very compact, lightweight turbines.[20]

Important as power plants were to warship development, it was probably the growth in the destructive potential of aircraft that most forcefully altered the designs of ships. The strengthening of deck armor against aerial bombs, the trend toward increased underwater protection against aerial torpedoes, and the installation of a new type of high-angle gun and high-angle gunfire director, as well as the retrofitting of all battleships and heavy cruisers to house, launch, and retrieve float-planes, were all evidence of how aviation had altered Japanese warship design.

AVIATION AS AN EMERGING COMPONENT IN JAPANESE NAVAL PLANNING

During the interwar decades, Japan developed the navy's air arm as a further means of overcoming the deficiencies in Japanese naval strength after the London Treaty. For Japan and the United States, naval aviation developed in an age of severely limited naval budgets of the treaty era, which was also a time of slow development in aircraft relative to other weapons alternatives, particularly the submarine. These considerations had much to do with the Japanese navy's moving rapidly ahead during the 1920s to develop the technology and doctrine for undersea warfare, even though it lagged in the development of naval aviation. The undersea emphasis was the exact reverse of the priorities of the U.S. Navy during the decade.[21]

During World War I the Japanese navy had learned a good deal about naval aviation through its contacts in the British navy, and Japanese naval aviation, both in technology and in doctrine, remained dependent on the British model for most of the 1920s. As discussed, Japan's first carrier, the *Hōshō*, had been largely designed with British advice, and the British naval aviation mission in Japan from 1921 to 1924 had provided guidance on training procedures and aircraft design. Moreover, the greater portion of aircraft that initially joined the fleet were land-based seaplanes whose main tasks were reconnaissance and antisubmarine patrols. At the outset of the treaty era, the navy had drawn up plans for the formation of seventeen squadrons of these aircraft, but budgetary considerations limited the units to eleven until 1931. The selection of land-based seaplane squadrons indicates that up to the mid-1920s, the Japanese navy had not been obliged to make a doctrinal choice between seaplanes and shore-based aircraft on the one hand and carrier-based aircraft on the other. The decision in favor of the latter was probably a result of the grand maneuvers of 1927, which demonstrated that the navy did not have the ability to project air power over the fleet.[22]

The most significant step in the navy's development of its air arm during the decade was its decision to add two large, fast carriers, capable of operating with the fleet. The navy could do so in large part because, under the terms of the Washington Treaty, which had called for the dismantling of all capital ships then under construction (except for those specially exempted), Japan was left with four large, uncompleted hulls. The navy decided to complete two of these as fleet aircraft carriers about the same time that the United States decided to use the hulls of the two canceled battle cruisers, the *Lexington* and *Saratoga,* for the same purpose. Work had begun in September 1923 on converting the battle cruiser *Amagi,* but the Tokyo earthquake of that month so damaged the hull that it was scrapped and plans for conversion shifted to the hull of the uncompleted battleship *Kaga.* In November of that year, work also began on converting the hull of the *Amagi*'s sister ship, the *Akagi.* The *Akagi* was completed in 1927, and the *Kaga* a year later. Although both ships initially incorporated design features that proved sufficiently unsatisfactory to require their major reconstruction in the mid-1930s, the addition of these two carriers and their aircraft made it possible to consider naval aviation as a significant element in strategic planning for the fleet, about the same time that the *Lexington* and *Saratoga* marked a similar evolution in the U.S. Navy.

By 1927, Japanese naval aviation had grown sufficiently in size and complexity that it was necessary to centralize the administration of its various peacetime activities, heretofore divided between the Navy Ministry and the Navy Technical Department, into a single Naval Aviation Department.[23] In 1932, an independent Naval Air Arsenal was established to centralize the testing and development of aircraft and weaponry. During their early years, these organizations were under the command of able and articulate air enthusiasts, which played no little part in the rapid expansion of Japanese naval aviation during the succeeding decade. Equally important, the new limitations imposed on warship construction by the London Naval Treaty of 1930 caused the Navy General Staff to view naval aviation as a new and important means to make up for the deficiencies in the navy's surface forces.

In 1931, therefore, the navy finally pushed through its demand for establishing the remainder of the seventeen air squadrons that had been projected in the 1923 expansion plans. These were eventually combined into six *kōkūtai* (air groups) located at six bases around Japan. The Circle One and Circle Two naval expansion programs, moreover, featured an additional twelve air groups, the development of certain aviation technologies, and the acceleration of air crew training.[24] The Circle One plan concentrated on developing new aircraft types, including large flying boats and land-based attack planes, as well as the building of seaborne air units—both floatplanes and carrier aircraft. The Circle Two plan continued the buildup in naval aircraft and authorized the construction of two carriers.

Added to the increasing attention given to the training of air crews, the development of dive-bombing and aerial torpedo tactics, the design of more powerful

aerial bombs and torpedoes, and the mounting of floatplanes on an increasing
number of larger warships, these initiatives rapidly increased the value of naval air
units in the eyes of the Navy General Staff. Aircraft were now seen as powerful
weapons against enemy warships when used in conjunction with the heavy guns
of the main fleet. But, as the 1934 revision of the Battle Instructions emphasized,
naval air units were expected merely to facilitate the main fleet action and were
not yet seen as capable of acting on their own against the enemy's main force or
his carriers.[25] Such caution was undoubtedly well placed, since carrier aircraft
probably then did not have the capability to do otherwise and could not have discharged an independent role.

OUTRANGING THE ENEMY

The sudden surge for aviation within the navy in the 1930s must be seen within
the tactical context of Japanese attempts to "outrange"the enemy.[26] That is to say,
by using superior weaponry or techniques, the Japanese wanted to strike the
enemy at the outset of the decisive encounter at a distance from which he could
not retaliate.[27] The concept began with the possibilities of long-range naval gunfire, but eventually came to be applied to the use of torpedoes, submarines, and,
of course, naval aircraft.

The idea of outranging had its origins in the "big ships, big guns" obsession of
the navy. The enemy would be defeated by the main batteries of the Japanese battle line that would deliver *shūchū dai enkyori shageki* (very long range, concentrated fire) and thus overwhelm the vanguard of the enemy fleet at the outset of
the decisive engagement. The concept first appeared to be possible in 1910 with
the launching of the battle cruiser *Kongō*, whose 36-centimeter (14-inch) guns, at
the time she was laid down, could fire a shell a greater distance—over 25,000
meters—than any warship then afloat. The concept then hardened into a combat
principle in the Japanese navy around 1917, when Japan was attempting to
assemble an eight-eight fleet. Over the next two decades, through simultaneous
development of several technological improvements in gunnery, "outranging" (in
the form of long-range concentrated shellfire) was confirmed as a basic doctrine
of the Japanese navy.[28]

The first improvement was in the field of gunnery. As outlined in chapter 6, the
evolving consolidation, integration, and mechanization of the various components
of fire control systems made it increasingly possible to coordinate long-range fire of
heavy guns. By 1920, the surface fire control problem was well understood in most
major navies. Still to be solved, however, were certain aspects of the problem—
further consolidation of plotting functions in a single and protected plotting room,
predicting future target position, accelerating internal communications, correcting

for the relationship between the gun platform and the plane of the sea at the moment of firing, and automating the movement of heavy guns.[29]

During the interwar years, the British and American navies began to deal with most of these problems. First, there were variations between the two navies, of course, in the progress of gunnery, particularly relating range. The British relied more on director-controlled fire, and the Americans more on the plotting room, in which data from range finders, director, and spotters could be processed. Second, although the Royal Navy had taken the lead in developing fire control in the years before World War I, the U.S. Navy caught up and surpassed the British during the interwar decades. By the late 1930s, the American navy was on the way to achieving a second gunnery revolution through several innovations. The most important were the establishment of a stable vertical and accurate, high-powered servomechanisms. The ship maintained a stable vertical by a gyroscope-based instrument that could continuously sense the relationship between the ship and the plane of the sea. Accurate, high-powered servomechanisms were electric motors that allowed remote control of the train and elevation of large guns. With these innovations, continuous aim could be achieved without human intervention in all but the heaviest seas, when firing at specified level and cross-level was invoked.[30]

The Japanese navy had followed a course of technological development that dealt with these same problems in naval gunnery, but at a slower pace than in the British and American navies. Although the Japanese had experimented with range clocks and change-of-range calculators between 1915 and 1930, fire control instrumentation had remained fragmented until 1926. In that year, realizing that its fire control systems were outdated, the navy had acquired from Barr and Stroud very sophisticated fire control tables for the battle cruiser *Kongō*. Besides being used in the *Kongō*, these tables were studied intensively and probably provided a basis for the fire control tables developed by the Aichi Company in the 1930s, the first manufactured in Japan.[31]

The principal Japanese innovation in fire control during these years was a unique Japanese instrument, the *sokutekiban*. The term's literal English translation (gauging-the-target-calculator) is less useful than a description of its function: the computation of target course and speed by use of an inclinometer (which took the angle between the target's course and the line of bearing to the target) and by timed changes in bearing. This information was, in turn, used to calculate range rate and bearing rate and subsequently, when combined with other data, to provide sight settings. By the 1930s, the *sokutekiban* was incorporated in all Japanese fire control systems except those on the *Mogami* and *Tone* classes of heavy cruisers (in which the target inclination angle was measured and delivered as an input to the fire control table, which calculated target course and speed).[32]

The *sokutekiban* represented the state of Japanese fire control in the interwar period. All its instruments were excessively heavy and manpower-intensive, using manual follow-up systems rather than incorporating automatic inputs. The navy's adherence to these systems may have reflected the contemporary Japanese lack of technical resources for the development of smaller, lighter, and more complex computing devices like those used by the British and American navies. Neverthe-less, there were several excellent points to Japanese fire control and gunnery in this period. The navy's optics were very good; the range-finder averaging on some fire control tables apparently produced very accurate range; and Japanese gun crews were sufficiently trained to shoot accurately. In any event, deficiencies of interwar fire control instrumentation did not prevent Japanese gunnery from more than holding its own in the surface engagements of the first year of the Pacific War.[33] Once the U.S. Navy fully exploited fire control radar and high-power servomechanisms for gun control midway through the Pacific War, the Japanese gunnery could no longer hold its own against the Americans.

The coordination of naval gunfire by the 1920s had made it obvious that gun-fire range could also be extended if the fire control officer could see farther, a pos-sibility realized by placing the fire control station as high in the ship as possible. The "director system" of fire control, pioneered by the British navy around 1912, laid all the guns from a position usually atop the bridge superstructure, which was also away from the smoke and noise of the main batteries themselves. From this position, the fire control officer, ranging salvos against the target, transmitted the necessary elevations and angles of train to the individual guns. Thus, the director system noticeably altered warship design as the fire control mechanisms came to be located high in the bridge superstructure of capital ships. To these mechanisms were added other instruments to extend the range and accuracy of naval gunfire—range finders, searchlight-directing equipment, and (used by the Japanese navy after 1923) a combination of the *shagekiban* (firing calculator) and the *sokutek-iban*. This combination computed gun orders and thus collectively served the same functions as the U.S. Navy's combination of the stable vertical and range keeper. (The separate elements of the Japanese and U.S. systems did not, however, perform the same functions.) Thus the bridge superstructures of all warships grew taller and more complicated and, as the Japanese were determined to outrange all other navies with control systems more complicated (but not necessarily better) than those of British and American ships, the huge "pagoda" masts of their capi-tal ships became the tallest and most cluttered of all, looking bizarrely top-heavy.[34]

Now that guns could aim at greater ranges, they only needed to shoot farther. One way to accomplish this was by increasing the maximum elevation of the main batteries of a capital ship. Standard maximum elevations of capital ship main bat-teries in most navies at the outset of World War I were between 15 and 20 degrees,

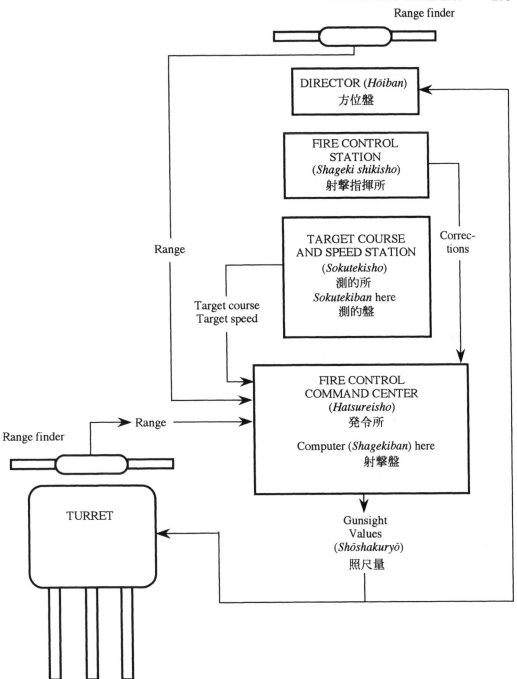

Range finder

DIRECTOR (*Hōiban*)
方位盤

FIRE CONTROL
STATION
(*Shageki shikisho*)
射撃指揮所

TARGET COURSE
AND SPEED STATION
(*Sokutekisho*)
測的所
Sokutekiban here
測的盤

Range

Corrections

Target course
Target speed

FIRE CONTROL
COMMAND CENTER
(*Hatsureisho*)
発令所

Computer (*Shagekiban*) here
射撃盤

Range finder

Range

TURRET

Gunsight
Values
(*Shōshakuryō*)
照尺量

Fig. 8-3. Fire control organization, 1930s. (Adapted from *KH*, 260)

but ships built toward the end of that conflict were completed with guns capable of considerably higher elevation: The guns of the British battle cruiser *Hood* could be elevated to 30 degrees, and those of American battleships then under construction were supposed to reach 40 degrees.

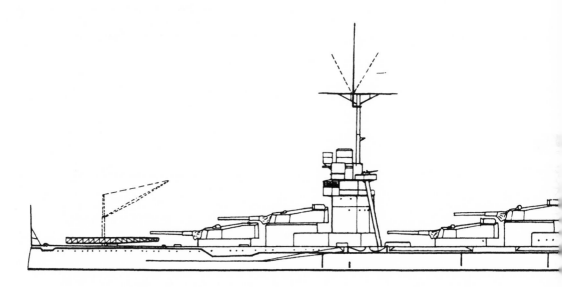

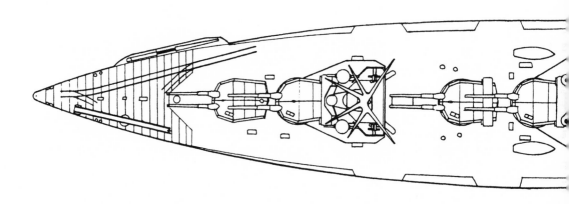

Fig. 8-4. The battleship *Ise* as reconstructed, 1937.

Under these circumstances, the Japanese navy, from the mid-1920s to the mid-1930s, undertook the series of refittings and major reconstructions of its capital ships. In addition to installing oil-fired boilers, adding torpedo bulges, and strengthening armor, the navy made radical modifications of turret structures to

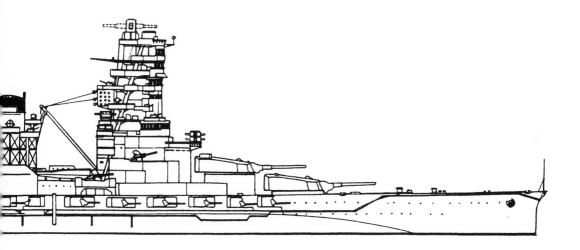

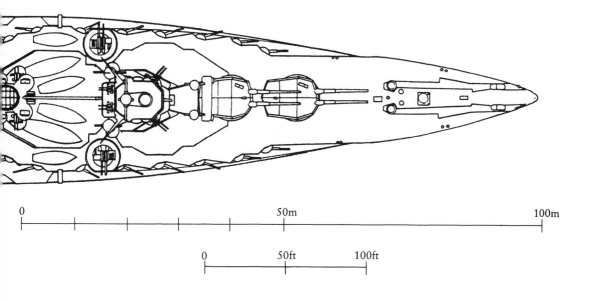

0   50m   100m

0   50ft   100ft

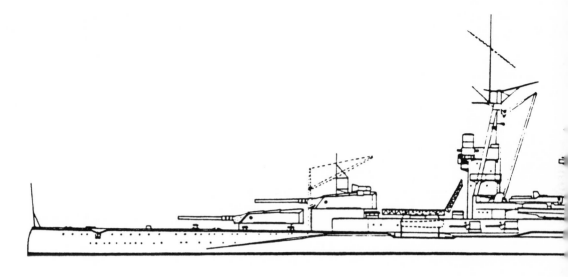

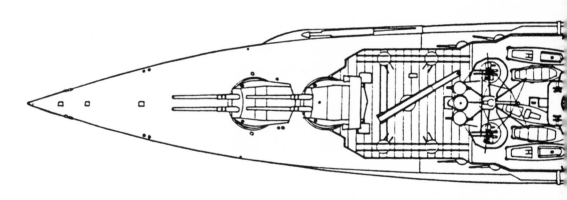

Fig. 8-5. The battleship *Mutsu* as reconstructed, 1936.

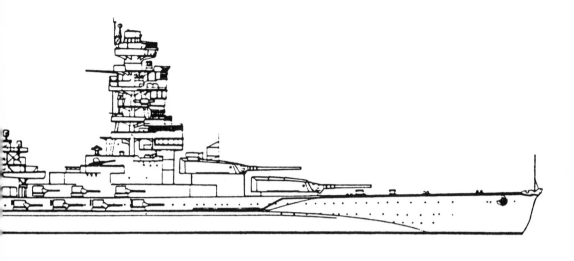

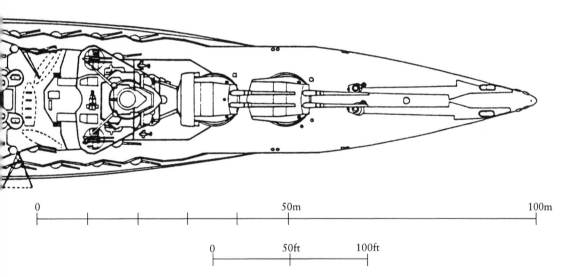

| 0 | | | | | 50m | | | | 100m |

| 0 | 50ft | 100ft |

increase the elevations of the guns.[35] By this means most of the navy's heavy guns had been repositioned to attain 43 degree maximum elevation, with a consequent increase in maximum range to 33,000 meters.

Increasing the armament of battleship main batteries was, of course, an obvious means by which Japanese gunfire could be made to outrange that of potential enemies. But this improvement was outlawed by the naval limitation treaties

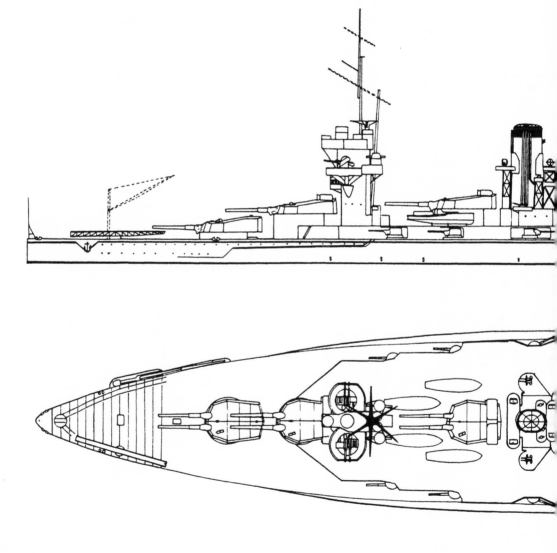

Fig. 8-6. The battleship *Fusō* as reconstructed, 1934.

and thus could not actually be undertaken by the navy. Such agreements, however, did not specifically prohibit Japanese tacticians and builders from *planning* warships that mounted batteries of a size unprecedented in the Japanese navy.

Meanwhile, there were other ways by which long-range concentrated fire of the navy's existing heavy ordnance could be improved. One of these was a better naval shell. The navy began manufacturing the first Japanese-designed shells at Kure

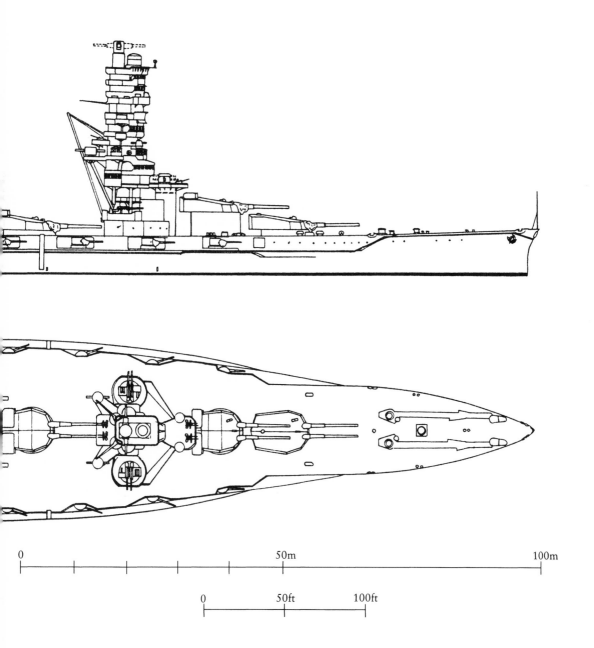

0   50m   100m

0   50ft   100ft

upon the outbreak of World War I, but after the Battle of Jutland demonstrated the capacity of European, particularly German, naval shells for range, high-angle trajectory, and fuse delay, the navy set about improving its own projectiles. In 1925, after extensive research and testing, the navy officially adopted the type 5 AP (armor-piercing) shell (in 8-, 14-, and 16-inch sizes), based on a British design that incorporated the ballistic lessons of Jutland, particularly in its blunt head for maximum penetration under a tapered cap for aerodynamic performance. It was designed to be resistant to premature detonation. After its adoption, however, the shell was found to have a faulty fuse delay, and within a few years, the navy developed another shell while experimenting with "underwater shots." It was the type 88 AP shell, which had an improved time delay in its fuse, a better armor-piercing performance, and a smoother trajectory through the water.[36]

Further improvements in ballistic performance followed. Ordnance designers had long known that a "boat-tailed" shell, that is, one slightly tapered at its base, would attain greater range, but at the price of accuracy. For some years, the Japanese navy had resisted the adoption of such projectiles, since it placed the greatest value on achieving the most concentrated salvo. But this priority changed after the Washington Treaty, and the navy's new interest in outranging grew. Even though it meant refitting turrets and magazines, the navy decided to build a new long-range shell. The result was the adoption, in 1931, of the type 91 AP shell, whose principal features were a boat-tailed shape, a fuse with a longer delay, security against premature detonation, and a blunt cap over the shell, surmounted by a pointed nose cone for streamlining (fig. 8-7). With the proper charges and with maximum elevation of the main batteries of its largest capital ships, the Japanese navy obtained ranges of 35,500 meters (38,800 yards) with 14-inch shells of this type and over 38,000 meters (41,500 yards) with the 41-centimeter (16.14-inch) version.[37]

Another important method of obtaining greater effective gunnery range was through the use of naval aircraft, principally floatplanes carried aboard battleships and cruisers as spotters to mark the fall of shells, thus achieving observation heights not attainable from the mast of any warship. Starting in 1932, this technique, with which other navies were also beginning to experiment, was increasingly used with the laying down of a heavy smokescreen to shield Japanese ships from enemy fire. In the naval maneuvers of 1933, the Combined Fleet carried out such *enmaku chōka shageki* (supra-smokescreen fire) with considerable success, and after 1935 the navy could achieve a high rate of hits, using this method, at ranges of over 30,000 meters. The navy practiced this tactical innovation repeatedly in succeeding years, and it was incorporated into Japanese planning for the decisive gunnery duel. The tactic substantially contributed toward an increasing emphasis on naval aviation, since the use of aircraft as spotters

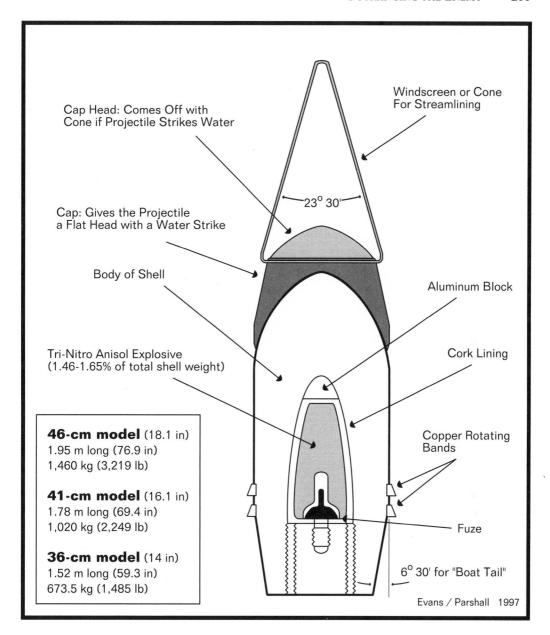

Cap Head: Comes Off with
Cone if Projectile Strikes Water

Windscreen or Cone
For Streamlining

23° 30'

Cap: Gives the Projectile
a Flat Head with a Water Strike

Body of Shell

Aluminum Block

Tri-Nitro Anisol Explosive
(1.46-1.65% of total shell weight)

Cork Lining

46-cm model (18.1 in)
1.95 m long (76.9 in)
1,460 kg (3,219 lb)

Copper Rotating
Bands

41-cm model (16.1 in)
1.78 m long (69.4 in)
1,020 kg (2,249 lb)

Fuze

36-cm model (14 in)
1.52 m long (59.3 in)
673.5 kg (1,485 lb)

6° 30' for "Boat Tail"

Evans / Parshall 1997

Fig. 8-7. Type 91 AP shell, large caliber.
(Sources: *KH,* 48; and U.S. Naval Technical Mission to Japan, "Japanese Projectiles: General
Types," NTJ-L-O-19, [1946])

could obviously not operate without Japanese control of the air over the contending fleets. Thus, by the mid-1930s, the decisive surface engagement came to be seen as preceded by a battle for control of the airspace over the contending fleets, though clearly, Japanese doctrine viewed such air superiority not as a means of developing an independent air strike mission, but as a means of support for the Japanese battle line.[38]

The Japanese navy had not developed outranging into an infallible tactic, however. There were, to begin with, concerns that outranging might use up too much ammunition in the early phase of the battle or that through a combination of circumstances, the Japanese battle line might then not be able to get sufficiently close in to finish off its enemy. There was also the recognition that standardized gunnery instructions for the fleet had not caught up with the rapid advances in ordnance and fire control. Indeed, it was not until 1930 that the navy distributed a fleet gunnery manual that included, among other things, the proper ranges for the decisive gunnery battle and the respective capabilities of various AP shells. Moreover, by the mid-1930s, these instructions had become outdated. They did not take into account the 18-inch guns to be installed on the monster battleships that the navy then had under design.[39]

Nevertheless, by the mid-1930s, the Japanese had sufficient confidence in their guns and gunnery that their main force units would outrange those of the U.S. battle fleet by 4,000 to 5,000 meters. With the firepower that the Japanese navy planned to have available, the Naval Staff College estimated that the Japanese battle line could begin to track the enemy at 40,000 meters (21.5 miles) and could seize the initiative by opening fire at around 34,000 meters, dealing the vanguard of the American fleet a devastating blow before the latter could retaliate. Subsequently, having crippled the enemy at long range, the main force would rapidly close to much shorter range to complete the enemy's destruction.[40]

In 1938, while the superbattleships *Yamato* and *Musashi* were still under construction, the navy, using the 16-inch guns of the *Nagato*, the largest mounted in a Japanese warship to that date, opened fire at a range of 34,600 meters (18.7 miles). The next year, using spotting aircraft and indirect fire, the navy reported direct hits for 12 percent of the shots at 32,000 meters, superb marksmanship for the time.[41]

It can be argued, of course, that although the Japanese navy was attaining some quite remarkable marksmanship for its heaviest guns, even greater strides were being made by the U.S. Navy because of the American innovations mentioned earlier. The Japanese navy could achieve Western standards of gunnery efficiency by the most rigorous training, costly increases in the number of guns, increasing displacement to carry them, or by the development of night combat, where American advantages in fire control would be offset, at least until the advent of radar.[42]

SUICHŪDAN (Underwater Shots)

Another—and quite unexpected—gunnery technique that had little to do with outranging was developed in secret by the Japanese navy during the interwar period. It emerged from the series of firing tests conducted in 1924 on several obsolete or unfinished battleships. The use of the unfinished battleship *Tosa* afforded the navy the first and only chance to test the armor of the newest type of battleship to see what sort of punishment it could take.

Up to this time conventional naval wisdom held that the only damage that could be inflicted on a warship below the waterline was by torpedoes and mines and thus only antitorpedo bulges and other bulkheads were necessary to protect the subsurface hull. Shells aimed at this "soft" part of a warship would be ineffective, presumably because, on striking the water, they would be so greatly reduced in velocity as to cause little damage. But during the firing tests on the *Tosa* in the summer and fall of 1924, ordnance officers found that a 16-inch shell fired at 20,000 meters and entering the water 25 meters in front of the target penetrated the hull below the armor, easily passed through the torpedo bulges, and burst in the engineering spaces, causing great damage (fig. 8-8).[43] Later tests showed that a properly designed shell—one with a flat head—could hit the water as far as 80 meters short of the target and still penetrate the hull as long as it entered the water at the optimum angle of 17 degrees. At 40 meters the underwater trajectory was best, and damage at a maximum.[44] Higher angles of incidence, up to 25 degrees, also allowed effective hits if no more than 20 to 25 meters short (fig. 8-9). As a result of these and later tests, the type 91 AP shell was designed as a dual-purpose projectile. If it fell on armor, it was capped to penetrate; if it fell on water, the windshield and cap would be torn off and the shell, now flat-ended, would follow a smooth and shallow submarine trajectory to the enemy ship's hull. Japanese fire control doctrine came to stress the desirability of getting short misses (rather than over misses), if not direct hits, since gunnery specialists believed that such misses would actually be hits. Type 91 shells would penetrate the hull and cause grave damage. Even plowing under an enemy ship, they would explode under the keel because the time-delay fuse would have been activated at the instant of impact with the water. The mining effect of the detonating shell would thus buckle the keel and cause even greater damage than a penetrating shot. The technique and results achieved by these *suichūdan* (underwater shots) were quickly classified as top secret, particularly since navy men believed that the tactic would be an important advantage for the Japanese battle line once it closed range for the annihilation of the American battle force.[45] There were, however, some major shortcomings in this technique. In the first place, as it was top secret, it was never practiced in peacetime training. Second, such shots were not effective unless fired at a range of about 20,000 meters for large guns and about 18,000 meters for 20-centimeter guns.[46]

American naval technicians are skeptical that even if the Japanese navy had used the "underwater shot" method, it would have achieved much success. The shell's long fuse delay was a major defect; it allowed time for the underwater trajectory but caused shells that hit the target ship directly to pass through it without exploding.[47] The U.S. Naval Technical Mission sent to Japan after the war concluded that the Japanese "sacrificed the effectiveness of their AP projectiles on occasions of direct hitting (particularly against large cruisers) in order to achieve a doubtful hit through the water or a mining effect, for which the AP shell is singularly poorly designed."[48] In the 1930s, however, American designers became aware of the danger of

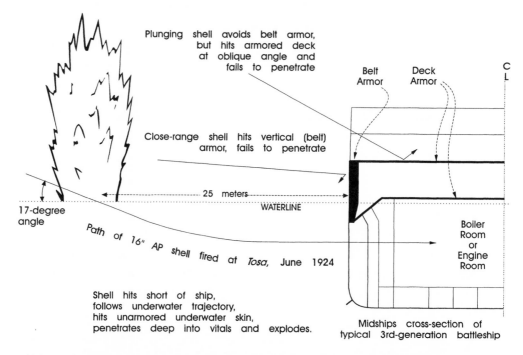

Mark A. Campbell

Fig. 8-8. The advantage of underwater attack. (Based on diagram in *KH*, 46)

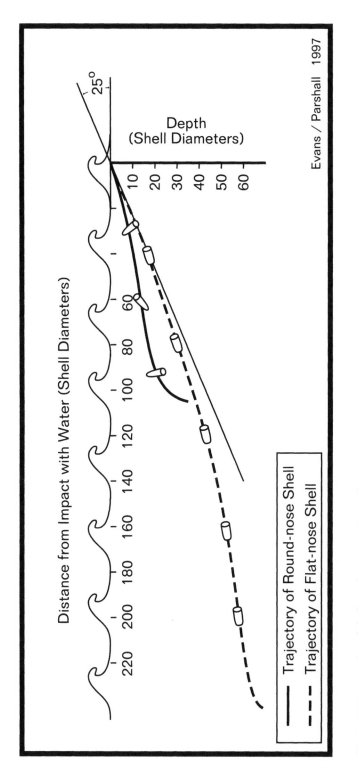

Fig. 8-9. Trajectories of shells underwater. (From diagram in *KH*, 46)

underwater hits (though apparently unaware of the Japanese shell) and applied special armor patches to the battleship *North Carolina* to defend against them. The battleships of the later *South Dakota, Iowa,* and *Montana* classes were all designed to resist underwater shell hits.[49] If evidence of underwater hits by the Japanese in the Pacific War is scant, the reason is that there were few gun battles at the required ranges. At the Battle of Cape Esperance in October 1942, the U.S. cruiser *Boise* was holed 9 feet below the waterline by a Japanese shell, with near-fatal results. There is, as well, evidence from the famous battleship encounter of May 1941 in the Atlantic. Both *Prince of Wales* and *Bismarck* may have been damaged by opposing underwater shots. According to a recent authoritative study, "the fatal shell hit to the *Hood* could have come from a shell with such a trajectory."[50]

THE OXYGEN TORPEDO AND LONG-RANGE CONCEALED FIRING

As noted, after the big gun, the torpedo had traditionally been the Japanese navy's weapon of choice, a preference reinforced by the limitations on heavy ordnance after the Washington Treaty. But unless torpedo attacks were restricted to night operations, the losses incurred by torpedo flotillas would be prohibitive. Although the navy was constantly involved in rigorous training in night torpedo attacks to increase the likelihood of their success, a system that would enable Japanese destroyers and cruisers to fire torpedoes at long range during either daylight or nighttime hours would obviously be a great tactical advance. By the second half of the 1930s, the Japanese navy believed it had hit upon just such a system and the weapon that would make it work: the oxygen torpedo.[51]

Most torpedoes were powered by steam engines that ran on a mixture of compressed air, fuel, and water (flashed into steam) from a combustion chamber. Using oxygen in place of air allowed a considerable weight saving that could be used for extra range or an increased payload in a torpedo of a given size. Also, the oxygen torpedo's combustion products—carbon dioxide, carbon monoxide, and water—are highly soluble in water, making it a wakeless torpedo. (The nitrogen in the exhaust of a conventional torpedo produced a visible wake.) This much had been known to the world's navies for some time, and indeed, both the British and the Americans had experimented with oxygen or oxygen-enriched torpedoes over a considerable period, but eventually dropped the project as unworkable.[52]

The rejection of the oxygen torpedo by the United States and Great Britain is easy to understand. Pure oxygen reacts spontaneously and very energetically with many materials, particularly hydrocarbons (e.g., oils and greases), and the reaction may be explosive. Pure oxygen is thus very dangerous in the shipboard environment and particularly so in torpedoes. The confined spaces of a torpedo require small-radius bends in all piping, including pipes supplying oxygen to the combustion chamber. Such bends and any form of surface roughness on the interior of the oxygen tubes impedes the flow. This local slowing causes compression and heating of the oxygen. In extreme cases, the temperature can be sufficient to oxidize metal chips or a rough surface. The real danger, however, is that the oxygen pipes may contain residual oil or grease that would ignite spontaneously when exposed to pure oxygen even at low temperature. The combination of very careful polishing and cleaning during manufacture would minimize this problem. The difficulty of lubricating the moving parts of an oxygen torpedo poses problems for exactly similar reasons.[53]

The Japanese began experimenting with oxygen-driven torpedoes about 1924, but gave up after numerous explosions and failures. Then, in 1927, an eight-man Japanese naval delegation went to the Whitehead Torpedo Works at Weymouth to study and buy a regular version of the Whitehead torpedo. While there, they believed that they had stumbled onto evidence that the Royal Navy was secretly experimenting with oxygen torpedoes. Although they were mistaken, the Japanese delegation was so impressed with the information they had gathered that they sent an extensive report back to Tokyo in 1928. By the end of that year, intensive research and experimentation had begun at the Kure Naval Arsenal on a workable oxygen torpedo. Starting in 1932, this effort was led by Capt. Kishimoto Kaneharu. [54]

Step by step, Captain Kishimoto and his colleagues began to attack the problems inherent in the design of such a weapon. Explosions were minimized by using natural air at the start of the engine's ignition, and oxygen was let in gradually to replace it. The men also took certain precautions to avoid contact between the oxygen and lubricants used in the torpedo's machinery. Particular care was given to the fuel lines. They were cleaned with a potassium compound to eliminate oil and grease and were redesigned to round out all sharp angles, and their linings were finely ground to eliminate all tiny pits where any residual oxygen, oil, or grease could accumulate.[55] The first test firings of the system, incorporating an engine of standard Whitehead design but using oxygen in place of air, were successfully carried out in 1933. That year, the navy formally designated the weapon as the type 93 torpedo, which has become known in the West as the "long-lance" torpedo.[56]

The first trials of the complete torpedo from the cruiser *Chōkai* at the Yokosuka Torpedo School demonstrated that the navy had indeed produced a formidable new weapon. A very large torpedo, it weighed 2,700 kilograms (just short of 3 tons), had a diameter of 61 centimeters (24 inches), a length of some 9 meters, and a payload of nearly 500 kilograms (over 1,000 pounds) of explosive in its warhead. It was capable of speeds up to 48 knots and ranges of up to 40,000 meters, depending on the combination of speed and range desired. (For speed and range combinations, and for comparison with the standard U.S. Navy torpedo, see figure 8-11). The torpedo left practically no visible wake.[57]

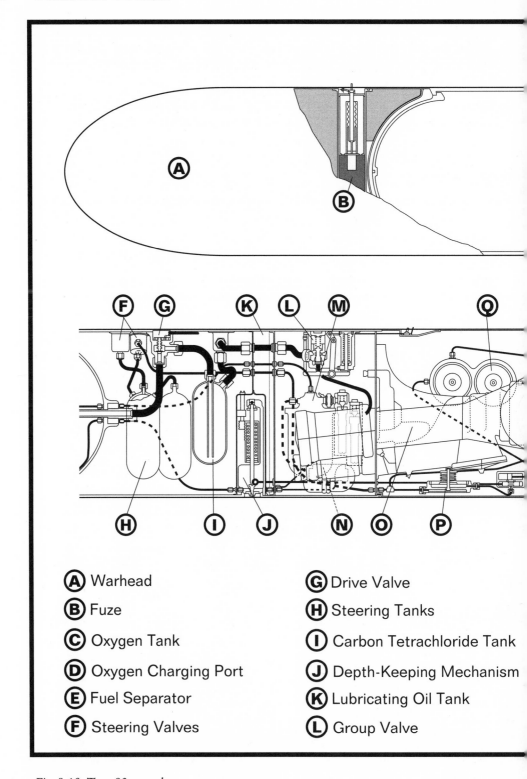

Fig. 8-10. Type 93 torpedo.

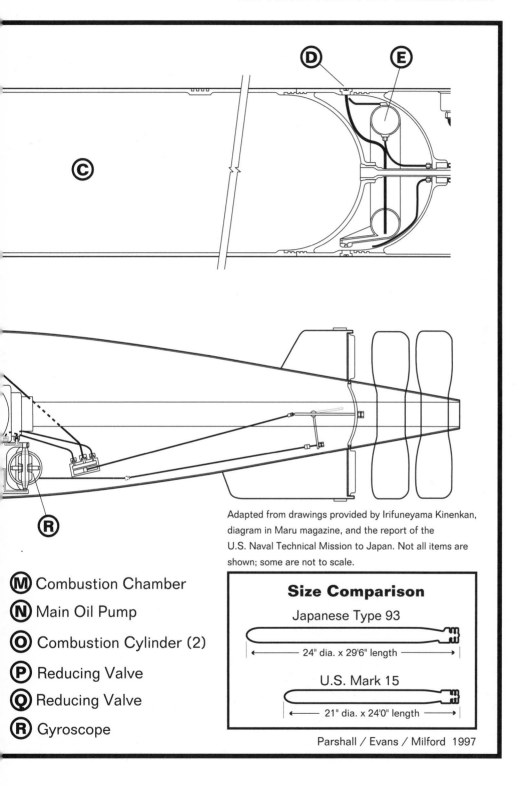

Adapted from drawings provided by Irifuneyama Kinenkan,
diagram in Maru magazine, and the report of the
U.S. Naval Technical Mission to Japan. Not all items are
shown; some are not to scale.

Ⓜ Combustion Chamber

Ⓝ Main Oil Pump

Ⓞ Combustion Cylinder (2)

Ⓟ Reducing Valve

Ⓠ Reducing Valve

Ⓡ Gyroscope

Size Comparison

Japanese Type 93

← 24" dia. x 29'6" length →

U.S. Mark 15

← 21" dia. x 24'0" length →

Parshall / Evans / Milford 1997

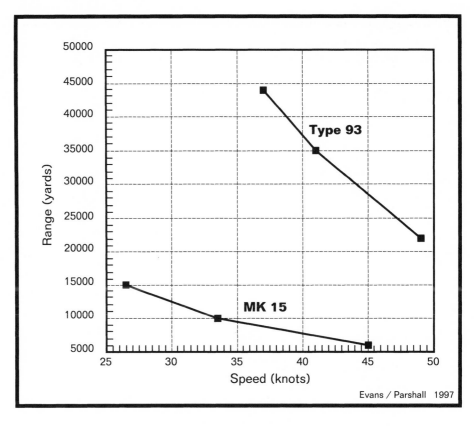

Fig. 8-11. Range and speed of IJN type 93 and USN MK 15 torpedoes.

In November 1935, the type 93 was adopted for surface use and was installed on A-class cruisers within three years. In 1940, an improved version was placed on the latest destroyers.[58] An aerial version of the torpedo, the type 94, and a submarine version, the type 95, adopted in 1935, were also developed, with varying degrees of success.[59] In view of the tremendous potential of the type 93, every precaution was taken to keep it secret. Even though in maneuvers the torpedoes were fired without warheads, recovery of every type 93 torpedo was obligatory after exercises at sea. One participant in such maneuvers recalled after the war that the entire fleet would comb the ocean to recover a stray torpedo and occasionally maneuvers were even canceled in bad weather for fear of losing one of the weapons.[60]

For the Japanese navy at the time, these precautions seemed only sensible since in speed, range, explosive power, and stealth, the type 93 was apparently the ideal weapon for outranging the American enemy. Exploiting the potential of the new weapon, Japanese naval tacticians now worked out a new torpedo tac-tic—*enkyori ommitsu hassha* (long-distance concealed firing)—which called for Japanese advance units, cruisers in particular, to be in contact with the enemy during daylight before he began to deploy for battle. Firing between 120 and 200 of the new wakeless torpedoes from a distance of at least 20,000 meters, the cruisers could deal the enemy a severe blow at the outset before he even knew he was in danger and before he even thought of evasive maneuver.[61] Japanese torpedo men assumed that in firing at such a range against moving targets, many torpedoes would go wide of the mark. Yet, if only 10 percent made hits against the enemy battle line, there would be between twelve and twenty hits on American capital ships and cruisers, throwing the foe into panic and confusion.[62] Such a prodigious expenditure of torpedoes would, of course, require commitment of a considerable number of lighter vessels. But in 1936, the idea gained currency that the same torpedo broadside could be achieved by refitting a number of the *Kuma*-class light cruisers as *jūrai sōkan* (torpedo cruisers), capable of firing 20 torpedoes at once. In any event, however, only two of the class, the *Ōi* and *Kitakami*, were so reconstructed, and their conversion was not begun until 1938.[63] Even before this, cruisers were counted upon to play a major role in both night combat and the decisive daylight fleet encounter.

With the advent of the type 93 torpedo and the concept of long-distance concealed firing, Japanese naval tacticians began to plan surface daylight torpedo warfare in two phases, beginning with long-range torpedo salvos by cruisers in the Japanese vanguard before general deployment of the fleet into battle formation,

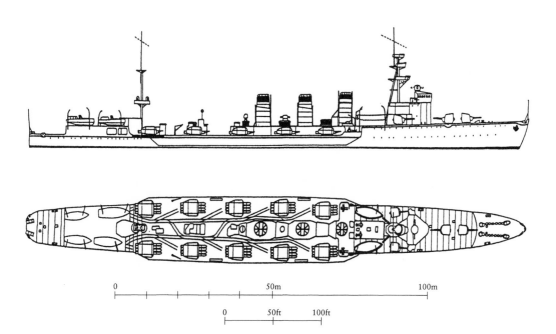

Fig. 8-12. The light cruiser *Kitakami* as converted to a torpedo cruiser.

followed by a close-in assault of torpedo (destroyer) flotillas. As it was recognized that both required a high degree of coordination by all elements of the fleet, from the main forces on down, torpedo training in the Japanese navy in the latter half of the 1930s meant not just practice in basic maneuvers and in technical skills in loading, aiming, and firing by individual ships attached to the torpedo forces, but also practice in "applied maneuvers" employing large formations in both day time and night combat. To insure that long-range torpedo firing would be entirely undetected by the enemy, various matters had to be considered, such as how to maneuver at the time of firing, the laying of smokescreens, beating back enemy cruiser groups, and preventing the possibility of an enemy withdrawal. All these problems were given detailed attention in repeated exercises.[64]

By the mid-1930s, the development of the type 93 torpedo and continued and rigorous practice in long-range torpedo operations gave the navy confidence that in cruiser-versus-cruiser encounters, the torpedo would be decisive. Japanese cruisers would be heavily armed with this weapon, and Japanese doctrine emphasized its dominance. During the same period, the U.S. Navy held to quite a different principle: the primacy of long-range gunfire. Lacking information on either Japanese torpedoes or torpedo tactics, American tacticians conducting the war games at Newport, Rhode Island, in these years mistakenly assumed that torpedoes would be ineffective in a long-range gunnery duel. Similar conclusions among American theoreticians that the torpedo was essentially a destroyer weapon, not appropriate for cruisers, had led the U.S. Navy to remove torpedo mounts from all its cruisers by mid-decade. This was a serious mistake. The differences in cruiser doctrine and weapons configuration largely accounted for the series of Japanese victories in the cruiser battles during the first year of the Pacific War.[65]

MIDGET SUBMARINES

The Japanese navy was perfecting another "secret weapon" and another tactic in the belief that they would provide Japan with an early advantage over the numerically superior American fleet. The first involved a new type of submarine, small and inexpensive, but with a high underwater sprint speed, which could be used in sizable numbers, either to attack the main American battle fleet or to blockade enemy bases. Under the leadership of Capt. Kishimoto Kaneharu, who had directed the effort on the oxygen torpedo, in the mid-1930s the navy began experimenting at the Submarine Section of the Kure Naval Yard with these midget submarines.

From its beginnings in a special closed shop at Kure, the project was pursued in the closest secrecy. During the design and construction of the first prototypes in 1934, they were innocuously referred to in all documents as "Metal Fittings *(kanamono)*, Type A." After prototypes underwent extensive testing in 1934–35, finally, in 1939–40, thirty-six "A"-class production models of these small, cigar-shaped submersibles were built at a special factory at Ōurazaki on Kurahashijima, just south of Kure. These boats, displacing 46 tons and manned by a two-man crew, were armed with two 45-centimeter torpedo tubes and were driven by bat-tery-powered engines that could propel them for fifty minutes underwater at 19 knots or for thirteen hours on the surface at 6 knots. Once they joined the fleet they were still kept under wraps. It was hoped that their small size, shape, and cover designation *(kō hyōteki*—"A" target) would so effectively disguise their purpose that the uninitiated would believe them to be target boats to be used by submarines in firing practice.[66]

Initially, these submarines were to be carried into a forward area by special tenders. The seaplane carriers *Chitose* and *Chiyoda* were converted for this pur-pose by the end of 1940; their sister ships the *Mizuho* (completed in 1939) and the *Nisshin* (1942) were built as midget tenders.[67] Each ship could carry twelve midget submarines. The tenders would sail toward the decisive battle area and, before reaching it, release their forty-eight midget subs, armed with a total of ninety-six torpedoes, for an attack on the main American fleet.[68] Thus, while other nations developed midgets for local defense and special operations, only the Japanese developed them for offensive use in main-force battle. Right before the war, more-over, the navy began contemplating use of these tiny submersibles in attacks far into enemy waters; J submarines were refitted to carry and launch them close to American bases.[69]

NIGHT COMBAT

By the mid-1930s, therefore, the Japanese navy had planned or had in place sev-eral technological and tactical innovations—the 8-inch-gun cruiser, the heavy destroyer, the oxygen torpedo, long-range concealed firing, underwater shots, the torpedo cruiser, and midget submarines—designed to make up for the navy's infe-riority in heavy ordnance imposed by the naval limitation treaties. At the same time, the Navy General Staff was constantly reviewing the scenario for the deci-sive fleet engagement, not only in light of Japan's own technological and tactical development, but also in light of what was known about the current strength of the U.S. Navy.

These reviews led to the general staff's renewed emphasis on night combat.[70] Throughout most of the 1920s, the staff had regarded night operations preceding the decisive daylight encounter as the province of the navy's lighter forces, in par-ticular the torpedo flotillas, whose task would be to cripple the enemy's battle line to leave it vulnerable to the coup de grâce by Japan's own battleships and battle

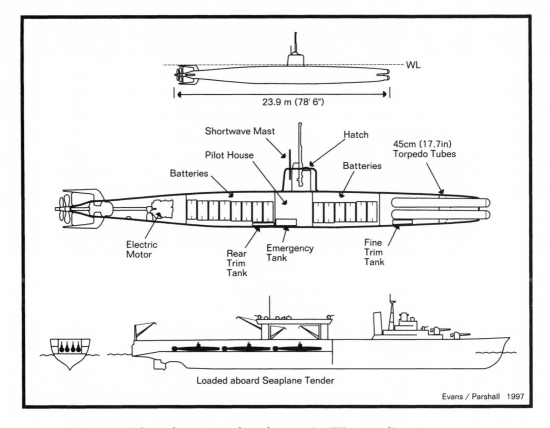

Fig. 8-13. Midget submarines and seaplane carrier. WL, water line.

cruisers. The fourth revision of the Battle Instructions had held that these heavier units were not to be committed to night combat, partly to avoid revealing the position of the main force until the last possible moment, and partly because the numerical size of the main force would make it difficult to maneuver at night. Up until the 1930s night operations were seen, therefore, as only the prelude to decisive naval combat. By the beginning of that decade, however, several developments had caused the general staff to place new emphasis on such operations.[71]

The first development was the increasing strength of the United States in heavy cruisers, particularly the six ships of the powerful *Northampton* class, whose imminent completion would so formidably strengthen the American "ring formation" that the Japanese navy would have to find means to disrupt it during the hours of darkness. The other development was the Japanese navy's increasing ability to detect enemy warships during night hours through the acquisition of superior visual equipment.

As already mentioned, Japanese progress in optics greatly advanced their submarine development. Prior to World War I, the navy had relied completely on imported optical equipment, since Western nations were ahead in this field. After the war, however, following a brief venture by the navy in the design and manufacture of optical equipment, Japanese private industry began to supply the navy with all its needs.[72] During the 1920s and 1930s, the Japan Optical Company, Limited (Nippon Kōgaku K.K.) produced a steady stream of optical devices— range finders, binoculars, periscopes, and aiming telescopes—that were among the world's finest. Particularly noteworthy were binoculars of powerful magnification and light-gathering capacity, featuring lenses as large as 21 centimeters. Among the most popular were those with lenses of 12 centimeters. The type 88, Model 1, adopted in 1932, was considered especially effective in enhancing night vision. By the start of the 1930s, Japanese navy men believed that their optics were superior to those of other naval forces.[73]

New equipment for illumination also improved the nighttime identification of friend and foe. Up to World War I the navy had depended exclusively for this purpose upon searchlights that gave a steady and continuous beam but that revealed their points of origin and thus put at risk the ships that carried them. In 1921, experiments were undertaken with star shells designed to illuminate an enemy target from above. The initial ammunition of this type provided great illumination radius, but only for a very short time. These problems were essentially solved by the adoption, in 1935, of parachute-suspended star shells that proved highly effective in maneuvers. By the end of the decade, the Japanese navy thus had more powerful, more effective, and more dependable night fighting equipment than did any other navy in the world.[74] The great exception, of course, was radar (see chapter 11).

It was, therefore, for reasons of both necessity and capability that the Japanese navy began to consider deploying elements of the main fleet in night actions. Cruisers and destroyers, of course, would still be the principal warships to undertake these operations, but they would be organized into more powerful night combat forces than heretofore. To each torpedo flotilla was added at least one division of heavy cruisers that would add punch to the destroyer forces, assisting them in penetrating the enemy's center. Such a force would now make up a *yasengun* (night combat group), four of which would be formed in wartime. But the navy now placed such importance on night combat that it determined to assemble an organization of capital ships capable of keeping up with the night combat groups and lending them big gun firepower. Constrained by treaty from building any new battleships for this purpose, the navy turned to its *Kongō*-class battle cruisers. These had, in 1927–32, already undergone major improvements in strengthened deck armor, increased maximum elevation of main batteries, addition of torpedo bulges, and provision of floatplanes. Over a seven-year period (1933–40), three of this class, the *Kongō, Haruna,* and *Kirishima,* were rearmed and reconstructed as fast battleships.[75] New oil-fired Kampon boilers and new Kampon turbines more than doubled their horsepower; these additions, along with the lengthening and reshaping of their sterns, increased their speed from 26 to 30.5 knots. Other improvements included new fire control systems and improvements of the secondary batteries. Formerly the main force of the Second Fleet, these ships now became the Third Division of the First or Battle Fleet. In their place, most of the heavy cruisers recently completed or nearing completion were assigned to the Second Fleet, whose commander now became responsible for night combat operations.[76]

While the navy had begun to acquire sufficiently powerful warships and to organize the most appropriate battle groups for night combat, the proper deployment of such forces and the timing of such operations in relation to the decisive daylight encounter remained matters of heated debate on the Navy General Staff and at the Naval Staff College from 1934 onward. A major feature of the fifth revision of the Battle Instructions in 1934 was the prominent place given to night battle. The instructions specifically underscored the importance of the destroyer (torpedo) flotillas as the main weapon in night combat and held that it was best to avoid employing capital ships in those operations, though the document also spoke vaguely of the role of the navy's battle cruisers (soon to be fast battleships) in repelling the enemy's guard forces and "promoting the forward movement of friendly cruiser and destroyer flotillas." The 1934 Battle Instructions, on the other hand, called for a twilight attack, followed by night combat with all forces, if visibility allowed, and culminating in the grand finale the next morning. There had even been serious discussion of a *hakubo kessen* (decisive twilight battle). But by 1935, Japanese doctrine about night combat became a good deal more cautious, leaving open the matter of night attack by main battle units.[77]

In any event, it is clear that by 1936 the Japanese navy considered night operations not as a mere preliminary skirmishing, but as a large-scale introduction to the decisive battle. That year had seen the formation of a new and much larger force, the Yasen Butai (Night Battle Force), also designated the Zenshin Butai (Advance Force), which broadly corresponded to the Second Fleet. The force would also incorporate all the night combat groups, thereby employing all heavy cruiser divisions and torpedo flotillas of the First and Second Fleets, supported by the fast battleship division. The principal task of the Night Battle Force was to break through the outer defense ring of the American fleet, so that the torpedo flotillas could deliver the main torpedo assault against the enemy battle line. During 1936, this general scenario of night combat was made the focus of the annual maneuvers of the Combined Fleet, which the newly reconstructed fast battleships *Haruna* and *Kirishima* had by then rejoined.[78]

In setting the doctrine for night combat in the mid-1930s, the Navy General Staff envisaged several scenarios. One such scenario gives the reader a sense of the pace and phasing of that doctrine.[79] To begin with, three prerequisites were deemed essential for a Japanese night offensive against the main force of the enemy: first, the enemy main force should be sighted by sundown; second, Japanese forces should be within 60 kilometers (about 33 miles) of that force (so that Japanese units could catch the enemy by midnight even if he made an effort to withdraw); and third, Japanese units should keep in contact with the enemy by any means possible, even by noncommittal skirmishing if need be, to determine the enemy's course and speed.

Upon sighting the enemy, the Japanese force was to abandon its search formations, and the Japanese Night Combat Force commander would immediately order all units into predetermined positions for encirclement (fig. 8-15), seeking to avoid observation by enemy screening forces while doing so. Once the commander had determined that all units were in position, he would order long-range concealed torpedo firing by the torpedo cruisers and by all cruiser divisions except the Fourth. A cross-weave of 130 torpedoes, virtually wakeless, would now be streaking toward the enemy. After having received firing reports from all units, the commander would then order, "close the range and prepare for attack." To prevent the Americans from reversing course, the Fourth Cruiser Division would divide into two halves, moving into positions obliquely astern of the port and starboard sides of the enemy's rearmost ships, which the Japanese would keep illuminated by searchlights and star shells. At the command *"zengun totsugeki"* ("all forces attack"), the night combat forces would work together in an all-out assault, guided by aircraft reports of enemy movement, parachute flares above the enemy capital ships, and floating flares dropped ahead of the enemy course. Within a few moments of this order, the mass of torpedoes fired earlier would now converge from two directions and begin to explode against the hulls of the enemy. Estimating the proportion of on-target torpedoes as low as 15 percent, the general staff was confident that some 20 torpedoes would strike home and at least ten ships of the enemy's inner ring would be destroyed or damaged.

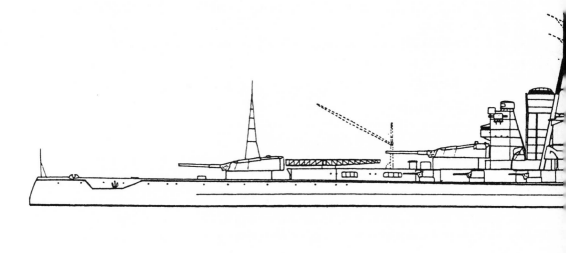

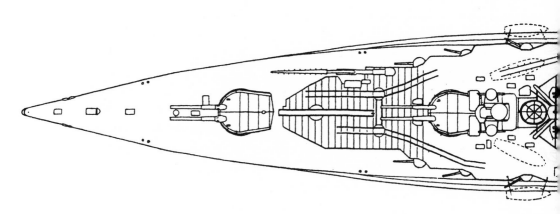

Fig. 8-14. The fast battleship *Kongō* after conversion, 1937.

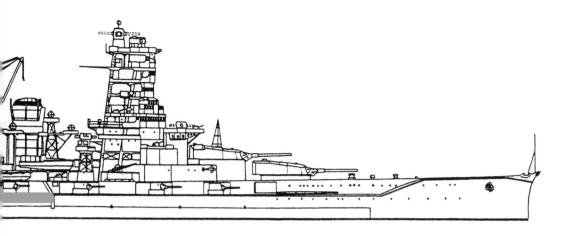

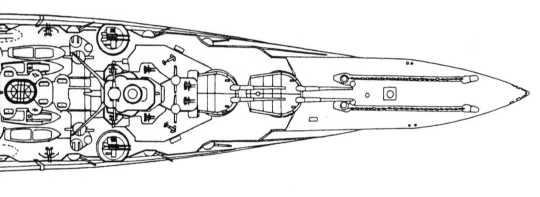

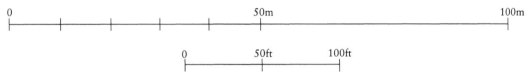

The heavy cruisers, including those of the Fourth Division, along with the fast battleships, would now race forward to crash through the American inner ring, making every effort to insure the success of the torpedo flotillas, even at the risk of sacrificing themselves. The final stage of the action, the most critical moment of the night engagement, would be the assault of the torpedo flotillas, conducted, ideally, in unison by all the destroyer forces. It was to be carried out by the destroyers led by light cruisers in the traditional "close in, strike home" manner, the divisions taking 2,000 meters as their standard distance for aiming and firing. After the initial attack, the division flagships were to collect the destroyers, which were in the process of reloading, to launch successive attacks until all the destroyer torpedoes were exhausted.[80]

The entire night action described, from initial deployment into encircling formation to the end of the operations of the torpedo flotillas, was expected to take three hours. The Navy General Staff recognized, however, that circumstances might drastically alter the sequence or timing of the action. While it was planned as an offensive under the firm control of the night combat commander, should conditions change, the general staff expected commanders of subordinate fleet elements to make the most of whatever fleeting opportunities the battle might present.

To the student of Western naval tactics, two things are striking about this plan. The first is the complexity of the initial long-range torpedo attacks that were designed to catch the American main force in a cross-weave of torpedo tracks. The other is that in this tactical scheme, major units—heavy cruisers and even battleships—were to be sacrificed to the mission of the destroyers, a stunning reversal of Western tactical doctrine in which destroyers were traditionally seen as expendable and heavier ships were to be protected at all costs.[81]

Notably, no elements of the main Japanese battle force were included in the plan. By 1936, the general staff had come to the conclusion that the main force should not participate in night actions other than in the most exceptional circumstances, such as the success of the Night Combat Force on so great a scale that it only needed the participation of the main fleet elements to insure the utter destruction of the American main force. In that case, the Japanese Night Combat Force would persist in its attacks and the Japanese main force would not wait for a daylight encounter, but would join the fray, annihilating the enemy's remaining units. But usually, the main force should maneuver away from the scene of the night action and prepare to fight at dawn. If necessary, some units of the Night Combat Force should be held back to reinforce it. If the overall commander in chief decided to engage the enemy at dawn, the Night Combat Force would gradually withdraw from battle about three hours before sunrise. An hour before daybreak, however, it would have to be back with the main force as part of the daylight battle formation.[82]

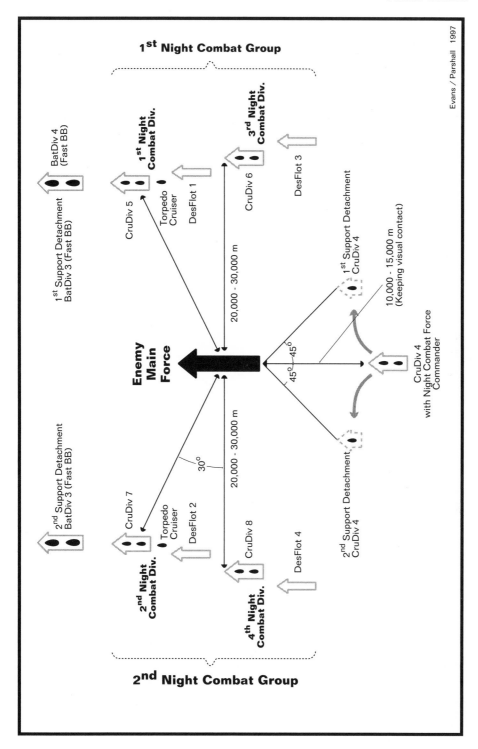

Fig. 8-15. Example of disposition for encirclement in night attack, mid-1930s. (Based on diagram in *KS*, 509)

THE DAYLIGHT FLEET ENGAGEMENT

While Japanese tacticians in the mid-1930s believed that an aggressively pressed night action might send an enemy reeling and would open the way to victory, the navy's orthodoxy still held that battleship main batteries would have to fight the decisive fleet engagement. The revised Battle Instructions of 1934 left no doubt on this score: "The battleship divisions are the main weapon in a fleet battle and their task is to engage the main force of the enemy."[83]

It was therefore the battleships that were to break the back of the enemy, opening fire at a distance at which the Americans would be outranged. Once the enemy line had been weakened, they would close in for the annihilating battle. But it would be other forces, properly coordinated with the battle fleet, that would cripple the enemy in the early stages of the encounter. At any cost, naval air units were to establish air superiority before the outset of any action, even to the point of one-way strikes of aircraft to ensure that the enemy would be outranged and the predetermined sacrifice of carriers to ensure the destruction of their American counterparts.[84] Cruisers and destroyers were to assist the battle line offensively with powerful torpedo attacks, first at extreme distance, before the Americans would suspect that they were within range, and later at close range. Fleet submarines, stalking the enemy fleet well before the main action began, would plunge in to assist other forces with their torpedoes, and midget submarines would be released at the critical moment to surround the American battle line.

These, in brief, were the principal elements in the plans of the Navy General Staff for the decisive daylight battle. Today, it is difficult to describe it in exacting detail, for the existing documentation is inadequate. What records are still available often avoid critical specifics and make only vague references to "attacking appropriately" or "maneuvering in response to the situation." In particular, information is wanting as to how, precisely, the Japanese fleet was to get into position before the battle. With the records that do exist, however, at least the outline of a scenario for the decisive daylight engagement can be constructed. What follows is a composite for such a plan, drawn from several sources.[85]

Apparently, the Japanese main battle force was to consist of six battleships that would be divided into two battleship divisions: the First, composed of the two *Nagato*-class battleships, and the Second, comprising the *Fusō* and *Ise* classes. These heavy units would be accompanied by one or two divisions of cruisers and two torpedo flotillas of destroyers. The vanguard force would be composed of four fast battleships of the *Kongō* class, as well as three to four divisions of heavy cruisers, two torpedo flotillas, and two torpedo cruisers.

Aircraft carriers, operating at a considerable distance from the main force, would have the task of achieving air superiority before the fleet action could begin. Deployed singly and widely separated, "so as to surround the enemy" *(hōi suru gotoku haibi suru),* they would launch their aircraft against the American carriers before they came within range of enemy planes. To do this, the Navy General Staff assumed that their aircraft would need a range advantage of 150 miles. If planes with this capability were not already operational with the fleet, then extreme measures would have to be taken with available aircraft: reduction of ordnance loads, refueling en route, or launching one-way air strikes with the hope that aircrews could be rescued after ditching.[86]

Once air superiority was achieved, the Japanese fleet would assume a course roughly parallel to, slightly ahead of, and about 40,000 meters distant from the American battle line. The commander in chief would issue a preliminary order for deployment *(tenkei yorei),* specifying the battle formation and compass heading to be assumed for the attack. The vanguard, some 20,000 meters in advance of the main force, would then receive the order for long-distance firing of torpedoes. Its fast battleships would close the enemy's advance guard and attack with their guns. This action, presumably, would open a corridor between the enemy's battleships and the vanguard's heavy cruisers, torpedo cruisers, and destroyers. In this situation, some 35,000 meters ahead and to one side of the lead American battleships, the Japanese torpedo cruisers and destroyers would supposedly be in an optimum position to launch torpedoes at the American battle line, whose big guns still could not reach them. Taking advantage of the opening provided, the cruisers and destroyers would launch a total of 280 torpedoes in two salvos. The navy staff considered that this devastating thrust would be concealed in several ways: The gunfire of the fast battleships would divert the attention of the enemy from the torpedo salvos; fleet units could make smoke to hide the launching of the torpedoes; and the Americans, having no knowledge of the type 93 torpedo, would not expect a torpedo attack at such extreme range. Moreover, the navy staff assumed that the Japanese main force would have little to fear from American torpedoes. Correctly calculating that the American advance force had little capacity for torpedo attack, the staff believed that the enemy would confine itself to forming a defensive screen for the main battle line.

As the torpedoes sped toward their targets, the Japanese fleet would take up its final disposition for the gun battle (fig. 8-16). The fast battleships, cruisers, and destroyers would fall back to a position ahead and to the engaged side of the main battle force, some 10,000 meters from it. The cruisers and destroyers of the main force would also shift position, taking up station to the rear and on the engaged side to prevent the American fleet from reversing course and escaping from the torpedo trap.

The staff plans assumed that Japanese torpedoes would begin to strike the oncoming American heavy ships about twenty minutes after the vanguard fired its

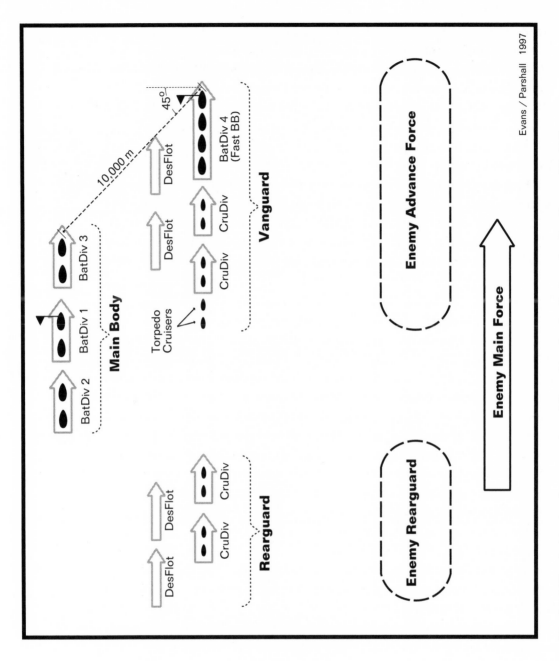

Fig. 8-16. The decisive battle: one version of disposition for the final gun battle. (Source: KS, 505)

torpedo salvos. At that moment, Japanese battleships, having approached to within 35,000 meters of the American battle line, would open up with their main batteries. Using aircraft as spotters, the *Nagato* and her sister ship, the *Mutsu*, could inflict significant damage, the navy staff concluded, starting at 35,000 to 34,000 meters, while the American battle line would not be able to respond until about 31,000 meters, the assumed range of the *Colorado* class.

At this point, the staff planners believed, the combination of torpedo hits and gunfire would begin to inflict enormous damage on the enemy. They estimated that Japanese torpedoes alone would cripple or sink about ten U.S. capital ships. Japanese gunfire, assumed to be more accurate, would extend this toll. Once the American fleet was thrown into confusion, the Japanese battle line would close to approximately 22,000 to 19,000 meters—the optimum range for underwater shots from Japanese 16- and 8-inch guns—and from that distance would hurl down its final blows upon the enemy. In this coup de grâce they would be assisted by Japanese supporting forces. Cruisers would blast open a path for the destroyers, which would then race in against the enemy in a furious, if sacrificial attack, launching their remaining torpedoes at ranges of less than 5,000 meters. In theory, each destroyer division should be able to take out at least one enemy battleship. Therefore, if all the destroyers—forty-eight ships in four torpedo flotillas—were thrown against the enemy, they should be able to sink sixteen American capital ships.

In the midst of this fierce surface battle, submarines would also come into action. Three fast submarine tenders would dash ahead of the enemy fleet and release their load of twelve midget submarines. These tiny submersibles would then submerge and await the arrival of the American battle line. At that point, using their considerable underwater speed, they would unleash their torpedoes, a total of seventy-two from all these small craft. Fleet submarines would also concentrate at the scene of battle and carry out torpedo attacks on the enemy.

The Navy General Staff also worked out a scheme for an alternative to the scenario outlined above, in case the Japanese could not outrange the enemy at the outset of battle. This was the "Z" tactic, which called for Japanese battleships to take up a position parallel to the American battle line and distant about 31,000 meters, judged to be the limit of the American main battery range.

Destroyers from the Japanese vanguard would run back down the Japanese line, laying a smokescreen to shield the entire Japanese force. A classic gun battle on parallel courses would then presumably ensue, the Japanese battleships slugging it out with the American, and the Japanese vanguard and rearguard, from positions slightly to the engaged side at 28,000 meters, firing on their opposite numbers. Japanese aircraft would also make smoke, flying through the center of the American formation to throw it into disorder (fig. 8-17).[87]

Reflecting on the Navy General Staff plans some sixty years later, one is struck by two glaring defects: their complexity and their optimistic assumptions about the enemy's dispositions. Although other navies of the interwar period had a similar tendency to work out elaborate tactical schemes,[88] Japanese battle scenarios seem to have surpassed all others in their intricacy. Japanese planners clearly indulged in wishful thinking about the degree of precise timing and coordination that the navy's forces could achieve in carrying out these complicated movements. Moreover, staff tacticians made surprisingly naive assumptions that the American enemy would passively stand by while the Japanese tactics unfolded. In reality, the U.S. battle line would hardly steam obligingly into the Japanese trap, and American precautions would make it extremely difficult for Japanese forces to achieve the correct positioning beforehand. American plans of the 1930s, for example, called for pickets as far out as 75–100 miles from the fleet center (fig. 8-18).[89] A few Japanese navy officers noted and disparaged this tendency toward self-deluding formalism in the evolution of Japanese strategy and tactics. After the Pacific War, Hori Teikichi, a prominent officer of the period, recalled that map maneuvers and plans of operation against the United States always assumed that the enemy would act according to predetermined conventions.[90]

Less obvious today is that even as these plans were drawn up, the Japanese navy was unready to carry them out. Some weapons to be employed in the battle, such as the midget submarines, were still under development.[91] Moreover, the intricate combinations of fleet elements called for by the tacticians had not been tested in fleet exercises. Yet the tradition of heaven-sent victory exemplified by the Battle of the Japan Sea evidently exerted a powerful influence on Japanese planners. Some planners took an almost mystical approach to the probability of success in the great sea battle and, sweeping aside the practical difficulties, apparently assumed that *ten'yū* (the grace of heaven) would once again provide the right conditions for victory.

JAPANESE NAVAL STRATEGY, 1930–35
From Close-in to Distant Defense

These tactical scenarios took place, of course, within the wider context of Japanese strategic planning for a possible Japan-U.S. war. In 1930, tacticians still planned on an essentially close-in defense predicated on the assumption that the American expeditionary force would move into the western Pacific across one or the other of two central routes. The planning was centered on the strategy of interception and attrition to reduce the enemy's numbers before the decisive battle. In that year, a Navy General Staff plan called for the distribution of the most powerful Japanese warships over two fleets, the First and the Second.[92] The First Fleet,

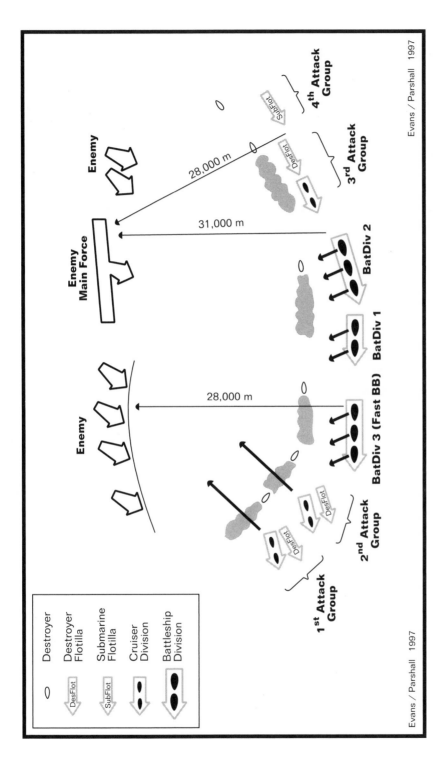

Fig. 8-17. The "Z" tactic: making smoke in the decisive battle. From a Naval Staff College study of 1936. (Source: *KG1*, 173)

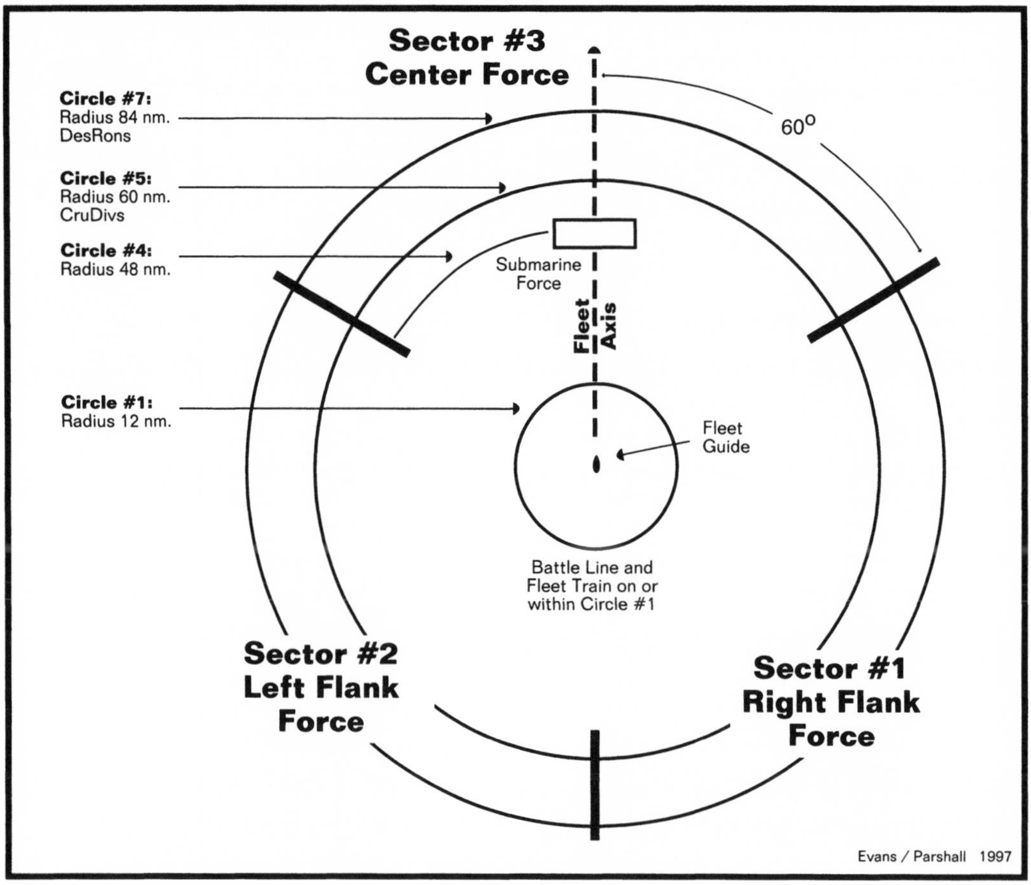

Fig. 8-18. U.S. Navy circle formation, 1934 (cruising disposition no. 3V). This formation was a disposition "suitable to obtain early information of the approach of hostile aircraft." It was considered "not suitable for other purposes." The number of screening vessels available and weather conditions determined the radii of the circles of the screen, but it was considered desirable that the radius of the outermost pickets be from 75 to 100 miles.
(Source: U.S. Navy, Chief of Naval Operations, *General Tactical Instructions, United States Navy. Fleet Tactical Publication Number 142,* Washington, D.C.: U.S. Government Printing Office, 1934)

or "main force," would include all nine active battleships (the battle cruiser *Hiei* having been demilitarized under the terms of the London Treaty), two heavy (8-inch gun) cruisers, an aircraft carrier division (two carriers), plus two destroyer divisions and two submarine flotillas. The Second Fleet, or "advance force," would contain most of the heavy cruisers, two torpedo (destroyer) flotillas, and two submarine flotillas. At the outbreak of hostilities these two fleets would join to form the Combined Fleet, whose mission was to reduce and then defeat the enemy somewhere between the Ryukyu and Bonin Islands.

Most submarines of the First and Second Fleets would be positioned along a great curve stretching south from the Izu Islands and westward to the Marshall Islands to scout and attack the westward-advancing enemy. Behind this line, the Second Fleet and part of the First Fleet—including the two heavy cruisers, a carrier, and a destroyer flotilla—would be prepared to carry out night torpedo attacks east of the Bonins. Finally, the bulk of the First Fleet was to take up its station just east of the Ryukyus to await the showdown against the American main force, estimated to arrive at the decisive battle area about forty-five days (in a worst-case scenario) after the opening of hostilities. Presumably, the American force would be greatly reduced by the attrition operations of Japanese submarines and elements of the advance force.

Meanwhile, the Third Fleet, composed of light (6-inch gun) cruisers, a torpedo flotilla, and several submarine flotillas would sweep aside the Philippine-based American Asiatic Squadron, now rated as rather feeble, and go on to support the Japanese army landings in those islands. The navy estimated that these operations should be completed in about thirty days, time enough to allow the Third Fleet to steam northward to contribute to the final defeat of the enemy main force.

Throughout the 1920s, the Combined Fleet, as a tactical command, was assembled briefly once a year for the purpose of coordinating the two principal fleets during the annual grand maneuvers. For the rest of the year, it existed only on paper, for planning purposes. In the early 1930s, however, international tensions suddenly increased, as did the possibility that Japan might go to war with the United States. The navy decided that it was critical to operational planning to bring its peacetime fleet organization as much as possible into line with requirements of projected wartime operations. Thus, in 1933, for the first time since it had been disbanded by Tōgō in 1905, the Combined Fleet was established as a permanent force. The First Fleet commander served as commander in chief, in whose hands would rest decisions concerning the phasing and timing of the interception, attrition, and decisive battle phases of the Japanese strategy.[93]

By mid-decade, advances in naval technology, particularly in the ranges and capabilities of both aircraft and submarines, had begun to recast perceptions of American strategy, as well as the best means with which to counter it. Because

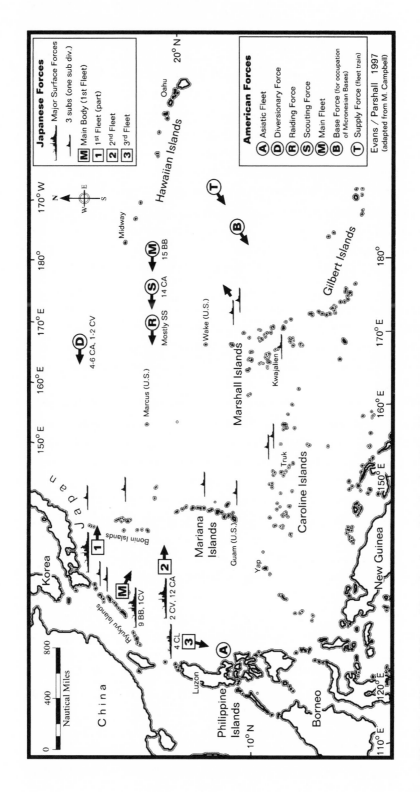

Map 8-1. IJN plan of dispositions for the decisive battle, 1925–30 (Source: *KG1*, 159)

land-based aircraft were now capable of well over a thousand miles, the Japanese navy became convinced that the American expeditionary force would attempt to establish island air bases at Wake Island, in the northern Marianas, in the Bonins, and in the Ryukyus. From there, the U.S. force could attack Japanese surface units and, eventually, the Japanese home islands themselves. Soon the conviction grew that the United States might try the most rapid and feasible means to launch a surprise attack by naval and air forces on the Japanese industrial and urban heartland (stretching from Tokyo to Kobe).[94] American submarines, too, were viewed as a direct threat to Japanese naval forces operating near the home islands. Japanese planners began to assume that U.S. boats would be capable of operating in Japanese waters where, positioned off Japanese ports and harbors, they would attempt to harass Japanese naval movements to and from those places.[95]

But if American aircraft and submarines could operate at far greater distances than those of a decade before, so too could their Japanese counterparts. Thus, at mid-decade, Japanese strategic planning, while still essentially defensive, began to take on a significant offensive coloration. The operational plan of 1935, for example, called for submarines of the First and Second Fleets to be sent at the outset of hostilities to Hawaii and the American west coast for offensive operations against American naval units. In 1936, plans were set afoot to organize a Fourth Fleet that would be sent to Micronesia to maintain reconnaissance of the enemy and to attack any forward bases the enemy might have established in the islands.[96] By that year, too, the navy had begun plans to base its new twin-engine Mitsubishi G3M Medium Bomber in Micronesia for offensive raids against enemy fleet units and advanced bases in that part of the Pacific.

The increasing emphasis on distant operations was meant to prevent the enemy from quickly bringing the war to Japan's doorstep. This emphasis also continually pushed eastward, in Japanese calculations, the locus of the projected theater of operations for the decisive battle. From about 1910 through the 1920s, the theater had been near the Ryukyus; in the early 1930s, just east of them; in the mid-1930s, somewhere on a line between the Bonins and the northern Marianas; and by 1940, it was placed as far east as the Marshall Islands (map 8-2).[97] But little attention was paid to the fleet train, oilers, supply ships, tugs, repair ships, and so on, required by the distances involved in this eastward shift in the site of the decisive battle.

New weapons and new strategies, particularly those involving naval aviation, thus influenced Japanese naval planning to defeat the American enemy. At mid-decade, however, Japanese naval orthodoxy still held that the final showdown with the American fleet could only be won by the principle of "big ships, big guns." To realize that principle, the Japanese navy now planned to build the biggest ships with the biggest guns that the world had ever seen.

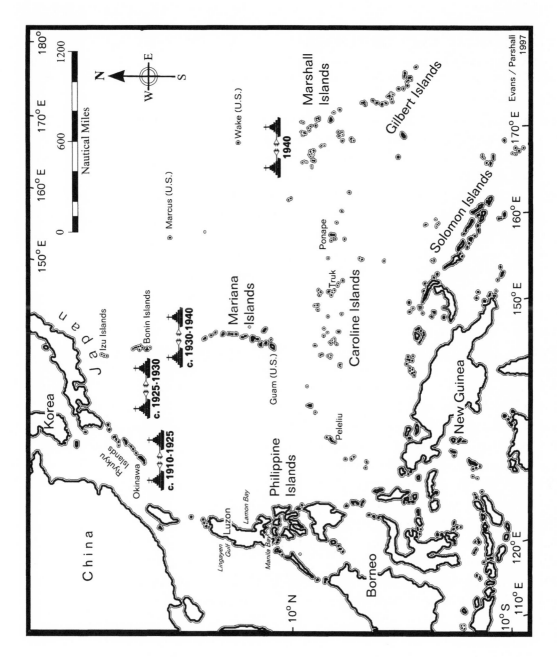

Map 8-2. Planned locations for the decisive battle, 1910–40

THE JAPANESE NAVY BIDS FOR SUPERIORITY
The Superbattleship Strategy

A remarkable feature of Japanese battle scenarios is that despite the navy's constant training and practice in naval combat, they remained largely theoretical. In fact, the Japanese navy never comprehensively and simultaneously tested the full range of coordinated operations in the twilight-night-daylight sequence of combat against the projected American enemy. The grand plan for the decisive battle had instead been largely worked out on the Naval Staff College's war-gaming tables and in the offices of the Navy General Staff, but the annual grand maneuvers of the Combined Fleet tested only discrete elements of these plans.[98]

The navy did not test the concept with comprehensive exercises, for several reasons. In addition to restrictions on fuel supplies—a problem that dogged the Imperial Japanese Navy from its beginnings until its end—there were limitations on new weapons systems, like the type 93 torpedo, which was not yet available to the fleet in any great numbers. Finally, at mid-decade, several weapons systems critical to the success of Japanese plans were either still in the planning stage or still under design or construction. The midget submarine would not be available in any numbers until the very end of the decade; only two of the four *Kongō*-class battle cruisers had been reconstructed as fast battleships; and the torpedo cruisers on which the navy counted heavily in its plans for long-range concealed firing would not be refitted until 1941. But the most important element in the navy's decisive battle scenario, which was as yet missing from its arsenal, was a new class of superbattleships mounting guns of unprecedented size that according to the Japanese tactical orthodoxy of the time, would demolish the American battle line while still out of the latter's range.

Japanese precedents for such enormous firepower went all the way back to the eight-eight fleet concept. In 1920, guns 48 centimeters (almost 19 inches) in caliber had actually been test fired, with the idea that they would be mounted in a new class of fast battleships that would complete the eight-eight fleet. Realization of these plans had been halted by the Washington Treaty, and for the rest of the decade the navy had been forced to abandon the means to outrange the enemy through bigger guns. But the treaty did not prohibit speculation and even *planning* for this purpose. Thus, early in the 1920s, on the assumption that the Washington Treaty would not be renewed once it expired in 1932, the navy had begun to consider plans for the replacement of the four *Kongō*-class battle cruisers. In 1930, it had reviewed various plans for four 35,000-ton battleships carrying 16-inch guns. Though Japan's participation in the London conference and its treaty had obliged the navy to discard these plans, that same year, it had begun to experiment with 18-inch ordnance. In 1933, under the cover of testing a 40-centimeter gun, the Kure Naval Arsenal actually produced several pieces of 18-inch caliber.[99] In October that same year, Comdr. Ishikawa Shingo, a former member of the Navy Technical Department and a rising star in the navy's virulently anti-treaty "Fleet Faction" of officers, submitted to Chief of Staff Fushimi a memorandum outlining his proposal for a ten-year naval construction plan based on the assumption that the limitations treaties would be terminated and Japan would find itself in an unchecked naval race.

The general thrust of Ishikawa's expansion plan was to reemphasize the decades-old Japanese inclination to achieve qualitative superiority over their competitors. Among the various recommendations he made, Ishikawa proposed the acquisition of four heavy cruisers, to be twice the size of existing ships of their type, carrying twelve 12-inch guns, protected by armor capable of withstanding hits from 8-inch shells, and capable of speeds up to 40 knots, specifications that would be nearly impossible to include in one design. But the centerpiece of his scheme was the construction of five superbattleships mounting 20-inch guns and provided with underwater protection sufficient to withstand ten torpedo hits. The acquisition of such firepower, Ishikawa pointed out, would enable the Japanese navy, in one mighty leap, to surge from a position of inferiority as compared with the American battle line to a position of stunning superiority. It would provide the navy with a weapons system that could deliver the death blow to an already battered American fleet in the decisive daylight encounter.[100]

The beauty of Ishikawa's proposal, as the Navy General Staff saw it, was that the United States would not soon be in a position to respond effectively to such a Japanese gambit. For the United States to undertake a construction effort that would quantitatively outstrip the proposed Japanese naval expansion plan would require enormous expenditures for the expansion of shipyard facilities, not to mention the fact that an expanded American fleet for trans-Pacific operations would require the construction of a vastly increased fleet train. Such an effort would be beyond American industrial capacity for the time being. While the overall industrial potential of the United States, including its capacity to turn out major armaments, was normally far greater than that of Japan, the American economy of late had been badly weakened, whereas the acquisition of the industrial resources and facilities of Manchuria had greatly augmented Japanese industrial strength. Most telling of all, should the Americans try to respond qualitatively to the Japanese superbattleship initiative, they would immediately face a nearly insuperable obstacle: The locks in the Panama Canal were too narrow to admit warships of the size Japan now contemplated. Indeed, staff studies assumed that the biggest warship that could pass through the canal could have no greater displacement than 45,000 tons, a size inadequate for mounting anything larger than 16-inch guns. A more immediate rationale for bigger Japanese guns was that, with only the existing 16-inch main batteries to rely on, it would be difficult for Japanese shells to penetrate the armor decks of U.S. battleships of the day. Thus, if Japan took the lead in developing guns of great size (18-inch ordnance seemed more feasible than 20-inch) and kept this fact secret for as long as possible, it might be able to keep this lead for some years, during which time these monster guns could outrange any American naval ordnance and destroy American battleships. Certainly, it would be five years before the United States could build a comparable battleship and by then the Japanese navy would be on its way to acquiring warships of even greater size and firepower.[101]

In August 1934, the Navy General Staff secretly decided to move ahead with plans to build four superbattleships. In October 1934 it passed to the Navy Technical Department a request to produce a design study for the new class.[102] Among the staff requirements for these new battleships were nine 46-centimeter (18.11-inch) guns (downgraded from Ishikawa's 20-inch main ordnance), armor capable of withstanding 18-inch shells fired at a range of twenty to 30,000 meters, 30 knots top speed, and a cruising range of 8,000 miles at 18 knots.[103] With these instructions the department's naval constructors set to work on a design project of yet unprecedented scale and difficulty for any navy.[104] In their task, however, they could call upon the navy's decade of testing, research, and observation that had included exhaustive review of the lessons of Jutland, the ordnance experiments of 1920, the numerous tests carried out on the hull of the *Tosa* in 1924, the insights gained from the abortive battleship designs of 1929, and the ongoing experience of reconstructing and refitting Japan's existing heavy units, particularly the battleship *Hiei*.[105] By the autumn of 1935 preliminary research for the design of the new class had been completed, but some twenty-three successive plans of unparalleled complexity were eventually drafted before the final design was approved in March 1937.

Simultaneously, in 1935, discussions took place between the Navy General Staff and the Navy Ministry concerning actual authorization for a new round of naval construction, eventually dubbed as the Circle Three program, which was approved in 1936 and scheduled to commence in 1937. At the heart of the Circle Three program was the authorization for the first two projected superbattleships, to be named *Yamato* and *Musashi*, the ultimate weapons systems to outrange the enemy and the apotheosis of the navy's "big ships, big guns" tradition. The Navy General Staff's decision in the summer of 1934 to have superbattleships built was symbolic of Japan's new confidence in facing an unrestricted race in naval armaments should the treaty system collapse.

THE JAPANESE NAVY AND THE END OF THE TREATY ERA

By 1934, the breakdown of the treaty system had become a distinct possibility. The signatory powers had come to a crossroads, since any one of them wishing to abrogate the treaties would have to announce its intention by the end of the year, which in turn would trigger a conference in 1935, necessary in the absence of a prior renegotiation of the treaties among the powers. Britain had proposed preliminary talks in London in 1934 to review the issue of naval arms limitation as a whole.

In the Japanese navy, there was extreme discontent with the system as it currently existed, especially among the hard-liners of the "Fleet Faction" centered on admirals Katō Kanji and Suetsugu Nobumasa.[106] In their view, Japan must be granted naval parity or must abrogate its treaty obligations altogether. A less hawkish group of officers, some of whom were allied with the so-called Treaty Faction, held essentially the same views on the limitations system that Katō Tomosaburō had articulated over a decade before: While it might be somewhat disadvantageous to Japan and might injure Japanese national pride, its continuation was better for Japanese security than an all-out naval arms race.

In the early 1930s, the growing atmosphere of international crisis in East Asia greatly strengthened the position of the antitreaty faction in the navy. Of course, the climate of tension was largely of Japan's own making. The invasion of Manchuria by the Japanese army in 1931, the outbreak of fighting in Shanghai provoked by the Japanese navy in the late winter of 1932, the army's conquest of Jehol Province in China, the fighting along the Great Wall in 1933, and the Japanese withdrawal from the League of Nations that same year, all served to inflame Japan's relations with China and to threaten the interests of the Western powers in East Asia. The measured American response to these Japanese initiatives, including the decision to leave the Scouting Fleet on the American west coast after the annual fleet exercises of 1932 and the passage in 1934 of the Vinson-Trammell bill designed to bring the U.S. Navy up to its treaty limits within eight years, only served to promote in Japan a heightened atmosphere of crisis. This unease was manifested publicly by a resurgence of "war scare" literature in the Japanese press,[107] and was exploited fully over the next few years by the Japanese navy.

Within the navy itself, several developments strengthened the hand of the hard-liners. A number of senior officers known to favor continuation of the treaty system were purged in 1933 by the navy minister. More critically, the Navy General Staff gained virtually unchecked authority through the appointment of Prince Fushimi Hiroyasu as chief of staff, which gave to its decisions the exalted aura of the Imperial House. Moreover, the redrafting of administrative regulations established the Navy General Staff's supremacy over the Navy Ministry.[108] Throughout the country at large, beginning in 1933, the navy undertook to wage a propaganda campaign to drum up public support for a fundamental reorientation of governmental policy toward the treaty system. So effective was the navy in shifting press and public opinion on the issue that the Japanese government, bowing to the pressure, agreed to accept a basic policy that sought to end the current "unequal" restrictions on naval armament and to substitute a system of parity among the leading naval powers.

As noted in chapter 7, the navy's agitation over the treaty system was provoked more by the standard of Japanese inferiority it stipulated than by the actual ratio of forces that existed during the treaty era. The navy sought a 10-to-7 ratio at Washington in 1922 and at London in 1930, and by 1934, Japan's total naval tonnage stood 10 to 8 in relation to the U.S. Navy, because Japan had built up to its treaty limits, while the United States had not. To the Japanese navy, which had expected to maintain this comfortable margin through 1936, the Vinson-Trammell bill came as a rude shock. Thus the new American expansion program made the limitations system even more distasteful. The navy now became adamant that the treaties should be drastically altered or abandoned altogether. Publicly, the navy declared that it sought parity; in private, its leadership, now confident of Japan's ability to maintain qualitative superiority in a naval arms race, hoped for the abrogation of the treaty system pure and simple.

To head the naval component of the Japanese delegation at the preliminary talks held in London in the fall of 1934, the navy selected Rear Adm. Yamamoto Isoroku, possibly because his relatively modest rank conveyed the navy's disdain for the whole process, but more likely because his knowledge of English, his participation in the earlier London conference, and his reputation for steady judgment and quick thinking made him an effective representative for the navy's interests. In these preliminary discussions Yamamoto made the Japanese position quite clear: a demand for parity with the United States and Britain and the reduction of overall tonnage to a common upper limit for the three major navies, as well as a proposal for the total abolition of battleships, carriers, and cruisers. Further, the Japanese delegation insisted that without prior agreement on quantitative limitations for the three naval powers, it was not prepared to enter into any discussions on qualitative restrictions on warship types.[109]

No doubt the Japanese delegates were well aware that their stand would be unacceptable to their British and American counterparts, who indeed protested that naval parity and naval security were not the same thing. The Japanese stipulations were rejected by the United States, which argued that the existing system of ratios was the best guarantee of the security of all maritime powers. After a failed attempt at compromise, the stipulations were also turned down by the British, who insisted that a system of parity, linked to a common low level of naval strength, would imperil the scattered territories of the British Empire. Over months of discussion in 1934 the three delegations repeated their various arguments ad nauseam without a major shift in their positions. The Japanese government announced its renunciation of the treaties in December 1934.

Thus, when the delegates met in formal conference in December 1935 with the hard-lining Adm. Nagano Osami taking over from Yamamoto as the ranking naval officer of the Japanese delegation, the last possibilities for agreement had already been foreclosed. When Nagano restated the Japanese position and it was rejected, the Japanese delegation withdrew in 1936, leaving the remaining delegations to haggle over a vestigial and meaningless limitations system. Though the Washington Treaty would technically remain in force until January 1937, for all practical purposes the system was already dead. Japan now prepared to strike out on a new, ambitious, and dangerous course of naval autonomy. The prime symbols of that determination were the monster battleships *Yamato* and *Musashi*, soon to be laid down at Kure and Nagasaki, respectively. Yet the truth of their construction was that as critical weapons of naval combat, they were obsolete by the time they were completed, and the great surface engagement in which they were to play the decisive role had become ever more unlikely. The new dimension of naval power was the air space above the fleet. Ironically, it was the Japanese navy that had done so much in recent years to make it so.

9

TO STRIKE
—*from*——————
THE SKY

Japanese Naval Aviation, 1920–1941

During World War I, the future roles of naval aviation had been demonstrated on one or more occasions. The roles included fleet reconnaissance, spotting for naval gunnery, aerial attack (against both maritime or land-based targets), and aerial protection of friendly forces at sea or ashore. Such was the promise of aircraft to project naval power beyond the range of shipborne weapons that the world's major navies felt impelled to develop a naval air arm in one form or another. By the early 1920s each had begun to develop land-based, sea-based, and carrier-based aircraft and had included in its roster of warships at least one prototype of aircraft carrier.

Yet none of the trials of naval aviation in the recent war had proved decisive. Much of the new arm's future lay in the realm of speculation rather than experience. On the basis of recent history, there was little evidence to shake the faith of naval establishments in the continued primacy of the big-gun battleship. During the 1920s, the battleship-oriented brass in all navies viewed the average aircraft of the day with some skepticism if not derision. Early naval aircraft were small, fragile, and capable of only short ranges. They had no adequate means of communication with ships or shore bases and were equipped with only the crudest navigation systems. They were incapable of delivering their bombs with any accuracy and were subject to grounding in any sort of bad weather. Thus naval aircraft had few capabilities to make them a serious threat to surface ships. Although heavy bombers of the U.S. Army Air Corps had sunk an old German battleship anchored off the Virginia Capes, the dubious conditions under which this test was conducted made its outcome inconclusive.

Until the mid-1930s, the naval aircraft's modest performance—in speed, range, ceiling, and payload—and thus modest potential, meant that in all three major navies, "command of the air" was seen only in relation to the decisive surface engagement. In the early 1920s, battleship and cruiser floatplanes were used as scouts for the fleet. By the end of the decade they were employed as spotters for fire from the battle line, a task shared by carrier aircraft as they later began to appear in greater numbers. Though there was a growing certitude about the vulnerability of carriers themselves to air attack, naval professionals doubted that carrier attack aircraft could actually sink a capital ship.[1]

After about 1935, high-performance aircraft began to enter service. They boasted large radial engines, fuel injection, variable-pitch propellers, all-metal construction of monoplane configuration, flush riveting, and retractable landing gear. Although these innovations were incorporated into all aircraft types, they seemed to provide a significant advantage to the bomber (an offensive weapon) over the fighter (an essentially defensive weapon) and thus made the former an increasingly dangerous threat to naval surface units.

Hence Japanese naval aviation remained tentative even into the late 1930s. But its first steps in the twenties, uncertain as they were, are nevertheless important to explore, if only to explain the extraordinary development in the field as the Pacific War approached.

THE NAVY'S PERSPECTIVE ON AIR POWER IN THE 1920s

During the 1920s, Japan was of two minds about the strategic implications of aviation. On the one hand, like a number of European powers, Japan exaggerated the capabilities of air weapons as they then existed. Drawing upon the "lessons" of early aerial bombardment during the world war, the Japanese military and political leadership came to fear the consequences of an aerial campaign against Japan. Eventually, Japanese representatives at the 1932 Geneva Naval Conference were to seek international agreement to eliminate the aircraft carrier as an aggressive weapon, or at the very least, to bring about severe restrictions on its construction.

Nevertheless, the Japanese navy was not slow to grasp the significance of the new aviation technology and, before the end of World War I, had even begun to manufacture some of its own aircraft. In these early years of Japanese naval aviation, however, the nucleus of Japanese aircraft designers and manufacturers was neither sufficiently large nor sufficiently advanced technologically to keep up with the rapid pace of aviation development elsewhere in the world, let alone to pursue its own innovations in aviation. During the world war, the gap in aviation technology between Japan and the West had widened considerably as the European belligerents gained valuable experience in the mass production of aircraft and as they developed aircraft with dramatically greater performance than that of prewar manufacture. The postwar decade in Japanese aviation technology was therefore marked by two related and intensive efforts: the infusion of considerable amounts of Western technological assistance and, at the same time, an effort by Japan to establish its own fledgling aircraft industry.

For the Japanese navy, such initiatives were impelled by critical matters of competition both abroad and at home. On the one hand, the navy had to be concerned with recent advances in naval air technology in the American and British navies that threatened to drop Japan into a distant third place as a modern naval power. On the other, the navy had reason to be chagrined at the rapid advances in Japanese military aviation made possible by the arrival of a French air mission invited to Japan in 1919 at the behest of the Japanese army.

For these reasons, the Japanese naval leadership decided in 1920 to seek the assistance of the British navy in improving the proficiency of its naval air arm. The next year, despite the reservations of the British admiralty about granting Japan unrestricted access to British technology, the British government sent an unofficial civil aviation mission to Japan. The mission was headed by Sir William Francis-Forbes (later Baron) Sempill, a former officer in the Royal Air Force experienced in the design and testing of Royal Navy aircraft during World War I. It arrived at Kasumigaura Naval Air Station in November 1921.[2] Its twenty-seven members were largely men with experience in naval aviation and included pilots and engineers from several British aircraft firms. As important as the training that the mission brought to the development of Japanese naval aviation was the access to the latest aviation technology that it provided. Not only did the trainees become familiar with the newest aerial weapons and equipment—torpedoes, bombs, machine guns, cameras, and communications gear—but the mission also brought to Kasumigaura well over a hundred aircraft, comprising twenty different models, five of which were currently in use in the Royal Navy's Fleet Air Arm. These planes eventually provided the inspiration for the design of a number of Japanese naval aircraft. By the time the last members of the mission had returned to Britain, the Japanese navy had acquired a reasonable grasp of the latest aviation technology.

JAPANESE NAVAL AIRCRAFT DESIGN AND MANUFACTURE

The Sempill Mission was not the only source of foreign air technology imported by Japan in the postwar decade, nor was the navy the sole beneficiary. Until then, Japanese naval aviation had mostly depended on the purchase of foreign-manufactured engines and airframes, or on their manufacture in Japan under foreign licensing arrangements. At the beginning of the 1920s, however, Western technological assistance began to work to Japanese advantage by providing the basis for the development of an independent Japanese aircraft industry.[3] As early as 1914, the Naval Arsenal at Yokosuka (Yokosuka Kaigun Kōshō, or Yokoshō, for short) had begun turning out a few seaplanes, the design for which had been based on foreign airframes, but which had used Japanese-designed engines. In 1920, at the Hiro branch of the Kure Naval Arsenal, the navy began the production of flying boats with the assistance of the Short Brothers, a British manufacturer.[4]

In their scramble for participation in an increasingly lucrative business, private Japanese firms were not far behind in the design and manufacture of aircraft. Established commercial and industrial enterprises began to build research and testing facilities, including wind tunnels and water tanks to study lift and drag. To master the new developments in aeronautical science in the West the Japanese companies hired foreign technicians, sent their engineers abroad, and purchased foreign aircraft for intensive study and analysis. Mitsubishi was especially fortunate at the outset of its aircraft ventures in the early 1920s. Obtaining the service of a British design team, it quickly secured a navy contract for the design, development, and production of three different types of aircraft—a fighter plane, a reconnaissance aircraft, and an attack plane—for use with Japan's first carrier, the Hōshō, then nearing completion. Another aircraft manufacturer, Aichi, made arrangements with the Heinkel Company in Germany, which provided technical assistance in the design of a new generation of naval aircraft. The most successful of these was an outstanding carrier dive bomber.[5]

Nakajima, founded in 1917 by Nakajima Chikuhei, one of the navy's pioneer pilots and later a formidably influential industrialist and politician, was unique among Japan's early aircraft manufacturing firms. From the beginning, it used its own engineers and designers rather than hiring foreign expertise. The firm became enormously successful during the 1920s, when it produced a range of first-rate aircraft types for both the Japanese army and navy and excelled in the design and manufacture of aircraft engines.

Another new firm, Kawanishi, became strongly identified with the navy because so many of its staff were former naval officers. Established in 1928 in cooperation with the Short Brothers, it began work on a number of highly successful flying boat designs that it undertook on contract with the navy.[6]

Although Yokosuka remained the center for the direction of aviation technology through the end of the Pacific War, as early as the outset of the 1920s the navy moved toward a division of labor in aircraft production. In 1921, the Navy Technical Department was given the authority to issue design competitions for the design of aircraft according to specifications called for by the Navy General Staff. Private firms like Mitsubishi, Aichi, Nakajima, and Kawanishi would submit the designs, and after testing the prototypes by the navy, contracts would be awarded to those firms most successfully meeting the navy's requirements. Under these arrangements a series of design competitions of the late 1920s produced some of the world's best reconnaissance aircraft, carrier bombers, and carrier fighters that would come into service in the next decade. For its part, the navy, while continuing to design and manufacture a few aircraft types in which it believed that it should lead, used its limited facilities for the testing and modification of aircraft prototypes. Thus, under the new arrangements, the navy conducted much of the research, and private enterprise undertook most of the production.[7]

With the increase in the scale and complexity of naval aviation, there was an obvious need for a single organization to coordinate its technology and training. Consequently, in 1927 the navy created the Naval Aviation Department. It was located in Tokyo, was directly responsible to the navy minister, but remained outside the ministry itself. In addition to having responsibility for the development of airframes, engines, ordnance, and equipment relating to naval aviation, the department was given charge of all training, except for air combat training, which remained in the hands of the various air groups.

The navy also attempted to consolidate its aviation research by bringing its technical research facilities together with tactical training facilities already in existence at Yokosuka. In 1936, the Naval Air Arsenal (Kaigun Kōkūshō, or Kūshō for short) was completed and placed under the command of the Yokosuka Naval Base. The creation of the arsenal brought together for the first time all work in aircraft design and flight testing, as well as the construction of prototypes not under contract with private firms. The aircraft prototypes that met the navy's basic safety and performance requirements at the arsenal were passed on to the Yokosuka Naval Air Group, which tested their combat capabilities and suitability for carrier operations. Considering the importance of the many aircraft designs that it evaluated and the outstanding success of some of these designs by 1937, the establishment of the Naval Air Arsenal as an advanced aviation engineering center marked a giant step forward for Japan as one of the world's leading aircraft producers.[8]

In 1932, the Naval Air Arsenal undertook a significant innovation. It was the "Prototypes System," a managed competition in the design and development of naval aircraft by the Japanese aircraft industry. By it, aircraft manufacturing firms were paired in the competition for orders for various types of aircraft to be designed and produced according to navy specifications. The firm whose prototype most successfully met these specifications was awarded with a production contract; the losing firm would be expected to produce its competitor's design, or to produce the engines for the aircraft as a second-source supplier. In this way, the navy coaxed the best competitive energies from private industry, and once the best design was selected, there was a synthesizing and sharing of the technologies involved. Not only did the Prototypes System provide guidelines for a series of outstanding naval aircraft, the first wholly designed by Japanese aircraft engineers, it also laid the basis for a military procurement system that exists in Japan to this day.[9]

Beginning in 1932, with a decade of apprenticeship and experience in aircraft production behind it, the navy moved decisively to become self-sufficient in aircraft design and manufacture. The establishment of the Naval Air Arsenal had much to do with this, but the driving force behind this new policy came out of the Naval Aviation Department itself. There, in 1932, Rear Adm. Yamamoto Isoroku, chief of the Technical Division of the department (1930–33) and chief of the department itself (1935–36), pushed through a plan to break the dependence of the navy, and by extension, the Japanese aircraft industry, on foreign aircraft design. The plan provided for autonomous production of naval aircraft based essentially on Japanese design, on the navy's emerging operational needs, and on the mobilization of civilian aircraft companies.

Japanese aircraft manufacturing never achieved total independence from foreign aircraft technology, of course. During the rest of the 1930s, the Japanese aircraft industry imported equipment, engines, and even aircraft, largely from the United States, and during the Pacific War, it received at least a trickle of such matériel from its Axis allies.[10] Yet, Yamamoto's initiative at the Naval Aviation Department, combined with the Naval Air Arsenal's Prototypes System, started a remarkably effective process in the design, development, and production of naval aircraft.[11] During the course of the 1930s, through the synergism of strong navy guidance and active private initiative, the Japanese aircraft industry not only began to join the technological revolution in military aircraft design and construction mentioned earlier, but in certain fields began to take the lead. By the end of the decade of the 1930s, the Japanese navy had acquired some of the finest combat aircraft in the world and was a leading participant in the world transformation of naval aircraft that moved them from the margins of naval power to its very center. What follows is a brief review of the most important of these aircraft in service with the Japanese navy at the opening of the Pacific War.

During the 1920s and early 1930s, the navy had acquired a series of excellent carrier fighters. But by the latter period, these aircraft had fallen behind land-based bombers in speed and range, a manifestation of a worldwide development in military aviation of the time. In 1934, accordingly, the navy began a search for a new single-seat aircraft to replace its current standard biplane carrier fighter. Its specifications called for high speed, low weight, and excellent control.[12] Even when great strides were being made in aviation technology—in increased engine power and more streamlined configuration—the design of carrier aircraft posed particular problems. These arose from the restrictions imposed by carrier operations; carrier aircraft needed good cockpit visibility, low landing speed, and small dimensions conforming to flight elevators. Given these restrictions, the design of a successful carrier fighter required a careful selection of performance priorities within the specifications set forth by the authorities.

The navy ultimately chose a design by Mitsubishi. Completed in 1935, it was the A5M (type 96, "Claude") carrier fighter. It was a radical aircraft for the time: a waspish-looking, all-metal, open-cockpit monoplane, powered by a 500-horsepower radial engine and armed with two 7.7-millimeter machine guns mounted in the upper engine cowling. Its smooth contouring, aluminum monocoque construction, and flush rivets minimized air drag so that fixed landing gear could be retained. Demonstrating an ability to climb to 5,000 meters (16,500 feet) in less than six minutes and reaching a level speed of 243 knots (280 miles per hour), it far exceeded navy specifications in both categories. Its superb maneuverability underscored the emphasis the navy placed on dogfighting in aerial combat, as opposed to reliance on pure speed and fire power (an issue that had been a cause of heated controversy among the navy's top fighter pilots in the first half of the decade). In the first years of the China War the fighter repeatedly shredded Chinese fighter opposition and showed itself to be an aircraft of great effectiveness.[13] But most important, its appearance and that of the G3M medium bomber (see below), marked the culmination of Yamamoto's ambitious program of aircraft reequipment for the navy and signaled the entry of Japanese aviation into an era of self-sufficiency.

Aviation technology was accelerating so fast, however, that even as the A5M was being distributed to the navy's carrier and land-based units in the spring of 1937, the Naval Aviation Department was initiating plans for a plane that would surpass it in performance. In the view of the navy's front-line pilots in the China War, the need was for a fighter with the speed and firepower to destroy an enemy bomber, the range and endurance to escort the navy's medium bombers on long-range missions into the heart of China, and the maneuverability to deal with any fighters it might meet on the way.

With these considerations and the needs of carrier operations in mind, the Naval Aviation Department proposed a new carrier fighter with specifications of unprecedented difficulty. The extraordinary range and armament requirements

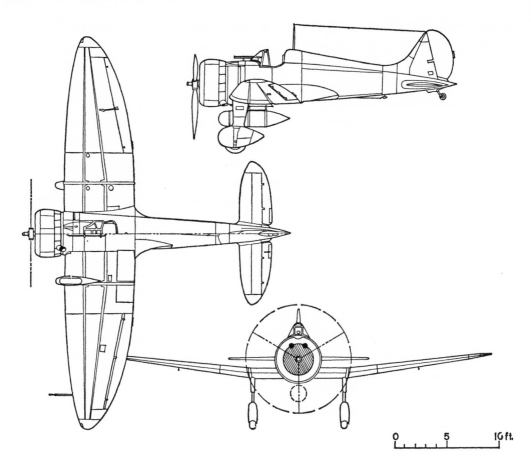

Fig. 9-1. Mitsubishi A5M (type 96, "Claude") carrier fighter.
(Source: René J. Francillon, *Japanese Aircraft of the Pacific War*, Annapolis, Md.: Naval Institute Press, 1987)

presupposed a large and heavy aircraft, whereas the speed and maneuverability requirements argued for a small and light airplane driven by a light and powerful engine. The Mitsubishi team that designed the A5M eventually won the competition for this aircraft. Headed by Horikoshi Jirō, the team solved the competing priorities by various means. They reduced weight through the use of lighter-than-usual structural components. They achieved aerodynamic design through the use of flush riveting, the adoption of retractable landing gear, the incorporation of a cockpit canopy, and the design of a streamlined fuselage. Innovations included a detachable auxiliary fuel tank, generous wing area, large ailerons, a variable-pitch propeller, and an 870-horsepower Mitsubishi Zuisei engine.[14]

The result of Horikoshi's team effort was the A6M (type 0, "Zeke") carrier fighter. The Mitsubishi "Zero," as it came to be known, was adopted by the Japanese navy in 1940. It was undoubtedly one of the most ingeniously designed fighter planes in aviation history. When the "Zero" appeared, it was an aircraft of high speed (288 knots, 332 miles per hour) and phenomenal range (1,000 miles); it could turn inside any fighter plane then in production; its rate of climb was faster than any contemporary aircraft; and in most situations it provided a remarkably stable gun platform. When it first entered combat its flaws—for example, its sluggish controls at high speed and inadequate dive speed—were scarcely perceptible. It was initially thrust into the thick of the fighting in the skies over China, where it provided long-range escort to Japanese bombers and quickly decimated enemy air units. Its weaknesses would not become fully apparent until it met the more rugged, more powerfully engined American aircraft of the Pacific War.[15]

Like its American and British counterparts, by the 1930s, the Japanese navy had developed two types of ordnance-carrying aircraft—torpedo bombers and dive bombers—though in each case the navy used different terms ("attack aircraft" and "bombing planes," respectively). Torpedo attack was the first of the two offensive systems developed in the Japanese navy. Torpedo bombers had been flying off Japanese carrier decks since the 1920s. But by 1937, the navy had acquired a carrier aircraft that could undertake multiple roles: torpedo attacks, high-level bombing, and reconnaissance. This was the B5N (type 97, "Kate") carrier attack aircraft, a cleanly designed three-seat monoplane built by Nakajima. It was capable of about 200 knots (230 miles per hour) and could carry an 800-kilogram torpedo or an equivalent bomb load. Though it almost immediately went into carrier service upon its adoption, it was also allocated to the navy's land-based air groups in China, where, accompanied by A5Ms, it performed well in support of ground forces. When the Pacific War broke out, an improved model was in service. At Pearl Harbor it helped to destroy the American battleship force, and it was undoubtedly the world's best torpedo bomber at the time.[16]

Remarkably rugged for a Japanese aircraft was the D3A (type 99, "Val") carrier (dive) bomber,[17] developed in the mid-1930s by Aichi and largely modeled on contemporary Heinkel aircraft. It had a fixed undercarriage, large elliptical wings, and dive brakes under each wing. Of the same generation as the German Stuka and the American Douglas Dauntless, the D3A was generally the equal of both in structural integrity, range, and speed, though in bomb load and range it was inferior. Its combat results were outstanding. Participating in all major Japanese carrier operations in the first year of the Pacific War, the D3A sank more Allied warships than any other type of Axis aircraft.

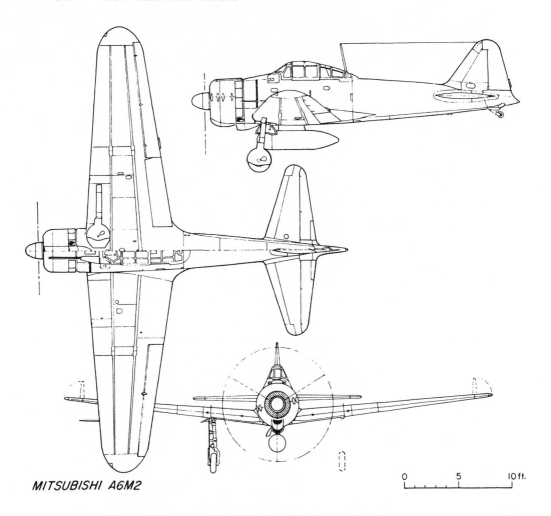

MITSUBISHI A6M2

Fig. 9-2. Mitsubishi A6M (type 0, "Zeke") carrier fighter.
(Source: René J. Francillon, *Japanese Aircraft of the Pacific War,* Annapolis, Md.: Naval Institute Press, 1987)

The development of an effective land-based long-range bomber was one of the first priorities of Yamamoto Isoroku when he took over as director of the Technical Bureau of the Naval Aviation Department in 1930. The impressive capabilities of a Mitsubishi prototype, the G1M, a long-range reconnaissance aircraft, had provided a real basis for Yamamoto's conception of such a bomber.

During a twelve-month period (1935–36), Mitsubishi kept testing improved prototypes until June 1936, when the navy finally accepted an advanced model,

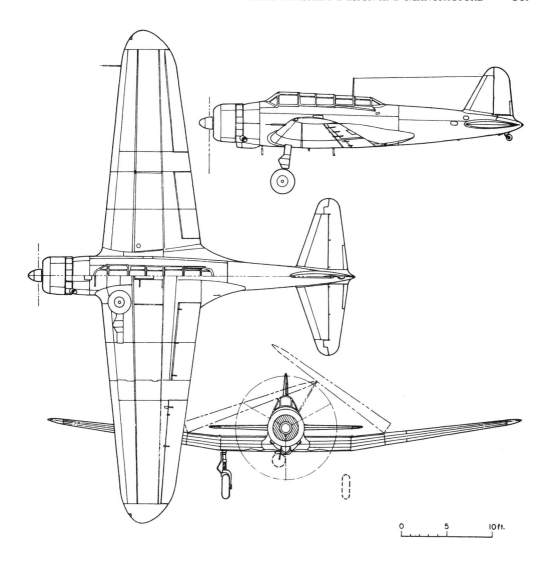

Fig. 9-3. Nakajima B5N (type 97, "Kate") carrier attack bomber.
 (Source: René J. Francillon, *Japanese Aircraft of the Pacific War,* Annapolis, Md.: Naval Institute Press, 1987)

the G3M (type 96, "Nell") land-based attack aircraft.[18] The G3M was a sleek, all-metal monoplane bomber whose slender shape was made possible by excluding internal bomb bays from the design. Its 800-kilogram bomb load or single torpedo was slung from racks fitted beneath the fuselage. Powered by two air-cooled radial engines, it was armed with two machine guns mounted in dorsal turrets and

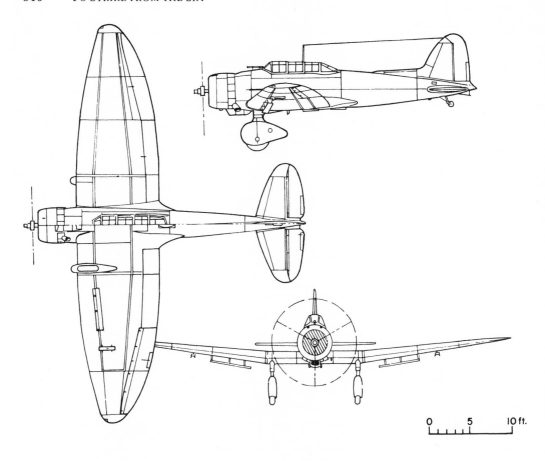

Fig. 9-4. Aichi D3A (type 99, "Val") carrier dive bomber.
(Source: René J. Francillon, *Japanese Aircraft of the Pacific War,* Annapolis, Md.: Naval Institute Press, 1987)

one in a ventral turret. In range (over 2,300 miles), speed (200 knots, 230 miles per hour), service ceiling (9,130 meters, almost 30,000 feet), and payload, the G3M was an unprecedented Japanese aircraft and, at the time, was surpassed only by the prototype of the Boeing B-17. The G3M's weaknesses—mainly the absence of protective armor and inadequate defensive armament—would only gradually be revealed as it was tested in the fire of combat over China.[19]

Even as the G3M undertook its first long-range missions in the China War, the navy was searching for a successor with increased engine power; greater speed, range, and payload; and better armament than the slender figure of the

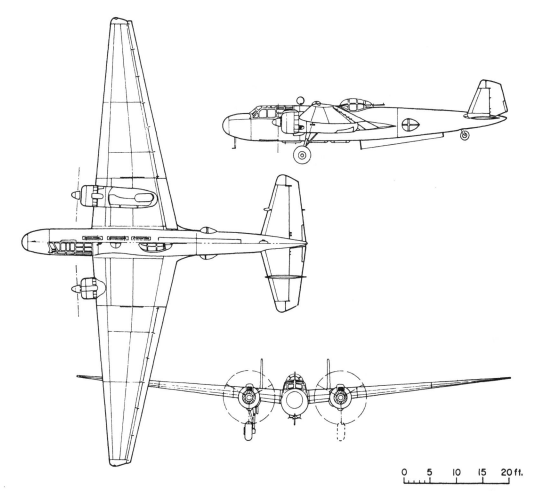

Fig. 9-5. Mitsubishi G3M (type 96, "Nell") land-based attack plane.
(Source: René J. Francillon, *Japanese Aircraft of the Pacific War,* Annapolis, Md.: Naval Institute Press, 1987)

G3M could accommodate. In September 1939, Mitsubishi produced a prototype, a twin-engined, cigar-shaped medium bomber with an airframe with an internal bomb bay and more defensive armament than the G3M (four machine guns in the nose and port and starboard waist positions, and two cannon in the dorsal and tail turrets). Early in 1940, the navy accepted it as the G4M (type 1, "Betty") land-based medium attack aircraft. In actual range it turned out to be inferior to the latest model of the G3M, but improvements enabled it to be used successfully on long-range missions deep into central and southern China in 1941. During the first six months of the Pacific War, the G4M ranged throughout Southeast Asia and the Pacific with impunity, but it proved so vulnerable to explosion under enemy fire that it earned the grim sobriquet of "The Flying Lighter" among its crews.[20]

The earliest role for aircraft in the Japanese navy had been patrol and scouting for the fleet; in the 1920s, the navy employed various seaplanes for those purposes. But in the early 1930s, when aircraft began to be used for spotting for surface gunnery, the navy developed a series of catapult-launched floatplanes for use both as spotters and scouts. By the late 1930s it had developed new reliable aircraft for these purposes that had an important role in the Pacific War. Mitsubishi built the F1M (type 0, "Pete") observation seaplane, a single-float biplane; its maneuverability led to its use in combat roles in the Pacific. Aichi developed the E13A (type 0, "Jake") reconnaissance seaplane, a twin-float aircraft, which was likewise used in a variety of combat, transport, and air-sea rescue roles in the war.[21]

During the interwar period, both the Japanese and American navies recognized the need for long-range over-water reconnaissance. For this purpose both navies developed the large flying boat (in the mid-1930s supplemented in the Japanese navy by its land-based medium bombers). Kawanishi's experience in the development of this type led to the design of the H6K (type 97, "Mavis"), adopted by the navy in 1938. It was a parasol-winged aircraft powered by four air-cooled radial engines. Its range of 2,200 miles gave it a remarkable reach over the vast distances of the Pacific, and early in the Pacific War it scored several bombing and reconnaissance successes. But the H6K's vulnerability to enemy fighter attack eventually led to its withdrawal from a combat role.[22]

Its hardier successor, the Kawanishi H8K (type 2, "Emily") flying boat, entered Japanese naval service in 1941. It surpassed the H6K in speed and range, and its added armor and armament made it far more resistant to attack. An outstanding representative of its type, the H8K had been conceived as a reconnaissance aircraft, but its speed and range led the navy to consider it as an attack aircraft. Occasionally, it served in both roles in the Pacific War.[23]

By the eve of the Pacific War, these aircraft constituted, as a group, some of the most advanced aviation technology in the world. For speed and maneuverability, for example, the Zero was matchless; for range and speed few bombers surpassed the Mitsubishi G3M; and, in the Kawanishi H8K, the Japanese navy had the world's best flying boat. Flown by highly skilled air crews, these aircraft, and the others mentioned, collectively constituted an immensely dangerous offensive weapon, an aerial rapier, so to speak. A rapier is brittle, however, and can snap if sufficient pressure is brought to bear.

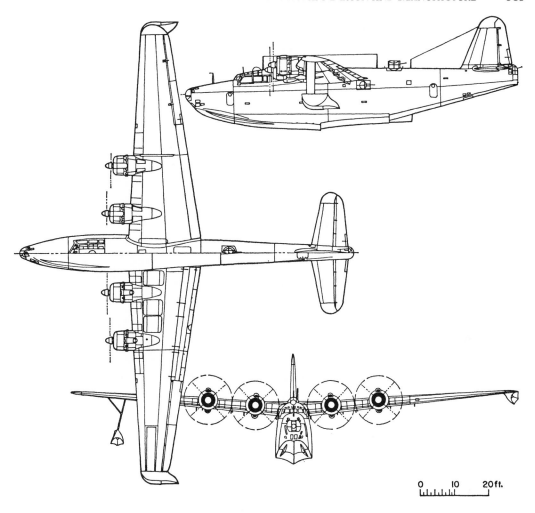

Fig. 9-6. Kawanishi H8K (type 2, "Emily") flying boat.
(Source: René J. Francillon, *Japanese Aircraft of the Pacific War*, Annapolis, Md.: Naval Institute Press, 1987)

So too was Japanese naval air technology. One major problem in Japanese aircraft manufacture as a whole was the failure of Japanese industry to keep up with the West in the development of aircraft engines, a consequence of the inaccessibility of strategic alloys, an insufficient research and development base in Japan, and the pressures of wartime replacement needs. Japan's failure to keep up was, at all events, a major reason for the increasing losses of Japanese naval aircraft in combat with American air forces as the Pacific War progressed. Another major problem in the design of Japanese naval aircraft was the imbalance between offensive and defensive considerations. Essentially, of course, naval aviation is an offensive force. But the design and construction of most Japanese naval aircraft were so shaped by offensive considerations—speed, maneuverability, and range—that they lacked all but the most minimal defensive protection. Their deficiencies of armor, defensive armament, self-sealing gas tanks, and the like, became apparent as they met their sturdier American competitors in the Pacific. The result was that air crews began to suffer huge losses. If the Japanese navy had been able to draw upon a sizable manpower pool, this would have been a manageable wartime problem. But Japanese naval air officials sharply limited the number of personnel by enforcing high admission standards for air crews, particularly for pilots. In combination, the vulnerability of Japanese naval aircraft and the limited number of trained air crews had fatal consequences during the Pacific War.

JAPANESE CARRIER DESIGN AND CONSTRUCTION, 1920–41

At the dawn of the age of carriers, designers of this new type of warship faced many difficulties. To begin with, they confronted problems of propulsion, hull structure, seakeeping, crew accommodation, and compatibility with shore facilities that builders of all naval vessels faced. Obviously, the designers also had to deal with a host of difficulties posed by flight operations. The carriers needed long decks for takeoffs and landings, aircraft control centers, and hangars and maintenance facilities. The ships' designers had to arrange storage and delivery systems for particularly hazardous materials: aviation fuel and ordnance. In addition to these new challenges, the naval limitation treaties restricted the displacement tonnage of carrier construction to 23,000 tons, although, as discussed, Japanese and American navies were allowed the conversion of certain capital ships to carriers (the *Akagi* and *Kaga,* and the *Lexington* and *Saratoga*).[24]

But two problems in particular bedeviled carrier design in this period. The first was the rapid development of aircraft technology, manifested in the increasing weight and speed of aircraft that required increasing flight deck length for takeoff. The second was the still uncertain function of the carrier and its place relative to the battle line. These ambiguities, for a while at least, seemed to argue for the installation of heavy guns on carriers for defense against cruisers and destroyers. Given these problems, it is not surprising that carrier design in these years was a matter of trial and error and that, in all three major navies, the design of the first warships of this type contained certain features that proved impractical in the long run.

These problems are evident in the history of the *Hōshō,* Japan's first and essentially experimental aircraft carrier. From the perspective of later years, the *Hōshō,* at less than 8,000 tons and with a flight deck of only 552 feet, was a very small carrier. She had a small island-type bridge on the starboard side from which the ship was conned and flight operations were controlled. The boiler uptakes were vented on the starboard side into three stacks that were hinged so that they folded over during flight operations. The hangar deck took up the full beam of the ship at the fantail, but narrowed amidships, stopping just forward of the island bridge. This configuration permitted the embarkation of only twenty or so aircraft: fighters, torpedo bombers, and attack aircraft used for reconnaissance. Within several years of her launching, the ship was remodeled to make a flush deck, and later, her stacks were permanently fixed at an angle downward over the ship's starboard side. But no alterations could remedy the vessel's main defect, her small size. This became increasingly apparent in the 1930s, as larger and faster attack aircraft were developed. When the Pacific War approached, the Hōshō's aircraft complement was limited to fighters, and her function was restricted to training, or at best, for defensive cover for the fleet. But the carrier had proved valuable as a laboratory for carrier design, construction, and flight operations.[25]

On the other hand, in the late 1920s, the addition to the fleet of the large carriers Akagi and Kaga and their more than 150 aircraft created new strategic as well as tactical possibilities for the navy. Their initial design, which incorporated a flush-top flight deck, two shorter flight decks below it, and 8-inch surface guns, demonstrated contemporary uncertainties about the function of carriers and an underestimation of the rapidity of change in naval aviation. As noted earlier, both were originally laid down as capital ships and were finished as carriers, a change in function that required more than just building a flight deck in place of an armored deck and superstructure. Modifications included the lowering and reduction of armor belts and the modification of torpedo bulges. The disposal of boiler exhaust was particularly troublesome; designers built huge shafts canted down over the sides of the ship, one large funnel on the port side of the Akagi and 300-foot long tubes on each side of the Kaga.[26]

By the mid-1930s, operational experience, changes in naval opinion, and increases in the size and power of naval aircraft led to the reconstruction of both the Akagi and Kaga. A small island was installed on the port side of the Akagi, but on the Kaga it was located on the starboard side. The 8-inch guns were retained in the Akagi and reduced in the Kaga as navy planners came to the conclusion that a carrier's attack aircraft were more important in defense against surface attackers than were guns. Most important, the three-level flight deck arrangement of these ships was eliminated and replaced by a single extended upper flight deck that projected over the stern and reached almost to the bow. This alteration allowed for more hangar space and thus a considerable increase in aircraft capacity (from sixty to ninety). Among the other significant alterations for both carriers were the addition of a third aircraft elevator, the trunking of boiler intakes into a single funnel canted over the starboard side, and the installation of completely oil-fired boilers.[27]

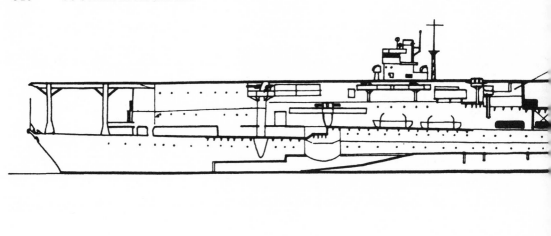

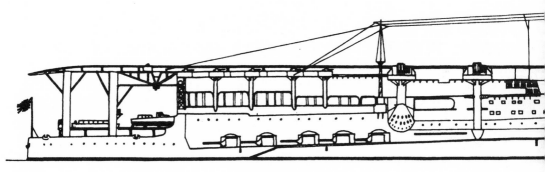

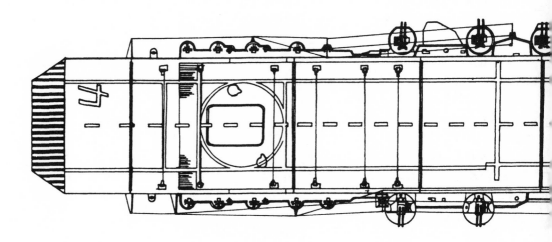

Fig. 9-7. The carrier *Kaga*, 1935.

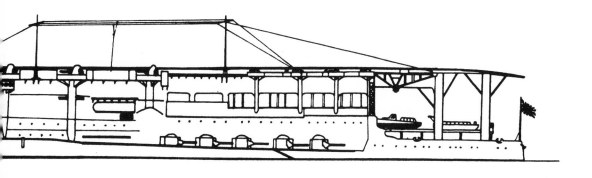

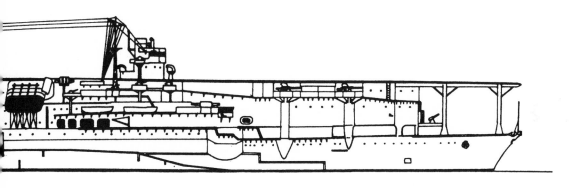

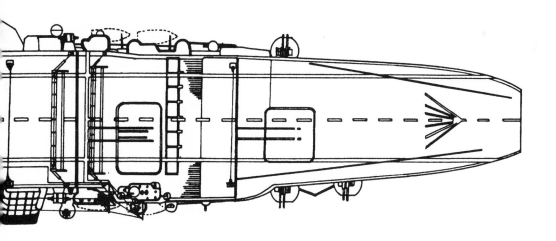

The great potential of carrier aviation became apparent when the *Akagi* and *Kaga* joined the fleet in the late 1920s. But design options for new carriers were narrowed by budgetary limitations and the fact that the *Akagi* and *Kaga* had already accounted for 54,000 of the 81,000 tons allocated to Japan for carrier construction under the limitation treaty. Accordingly, the navy attempted to build a carrier at under 10,000 tons. At this size, it would be exempted, along with the *Hōshō*, in the calculation of Japan's allowed carrier tonnage. The result was the *Ryūjō*, a flush-deck carrier with almost no armor protection and only one hangar. She was the smallest carrier built before 1941, and from the date of her laying down in 1929, she was beset with problems. A navy panel judged the *Ryūjō*'s aircraft complement to be too small, and a second hangar was constructed. The addition not only increased her displacement to 12,000 tons (a fact kept secret at the time) but made her less stable. In consequence, the carrier was twice in drydock between 1934 and 1936 for structural changes to improve her stability.[28]

These alterations did little to improve the *Ryūjō*'s overall efficiency, though the lessons learned were applied to the next carriers, the *Sōryū* class. The two ships of that class had originally been planned in 1931–32 as hybrid warships, part cruiser and part carrier, to circumvent the treaty limitations on total carrier construction. When the Navy General Staff realized that Japan would withdraw from the treaty system, the two were built as pure carriers. They retained cruiser hull configurations and propulsion systems, however, and were thus capable of an impressive 35 knots. The *Sōryū*, completed in 1936, was a carrier of nearly 16,000 tons, with double deck hangars accommodating sixty-eight aircraft, the lower hangar being placed within the hull for greater stability. In what was becoming a trademark of Japanese carriers, the boiler uptakes were trunked in two funnels over the starboard side amidships. Just forward of these, on the starboard side, was a small island superstructure.[29]

The design of the *Hiryū*, laid down in July 1936, six months after the *Sōryū*'s launching, incorporated changes suggested by experience and research. Damage to the Fourth Fleet in the great storm of 1935 made clear the need for better stability in the navy's ships. Accordingly, builders strengthened the hull, raised the forecastle, and increased the beam of the *Hiryū*. The other structural difference from her sister ship was that, like the *Akagi*, her island superstructure was located on the port side, though this arrangement was eventually found to be similarly troublesome for flight operations. The *Hiryū*'s maximum aircraft capacity, seventy-three, was slightly larger than that of the *Sōryū*.[30]

The end of the treaty era in December 1936 allowed Japan to build ships of all classes, including aircraft carriers of unprecedented size and performance. Thus, during the five years before the onset of the Pacific War, the navy added the finest carriers that Japan ever built: the *Shōkaku* and *Zuikaku*. Ordered under the Circle

Three program to counter growing U.S. carrier strength, the *Shōkaku* class was a carrier group capable of operating with the monster *Yamato*-class battleships, a mission that called for large, fast carriers capable of embarking a powerful aerial strike force and able to defend themselves effectively. Navy General Staff specifications called for the same aircraft complement as the remodeled *Akagi* and *Kaga* (ninety-six), the same speed as the *Sōryū* (35 knots), and a greater radius of action (10,000 miles at 18 knots). Because of armor on their main decks above their machinery, magazine, and aviation gas spaces, these carriers were 10,000 tons heavier than the *Sōryū*, yet they had excellent stability. Their engines delivered 160,000 horse power, 10,000 more than even the superbattleship *Yamato*. By the time of their participation in the Hawaii strike, the *Shōkaku* and *Zuikaku* provided the navy with a formidable offensive punch: each carried twenty-seven dive bombers, twenty-seven torpedo bombers, and eighteen fighters—seventy-two aircraft in all, not counting twelve reserve aircraft.[31]

The *Shōkaku* and *Zuikaku* were critical additions to the Japanese carrier fleet. In performance and capability they exceeded all American carriers until the wartime appearance of the *Essex* class. So valuable were these two warships that the decision to mount a Pearl Harbor attack was based in part on their availability to the mobile task force organized for that operation. Moreover, their absence from the Midway campaign may well have proved the margin of defeat for the Japanese navy.[32]

In this survey of the Japanese carrier fleet, from its origins immediately after World War I to the eve of the Pacific War, not yet mentioned are the aircraft carriers under construction as hostilities began in December 1941. None proved a durable asset to the navy in the coming struggle, but the most promising of the group were the *Shinano* and *Taihō*. The *Shinano* was laid down in May 1940 as the third of the *Yamato*-class superbattleships, but converted during the war to a carrier. An enormous platform for air operations and prodigiously armored, the *Shinano* was sunk soon after her completion in November 1944. The *Taihō*, laid down as a carrier in July 1941, was apparently patterned after the British *Illustrious* class, which she closely resembled. She was the first Japanese carrier originally designed to have an armored flight deck, but this protection was of no avail against the U.S. submarine attack that sank her in June 1944.[33]

In addition to the carriers completed under publicly announced construction programs, there were a number of carriers from a "shadow fleet" of auxiliary and merchant vessels. These were designed to be quickly converted into carriers in case of war. The navy had begun this semisecret building program even before the London Treaty, working particularly with the Nippon Yūsen Kaisha in the design of fast passenger vessels that could be easily converted to carrier configuration. Two of these ships were rebuilt as carriers prior to Pearl Harbor

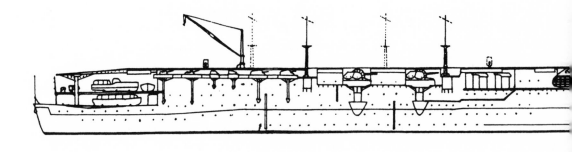

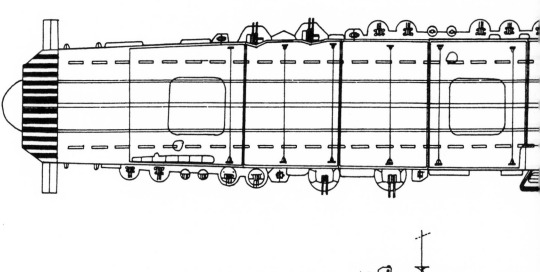

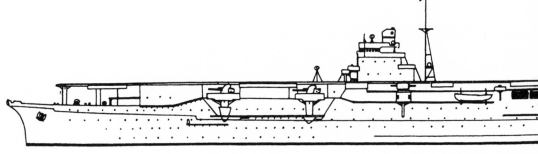

Fig. 9-8. The carrier *Shōkaku*.

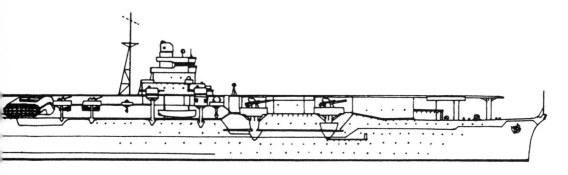

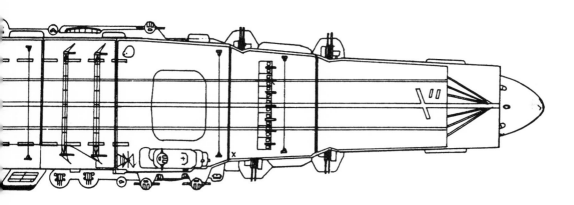

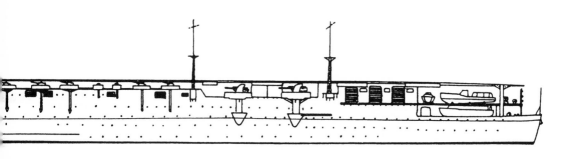

0				50m			100m

0	50ft	100ft

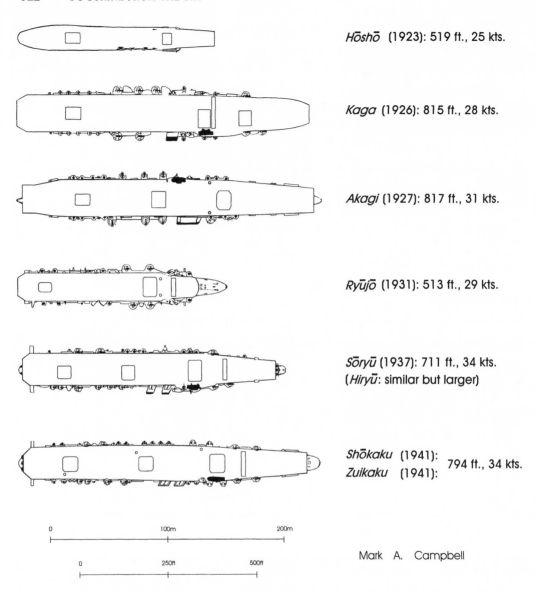

Hōshō (1923): 519 ft., 25 kts.

Kaga (1926): 815 ft., 28 kts.

Akagi (1927): 817 ft., 31 kts.

Ryūjō (1931): 513 ft., 29 kts.

Sōryū (1937): 711 ft., 34 kts.
(*Hiryū*: similar but larger)

Shōkaku (1941):   794 ft., 34 kts.
Zuikaku (1941):

Mark A. Campbell

Fig. 9-9. Japanese carrier development, 1922–41. Carriers are shown as they appeared in late 1941, after reconstruction. The date in parentheses is the year of completion of the carrier; "ft." is the length in feet of the flight deck; and "kts." is the carrier's nominal maximum speed in knots (operation maximum speed was almost always considerably less).

and were commissioned as the *Zuihō* (in 1940) and the *Shōhō* (in late 1941). Conversion work was begun on two other "shadow" carriers in 1940, and nine other such vessels after the Pacific War had broken out. But as a group these conversions were unsuccessful. Their slow speed and inadequate power, their small aircraft capacity, and their minimum protection made them ineffective as fleet carriers.[34]

By the eve of the Pacific War, the Japanese navy had ten carriers in commission (though one of these was only a light carrier). Like their opposite numbers in the U.S. and Royal navies, they collectively represented the evolution of carrier design between the world wars: the small initial aviation platforms, largely flush deck in configuration; the inclusion and later abandonment of surface armament; the use of capital ship hulls for two early large carriers (in the U.S. and Japanese navies); and the experimentation with small carriers (the *Ryūjō* and the USS *Ranger)* before the return to larger hulls. In many ways the Japanese were in the forefront of carrier design, and in 1941, the two *Shōkaku*s—the culmination of prewar Japanese carrier design—were superior to any carrier in the world then in commission.

Japanese and American carriers both sacrificed armored protection in order to maximize the offensive potential of their aircraft. In Japanese carriers, armor was limited to the hull in the largest carriers. There was modest protection over machinery, magazines, and aviation gasoline tanks. The *Hōshō* and *Ryūjō* had virtually no armor. Like the American carriers, the flight decks were for the most part simply superimposed upon the hull rather than constructed as a strength deck supporting the hull, as in contemporary carriers of the Royal Navy. The Japanese decks were unarmored, consisting merely of wooden planking laid lengthwise over thin steel decks. Like American carriers, hangars also were unarmored.[35]

There were, however, three distinct differences in Japanese and American carrier design and construction. The first was maximum aircraft capacity. In the Japanese navy, as in the Royal Navy, aircraft capacity was determined by the size of the hangar rather than the size of the flight deck. From the beginning, American carriers normally parked most of their aircraft on the flight deck and used the hangars below only for repair and maintenance. Japanese carriers, on the other hand, used their hangars as their main storage area as well as for servicing, refueling, and loading ordnance. Because hangars generally provide less storage space than do flight decks, Japanese carriers of roughly the same displacement as American carriers usually had smaller carrier air groups. (Given their use of carrier hangars for aircraft storage it is curious that the Japanese did not put more emphasis on folding wings for greater aircraft storage.)[36]

The second difference was that hangars in Japanese carriers were enclosed by storerooms, so that their aircraft and ready crews were shielded from wind and weather. Such arrangements would be lethal. In the Pacific War, when enemy bombs penetrated the unarmored flight decks and exploded in the hangars, the resultant blast pressures would be disastrous: flight decks were blown apart, and the hangar sides buckled. The enclosed spaces also prevented rapid disposition of fuel and ordnance over the side and easy insertion of fire hoses from screening ships to fight a fire. One of the most serious deficiencies of Japanese carrier design during this period was the vulnerability of aviation fuel systems, a defect that undoubtedly contributed to the loss of the *Sōryū* and the *Hiryū* by fire at Midway.[37]

The third difference lay in flight operations. The American carriers used crash barriers to separate parked and landing aircraft, whereas the Japanese needed clear flight decks during all flight operations. After each Japanese aircraft landed, it had to be stowed below before the next aircraft could land. This mode of operations kept Japanese flight decks clear and permitted a fairly rapid launch of aircraft, but during continuous flight operations, elevator cycles governed launch and recovery speeds. In consequence, more time was required to refuel and rearm planes than it would have taken on the flight deck. In urgent combat situations, an attempt to speed up the flight cycles of Japanese carriers was apt to lead to careless rearming and refueling. Indeed, the often-told loss of the *Akagi* and the *Kaga* at Midway is testimony to this ominous problem.[38]

JAPANESE NAVAL AIR RECRUITMENT AND TRAINING

As the Japanese navy acquired more and better aircraft and, through a process of trail and error, built a carrier fleet, it also set about the difficult task of recruiting and training skilled air crews. In the earliest years of Japanese naval aviation, pilot and observer recruitment was largely restricted to Naval Academy graduates. But with the increase in the number of land and carrier air groups in the late 1920s and early 1930s, the number of academy graduates volunteering for service was inadequate and their lengthy training for service in the surface fleet largely irrelevant to naval aviation.

To deal with these problems, the navy established two parallel programs that greatly expanded the pool of aviation trainees by drawing candidates from outside the officer corps. The Pilot Trainee Program, created in 1928 and known best by its contracted Japanese designation, the *Sōjū* system, recruited noncommissioned officers in fleet service. The Flight Reserve Enlisted Training Program, established in 1929 and also known by an abbreviated name *(Yokaren),* drew its candidates directly from civilian life. It recruited youngsters fifteen to seventeen years old who had finished primary school, were superior physically, and had excelled academically. After three years of general naval training including a short stint at sea, the recruits were sent to the Yokosuka Air Group for basic aviation training, either as pilots or observers. In 1937, to increase the caliber of navy pilots, the *Yokaren* system was upgraded to emphasize recruitment of middle school graduates (who now had to spend only about a year in general naval training).[39]

Although a few aviation trainees still continued to be drawn from volunteers of officer rank, up through the Pacific War, the great majority of Japanese naval pilots and observers were products of the *Sōjū* and *Yokaren* systems. This high ratio of enlisted men in the cockpits of Japanese naval aircraft—about 90 percent at the opening of the Pacific War—was due to the lack of incentive for an officer to volunteer for flight training, since future command prospects for naval aviators were limited. The Japanese navy, unlike its American rival, did not require its air group commanders or carrier captains to be qualified naval aviators.[40]

From its earliest days, the Japanese naval air service for the most part used operational facilities for training its personnel rather than specialized schools. In 1916, the Yokosuka Naval Air Group had been established for such a purpose; in 1921, naval air training had been moved to Kasumigaura, leaving Yokosuka as the training unit for lighter-than-air craft. In 1930, with the navy's essential abandonment of lighter-than-air craft, the Kasumigaura Naval Air Group became the unit for basic flight training of student pilots (succeeded in 1940 by the Tsuchiura Naval Air Group). The Yokosuka Naval Air Group became the training unit for *Yokaren* students and for advanced training in aerial combat. As the navy expanded its recruitment of *Yokaren* personnel, new training air groups were established up and down the Japanese home islands. After graduating from these units, future fighter pilots were sent on for further training at one of three operational air groups (Omura or Ōita on Kyūshū, or Tokushima on Shikoku), where they mastered carrier flight operations, acrobatics, formation flying, and air combat maneuvers. After this, the pilots were posted to combat air groups, either carrier or land-based, for a final year of intensive training. The best pilots were attached to carriers. Starting in the summer of 1937 and the outbreak of the war in China, the searing experience of air combat became part of the education of naval air crews. Carrier pilots were rotated to land bases in China specifically to give them combat experience. Beginning in 1938, the air crew in bombers (level bombers, dive bombers, and torpedo bombers) received nine months of intensive instruction in bombing, observation, and communications.[41] Hence, by 1941, in training and experience, Japan's naval aviators, were undoubtedly the best among the world's three carrier forces. For the first six months of the Pacific War Japanese naval pilots fought and flew supremely, jinking about the skies over Southeast Asia and the western Pacific and using their Zeros like rapiers against less experienced Allied airmen flying inferior aircraft.[42]

By the end of 1942, however, the navy's air squadrons had begun to go down in defeat. Several factors caused this decline, but chief among them was that in the years before the Pacific War, the navy had simply produced too few fliers. During the 1930s, the rigid screening and expulsion practices of Japanese naval air training reduced the thousands of qualified students to the ridiculously low annual average of a hundred or fewer graduated pilots.[43] Though this number substantially increased as the Pacific War approached, in late 1941, the Japanese navy probably had on hand not much more than six hundred *outstanding* fighter pilots (mostly on carriers, each with about 800 hours of flying time), while the *good* pilots in the United States constituted a far larger pool.[44]

The U.S. Navy's case provides an instructive contrast. About three years before the Pacific War, the U.S. Navy made a basic decision to expand pilot training and the production of training aircraft even at the cost of combat aircraft and personnel in operational air units. Hence, American pilot losses in the first year of combat were replaced by the end of 1943 without great difficulty. But the Japanese navy made no such decision until 1941, when it began to plan for the training of 15,000 pilots annually. Unfortunately for the Japanese navy, the outbreak of the war overtook this effort to build an adequate reserve of trained airmen, and the navy was forced to enter the war with only its cadre of elite pilots.[45] Once attrition took its toll in the great carrier battles in the spring of 1942 and in the Solomon Islands campaign that fall, there was no reserve of highly qualified aviators in the Japanese navy to take the place of those first line airmen who were lost. Moreover, despite the training it lavished upon the very best of its aviators, the Japanese navy probably undervalued them in practice, since the navy felt compelled, perhaps out of a consciousness of Japan's industrial and economic weakness, to pursue a policy of aircraft design in which safety factors (armor, self-sealing gas tanks, and structural integrity) were sacrificed for greater performance, speed, and maneuverability.

EMERGENCE OF THE NAVY'S AIR ATTACK TECHNIQUES

In the first decade of aviation in the Japanese navy, aircraft, whether land, sea, or carrier-based, had been considered useful in scouting and reconnaissance and, to a lesser extent, in fleet air defense. By the end of the 1920s, they also were employed in spotting for gunfire from the battle line. Although bombing and torpedo aircraft had been among the first naval aircraft types developed by the fledgling Japanese aircraft industry, for the most part, aviation was not seen as an offensive naval asset, largely because its reach and endurance were still so feeble. Then, in the 1930s, with the increase in aircraft performance, the navy began to consider using aircraft to attack an enemy fleet. Thus, for much of the decade, greater attention was given to the development of effective tactics and aircraft for offensive missions than for defensive interception of enemy aircraft.

The navy's first attempt at aerial bombardment against enemy surface units had been the horizontal bombing attack carried out at Tsingtao in the autumn of 1914, an operation undertaken without training or bombsights and thus without any significant results. After the war, the Sempill Mission had provided instruction in horizontal bombing *(suihei bakugeki),* along with British bombsight technology. But it was not until the publicity surrounding the American bombing tests off the Virginia Capes in 1921 that Japanese interest was aroused in this particular tactic. The Japanese navy emulated the American experiment with the bombing of an undefended hulk off Yokosuka in 1924, with similarly inconclusive results.[46] During the remainder of the decade, the navy annually carried out further experiments in horizontal bombing to improve equipment, aiming skills, and bomb release techniques. While accuracy became reasonably good at 2,000 to 5,000 meters (6,500 to 16,400 feet) against stationary targets, the attempt after 1930 to make such bombing exercises more realistic by directing them toward moving targets produced much poorer hit percentages. To improve the results, the navy tried bombing at lower altitudes and speeds and using larger formations of bombing aircraft. Although hit ratios were slightly improved, the lack of really accurate bombsights and the inadequate coordination between pilots and bombardiers were ongoing problems in horizontal bombing. Against moving targets, little progress was ever made, and by 1939, the navy had settled on two other bombing tactics that promised greater and more consistent success: aerial torpedo attacks and dive-bombing.[47]

Torpedo attack was actually the first method of aerial assault studied by the naval air arm. The method was in keeping with the navy's offensive tradition; it was tactically related to surface torpedo warfare; and it was technologically feasible.

Considerable impetus for the idea had been provided by a series of simulated night attacks by aircraft against fleet units at Tateyama Bay, south of Tokyo, in 1916. A number of the navy's early aviators argued for developing what they saw as the enormous potential of the new tactic.[48] The main obstacle to the rapid advancement of this tactical concept during these years was a lag in the development of aircraft to carry torpedoes, of the torpedoes themselves, and of the mechanisms to assure their steady course through air and water.

Over time, these difficulties were overcome by research along various lines. In the type 91 aerial torpedo, adopted by the navy in 1931, the Japanese acquired a formidable weapon, one that enabled Japanese torpedo bombers to maintain an air speed of 100 knots and to launch their torpedoes from a height of 100 meters.[49] The development of an aircraft to carry the new torpedo took a longer time. After years of testing, Mitsubishi developed an all-around carrier-based attack aircraft, which was adopted by the navy as the type 13, a single-engine three-seater biplane that remained the navy's main attack aircraft until the early stages of the China War. The aircraft was then replaced by the B5N described above. Solving the particular aerodynamic and hydrodynamic problems of dropping aerial torpedoes so that they would run at the proper depth and at the proper angles took the most time of all. The problems of drop angle, pitch, and roll of the torpedo in flight (which affected the course of the torpedo once it entered the water) tested the ingenuity of the engineers at the Naval Air Arsenal; some were not completely solved until the eve of the Pacific War.[50] But by the mid-1930s, breakthroughs in solving these problems made practical the tactic of aerial torpedo attack.

Along with these advances, there had emerged by then a coterie of dedicated, skilled torpedo pilots who, through constant practice in day and night attack methods, continued to improve the accuracy of the navy's aerial torpedo tactics. Not only were speed and launch heights increased (to heights of up to 200 meters and speeds of up to 120 knots by 1937), but accuracy against moving targets jumped to an average hit rate of 70–80 percent by 1935. Even allowing for the ineffectiveness of contemporary naval antiaircraft, fire-exercise umpires judged very few aircraft as downed—the high hit rates achieved by Japanese naval air crews during these years demonstrates their great skill and spirit.[51]

Dive-bombing was the third aerial attack technique developed by the Japanese navy. As aircraft carriers grew in importance, the Navy General Staff began to study the best aerial tactics to use against them. It soon came to two conclusions about any carrier-to-carrier engagement: First, the winning side would be the one that got in the initial blow. Second, it was less important to try to sink an enemy carrier (which could be accomplished with aerial torpedoes but probably not before the enemy could get off his own aircraft) than it was to destroy their flight decks at the earliest possible moment. For reasons already examined, horizontal bombing held out little prospect for success.[52]

Thus, at the outset of the 1930s, the navy seized upon the concept of dive-bombing, recently developed by the U.S. Marine Corps. Dive-bombing had some important advantages over high-level, horizontal bombing. The first was its accuracy. The dive-bomber released its payload at a far lower altitude relative to the target, and its pilot could easily adjust his bombing run to any evasive action by the target ship. Second, although at low altitude the dive-bomber was more vulnerable to antiaircraft fire, its rugged airframe could absorb more hits than other types of aircraft. All in all, given the accuracy of the technique and the vulnerability of carriers, the navy came to view dive-bombing as an essential element in its offensive repertoire. Beginning in 1931, the navy began a series of dive-bombing experiments on old hulks and mockups of American carriers, using structurally reinforced fighter aircraft from the First Carrier Division. The accuracy achieved in the new tactic was phenomenal. Some bombing runs scored 100 percent direct hits.[53]

As in the development of aerial torpedo attack, progress in dive-bombing was dependent upon the creation of specialized aircraft and specially trained air crews. The development of Aichi's rugged D3A carrier dive-bomber has already been described. By 1937, through constant and rigorous practice, the navy had also developed a highly skilled cadre of dive-bomber air crew, chief among whom was Lt. Egusa Takashige, destined to become the Japan's great dive-bombing ace of the Pacific War.

AERIAL SEARCH

From its outset, one of the foundations of Japanese naval aviation had been the desire to enhance reconnaissance capabilities. During World War I, shipborne (though not ship-launched) seaplanes had been used on several search missions, and after the war, long-range reconnaissance flights from to Okinawa and Korea had demonstrated the value of aerial reconnaissance for fleet operations. Japan's first carrier, the *Hōshō,* had been built with scouting and reconnaissance very much in mind.

The importance of scouting grew steadily as carrier aviation itself developed. In particular, the doctrine of a first strike against enemy carriers underlined the importance of reconnaissance. Yet the Japanese carrier strategists, focusing on offensive action, made little provision for carrier scouting. Unlike the Americans before the Pacific War, the Japanese navy perfected no specialized carrier aircraft for this purpose, wishing to maximize the number of attack aircraft embarked, and preferring to let its cruiser floatplanes and flying boats undertake this task. Although the navy developed many fine aircraft of these types, they were subject to serious limitations. Floatplanes, launched from catapults, were subject to damage by wind and salt spray, and their retrieval was difficult in heavy seas. Flying boats required calm waters for landings and takeoffs. Further, the low priority given to search as opposed to attack capabilities resulted in perfunctory training of Japanese air crews in reconnaissance tasks.[54] As a result, Japanese carriers, and Japanese task forces generally, had less reconnaissance capability than their American counterparts.

THE VICISSITUDES OF FIGHTER AIRCRAFT IN THE NAVY

Unlike the Japanese army, the navy gave surprisingly little thought in the 1920s and early 1930s to the value of the fighter as an offensive weapon or even to its use in fleet air defense. The army had concluded from studies of World War I that fighters were the main element in air power. During most of this period, therefore, the Japanese army developed air combat tactics while the navy's fighter arm, for the most part, did not progress much beyond the training provided by the Sempill Mission.

In the early 1930s, however, the navy began to take a number of steps—sending its better pilots to the army and even to Britain for training, holding training exercises that brought together pilots from carriers and land-based air groups, and employing RAF instructors—to improve the aerial combat skills of its fighter arm.[55] Building on these improved skills, the navy's best fighter pilots participated in the frequent exercises held by the Yokosuka Naval Air Group's fighter squadron. Out of this rigorous training environment emerged many highly skilled and motivated fighter pilots who shaped the navy's fighter doctrine by the late 1930s and who eventually commanded some of the navy's best air groups in the Pacific War. Of these men, none gained more attention than Lt. Comdr. Genda Minoru, who headed an aerial stunt team, the "Genda Circus," and became the single most influential naval airman of his generation. Thus, by the mid-1930s, the Yokosuka Naval Air Group became the Mecca of fighter pilots, and the naval air service began to pull even with the Japanese army in air combat capabilities.[56]

Even as the air combat skills of its fighter pilots were improving in the first half of the 1930s, however, the navy had begun to doubt the value of its carrier fighters. This was partly a consequence of the Japanese navy's traditional preference for offensive operations, for which the torpedo planes and dive-bombers were admirably suited and the fighter, in its defensive role, was not. Furthermore, all the world's air powers during these years believed that fighter aircraft had inferior performance—in speed and range and armament—in comparison to bombers. Japanese pilots believed that fighters without a margin of speed greater than 30 percent would have difficulty in carrying out the maneuvers necessary to bring down enemy bombers. This view intensified with the appearance in 1936 of the G3M medium bomber, whose speed and range surpassed any aircraft Japan had thus far produced. To many in the naval air service the appearance of this aircraft was proof that fighter aircraft ought to be abolished and carrier decks given completely over to attack aircraft.[57]

Some Japanese navy airmen, however, maintained that the fighter plane still had a role to play in air operations. They believed that its weaknesses could be overcome by changes in tactics, improvements in command and communications systems, and the development of new fighter plane designs. The superior speed of bombing aircraft could be overcome, they insisted, by attacking from the rear or aiming at the most vulnerable parts of the enemy bomber, its wing tanks. They also argued that an essential reason for the fighters' supposed ineffectiveness lay in the lack of an early warning system that would enable them to meet an approaching enemy in the sky. All the world's air powers shared this problem, which would not

Genda Minoru

be solved until the perfection of radar. Nevertheless, some Japanese pilots believed that intensive efforts in improving intelligence, aircraft communications, and command and control aboard aircraft carriers could increase the capabilities of fighters. In the meantime, much could be done to redesign the single-seat fighter by increasing its speed, maneuverability, and armament.[58]

Ultimately, in their search for optimum performance, Japanese fighter plane designers were forced to choose between these three capabilities. The choice, essentially shaped first by the test pilots at the Yokosuka Naval Air Group in the mid-1930s and then by the navy's fighter pilots in combat over China, was to emphasize maneuverability—a decision that profoundly influenced the design of both the A5M and its successor, the A6M (Zero). With the appearance of these two aircraft, from which designers also coaxed impressive speed, the fighter arm began to assume a major role in the Japanese naval air service. In the wild chaos of combat over China, the navy's fighter pilots, operating first from carriers and then from bases on the continent, displayed the capabilities of these high-performance aircraft. There they also demonstrated exquisite teamwork, reducing if not overcoming problems in airborne communications that had hampered fighter units in the past.[59]

In the four years before the Pacific War, the navy's fighter squadrons came to be regarded as essential for the navy both defensively and offensively. Adequate fleet air defense would continue to be a problem right into the Pacific War. But the Combined Fleet placed great hopes on its fighters to protect ships and bases from enemy bombers and on an elaborate system of patrols to cover its carriers. Though fighters comprised the core of fleet air defense, their role in the navy's growing offensive power was even more valued. The China War had demonstrated that the range and firepower of the Zero made it a formidable adjunct to any bombing force the navy could assemble. This belief was confirmed by the success achieved by Zero fighters in the first offensive operations of the Pacific War: Pearl Harbor, Northern Luzon, Darwin, Colombo, and Trincomalee.[60]

THE EMERGENCE OF JAPANESE CARRIER DOCTRINE, 1920–37

As discussed, in the early days of carrier aviation, the justifications for building carriers were uncertain and the designs for constructing them were necessarily experimental. The variety of carriers produced by the Japanese navy in this period is ample testimony to these conditions. Carrier doctrine was no less tentative. It developed incrementally on the basis of both the demands of the Navy General Staff for weapons and the practical results of Japanese carrier operations in these years.

When Japan's first carrier was launched, little thought was given to naval aircraft in an offensive role. Moreover, with only one carrier, there was scant consideration of carrier doctrine. In 1928, however, the First Carrier Division was formed with three carriers, and study of the role of carriers in a fleet engagement began in earnest. Because of the short range of carrier aircraft, of course, the navy high command, still very much surface oriented, viewed them as support for the main battle force, not offensive weapons. Carrier planes were to act as scouts, as spotters for naval gunfire, as layers of smoke screens for supra-smoke-screen fire, as fleet air defenders, and, finally, with the increase in aircraft performance, as attack craft directed toward battleships as priority targets.[61] Naval aviators, however, believing that a major air engagement to clear the space over the opposing fleets would precede the final surface battle, increasingly considered the enemy's carriers as the main target of carrier air power. Thus, early in the 1930s, the Japanese navy held no unified doctrine as yet about how carriers would be used in a fleet action and, for that matter, no clear vision as to the role of air power in naval warfare.[62]

With every increase in the range and power of carrier aircraft, however, carriers became recognized above all for their ability to strike at targets beyond the range of surface guns and surface torpedoes. Gunnery staffs as well as airmen became convinced that carrier planes should be used for a preemptive strike against the enemy's carriers to achieve air superiority in the vicinity of the surface battle. Thus, about 1932–33, the navy began to shift its aerial targets from the enemy's battleships to his carriers. By mid-decade, with the improved performance of bombing aircraft, particularly the dive-bomber, the destruction of the enemy's carrier force became the focus of Japan's carrier forces. The emerging concept of mass aerial attack shifted carrier air power away from the defense of the main battle force to attack on targets over the horizon.[63] Essential to the execution of such a tactic was discovery of the enemy before he found the Japanese carriers. Thus, it was important that Japanese naval aviation be able to "outrange" the enemy in the air, just as Japanese surface forces could by shell and torpedo. Throughout the 1930s, accordingly, the navy emphasized range in its specifications for new aircraft.

The concept of a preemptive carrier strike gave rise to a difficult problem, whether to concentrate or disperse carriers in battle. The nub of the problem was that although carriers possessed great striking power, they were also extremely vulnerable to aerial assault. Thus, while their offensive power was best realized by concentrating them for a mass aerial attack, in such a formation they could conceivably be annihilated at one blow. If they were dispersed, however, individual carriers would have a smaller air defense; their weaker formations of attack aircraft would be more vulnerable to enemy fighters, and because of factors of time and fuel, their attacks would become more sporadic. In the early 1930s, when the navy had only two fleet carriers, the relative merits of concentration and dispersal could be tested only by tabletop maneuvers. By 1936, however, on the basis of fleet maneuvers (with three fleet carriers) as well as map exercises, most Japanese tacticians had come to favor the doctrine of dispersing carriers while nevertheless attempting to concentrate their attack aircraft once airborne. The keys to success were judged to be mass attacks, delivered preemptively, and the "outranging" of the enemy by the attack force.[64]

The general composition of Japanese carrier air groups during these years reflected these ideas. In keeping with the offensive priorities of emerging Japanese carrier doctrine, carrier air groups were weighted in favor of attack aircraft— dive-bombers and torpedo planes—over fighters. Among attack aircraft, the emphasis was on torpedo planes until the effectiveness of dive-bombing was conclusively demonstrated. By early 1941, most Japanese carriers embarked roughly equal numbers of torpedo planes and dive-bombers, though still far fewer fighters.[65]

LAND-BASED AIR POWER
The Naval Air Groups

In addition to developing carrier-based naval air power, the Japanese navy maintained many shore-based contingents in keeping with the strategy of providing a rapid defense of the home islands against the possible westward advance of an American naval offensive. Indeed, it was land-based aircraft that provided the bulk of Japan's naval aviation up to the eve of the Pacific War. In this, the Japanese navy was unique among the three major naval powers during the interwar period. In the immediate prewar years, the only analogy to Japan's shore-based naval air units were the two air wings of the U.S. Marine Corps.

The creation of land-based naval air contingents had begun at the end of World War I, when plans had been drawn up for seventeen such units, but these plans were not fully realized until 1931. Located at six bases around the Japanese home islands—Yokosuka, Sasebo, Kasumigaura, Omura, Tateyama, and Kure— these units were composed of various types of aircraft, most of which were seaplanes.[66] In sheer numbers the navy's land-based aircraft provided the greatest growth in Japan's naval air power in the years before the Pacific War. The Circle One naval expansion program, advanced in 1927, had called for the creation of twenty-eight new air groups.[67] Although only fourteen groups were actually established by 1934 (a response to American naval expansion under the first Vinson plan), the Circle Two program called for eight additional air groups to be created by the end of 1937. They were to operate out of six new air bases at Ōminato, Saeki, Yokohama, Maizuru, Kanoya, and Kisarazu in the home islands and Chinhae on the southern coast of Korea.

The biggest surge in Japanese land-based naval aviation, however, was yet to come. Under the pressure of the second Vinson plan in the United States, the Japanese navy picked up the pace in building its shore-based air forces. Not only was the deadline for completion of the aviation portion of the Circle One expansion moved up to 1937, but soon an all-out effort was made to complete the air component of Circle Two by the end of the same year.[68] By 31 December 1937, the navy possessed 563 aircraft based ashore. Added to the 332 aircraft aboard its carrier fleet, the navy thus had a total of 895 aircraft and 2,711 air crew (pilots and navigators) in thirty-nine air groups.[69] While this last figure was considerably less than total American naval air strength for the same period, Japan's shore-based naval aviation was substantially larger. This discrepancy in force structure would have been meaningless at the outset of any encounter between the two

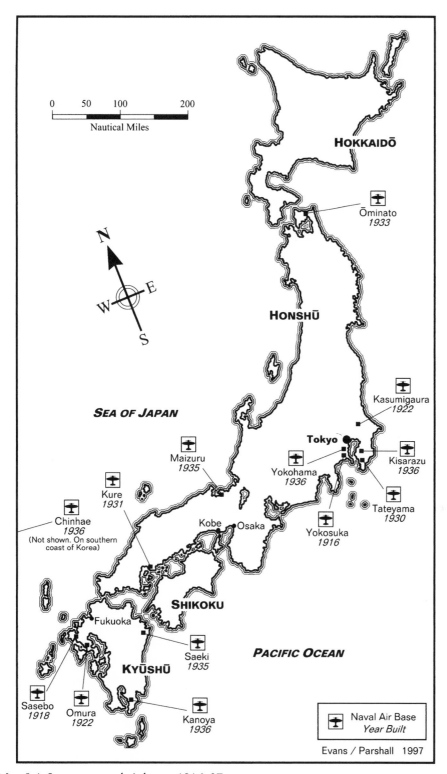

Map 9-1. Japanese naval air bases, 1916–37

naval powers in the 1930s. But the navy's substantial land-based air power worked to Japan's advantage when the nation went to war in 1937 with a land power, China.

The Development of the Land-Based Medium Bomber and Claims for "Air Power Omnipotence," 1927–37

During the interwar period, the evolution of the specific technologies, armaments, and tactics for a modern Japanese naval air service took place against the background of a broad and intensifying debate within the navy. The debate centered on the appropriate place of aviation in naval warfare generally. As in the U.S. Navy, the lines in this debate were drawn between the majority of officers in the fleet and high command who held that the main batteries of the Japanese battle line remained the final arbiter of victory at sea, and the much smaller group of air power enthusiasts who argued that the range, speed, and destructive capability of the airplane had substantially overturned the supremacy of the battleship. This debate was influenced by two factors. First, in Japan, as in other nations, the capacities of air weaponry were consistently exaggerated by its advocates during this period. In particular, governments assumed bomb-delivery aircraft capabilities that did not exist until World War II. In its initial phase, therefore, the aircraft versus gun debate was between visionaries who claimed for the airplane all the things that it could not yet do and realists who noted the enormous disparity in capabilities between air and surface units.

The second point is that in its later phase, the debate was not between a blindly obdurate battleship faction and a small clutch of airmen struggling to find a role for naval aviation. Rather it involved an argument between a battleship-oriented naval orthodoxy now sensitized to the potential of air power and a group of air-power radicals who believed that all future naval warfare would be decided by aviation. The former held that the offensive power that aviation had by then acquired should be exploited to insure victory by the surface fleet. The latter, centering their vision largely on the range and striking power of land-based heavy aircraft, advanced the theory of *kōkū bannō ron* (air-power omnipotence), which called for the scrapping of all capital ships.

In a sense, the debate began at the very dawn of Japanese naval aviation when, in January 1915, Engineer Lt. Nakajima Chikuhei, the future aircraft industry magnate, drafted a memorandum to the navy's Aeronautics Committee outlining his views on weapons procurement for the navy. The thrust of the memorandum was that even though the airplane was in its infancy, it was destined to be the decisive weapon of the future and that therefore the dreadnought battleship was now fatally threatened by the aerially launched torpedo and mine.[70] Given the relatively feeble capabilities of aircraft of the time, Nakajima's air power manifesto, the first of its kind in any country, was given short shrift in contemporary Japanese naval circles. Indeed, it had been the argument of a visionary; the realities of aircraft technology for the next several decades made it hardly likely that such frail machines could accomplish all that Nakajima and like-minded air-power advocates had expected of them.

Over a decade later this technological gap between air-power theory and air-power fact still hampered aviation proponents. Speaking at the Kasumigaura Naval Air Station in 1927 before a group of Navy General Staff officers, Lt. Comdr. (later Vice Adm.) Kusaka Ryūnosuke, destined to be one of Japanese naval aviation's most important figures, ticked off some obvious advantages provided by aircraft in naval combat, but was forced to admit the equally apparent limitations of most aircraft in naval warfare: They could not stay in the air for long periods of time; they had difficulty operating with the fleet over great distances; their operations were at the mercy of the weather; and, because they were still small, the bomb-carrying capacity of aircraft was too limited to cause substantial damage to an enemy fleet.[71]

To an extent, of course, the development of carriers and their aircraft solved some of these problems, but at a time when the Japanese government and armed services were concerned about the possibility of an enemy bringing *his* aircraft carriers close to Japanese shores, the range of those land-based aircraft then in service seemed insufficient. At the outset of the 1930s, several Japanese naval officers, including Yamamoto Isoroku, then head of the Technical Bureau of the Naval Aviation Department, argued for a new long-range capability for naval aviation and specifically for the development of a land-based bombing aircraft that could seek out and destroy an approaching enemy fleet while it was still far out at sea. Yamamoto was the one air-power advocate in the navy who had both the vision and the influence to make such an idea a reality for the defense of the home islands and beyond, out into the far reaches of the Pacific. Looking ahead to the day when Japan could use its demilitarized islands in Micronesia to create a chain of bases across the central Pacific, Yamamoto saw the tremendous "outranging" advantage of a long-range bomber operating from those bases. Shifting from one island base to another, such a flexible bomber attack would upgrade the Japanese navy's attrition strategy against the larger westward-moving American fleet.

With this concept in mind, Yamamoto initiated plans for the design of a land-based, all-metal, twin-engined monoplane with a range of 2,000 nautical miles and a 2-ton bomb load. The ultimate result of his initiative and of the efforts of the Mitsubishi Aircraft Corporation was the G3M.[72]

The land-based long-range bomber's appearance in the mid-1930s seemed to strengthen the arguments of the air-power supremacists in the Japanese navy. Their expectations were paralleled about the same time, however, by the hopes that the navy's so-called *teppō-ya* (gun club) placed on the plans for the construction of the superbattleships *Yamato* and *Musashi*. The conjunction of plans for these two opposing weapons systems—neither yet operational—fueled the sudden aircraft-versus-gun debate in the Japanese navy, a controversy little reported in the West at the time and largely overlooked by Western naval historians in the decades since.[73]

The debate was the result of two proposed solutions to the same problem: the numerical inferiority of the Japanese battle fleet in comparison to that of the United States. Japanese naval war games and maneuvers during these years had confirmed once again the inevitable victory of superior numbers in a collision between forces of similar composition. The solution of the "Gun Club" to this tactical dilemma was the construction of capital ships far more powerfully armed and armored than the enemy's. The solution of the air-power advocates, on the other hand, was to change drastically the composition of Japanese naval forces by making carriers, supported by lighter ships, the navy's main force, to circumvent and render irrelevant Japan's inferiority in capital ships.[74]

Among the first of the naval air staff to seize upon the appearance of the large land-based bomber as the harbinger of air-power supremacy was Capt. Ōnishi Takijirō, destined to become one of the navy's most forceful air-power advocates, a confidant of Yamamoto Isoroku, and the architect of the navy's desperate *kamikaze* strategy at the end of the Pacific War. During the 1930s, Ōnishi drafted several memoranda that set forth a radical critique of the navy's current battleship-oriented policies and called for the scrapping of all big gun ships and the placing of the navy's offensive capabilities mainly on aircraft, particularly on land-based bombers.[75] Other younger air-power advocates, restless under the battleship orthodoxy of the navy's high command, began to weigh in with similar opinions. Lt. Comdr. Genda Minoru, then a student at the Naval Staff College, drafted an essay proposing that the navy scrap its battleships and center its efforts on land- and carrier-based aircraft, with cruisers, destroyers, and submarines to be used in a supporting role.[76]

For his part, Yamamoto regarded the plans for the projected battleships as the height of folly. At first, he confined his opposition to sarcastic references to battleship orthodoxy in conversations with his colleagues and subordinates in naval aviation. At the talks preliminary to the London Naval Conference, despite his misgivings, he had followed his instructions and insisted upon parity for Japan in cruisers. But by the mid-1930s, the superbattleship project was under serious discussion as part of the Circle Three program. For that reason, he attempted to take the case for air power directly to the plan's powerful backers in the navy's upper echelons. Upon his return from London, he had met with Vice Adm. Koga Mineichi, chief of the Navy General Staff's Armaments Division; Capt. Fukuda Keiji of the Navy Technical Department, responsible for coordinating the design plans for the monster battleships; and Vice Adm. Nakamura Ryōzō, chief of the Navy Technical Department and one of the superbattleship project's most determined architects.

Fruitlessly, Yamamoto sought to demonstrate to these men the ultimate vulnerability and obsolescence of such warships. With detailed figures, he argued that the navy would gain far greater offensive power by spending the same amount of money on naval aviation.[77] The Japanese navy establishment adamantly defended the superbattleship project; its heated responses to criticism reflected a growing irritation at having its collective wisdom questioned. When Adm. Takahashi San-kichi, then commander of the Combined Fleet and still open-minded about the air-power-versus-battleship controversy, suggested to the ministry and general staff that perhaps the navy should concentrate on building its air power rather than building bigger battleships, he was told, in effect, to mind his own business. Despite his lofty command, Takahashi was from that time forward cut off by the general staff from any further information about the superbattleship project.[78]

The high command's rejection of the arguments of Yamamoto and the other air-power advocates was not just a matter of upper-echelon hubris. "Gun Club" officers believed that the concept of "air-power omnipotence" had serious flaws. As they pointed out, aircraft (in the mid-1930s) were still unreliable machines. Moreover, horizontal bombing had demonstrated no ability to sink a battleship under way. Conversely, they pointed out, both the offensive and defensive power of capital ships had increased: New techniques in spotting the fall of shot had supposedly doubled the accuracy of battleship main batteries, and the number and effectiveness of shipborne antiaircraft weapons had increased substantially.

It is, of course, the responsibility of military professionals not only to assay what is tactically feasible today, but also to anticipate what may be tactically feasible tomorrow. Their ability to read the future will be affected by the rapidity of technological change in any given era. In an age of slow progress, the prognosticator may appear to be a visionary. During World War I, at the dawn of naval aviation, the feeble capacities of aircraft lent an air of fantasy to the ideas of air-power enthusiasts like Nakajima Chikuhei. But by the mid-1930s, when Yamamoto Isoroku argued for the primacy of air power, the gap between air-power theory and technological reality was closing with a rush, and his predictions increasingly had the authority of coolheaded calculation.

Nevertheless, by the evidence available at mid-decade, the navy's battleship orthodoxy apparently had the greater logic in the controversy. The problem with

Yamamoto's arguments was that they still were more prediction than fact. Dive-bombing techniques and aerial torpedo tactics were still being worked out, and the new medium bomber had yet to be tested in any sort of combat, let alone employed to attack moving targets. Moreover, compared to the radical theories of air-power advocates like Ōnishi and Genda, who wanted to scrap all capital ships, the mainstream view that the navy needed both capital ships *and* aircraft, with the latter supporting the former, seemed a more rational balance of forces. The balance seemed to be confirmed by the adherence of the British and American navies to such a force structure and doctrine.

In any event, because the high command favored the superbattleship project, air-power advocates like Yamamoto were unable to halt it or to divert its resources to strengthening the navy's air power. In the years ahead, Japanese naval airmen would argue with increasing confidence for the primacy of air power, and a few even demanded its complete independence from the two established services. But at the outset of the post-treaty era, the capabilities of naval air power, to be convincing, would have to be demonstrated in actual aerial operations, not debated as part of an effort to downgrade the theoretical importance of the battle fleet. That opportunity would come within months over the skies of China.

Attacking a Continent
Japanese Naval Aviation in the China War, 1937–41

In Japan's war with China, 1937–41, the navy had two prime responsibilities. The first, support of amphibious landings on the Chinese coast by army ground forces, was a traditional role not only for the Japanese navy, but for naval forces in general and will not be discussed here. The second, the strategic aerial bombardment of Chinese cities, which was eventually carried deep into the Chinese interior, was unique in world naval history, since it was the first time that any navy had ever carried out such an effort. In summary, the campaign took place largely in the Yangtze River basin, beginning in the summer of 1937, with attacks on Chinese military installations along the Chinese coast by Japanese carrier aircraft. It reached its peak in 1938–39 with the ferocious bombardment of Chinese population centers deep in the Chinese interior by land-based medium bombers. The campaign concluded during 1940–41 with an attempt by the navy's tactical aircraft, both carrier and land-based, to cut Chinese communication and transportation routes in southern China. The 1937–41 air offensives utterly failed in their political and psychological aims (as did all strategic bombing campaigns prior to August 1945), though they did reduce the flow of strategic matériel to China and thus, for a time, eased the Japanese military situation in the central and southern parts of the country.

The Japanese air campaign against China strongly influenced the development of Japanese naval air power and Japanese naval thinking prior to the Pacific War. To begin with, despite the deeply rooted fixation of the Imperial Japanese Navy on warships as the decisive weapons of naval war, the navy's air war in China brought home to nearly its entire leadership the tremendous offensive potential of aerial weapons. In this sense, the war greatly altered the navy's assumptions concerning the use of air power. Aircraft had earlier been considered useful mainly in tactical roles, but the medium bombers' attacks on distant targets demonstrated their strategic value. Even fighter aircraft, envisioned as limited to a purely defensive role, came to be seen as offensive air weapons, particularly after the appearance of the A6M Zero.[79] Carrier fighter units, though trained for operations at sea, were found surprisingly effective in shooting up enemy airfield installations and aircraft on the ground. As a result, the navy began to experiment with the use of fighters to strafe surface targets at sea, particularly the bridges of enemy ships, to create confusion in the enemy command while carrier dive and torpedo bombers attacked hulls, decks, and main batteries.[80]

Just as important, the China War was of great value to the Japanese navy in demonstrating how aviation could contribute to the projection of naval power ashore. Quite probably, the air power assembled early in the war from Japanese carriers, along with that of the land-based air groups in Kyūshū and Taiwan, modestly prefigured the concentration of air power four and a half years later by the semi-independent carrier task group that undertook the Hawaii operation.

A corollary to the navy's recognition of the enormous potential, if not the primacy, of air power, was new thinking on the scale of aerial warfare. The air operations over China showed the tactical advantage of employing considerably larger units than had been contemplated before the conflict. Specifically, naval aviation leaders learned that because of Chinese fighter plane and antiaircraft defenses, the only way in which air strikes could be effective was to send up large formations of attack aircraft covered by a strong fighter force. Granted that air operations over land were different from operations at sea, the results of a concentration of air power in both situations were not all that different. If anything, they could be even more decisive at sea, where the destruction of a carrier was a permanent loss, whereas the crippling of an air base might be only temporary. Thus, the navy came to recognize the effectiveness of scale: The air group system had increasingly given way to the formation of combined air groups, and combined air groups brought about the concept of air fleets, with which the navy launched the massive hammer blows against Allied naval forces and facilities in the first months of the Pacific War.[81]

As a result of the air war over China, moreover, aircraft technology steadily improved as the lessons of air combat were effectively incorporated into aircraft design, either through the improvement of existing service models or the development of new types of aircraft. The coordination and integration of air combat experience with the capabilities of aircraft designers and production facilities would not have been possible, however, without the effective centralized institutions for research and development: the Naval Aviation Department, the Naval Air Arsenal, and the Yokosuka Naval Air Group. In the prosecution of the war these central command organizations, and research and testing units, were greatly expanded, and an improved system of combat supply and repair was initiated. These were important developments in the navy's preparation for the coming war with the U.S. Navy.[82]

Vital, too, was the tactical proficiency that the navy's fighter pilots gained during the China War. Before the conflict, the navy's air service was an organization without practical experience in modern air combat. As one veteran of the air war later pointed out, the exploits of individual fighter pilots during the Shanghai Incident of 1932 were colorful, but they really belonged to the Richthofen age of air duels rather than to that of modern air fighting.[83] Even the exercises of the Yokosuka Naval Air Group and the tactical experiments and innovations of veteran pilots in the mid-1930s could not begin to match in value the experience of furious combat over China. It was the skill of Japanese fighter pilots honed in air combat over China, 1937 to 1941, as much as the excellence of Japanese air weapons, that gave Japanese air power its potency in the first six months of the Pacific War.[84] Moreover, the Japanese naval air service had pioneered new roles for fighter aircraft. It was the world's first air force to use fighter planes as escorts on long-range bombing missions, a role not assumed by Allied fighter aircraft until 1943.[85]

The most singular progress in operational efficiency during the China War was made by the navy's land-based air groups. As a result of their missions deep into the interior of the continent, the medium bomber units gained confidence in long-range operations and demonstrated that the navy had a strategic as well as a tactical air arm, one capable of striking an enemy far behind the front lines on land or several hundred miles out at sea. Before the war, moreover, the navy's air power had been intended to sink enemy warships exclusively. But after the first year of the conflict, proficiency in knocking out enemy air bases and other land targets became an important gauge of the navy's combat readiness.[86]

Yet the air campaign over central and southern China, 1937–41, also worked to the detriment of the Japanese navy in general and its air service in particular. In the widest sense, it diverted the Japanese navy from its primary mission, the destruction of its American counterpart. Practice in air operations with the Combined Fleet had been halted or delayed. Except for air-to-air combat, few operations of the China air war—cooperation with army ground forces, bombardment of military and air facilities, interdiction of transportation and supply routes—involved missions of the sort that the navy had viewed as important. The effectiveness of naval air groups in China began to decline as they concentrated on land missions. This was particularly true of medium bomber units, since level bombing of land targets (particularly the random terror-bombing of cities) did not demand the same kind of accuracy necessary in bombing ship targets at sea. Moreover, though the navy periodically recycled most of its air groups back to service with the Combined Fleet during the China War, training in ocean reconnaissance, carrier flight deck operations, and attacks on surface vessels actually declined during this period. Another reason for this decline was the sudden expansion of naval air power in the years before the Pacific War. It forced the navy to spread both its budget and its instructor cadres over more naval air groups. Realistic training in carrier warfare—such as exercises in the concentration of carriers and their aircraft—was impeded. Thus, as the navy began to wind down its aerial operations on the continent in 1940 and 1941, the Combined Fleet had to train furiously to recover its naval air capabilities at sea.[87]

Nevertheless, in technology, fighting capabilities, and organizational efficiency, the Japanese naval air service was a far better combat arm in the summer of 1941 than it had been four years before. Indeed, if one can argue that by the summer of 1941, the Japanese naval air service was superior to its American counterpart in several major respects, then the differences stem from its experience and development during the China War.

COMING OF AGE
The Navy's Air Attack Tactics, 1937–41

Despite the distractions of the China War, the Japanese navy increasingly realized the importance of carrier air power and the growing probability of a clash with the U.S. Navy. To address these issues, the Japanese navy, in the years 1940–41 particularly, honed the tactics of its various carrier attack units and welded these units into an offensive system of great power and speed.

Of the navy's various aerial bombardment methods, horizontal bombing was given the most extensive trial during the China War. But although the navy's long-range, high-altitude bombing missions over China gave its air units useful experience in various aspects of such operations, they did little to improve the *accuracy* of the navy's bombers.[88] This was not a major concern for the Japanese navy until 1941, when, as part of its planning for the Pearl Harbor strike, navy tacticians concluded that success in attacking the U.S. ships in harbor could not be guaranteed by aerial torpedoes or dive-bombing by themselves, but would have to include horizontal bombing as well. To overcome the problem of inaccuracy of high-level bombing, navy tacticians reduced the drop altitude to 3,000 meters (9,800 feet) and instituted relentless training in tighter bombing formations. In the attack on Pearl Harbor, these improved tactics in high-altitude bombing paid off thunderously in an 80 percent hit rate and the sinking of the *Arizona*, though the navy never again achieved such success in the Pacific War.[89]

Dive-bombing tactics were also restudied and perfected during these years. Building on experiments in the mid-1930s and exploiting the advanced capabilities of the D3A dive-bomber, the navy began to work out a powerful formula for surprise attack on enemy ships. These called for dive-bombers to approach on a course opposite to the target, beginning their attack with a long, shallow dive, followed by a steep dive. After releasing their bombs at a height of 600 meters (about 2,000 feet) above the target and well before it, the dive-bombers ended with a sharp pull-up, using all possible maneuvers to avoid antiaircraft fire. When several bombing formations attacked at once they were to come in from different oblique angles to the target. By 1940, the navy adopted this technique as its standard dive-bombing tactic, one that achieved dramatic results in the first six months of the Pacific War, sinking two carriers (the *Hermes* and *Hornet*) and two heavy cruisers (the *Cornwall* and *Dorsetshire*).[90]

Though torpedo bombing played no part in the China War, the navy was nevertheless able to improve performance in this field through various innovations, constant practice at sea, and the acquisition of larger and more powerful torpedo aircraft. The navy ran experiments in massed attack, coordination of carrier and land-based torpedo operations, and night torpedo bombing. As in dive-bombing runs, Japanese torpedo bomber squadrons worked out a tactic for approaching the target bow on, dividing some 10–12 miles out, and attacking the target from opposite sides in a "hammer and anvil" technique. To minimize the possibility of collisions between attacking bombers, the navy set down rules that called for torpedo launches at greater heights and distances. Some naval airmen denounced the rules as too cautious, but the new methods reduced the hazards in training and caused improved hit percentages in aerial torpedo attacks.[91]

One final element in the evolution of aerial torpedo tactics deserves mention, since it played a decisive role in the opening hours of the Pacific War: shallow water attack. The Japanese navy's use of shallow torpedo attack on "Battleship Row" at Pearl Harbor was supposedly prompted by the British attack on the Italian fleet at Taranto in November 1940. The British assault may well have strengthened Japanese interest in such a tactic, but in fact the Japanese had already practiced this tactic in 1939 against their own fleet units anchored in the

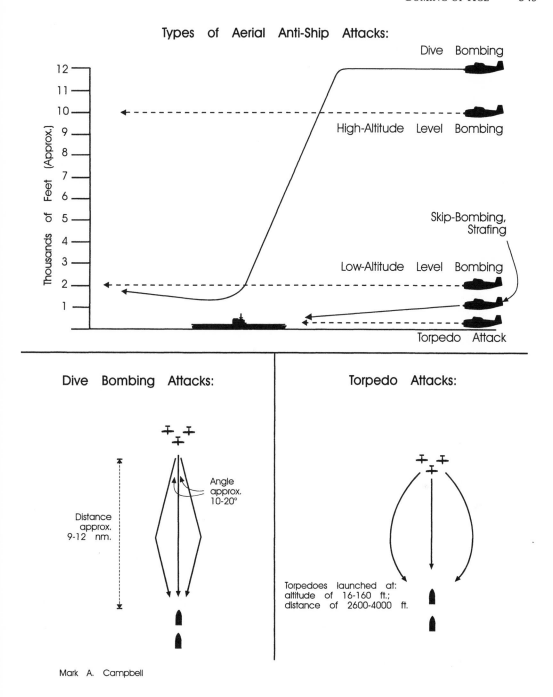

Mark A. Campbell

Fig. 9-10. Aircraft attacks against ships.
(Source: Joint Intelligence Center, Pacific Ocean Area, "Know Your Ememy: Japanese Aerial Tactics against Ship Targets," addendum to *CINCPAC-CINCPOA Weekly Intelligence,* 1 [October 20, 1944]: 19, 21–22)

shallow waters of Saeki Bay in Kyūshū. At the time, they did not have Pearl Harbor specifically in mind. The difficulties arising from this experiment had led the navy to study the problems of attack as it might be carried out in five major Asian and Pacific ports, including Pearl Harbor. The navy ultimately solved the problem by research and practice along two separate lines. The first was a series of innovations in the design of the type 91 aerial torpedo that stabilized it in flight, reduced its speed when it hit the water, and limited the depth of its initial plunge. The other was the relentless experimentation and practice in approaches and release techniques. These were carried out by torpedo pilots of the Yokosuka Naval Air Group over Kagoshima Bay in Kyūshū, led by Lt. Comdr. Murata Shigeharu, the navy's leading aerial torpedo specialist. The perfected tactics, as the world knows, were shatteringly successful at Pearl Harbor.[92]

In 1939, the Japanese navy began to devote much effort to melding all the air attack systems—horizontal, dive, and torpedo bombing, as well as fighter attacks—into a single system of massed aerial assault. The goal was to maximize the probability of carrier aircraft making hits on targets under way. Out of the research into this problem emerged an air attack doctrine that called for closely phased operations by fighters, dive-bombers, and torpedo aircraft. Some fighters would be used as escorts to the bombing aircraft; others would race ahead to strafe the bridges and decks of enemy carriers. These steps would immediately be followed by horizontal bombing attacks. Dive-bombing runs and a succession of torpedo attacks just above wave level would complete the coordinated assault.[93]

The execution of a scheme of such complexity and risk was difficult. It required an expanded tactical organization, meticulous planning, rigorous training, skilled air crews, and bold leadership. All these ingredients were essential, of course, to the preparations for the final realization of the scheme: the attack on the U.S. Pacific Fleet at anchor at Pearl Harbor.

FLEET AIR DEFENSE

The doctrine of a preemptive aerial strike on an enemy carrier force, naturally, raised issues of fleet air defense. In considering such a strike, Japanese tacticians assumed that the two strikes—one's own and the enemy's—would be launched about the same time. If so, how would they preserve part of the strike force to finish off the enemy after attacks on both sides? Also, how would they increase the defensive capabilities of their own carrier force to deal not only with the enemy's first strike, but also with his second?[94]

The Japanese navy was still wrestling with these questions as it plunged into the Pacific War. Generally speaking, the staff of the Combined Fleet had given scant consideration to the problem of fleet air defense prior to the conflict.[95] There were reasons for this neglect. The first, and probably the most important, was the navy's traditional fixation on offensive operations to the exclusion of all else.[96] Other reasons were practical. In the age before radar, detecting enemy fighters as they approached was extremely difficult. Lacking adequate radio communications (not to mention radar), organizing and directing an effective fighter cover was nearly impossible. Among the navy's air tacticians these considerations led to a general consensus that it would be impossible to defeat completely an enemy air strike. (This conclusion was shared by their counterparts in the U.S. Navy when it worked out the Fleet Problems of the 1930s.)

Japanese Carrier Doctrine, 1937–41

In the evolution of a system of integrated offensive operations by various types of naval aircraft, any operation involving massed aircraft could not have been even contemplated had not the navy first developed a system of concentrating its aircraft carriers. At the the outbreak of the China War, fleet maneuvers and tabletop war games had led the navy to favor the doctrine of dispersal for its carriers. But the first years of the war in China had demonstrated not only the improved performance of fighter planes, but also the importance of massing attack aircraft, both for bombing impact and for defense against enemy fighters. The navy soon concluded that bombers were only effective if they were massed and protected by substantial fighter cover. Extending these realities to air war at sea slowly but inevitably led to the conclusion that carrier forces must be concentrated.[97] But the question remained: If the carriers were concentrated would not this jeopardize all or most of the navy's carrier force if the enemy could get in the first strike?

By late 1940, the navy's tacticians hit upon a solution to this dilemma of tactical effectiveness versus strategic risk: a "box" formation of carriers. It provided not only more rapid massing of air groups for offensive operations but also a much larger combat air patrol and a greater concentration of antiaircraft fire than would be possible from any single carrier.[98] The next year, this innovation induced the Combined Fleet to undertake several operational experiments in the concentration of carriers. While these trials had some success, they demonstrated the need for a standing carrier command. Up to that point, the navy's carrier divisions (of generally two to three carriers each) were allotted to different fleets. Not only did both fleets and carrier divisions change from time to time, but there was little effort to work them together. There was thus no standardized carrier training program or any overall leadership for the kind of concentrated carrier tactics that seemed to offer the greatest offensive potential and defensive safety.

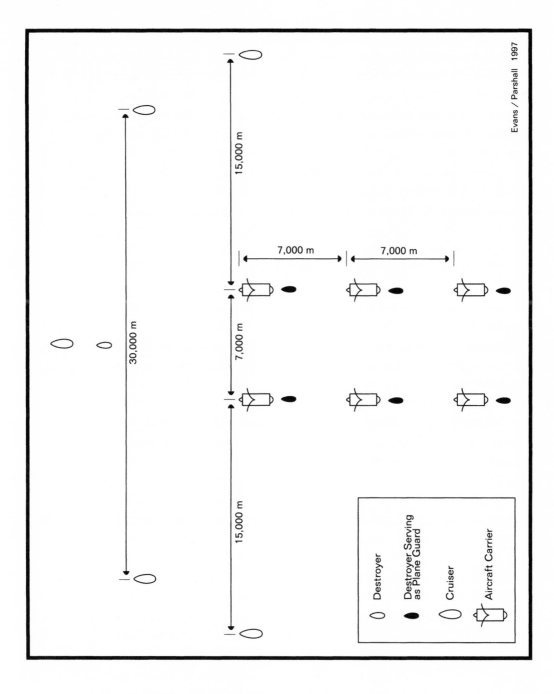

Fig. 9-11. Japanese "box" formation for carriers, 1941. (Source: Genda, *Shinjuwan sakusen*, 63)

It was Rear Adm. Ozawa Jisaburō who saw in the latent potential of the navy's scattered land-based air groups, as well as its dispersed aircraft carriers, a revolutionary means to achieve formidable offensive power. While not himself an aviator, Ozawa was well instructed in aviation matters, including carrier operations by his subordinates, who came to impress upon him the need to harness all the navy's air power under a single command. To that end, Ozawa undertook to persuade Admiral Yamamoto to form an "air fleet" within the Combined Fleet, so that all its air units—both carrier and land-based—would come together under a unified command. In late 1940 Yamamoto authorized the implementation of such a force, and in January 1941, the air fleet system was activated with the creation of the Eleventh Air Fleet. The fleet consisted of three air flotillas *(kōkū sentai*—the land-based equivalent of carrier divisions), comprising eight land-based air groups. In the coming conflict the components of this force would spearhead the navy's thrust into Southeast Asia in the winter of 1941–42.[99]

The real concentration of naval air power, however, came in April 1941 with the creation of the First Air Fleet, composed of three carrier divisions, two seaplane divisions, and ten destroyers.[100] When it was formed, the First Air Fleet was the single most powerful agglomeration of naval air power in the world, specifically including the U.S. Pacific Fleet. The First Air Fleet comprised all seven of Japan's commissioned fleet carriers and 474 aircraft: 137 fighters, 144 dive-bombers, and 183 torpedo planes (figures that include reserve aircraft). The First Air Fleet was not an independent tactical formation that could undertake a naval operation on its own, since unlike the later American task forces, it had no accompanying supply force or any significant surface escort. It formed only a component, though the single most important one, of the *kidō butai* (mobile [task] force or strike force) that Yamamoto sent across the Pacific for the Pearl Harbor strike. But in its massing of carriers, the First Air Fleet was revolutionary in strategic concept. The Pearl Harbor operation might not have been conceived, let alone executed, without the concept's existence.[101]

Although the First Air Fleet and the "box formation" of carriers had originally been formed to deliver a preemptive strike against enemy carriers, in the first six months of the Pacific War, when there was no significant Allied carrier force to challenge them, the fleet and carriers were used primarily against Allied land installations (the Indian Ocean raid and the Coral Sea campaign being the exceptions). In any event, at Midway, the First Air Fleet's concentration of carriers proved disastrous. After that battle, Japanese carrier doctrine adopted a compromise between concentration and dispersal. The navy's surviving and newly commissioned carriers were concentrated in divisions of three carriers each, but each division was widely separated from the others.[102]

Ozawa Jisaburō

Japanese Naval Air Power on the Eve of the Pacific War

By the late autumn of 1941, the Japanese naval air arm constituted the most potent offensive force of any of the three major navies, one whose flaws were not readily apparent at the time either to its foes or its own leadership. Indeed, one can argue that in assessing Japan's naval air power in relation to that of its most dangerous rival, the U.S. Navy, its weaknesses were the obverse of its strengths.

At this point, the navy's combat aircraft were among the world's finest and, with important exceptions, could generally fly faster and farther and could outperform their American counterparts. Most of these aircraft had fatal weaknesses, however, largely those of inadequate protection for their fuel tanks and air crews. In any event, in a struggle with a naval enemy backed by the wealth of industrial resources available to the United States, there were too few aircraft for anything but a short conflict.

By December 1941, the Japanese navy possessed over 3,000 aircraft (operational and reserve), of which about 1,800 were combat aircraft and a little over 500 were training aircraft.[103] This contrasts with the nearly 5,000 U.S. Navy aircraft available at the outset of the Pacific War, of which nearly half were trainers.[104] Generally inferior in performance to Japanese aircraft and dispersed over two seacoasts and island possessions, American naval aircraft appeared, collectively, to put the U.S. Navy at a major disadvantage at that time. Yet American technological skills and productive capacity would eventually alter these comparisons dramatically.

Japanese naval fliers were superbly trained, combat-experienced aviators, the best of whom were stationed on carriers. Behind these men, however, were few trained reservists. The U.S. Navy and U.S. Marine Corps, on the other hand, had a far larger pilot pool. If at that point these men lacked both the flight time and the combat experience of their Japanese counterparts, the U.S. Navy's ability to augment their numbers in the months to come would be a telling element in any extended conflict with the Japanese navy. At the beginning of the war, however, the superior quality of its air crews gave the Japanese navy a substantial initial advantage.

In the years immediately before the Pacific War, however, the Japanese navy had given insufficient thought to some of the most basic implications of its greatly augmented air power. The navy's leadership, which had for years planned the all-decisive encounter with the main force of the U.S. Navy, had scarcely considered the problems of naval air maintenance and replenishment. At great cost, the navy would learn how easily exhaustible both aircraft and personnel were in a major air battle. Moreover, the Japanese navy never really gauged the capacity of the United States to wage a protracted naval air war. At the opening of hostilities in December 1941, the technical skills of Japanese navy air crews and the quality of its aircraft, weapons, and equipment were superb. But the naval high command, without planning or forethought, plunged into the conflict. They did not accurately assess how these elements compared with those of the enemy or consider the enemy's prospects for improvement in these categories in the case of a protracted war.[105]

On paper, the Japanese carrier forces were superior to the U.S. and British forces in December 1941: For the ten Japanese carriers, there were six American (the *Hornet* was working up but not yet operational), of which only three were in the Pacific, plus a small British carrier in the Indian Ocean. But without doubt, the most potent aspect of Japanese naval air power at the onset of the Pacific War was the welding of its carrier forces into an effective administrative and operational unit. Though all three navies had experimented with carriers working together, the U.S. Navy having specifically done so during a number of its Fleet Problems of the 1930s, only the Imperial Japanese Navy had translated this practice into a permanent carrier force, the First Air Fleet, as contrasted with ad hoc U.S. carrier forces organized for exercises.[106] The pilots of the First Air Fleet had trained together intensively in the tactics of combined aerial assault. In December 1941, they stood poised to deliver a thunderbolt.

For all its striking power, however, the First Air Fleet was still not regarded by the Japanese naval leadership as the main element of the Combined Fleet. According to Japanese naval orthodoxy, that role was still reserved for "big ships and big guns." The next chapter discusses the navy's acquisition of the biggest warships and biggest naval guns the world had yet seen.

10

THE BATTLE
—of the—
SHIPYARDS

Japanese Naval Construction, 1937–1941

The international system of naval arms limitations legally remained in force until January 1937. In fact, however, a new naval arms race had begun in January 1936 with the failure of the second London naval conference after Japan's announcement that it would allow the treaties to lapse. As noted previously, by the early 1930s, the Japanese navy had developed a Janus-faced policy toward the treaties. To its Anglo-American rivals and the rest of the outside world, it advocated parity in all major warship types within the framework of the treaty system. Domestically, the navy, or rather its dominant antitreaty faction, confident of Japan's ability to maintain qualitative superiority in an arms race with the United States, had worked to undermine governmental and public support of the nation's further participation in the naval arms limitation system.

For its part, the United States had already embarked on a major naval construction program to make up for a decade of fiscal constraint and reliance on international agreements to guarantee its naval security. During this decade, 1922–32, Japan built more than twice the tonnage in warships that the United States built, and most of the other naval powers had also outdone the United States in naval construction.[1]

While the U.S. Navy had been authorized to acquire several new carriers and cruisers at the outset of the new decade, the first major effort to rectify America's weakness in relation to Japan and other naval powers—the Vinson-Trammell bill of 1934, sometimes called the first Vinson plan—was directed at bringing the navy up to its treaty limits by the construction of 102 ships over an eight-year period, 1934–42. Because the American "treaty" navy, like its Japanese counterpart, was built around a battleship force supported by other warship types, it is not surprising that a subsequent naval bill, signed by President Roosevelt in June 1936, authorized the construction of two capital ships as soon as such replacements in this category were permitted by the treaty. Believing that the treaty system might soon be moribund, American designers had been instructed to draft plans for the two battleships in any event. Laid down in June 1937 and completed in 1941, the 35,000-ton *North Carolina* and *Washington* represented an enormous advance in speed, armor, and fire control over *West Virginia,* the last American battleship constructed before the treaty era.[2]

But American naval leadership during the interwar years had remained convinced that maintaining a balanced fleet was critical to defeating Japan. The battleship force could not fight its way westward across the Pacific by itself; it needed a sufficient number of supporting arms and auxiliary vessels. Given the increasing complexity of naval armaments, therefore, the United States was obliged to spread its expenditures over a growing number of warship categories essential to the security of the battle line.[3] Thus, during the great expansion of American naval strength during the 1930s, what is noteworthy is not the augmentation of the U.S. battleship force, but the increase of other and sometimes new elements of sea power: the strengthening of the naval air arm, the modernization of the submarine fleet, the substitution of carrier aircraft and long-range reconnaissance planes for cruisers in the scouting role, the improvement of the navy's logistical capacities through the construction of high-speed tankers, and the development of effective techniques for refueling at sea, to name the most significant.[4]

In the late 1930s, worsening relations between Japan and the United States led to a further expansion of the U.S. Fleet. Japan invaded China in the summer of 1937, and in December of that year, Japanese navy planes sank the U.S. gunboat *Panay,* which had been on station in the Yangtze. These developments lay behind the so-called second Vinson plan of 1938, which authorized an increase of 20 percent in overall tonnage. Then, following the construction of the treaty carriers *Yorktown* and *Enterprise* and the light carrier *Wasp,* the navy turned once again to adding battleships. In November 1938, the Navy Department announced plans for the construction of four *South Dakota*-class battleships, along with nine light cruisers, twenty-three destroyers, two submarines, a thousand naval aircraft, and the modernization of several older warships.[5]

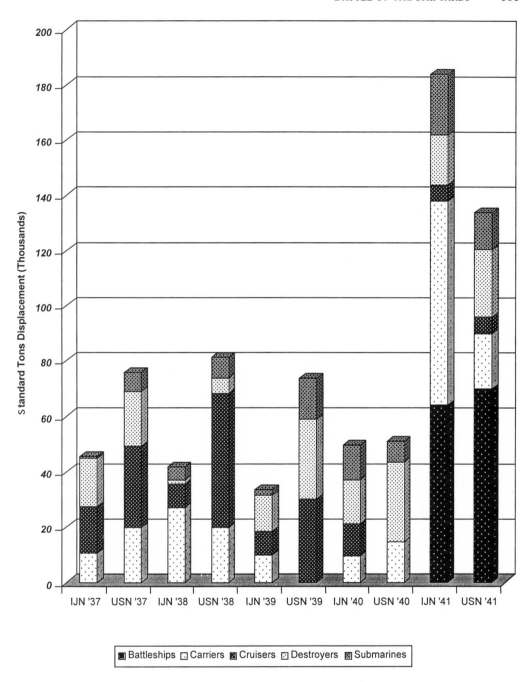

Fig. 10-1. U.S. and Japanese naval shipbuilding, major combatants completed, 1937–41.

In 1940, American naval power made a number of formidable advances. In early June, Congress passed yet another expansion bill authored by Carl Vinson, this one providing for an 11 percent increase in naval tonnage and for a great expansion of naval aviation. But events overtook this bill even as it was being passed. Galvanized by the threat posed by the enormous German victories in Europe , and realizing that Japan might move into Southeast Asia, in mid-June, the United States announced a huge building program—the "Two-Ocean Navy" Act. The act aimed at allowing the navy to conduct simultaneous major operations in European waters and the Pacific by creating two separate and balanced fleets. Then in July, following the recommendations of Adm. Harold Stark, Chief of Naval Operations, Congress passed a vastly expanded Two-Ocean Navy bill. Sometimes called the Stark plan after its prime mover, this unprecedented building program would increase the size of the navy by 70 percent and would take eight years to complete. Stark himself estimated that it would require about 18 fast aircraft carriers and 200 ships in other categories: battleships, small carriers, cruisers, destroyers, submarines, and an enormous fleet train, in addition to the 3,000 aircraft called for in the plan.[6]

With the enactment of this enormously ambitious naval construction program the United States, in effect, made a bid to become the world's largest and most powerful navy. But the Two-Ocean Navy Act was not an unrealistic flight of American naval ambition. Behind the act, and ready to produce the great arsenal of ships and aircraft it called for, stood the enormous industrial might of the United States. Against this hugely expanding American industrial capacity, which by 1940 had fully recovered, and renascent American naval power, the Japanese navy was obliged to shape its own expansion in the five years between the end of the treaty era and the onset of the Pacific War.

JAPANESE NAVAL CONSTRUCTION PLANS, 1937–41

Japan, having abrogated the naval arms limitations agreements and freed itself from the Anglo-American imposition of a 60 percent ratio in major warship construction, believed that it had at last recovered the essential element of its naval security—the ability to build up to at least 70 percent of the U.S. Navy's naval tonnage. A world without a treaty, however, proved more threatening to Japan than its naval leadership had foreseen. The United States, freed from treaty restrictions as well, could now not only build up to the old treaty limits, but put its industrial might into naval rearmament that surged far beyond those limits. The successive American naval expansion plans eventually extinguished Japanese hopes of attaining a 70 percent ratio (let alone parity), and Japanese naval leaders began to fear that their naval strength might even sink below 60 percent vis-à-vis the United

States. Given that ominous possibility, the Japanese navy's only recourse, as its leaders saw it, was exceptional weapons, further improvement of skills, and "making up for quantity by means of quality."[7] In the navy's post-treaty era, this conviction led to some basic decisions concerning naval construction, of which its superbattleship strategy is only the most famous.

In October 1935, representatives of the Navy General Staff and Navy Ministry met to shape a program of naval construction in the new period of complete naval autonomy. In 1937, as a result of these consultations and of the subsequent discussions and planning over the next several years, the navy began the Circle Three plan, its third major naval building program since 1930. Circle Three was a six-year building project that not only gave expression to the liberation of the Japanese navy from the old treaty restrictions, but concentrated its efforts on qualitative superiority to compensate for its quantitative deficiencies compared with the United States.[8]

While the heart of Circle Three was the construction of the two superbattleships *Yamato* and *Musashi*, it also called for the construction of the two *Shōkaku*-class carriers (chapter 9), along with sixty-four other warships in other categories. The navy realized that modernization of existing ships was one of the least expensive means of dealing with the anticipated American quantitative lead in major fleet units. Circle Three consequently also called for the rearming of the demilitarized battleship *Hiei* and the refitting of her sister ships, the *Kongō*, *Haruna*, and *Kirishima*. The navy similarly hastened to upgrade the four *Mogami*-class cruisers by replacing their 6-inch main batteries with 8-inch guns. The two *Tone*-class cruisers under construction were similarly completed. In aviation, Circle Three aimed at maintaining parity with American naval air power by adding 827 planes to be allocated to fourteen new land-based air groups and by increasing shipborne aircraft by nearly 1,000. Along with the sharp rise in the number of aircraft, the plan called for several new airfields to be built or expanded and for a significant increase in the size of the navy's production facilities for aircraft and aircraft weapons.[9]

In the summer of 1937, just as the first construction contemplated under the Circle Three program had begun, the navy found itself embroiled in the expanding conflict on the China mainland. To accommodate the sudden diversion of substantial naval forces to meet this new crisis and to deal with the worsening international climate, the navy had to undertake four *sembi sokushin keikaku* (armament accelerations plans) that hastened certain projects in Circle Three. Two plans were instituted in the summer and early fall of 1937, one in 1938, and one in September 1939. The first three plans provided for the rapid modernization of certain larger fleet units, but their main emphasis was the construction or refitting of smaller warships and the conversion of merchant ships for fleet service.

The fourth plan, instituted upon the outbreak of the war in Europe, speeded up still further the refitting projects throughout the fleet that were deemed necessary to the commissioning of all serviceable warships.[10]

In 1938, with the construction of Circle Three under way, the navy high command had begun to consider preparations for the next major expansion, tentatively scheduled for 1940. But the quantum leap in American naval power projected by the second Vinson plan pushed the general staff into accelerating its planning schedule, lest in five years the navy find itself quantitatively inferior by 300,000 tons and a thousand aircraft. A furious round of staff-to-ministry consultations ensued, the product of which was the Circle Four six-year expansion program, approved in September 1939. Circle Four called for the building of two more *Yamato*-class superbattleships to replace the aging *Haruna* and *Kirishima,* a fleet carrier (which became the *Taihō),* six of a new class of planned escort carriers, six cruisers, twenty-two destroyers (to start the replacement of the *Akizuki* class, which would be overage by 1943), and twenty-five submarines (ten of which were to be replacements for those I-class submarines, also expected to be overage by 1943).[11]

The real emphasis, however, was on naval air power, in which the Japanese navy hoped to take the lead. Circle Four called for the acquisition of 175 ship-based aircraft and nearly 1,500 aircraft to be allocated to seventy-five new land-based air groups. Upon completion of its air expansion under Circle Four, the Japanese navy would have 874 ship-based aircraft and 3,341 aircraft in 128 land-based air groups, 65 of these being combat air groups and 63, training groups.[12] With its goal of doubling Japan's naval air strength in just five years, Circle Four was a ferociously ambitious program aimed at achieving air superiority in East Asia and the western Pacific. In attempting this objective the navy realized that its success or failure greatly depended on how rapidly the nation's civilian industrial capacity could meet the challenge. Using the momentum of the stepped-up aircraft production required under the Circle Three program, the navy hoped to promote a greatly accelerated expansion of what was still a very young aircraft industry. In any event, aircraft production by civilian manufacturers did increase; 5,088 military aircraft were produced in 1941. However, this was not sufficient to overtake the American aircraft industry, which produced 19,433 military aircraft during the same year.[13]

In the fall of 1939, with the outbreak of the war in Europe, the representatives of the Navy General Staff and Navy Ministry began preliminary consultations on the scale and content of the next round of naval construction, the Circle Five program. These discussions continued into 1940, but by then Japan's naval leaders had become increasingly pessimistic about their nation's ability to maintain its 70 percent ratio of naval strength in competition with the United States. (They were determined, however, to maintain parity in aircraft carriers and thus turned to the conversion of the "shadow fleet" of merchant liners discussed earlier.) As usual, the Navy General Staff weighed in with a wish list that was extreme in its demands: three more superbattleships, three carriers, two "supercruisers," thirty-two destroyers, forty-five submarines, sixty-seven land-based combat air groups (1,320 aircraft) and ninety-three training groups (2,138 aircraft). The Navy Ministry, considering the financial, material, and industrial limits of Japan, including the fact that Japanese shipyards were already filled with orders placed under Circle Three and Circle Four, believed that such an expansion schedule for major fleet units would take at least nine years to complete. For that reason, the ministry argued that work should be begun on the aviation portion of the program, a task that could be completed far faster than would warship construction.[14]

The projected increase in the number of American naval aircraft made public in the spring of 1940, as well as continuing Japanese losses in the air war over China, made it impossible for the Japanese navy to maintain parity in naval aviation. Given speculation that in the event of Japan-U.S. hostilities, the United States might attempt to deploy a sizable number of aircraft in Asia, most probably in the Philippines, the American naval air lead seemed more ominous than ever before. On the other hand, the navy believed (to its eventual sorrow) that American air power had a low level of effectiveness and that Japanese naval air mobility could be enhanced by a suitable distribution of air bases in Asia and the western Pacific, which might make up for numerical inferiority. Thus Japan needed only to maintain air strength sufficient to trap these forward American air units in the event of war. Such, at least, was the Japanese thinking at the time.[15]

The staff and ministry officers were putting the finishing touches on the Circle Five expansion plan when they received intelligence providing details of the awesome American Two-Ocean Navy program. Shocked, the Japanese naval high command hastily reconvened its meetings to consider how to face the new American challenge. While the Circle Five program was undergoing revision in light of the Stark plan, the Navy General Staff therefore began pondering a sixth expansion program to narrow the gap in projected American and Japanese naval power. Once again, the staff solution was to add more superbattleships to the fleet. Whereas Circles Three and Four called for four such monsters, Circles Five and Six spoke vaguely of laying down *seven* more, each armed with 50-centimeter (nearly 20-inch) guns.[16] The unrealism of such schemes, given that the nation's shipyards were already working at full capacity and its material and financial resources were strained to the utmost, reveals a growing insubstantiality and incoherence of the navy's construction plans under the pressures of approaching war and the American industrial challenge.

In May 1941, a draft of the Circle Five plan was hammered out by the Navy General Staff and handed to the Navy Ministry for execution. The Navy Ministry then entered into negotiations with the Finance Ministry and the Cabinet Planning Board, as well as the Army Ministry, for the necessary funding, industrial capacity, and interservice cooperation. The last was particularly important. The unprecedented scale and cost of this expansion program meant that budgetary priorities had definitely shifted to the navy. In June, the Navy General Staff asked the support of the Army General Staff for allocations of matériel required for the construction the navy envisaged under the plan. The latter gave its provisional and reluctant approval, but its serious qualifications ultimately led to fierce squabbling between the two staffs over national armaments production, still another manifestation of an old problem becoming increasingly dangerous to Japan's security.[17]

In any event, Circles Five and Six were destined to become empty schemes for the massive and long-range augmentation of the Japanese navy, overtaken by the more immediate necessities of the Pacific War. Few ships planned under Circle Five were ever completed, and planning for Circle Six never got beyond initial studies. After the Battle of Midway in June 1942, Circle Five was completely canceled and replaced by a "Revised Circle Five" construction program that gave greater priority to carriers and submarines.[18]

In 1941, while the navy was grappling with the problems of long-range planning for the construction of major naval units, it discovered that there were far more immediate needs across a range of warship types, many of them auxiliaries: minelayers, minesweepers, supply ships, and such. That year, to make up for these deficiencies by 1943, the navy undertook three special circle plans, each of which was designated by a different ideogram identifying it by name: the Circle *Rin* (provisional) program, which provided for the construction of nearly 60,000 tons of auxiliary vessels; the Circle *Kyū* (emergency) program, which hastened construction of two carriers, twenty-six destroyers, and thirty-three submarines of various types; and the Circle *Tsui* (follow-up) program, which was simply an advance on, and a supplement to, Circle Five for a few auxiliary vessels.[19]

By the eve of the Pacific War, by dint of tremendous effort, the Japanese navy had completed nearly all the construction itemized under the Circle Three program; half of the Circle Four and half of the "provisional" program were well under way; a portion of the "follow-up" program was completed and a portion of the "emergency" program had been begun, for a total of 230 warships and 160 other vessels.[20] When the war finally came, however, the ships that these building programs provided would be too few and too many of the wrong kind.

Another category of measures, the *suishi jumbi,* was instituted in 1940–41 to put the navy on a wartime footing. The term *suishi jumbi,* dating from the Sino-Japanese War of 1894–95, is best translated as "preparatory fleet mobilization." The origin of such measures lay in the fact that, for reasons of economy, a significant portion of the Japanese navy remained in reserve status during peacetime. Not only were some officers and enlisted men on half-pay reserve, but many warships, even first-class units, were designated as reserve, with downgraded personnel, fuel, and ammunition—conditions that made them unready for combat.[21] There were, as well, merchant ships, like those of the "shadow fleet" whose construction had been subsidized by the navy in the 1920s and 1930s, which operated in a civilian capacity during peacetime. During a period of hostilities, however, the navy could legally lay claim to their use.

The *suishi jumbi,* therefore, comprised standing instructions during peacetime, reviewed annually and revised as needed, to convert the entire navy to a wartime footing should hostilities appear imminent. The measures originated with the Navy General Staff and were passed on to the Navy Ministry, which then submitted them to the cabinet for approval. The plans included the recall of all reserve personnel to active duty, the reactivation of all reserve fleet units (mustering complete complements for each ship, cleaning all boilers, topping off fuel bunkers, loading necessary ammunition, testing all machinery, etc.), expropriation of civilian merchant vessels and converting them as needed for naval service, and all other measures necessary to bring the fleet to a state of full combat readiness. The activation of such plans would be a giant step toward taking the navy into full-scale hostilities. For that reason, instructions for such activation in 1940 and 1941 were held in the tightest secrecy by the navy. They were also the subject of the most intense consultation and negotiation with the army and the cabinet. The instructions included a major revision, in favor of the navy, of the standing arrangements for the allocation of strategic materials, as well as the requisition and conversion of merchant ships.[22]

While new construction was continuing during the five years before the Pacific War, the navy was also energetically pushing through refitting projects for warships in need of modernization. The navy's modernization program began in 1936 and reached its height in 1939 and 1940. By the beginning of the Pacific War, only a single vessel—a destroyer—was deemed in need of a major overhaul.[23]

All these modernization and new construction projects were undertaken by the navy's own four yards—Yokosuka, Kure, Sasebo, and Maizuru (a fifth, at Ōminato, only handled major repair work)—and eight major commercial yards. As discussed in earlier chapters, private yards had played a major role in Japanese naval construction ever since the late nineteenth century. Their prime position stemmed from the Japanese navy's consistent support of the nation's commercial yards as a vital strategic industry. In subsequent decades, the navy had placed a considerable portion of its construction orders with private shipbuilders, not only to make up for its own inadequate shipyard capacity, but also to maintain and improve the technical skills of that industry's labor force.[24] To facilitate further experience in naval construction, the Navy Technical Department allotted construction of particular categories of warships to specific shipyards, both navy and commercial (table 10-1).

Table 10-1

JAPANESE NAVAL CONSTRUCTION BY WARSHIP CATEGORIES ALLOCATED TO PRINCIPAL
SHIPYARDS, CIRCA 1941

Warship category	Shipyard
Battleships, *fleet carriers,* heavy cruisers, submarines	Yokosuka Navy Yard
Battleships, heavy cruisers, submarines	Kure Navy Yard
Light cruisers, destroyers, submarines	Sasebo Navy Yard
Destroyers, submarines	Maizuru Navy Yard
Battleships, cruisers	Mitsubishi (Nagasaki)
Submarines	Mitsubishi (Kobe)
Special ships	Mitsubishi (Yokohama)
Carriers, cruisers, submarines	Kawasaki
Destroyers, smaller craft	Ishikawajima
Destroyers, smaller craft	Uraga
Destroyers, smaller craft	Fujinagata
Submarines, smaller craft	Mitsui

Italics show that more ships of this category were built at the particular shipyard than at any
other yard or that the first of a class of ships was built at that yard, which then had the responsibility of establishing uniform blueprints and procedures for other yards constructing ships
from the class.
Source: *SZ*, 1: 738.

Over the years, commercial yards came to occupy an increasingly important
role in the navy's construction schemes. Of the 1,794,000 tons of naval construction launched in Japan from 1926 to the end of the Pacific War, 1,056,000 tons,
or 59 percent, were built in commercial yards, and 737,800 tons, or 41 percent, in
navy yards. In the five years of the post-treaty era before the Pacific War, naval
construction even more clearly depended on the private sector (table 10-2).[25]
During the war, this dependence on the private shipbuilding industry for naval
construction posed a terrible dilemma for the nation. The navy's increasing
demands on commercial yards (which were, after all, the only source of merchant

ship construction) made it extremely difficult to replace merchant ship losses resulting from enemy submarine and air action. Japan simply did not have the shipyard capacity to built both the warships and merchant vessels needed to fight a war with the United States.

COMPARING U.S. AND JAPANESE NAVAL CONSTRUCTION, 1937–41
Destroyers

We have alluded to the unreality of Japan's naval augmentation plans pushed forward in the last year or so before the outbreak of the Pacific War. Not only were the most ambitious schemes beyond the capacity of Japanese industry to realize within the time projected, but they were doomed to be overtaken in the post-treaty period and overwhelmed in the war years by both the size and the efficiency of the American shipbuilding industry.

The scale of the Japanese problem can be seen from the data on U.S. and Japanese naval construction shown in tables 10-3 and 10-4. America's preponderance is indicated by a few salient facts. When Japan decided to commence hostilities in December 1941, the United States was building eight new battleships and five new *Essex*-class aircraft carriers. At the end of those hostilities, the United States possessed ninety-eight carriers, of which twenty-eight were fleet carriers, to Japan's

Table 10-2

NAVAL CONSTRUCTION IN THE JAPANESE NAVY AND COMMERCIAL YARDS
1937–41

YEAR	TOTAL CONSTRUCTION	CONSTRUCTION IN NAVY YARDS	PERCENT	CONSTRUCTION IN PRIVATE YARDS	PERCENT
1937	59,990	33,350	56	26,640	44
1938	50,300	18,400	37	31,900	63
1939	109,840	50,200	46	59,640	54
1940	210,810	85,900	41	124,910	59
1941	120,420	24,300	20	96,120	80

The figures are given in launched, not delivered, tonnage.
Source: *SZ*, 1: 738.

remaining four (only two of which, the *Hōshō* and *Katsuragi,* could be considered even remotely operational). The most dramatic comparison comes from H. P. Willmott, who pointed out that "Such was the scale of American industrial power that if during the Pearl Harbor attack the Imperial Navy had been able to sink every major unit of the entire U.S. Navy and then complete its own construction programs without losing a single unit, by mid-1944 it would still not have been able to put to sea a fleet equal to the one the Americans could have assembled in the intervening thirty months."[26]

The primary reasons for the huge discrepancy between the productivity of American and Japanese shipyards lies, of course, in the enormous difference in financial wealth and industrial resources available to the two nations. A detailed elaboration of all factors involved, particularly since they have been the subject of other comprehensive studies on the relative war potentials of the great powers on the eve of World War II, is beyond the scope of this book.[27] Of note here, however, is that of the $68 billion of the national income of the United States in 1937 only 1.5 percent was being spent on national defense, whereas in the same year Japan was already devoting over 28 percent of its relatively puny $4 billion national income to the same purpose. The industrial resources available to each power were correspondingly disproportionate. Steel, the central component of naval construction, demonstrates this clearly. Production of ingot steel in the United States in 1940, for example, was 61 million metric tons; in Japan, 7.5 million metric tons.[28]

But explanations of a superior American ability to build ships in quantity go beyond matters of greater wealth and industrial resources. To understand the nature of the quantitative American superiority in naval construction it is useful to compare American and Japanese construction in one particular category of warships. Destroyers will serve as an example.[29]

Until the end of World War I, the Japanese navy had significantly more destroyers than did the U.S. Navy, but the huge American naval building program at war's end reversed this situation. By 1921, the U.S. Navy had about 300 destroyers, compared with just under 100 for Japan. With such numbers, the United States felt no need to lay down additional destroyer hulls until the early 1930s. On the other hand, the Japanese navy during the 1921–32 period undertook a significant destroyer construction program, laying down 57 such hulls during these years. Some of these vessels, particularly the *Fubuki* class, possessed outstanding qualities. Beginning with the hull of the first of the 8-ship *Farragut* class, laid down in 1932, the United States began a major effort to catch up and eventually overtake Japan in destroyers. The number in each class generally increased through the decade: for example, the *Benson* class, built between 1937 and 1940, comprised 32 ships; the *Livermore* class, launched between 1938 and 1941, had 64; and the *Fletcher* class, the first of which was laid down in 1940,

Table 10-3

U.S. AND JAPANESE MAJOR COMBATANTS: COMPLETIONS AND COMMISSIONINGS BY YEAR 1937–41

	BATTLESHIPS		CARRIERS		CRUISERS		DESTROYERS		SUBMARINES	
	USN	IJN	USN	IJN	USN	IJN	USN	IJN	USN	IJN
1937	—	—	19,900 (1)	10,500 (1)	29,350 (3)	17,000 (2)	19,850 (13)	17,340 (12)	6,770 (5)	700 (1)
1938	—	—	19,900 (1)	27,000 (3)	48,500 (5)	8,500 (1)	5,500 (3)	1,500 (1)	7,250 (5)	4,755 (3)
1939	—	—	—	10,050 (1)	30,000 (3)	8,500 (1)	28,920 (19)	13,000 (7)	14,750 (10)	2,180 (1)
1940	—	—	14,700 (1)	9,500 (1)	—	11,600 (2)	28,900 (18)	16,000 (8)	7,375 (5)	12,640 (6)
1941	70,000 (2)	64,000 (1)	20,000 (1)	74,000 (5)	6,000 (1)	5,800 (1)	24,450 (15)	18,160 (9)	13,400 (10)	21,930 (11)

The table shows ships commissioned (USN) or delivered (IJN) by year. The first figure shows aggregate standard tons; the second (in parentheses), the number of ships of the type. U.S. data is based on the calendar year, Japanese on the Japanese fiscal year (April to March).
Sources: *Dictionary of American Naval Fighting Ships*, vols. 1 and 2; Fahey, *Ships and Aircraft of the U.S. Fleet*, war edition; and U.S. Strategic Bombing Survey, Military Supplies Division, *Japanese Naval Shipbuilding*, appendix A, 15.

Table 10-4

Total Wartime Completions and Commissionings of Principal Naval Vessels, 1942–45

	U.S. Navy	Imperial Japanese Navy
Battleships	320,000 (8)	64,000 (1)
Escort aircraft carriers	670,000 (82)	53,490 (3)
Destroyers	737,420 (354)	106,620 (61)
Aircraft carriers	703,900 (30)	190,900 (7)
Cruisers, light and heavy	558,200 (48)	34,772 (5)
Submarines	310, 070 (203)	144,182 (121)

The table shows ships commissioned (USN) or delivered (IJN). Sizes are given in standard tons displacement and in number of ships, the latter shown in parentheses. U.S. data is provided by calendar year; the Japanese data by fiscal year, that is, 1 April of one year through 31 March of the next. The wartime data calculations for the U.S. Navy are carried to the end of the calendar year 1945, but for the Japanese navy they extend only through July 1945. Figures for destroyers include the Japanese *Matsu* class, which some authorities cite as destroyer escorts. Sources: *Dictionary of American Naval Fighting Ships,* vols. 1 and 2; Fahey, *Ships and Aircraft of the U.S. Fleet,* war edition; U.S. Strategic Bombing Survey, Military Supplies Division, *Japanese Naval Shipbuilding,* appendix A; and Frederick J. Milford, letter to authors, 15 May 1994.

totaled 119. During the Pacific War, construction of the *Sumner* and improved *Fletcher* classes added 126 more destroyers to the navy. Between 1932 and 1945, therefore, the U.S. Navy acquired 502 destroyers, built in twelve commercial and seven navy yards.

American destroyer building programs not only turned out many ships, but did so speedily. The most experienced yards reduced the time on the ways of 2,100 and 2,200-ton destroyers to as little as four months, and five months became routine. Less experienced yards took significantly longer, of course, but the average time on the ways for American destroyers was still only about six months.

It is not hard to determine the reasons for the remarkable speed at which American shipyards developed. To begin with, the lessons of the mass production programs of World War I were not forgotten. The learning time in construction techniques was spread out over large numbers of ships. In part, this was due to the small number of destroyer designs (classes) that came off American drawing boards and the large number of destroyers ordered for each class. In part, it resulted from the very few shipbuilding firms that contracted to build a large

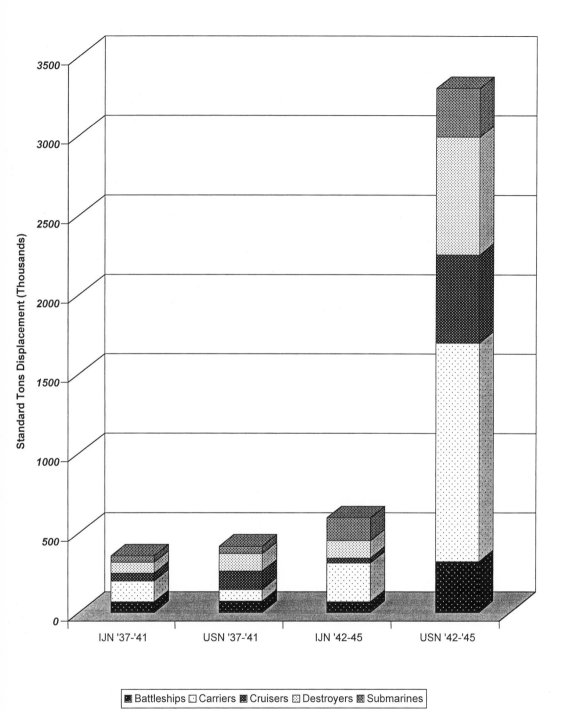

Fig. 10-2. U.S. and Japanese naval shipbuilding: major combatants built, 1937–41 and during World War II.

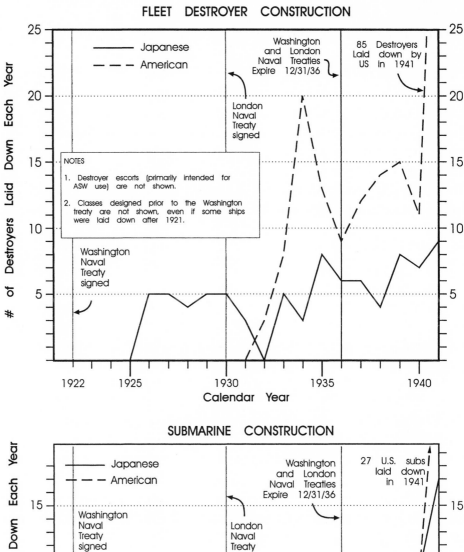

FLEET DESTROYER CONSTRUCTION

NOTES

1. Destroyer escorts (primarily intended for ASW use) are not shown.

2. Classes designed prior to the Washington treaty are not shown, even if some ships were laid down after 1921.

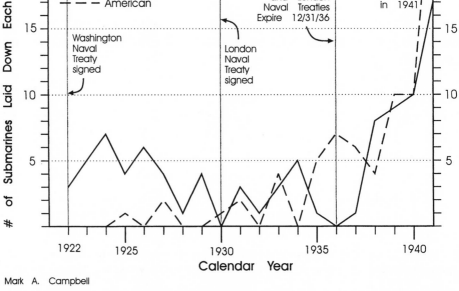

SUBMARINE CONSTRUCTION

Mark A. Campbell

Fig. 10-3. IJN and USN fleet destroyer construction and submarine construction, 1922–41.

number of destroyers. Just three firms built over 60 percent of the American destroyers laid down between 1932 and 1945. Furthermore, many yards took to building several destroyers at once, and after 1937, new keels were typically laid within a few days of the previous hull's launching. To speed work further, American designers simplified hull configurations, providing them with flush decks and avoiding unnecessary curves in the designs. The introduction of all-welded hulls in the early 1930s also contributed to shortened construction times. Moreover, machinery and armament were standardized for the largest classes of destroyers. The engineering plants of destroyers subsequent to the *Benson* class were so similar, for example, that the Bureau of Ships could issue a single operation manual for 331 destroyers.[30]

The 177 destroyers produced in Japan from 1921 to 1945 were, on the whole, very good warships, notwithstanding certain stability problems and the bulkiness of their engineering plants, which were somewhat less efficient than those of American destroyers. The real problem lay in their comparatively small numbers. The most immediate causes of limited construction were twofold: there were too few ships of any particular design (class) and too few ships per yard. Only the combined and closely related *Asashio, Kagerō*, and *Yūgumo* classes (48 ships) yielded single-yard production runs of over 10 ships. The second problem is exemplified by the fact that only two Japanese commercial yards (Fujinagata Shipbuilding Company and Uraga Dock Company) and one navy yard (Maizuru) built more than 20 destroyers of any type. Even in these more experienced yards, production was generally limited to 5 or 6 hulls of a given class. In the construction of destroyers, therefore, Japanese shipyards did not develop efficiencies of construction as rapidly as did their American counterparts, which translated into markedly longer completion times for the Japanese. The Fujinagata yard in Osaka eventually reduced the time on the ways for the 15 hulls of the *Asashio, Kagerō*, and *Yūgumo* classes from eighteen months to an average of seven months for the last 3 ships of the class, but the overall average time for the entire class was twelve months.[31]

The more indirect and long-range causes of the comparatively limited production of Japanese destroyers were multiple. Shortage of steel and other strategic materials was one factor, along with inadequate transportation systems to get them to Japanese shipyards in sufficient quantity. Clearly, too, Japan started with significantly fewer shipyards and thus smaller space devoted to slipways and graving docks than existed in the United States. Moreover, building capacity in most yards was simply inadequate even for the building programs that the navy actually undertook, and construction schedules for one type of warship were frequently delayed by those of another. The expansion of shipbuilding facilities from 1937 to 1941 was quite modest in light of the national emergency and (with the exception of the navy yard slipways at Kure and Yokosuka for the construction of the *Yamato* and *Shinano)* affected only existing commercial yards, which increased by 8.2 percent of floor space and by 8.1 percent in length of ways.[32] The limited expansion of shipyard facilities was made difficult by Japan's topography and urban patterns, both of which restricted the number of possible shipyard sites. The mountainous terrain of much of the Japanese islands and the rugged coasts along them meant that there was very little level land alongside deep water. The older shipyards where such land did exist were located in port cities, usually on the waterfront where it was difficult and expensive to clear space for shipbuilding.[33] The main reason for the lack of new shipyard development, however, was that Japan simply did not have the economic resources to build the new shipyards needed. The larger yards had difficulty recruiting enough skilled labor. In some places, heavy machinery was inadequate and machine tools may have declined in quality. In any event, there were critical problems with the older yards that had grown piecemeal over the decades. They were congested, poorly organized and too often devoted to clumsy and antiquated construction methods. These difficulties, all of which made mass-production techniques impractical, were exacerbated during the Pacific War. New ship types had to be developed to respond to the changing tactical situation; combat losses had to be made up, and repair work was constantly necessary. These requirements threw regular building schedules into disarray.[34]

At all events, during the Pacific War, the limited Japanese production of destroyers, when combined with the soaring construction figures for destroyers built in American yards, is emblematic of disastrously inferior Japanese naval strength. Despite the superior quality of Japanese destroyers built during the interwar period, it was ultimately quantity rather than quality that proved decisive. This dominance of quantity over quality ruled other aspects of the Japan-U.S. naval confrontation. While the number of American destroyers roughly doubled during the war, despite combat losses and conversions, the number of Japanese destroyers declined by four-fifths due to war losses and to a building program that simply could not keep up with the American enemy.

THE SUPERBATTLESHIPS, *YAMATO* AND *MUSASHI*

Of all the Japanese navy's efforts to use its qualitative superiority to match the growing strength of a resurgent U.S. Navy, none was more dramatic than the "superbattleship" strategy. The Brobdingnagian result of this effort was the construction of the two largest, most powerful battleships ever built: the *Yamato* and *Musashi*.[35] Beginning in the autumn of 1935, plans for the new class went through

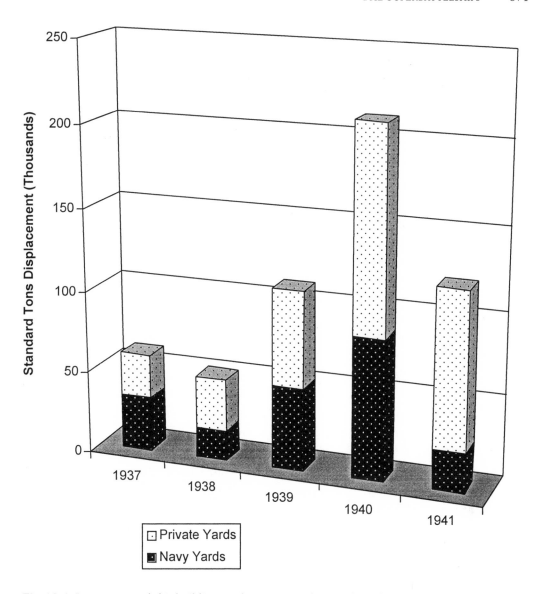

Fig. 10-4. Japanese naval shipbuilding yards: major combatants launched, 1937–41.

twenty-three designs before the final design was accepted in July 1936. Some earlier schemes had called for an even larger class of ship than was finally approved, but the initial plans of Hiraga Yuzuru and Fukuda Keiji, the principal architects, had been judged too ambitious and expensive even by the Navy General Staff. Still, the revised staff requirements—nine 18.1-inch guns, armor capable of withstanding the same caliber of shells fired at ranges of 20,000–35,000 meters, underwater protection capable of resisting a torpedo explosion of 300 kilograms (660 pounds) of TNT, a top speed of 27 knots, and a cruising range of 8,000 miles at 18 knots—inevitably meant an unprecedented displacement, some 69,000 tons, nearly twice that of any other battleship afloat.[36]

In addition to the actual specifications provided by the Navy General Staff, Hiraga and Fukuda were guided in their work by principles laid down by the staff and by the realities of naval architecture. To begin with, given the rationale for the navy's superbattleship project, it was important to design a warship that would prove superior in any gun battle with enemy capital ships. In pursuit of this objective, the design had to provide superiority in armor as well as armament. But at the same time, it was vitally important to reduce armor weight. The solution to that problem, as it was for many battleship designs, was to concentrate armor protection in one section of the ship, the most obvious place being the center section, where the vital machinery and magazine spaces were located. For that reason, it was critical that these vital, vulnerable parts of the ship be concentrated in order minimize the longitudinal area that the armor would have to cover. This was particularly important in a ship that had machinery spaces the size of those in the *Yamato* and *Musashi*. Such a concentration could thus only be achieved within a hull configuration of unprecedented beam, rather than a long, narrow one. Finally, Hiraga and Fukuda, like all naval architects, were obliged to make choices as well as compromises in their design. Just as armor would have to be strong in some places and slight or virtually nonexistent in others, the defenses of the ship could not be equally effective against all possible kinds of attack. In drawing up their design Hiraga and Fukuda accepted the staff priority given to superiority in surface battle.[37]

When the final design was completed there were no Japanese dockyards capable of handling the construction of such enormous hulls, and only four—Kure, Nagasaki, Yokosuka, and Sasebo—judged suitable for the necessary enlargements and alterations that would make such construction possible. At the Kure yard, where the first of the class, the *Yamato*, would be laid down in 1937, the dock was deepened and the gantry cranes over the dry dock strengthened to lift the outsized armor plates that would be employed in building the ship. At the Mitsubishi dockyard at Nagasaki, which was to be the birthplace of the *Musashi* in 1938, the slipway was lengthened by about 15 meters by digging into the hillside. Several years later, a huge new dry dock, capable of accommodating ships of up to 80,000 tons, was constructed at Yokosuka, where the *Shinano* would be laid down in 1940 as a sister ship (but completed as a carrier). A drydock of similar size was built at Sasebo, where the fourth sister ship of the class was laid down but never completed.[38]

Given the tremendous importance that the Japanese navy attached to its super-battleship strategy and thus to maintaining absolute secrecy, it is not surprising that the security precautions involved were probably the most stringent of any prewar military construction effort. Because of the size of the hulls to be hidden while under construction, the precautions were most difficult and complex. At Kure, cradle of the *Yamato,* a huge fence was erected around the dry dock, pierced by only one heavily guarded entrance; high zinc fencing was placed at higher points overlooking the port and guards posted there to keep away the curious, and the windows of all the trains passing through Kure City were covered on the side facing the harbor.

At Nagasaki, the task of concealing the *Musashi* was even more daunting, since the harbor was surrounded on three sides by mountains and the sloping streets of Nagasaki overlooked the dockyard. The city, moreover, not only contained a large Chinese population but also served as the terminus of the Shanghai Steamship Company. The location of the American consulate near the harbor was a further complication. The navy found a solution to these problems by suspending a series of huge rope curtains from the gantries over the slipways, and as an added precaution, a long two-story warehouse was built to block the view of the harbor from the American consulate. At both dockyards all those concerned with the design and construction of the ships were carefully screened and obliged to have numerous personal references; their entrance into the dock area was permitted only with photographic identification. The few outsiders allowed to visit the construction sites had to have written authorization personally signed by the navy minister. The use of blueprints was restricted on a need-to-know basis. Few people were permitted to see the entire layout of the ships, and then only in a specially guarded room under close supervision. The launching ceremonies for each ship (August 1940 for the *Yamato,* November the same year for the *Musashi)* were brief, austere, and held in secret. Finally, following the launching of each ship, various precautions were undertaken to shield a portion of the ship from public view so that it would be difficult to ascertain its exact length.[39]

These security measures were eminently successful. Almost to the end of the Pacific War the navy maintained its curtain of secrecy around the two ships. Prewar American and British naval intelligence on Japanese naval rearmament in general was quite deficient, and particular information concerning these battleships was virtually nonexistent. The poor intelligence of the British and Americans stemmed partly from the Japanese security precautions and partly from the inability of British and American naval analysts to conceive that the Japanese had the capability of building warships of such size and complexity.[40]

Had they had the least information on some of the configurations and capabilities of these two superbattleships in the years before World War II, intelligence officers in the British and American navies would have been surprised, if not alarmed. At the heart of the battleships' design, of course, were the nine 18-inch guns of their main battery, the most powerful guns ever placed aboard a battleship.[41] Only the German siege guns at Sevastopol in World War II and a few outsized mortars were

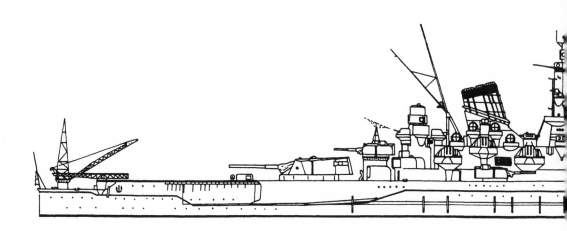

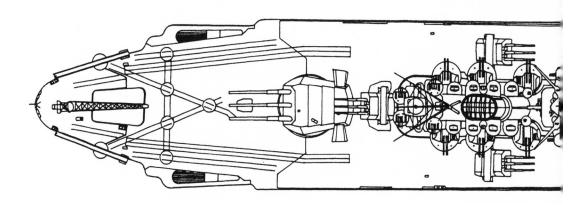

Fig. 10-5. The battleship *Yamato* as completed.

of larger caliber. Each gun of the *Yamato*-class battleships weighed 162 tons, and each triple-mount turret that housed them had a rotating weight of approximately 2,774 tons, a greater weight than most destroyers of the time. The shells fired by each main battery gun weighed about 1.5 tons (actually 3,219 pounds or 1,460 kilograms), and the designed rate of fire was 1.5 rounds per minute at maximum elevation, though better rates of fire were possible at lower elevations.[42]

The *Yamato* and *Musashi* also had secondary batteries of twelve 6.1-inch guns in four triple turrets, one each superimposed forward and aft of the main battery

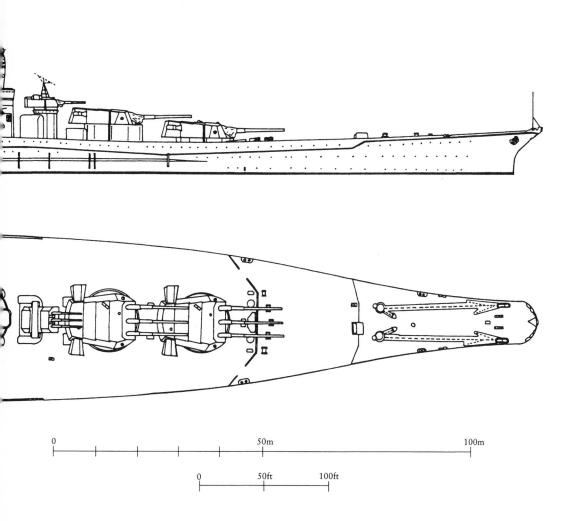

0   50m   100m

0   50ft   100ft

mounts, and one on each beam amidships. Although these were excellent weapons against surface targets, their slow rate of fire made them ineffective anti-aircraft weapons, and for that reason, during the Pacific War, the beam 6.1-inch turrets were removed. For long-range antiaircraft defense, the primary battery consisted of twelve 5-inch guns placed in three twin mounts on each side, grouped together amidships. When the ships were designed, the twenty-four 25-millimeter cannon (the Japanese navy's light antiaircraft weapons of choice) in triple mounts clustered amidships and the four 13-millimeter machine guns on the forward bridge tower were deemed sufficient for short-range antiaircraft protection, but the aerial threat grew so great during the Pacific War that the *Musashi* was refitted with nearly eight times and the *Yamato* twelve times the number of 25-millimeter cannon originally installed on these ships.[43]

As one might expect from the design priorities just mentioned, a singular feature of the *Yamato*-class battleships was their extremely broad beam (127.7 feet) in relation to their waterline length (839 feet) and their relatively shallow draft for ships of such enormous displacement. When fully loaded, however, the ships reached a depth of 35.4 feet (10.8 meters), which necessitated the dredging of certain harbors designated for potential use by these monsters. Numerous tests concerning hull resistance and propulsive efficiency undertaken during their design had led to the development of another singular hull configuration of the class: a narrow prow, ending in a giant, bulbous bow. This shape, together with improvements in the bilge keels and the brackets for the propeller shafts, resulted in a remarkable propulsive efficiency of 58.7 percent at a standard rate of 18 knots, one of the highest in any warship of Japanese design.[44]

In designing a hull with such a great beam, the architects of the *Yamato* class reaped the advantages in armor protection sought by the general staff. Her broad beam allowed the four main turbines and their associated boilers to be placed side by side across the hull, instead of in tandem along its length. This meant that the space required to protect the vital main machinery areas was limited to a surprisingly short section of the hull, just 53.3 percent of its waterline length. The reduced length of the armored citadel or "box" in the center of the ship provided a great saving in the total amount of armor needed for the ships and thus allowed armor of unprecedented thickness.[45] The "box" itself employed 410-millimeter (18-inch) steel. Deck armor consisted of 7.8-inch steel, capable of withstanding armor-piercing bombs of up to 1,000 kilograms dropped from a height of 1,000 meters. The front armor of the barbettes consisted of armor plates 22 inches thick; the sides, of 16-inch armor plates, were both specially hardened. To protect the inside of the ships from flying bolts and rivets when the armor deck was struck by bombs or shells, the designers provided the ships with 9-millimeter Ducol steel plates running underneath the armor deck. Finally, the bottom of the ships, or rather those portions below the magazines and main machinery, were protected by 2- to 3-inch armor plates to shield them from torpedo or mine explosions. To save weight and at the same time to provide for added strength, the design called for some of the armor to be fitted as hull strengtheners, the lower side armor being placed to provide longitudinal strength. All in all, the *Yamato* and *Musashi* were the most massively armored ships ever built. Their armor defenses, however, were dangerously compromised both by defective armor joints and by armor distribution.[46]

To achieve the unprecedented protection to the central citadel, the designers of the *Yamato* class were obliged, of course, to make certain sacrifices in armor elsewhere in the ship. Specifically, this meant leaving the underwater bow and stern sections unprotected. To compensate for the lack of armor in these areas, however, they devoted a great deal of attention to increasing watertight compartmentation and provided a remarkable reserve buoyancy (57,450 tons). This was believed to be sufficient to keep the ship afloat and fairly stable in a damaged condition, and as long as the protected portions of the ship remained buoyant, the ship would maintain its stability up to a list of 20 degrees. Further, the flooding and pumping systems built into the ships of the class supposedly enabled a recovery to an even keel from a list of 18.3 degrees and allowed the ships to function even if the freeboard at the bow was reduced 4–5 meters by complete destruction and flooding of the forward part of the ship.[47] Experience would show, however, that the stability and damage-control calculations were optimistic and that the armored citadel was not invulnerable.

Along with firepower and armor protection, speed was the third critical element in the design of the *Yamato* class. In addition to the improvements to the hull, the selection of a propulsive plant of maximum efficiency was vital in attempting to meet the general staff requirement of 27 knots' top speed. A few early designs had called for either completely diesel or mixed diesel-steam plant propulsion, but later, at Hiraga Yuzuru's insistence, the idea of diesel propulsion was dropped altogether.[48] In its place, the designers substituted steam turbine propulsion. Steam was provided to four Kampon-geared turbines by twelve Kampon boilers arranged, across the hull, in four longitudinal rows of three boilers, each boiler with its own fire room. Each row of boilers provided steam to one of the turbines which, together, produced a nominal total of 150,000 shaft horsepower to the four propeller shafts. At the time of her launching, the *Yamato* was the most powerfully propelled battleship afloat. At 27 knots (28 knots during her trials), she was matched at the time of her commissioning only by the American *North Carolina* and the British *King George V* classes.[49]

Maneuverability and habitability were several other notable features of this famous class of warships. The turning ability of the *Yamato* and *Musashi* was excellent, superior to any other battleships afloat at the beginning of the Pacific War. Their small heeling angle (9 degrees at a rudder angle of 35 degrees at a 26-knot speed) was a great advantage in taking evasive action from torpedoes and bombs and in producing the steadiest possible platform for gunnery. When commissioned, the *Yamato* and *Musashi* were also the most comfortable ships in the Japanese navy (though in terms of space per crew member, Japanese habitability standards were still below those in Western navies). The *Yamato* was the first Japanese warship equipped with air conditioning (though it did not extend to all living quarters), and so luxurious were her accommodations by Japanese standards that during the Pacific War, she earned the nickname "The Yamato Hotel."[50]

The profile of the *Yamato* design—the long, undulating sheer line (a characteristic of the larger Japanese warships in the interwar period), the sweeping upward curve of the bow, the two main battery turrets squatting before the massive forward tower, the single raked funnel, and the third main battery turret pointing aft—all bespoke of speed, power, and fortresslike strength. From the photographs of the *Yamato* taken on her trials in the autumn of 1941, one can guess that to have actually seen her pounding along through the seas must have been one of the most impressive spectacles in Japanese naval history. Indeed, the potency of this sort of image was not lost on Japanese navy men at the time. In his arguments with air-power advocates, Capt. Fukutome Shigeru, chief of the Operations Section of the Navy General Staff, described the *Yamato* and *Musashi* as "symbols of naval power" that provided to officers and men alike a profound sense of confidence in their navy.[51] Strengthening this symbolism were these warships' names, which had a special meaning for Japanese. Yamato had been the cradle of Japanese civilization and one of the earliest names for Japan; Musashi was the name of an ancient plain on which the modern city of Tokyo was located. Like the poetic "Columbia" for Americans and "Albion" for Britons, these names conveyed to all Japanese a sense of historical mystique.[52]

In planning the *Yamato*-class battleships the Navy General Staff and the design team had attempted to produce a battleship superior to all other capital ships for years to come. Yet the design and the capabilities of the two ships were flawed in ways that ranged from severely limiting to fatal. Some defects were inherent in the design itself; others were simply due to rapid and inevitable advances in technology. Those advances eventually overtook the assumptions upon which the superbattleship strategy and design had been based. To understand these problems as they evolved it is worthwhile to identify them in the context of the service histories of the two warships.[53]

Both ships spent the first half of their careers serving, successively, as the palatial headquarters for the Combined Fleet, anchored at Truk in the central Caroline Islands. The *Yamato* filled this role from 1942 to 1943 as Yamamoto

Isoroku's flagship; the *Musashi* served in the same capacity from 1943 to 1944 for Koga Mineichi until his death. Neither ship played any role in the great naval battles around the Solomons in 1942 and 1943, probably because they were being saved for the "decisive" gun-to-gun encounter still envisioned by the Japanese high command and possibly because their fuel consumption was so prodigious.[54] Few historians have failed to comment on the idleness of these two great ships during the critical early stages of the Guadalcanal campaign. So rare were the occasions that seemed to offer an opportunity to seek out and destroy an American battle force and so great became Japan's other strategic needs in the Pacific, that on one occasion the *Yamato* was pressed into service as a troopship, a function that must have been one of the most wasteful expenditures of sophisticated technology in World War II.

Both ships had been hit by a single torpedo from an American submarine: the *Yamato* in December 1943, at the main armor belt on the starboard side aft; the *Musashi* in March 1944, on the port side forward. In both cases, the detonations caused far more flooding than had been anticipated during the ship's design stage. Though not fatal, the damage was ominous; it revealed major flaws in the design and construction of the ships. For the *Yamato*, it was a serious failure in the massive side protection because of a defective joint at the upper and lower side belts.[55] The *Musashi*'s flaw was the vulnerability of the unprotected bow and stern areas, the bow in particular, in which large compartments led to excessive flooding and list. The pumping system, intended to provide an augmented counterflooding capability, proved to be inadequate.[56] But what is singular about the damage in each case is that it was caused by a single torpedo armed with a powerful new American explosive, Torpex.[57]

The abortive role of the *Yamato* and *Musashi* in the great Leyte Gulf campaign of October 1944 or, more exactly, as members of Adm. Kurita Takeo's strike force in the battles of the Sibuyan Sea and off Samar, illuminated further flaws in the design of these ships. In the Battle of the Sibuyan Sea, the *Musashi* was subjected to ferocious assault by American carrier aircraft, against which her antiaircraft defenses, largely composed of multiple 25-millimeter machine guns, were generally unavailing. During the course of the battle, American bombing and strafing attacks reduced the *Musashi*'s antiaircraft defenses by three-fourths. Although the seventeen bomb hits scored on the *Musashi* caused great damage to her deck and superstructure, they did not threaten the ship's survival. Rather, her destruction was due to the last eleven of twenty torpedo hits. These flooded the compartments beneath the magazines and exploited the structural flaws on both sides of the main belts beneath the waterline.[58] In the battle off Samar the next day, the *Yamato,* which had been only slightly damaged by several bomb hits, fired on surface targets—destroyers protecting a group of American escort carriers—for the only time in her career, but was forced to break off action when threatened by destroyer torpedoes.

The *Yamato*'s dramatic destruction took place near the end of the war, when she was the only battleship still in service and the flagship of a pitiful remnant of the Japanese navy. She was the principal unit of a force sent, without air cover, on a suicide mission to strike American naval forces and shipping off Okinawa in early April 1945. Well over two hundred carrier aircraft attacked her southwest of Kyūshū. In these actions, she was struck by numerous bombs and between ten and twelve torpedoes, the latter mostly on the port side. Again, while the bombs created fearful havoc topside, it was the torpedoes that finally caused her to capsize and, as she did so, to blow up in a fearful explosion when one of her magazines ignited.

In assessing the destruction of these two monster battleships, a few major conclusions seem reasonable. First, given the crushing aerial bombardment to which they were subjected, it is doubtful that a warship of any design could have survived them. By the time that the *Musashi* was sent to the bottom in 1944 and the *Yamato* in 1945, the destructive power of numerous U.S. Navy carrier aircraft and the combined weight of bombs and torpedoes they could hurl against any surface target would have obliterated the ships planned by any naval architects of the 1930s.

The specific design of the *Yamato*-class battleships nevertheless clearly demonstrated the dangers involved in the all-or-nothing concept of armor distribution. By itself, this type of armor distribution would have not necessarily proved fatal in the aerial assaults upon them. In combination, however, with inadequate compartmentation (bow and stern compartments were too large, and therefore flooding even a single one required major damage control efforts), an inadequate pumping system, and weak connections between the massive side belts, the armor design hastened the foundering of both ships. The concentration of armor around the central citadel provided the heaviest possible protection to that vital area, but exposed too great a portion of the hull to torpedo damage. The watertight compartmentation proved inadequate to prevent excessive flooding, and the pumping system could not check it. Although the ship was supposed to remain stable even if all the areas beyond the citadel were flooded, the designers assumed that the citadel would remain intact. When the defective side belt armor—truly the Achilles heel of these ships—gave way, the armored citadel itself was fatally compromised.

Raising these observations to a more general level, defects in the armor arrangements for the *Yamato* and *Musashi* were the result of two realities, one known to their designers and one less obvious to them at the time: first, the necessity to make choices in the design of any warship, and second, the inability to foresee the direction or pace of naval technology, which together may overturn the assumptions behind any design.[59]

The original design decision emphasized the need to protect the ships against shell fire and bomb detonations above the waterline, rather than torpedo damage below it. That decision reflected the general staff's preoccupation with the great gun battle, which in turn, reflected the fact that *any* design that might have been chosen would have represented a series of compromises away from an "ideal" set of specifications, since the "perfect" warship design is an impossibility. A different set of compromises would have undoubtedly have created a different set of problems. Had the armor been distributed more evenly, for example, it would have been thinner and thus less effective anywhere in the ship.[60]

Unfortunately for the fate of both these ships, their designers tended to neglect the threat posed by torpedoes. Protection above the waterline had priority, and below the waterline, diving shots of enemy shells were considered just as serious a danger as torpedoes. Greater attention was given to providing strong armor—which extended all the way down to the keel—than to constructing the voids that would absorb torpedo blasts. During construction of the two ships, tests showed that the hull could stand the explosive force of 400 kilograms (880 pounds) of TNT. This exceeded the force that any American torpedo, whether air- or sea-launched, could then supply. During the war, however, American advances made the torpedo more lethal and this fact, coupled with the ships' defective armor joints, does much to explain the destruction of both the *Yamato* and *Musashi*.[61]

Nevertheless, the resistance of these two ships to battle damage is the best testimony to the general success of their design. The number of bombs and torpedoes required to sink the *Musashi* and *Yamato* amazed both the fliers who destroyed them and the analysts who studied their destruction. One can only wonder what sort of fearful punishment they could have survived and still have remained combat effective had they ever been used in the great gun duels for which they had been intended. In this sense, despite their drawbacks, they were indeed the "most formidable battleships ever built."[62]

The general weakness of the antiaircraft defenses of the *Yamato* and *Musashi* also reflect the rapid and often uneven advance of technology. The plans for these ships as they were commissioned seem to bristle with close-range antiaircraft weapons, and wartime refitting of the ships added many more. When the ships were designed, the 25-millimeter cannon, the most numerous antiaircraft armament aboard the ships, were suitable defenses against the slow, lightly built aircraft of the day. By the third year of the Pacific War, as faster, more rugged American aircraft appeared, firepower of these particular antiaircraft batteries proved feeble, and by then the Japanese navy had no suitable replacement weapon available.[63]

The long-range antiaircraft defenses of these ships were also shown to be ineffective by midwar. Lacking the devastating proximity fuses that the Americans had developed, the gun crews of the 5-inch high-angle cannon on the *Yamato* and *Musashi* were trained to concentrate their fire as a barrage at the estimated height of the attacking enemy aircraft. While this tactic was relatively effective against high-altitude bombers, it was by 1944–45 almost useless against carrier aircraft, which were far more elusive.[64]

Last, criticisms can also be raised about the 18-inch guns that were supposed to be the key elements in the *Yamato* class. There is, of course, no sure way to assess their true effectiveness, since neither of the two ships ever used her main batteries against enemy capital ships. But several studies suggest that despite the prodigious time and cost devoted to the research, design, and manufacture of these huge guns, the results achieved (armor penetrations at set ranges) may not have been commensurate with the effort expended.[65]

Hindsight has not been kind to either the concept behind the "superbattleship strategy" or its apotheosis, the *Yamato* class of battleships.[66] Much ink has been devoted to the apparent uselessness of the capital ship over time; a recent popular work has heaped ridicule on them as objects of almost religious veneration by naval professionals.[67] Because the *Yamato* and *Musashi* were the largest capital ships ever built, were never used for the purpose for which they were constructed, and were sent to the bottom under a rain of aerial bombs and torpedoes, and not by the salvos of other battleships, the folly behind their original conception has been confirmed for many historians. Even Japanese navy men, looking back on the ships' birth and death, came to believe that "the three greatest follies of the world were the Great Wall of China, the Pyramids, and the battleship *Yamato*."[68]

A closer look may show, however, that the superbattleship strategy that the Navy General Staff first conceived in the early 1930s was a rational policy. As a contemporary alternative to an economically ruinous quantitative race with the United States in battleship construction—a competition that Japan was bound to lose—the construction of the superbattleships can hardly be called an act of folly. Furthermore, neither the idea of the battleship nor its concrete manifestations were obsolescent when the plans for the *Yamato* class were drawn up. Much has been made of the threat of the airplane to surface warships before World War II; the pronouncements of air-power advocates like Giulio Douhet, "Billy" Mitchell, and Nakajima Chikuhei have been cited as holy prophecy by air-power historians. Eventually, they were proven at least partially correct and the battleship did become shockingly vulnerable to the dive and torpedo bomber. As late as the mid-1930s, however, neither the flimsy aircraft of the time nor the puny ordnance they carried posed overwhelming threats to a battleship's active or passive defenses. The designers of the *Yamato* class could not know that future technological developments would obliterate their plans, nor could they have guessed how rapidly such developments, particularly those concerning aircraft and aircraft-carried ordnance, would overtake the much slower progress of capital ship design. Unknown to them, this category of naval architecture was approaching its terminal point.

The most relevant criticism of the Japanese navy's superbattleship strategy does not concern the building of the superbattleships themselves, but the consequent diversion of the navy's attention and the nation's resources from one of the most critical strategic problems that the navy faced: its utter dependence on its overseas sea routes and the need to acquire the ships, to form the organization, to shape the doctrine, and to develop the training that would be the most effective in protecting those sea routes.

OTHER NAVAL CONSTRUCTION, 1937–41

Because of its heavy investment in cruiser construction during the 1920s and early 1930s, the Japanese navy was convinced that it could, for the present, maintain a 70 percent ratio with the United States in heavy cruiser construction. Japan considered it essential, however, to maintain a qualitative lead in speed, firepower, and torpedo armament in ships of this category.[69] This was particularly important because of the role that the navy continued to assign to cruisers in the deployment of its destroyer squadrons. As described in chapter 8, aggressive torpedo attacks by destroyer forces were an essential preliminary to the decisive gun battle between opposing battle lines. Navy tacticians had planned that these forces would be led into battle by light cruisers acting as flagships for the torpedo squadrons. By the end of the 1930s, in light of the advanced performance of Japanese destroyers, the navy was seeking to replace the old 5,000-ton *Kuma* class that had served in this capacity for nearly two decades. Authorization for four such cruisers of a new design was obtained in 1938, but bickering over the specifications between the various naval branches delayed until 1940 the laying down of the first of these ships, the *Agano*, a 6,652-ton cruiser armed with six 6-inch/50 guns in three twin turrets, two forward and one aft.[70] Two quadruple 24-inch torpedo tube mounts with quick reloading gear were placed on the centerline between the funnel and the rear mast. Although the speed and gun armament of the *Agano* and her sister ships was no greater than the *Kuma* class they were meant to replace, their torpedo armament was more powerful and their facilities as command ships were obviously superior. Yet, because of the press of other construction work at the Sasebo Navy Yard, where three of the four were built, none of the four ships of this class (the *Agano, Noshiro, Yahagi,* and *Sakawa)* was ready by the time the Pacific War broke out. Hence, in the early surface battles of 1942, Japanese destroyer squadrons were obliged to go into action with the old 5,000-tonners as flagships.[71]

About the same time that the *Agano*-class cruisers were being planned, the navy decided to enhance the role of cruiser and fleet-type submarines in the attrition of the U.S. battle force. As early detection of the American fleet's anticipated westward movements would obviously be of significant help in this mission, the general staff conceived of the formation of a combined submarine-surface force composed of a squadron of large submarines and a fast cruiser flagship. This flagship would be a hybrid, combining reconnaissance and command missions. She was to be capable of a large radius of action and equipped with a number of high-speed reconnaissance floatplanes of advanced design. Supposedly, the aircraft would scour the ocean, locating enemy surface targets and report back to the flagship when targets were found. The flagship would then coordinate the attack of the submarines, guiding them to the target, by radio, presumably. The cruiser planned for this purpose was similar in design to the *Agano* class, but 1,500 tons heavier and armed with six 6.1-inch, rather than 5.9-inch guns. The *Ōyodo* (only one of her class was built) was laid down early in 1941 and was commissioned midwar. Her main batteries were mounted forward to allow the installation aft of a powerful catapult and large derricks to handle the ship's planes. She was the only Japanese cruiser ever built with no torpedo armament, and her protection was generally sacrificed to allow high speed. As a mark of the utter failure of the Japanese submarine campaign during the war, however, the *Ōyodo* never operated in her intended role. Nor were the new aircraft, which were to be the eyes for the planned submarine attack group, ever produced.[72] Instead, the *Ōyodo* languished in home waters, where she was repeatedly subject to American air attacks, finally capsizing at Kure, March 1945.[73]

At the beginning of the post-treaty era, the Japanese still maintained a 70 percent ratio in relation to the destroyer forces of the U.S. Navy. True, successively large American construction programs and the greatly shortened construction time of U.S. destroyers did provoke some concern that the gap in Japan-U.S. strength in this category might soon widen. Nevertheless, the Japanese navy's confidence in the striking power of its destroyers in torpedo armament and in their effectiveness in night combat led the navy to conclude that the superiority of its large destroyers could offset an increase in American warships of this type.[74] The need, therefore, was to maintain superiority in design as new destroyer classes were planned to replace the old. With no tonnage or armament restrictions to hamper its planning, the general staff could now draw up the specifications for a new class of fast fleet destroyers, designated initially as "Type A."

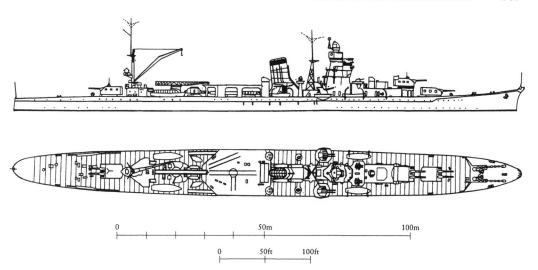

Fig. 10-6. The cruiser *Agano*.

The result was the *Kagerō*, laid down in 1937 and completed in 1939, the first of eighteen ships of her class, fifteen ordered under the Circle Three program and three under Circle Four, but all of them commissioned and in service by early 1941. Not unlike the "Special Type" *Fubuki*-class destroyers in configuration, the *Kagerō*, at a little over 2,000 tons, was slightly heavier than the reconstructed *Fubuki*, but was significantly more stable. Her beam and the draft had been increased, and the torpedo mount arrangement made more efficient. Capable of 35 knots, the *Kagerō* had approximately the same maximum speed as the *Fubuki*, but possessed a higher cruising speed (18 knots) for a similar range of action of 5,000 miles. The power output was increased to 52,000 shaft horsepower, and the machinery (three Kampon boilers and geared turbines that drove two propeller shafts) was improved, lightened, and made more efficient. Quantitatively, the firepower was essentially the same: a main battery of six 5-inch guns in three twin turrets, one forward and two aft, and eight 24-inch torpedo tubes, though the latter were now grouped in two quadruple mounts amidships along the centerline.[75] With these ships the Japanese navy maintained its qualitative lead over British and American destroyers of the same period, particularly in gun and torpedo armament. They gave a good account of themselves in the fiercest gunfire engagements of the first several years of the

Pacific War. One ship, the *Yukikaze*, became the most famous small ship in the Japanese navy. During the three and a half years of the war, she logged well over 10,000 miles on combat missions, took part in nearly every major gun battle, and survived the war without receiving a single hit from shell, bomb, or torpedo.[76]

In 1939, under the Circle Four program, the Japanese navy ordered twelve destroyers of a very similar design. The first of this class of twenty ships and its namesake, the *Yūgumo*, commissioned just before the outbreak of the war, was slightly larger and faster than the *Kagerō* class. The major improvement, however, was the fitting of a 5-inch main battery that could elevate to 75 degrees to provide antiaircraft fire. Only two ships of this class, the *Yūgumo* and *Akigumo*, were in service at the start of the war, and the last of this class was not put into commission until March 1944.[77]

The origins of the last destroyer class to be planned prior to the onset of the Pacific War lay in the need to strengthen the antiaircraft and antisubmarine warfare capabilities of the escorts for Japanese carrier divisions, which were increasingly operated separately from the main force. As carrier escorts, most pre-*Fubuki* destroyers were inadequate: their armament was too feeble, their radius of action was too limited, and they were insufficiently seaworthy. In 1938, therefore, the Navy General Staff set out the specifications for a new escort: a maximum speed of 35 knots, a radius of action of 10,000 miles at 18 knots, and eight high-angle guns. The result was the *Akizuki*, the first of a twelve-ship class of 2,700-ton destroyers that featured four fully power-operated turrets, two forward and two aft, each mounting two new high-velocity 3.9-inch antiaircraft guns. These could elevate to 90 degrees, could fire fifteen to twenty rounds per minute, and had a vertical range of over 14,000 yards and a horizontal range of 20,000 yards. To increase their effectiveness, separate fire control positions were located fore and aft. This was the most formidable antiaircraft armament of any destroyer then afloat. To give them offensive punch against surface targets, the *Akizuki* and her sister ships were armed with a quadruple 24-inch torpedo tube mounting amidships. Four ships were laid down in 1941, but none was commissioned by the start of the war.[78]

The Japanese thus entered the Pacific War with some of the finest destroyers in any navy. But because of the surge in American destroyer construction just prior to the war and because many Japanese destroyers had been built in the 1920s and early 1930s, Japan's destroyer force was composed of relatively older ships.[79] Moreover, as a whole, they lacked adequate antiaircraft and antisubmarine defenses, and most ruinously, like most Japanese warships for much of the war, they lacked both high-quality search and fire control radar. Yet, in some of the fiercest combat in Southeast Asian and western Pacific waters, 1942–43, they more than held their own. That their numbers diminished in these campaigns says

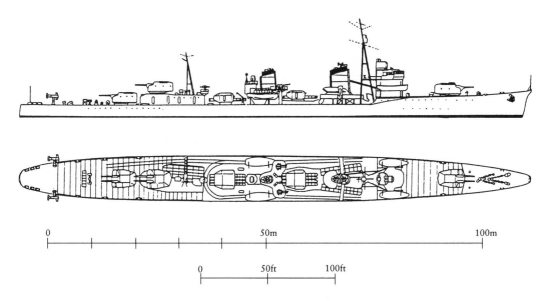

Fig. 10-7. *Kagerō*-class destroyer.

more about the high-risk nature of their missions, the sacrificial aggressiveness of their captains and crews, and the growing power of American carrier aviation and submarine warfare than it does about any shortcomings in their design.[80]

In oceangoing submarines the Japanese had been ahead of the U.S. Navy in both quantity and quality for much of the 1930s, though this situation changed dramatically with the appearance of the American fleet submarines. During the decade, Japanese submarine doctrine for both the "ambush" strategy and the decisive fleet engagement had called for the deployment of a comparatively few, large submarines. Indeed, the midget submarines had been seen as a means of compensating for the limited number of larger submersibles.[81]

In the mid-1930s, the Navy General Staff had begun to work out tactical schemes for the coordinated deployment of squadrons of submarines. As mentioned, these ideas had been the rationale for the design of the cruiser *Ōyodo* as a submarine flagship. Even before this, however, the staff had projected three new types of submarines, each of which was to be a specific component in the formation of long-range attack groups. The first of these was a cruiser submarine, type A1, designed to act as a command ship, coordinating the attacks of other submarines within the squadron. It was a large craft (2,434 tons, 343 feet long) whose design included additional space for the greater number of crew members, extra room for more elaborate telecommunications equipment, accommodations for the squadron commander, and a hangar faired into the superstructure, which housed a reconnaissance floatplane. Its diesel engines were given somewhat greater power (6,200 shaft horsepower) than earlier Japanese submarines, which gave it a surface speed of over 23 knots. Consistent with its function, this submarine was equipped to stay three months at sea, and its radius of action was extended to 16,000 miles. For the task for which it was conceived, the design of this submarine appears to have been adequate. Only three were ever built, however: two were laid down in 1938 and were completed in 1941; a third was completed in 1942.[82]

The second planned component of the projected long-range attack groups was the type B1 submarine, designed as a scout for the squadrons. Developed from the type KD6, the B1 submarines had the same machinery as the type A1s, but were smaller and had a slightly more limited range of action, though they too were equipped with seaplanes for reconnaissance. Six submarines of this type were ordered under the Circle Three program and fourteen under Circle Four. The first was launched in 1939 and completed in September 1940; the last was completed in 1943.[83]

The actual teeth of the long-range submarine attack groups were supposed to be the type C1 attack submarines. These were almost identical to the B1s, except that they carried no seaplanes, and their armament was increased from six to eight 21-inch torpedo tubes. Although the smallest of the three designs developed for the long-range attack strategy, they were large enough to carry a midget submarine as needed. Six of these submarines were ordered under the Circle Three program, the first being laid down in 1937 and four more being completed by 1941.[84]

Two medium-range attack submarine types complete the list of those Japanese submersibles under construction by the eve of the Pacific War: the ten type KD7 submarines of 1,630 tons ordered under the Circle Four program and the eighteen type KS submarines, ordered under the Special Circle plans of 1941 and designed for coastal defense operations, particularly for the defense of Japanese air bases in Micronesia.[85]

American submarine design during the immediate prewar years illuminates some of the basic flaws in the Japanese navy's submarine program. Having determined by the early 1930s that it needed an all-purpose, powerfully armed submarine with excellent sea-keeping abilities, fast enough to act in concert with battleship squadrons yet also capable of undertaking patrol and attack missions over the vast distances of the Pacific, the U.S. Navy concentrated on the design and construction of a single, standard type. The result was a long-range submarine of great endurance and habitability, powered by reliable and economical engines. This submarine was known generally as the "fleet boat." The advantages of scale and cost stemming from that decision enabled American shipyards to produce it in great quantity.[86]

The forces that shaped the Japanese submarine fleet were profoundly different. Over time, the missions assigned to Japanese submarines—fleet attacks, ambush attacks, scouting, picket duty, coast defense, and commerce raiding—were varied and divergent. Inevitably, this led to a scattering of various designs, each drawn up for a particular mission, but few actually produced in large numbers. The Navy General Staff and Japanese naval architects seemingly skipped from one design to another, always in search of the optimum design for a particular function, but never staying with one design long enough to produce it in mass quantity or to test it adequately in fleet service. The core of this technological inconsistency, of course, was that the requirements of Japanese submarine doctrine could not be satisfied with a single set of design specifications. The designs drawn up for the three different types of submarines operating in the long-range attack groups are a case in point. The navy could not decide whether these would be directed by a submarine flagship or by a surface flagship and so built both the three A1 submarines and the cruiser Ōyodo. In any case, neither the submarines nor Ōyodo was ever used for the purpose intended, largely because the long-range attack groups never materialized. Given the limited construction facilities available to the Japanese navy, this was a scandalous waste of Japanese industrial resources.

The remaining ships used in the Japanese navy were several lesser warship types. The river gunboat was the one warship type in the Japanese navy whose design and function lay outside the navy's general strategic and tactical concerns. Its existence was due to Japan's interests in the Chinese interior and the consequent maintenance of a naval presence on the Yangtze along with the other treaty port powers since the beginning of the century. By the eve of the Pacific War, Japanese gunboats were the most numerous on the river, and the navy's two latest additions, the Fushimi and Sumida, undoubtedly had the best speed and range of the river gunboats of any navy.[87]

Despite its durable emphasis on torpedo warfare and its long tradition of "press closely, strike home," the Japanese navy never really gave serious attention to the "fast fighting boat" of less than destroyer size. Perhaps this was because the navy concluded that the motor torpedo boat could play no role in the decisive encounter at sea and Japanese strategic plans did not give priority to the defense of the nation's coastline. Whatever the reason, on the eve of the Pacific War, the navy possessed only a few of these craft, a couple of foreign-built vessels, purchased or captured in China, and about thirty-eight shallow-draft wooden boats intended for use on Chinese rivers, none of which remotely approached the American PT boats in performance or capabilities. The prime justification of a motor torpedo boat is speed, and speed is derived from engine power. But for the same reasons that the navy ran into problems with its aircraft engines, the marine engines for these small craft were so underpowered that they were motor launches rather than motor torpedo boats. Because the preparatory research, design, and testing of engines and hulls had not been undertaken in peacetime, subsequent wartime efforts to develop a motor torpedo boat force ended in failure. Lacking the fast-striking small vessels like those of the U.S. torpedo boat force, the Japanese navy was at a significant disadvantage in the struggle for the Solomon Islands, 1942–43.[88]

In the twentieth century, of course, the capabilities of any navy are measured not just in the construction of its warships, be they 60,000-ton battleships or 18-ton motor torpedo boats. Its capabilities in transport and supply, its effectiveness in gathering and correctly analyzing information about the enemy, its capacity to wage war upon the enemy's supply and communication lines, and its ability to project its force ashore are all essential elements in naval power. These elements in the Japanese navy on the eve of war will be addressed in the next two chapters.

11

BEHIND
—*the*——————————
FLEET

Collateral Elements of the Japanese Navy, 1937–1941

For all the major navies, the conflict at sea during World War II was as much affected by noncombat activities—economic, industrial, and organizational—as it was by the number and type of warships and aircraft that each threw into the battle. Because of the existence of their authoritarian governments, the Axis powers seemed, at the outset of hostilities, to be in a position to employ these sinews of war more rapidly and effectively than the Anglo-American maritime nations. But Axis convictions about the superiority of their own military systems, their assumptions that the conflict would be short, and their consequent failure to mobilize effectively their industrial, technological, and scientific resources for a prolonged struggle created enormous problems once war was upon them.

Admittedly, the Allied powers had, to a great extent, similarly neglected to plan adequately for these aspects of naval warfare by the eve of World War II. For example, despite all its planning over the decades for carrying out a transoceanic campaign against Japan, the U.S. Navy had taken few concrete measures to insure the creation of an adequate logistic structure for such a strategy.[1] Until shortly before the Pacific War, many of the U.S. Navy's fleet problems rested on untested and often false assumptions. American strategic plans called for the creation of advanced bases in the Pacific, as well as the supplying of the fleet over vast distances. On the eve of war, however, the navy had not yet pulled together the material, the organization, or the personnel to undertake these tasks.

Two American strengths enabled the U.S. Navy to make up, rapidly and massively, for this prewar neglect of a logistical base for its strategy. The first was the tremendous productive power of American industry, and the other was the American talent for improvisation and organization. Once fully exploited, American industry could disgorge a seemingly endless flow of war matériel. Once tapped, American research could develop effective logistic techniques, such as underway replenishment of fuel, ammunition, and provisions. The U.S. Navy created organizations like the Construction Battalions—or Seabees—which, with a wealth of civil engineering equipment and human talent at their disposal, provided a flexible capacity for advanced base construction. Furthermore, the U.S. Navy could coordinate, under a single government agency, shipping for both military operations and the ongoing needs of the civilian economy.

During the interwar period, neither Britain nor the United States renovated and strengthened their merchant fleets as the Japanese did. Nevertheless, as maritime powers, they had a great advantage in sheer size, commanding some 30,000 million tons at the start of the war and having the resources to charter or purchase more tonnage if necessary. A revived German U-boat fleet and a new doctrine of mass surface attack threatened the British at the start of the war. But Hitler had squandered time and money on the construction of capital ships and had neither sufficient submarines nor crews to savage British merchant shipping in this critical period. The United States was eventually able to supply two transoceanic fronts once it entered the conflict, because of its vast resources, productive power, and capacity for technological innovation. The development of the Liberty ship was emblematic of these strengths, since with it, the United States eventually more than made up for losses and met the increasing wartime demands for shipping. Built of prefabricated parts, quickly constructed, and easily operated, the first Liberty ship slid down the ways in September 1941. Mass production techniques allowed the construction of 2,700 sister ships by 1945, and beginning in 1943, 531 Victory ships of similar size, but 50 percent faster, were an enormous contribution to the supply of a two-ocean war.

One miscalculation made by the Axis powers in World War II concerned their underestimation of the ability of the Allies, particularly the United States, to mobilize military manpower with sufficient speed and in sufficient numbers to resist Axis campaigns of conquest. They assumed that the United States could not—in the necessary time—create an officer corps and a pool of technical specialists capable of employing the vast output of arms and equipment produced by American industry. In making this miscalculation they overlooked both American organizational genius and the enormous potential of American educational institutions to contribute to the rapid expansion of qualified personnel. Throughout the war, special reserve officer training programs and special technical schools held at hundreds of American colleges and universities supplemented, by hundreds of thousands, the existing numbers of service academy and ROTC graduates. In the V-12 program alone, more than sixty thousand U.S. Navy and Marine Corps officer candidates received their training and commissions in anywhere from eight months to two years. In the midshipman schools, many with college diplomas in hand were trained in as little as three months—the "ninety-day wonders" of the wartime navy. All these programs were based on a typically American assumption that given the right methods of training, anyone with sufficient preparatory education and reasonable intelligence could acquire a satisfactory capacity to do a required task.[2]

One problem that never posed a global concern to the U.S. Navy before the Pacific War was the availability of fuel for the fleet. The nation was entirely self-sufficient in petroleum, and the navy itself owned major untapped oil fields in Wyoming and California. So great was this strategic resource that during the 1930s, oil was exported to Japan from California, where the U.S. fleet was based. The U.S. Navy's only concern in these years was the delivery of oil to its fleet units far out at sea. In the 1920s, the navy estimated that 83 percent of American civilian tanker tonnage would be needed for the fleet's trans-Pacific crossing to the Philippines. While existing civilian tankers were slow, from 1936, the fast-tanker building program, subsidized by the Maritime Commission, provided the navy with a fairly good oil transport capability. Moreover, cognizant of the logistical challenges of trans-Pacific operations, the U.S. Navy had begun to experiment with underway refueling as early as 1936 and was perfecting the technique for refueling heavy fleet units by the end of the decade.[3]

Military technological innovation was far more prevalent in World War II than World War I. The research laboratory was the birthplace of the two most decisive military technologies of World War II: electronics and atomic weapons. Here again, authoritarian regimes like Germany, Italy, and Japan, with their powerful bureaucracies, should have had the greater ability to harness the work of the scientific researcher to the requirements of the military commander. As several thoughtful post–World War II studies made clear, democracies (unlike their more authoritarian counterparts) encouraged basic research and enjoyed the synergism of various researchers working separately but cooperatively on scientific and technological problems. Democratic nations could better link strategic imperatives with the principles of free discussion and creative thinking. Thus, the democratic freedom in scientific inquiry won the race for the development of military technologies.[4]

The development of radar in Britain and the United States, or more particularly, its application to searches at sea and to fire control, is an example of such success. Although radar research had begun separately and secretly during the 1930s in Britain, the United States, Germany, and Japan, by the eve of World War II, it was the British and Americans who had made the greatest advances in this technology.

In the mid-1930s, pulsed radar was under active investigation in both countries, and cathode-ray radar scopes, able to depict range, had been developed in the United States. Both technologies were successfully demonstrated in the U.S. Naval Research Laboratory and aboard fleet units in 1936. Early in 1938, a search radar was installed on a battleship and was exhaustively and successfully tested in fleet maneuvers in the Caribbean in the winter of 1939. The device detected aircraft at nearly 50 miles. Over the next two years, improved search radars were installed on all seven American carriers, five battleships, six cruisers, and two large seaplane tenders. The development of naval fire control radar began in 1937, and after the delivery of the first set to the navy, substantially improved fire control radars were installed aboard cruisers before Pearl Harbor. By the eve of the Pacific War, therefore, primitive though the systems may have been by later standards, the U.S. Navy had operational radar systems that greatly aided its fleet in the early detection of approaching enemy air and surface forces and the directing of gunfire against enemy air and surface targets at all hours and in all weathers.

Matching radar in its tactical implications was a much earlier, yet related technology—radio—which had already provided to any commander the rapid means of communication with his forces and thus tighter tactical control over them. Conversely, its principal weakness, the vulnerability of its communications to interception, also became an increasingly critical source of intelligence, the key element in the strategic planning of opposing forces. The attempt to protect radio communications through the encoding or encryption of messages inevitably summoned forth counterefforts by other governments and military establishments toward the decoding and decryption of those messages.

Within the past decade, a growing body of literature has traced the course by which the Anglo-American maritime nations attempted, fitfully in the early 1930s, and then with increasing competence and sophistication by the end of the decade, to read the secret radio traffic of Germany, Japan, and Italy. By the end of 1941, the scale, continuity, rapidity, and currency of signals intelligence gleaned by the Anglo-American maritime nations from Axis sources was such that a recent scholarly study has termed it an "intelligence revolution."[5] As is now known, ULTRA and MAGIC, the principal intelligence by which the Allies successfully read a critical amount of the highest-grade Axis codes and ciphers, eventually employed an enormous mobilization of interdisciplinary military and civilian talent. This cryptanalytic establishment displayed great ingenuity in developing techniques for solving complex codes and ciphers.

Signals (radio) intelligence came to yield an increasing amount and diversity of information about the movements, composition, and intentions of any fleet at very little cost. Radio direction-finding made it possible to monitor the daily activities of another fleet. By taking cross-bearings on the radio signals of any warship, one could pinpoint the location of that ship and even plot its course and speed. Analysis of the radio traffic of another fleet made it possible to deduce the chain of command of a fleet by ascertaining which radios talked to which. Analysis of the volume of radio traffic could also produce educated assessments of the imminence of fleet movements, since an increase in such traffic usually preceded important operations. The most difficult, yet potentially most rewarding, element of signals intelligence was cryptanalysis, the varied methods of discovering the clear meaning of any code or cipher.

Through the 1920s and 1930s, the U.S. Navy worked diligently to solve Japanese navy codes and ciphers. The effort was sometimes assisted by surreptitious entry and the photographing of codes and ciphers. In other cases laborious cryptanalysis, extending over many years, finally led to useful intelligence. By the late 1930s, the U.S. Navy had a cadre of very experienced and capable cryptanalysts. But the key ingredient in the ultimately successful breaking of the most important Japanese codes—as it was in Britain, where the German Enigma ciphers were broken—was the recognition that solutions could not be found by military personnel alone: that it would take the talents of a host of specialists, civilian and military, mathematicians and linguists, to solve a problem that was, after all, hydra-headed.

THE NAVY AND THE MERCHANT MARINE
Subsidies and Requisitions

The Japanese navy's expansion plans for the post-treaty period included not just construction of new warship hulls, but also the requisitioning of ships from the civilian merchant marine either for conversion into warship auxiliaries or for additional transport capacity for the fleet. Such requisition programs were the advantageous end product of a system of government, particularly navy, support for Japanese civilian shipping.[6]

While the Japanese merchant marine had grown enormously during World War I, the postwar depression had left the Japanese shipping industry, and the shipping industry worldwide, in a slump that persisted for most of the 1920s. Naturally, with a glut of shipping, maritime construction sharply declined. For the Japanese government as a whole, the empty civilian yards swelled unemployment

numbers and added to the parlous state of the Japanese economy, a situation exacerbated after 1930 by the London Naval Treaty, which further reduced the orders
for naval construction coming to both government and private yards.[7]

In the early 1930s, working together, the civilian government, the navy, and
private industry undertook to strengthen both Japanese maritime construction
and the shipping business by a subsidy program that benefited the Japanese economy and, in the long run, the Japanese navy. Under its "scrap and build" program, the government agreed to subsidize those Japanese shipping companies
willing to scrap 2 tons of old shipping (over twenty-five years old) for every ton of
new shipping added, as long as the new merchant vessels were over 4,000 tons
and were able to make 13.5 knots. In 1936, the subsidy was available across a
range of merchant ship types (though the requirements were raised to 6,000 tons
and 19 knots), and that year the government offered subsidies for new construction without the scrapping requirement.[8]

The result of these programs was a surge in Japanese ship construction and a
consequent expansion in the Japanese merchant fleet from just over 4 million tons
in the early 1930s to more than 6 million on the eve of the Pacific War. Far more
important, however, was the tremendous improvement in the quality of the
Japanese seaborne transport in modernity, speed, and fuel efficiency.[9] "By 1940,"
Mark Parillo concludes, "Japan possessed a merchant fleet ranked third in the
world in size and perhaps second to none in efficiency."[10]

For the Japanese navy and army, there were obvious benefits derived from this
qualitative superiority of the merchant fleet, given their past history of commandeering civilian shipping for their wartime operations (in the Sino-Japanese and
Russo-Japanese wars). For the navy, it was particularly advantageous, moreover,
since many of these newer vessels could be converted, in wartime, for use as naval
auxiliaries. Several were designed according to navy specifications for ease of conversion and thereby constituted clandestine naval units. Such arrangements were
the basis of the navy's projected "shadow fleet" of aircraft carriers masquerading
in the 1930s in their original guise as fast passenger liners (see chapter 9). The
Kasuga-maru of the NYK Line, for example, became the escort carrier *Taiyō*; her
conversion was completed in time for her to participate in the invasion of Southeast Asia. In the year or so immediately before the Pacific War, other civilian vessels built under government subsidy were converted to auxiliary cruisers, gunboats, minesweepers, patrol boats, and the like.[11]

As for seaborne transport, however, there were no civilian ships more vital to
the Japanese navy than tankers. When the navy had initiated an oil reserve policy
in the late Meiji period, it had no tankers of its own, depending entirely on civilian
shipping to transport its fuel. In 1916, it had constructed the first of its own
tankers and, in the years immediately after the World War I, the navy had switched

to using its own ships to supply oil to the fleet, employing civilian tankers only as a reserve. Central to this policy had been the construction, from 1920 to 1923, of a class of ten high-speed tankers, the *Shiretoko* class, capable of 14 knots, each having a capacity for 8,000 tons of oil. (An eleventh ship of this class was converted to the seaplane carrier *Notoro* even before leaving the ways.)[12] But in the 1930s, the building of navy tankers stopped except for a few that could be converted to other functions (as aircraft carriers, submarine tenders, and the like). Instead, the navy supported subsidies for the construction of newer, even faster and more efficient civilian tankers that it could charter to supply petroleum in peacetime (at much higher than customary civilian charter rates) or commandeer in the event of war. With this sort of backing and with the steadily growing navy demand for oil as its major market, the Japanese tanker industry expanded vigorously. From 120,000 tons in 1934, Japan's tanker tonnage grew to 364,000 tons in 1940; the annual carrying capacity grew from 1 million tons in 1934 to four times that in 1940. Moreover, quality increased along with quantity. Private companies were willing to build 10,000-ton tankers, the largest in the world at the time, and by 1940, thirty-three of Japan's oceangoing tankers could make at least 16 knots.[13] Nevertheless, by the late 1930s, Japan's skyrocketing need for oil, provoked chiefly by the China War and the navy's strenuous efforts to stockpile oil, left the size of the civilian tanker fleet of forty-nine ships inadequate for the nation's needs.[14]

Even before the war, the ravenous demands on all civilian shipping by both military services put them in competition with the needs of the civilian economy, to the great detriment of the latter. As mentioned, the requisition of merchant shipping had been a practice of both services in earlier wars. Of this *chōyō sempaku* (requisitioned shipping) the army usually sought transports and the navy needed both transports and ships for conversion to auxiliary warships. A new spate of government requisitions had gone into effect with the outbreak of the China War in 1937, the navy commandeering some 600,000 tons of merchant shipping that year. Other requisitions followed, but real pressure on civilian shipping was not exerted until the three *Sempaku tairyō chōyō* (large-scale mercantile shipping requisitions) of 1940–41. The first occurred in November 1940 when the navy commandeered some 550,000 tons of merchant shipping for naval service, including conversion to auxiliary warships; the second was part of the navy's "emergency" construction program in August 1941, which included the conversion of two fast liners, *Aikoku Maru* and *Hōkoku Maru,* into armed merchant cruisers for commerce raiding purposes.[15] The third requisition came in November 1941, when the navy requisitioned an additional 550,000 tons. By the time that the Pacific War began, the navy had taken over 482 merchantmen comprising 1,740,200 tons, or 30 percent of the merchant marine.[16]

In the short run, the navy was thus able to reap the benefit of a rapid increase in its sea transport capacity provided by some of the world's finest merchant shipping and a rapid augmentation of its auxiliary forces at a cut-rate cost. But these almost heedless demands on Japanese civilian shipping by the navy (and the army) had disastrous consequences once Japan found itself at war. Not only were there too few ships to support Japanese civilian needs in the home islands and throughout the formal colonial empire, but the mobilization of all reservists, chiefly composed of experienced merchant seamen, left the remaining civilian merchant marine to be manned by inexperienced crews that often performed poorly when their ships came under attack.[17]

There was, in addition, another critical problem that affected the maintenance of a first-rate merchant marine. Commercial shipyards held a preponderant position in Japanese naval construction in the years immediately before the Pacific War. By the eve of the war, those yards were working to full capacity, if not maximum efficiency. These conditions presented Japan with a critical choice between maritime and naval construction, since neither the nation's resources nor its shipbuilding facilities could be used extensively and simultaneously for both. Building capacity was increased during the war, and control and responsibility for merchant construction passed to the navy, which gave somewhat greater attention to commercial vessels than before. Yet the tension between demands for naval construction and merchant building grew worse as losses mounted from enemy air and submarine attacks.[18]

The destruction of Japan's merchant fleet ultimately had its origin in the navy's surprising failure to give priority to the problems of commerce protection and antisubmarine warfare in the interwar decades. We say "surprising" because Japan, as an industrial nation with few natural resources of its own, had become increasingly dependent on its seaborne trade, and because World War I had demonstrated with awesome clarity the desperate circumstances to which an island trading nation could be reduced by a ruthless submarine campaign.

LOGISTICS
The Consequences of Planning for a Short War

As early as the first decade of the twentieth century, Akiyama Saneyuki had spoken of the importance of *semmu*—the conduct of war other than strategy, operations, and tactics. Though Akiyama had broadened the term's meaning beyond logistics, at its heart was a concern for matériel—the arming, fueling, provisioning, and manning of a navy—as well as the procedures—transport, construction, and transfer techniques—that kept that matériel flowing to the navy's warships and bases. These are obviously elements without which any navy cannot maintain itself in a state of readiness in peacetime, let alone fight effectively in war. Though little detailed information exists today about logistics of the Japanese navy, it would appear that in its two tests in combat—the Sino- and Russo-Japanese wars—the navy's logistical requirements were simple and adequately met.

These were conflicts of short duration, however, against naval enemies that were close at hand. Even during World War I, most naval operations of the major combatants covered comparatively short distances. The sites for naval bases were fixed, and fleets sortied out of them for a few brief days and then returned. Under such conditions there was no need for a fleet train, nor was there much concern about a restriction of the fleet's movements because of fuel. A Japanese naval war with the United States decades later would confront the Japanese navy with far greater logistical problems, fought as it would be over vast distances, against a foe formidably supplied by an enormous industrial base. Moreover, it would be fought in an age in which new weapons, like the airplane, created new and unprecedented demands for fuel, spare parts, and maintenance.[19]

Among the unanticipated logistical problems that the navy faced in planning the opening moves in the Pacific War was that of underway refueling at sea. The U.S. Navy, necessarily more cognizant of the logistical challenges of trans-Pacific operations, had begun to experiment in underway refueling as early as 1936 and was perfecting this technique for refueling heavy fleet units in the late 1930s.[20] The Japanese navy, however, which had traditionally thought of fighting its decisive battle in its home waters and had thus designed its ships for speed rather than for radius of action, faced an unprecedented challenge in refueling and replenishing the fleet during the 6,000-mile round trip Hawaiian operation and during the naval operations supporting the invasions of Malaya, the Philippines, and the Netherlands East Indies. By mid-1941, however, the fleet was beginning to work out underway replenishment for fuel oil. The fleet practiced both: the "alongside" system of refueling, in which tanker and ship being refueled steamed side by side, and the "astern" system, in which the tanker and the ship being replenished were in tandem. For refueling destroyers and cruisers, both methods were employed. For battleships and carriers, whose power and inertia made it more difficult for them to maneuver and thus more likely to snap the refueling hose in the "astern" system, the position of tanker and ship being refueled were reversed. In any event, the Hawaii task force's successful refueling in the treacherous waters of the north Pacific speaks highly of Japanese seamanship in performing this essential logistical task.[21]

Turning to the larger problems of matériel in a war with the United States, the Japanese navy clearly gave too little thought to them. This first became apparent in the efforts to carry out the navy's *suishi jumbi* (preparatory fleet mobilization) just prior to the Pacific War. Other than the question of fuel stocks, an ammunition shortage was the most serious logistical problem the navy faced in making these preparations. The navy soon discovered that the demands of fleet units for ammunition far exceeded the reserves stockpiled during peacetime.[22]

In particular, the navy was confronted by a critical shortage of aviation ordnance, possessing only 10–30 percent of the anticipated needs for type 91 aerial torpedoes and 20-millimeter aircraft cannon ammunition. Since current production of this ordnance was fairly low, the navy recognized that unless the shortages were made up rapidly and drastically, the fleet would probably exhaust the stocks of these items within a few months after the start of hostilities. Moreover, at the outbreak of the war, the navy's warships got under way from their various bases with full loads of ammunition, but thereafter, the magazines at Yokosuka, Sasebo, and Kure ran out of 25-millimeter shells. At the last moment, to deal with this and related problems in matériel, the navy undertook an emergency program in industrial mobilization to coordinate logistical planning and to oversee the increased production of needed material. This unprecedented effort involved the conversion of major ordnance facilities and basic changes in the use of raw materials, parts, and machinery. Although the navy succeeded in preventing the interruption in the flow of ordnance at the start of the war, throughout the remainder of the conflict, it was haunted by ammunition shortages.[23]

Another logistical element unanticipated by the navy high command in the interwar years was the need for civil engineering in the construction of forward bases. Indeed, Yamamoto Isoroku had been one of the few who had foreseen the importance of base construction in a future Pacific conflict. "As I see it," Yamamoto has been quoted as declaring about 1936, "naval operations in the future will consist of capturing an island, then building an airfield in as short a time as possible—within a week or so—moving up air units, and using them to gain air and surface control over the next stretch of ocean."[24]

At the time, however, the Japanese navy lacked the organization, the training, and the equipment of construction units to make this possible. The navy (like the nation as a whole) lagged badly in the development of civil engineering. In particular, it lacked the requisite machinery—bulldozers, earthmovers, and steam shovels—and nearly all of its construction was done by hand.[25]

In the first few months of the war, as Japanese forces rolled through Southeast Asia and the southwest Pacific, the construction of advanced bases was the responsibility of combat units themselves. In those combat theaters, the Japanese forces had generally managed to occupy or to repair the naval bases and port facilities of their retreating enemies. But within a few months, as the tide of the Japanese advance swept through undeveloped atolls of the central Pacific, the navy recognized the need for specialized units to build airfields and other advance base facilities. The first such units, *setsueitai* (construction units), had been organized in November 1941. Composed mostly of Koreans or Taiwanese, with a sprinkling of Japanese officers with command authority and Japanese civilians with engineering experience, the units were only semi-military in character and had limited combat value. Nevertheless, these special construction units were rushed to the Pacific, along with labor battalions whose ranks were even more unskilled, and were frequently landed with the first wave of operational units that came ashore. But the *setsueitai* never possessed the expertise, the training, or the equipment possessed by the U.S. Navy Seabees. Because the Japanese naval high command understood neither the limitations of the *setsueitai* nor sound civil engineering principles very well, the *setsueitai* were often given impossible construction tasks. Ultimately, as the tide of the Japanese advance slowed and then stopped, their mission and equipment were directed toward the construction of defensive works—tunnels, fortifications, gun emplacements, dispersed machine shops, and the like. Later, the *setsueitai* were often incorporated into larger *konkyochitai* (base defense units). Overwhelmed in a series of futile defenses as the American counteroffensive began to roll through the central Pacific, the *setsueitai* were immolated in the bunkers they had helped construct.[26]

The single greatest cause of the Japanese navy's prewar failure to recognize in advance the logistical problems of a war with the United States was, once again, the navy's overriding concern with the decisive battle. The problems of "bullets, beans, and black oil" could not hold the attention of either staff or line officers fixated on the dramatic strategies and tactics of the great encounter at sea. Only those officers judged less capable or physically limited were assigned to grapple with the difficulties in transport, supply, or construction. As there was no exchange of personnel between these two groupings, each group understood little of the other's difficulties or circumstances. The result, one former navy officer has recalled, was that during the Pacific War, there was constant friction between those directing the navy's operations and those responsible for supplying the operations. The former tended to frame their plans without relation to logistical resources. Assuming that the manpower and material were already at hand, they discovered that it often took unanticipated weeks or even months to provide supplies for their operations. And, as maritime transportation facilities started to shrink through destruction of the nation's merchant fleet, this situation only worsened.[27]

MANNING THE NAVY
The Perils of Elitism

Manpower is as critical a problem in naval logistics as ammunition, supplies, fuel, victualing, transport, or engineering. There are, of course, two basic ways to deal with the problem, depending upon the size of a nation's population and the navy it intends to maintain. The first is to rely, both in peace and war, on a small, highly trained cadre of career officers and men—in other words, to fight with the resources and manpower at hand. The other is to create a professional core of naval personnel in peacetime, backed by a much larger reserve of officers and men who have been given some training and who can be mobilized to swell the ranks to meet wartime needs.

With modifications, the Japanese navy, from its earliest years, had taken the first approach. Consistent with its views on the most appropriate force structure for the fleet and on the most appropriate tactics and strategy to apply to it, the navy had pursued *shōsū seiei shugi* (a policy of small numbers, but a high state of readiness), that is, quality over quantity.[28] Over the decades, the navy had succeeded in building a small, elite force of some the most experienced, best trained,

Table 11-1

OFFICERS AND MEN IN THE IMPERIAL JAPANESE NAVY, 1928–42

Year	Officers	Noncommissioned officers and men	Total
1928	7,849	72,746	80,595
1929	8,016	68,208	76,224
1930	8,095	71,298	79,393
1931	8,096	70,334	78,430
1932	8,184	75,638	83,822
1933	8,514	80,394	88,908
1934	8,873	84,196	93,069
1935	9,310	89,586	98,896
1936	9,749	97,718	107,467
1937	11,029	122,984	134,013
1938	12,719	146,414	159,133
1939	15,040	175,058	190,098
1940	18,113	205,060	223,173
1941	23,883	287,476	311,359
1942	34,769	394,599	429,368

Figures as of 31 December.
Source: *KG1*, 638–39.

best disciplined, and best motivated naval professionals in the world. With such a core of career officers and men, the navy had won two major naval wars in the first thirty years of its history.

The navy's internal dynamics, as well as its operational emphasis on quality over quantity, also served to limit the number of its officers. A solicitous navy scheme of promotion sought to guarantee that every graduate of the Naval Academy who was healthy and reasonably competent would reach the rank of captain. Consequently, the number of officers admitted to the academy had to be kept to a bare minimum, which was a major cause of its ferocious entrance requirements.[29] Such a personnel policy was based on assumptions of stability, continuity, and settled careerism, and, during the quieter decades immediately after the Russo-Japanese War, may have been appropriate to the manpower needs of the Japanese navy.

The trouble began in the mid-1930s, when the navy launched its expansion programs following the lapse of the limitation treaties. In 1936, there were fewer than 10,000 officers and not quite 98,000 enlisted personnel to man not only the rapidly growing surface fleet, but also an expanding air force, sizeable naval landing forces, and a shore establishment, including shipyards, port facilities, naval and air bases, schools and research centers, both in the home islands and in China. At least half this total of nearly 108,000 men served aboard ship or in operational air units; the rest served ashore—a ratio of "teeth" to "tail" (in current military parlance) that was in keeping with the navy's traditional orientation toward battle, but ultimately harmful to the navy's overall ability to wage modern naval war.[30]

In these years of rapid expansion the great difficulty was training enough officers. At the time, the number of officers accepted at the Naval Academy (as well as the numbers of enlisted personnel) was based upon the size of the fleet at hand. It was Japanese navy practice to determine personnel requirements only after the question of armaments budgets had been settled. Thus, not until a plan for new ships and aircraft had been approved did the navy begin to increase the number of officers admitted to the academy and to recruit new enlisted personnel. In a navy that supposedly took ten years to develop a truly capable lieutenant and twenty years for a commander, training should have anticipated the numbers of officers and men required by the level of armaments ten years on.[31] Except for all but the largest naval units, the necessary lead time for adequate training and experience was deemed to be far longer than the average construction period for the navy's ships.

As the navy began to pile one expansion plan on top of another, this situation worsened. Between 1936 and 1941, the navy estimated that it was roughly eight hundred to a thousand officers short. According to one estimate, the navy went

Table 11-2

Shortages of Officers in the Imperial Japanese Navy, 1934–41

Year	Billets authorized	Officers available	Shortfall
1934	4,917	4,501	416
1935	5,030	4,735	295
1936	5,469	4,663	806
1937	6,185	5,164	1,021
1938	6,824	5,922	902
1939	7,751	6,642	1,109
1940	9,013	8,326	687
1941	12,045	10,894	1,151

Source: *KG1*, 650–54.

into action in late 1941 short at least two thousand combat and engineer officers.[32] The real trouble came, of course, during the Pacific War itself, when the difficulty in manning new naval construction was compounded by mounting combat fatalities and injuries. The navy could make up for losses in the most junior officer ranks by expansion and by an acceleration of training in the academy, but officers lost in the middle ranks, particularly those of commander and lieutenant commander, proved impossible to replace. Various expedients were tried: calling up more reserves, promoting warrant and special duty officers, and putting lieutenants into lieutenant commander and commander billets.[33] But the officers called in to cover these midlevel shortages often proved unqualified and thus generally lowered the navy's efficiency.[34]

By the middle of the war, when the many of the midlevel officers had been killed, the problem reached crisis proportions. It was only after the combat losses of the Solomons campaign, however, that the Navy Ministry's Personnel Department began to reconsider its manpower policies. By then, the ministry realized, it was already too late to do anything effective about the problem. "At present there is no way to solve our serious personnel restraints, and the prospects are for the situation to get worse, not better," the chief of the department reported in early

1943. "We are now faced with a situation in which we cannot relieve fatigued men on the front lines and cannot fully replace men who are lost [in combat]." A fundamental cause of the navy's disastrous personnel predicament, he admitted, was the nature of its manpower policies: "Of all the nations fighting in this war, Japan has been the slowest and least thorough in mobilizing its men."[35]

The creation, in the prewar decades, of a strong, reasonably trained reserve would have considerably altered this situation. Not only had the Japanese navy failed to take this precautionary step, but it had given relatively little consideration to planning a personnel force that could be rapidly expanded in time of war.[36] There was a reserve, indeed, but it was confined to the few graduates of the Merchant Marine Academy and the Merchant Marine School, and, naturally, most of these officers were needed to man the merchant fleet. Only slowly did the navy begin to expand its reserve, setting up reserve categories in the medical and pharmacy branches and, in 1934, creating a student reserve system in naval aviation. These programs, however, trained only a few officers until after the China War began.

The shortages that developed in trained noncommissioned officers and ratings proved almost as serious as the shortage of officers. The navy's manpower needs were nearly always met in sheer numbers, because if there were not enough volunteers, men were conscripted. The problem was quality. Naturally, the navy wanted the largest possible number of volunteers, since, quite apart from questions of morale, volunteers served longer (five years, as opposed to three years for conscripts) and could therefore be better trained and could better maintain the high level of technical proficiency the navy required. From 1927 to 1942, volunteers constituted about one-third of the navy's enlisted personnel each year; by 1942 the number of volunteers and conscripts entering the navy was about equal (but, since volunteers served longer, their proportion overall became greater). Conscription presented certain difficulties for the navy. Conscription was administered by the army, often to the pronounced disadvantage of the navy. When the navy needed men, it had to consult with its sister service, which, with its own manpower needs to satisfy, could refuse to meet navy requisitions. There is strong evidence that during the Pacific War, the army not only began sending conscripts of inferior quality to the navy, but began to draft into its own ranks civilian employees of the navy.[37]

The essential cause of the Japanese navy's crippling personnel policies was lack of foresight pure and simple.[38] A policy that relied on entering into combat with a small elite of highly trained professionals undoubtedly suited the kind of short war centered on a single battle that the navy planned to fight; it was a fatal defect in waging the extended war of attrition that the navy was actually obliged to fight.

LIFEBLOOD
The Navy's Oil Problem

No aspect of the navy's logistics had become more critical to the Japanese navy by the mid-1930s than oil.[39] The problem had begun with the switch-over from coal to petroleum as the navy's principal fuel shortly after World War I (see chapter 6). With the addition of new oil-burning warships—carriers, cruisers, destroyers, and submarines—in the 1920s and the retrofitting of a number of the navy's capital ships as fast battleships in the 1930s, the problem of maintaining adequate petroleum supplies for fleet training and exercises became severe. With the advent of a sizable naval air force and the need for high-octane fuel it became critical.

About the time of the Washington Treaty, the navy had calculated that it needed about 10,000 tons of bunker fuel to operate the entire fleet, steaming at 24 knots, for twenty-four hours.[40] Working from this figure, the navy judged that in wartime, it would consume at least 3 million tons of fuel oil per year.[41] The navy's predicament was that the paucity of domestic sources of petroleum made it extremely difficult to maintain sufficient petroleum stocks to meet such emergency requirements.

To deal with the situation, the navy had attempted two solutions: the development of synthetic fuels, and an aggressive program of stockpiling oil. The first program had been less than successful, however. Collaboration with the South Manchuria Railway to produce oil from shale had begun at Fushun, Manchuria, in 1926, and another plant had been established six years later on the Korean-Manchurian border. Yet the nearly half-million tons of oil that the navy hoped for from this source never materialized and the trickle of 10,000–11,000 tons a month was negligible in comparison to the projected consumption in case of a national emergency.[42]

The other measure was to accelerate the stockpiling of oil in peacetime. By adding continually to its storage tank capacity and making offshore purchases, the navy had been able to store approximately 1.5 million tons by 1926. During a time of tight naval budgets, the money for both imports of foreign oil and storage tank construction had been hard to acquire. Yet from 1925 to 1930, using funds earmarked for naval construction, the navy managed to store some 300,000–400,000 tons annually, so that by 1931 it had a stockpile of 3 million tons, a fact it chose not to share with its sister service or the Japanese civilian government.[43]

Although the Japanese navy's fuel policy had for several decades concentrated on building up reserves in heavy (bunker) fuel, with the increasing scale of naval aviation, it became just as important to develop and store aviation fuels and lubricants. The navy had begun to research and test these materials in the 1920s and early 1930s at several of its fuel depots and air arsenals, but the materials were not a priority until the mid-1930s, when the increasing performance of aircraft engines demanded the use of higher-grade fuels. Thus, while the navy was building up supplies,[44] fuel research was advanced, particularly toward the production of high-octane gasoline. One difficulty in the development of such fuels and lubricants was that along with the crude oil from which these substances were made, much of the technology and manufacturing equipment came from the United States. Thus, in 1937, when the China War broke out and Japanese carrier and land-based air units were rushed to the mainland, the Japanese navy was obliged to undertake a emergency program to import 4,300 tons of 100-octane aviation fuel from the United States. Because of the scale of its air operations in China, the navy's consumption of high-grade aviation fuels skyrocketed, and in early 1938, it imported another 43,400 tons of American fuel, including some isooctane for use as an additive. These imports were a further spur to advance the research necessary to make the navy self-sufficient in aviation fuels. In fact, however, because of the continuing demands of the China War, the successive restrictions on imports from the United States after 1939, and the mounting threat of a full-scale naval war after 1940, the navy never really caught up.[45]

Several difficulties faced the Japanese navy in its effort to bring its petroleum supplies into balance with its current and projected consumption. It had to worry about the ability of Japan to obtain oil in the increasingly uncertain international petroleum market. The navy was also concerned about competition with its sister service, the civilian sector, and private industry in obtaining sufficient petroleum allocations from the government. In 1933, to deal with the first problem, the navy had sponsored the establishment of an interministerial National Petroleum Policy Council. Then, in 1934, discovering with dismay that the private sector was apparently counting on naval fuel stocks to supply its needs in case of a national emergency, the navy persuaded the government to pass the Petroleum Industry Law, which provided that each oil company was obliged to keep one-half of its annual petroleum imports in stored reserve.[46]

By 1936, thanks to the passage of this law, the navy brought its stockpile up to approximately 3.5 million tons of oil.[47] With the outbreak of the China War, however, the nation and the navy were faced with a new energy crisis, not so much because of the immediate drain on current fuel stocks, but rather because the war, in combination with the tightening international situation, raised the prospect of an increasingly uncertain strategic future.[48] In these years the navy was consuming approximately 800,000 tons of oil annually out of the approximately 1.2 million tons that it imported: 550,000 tons went for fleet training and maintenance; another 100,000 tons went for air operations over China and naval operations off the China coast cost; 100,000 tons for training ships and coastal patrol craft; and an additional 50,000 tons for reserve ships at home ports.[49] But despite the navy's combat operations in the skies over China, the navy recognized that the China War was a sideshow, a strategic digression from its blue-water mission in the Pacific. In a real naval war with the United States, the navy now calculated that it would expend 3,590,000 tons of heavy oil and 440,000 tons of aviation gasoline annually. Given that domestic production of oil was only 397,000 tons in 1937, an aggressive program of oil imports and stockpiling was more than ever an urgent matter.[50] Working to the advantage of the navy was a series of emergency appropriations passed in the Diet that facilitated the stockpiling of oil and made it possible to divert funds from one expenditure to another. These appropriations further enabled the navy to conceal its stockpiling of oil and construction of fuel tanks not only from foreign agents, but also from the army and other government agencies.[51]

But such petroleum stores were still being amassed largely through purchase from the United States, an increasingly hostile provider. In 1939, the abrogation of the U.S.-Japan Commercial Treaty placed the export of petroleum and petroleum-manufacturing equipment and technology under U.S. government control. In the months following, successive restrictions were placed on all these items, most importantly, on high-octane aviation fuel. In 1939, the American abrogation of the treaty reduced the import of high-octane fuels, and in 1940, these reductions were followed by an American embargo of oil-refining equipment and tetraethyl.

As Japan had depended on the United States for 80–90 percent of its oil imports, these restrictions posed a severe blow to the Japanese navy, despite its best efforts to become fuel-independent. More than anything else, the restrictions made the navy realize the tremendous vulnerability of its fuel supplies. Increasingly, the oil fields of the Netherlands East Indies and British North Borneo seemed to be the outstanding substitute for the narrowing stream of oil from America, on which the navy had so long and so perilously depended.[52] With the collapse of France and the Netherlands and the siege of Britain in the spring of 1940, the way seemed open to bring those territories and their resources under Japanese control.

The circular reasoning of the Japanese navy, however, predicated any Japanese military and naval initiative toward the Indies on the risk of war with the United States. In turn, assessment of Japanese success in such a conflict was based on the assumption that the navy would have to have access to the huge fuel resources of the Netherlands East Indies. In August 1940, the navy brass met to discuss the logistical risks involved and concluded that with its current petroleum reserves, Japan could not fight for more than a year.[53] In an interministerial conference that September, Prince Fushimi, chief of the Navy General Staff, confirmed that the navy did not have enough fuel to undertake a protracted war with the United

States. By 1940, moreover, with the loss of its oil supplies from the United States, the navy, which was consuming about one-quarter of the petroleum used in Japan at that time, had started digging into its petroleum stocks, the largest in Japan.[54]

In 1941, as Japan edged toward a naval war with the United States, the key role that oil would play in such a war was the focus of reviews by several bodies both inside and outside the navy. Meeting in June was the First Committee (perhaps the most powerful specialized committee of middle-echelon officers that had come to dominate Japanese naval policy in the 1930s); in November, the Ministry's Naval Affairs Bureau; and that same month, the Cabinet Planning Board (an interministerial body charged with collating resource data for strategic planning purposes). While their calculations differ in some significant respects, the three bodies clearly shared some conclusions. First, they all assumed a three-year war, largely because they all judged that to be the maximum length of Japan's endurance to fight an industrial war with the United States. Second, they all assumed that the navy would have sufficient fuel resources to fight effectively for one year, but that the second year would be critical from the perspective of fuel supplies, and a third year fraught with disaster. And last, all assumed that Japan would have control of the oil-rich resources of the Netherlands East Indies and British North Borneo.

By the summer of 1941, this last condition had become a bedrock of Japanese naval strategy. In these immediate prewar years, however, Japanese naval planners apparently never thought through the logistical and strategic requirements that would be involved in the successful seizure and exploitation of the petroleum and other resources of Southeast Asia. To begin with, the oil fields of the region either would have to be captured intact or, if damaged, would have to be quickly restored to full operation very quickly. But of far greater importance was the question of transporting these materials from Southeast Asia to Japan. At the heart of this task lay, once again, the problem of tankers. Although Japan had well over 300,000 tons of tanker capacity by the opening of the Pacific War, the navy requisitioned some 270,000 tons of that, leaving only about 30,000 tons for nonoperational purposes, plus whatever new tanker construction could be made available.[55]

Early on in the Pacific War, it became clear that despite the navy's efforts to subsidize civilian tanker construction, Japan would have inadequate tanker capacity to transport the oil resources that were the chief object of its strategic ambitions in 1940–41. In the opening moves of the war into Southeast Asia, moreover, this tanker shortage was another cause of friction between the army and the navy. And, by the third year of the war, this initial tanker deficit was enormously compounded by the staggering losses of oil tankers to American submarine and air attacks. How to protect the long shipping route once hostilities commenced was a problem that few Japanese navy men considered in the years when the navy was exerting maximum pressure for the "southward advance" of Japanese power and influence.

Nevertheless despite the alarms raised within the inner councils of government during the last months before Japan opened hostilities, the Japanese navy badly miscalculated both the scale and the nature of the problem. As of 1 December 1941, the navy had on hand 6,500,000 tons of petroleum, enough to last for two years of wartime operations, it estimated: 1,435,000 tons of crude; 3,634,000 tons of bunker fuel; 473,000 tons of aviation gasoline; 27,000 tons of isooctane; 6,400 tons of aircraft lubricants; 13,600 tons of ordinary lubricants; and 921,000 tons of various fuels already distributed to ships and bases outside the home islands.[56] The navy calculated that after the start of hostilities, on average, it would consume about 233,000 tons of fuel monthly, of which 200,000 tons would be bunker fuel and 20,500 tons aviation gasoline, for an average annual expenditure rate of not quite 2,800,000 tons. In fact, during the Pacific War, despite extreme economy measures, the navy consumed well over 12,000,000 tons of petroleum. This was about 4,400,000 tons more than anticipated: 4,850,000 tons in the first year of the war; 4,280,000 in the second; and 3,180,000 tons in the third. In all, it amounted to a staggering 60 percent of Japan's total consumption of petroleum during the war, by one estimate (table 11-3).[57]

As it turned out, it was indeed oil from Southeast Asia that both literally and figuratively fueled the navy's operations during the Pacific War.[58] By 1943, however, the Combined Fleet had become tethered to its Southeast Asian oil spigot. Very little of that oil could get through to the home islands or other ports in the empire because of attacks by American submarines. In its obsession with the tactical details of the "decisive battle" the Japanese navy had given too little thought to the question of fuel and thus to the cruising radius of its ships, a problem that came back to hobble the navy again and again during the war.[59] Moreover, as it transpired, the naval surface war turned on not a single "decisive battle," which the navy had estimated would consume 500,000 tons of fuel oil, but on at least three major encounters: Midway, the Philippine Sea (the Marianas), and the combined battles off the Philippines, which together cost the navy a total of 1,150,000 tons of fuel.[60] Finally, in its position as the nation's chief consumer of fuel and in its narrow concern with only its own interests, the navy gave little thought to the fuel requirements for Japan as a whole. With the onset of the Pacific War, as the fuel supplies of the army, the civilian government, and private industry began to give out, the navy, as holder of the nation's largest supply of petroleum, was occasionally obliged to accommodate these other sectors out of its own stockpiles.[61]

For the Japanese navy in 1941, oil was the single most important reason for undertaking the risk of war. Gambling that war would yield a vast harvest of oil, the navy (and, for that matter, the army) miscalculated on a disastrous scale. The situation became so desperate that by 1944, the navy would be investigating the possibilities of extracting aviation fuel from pine roots.[62] The Japanese navy's failure to think through the problem of oil as a critical resource in naval war was demonstrated on the very first day of the Pacific conflict. Neither in the planning nor in the execution of the Pearl Harbor strike was any attention paid to the large oil storage facilities at Pearl Harbor, destruction of which could have crippled American naval operations in the Pacific for months.

THE EVOLUTION OF JAPANESE RADAR
Too Little and Too Late

Of all the fields of naval technology that were critical to the relative performances of the Japanese and United States navies in the Pacific War, electronics was the most vital. Disastrously for the Japanese navy, its development of electronics, particularly radar,[63] was a case of too little and too late. Ironically, Japanese researchers had begun exploring this field almost as early as their counterparts in Britain and the United States, but official indifference, haphazard mobilization of scientific talent, and—as always—the absence of interservice cooperation fatally delayed the practical military application of Japanese radar research.

That research had begun in the early 1930s in a number of fragmented and isolated endeavors: a conference in which the two armed services joined the Communications Ministry to explore electromagnetic radiation; research at the navy's Technical Research Center by a young navy lieutenant, Itō Yūji, on the use of magnetrons to detect targets by radio waves; further studies along these lines by Constructor Capt. Tani Keikichirō; and, by 1936, the discovery, at Osaka University, of an electronic method of detecting passing aircraft. In 1937, in cooperation with the Japan Broadcasting Company, the navy began to experiment with frequency-modulated continuous-wave radio signals, and, in 1939, at a naval review in Tokyo Bay, ships were detected at ranges of up to 5 kilometers using a device with 10-centimeter waves. All these initiatives seem to have been undertaken independently from similar research in Britain and the United States, but none was pushed along very rapidly. Nor do their implications seem to have energized the high command into accelerating their practical application for the navy.[64]

The outbreak of the war in Europe, however, and the recognition by the Japanese navy of some of the advances in radar in the West led to an accelerated interest in this new technology. Early in 1941, Itō Yūji, by then a prominent member of the Technical Research Center, went to Germany with the navy's technical mission (headed by Adm. Nomura Naokuni). Itō was able to inspect German radar and acquire German technical reports. Through Itō's full report and through detailed accounts of British antiair radar defenses from Hamazaki Ryō,

Table 11-3

TWO ESTIMATES OF NATIONAL PETROLEUM SUPPLY VERSUS ACTUAL CONSUMPTION
DURING THE PACIFIC WAR (IN MILLIONS OF KILOLITERS)

FIRST YEAR OF THE PACIFIC WAR

	Navy estimate	Cabinet Planning Board estimate	Actual
Reserves at the start of the year	9.4	8.4	8.4
Japanese domestic production	0.2	0.25	0.26
Synthetic production	0.3	0.3	0.24
Imports from S.E. Asia	0.3	0.3	1.49
Total supply	10.2	9.25	10.39
Consumption	5.4	5.2	8.25
Navy's consumption	?	2.8	4.85
Remainder at year's end	4.8 (2.5)*	4.05 (2.55)†	2.14

SECOND YEAR OF THE PACIFIC WAR

	Navy estimate	Cabinet Planning Board estimate	Actual
Reserves at the start of the year	4.8	4.05	2.14
Japanese domestic production	0.2	0.2	0.27
Synthetic production	0.7	0.4	0.27
Imports from S.E. Asia	2.44	2.0	2.65
Total supply	8.14	6.65	5.33
Consumption	5.4	5.0	6.62
Navy's consumption	?	2.7	4.28
Remainder at year's end	2.74 (0.44)*	1.65 (0.15)†	−1.29

THIRD YEAR OF THE PACIFIC WAR

	Navy estimate	Cabinet Planning Board estimate	Actual
Reserves at the start of the year	2.74	1.65	−1.29
Japanese domestic production	0.4	0.3	0.25
Synthetic production	1.5	0.5	0.22
Imports from S.E. Asia	4.77	4.5	1.06
Total supply	9.41	6.95	0.24
Consumption	5.4	4.75	4.68
Navy's consumption	?	2.5	3.18
Remainder at year's end	4.01	2.2	−4.44‡

Table 11-3 (cont)

Sources: Figures for the navy estimates (by the Naval Affairs Bureau of the Navy Ministry, 1 August 1941) and the Cabinet Planning Board estimates (22 October 1941) are from Japan, Bōeichō Bōeikenshūjo Senshishitsu, *Kaigun gunsembi, ichi, Shōwa jūrokunen jūichigatsu made* [Naval armaments and war preparations, no. 1, up to November 1941] (Asagumo Shimbunsha, 1969), 730–32. Figures for actual production and consumption are from Japan, Bōeichō Bōeikenshūjo Senshishitsu, *Dai Hon'ei Kaigunbu, Rengō Kantai (roku), dai sandan sakusen kōki* [Imperial General Headquarters, Navy Division, Combined Fleet, no. 6, the latter period of third-stage operations] (Asagumo Shimbunsha, 1971), 114–15. See also Michael A. Barnhart, *Japan Prepares for Total War: The Search for Economic Security, 1919–1941* (Ithaca, N.Y.: Cornell University Press, 1987), 261; and Minoru Nomura, "Japan's Plans for World War II," *Revue Internationale d'Histoire Militaire* 38 (1978): 208–13.

*Estimate of national petroleum supply setting aside 1.0 million kiloliters for private sector reserve, 0.8 million kiloliters for dead remainder in tanks, and 0.5 million kiloliters for major sea battle.

†Estimate of national petroleum supply setting aside 1.5 million kiloliters as a minimum reserve.

‡ Before the war, neither research analyses nor war plans had taken into account the possibility of using petroleum from Southeast Asia without first transporting it to the home islands. However, a large quantity of Southeast Asian petroleum was actually used in this way—navy vessels often fueled at Palembang, Sumatra—and this probably accounted for the difference between supply and consumption. See Minoru Nomura, "Japan's Plans for World War II," referenced immediately above, 208.

a naval constructor commander in London, the Japanese navy was apprised, for the first time, of the fact that pulsed radar was being used by the combatants in the European war.[65] The naval high command was clearly alerted to the implications of radar and to the urgent need to facilitate research in that field. Capt. Yanagimoto Ryūsaku, chief of the Armaments Section of the Navy General Staff, for one, asserted that without radar, the navy simply could not enter the war.[66] A navy ministry instruction of 2 August 1941 finally ordered a crash program of radar development.[67]

By late 1941, definite progress had been made. With the encouragement of the general staff, the Navy Technical Department, and interested elements of Japanese private industry, Captain Itō and his staff made advances in meter-wavelength radar, which led to the testing of land-based air-search sets at several sites on the west coast of Honshū. The first production model, the No. 1, Model 1 air search radar, was ready in late November 1941. Electrically and mechanically crude by Western standards, it had a range of not much more than 35 miles. When used in the Southwest Pacific early in the war, it was subject to frequent breakdowns, as it had not been designed for use in the humidity of the tropics. Improvements in later models during the war reduced these malfunctions and greatly extended their effective range, but the radar models were never on a par with Allied radar sets.[68]

At all events, at the outset of the Pacific War, the navy had no shipborne surface search or fire-control radar or any radar that could be installed in any of its aircraft.[69] Confident in its night combat doctrine and equipment (powerful optics and searchlights), a year into the Pacific War, the Japanese navy found itself fighting like a man blindfolded. By the autumn of 1942, the navy would begin to understand the tremendous advantage radar provided to the American enemy.[70] With this recognition would come urgent demands by the Navy General Staff for accelerated development of the new technology. Yet, for the navy's research laboratories and centers, the greatest single problem, from the beginning of its radar research to the end of the war, was the inability to develop high-power centimeter-wavelength transmitting tubes—magnetrons—that were essential to accurate surface search and fire-control radar as developed in the United States. Moreover, the severe staff specifications for radar sets—small size, light weight, reliability, a range of 100 nautical miles, and an ability at 50 kilometers to read a bearing on a target within one-tenth of a degree—would prove impossible for the navy's research staffs to satisfy in the time they were given.[71] If ever there was a case of too little too late, the Japanese navy's attention to radar technology merits that judgment.

Given that the Japanese navy had begun its radar research approximately at the same time that the West did, what accounts for the Japanese inability to match the progress of research in Britain and the United States? Among the catalogue of failures, several reasons stand out. To begin with, there was little nationwide effort to mobilize the scientific and technical expertise in academe, industry, and the military to attack the critical technical problems involved in the development of useful naval and military radar systems. With such cooperation, the importance of microwave (centimeter-length) radar might have been more quickly recognized. Behind the rather leisurely prewar approach to the possibilities and requirements for radar was the navy's confidence in its optical sights and its assumption that radar would remain simply an auxiliary device to targeting the enemy. It has also been asserted that the navy's failure to make real progress in acquiring radar technology was due to a misguided belief in some quarters that any use of radio waves would do more to compromise Japanese movements than it would help Japanese naval units to discover the enemy.[72] Moreover, the navy was clearly reluctant to invest significant resources in pure research; the Navy General Staff consistently demanded technology that had immediate practical use.[73] It is also possible, though not demonstrable, that radar was seen as an essentially defensive technology and thus of lesser interest to a navy that was offensively minded. Once the importance of radar was recognized, however, progress in its development was delayed by a host of other problems. Chief among these was the age-old inability of the two services to work together; the conduct of totally separate research in electronics inevitably led to a duplication of effort and wasted time. Apparently, too, the navy's overzealous secrecy prevented civilian scientists and technicians from going aboard warships on which radar sets had been installed and from understanding how the sets actually functioned at sea. Further, Japan's electronics industry was minuscule in comparison with those of the Western powers; expertise and resources were simply inadequate. Once the tide of war turned against Japan, shifts in the military situation led to chaos in the production, transportation, and installation of radar in the navy's ships and aircraft.[74]

All this would have been serious enough had the Japanese navy been able to fight against an enemy similarly handicapped electronically. But the enormous Allied advances in electronics during the Pacific War meant that darkness would no longer be the safe realm of Japanese surface units, submarines, and aircraft. To the contrary, increasingly, they would be identified, targeted, and attacked by the enemy before they could get in a blow.[75] Without doubt, the prewar American advance in radar and the Japanese failure to match it were some of the principal reasons for American naval victory and Japanese naval defeat in the Pacific War.

JAPANESE NAVAL INTELLIGENCE

The navy's intelligence capabilities and limitations were central to Japanese naval victories at the opening of the Pacific War and to the navy's greatest defeats thereafter. At the highest level (that of the Navy General Staff), the navy's intelligence responsibilities were divided between the Third (Intelligence) Division, whose antecedent was founded shortly after the Sino-Japanese War and which performed most standard intelligence functions, and the Fourth (Communications) Division, established during the Russo-Japanese War and charged with communications security and cryptanalysis.[76]

There were several anomalies in the status and structure of the navy's intelligence organization. The first was the limited role and influence of the Intelligence Division in the formation of Japanese naval strategy and policy. The principal function of the Intelligence Division was to provide operationally relevant information to the Operations Division. Combining such information with communications intelligence from the Communications Division and with tactical intelligence from various fleet units, the Operations Division would then shape its estimates of enemy capabilities and intentions. But in providing this service, the Intelligence Division itself apparently did not evaluate the information that it had gathered, amazing as that may seem.[77] It is little wonder, therefore, that the Intelligence Division had little influence elsewhere within the Navy General Staff or the Navy Ministry. Surprisingly, however, even within the Operations Division, information supplied by intelligence was often ignored as suspect or irrelevant. Operations, fixated on its own agenda, sometimes initiated plans without consulting the Intelligence Division.[78]

The second peculiarity in Japanese naval intelligence relates to the first. Because the Intelligence Division, particularly after 1937, became for all practical purposes an able, if understaffed, adjunct to the Operations Division, it never developed into a coordinating organization capable of collecting, processing, and disseminating useful intelligence throughout the navy at all levels. The Combined Fleet, for example, received intelligence from the General Staff, not from Intelligence. The single intelligence officer in Combined Fleet Headquarters who supervised a small team of enlisted men engaged in radio intercepts, gathered information strictly for the fleet commander's use and did not necessarily share it with subordinate units or with the Navy General Staff. Each of the five fleets comprising the Combined Fleet had a single intelligence officer, but he received no regular intelligence briefings from Combined Fleet Headquarters. For the rest of the navy, below fleet level, intelligence was regarded as a secondary function; there existed no offices or officers whose sole responsibility was intelligence collection, analysis, and dissemination. The result of this headquarters concept of intelligence was that although much information was collected at the high command level, too little of it was disseminated to the navy's tactical elements.[79]

Last, although highly capable officers staffed the Intelligence Division, there were too few of them and little effort was made to augment their numbers or improve their skills. There were, in fact, no counterparts to the army's noted (and notorious) Nakano Intelligence School, no special training courses given by the navy to assist officers assigned to intelligence billets, or any courses available in intelligence techniques and methods. By and large, assignment of intelligence personnel at the high command level was made on the basis of foreign language proficiency, experience abroad, personal preference, or exemption from fleet duty because of physical disabilities.[80]

Like most intelligence organizations, the Intelligence Division obtained its information from a multiplicity of sources. Traditionally, it depended on the translation of foreign books and periodicals as well as the placement of naval attachés and clandestine operatives abroad. In China, the Intelligence Division kept foreign establishments and agents under surveillance through a network of *tokumu kikan* (special service organs), which were navy-run espionage centers, the largest of which was located in Shanghai. These were of little actual use in providing operational intelligence to the navy. In places like Shanghai, Singapore, and Surabaya, however, the navy also relied on reports from Japanese consulates regarding foreign ship movements.[81]

But the single greatest source of intelligence available to the navy was foreign, particularly American, radio traffic. At the highest level, radio intelligence was the responsibility of the Fourth Division of the Navy General Staff, first established in 1929 as a small branch office of cryptanalysis at Hiratsuka, south of Tokyo on Sagami Bay. Following signals intelligence coups in connection with the Shanghai Incident of 1932, the Fourth Division was expanded to include all aspects of communications intelligence. Renamed the Tenth Division, it was divided into offices of plans, operations, research, training, and materials collection. As war approached, in late 1940, the chief of the Navy General Staff recognized the section's importance by making it directly subordinate to himself, upgrading it to the status of a division, and renaming it the *tokumu han* (Special Division).[82]

Within the Special Division was a code-breaking research branch and a communications unit located at Owada, in Saitama Prefecture, outside of Tokyo. The Owada listening post, which became the navy's chief radio intercept center, gradually grew in size. By the Pacific War it comprised well over a hundred communications personnel who analyzed ship call signs, differentiated foreign codes, and otherwise monitored all seaborne radio traffic.[83] In 1937, its sophisticated radio direction-finding equipment enabled the Japanese navy to track the maneuvers of the U.S. Navy's Fleet Problem 18. Two years later, with the aid of a Japanese intercept site on Jaluit Atoll in the Marshall Islands, operators at Owada were able to identify individual ships involved in large-scale maneuvers off Hawaii.[84]

Since the 1920s, the Japanese navy had also begun to experiment with fleet tankers as clandestine, floating intercept stations. In 1924, it despatched the tanker *Sata*, crammed below decks with electronic gear, to Hawaiian waters to monitor portions of the U.S. Navy's fleet problems there, but because of equipment failure, the effort had only limited success. In 1932, with equipment capable of intercepting American shortwave transmissions, a sister ship, *Erimo,* loitering off Hawaii, obtained a fairly precise understanding of Fleet Problem 13 (and approached so closely that it could observe simulated attacks by U.S. Army bombers on the carrier *Saratoga)*. From an analysis of the radio traffic collected during these maneuvers, the Japanese navy was able to solve the U.S. Navy's two-digit cipher. In 1939, another sister ship, *Irō,* monitored the radio traffic of American fleet units in American west coast ports and intercepted medium-wave signals between California and Hawaii.[85]

The U.S. Navy made parallel efforts in signals intelligence in the Pacific.[86] For the United States, confronting a racially homogeneous society into which it was difficult to place agents, such means were particularly critical. The U.S. Navy and Marine Corps undertook several measures to enhance the radio intercept capabilities of their stations and ships in East Asia and the western Pacific. Listening posts were established in Peking, Shanghai, and Manila, as well as by American gunboats on the Yangtze River.[87] But both navies considered most valuable the monitoring of the other's signal traffic while the main fleet was at sea, particularly during its annual naval maneuvers. To that end, the U.S. Navy occasionally dispatched ships of its Asiatic Fleet to Japanese waters when adequate cover could be provided for such visits. One such foray was made by the American cruiser *Marblehead* in the fall of 1927. While in charge of a navy radio intercept post at the U.S. Consulate General in Shanghai, Lt. Comdr. Ellis Zacharias noted a sudden and unusual surge in the Japanese navy's radio traffic. Concluding that particularly important Japanese naval maneuvers were about to take place, he informed his superiors in Washington. Knowing that the Japanese navy had just acquired the *Akagi* and believing that she would participate in the maneuvers, the Navy Department immediately dispatched Zacharias and all his equipment to the *Marblehead,* which was about to depart Shanghai for Kobe on a courtesy visit. On her way to Kobe, the *Marblehead* passed through the area of Japanese fleet maneuvers and thus collected extensive intelligence data from the airwaves, some of which proved valuable in understanding Japanese fleet composition and tactical readiness.[88]

The U.S. Navy also sent ships that could establish routine sailings between various East Asian ports and thus reduce Japanese suspicions when they traversed seas adjacent to Japan. One of the most successful of these operations was an effort to monitor the Japanese Grand Fleet maneuvers in the early 1930s. The code name of this operation was that of a U.S. Navy cargo ship, *Gold Star,* based at Guam, which transported most of the island's imports and exports to and from various East Asian ports, including those of Japan. The ship thus had excellent cover as it cruised through Japanese waters during the most active period of Japanese maneuvers, collecting considerable information from the airwaves as it went.[89]

The United States was not alone in its efforts to keep the Japanese navy under surveillance, of course. The British and Dutch navies also monitored Japanese signals traffic, particularly when the fleet was on maneuvers: British espionage agencies, military and civilian, working out of Hong Kong, Shanghai, and Singapore kept track of Japanese ship movements in and out of these ports, and British submarines occasionally penetrated anchorages used by the Combined Fleet.[90]

The Japanese navy also established active signals intelligence operations on foreign soil. By 1940, complementing the various radio intercept units it had established at Japanese embassies in the major European capitals, the navy greatly expanded its electronic surveillance of American naval movements by the completion of a network of land intercept stations across the Pacific. The most successful of these was a five-man unit in Mexico known as the L *Kikan* (L Organization), which monitored radio frequencies used by the U.S. naval forces in the Atlantic. With this network of monitoring stations, supplemented by air reconnaissance squadrons in Micronesia, and with its relatively sophisticated radio direction-finding techniques, the Japanese navy was confident that no American naval force could move into the western Pacific undetected.[91]

Thus, through most of the 1920s and 1930s, the Japanese and American navies played the most intensive intelligence cat-and-mouse games. Through such reciprocal electronic espionage during the mid-1930s, the United States and Imperial Japanese navies apparently had a reasonable understanding of each other's current tactics and, to a large extent, of each other's current strategies. Each navy also probably had fairly good reason to believe that the other side had such knowledge. For its part, Japanese communications intelligence provided the navy with information on a wide range of American operational procedures. In the long run, however, the Japanese navy lost ground in the communications intelligence war because its code-breaking efforts failed to match its success in signals traffic analysis and because its own crypto systems proved vulnerable.

Ever since 1929, Japanese navy cryptanalysts had been working to break American and British naval and related diplomatic codes. By the 1930s, the personnel of the Communications Division could solve and read the U.S. Navy's two-digit AN-2 code and a simpler and less important State Department code, but failed completely to read the U.S. Navy's two-part "Brown" code. In the months before the outbreak of the Pacific War, the navy belatedly recognized that it had insufficient personnel. As a last-minute effort it recruited dozens of promising graduates from universities and commercial schools and gave them accelerated training. In this way, the communications intelligence offices of the navy expanded.[92]

Still, with the exception of one or two breakthroughs (such as the partial solution of the Allied merchant ship code) the Japanese navy was unable to make any headway in reading American radio traffic during the Pacific War, even the midlevel systems being beyond the abilities of Japanese cryptanalysts. Of particular difficulty were the U.S. Navy's "strip ciphers" (systems made more complex by adding a mix of cipher alphabets to the existing code by means of sliding paper or metal strips to an encryption mechanism), which so frustrated the navy's cryptanalysts that in effect, they gave up on decryption and simply resorted to traffic analysis.[93]

When one considers the stunning success of the United States and Britain in solving several critical Japanese codes and ciphers on the eve of the Pacific War and the Allies's ability, jointly, to read nearly all of them during the course of that conflict, the incapacity of the Japanese armed services to do the reverse requires some explanation. The prewar Japanese navy, to begin with, lacked the appreciation of the importance of the "intelligence revolution" wrought by radio communications and thus failed to devote sufficient resources—especially human resources—to the task of keeping up with it. As in the development of Japanese radar technology, Japanese success in cryptanalysis was hampered by the tardy mobilization of civilian talent—in this case mathematical skill—which would have speeded its progress. There was, as well, no effective collaboration between the Japanese army and navy in apportioning cryptanalytic responsibilities, a failure that resulted in frequent duplication of decryption attempts and thus a prodigious waste of time and effort.[94] Nor did Japan receive much help from its Axis partners. Though often willing to share critically important strategic and tactical information derived from their own cryptanalytic successes, Japan's partners were reluctant to relay the procedures by which they were derived.[95] Finally, American encryption mechanisms were enormously superior. At no point before or during the Pacific War were the Japanese able to capture or reconstruct any of these devices used by the Allies for their highest-level communications. For that reason, none of the Axis nations could ever read such communications during the course of World War II.[96] The formidable Allied encryption systems, in any event, would have proved an insurmountable barrier to the Japanese navy's cryptanalytic efforts during the Pacific War, though a greater expenditure of effort and resources in the interwar period might have yielded significant results.

Unfortunately for the Japanese navy, the U.S. Navy was superlatively successful in breaking Japanese codes and ciphers during these years. The damage had begun with the now famous break-in at the Japanese Consulate General in New York and the copying of Japanese diplomatic codes by U.S. Naval Intelligence agents in 1921. Throughout the 1920s and 1930s, the U.S. Navy had worked to solve Japanese naval codes and, with the considerable amount of raw material drawn from intercepts during the annual fleet maneuvers, had been quite successful in cracking the Japanese naval codes used for tactical communications between surface forces.[97] An American naval officer involved in these efforts recalled decades later that "the only limits to our detailed knowledge of what was going on in the Japanese navy was the acute shortage of translators and the fact that sometimes the Japanese did not entrust important secret matters to radio communications."[98]

One of the problems for the Japanese navy was that it had too many codes.[99] In addition to the navy's high-level systems, there were codes for various units, branches, and functions of the service, as well as for various operational theaters. Few of them were particularly secure, even though they differed from one geographic area to another and were changed regularly. Before and especially during the Pacific War the navy's cryptography was fatally undercut by poor administration, lax security, and chaotic distribution.[100]

Two strategic crypto systems resisted easy solution, the navy's "Ko" and "Ro" systems. The former was the Japanese navy's "flag officer code" (called AD by the U.S. Navy), a four-number super-enciphered code used by the navy for its highest-level communications. In the years before the Pacific War, American cryptanalysts worked hardest on "Ko," but they never broke it. Within days of the outbreak of hostilities, the U.S. Navy discontinued its efforts to read it in order to concentrate on the numbered fleet codes of the enemy and, by 1942–43, the Japanese navy had itself abandoned the "Ko" code as too complex, too slow, and too vulnerable. The "Ro" (or D) code, called JN-25 by Americans, was the Japanese navy's most widely used fleet cryptographic system. A super-enciphered, two-part code, it carried 70 percent of all the navy's communications and was the object of the most intense American efforts during the Pacific War.[101] The original version, JN-25-A1, was effective from June 1939, ran through three additive tables, and was succeeded in December 1940 by JN-25-B. (JN-25-B used the last additive table of JN-25-A, which was a significant cryptographic blunder by the Japanese navy.) As mentioned earlier in the chapter, the U.S. Navy was reading some editions of JN-25-A by the end of 1940, but did not really make much progress in solution of its current edition until the spring of 1942.[102] The partial solution of the current edition of JN 25,[103] in combination with Japanese tardiness in changing it, provided the U.S. Navy with intelligence sufficient to assist in the surprise of the Japanese task force at Midway, perhaps the greatest intelligence coup of the entire Pacific War.[104] The fatal Japanese error in this case, as it was before the war, was in thinking that their codes were unbreakable. Since the Japanese navy's crypto systems were targeted by several American teams comprising some of the most brilliant cryptanalysts of the time, this misplaced confidence constituted the most disastrous lapse of all in its communications security.[105]

The lack of a uniform, navywide system for collection, processing, and disseminating intelligence was a failure for which the Navy General Staff and Combined Fleet were responsible. This weakness was the more pronounced at the tactical level, where, in the absence of any pressure from higher command to do so, few resources were devoted to the development of combat intelligence.[106] This was particularly true of the navy's air units. Aboard the navy's carriers, concern for combat intelligence varied according to the degree of importance attached to it by the individual carrier commanders. In many cases, combat intelligence duties were haphazardly undertaken and were almost always secondary to other responsibilities of air group personnel. Preoperational briefings, though cursory, were perhaps the better of the two phases of combat intelligence. They were usually undertaken by the air group commander, who supplied air crews with as much information as possible concerning the target, navigational data, method of attack, and relevant instructions concerning communications. Postmission reporting appears to have been imprecise, to say the least. Interrogations of air crew were conducted by the carrier's air officer, after which a report was submitted by the flight leader, who, lacking intelligence training, had little skill or even interest in submitting a report sufficiently detailed to support claims as to destruction or damage inflicted on the enemy. In combination with the overconfidence of combat air crews (at least during the first half of the Pacific War), this carelessness in reporting often resulted in overstated claims of enemy losses.[107] In fairness, one should remember that air crews of all air forces of World War II tended to exaggeration in their reports.

Considering that photo reconnaissance had been used with relative success in the navy's air war over China, it is somewhat surprising to learn from American assessments of Japanese intelligence made after the Pacific War, that Japanese naval officers "didn't consider photography to be useful operationally beyond the immediate tactical phase and apparently made no effort to use photos in planning or anticipating new offensives." Further, the same report concludes that by American standards, Japanese photo intelligence, even by the end of the war, was still primitive.[108] The principal deficiency, however, was probably less one of technological competence than one of the failure by higher commands to establish uniform requirements and procedures, as well as the absence of a top-to-bottom organization to develop and disseminate photo intelligence.

Japanese neglect of photo reconnaissance was merely part of the wider neglect of aerial reconnaissance in general (see chapter 9). Since air reconnaissance had never been made a navywide priority, higher commands had difficulty in initiating operations to collect combat intelligence. Without sufficient training, aircraft, or specialized reconnaissance units, moreover, the intelligence reports sent from tactical units to higher commands were often too brief and fragmented for use in operational planning. But even burdened with technical deficiencies, some effort in the Pacific War to mount regular and thorough air searches might have prevented or at least modified some of the unpleasant surprises that suddenly confronted Japanese naval forces, of which Midway is only the most famous.

In any case, the question arises: If the Japanese Navy's intelligence system suffered from all the defects enumerated, how does one explain its remarkable success in correctly planning the opening moves of the Pacific War? The answer probably comes in two parts. To begin with, the Japanese navy was able to place its human intelligence assets in Hawaii and Southeast Asia months before the war. Thus, with time to collect, collate, and analyze all information relevant to the operations it was planning, the navy was able to form very accurate assessments of Allied naval, ground, and air forces in the Hawaiian islands, the Philippines, Malaya, and the Netherlands East Indies. But, once the war broke out, such sources were obviously neutralized, and the navy had very little operational or communications intelligence to take their place. As the war proceeded, the navy became increasingly starved for intelligence of any kind. Lacking such information, the navy too often had to make choices based on its best professional speculation.[109]

The second point is that during the years before the Pacific War, the tedious effort of the Intelligence and Communications Divisions to sift through masses of material to collect strategic intelligence did indeed contribute significantly to Japanese understanding of Allied force structures, military capabilities, and political weakness in the western Pacific and Southeast Asia in the months before the war. In this, the navy was also greatly aided by inter-Axis intelligence cooperation that yielded some enormously important information.[110] Japanese naval intelligence was thus able to provide the nation with a clearer picture of its enemies' strategic situation than its enemies had of Japan. To this extent, Japanese naval intelligence performed valuable service for the nation and the navy. But it was in the realm of larger issues, such as the assessments of the national character and psychology of foreign countries and the strength of national economies, that Japanese intelligence, specifically Japanese naval intelligence, missed by a mile. This failure was largely because the reports of the Intelligence Division were written for the Operations Division, which fixated on its own offensive agenda and had little use for such nonoperational intelligence. Thus, what the Navy General Staff (and the rest of the Japanese high command) overlooked was not the operational strength of enemy forces, but rather two matters of overwhelming strategic importance: first, the recuperative powers of the Allies, particularly the United States, after they had absorbed the first Japanese blows, and second, the vastly superior American military and industrial capacity that in the months to come would enable American forces to launch counterblows with speed and strength that the Japanese did not anticipate. The failure to understand these elements was a fatal weakness in the navy's assessment of the probable American response to the navy's tactics and strategy to open the Pacific War.[111]

12

UNEVEN
WEAPONS

Submarine, Antisubmarine, and Amphibious Warfare
Capabilities in the Japanese Navy, 1937–1941

The 1920s and 1930s had seen much submarine construction notwithstanding efforts to outlaw or curtail submarine operations by international law.[1] Britain, in spite of its determination to abolish the submarine as more a threat than an asset to its maritime security, had continued to build submarines and to experiment in their design. The United States maintained a growing number of submersibles, though until the mid-1930s these were mostly smaller boats for coastal defense. Lesser naval powers saw the submarine as a means of compensating for the modest size of their battle fleets. France remained the foremost advocate of the submarine, seeing it as a fleet equalizer, and had embarked upon a considerable submarine construction program, which included the construction of the huge *Surcouf*. Germany had begun secret preparations to rebuild its submarine fleet in the 1920s, an effort so successful that in 1935, less than a week after signing an accord with Britain that generally freed it from restrictions on construction in this category, German launched its first submersible. Japan had led the way in the construction of oceangoing submarines, predicating its submarine policy on the strategic principles set forth by Admiral Suetsugu.

If the pace of submarine construction quickened in the 1930s, at the end of the treaty era, naval strategists worldwide held no consistent views about the most advantageous use for submarine fleets. Certainly, none of the submarine strategies of the former maritime Allies of World War I was shaped by the evidence of the awesome destructiveness of the submarine as a commerce raider. Officially, the United States, up to the outbreak of the Pacific War, continued to view the submarine primarily as an element of fleet operations, though influential submariners in the U.S. Navy appear to have privately advocated a policy of aggressive commerce raiding in the event of war with Japan.[2] Though Britain was determined to stay abreast of the latest developments in submarine design and technology, it failed to develop a coherent submarine strategy, partly because of financial stringency and partly because of the Royal Navy's continuing priority on the battle fleet. In the Pacific, this left Britain with a submarine force inadequate in numbers and range to carry offensive war to Japan. The submarine force was thus relegated to the defense of the base at Singapore, though World War I offered little evidence that submarines were effective in a defensive role.[3] Given the political and military realities of the time, particularly the near-at-hand Italian threat in the western Mediterranean, French thinking behind the construction of *Surcouf* seemed, by the late 1930s, quite misconceived. Among the Western maritime powers, only the small but resurgent German navy began to assemble a submarine force whose principal objective was the destruction of enemy commerce. Against the convoy system, which had finally turned back the German U-boat offensive in World War I, Comdr. Karl Dönitz now devised new wolf-pack tactics that called for the massing of submarines at night and on the surface.

In part, the coordination of such tactics was made possible by greatly improved communications between submarines and shore command. High-frequency radio transmitters ashore now made it possible to send messages to submarines at great distance from the land, and extremely powerful, very low frequency (10–20 kilohertz) signals could be received even by submerged submarines. Though the vessels had to surface to transmit, these new developments in radio communication not only enhanced the value of the submarine for reconnaissance, but allowed more effective control of submarine fleets. Of course, radio direction finding, perfected during the late 1930s, enabled an enemy to detect the location of a submarine transmitting messages, which was a key element in the development of antisubmarine warfare (ASW) in World War II.

Between the world wars, however, ASW had progressed very little beyond its development at the end of World War I. One reason was the financially tightened circumstances in which most navies found themselves in the 1920s and 1930s. The slow progress was also related to the priorities most major naval establishments placed on the capital ship and to the misplaced confidence among these establishments that if need be, the tactics, technologies, and force structures of World War I could be reconstituted to defeat the submarine once again. The use of asdic, or sonar, as it was later called, had proved effective in detecting the direction if not the depth of submerged targets, but its various limitations had not been addressed in the years since its first appearance. Britain, which had pioneered the development of asdic, was so confident of its lead in this technology that it placed no great priority either on asdic's radical improvement or on the perfection of those complementary elements of ASW—the convoy system, the escort vessel, and the patrol aircraft specifically dedicated to ASW—that had proven effective in World War I.[4] During the interwar years, deficiencies in these tactics, technologies, and force structures were also manifested in the U.S. Navy, second only to Britain in its experience in ASW in World War I. The United States would learn the consequences of its neglect of these elements of ASW in the stunning losses it sustained during the German U-boat offensive along the American east coast in the spring of 1942.[5]

If submarine warfare and ASW warfare had provided obvious evidence of major successes in World War I, amphibious warfare apparently had not.[6] The most ambitious amphibious operation of the war, the landing at Gallipoli, had also been its most disastrous failure. It had, moreover, been one of the few amphibious operations undertaken in the face of determined opposition ashore (the assault on Zeebrugge being the other notable amphibious operation under such conditions). After the war, most military and naval establishments sifting the evidence of Gallipoli found it less a sorry record of mistakes that might be corrected by better planning, organization, and performance, than a confirmation of the difficulty, if not impossibility, of conducting a landing from the sea in the face of entrenched and presighted automatic weapons and artillery.

Early in the interwar period, the Washington Treaty had given each of the three major maritime powers a rationale of sorts to maintain an amphibious capability in the Pacific. As the treaty had prohibited the construction of new bases in the western Pacific or the strengthening of existing bases there, a successful strategy in any conflict between the three powers would require the occupation of enemy bases or the recapture of bases lost to the enemy. But by the 1930s, to Britain, the danger seemed to come from the air and ground forces of an enemy much closer to home. In such a strategic context, it was difficult enough to get funds for the navy, let alone the expansion of the Royal Marines as an amphibious force. During these years, professional conservatism, budgetary restraints, and the discouraging conclusions about the Dardanelles campaign also limited the development of amphibious war capability in the British armed forces to the realm of staff studies and the testing of landing craft, vehicles, and equipment in exercises that were theoretically unopposed. Finally, in this period, Britain had no enemy against which amphibious operations would be required. Under such conditions,

Britain understandably failed to develop either the doctrine or the forces for amphibious operations.

Of the three major naval powers, the United States had the strongest motivation to develop an amphibious warfare capability, since the Japanese occupation of Micronesia at the outset of World War I had placed Japan directly athwart the path of any American fleet crossing the central Pacific to rescue or retake the Philippines. Japan had been forbidden by the treaty to fortify the islands of the Pacific. But this prohibition in no way lessened the American conviction that the islands would have to be taken by force, strengthened by strong but mistaken suspicions that Japan, prior to the late 1930s, had fortified the islands in violation of its treaty pledge. Thus, with a specific enemy and a specific theater of operations in mind, the U.S. armed forces, through landing practice and staff study, gradually built up an amphibious warfare capability. In this effort, both the major services participated to some extent: the army and navy periodically joined in fleet landing exercises of some scale in both the Pacific and Caribbean in the 1930s and made limited contributions to the drafting of the tactical manuals that served as doctrinal guides for amphibious operations.

But because the tactical priorities of the two services lay elsewhere, the U.S. Marine Corps was left to develop American amphibious warfare doctrine and thus carve for itself a mission and a professional raison d'être, which the corps has never relinquished. The development of that doctrine and the weapons, equipment, and force structure to support it have been discussed in other publications and are beyond the scope of this book.[7] Suffice it to say that the Marine Corps' recognition of the terrain and configuration of the Micronesia beaches, which it had targeted for its operations, forced upon the Marine Corps tacticians the doctrinal realities that their British and Japanese counterparts were not obliged to confront in the interwar period. The narrowness of the low islands of Micronesia ensured that landing operations would be met with fierce enemy opposition at the water's edge and would therefore require the most careful planning, the most effective transport loading, and the most precise coordination with naval gunfire to be successful. The traversing of the coral reefs surrounding most such islands would necessitate the employment of transports and amphibious vehicles not yet in the arsenals of any maritime power. The flat terrain of the Micronesian atolls meant that even high-velocity and flat-trajectory gunfire might not destroy the low bunkers dug into the atolls' coral and sand. In time, the elements of the Marine Corps' amphibious warfare capability—unified command, combat loading, adjustments in naval gunnery, closely controlled ship-to-shore movement, amphibious landing craft, and specialized air support—came together and found expression in the kind of war that neither the British nor the Japanese armed forces had seriously considered.

JAPANESE SUBMARINE STRATEGY AND TACTICS, 1937–41

In the mid-1920s, Adm. Suetsugu Nobumasa had given the Japanese submarine force several missions that transformed it, in theory, into a long-range offensive system. The missions assigned to this system were the extended surveillance of the enemy battle fleet in harbor, the pursuit and shadowing of that fleet when it sortied from its base, and the ambushing of the enemy by pursuing submarines that would destroy a number of his capital ships and thus reduce his battle line just before the decisive surface encounter with the Japanese battle fleet.

By 1930, this strategy, embodying the principles of extended, long-range surveillance, pursuit, ambush, and attrition of the enemy, had become, like the 70 percent ratio in the 1920s, an article of faith in Navy General Staff planning for war with the U.S. Navy. Yet, surprisingly, for reasons not entirely clear, the strategy had never been subjected to the trial of its various tactical elements. This failure stands in marked contrast to the navy's rigorous testing of other tactical matters. At all events, late in the decade, with the acquisition of large submarines with high surface speed, starting with the J3 type, the navy finally began frequent and intensive training in the tactics of surveillance, pursuit, shadowing, and ambushing of enemy fleet units.

Such training began in 1938 with a series of exercises designed to test the efficiency of submarines and crews for intense periods of patrol near the enemy.[8] The next year, the navy began serious practice in submarine attack doctrine, beginning with close surveillance of tightly guarded heavy surface units, both those in harbor and those under way. The results were disconcerting, to say the least. Trying to get near to fleet targets, some submarines taking part in the exercises strayed within waters patrolled by destroyers and were judged to have been sunk; others apparently gave away their positions through radio transmissions. Still others, which had remained undetected while submerged during the periods of most intense antisubmarine activity by destroyers and aircraft, nevertheless missed important radioed instructions.[9]

From these exercises the navy drew several conclusions that eventually were translated into standard operating procedures during the Pacific War. Unhappily for the Japanese submarine force, none made for effective submarine strategy, and some were downright disastrous. The great stress on concealment during extended surveillance operations in enemy waters seems commonsensical, but during the war it contributed to the extreme caution of Japanese submarine commanders off American shores. It also explains the Japanese wartime practice of using submarine-borne aircraft, particularly during moonlight nights, to reconnoiter enemy harbors and bases in place of submarines themselves. (While this technique was used during the war for reconnaissance over several Allied bases, it failed to produce any significant operational results.) Undoubtedly, however, the most significant lesson to come out of the 1938 exercises was the extreme difficulty in maintaining close submarine surveillance of a distant and carefully guarded enemy base. This was the first of many revelations pointing to the clear unworkability of accepted Japanese submarine doctrine.[10]

The key to the success of the actual interception operations was the proper deployment of submarines for the best possible torpedo shots against an advancing enemy fleet. Experience had shown that the best position for a torpedo shot was a 50- to 60-degree angle off the bow of the target at a distance of about 1,500 meters (1,650 yards). Even if the submarine commander was slightly off in his estimates of target course and speed, and even if the target changed course, the likelihood of a hit was greatest with this position. For a submarine to arrive at this optimum point, it needed maximum freedom of movement, so as to locate itself across the enemy's intended course. Where the enemy's course was known, interception operations called for pursuing submarines to race ahead of the enemy fleet to a spot where they could lie in wait and maneuver themselves into an ideal firing position. Where the enemy's actual course was unknown, a picket or ambush line was to be thrown across the track that the enemy seemed most likely to follow.[11]

In 1939 and 1940, as part of a series of maneuvers held in the western Pacific from Honshū to Micronesia, Japanese submarines began to practice these tactical requirements for long-distance interception operations. In these exercises an "A Force" was usually designated to defend Micronesia from an invading "B Force" coming down from Japan. Once B Force had sortied from its home base, A Force was supposed to "acquire" it, pursue it, maintain contact with it, and then destroy it in ambush. To their dismay, the A Force submarine commanders discovered that despite their surface speed, they could just barely maintain contact with the advancing B Force. It proved difficult to race ahead of the enemy and then lie in wait in an ideal firing position, particularly since they were obliged to fire while submerged and, once underwater, they were practically stationary. The surface targets all too often raced by unscathed. Firing on the surface seemed out of the question, since the submarines were easily spotted not only by patrolling destroyers but by carrier-borne aircraft used in an ASW role.[12]

These maneuvers also supplied the navy with one irrelevant "lesson" and another a good deal more ominous. Because of the activity of submarines as well as land-based bombers and flying boats in the defense of Japanese-held atolls in Micronesia, the navy became convinced of the value of both submarines and aircraft in the defense of Japanese island bases in the western Pacific.[13] In fact, submarines were little use in island defense in the Pacific War, except as supply ships for stranded garrisons, and of Japanese aircraft there were never enough, once the American amphibious wave crashed into Micronesia late in 1943. More to the point, the maneuvers demonstrated to individual submarine captains the near impossibility of the pursuit-contact-annihilation elements of the interception strategy, as well as the hazards of these tactics, so long the mainstays of Japanese submarine strategy.[14]

Because the Japanese navy never did assemble its projected long-range attack groups, it is impossible to know what sort of tactics and command structure might have developed out such a combat organization. What is clear from the maneuvers of 1939–40 is that although the navy held exercises bringing together groups of submarines, it never developed the idea of concerted attack. Specifically, the German (and American) "wolf pack" concept—whereby an embarked commander directed multiple attacks on common targets by submarines under his command—apparently never occurred to those directing the Japanese submarine forces. The Japanese approach to submarine operations, practiced in prewar maneuvers and carried out during the Pacific War, was to retain control of submarine forces from a shore command. The navy's failure to produce more than three type A-1 command submarines meant that the at-sea command concept built around Ōyodo-class cruisers never materialized. An ambush or picket line of submarines might be established across an anticipated course of enemy advance, for example, and submarines assigned stations along it, but once on station, a submarine was generally moved only by orders from ashore.[15] This failure of the Japanese submarine forces to develop either the concept of concerted attack or the skills and command structure to make it work is another reason for the meager results of Japanese submarine operations during the war.

The doctrine of concerted attack was developed by the German and U.S. navies for commerce raiding, not for attacks on major fleet units. Moreover, from Suetsugu's day forward, Japanese submarine doctrine clearly focused on the enemy's battle fleet, not primarily his sea communications and commerce. The Japanese navy, however, was not entirely unaware of the possibilities of commerce raiding. In maneuvers in October 1940, the Japanese navy actually deployed several submarines to patrol vital maritime corridors in the home islands—Tsushima Strait, between Honshū and Korea; Bungo Strait, between Shikoku and Kyūshū; and Uraga Strait, the entrance to Tokyo Bay. The submarines simulated attack on Japanese commercial vessels to determine how vulnerable the commercial fleet was to submarine raids. Because of inadequate Japanese antisubmarine capabilities and lack of attention to convoy escort, in only five days, 133 Japanese merchantmen were "sunk" by the submarines involved in these simulation exercises. Considering that four years later, these same waters were the scene of actual havoc and slaughter by American submarines, one can only wonder why the lessons of this exercise were not more salutary. Unfortunately for the Japanese, the principal conclusion drawn by those in command related not to the offensive potential of attacking submarines, but to their vulnerability to detection by radio direction finding.[16]

Not surprisingly, the Japanese navy's neglect of the extreme vulnerability of the Japanese home islands to submarine blockade was matched by its general disinclination to give priority to a submarine campaign against American coastal and trans-Pacific shipping. While the high command did acknowledge that threatening the enemy's sea lanes was an important part of naval warfare and that submarines should take part in such operations, it held that they should do so only as long as such operations did not greatly interfere with their primary mission of destroying enemy fleet units in battle.[17]

As discussed, a certain incoherence in Japanese submarine strategy was shown by the multiple submarine designs developed before the Pacific War. A further fragmentation of that strategy occurred in 1940–41, now reinforced by the difference in submarine types. It began with the reorganization of the submarine forces late in 1940. The navy created a separate submarine fleet, the Sixth, composed of the first three of the navy's seven submarine flotillas. The other flotillas were distributed to the Combined, Third, and Fourth Fleets. Each submarine flotilla began operational training according to the mission or missions it had been assigned.[18] As each flotilla was usually composed entirely of submarines of one type, that type differing from flotilla to flotilla, missions had to be shaped by the capabilities and limitations of the particular type. This tactical reality was demonstrated in exercises held in May 1941 that were designed to test different types of submarines in different operational situations. The cruiser submarines proved themselves sluggish but reliable and capable of great endurance. They were therefore confirmed as suitable for long-distance operations—attacks on enemy bases, disruption of enemy transport routes, and ambush operations—but were judged not likely to be effective in fast-moving fleet attacks. On the other hand, the Kaidai submarines, with their slightly greater speed, would be used to pursue, shadow, and attack a westward-moving American fleet or could be deployed in the vanguard of a counterattacking Japanese surface force once the enemy reached Japanese waters.[19]

Exercises undertaken by the Sixth Fleet's Second Submarine Flotilla from February to April 1941 in the waters between Honshū and Micronesia revealed further difficulties in the pursuit, contact-keeping, and attack formula so long the accepted submarine doctrine in the navy. The postexercise report of the flotilla's staff pointed out some major problems in the approved strategy. Chief among them were insufficient numbers in surveillance operations, the risk of discovery by antisubmarine forces, and inadequate submarine speed. The current strength of advanced submarine forces was simply insufficient to monitor effectively an enemy fleet in a distant harbor. Moreover, the report argued, submarines assigned this mission had to be positioned at sufficient distance to avoid antisubmarine patrols. Consequently, the enemy fleet often sortied from base undetected by the patrolling submarines. Once at sea, submarines in pursuit continued to have difficulty in maintaining contact with the enemy and even greater difficulty in getting into firing position to attack him. As in previous years, problems were encountered in setting up an ambush or picket line; once again, with submarines stationed along the line at extended intervals, the enemy too often slipped by. To deal with these various problems, the staff of the Second Submarine Flotilla recommended that in gathering information on fleet departures from enemy harbors, the navy should depend as much upon Japanese intelligence organizations as it did on submarine surveillance. To monitor the progress of a westward-moving American fleet, the navy should deploy lines of fishing boats across the enemy's anticipated track, backed up wherever possible by large flying boats, based, most likely, in Micronesia. These recommendations are a dismal commentary on the general failure of the interception concept by 1941. Certainly, the staff of the Second Submarine Flotilla no longer believed that submarines by themselves could significantly reduce an American battle fleet not yet within the range of Japanese naval and air bases.[20]

Further testing of equipment and training of crews in 1941 extended the scope of problems relating to the use of submarines in the decisive fleet encounter. In March and July, submarines of the Sixth Fleet and Fourth and Fifth Submarine Flotillas practiced close-in attacks on well-guarded fleet units. Again, however, such operations all too often caused the attacking submarines to be discovered because their periscopes were sighted. Some submarine officers suggested that because of the difficulties in carrying out such attacks, it would be better to carry out long-distance firing than to have the attacking submarines discovered and have the enemy turn away to avoid Japanese torpedoes. Though long-distance firing had been conceived in the 1920s, remarkably, its effectiveness had never really been tested. In any event, the concept of long-distance firing cut across the grain of the navy's traditional *nikuhaku-hitchū* spirit of close-in attack. This problem lay unresolved by the time the war broke out in December 1941.[21]

Accounts of the Japanese submarine exercises of 1939–41 clearly show that Japanese navy training attempted to be comprehensive, rigorous, and innovative in the development of the submarine as a weapon to attack regular fleet units. Tactical training was carried out at night as well as during daylight. Long- and short-distance operations were practiced. Coordination was attempted between submarines and aircraft. New weapons, like the type 95 torpedo, were tested, and novel techniques, such as "submerged firing," were practiced.

Japanese submarine commanders developed *zembotsu hassha* (submerged firing) because, although their boats had proper range finders and devices for ascertaining exact bearing, they could only be used on the surface. Preferring to stay submerged when attacking fleet units screened by destroyers, submarine commanders would submerge, expose the periscope for a final optical reading of bearing and range, keep the periscope down for the final closure to the firing point, and then fire on sound bearings.[22] This technique was hardly unique to the Japanese navy; American submarine commanders practiced something very much like it ("sound shots") before the war, but having little luck, dropped them.

Despite the navy's intensive training and development of new tactics, by the eve of the Pacific War, the navy had apparently not resolved the central problem of submarine tactics: the opposing requirements of self-preservation and aggressiveness. The essence of the submarine—and its preservation—is stealth. To be combat-effective, however, it must reveal itself at the moment of attack. "The trade-off between preservation and combat effectiveness," Norman Friedman has written, "is central to submarine tactics and submarine design."[23] Right up to the Pacific War, Japanese submarine forces held to the navy's traditional aggressive "close-in-sure-shot" torpedo tactics rather than switch to long-distance firing (and thus was a notable exception to the navywide obsession with outranging the enemy). At the same time, however, Japanese submarine commanders favored the contradictory and passive emphasis on concealment, which meant staying submerged for as long as possible, lying in wait for heavy enemy fleet units to come steaming by and present themselves as targets. By the time the war began, the concern for concealment proved stronger than the necessity for aggressive action, which, in the prewar exercises, appeared to lead all too often to discovery by antisubmarine surface and air forces. The result was a submarine force hobbled by conservative doctrine and aimed primarily at the destruction of naval targets. After the war, American naval interrogators were astounded at evidence of the timidity of Japanese submarine commanders on patrol. "It was frankly impossible to believe that [Japanese] submarines could spend weeks on the U.S. west coast 'without contacts,'" one analysis recorded caustically, "or spend more than forty days among the Solomons during the Guadalcanal campaign 'without seeing any targets.'"[24]

In fairness, it should be pointed out that before the war, U.S. submarine tactics showed a similar passivity. Submariners came to almost identical conclusions regarding the vulnerability of submarines attacking battle formations based on fleet exercises before the war. They believed, for example, that exposing the periscope in a fleet action was suicide, and they practiced firing on tracks based on bearings acquired by sound detection. The poor performance of U.S. submarines at the beginning of the war is partly attributable to these ingrained tactical lessons, and only the shock of American losses in the Pacific led to rapid adjustments in submarine doctrine.[25]

For the Japanese submarine forces, in any event, this excess caution undoubtedly stemmed from lessons of the exercises of 1939–41, which revealed the extreme difficulties of carrying out their longstanding missions. These difficulties arose in part from the design of the vessels themselves, but even more from the impracticability of the prescribed tactics for the various missions. In the view of one former submarine commander, the fundamental reason for the failure of the Japanese submarine forces in the Pacific War was that those who made the basic decisions on submarine tactics—staff officers in the Combined Fleet and on the Navy General Staff—were ignorant of both the capabilities and the limitations of submarines.[26] Typifying this lack of practical submarine knowledge was Admiral Suetsugu, who can be thought of as the father of Japanese submarine strategy. Because Suetsugu was a gunnery specialist, not a submariner, the essential strategies and tactics that he had devised for Japanese submarines were, in practice, unworkable. Individual Japanese submarine commanders knew that the tactics were impractical by the opening of the war, but being loyal and courageous officers, they did their job as best they could. During the war, this gap between staff ideas and combat realities grew even greater, and by war's end, despite enormous losses, the Japanese submarine force had substantially failed to affect the course of the war.[27]

THE ORIGINS OF DISASTER
Japanese Convoy Escort and ASW Capabilities

As discussed earlier, the Japanese navy was indifferent to the problem of protecting the nation's shipping lanes. As early as the Russo-Japanese War, this neglect had led to several serious yet avoidable injuries to Japanese sea transport. In the period between the conflict with Russia and World War I, commerce protection was still neglected by the Japanese navy, since the two greatest future threats to merchant shipping, the submarine and the airplane, were still in a primitive stage of development. From the outset of World War I, of course, the submarine caused enormous havoc. Ultimately, however, it was the great gun duel at Jutland, not the ravages of the U-boat, that had the greater impact upon the thinking of the Japanese naval high command. Much the same would be said of the British and American navies. Yet, as major participants in convoy escort and ASW in World War I, Anglo-American efforts in these tasks during World War II were aided at least partly by institutional memory at the high command level of the requirements for convoy protection.[28]

In contrast, Japanese understanding of the rigors of commerce protection against submarines was limited in time, distance, and practical experience. The singular exploits of a handful of Japanese destroyer men who served with the Special Service Squadron on convoy escort and antisubmarine patrol in the distant Mediterranean, 1917–18, had made little impression on the outlook of the Japanese Navy General Staff.

To be sure, the navy took several measures both during and immediately after World War I to keep itself informed on the techniques and technologies used by the Allies in defeating the German U-boats. To begin with, naval observers like Comdr. Suetsugu Nobumasa sent back reports on German U-boat warfare. Moreover, as part of a major study undertaken by a special research commission and by Japanese naval attachés in Europe, the general staff's Intelligence Division amassed voluminous materials on Britain's protection of its sea trade during the war. From these sources, the navy collected detailed information on the convoy system and the techniques of ASW, as well as on the British naval organization to deal with these problems, the last being the focus of a special report in 1922 drafted by Lt. Comdr. Niimi Masaichi of the Intelligence Department. After the war, based on the information gathered, the Naval Staff College held lectures and map exercises on commerce protection. But none of these studies and presentations did much to arouse interest within the navy as a whole. Even a memorial to the throne in 1929 by chief of staff Katō Kanji on the importance of protecting Japan's sea lanes failed to find any resonance in Japanese naval policy. Moreover, Admiral Katō failed to back up his general recommendation with specific proposals that would alter the navy's force structure to provide for greater commerce protection.[29]

Thus, on a theoretical level, the Japanese navy acknowledged the problems of protecting Japan's merchant shipping, but it failed to undertake any concrete measures that would make such protection effective. The reasons for this were several. To begin with, the restricted budgets in the 1920s and early 1930s (not unlike those of the U.S. and British navies) did not allow any deviation from the priority the navy had placed on the construction and modernizing of fleet units. Moreover, the failure of contemporary Japanese naval thinking to link commerce protection with the requirements of ASW derived considerably from the navy's view of its own submarine force. Seeing that force as directed primarily against American fleet units, the Japanese naval high command apparently assumed that their opposites in the U.S. Navy harbored similar plans, as indeed they did, up until the beginning of the war.[30]

Furthermore, while the navy considered protection of its vital sea lanes to be important, the geographic definition of which sea lanes were considered "vital" was quite limited. This limitation can best be understood by reference to the navy's operational plans. For example, in case of war with the United States, pre-1941 plans called only for commerce protection in the waters north of the Taiwan Straits and along the littoral of the northeast Asian continent. The China Sea and the waters of Micronesia were only provisionally included. With hindsight, the official history of Japanese escort operations points out that by so limiting the area of Japanese interest, the navy had virtually abandoned the idea of commerce protection in much of the ocean where the Pacific War would be fought.[31]

Essentially, the navy saw commerce protection as an extension of the problem of providing for coastal defense of the Japanese home islands. Immediately prior to the London Treaty both the Navy General Staff and the Naval Affairs Department of the Navy Ministry had done some careful study of the navy's needs for coastal defense. They had recommended building substantial light forces for this purpose, including escorts, submarine chasers, and land-based air groups. However, the restricted naval budgets of the treaty era aborted such plans.[32]

Undoubtedly, however, the overriding consideration in limiting the construction, training, and equipment devoted to commerce protection was the navy's absolute priority on the heavy ships with which the navy hoped to win the decisive surface battle. In combination with the interwar budgetary limitations, this fixation repeatedly set aside "lesser" considerations, such as the security of the nation's maritime transport. Indeed, until the Pacific War, the navy viewed the safety of Japanese merchant shipping as a matter of coastal defense, which the navy assumed would be indirectly guaranteed by Japanese battle forces in any event. The 1928 Nomura Report (see chapter 7) gave a clear priority to heavy warship construction and, with the exception of a few special units, left the matter of coastal defense to a few overage warships still in service. In the 1936 Imperial Defense Policy, references to the creation of an escort force for Japanese shipping were vague, feeble, and unrealistic: Preparations were to be limited in peacetime to the creation of a few core units; further study was to be made of the kind of training and ships that would be required for protection of Japanese shipping; and, in the event of hostilities, the navy would somehow undertake the rapid and wholesale construction of escort vessels as they were needed. The 1941 operational plan, for its part, did not make specific reference to the preparations necessary for commerce protection, these being subsumed under the problem of the general defense of the home islands. In the plan, sea communications in this rear area would be protected by first-line sea and air forces. Direct protection of coastal areas would be left to elements allotted from the navy's slender defense units, to wartime construction, and if necessary, to fleet units detached from first-line forces. The view of most Japanese naval officers reflected this official disdain for commerce protection. They had little understanding or experience in either convoy escort or antisubmarine operations and, trained as they were in the principles of decisive fleet action, had no interest in learning what seemed a marginal and unrewarding trade.[33]

At the highest levels of the navy there was Olympian complacency concerning the safety of Japanese shipping in the event of war. Civilian leaders were far less confident. In the summer of 1941, the Cabinet Planning Board had warned of dire shipping losses that might well exceed Japan's capacity to replace them. In important meetings that autumn, civilian cabinet members had tried to raise the issues of convoy protection, shipping safety, and the American submarine threat with chief of the general staff Adm. Nagano Osami. On such occasions, Nagano either replied with utter assurance about the navy's ability "to bring American submarines under control" or, under the pretext of national security, refused to discuss the navy's preparations to deal with these problems.[34]

Thus, on the eve of the Pacific War, the Japanese navy had given almost no thought to the possibility of a submarine campaign in its rear areas, and commerce protection, specifically including convoy escort, was a mission to be improvised as the need arose. These deficiencies in outlook would have been serious enough had Japan been planning to fight a defensive war within its home waters. But with the plans emerging in 1941 for a campaign of territorial aggrandizement, the potential difficulties for commerce protection increased enormously. The strategic rationale for the conquest of Southeast Asia was based on Japan's acquisition of the region's vast resources. This being the case, the occupation of the region would require not only the transport of sufficient military forces to bring it under Japanese control, but also forces for the defense of the area and the ships carrying strategic materials back to Japan. Both these operations, moreover, would require attention to the problem of escorts, as well as to the problem of shipping.[35]

As asserted in chapter 11, no aspect of this twin logistical-naval problem was more important than tanker tonnage and the means to protect it, but only a few Japanese naval officers seem to have grappled with these issues. If his memoirs are correct, Comdr. Ōi Atsushi was one of those who did. In the autumn of 1939, Ōi, then a lieutenant commander and a junior member of the Intelligence Division, studied the convoy system resurrected by the British navy at the outset of the war. He lacked the influence, however, to have his enthusiasm for it converted into concrete measures. Two years later, in an informal meeting, a handful of middle-echelon officers, including Ōi and several civilian petroleum specialists, met to discuss the problem of Japanese access to the oil of the Netherlands East Indies. Ōi argued that the issue was not getting the oil out of the

Indies, but getting it back to Japan. Pointing to the threat of British and American oceangoing submarines, Ōi noted the unwarranted complacency of the Navy General Staff and Navy Ministry concerning convoy escort in the face of this potential danger. Ōi's views led to an extended discussion of the number of tankers available for regular transport of East Indies oil back to Japan, the amount of naval strength sufficient for convoy escort for such shipping, and the expected losses of tankers to enemy submarines. Lacking an official forum, however, neither the views nor the concerns expressed by the participants in the meeting ever reached higher levels to affect policy. Thus, a month before the war, when the emperor queried Admiral Nagano about the ability of Japan "to obtain and transport oil without hindrance when faced with attacks by planes and submarines based in Australia" and what measures the navy would take to deal with the problem, Nagano was still unshaken in his complacency.[36]

Given the general neglect of the problem of commerce protection by the Japanese navy, it is not surprising that on the eve of the Pacific War, there existed very little in the way of organization, naval units, weapons, tactics, or training to deal with the tasks of convoy escort and ASW. To begin with, no organization within the naval high command had exclusive responsibility of planning for these missions. Such responsibility that existed was the concern of a single individual, and not his only concern at that. In the Second Section (Defense Planning) of the Operations Division of the Navy General Staff (much less glorified than the First Section, whose ten members dealt with the heady operational plans for the Combined Fleet), three or four officers were charged with an assortment of planning duties, including those for "rear area" defense. This last was the responsibility of a single officer and was considered to include, inter alia, the task of commerce protection. In 1941, with the imminent possibility of war, rear area defense was assigned to two staff officers. Yet only one of them had responsibility for commerce protection, and until October of that year, he held the concurrent position of aide-de-camp to the emperor.[37]

The actual direction of convoy escort and ASW was assigned to the naval districts, which were responsible for Japan's coastal defense. Not only did the district staff officers command few resources for this considerable task or even have much understanding of it, but also, by precedent and inclination, they were far more concerned with accommodating the tactical and logistical demands of the Combined Fleet.[38] Before the Pacific War, therefore, there was no major line command for commerce protection and none was established until the war was four months old. Even then, the quality and quantity of these forces were completely inadequate for the task at hand, and Combined Fleet headquarters became exasperated with having to detach destroyers and other fleet units for convoy escort. This would change only with the establishment of a full-fledged escort force in 1943.[39]

The marginal attention given by the navy to protection of sea transport was reflected in the quantity of warship construction devoted to it. Just before the London Treaty, the navy briefly considered building a sizable force of specialized craft for commerce protection, but budgetary considerations had aborted the plan. The meager result of this brief interest in escort ships was the building of four *kaibōkan* (coastal defense vessels) that had originally been designed for fishery protection and security tasks in Japan's Kurile Islands.[40] Proposed under the Circle One program and then again under Circle Two, the four ships of this *Shimushu* class were finally authorized under the Circle Three program when the navy concluded that they could fill the role of a general-purpose escort able to perform several coastal defense duties, including minelaying, minesweeping, and antisubmarine patrols. But the low priority that the navy assigned to commerce protection was reflected not only in the navy's originally laying down no more than four ships of this class, but also in the ships' reduction from a planned displacement of 1,200 tons to an actual 860 tons. The ships were reduced because a portion of the funds set aside to build them was used instead to help defray the costs of the *Yamato* and *Musashi*.[41] These *Shimushu* vessels were the closest thing the Japanese navy had to the British and American destroyer escorts. Sufficiently satisfied with the *Shimushu* class, the navy ordered fourteen more ships of an improved *Shimushu* design (the *Etorofu* class), but they took so long to construct, because of stringent naval construction standards, that none was completed when the Pacific War broke out. The *kaibōkan* were well designed and sturdily built to withstand the enormous stresses of the North Pacific. But their modest armament, few depth charges (none of which could be thrown forward), and their speed of less than 20 knots (slightly lower than the surface speed of the average U.S. fleet submarine) made these ships less than ideal as antisubmarine vessels. Ultimately, the most serious failure of the *kaibōkan* effort was that not enough were built.[42]

In addition to building the *kaibōkan,* the Japanese navy ordered the construction of vessels that, although constructed for other purposes, could serve as escorts (such as the minelayer-cruiser *Okinoshima*). Further, the navy converted several torpedo boats and older destroyers for escort work. Beginning in 1931, the navy also ordered a few submarine chasers averaging 250 tons and carrying two 40-millimeter antiaircraft guns and thirty-six depth charges. Finally, it commissioned about seventy-five auxiliary submarine chasers averaging 130 tons. But the auxiliary submarine chasers were only good for harbor and coastal patrol, because their 11-knot speed, feeble armament, and low freeboard made them ineffective for their intended purpose. Destroyers, of course, were the most formidable warships for both convoy escort and ASW, but the priorities of the Japanese navy made it reluctant to release fleet units for either of these missions.[43] In any

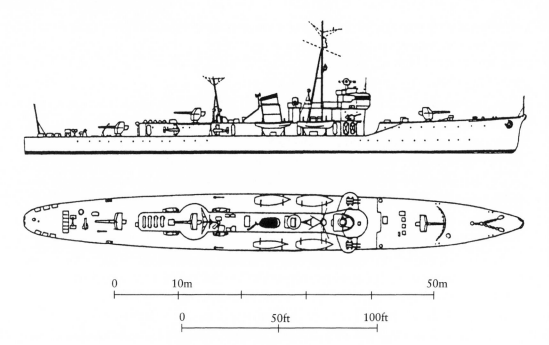

0   10m   50m

0   50ft   100ft

Fig. 12-1. The coast defense vessel *Shimushu*.

event, the number of ships assigned escort duty was wholly inadequate for the defense of Japanese shipping.

Not only was the quantity of these vessels wholly inadequate for their assigned missions, but their weapons and equipment were largely ineffective for such tasks. They were equipped with no forward-throwing ASW weapons, and their main armament was usually inferior to the larger deck guns of enemy submarines. Their depth charges were frequently set too shallow because faulty intelligence had underestimated the maximum diving depth of American submarines.[44]

In underwater detection, the Japanese navy had not greatly progressed beyond the technology developed during and immediately after World War I, much of which had been acquired from Britain and Germany. The navy had undertaken research on hydrophones in the 1920s and, in 1930, had imported the American MV-type hydrophone, from which it developed its own hydrophones, the type 93 and type 0. The former was the navy's standard underwater detection device throughout the Pacific War, despite its limited range of 1,000 yards. In the field of sound ranging—sonar—the Japanese had made some progress when the war broke out; about twenty destroyers had been outfitted with type 93 sonar.

Development of sonar continued throughout the war, but the pace of the program was slow, and Japanese sets remained rudimentary.[45]

Detection of submarines by interception of their radio communications offered promise. The Japanese navy had some experience in tracking American naval maneuvers through radio intercepts since the early 1930s. The slow collation of bearings, however, made the navy's otherwise efficient high-frequency-radio direction-finding (HF/DF) system of little use for the kind of quick response demanded by convoy escort and ASW operations in the Pacific War.[46]

In sum, the Japanese navy was ill prepared, in outlook, doctrine, training, ships, and equipment to deal with either commerce protection or ASW. The official history of the navy's maritime protection operations during the war recapitulates the reasons for this failure. First, the navy failed to foresee the protracted nature of the war and that it would inevitably involve the protection of sea transport over a vast area. Second, the navy's fixation on the decisive surface battle monopolized its armaments, its preparations, and its training, and left it blind to the possibility that destruction of the nation's commercial shipping might also be decisive. Third, the British and American advocacy of limitations on submarines at the London Naval Conference left the Japanese navy with the impression that submarines were a weak point in the U.S. Navy's force structure. This led to the fatal conclusion that the possibility of an American submarine campaign against Japan was slight. Last, the defensive character of both convoy escort and ASW, and the tiresome, repetitive duty that they entailed, gave them short shrift in a navy whose traditions had held that offense was the best defense.[47]

FROM SEA TO SHORE
Japanese Landing Capabilities

The development of an amphibious landing capability offers something of an exception to the otherwise dismal record of noncooperation between Japan's two armed services. Since nearly all of Japan's modern wars were fought outside the home islands, of necessity, the army's initial operations—landings on an enemy coast—required the navy's support, a fact remarked upon with some irony by Adm. Yamamoto Gombei (see chapter 1). Japan was thus one of the first nations to understand the importance of modern amphibious operations, without which it could not hope to establish a military presence on the Asian continent. The navy's cooperation in debarkation of army troops on Korean shores during the Sino-Japanese and Russo-Japanese Wars had set the tone for the amphibious operations of the future: unopposed landings, often at several landing sites simultaneously, undertaken at night to achieve surprise and to have control of the coastline by dawn.

Until the 1930s, however, neither service maintained a force that had landing operations for its primary mission, as did the U.S. Marine Corps.[48] The army's role in these wars was principally devoted to the great land battles inland, and therefore, its initial interest in amphibious operations was slight; it was the navy that maintained a modest capability to project its power ashore. Most Japanese warships had a portion of their crews (usually less than a third) designated for use as a *rikusentai* (naval landing party) composed of sailors who had been given a modicum of infantry and small-arms training and who could be put ashore should the need arise.[49] In riverine China, particularly at Shanghai and on the Yangtze, these shore parties were most often used. There, Japanese gunboats shared the rivers with similar vessels of Western nations in the protection of their nationals and their commercial interests at the treaty ports upriver. As early as 1897, at Shanghai, the navy had put these small forces ashore, ostensibly to quell some disturbance or meet some threat to Japanese lives and property.[50] *Rikusentai* had been among the first units ashore in the Russo-Japanese War, had been used in the occupation of the German-held islands in Micronesia, and had spearheaded the Japanese intervention at Vladivostok in 1918. But the naval landing parties were used most extensively in China, where they often performed garrison duty after securing a particular landing site. Notably, such a unit had formed a permanent garrison just outside the Japanese quarter of the International Settlement at Shanghai, beginning in 1927. In its weaponry, equipment, and combat skills, however, the unit could hardly be considered a formidable amphibious force.

Until World War I, the Japanese army had hardly thought about the problems of amphibious warfare. But the Allied disaster at Gallipoli, demonstrating the difficulty of landings on a well-defended coast, had changed the army's outlook sharply. Concluding that its future landings—in the Philippines and elsewhere—might have to be made in the face of enemy fire, the army began to insist on a more prominent role in amphibious planning.[51] For that reason, the army actively joined the navy in a series of exercises in amphibious warfare during the 1920s: on the Shikoku coast in 1922, at Ise Bay in 1925, at Niijima in the Izu Islands in 1926 (where the army tried out its first amphibious tank), and along the Wakayama coast in 1929. In these maneuvers, both services worked out problems of navy gunfire support, maps for joint bombardments, ship-to-shore communications and control, various kinds of landing craft, assaults by division-sized forces, the use of smoke shells, and the movement of troops over long stretches of water. From the experience gained in these maneuvers, the army and navy together developed a series of guidelines for amphibious operations. Among these, the *Tairiku sakusen kōyō* (Outline of amphibious operations) of 1932 became the permanent manual on the subject. The result of five years of inter-service deliberations, the document clearly set forth principles for army-navy cooperation in amphibious operations and delineated the responsibility of commanders at various levels.[52]

The eruption of fighting at Shanghai in 1932 brought about a shift in the relative attention and effort devoted to amphibious operations by the two armed services. In February, the permanent Japanese naval landing party clashed with Nationalist forces in the city streets and was badly bloodied in the process. Fearing that its garrison would be overrun, the navy called for army help in turning back the enemy. Although a mixed brigade was successfully landed to relieve the beleaguered landing party, the experience left much to be desired from the army's point of view. The first landings were made in navy vessels unequipped with armor or armament and carrying inadequate amounts of ammunition and weapons.[53]

The mediocre performance of the navy in the fighting at Shanghai in 1932 caused the navy to modify the way in which its naval landing parties were organized, armed, and employed. It was now perfectly willing to leave the development of a major amphibious capability to the army, including the design of docking ships, transports, and landing vessels. But in its determination to reduce its traditional reliance on the formation of ad hoc landing parties from warships on station, a measure which only depleted their complements and reduced their efficiency, the navy now decided to create permanent, specialized landing forces for limited, small-scale missions. Thus was born the Special Naval Landing Force, initially of battalion strength and armed with no more than small arms and mortars, but extensively trained in landing operations. Five units were formed in the 1930s, one at Shanghai and one each at the navy's principal bases in the home islands: Yokosuka, Kure, Sasebo, and Maizuru. Each domestically based unit was designed to be embarked on warships, usually light cruisers or destroyers, whose naval guns could support the limited, specialized missions projected by the navy.[54]

The army's dissatisfaction with its actions at Shanghai also led it to rethink its dependence on the navy for amphibious operations. As a first step, it sought navy assistance in the development of a specialized landing ship. The *Shinshū-maru*, designed and built by the navy to army specifications, was the first ship of any nation specifically conceived for amphibious operations, a prototype of the landing ship dock later developed by the U.S. Navy.[55] The army also went on to develop landing craft for tanks and to upgrade the training of several divisions specially earmarked for amphibious operations. Through these developments, the army became the dominant partner in the conduct of amphibious warfare even as the navy's role shrank to providing gunfire support and convoying army landing craft to the beaches.[56] Still, both services continued to cooperate in perfecting amphibious training and tactics.

Such training proved its worth when Japan's China War broke out in 1937. The first amphibious operation of that conflict, in August, at the mouth of the

Yangtze, reverted to the earlier arrangement of navy-directed landings in which the navy used its warships to bring the army's troops ashore. But larger army forces were landed by army vessels, including the *Shinshū-maru,* in a textbook operation that followed the principles set down in the "Outline of amphibious operations": a landing unopposed, at dawn, and at several places simultaneously.[57] Three other major landings involving divisional forces took place over the next fourteen months: at Hangchow Bay in November 1937; at Ta-ya Wan (Bias Bay) near Hong Kong in October 1938; and at Bocca Tigris (Humen) at the entrance to the Pearl River the same month. All followed the essential pattern of established Japanese amphibious doctrine.[58]

The Japanese landings in the China War provided excellent experience in working out the procedural and logistical problems of large-scale amphibious operations. While these operations, unopposed as they were, hardly put a strain on Japanese amphibious resources, in the words of a recent comparative study, they demonstrated that in amphibious warfare, "Japan entered World War II as well prepared as the United States, both in terms of operational forces and published doctrine."[59]

As discussed, in the 1930s the army had come to dominate the development of Japanese amphibious warfare, particularly in transport, equipment, strategic decisions, and the scale of forces directly involved. Yet, the army's major missions were the defeat of enemy ground forces and the occupation of large land masses. For this reason, the army never saw its amphibious function as paramount. The same could be said of the navy, because of its obsession with the decisive battle at sea. The navy, however, confronted with the problems of seizing British and American island possessions in the Pacific, continued to manifest a strong interest in improving its amphibious capability.

Thus, as the likelihood of a war in the Pacific approached, the navy began to enlarge, strengthen, and diversify both its landing forces and their missions. The special naval landing forces grew to enlarged battalions of about two thousand men, equipped not only with small arms but also with heavy weapons, including 3-inch naval guns and howitzers. After the outbreak of the war, the battalions were sometimes enlarged by combining two or more such units into a new type of organization designated the Combined Special Naval Landing Force. On the eve of the Pacific War, some officers were inspired to promote a powerful and semi-independent amphibian force, but the idea never received much interest from the navy brass, caught up as they were in the strengthening of the battle line.[60] Other proposals for extending the navy's power ashore were realized, however, chief among them the idea of vertical envelopment. The navy had recognized the possibilities of this new dimension of warfare after the German paratroop successes in Europe in 1940. Late that year, under the cover designation of "Experiment

1001," the Japanese navy began secret paratroop training for men selected from its special naval landing forces, and by the outbreak of the war had organized at least two paratroop units within those forces. The forces performed superbly in several combined operations that contributed to the rapid conquest of the Netherlands East Indies in the first months of the Pacific War.[61]

On the eve of the Pacific War, therefore, Japan had good reason to be supremely confident of its abilities to conduct amphibious operations.[62] This confidence was basic to its strategic decision to give military reality to the long-standing concept of *nanshin,* the southward thrust of Japanese power into Southeast Asia. Indeed, the first months of the Pacific War demonstrated how effectively the nation's armed services had mastered the logistical and doctrinal problems of amphibious operations. Japanese landings in Southeast Asia—often at night, by forces that landed separately but concentrated at the point of attack—were carried out with a speed, surprise, and economy of force that sowed confusion and consequent demoralization among their British, Dutch, and American enemies. In these operations, the navy's role was slighter than the army's, but the former's powerful covering forces, both distant and close, as well as its destruction of enemy air opposition, were necessary if not sufficient causes for the operations' success.[63]

With the end of the major Japanese offensives in the Pacific, however, the mission of the navy's land forces changed from mobile to positional warfare. Indeed, the precedent for the shift had been set as early as 1939, with the Japanese occupation of Hainan Island, off the South China coast. Its seizure had been largely a navy operation, and with its completion, the special naval landing forces involved had been transformed into a naval guard force whose mission was defense and internal security. With the occupation of an expanded circle of island territories in the central and southwestern Pacific early in the war, the navy was obliged to repeat this model. Its land forces were increasingly given defensive missions, and their organization was changed accordingly. Increasingly, the shipborne, quick-strike special naval landing forces were replaced with *konkyochitai* (base forces) and their subordinate *keibitai* (guard units), often hastily organized and hastily dispatched to defend the navy's advanced bases in the Pacific. Although some of these proved exceedingly resistant to attack, most were eventually annihilated by American amphibious offensives more powerful than any similar operations that Japan had ever mounted, or were simply bypassed and, by their isolation, rendered ineffective.[64]

Clearly, then, the particular skill mastered by the Japanese navy in projecting its power ashore was the ability to make *unopposed amphibious landings*—operations carried out against undefended or lightly defended coastlines. This facility was amply manifested in all Japan's modern wars. In these conflicts the navy, as well as the army, demonstrated mastery of the complex tactical and logistical problem of putting troops ashore in landings marked by stealth, deception, and dispersal.

What the navy never developed was a capability in *amphibious assault*. This term means the ability, such as that developed by the U.S. Marine Corps, to make an amphibious landing in the teeth of determined resistance by an alerted, fortified, and entrenched enemy. Indeed, the navy's one experience in such operations, the assault on Wake Island in December 1941, met with near disaster and revealed how unprepared were Japan's armed services to undertake them.[65]

One must recognize, however, that for the entire history of the Japanese navy, amphibious assault was irrelevant. From the Sino-Japanese War of 1894–95 through the first year of the Pacific War, the navy had no need of such a capability. By 1943, even had Japan's armed services developed the doctrine, training, forces, and techniques to conduct amphibious assault, its inability to establish local sea and air control in contested areas of the Pacific would have made such operations impossible.

13

THE GREAT GAMBLE

The Japanese Navy Plans for War, 1937–1941

In a book such as this about the strategy, tactics, and technology of the Imperial Japanese Navy before the Pacific War, a dilemma inevitably arises. On the one hand, a detailed discussion of Japan's drift toward war from 1937 to 1941, or even of the navy's role in that drift, is beyond the scope of this book and has been given ample and expert treatment elsewhere.[1] On the other hand, one needs at least a general appreciation of the navy's road to war to understand and assess its strategic planning immediately before the opening of hostilities. This chapter will therefore briefly review the issues, events, institutions, and personalities involved in the navy's fateful decision to lead the nation into war. This review is undertaken with the recognition that in the decisions leading to the outbreak of the Pacific War, the Imperial Japanese Navy was not the only actor, only the most important.

THE JAPANESE NAVY'S ROAD TO WAR, 1937–41

By the opening of 1936, the shifts of power in Europe and East Asia and the uncertainties of a treaty-less naval world were sufficient to cause the two armed services, in consort with the civil government, to review Japanese policy and strategy, considering the new perils and opportunities that appeared to confront the nation. The accepted means of reformulating grand policy and strategy was, of course, to revise the Imperial Defense Policy, a process begun in joint committee in February. This third and final revision of the nation's most important strategic statement largely repeated the effort to reconcile the essentially irreconcilable approaches of each service to Japan's basic security interests. Yet, new concerns apparently required a broader range of strategic commitments.

For the army, as usual, continental commitments shaped its policies. As in the past, Russia, greatly strengthened under the Stalinist Soviet regime in its position in Siberia, was the chief hypothetical enemy. But the rise of Chinese nationalism and its apparent threat to Japanese interests on the mainland caused the army to insist on China's inclusion as a second-level target of Japanese army planning. The navy saw no reason to change its fundamental purposes: domination of the western Pacific and the eventual defeat of the U.S. Navy. The Soviet Union[2] and China remained as secondary and tertiary enemies but, at all events, the navy kept to its strategic tradition: fighting one enemy at a time. By the mid-1930s, mostly because British naval forces in Southeast Asia might eventually prove an obstacle to the navy's growing interest in the region, the naval high command was ready to add Britain to its short list of hypothetical enemies (but only under the assumption that Japan would fight Britain alone, or at the most Britain and China).[3]

As mentioned previously, the navy maintained a policy of *nanshin* (southward advance), that is, an extension of Japanese power and influence into Southeast Asia and, to a lesser extent, into Melanesia. Through the first two decades of the twentieth century, in the navy's struggle with its service rival for budgets, preferment, and prestige, the *nanshin* concept had really only been a counterpoint to the army's advocacy of a *hokushin* (northward advance) onto the continent in northeast Asia. Then in the 1930s, while it continued to serve this purpose, the *nanshin* idea took on a new life in shaping actual navy policy. Induced by a concern for Southeast Asia's strategic resources, especially oil, which had been articulated particularly by a few middle-echelon activist officers, the navy had renewed its interest in the region.[4] Since almost all of Southeast Asia was in the hands of Western colonial powers, the navy initially had difficulty in defining what its strategic interests were in the region and how they would be obtained. In the next few years, however, circumstances at home and abroad considerably sharpened the navy's focus on Southeast Asia.

Of the two simultaneous and countervailing demands upon the nation's energies, moneys, and resources, one was continental and pointed toward a final showdown with Russia. The other was maritime and directed against the United States, while also seeking to open a new range of strategic opportunities in the tropics. Both demands inevitably affected the Japanese government's ability to redefine its strategic objectives. Once again, as in 1907, 1918, and 1923, the fundamental differences between the army and the navy in strategic priorities resulted in an Imperial Defense Policy (approved by the emperor in June 1936) that was positively vaporous in its generalities. Essentially, the United States was to remain the main hypothetical enemy of the navy, which was allowed to begin the major construction plans discussed in chapter 10 in return for an army buildup against the Soviet Union.[5] In any event, the Imperial Defense Policy, crippled by the disagreements of its creators, overtaken by events in Europe and Asia, and burdened by the cumbrous processes for approval of the throne, was by now too antiquated a mechanism to serve any longer as an effective guide for Japanese grand strategy. In the five years that remained before Japan initiated the Pacific War the defense policy was never even reviewed, let alone revised.

There were other attempts to coordinate the nation's military, naval, and foreign policies and to establish strategic priorities. Yet these too came to naught, largely because of the navy's burgeoning interest in Southeast Asia. In April 1936, Navy Minister Nagano Osami put before the inner cabinet (of principal ministers) a policy paper, *Kokusaku yōkō* (General principles of national policy), which stressed the strategic importance of the "southern areas."[6] That June, Nagano presented the inner cabinet with yet another document that vaguely spoke of a "southward advance," to be accomplished, supposedly, by peaceful economic means. Neither statement garnered much support from the army.

Finally, in August, both services attempted to reconcile their differences over budgetary and strategic priorities in a series of meetings, held chiefly between Capt. Fukutome Shigeru, chief of the Operations Section (of the Operations Division) of the Navy General Staff, and his opposite number on the Army General Staff, Col. Ishiwara Kanji. In the end, however, other than agreeing that current Japanese military and naval capabilities could not assure victory in the case of hostilities with more than one power, Fukutome and Ishiwara simply talked past one another. Fukutome argued for a "southward advance" and an augmented program of naval construction, and Ishiwara insisted on the necessity of buildup against the Soviet Union and the priority of strategic considerations in northeast Asia. This interservice wrangling over strategy was brought to the cabinet level and, in August 1936, after a series of meetings, resulted in a compromise statement, *Kokusaku no kijun* (Fundamental principles of national policy).[7] Since the statement simply restated the separate ambitions of the army and the navy and did nothing to integrate national strategies, however, it failed utterly to resolve the differences between the army and navy over budgetary priorities and the direction of future Japanese expansion. Basically, the policy standoff demonstrated the continuing hubris of each of the two services that, from first to last, defined national policy primarily in terms of its own needs and the budget required to support them.[8] As an index of the emerging thrust of Japanese naval policy, however, the "Fundamental principles" paper also demonstrated the navy's intention to realize its own strategic and economic interests in Southeast Asia (as counter to the army's interests in Manchukuo and China), as well as to undertake the construction of a fleet sufficient to dominate the western Pacific and, by implication, Southeast Asia.[9] This rationale had been basic to the Circle Three naval construction program.

The outbreak of the China War further complicated this issue, since Japan's broadening involvement on the continent threatened to violate the principle of fighting one enemy at a time, a basic axiom of Japanese grand strategy since before World War I. For its part, the army, focused as always on the Soviet Union but fully engaged in China, now wished to plan for the possibility of operations against two or more enemies. The navy initially insisted on adhering to existing policy. After protracted negotiations with its sister service, the navy, under the influence of its most belligerent elements, gave way. It agreed to a fundamental shift in traditional Japanese strategy: the possibility of hostilities against three powers at once, the United States, the Soviet Union, and China.[10] By the end of 1938, the navy was also willing to add a fourth enemy: Great Britain, which had already figured in its list of single enemies. Britain's relations with Japan had noticeably cooled, and Britain was the strongest obstacle to the extension of Japanese power and influence in Southeast Asia, mostly because of British efforts to strengthen its naval base at Singapore. It seemed natural to Japanese planners at the time, therefore, to count Britain in that array of nations it might have to challenge. For the navy, the fuel problem had now reached a level at which the establishment of some sort of future hegemony over Southeast Asia—economic or political—seemed worth such a confrontation.[11] At this point, however, far from there being any concrete studies or detailed planning for a war with Britain, there was hardly any military data on which to base such planning. Not until the annual operation plan of 1940 did the two services draw up such plans.[12] Indeed, so new to the Japanese navy was the idea of conflict with its "old friend" (Arthur Marder's term) that some on the general staff were not familiar with the geography of the British empire in South and Southeast Asia. From the outset, however, Japanese navy planners were confident that in the event of a war with Britain, the Japanese navy could dispose of British naval forces in Asian waters.[13]

The first years of the China War somewhat deflected the navy's efforts to reorient national policy toward a southward advance. The strategy was still due as much to the navy's obsession for place and preferment vis-à-vis competing army interests as it was to strategic or material necessity. Instead, the navy pursued a policy of opportunistic belligerence, manifested first by its provocation of fighting in Shanghai in August 1937, and then by its continuing efforts to acquire bases along the South China coast and in the South China Sea.[14] In the first two years of the war, the navy took the lead in occupying Amoy, Canton, and other ports on the South China coast. In February 1939, the navy seized Hainan and put it under navy control; in March, the navy occupied the Spratly Islands in the South China Sea. These actions positioned the navy for further advances southward should the opportunity arise.[15] Nor was the navy's exploitation of the China War limited to improving its strategic position. Except for its air operations, its role in the China conflict was smaller than the army's. The navy nevertheless also used the war to insist that the government increase allocations of strategic matériel, now seen as even more important than budgetary allotments.

In the summer of 1939, Japan seemed at once burdened by difficulty and blessed with opportunity. The China War dragged on without conclusion, and the worsening atmosphere of Japan-U.S. relations was symbolized by the abrogation of the long-standing U.S.-Japan Commercial Treaty. Yet some in the Japanese navy, undoubtedly inspired by memories of the freedom of action made available to Japan by the power vacuum in East Asia and the western Pacific during World War I, believed that opportunities for even more dramatic initiatives might be created by the outbreak of hostilities in Europe. The most flamboyant statement of this sort was made by Capt. Nakahara Yoshimasa, whose aggressive advocacy of the "southward advance," beginning with the Pakhoi Incident[16] while he was on the general staff, had earned him the sobriquet Nan'yō-ō (King of the South Seas). Early in the fighting in Europe in 1939, Nakahara wrote, "Finally, the time has come. This maritime nation, Japan, should commence its advance to the Bay of Bengal! Moss-covered tundras, vast barren deserts—of what use are they? Today people should begin to follow the grand strategy of the navy, altering their old bad habits. Japan must be brought back to its maritime tradition, placing the main emphasis on the development of the navy. (We should not hesitate even to fight the United States and Britain to attain that end.)"[17]

While these were the views of only the most militant *nanshin* advocates in the navy and certainly found no resonance in the army's viewpoint at this time, the Navy General Staff set in motion certain preparations that would enable the navy to move quickly toward whatever opportunities presented themselves. Among these were steps toward the reorganization of the navy to put it on a semiwartime footing and the creation of a new, independent command, the Fourth Fleet, assigned to the western Caroline Islands, which would put the navy in a position to move into the Netherlands East Indies if the situation warranted.

By the beginning of 1940, with the continuation of the "phony war" in Europe, the navy concluded that there would be no drastic change in the war situation there and thus for the time being no new opening in Southeast Asia.[18]

Then, in the spring of that year, tumultuous events in Europe appeared to present the navy with the opportunity to realize its long-sought ambitions in Southeast Asia. First came the rapid German invasions of Denmark and Norway in April, with their demonstrations of the overwhelming air power. Then in May, the Low Countries and France swiftly collapsed under the German tide, leaving Britain suddenly besieged. These calamities made the French, Dutch, and British colonial territories in Southeast Asia vulnerable to Japanese pressure and even outright conquest. Among these potential targets of opportunity none was greater than the Netherlands East Indies, first, because their treasure house of strategic resources was the richest, and second, because the forces defending them were the weakest.

These events presented the Japanese navy with a set of strategic ambiguities and seemed to offer a glittering opportunity to achieve a long-sought ambition. They thus drew the navy along a course of belligerence toward the West and renewed the navy's assertiveness toward its service rival. But aggressive moves to realize its ambitions in Southeast Asia might bring the navy into a dangerous confrontation for which it believed itself not yet prepared. In brief, the problem lay in undertaking naval operations against the Dutch in the Indies without provoking a war with either Britain or America. This dilemma emerged when the navy was still straining to match the massive building program of the U.S. Navy and was competing with the Japanese army for the strategic resources to do so. Worse yet, the dilemma came at a time when the navy realized that it might find itself embroiled in combat with *five* nations simultaneously—the United States, Britain, China, the Netherlands, and the Soviet Union—a mark of how far the navy had strayed from its strategic principle of one enemy at a time. For several years, these opposing tensions—opportunity and danger—created shifts in the policy and strategy of the Japanese navy that, to the Japanese army then and to historians long after, seemed sometimes reckless and sometimes pusillanimous.

As early as the beginning of April 1940 an influential middle echelon within the navy had urged that the time had come to occupy the Indies. In May, at the outset of the great German offensive in western Europe, the newly organized Fourth Fleet had been despatched to Palau, in Japanese Micronesia, to be in a position to occupy ports and bases in the Indies on the pretext of protecting their neutrality. That same month, the navy had held map exercises oriented to the larger strategic questions involved in naval operations in Southeast Asian waters. From these exercises the navy had concluded that in the event of a Japanese invasion of the Indies, it would be impossible to limit operations to Dutch military and naval forces alone. Inevitably, such operations would involve Japan in a war against Britain, the United States, *and* the Netherlands. The particular focus of concern was the likelihood of a protracted war with the United States, which the exercise participants saw little chance of winning if it lasted more than a year and a half. Added to this concern was the question of the security of the sea routes between Japan and Southeast Asia, without which it would be impossible to maintain access to the petroleum and other resources of the Indies.[19]

Two important consequences flowed from these considerations. One was the navy brass's conviction that any hope of victory in a war with its prime enemy would require not only time for extensive preparations, but also a far greater share than formerly of the nation's strategic resources to make these preparations possible. The other consequence was a circular chain of navy reasoning (particularly by the Operations Section of the general staff) that linked the problem of Southeast Asian oil to the inevitability of a war with the United States. In the worsening climate of Japan-U.S. relations, so the line of argument went, the United States would most probably reduce or entirely ban its export of oil to Japan. Since the United States had supplied the navy with most of its petroleum needs, the navy would be obliged to look to the Netherlands East Indies, the only other source that could supply the navy's requirements in like quantity. But to take the oil fields of the Indies by force would embroil Japan in a war with the United States, which Japan could not possibly win without access to those very same sources.[20] Very little evidence suggests that the Japanese naval leadership ever questioned the circularity of the argument by seeking policy alternatives that might have made it less necessary to consider war with the United States.

In any event, these two basic assumptions greatly complicated the nation's decision-making processes as Japan drifted toward war. By July 1940, these processes were further complicated by a volte-face by the Japanese army, which suddenly announced its own interest in a "southward advance." The army now saw such a strategy as helping create a vast, economically self-sufficient Japanese sphere stretching from Manchuria to the waters north of Australia and from the Indian Ocean to Melanesia. The first step in the creation of such a sphere would be the occupation of the bases in Tonkin, French Indochina. The army, however, clearly made quite different assumptions from those of the navy. To realize its ambitions, the army was willing to go to war with the colonial government of the Indies and even with Britain, but assumed that in the process of doing so, Japan could avoid conflict with the United States.

To the navy, such an arrangement was unthinkable. In the first place, the army's sudden policy shift meant an intrusion into the navy's long-standing schemes of a "southward advance." Second, exclusion of the United States from Japanese war plans meant that the navy, which for decades had justified its existence by an American naval threat, would have only a very minor role in a Southeast Asian campaign. And third, by accepting such a role, the navy could hardly lay claim to the greater allocation of strategic materials required for its major expansion plans.

For a brief period in the summer of 1940, these considerations caused the navy to reverse course. It refused to prepare for an invasion of the Netherlands East Indies and urged that Japan obtain its strategic resources through diplomatic means. But upon learning of the threat of an American embargo should Japan resort to force in Southeast Asia, the navy resumed its "circular, conspiratorial logic" (the words are Henry Frei's). It again veered toward an attack on the Indies. In early August, the navy judged that the combat readiness of its principal fleets over the next thirty days was low and predicted that it could fight no more than a year should the United States cut off all oil supplies to Japan. Nevertheless, the navy began planning for a full-scale naval war by undertaking the first measures involved in the mobilization of the fleet, specifically, "preparatory fleet mobilizations" and "emergency war programs" (see chapter 10). These measures were the first serious step toward war with the United States, one taken even before relations with the United States had begun to deteriorate.[21]

In late August, the navy believed that war with the United States should be initiated in either of two situations: if a "favorable opportunity" presented itself, or if hostilities were deemed "inevitable" because Japan had been driven into a corner by Anglo-American embargoes or other measures that threatened Japan's very existence. The navy nevertheless continued to assume that the outcome of such a conflict would turn largely on the question of whether the navy could prepare for it by amassing the necessary weapons and resources.[22] One can scarcely think of a set of strategic postulates longer on risk and shorter on logic and careful calculation of alternatives.

The Japanese navy was thinking less in long-range terms than it was of its immediate interests. Against the judgment of a number of its most senior and experienced officers, the navy leadership agreed to support the army's insistence on the signing of the Tripartite Pact with Germany and Italy, in return for a far greater share of resource allocations. Emboldened by this priority claim on war material, the navy, in the autumn of 1940, pressed ahead with its preparations: It accelerated warship construction and retrofitting; mobilized reserve personnel; stockpiled matériel; and equipped and stocked airfields, ports, depots, and bases, especially those in Micronesia. Overlooked was the fact that by signing the Tripartite Pact,[23] Japan had not only further antagonized the United States, which supplied the bulk of the navy's strategic materials, but had tied itself to the military ambitions of two nations that, half a world away and with desperate resource needs of their own, were not in a position to supply any strategic materials to Japan.

As 1941 began, however, the two services still disagreed about how far and how fast to push toward war. The army, bogged down in its struggle with China and unable to end it either by force or by secret negotiations with the Nationalist government, had in the previous autumn occupied French bases in Tonkin. This move came not only as part of the army's effort to cut off China from outside assistance, but also as the first step toward a possible full-scale invasion of Southeast Asia. The army nevertheless continued to insist that such a campaign be limited in time and scope: a brief campaign to seize Malaya and the Netherlands East Indies, preceded by further pressure on the French colonial government to admit the stationing of Japanese forces in southern Indochina. The navy continued to insist on more time (and matériel allocations) to prepare for such a conflict, convinced as ever that an attack on British and Dutch colonial territories would inevitably involve Japan in a longer war with the United States. In the late winter of 1941, the navy now also insisted that "a favorable opportunity" was no longer sufficient as a trigger for offensive operations in Southeast Asia. Such operations should now be undertaken only if war became "inevitable," either by a direct threat to Japanese security, such as a major Anglo-American fleet movement, or by an indirect threat, such as a complete embargo on petroleum shipments to Japan.[24]

To army leaders, this navy backtracking was further evidence that the navy was playing a double game: even as units of both services were practicing joint assaults on the beaches of Kyūshū for the invasion of Malaya, the navy appeared more interested in hogging huge allocations than in committing itself to any sort of concerted action. Ultimately, however, in the planning for most offensive operations outside French Indochina, the navy held all the cards: without naval transport and protection the army could go nowhere. The army thus acceded to the navy and temporarily shelved its plans for imminent operations in Malaya or the East Indies.[25]

For its part, Japan's naval leadership had decided by the spring of 1941 that war with the United States was indeed inevitable; it only sought to control the timing of hostilities and the preparations for them. Spurred by the emergent influence of its aggressive middle echelon, the navy's stance became increasingly bellicose. "We must build bases in [southern] French Indochina and Thailand in order to launch military operations," Adm. Nagano Osami, the chief of staff, insisted at an Imperial Liaison Conference, 11 June 1941. "We must resolutely attack anyone who tries to stop us. We must resort to force. . . ."[26] Yet, even Nagano recognized that a delay in a full-scale invasion of Southeast Asia would give the navy more time to complete its preparations for war. Caught in the awkward position of urging war and not wishing to admit that the navy was not really ready for it, the Navy General Staff and Navy Ministry supported the movement of Japanese troops into Annam, Cochin China, and Cambodia in July 1941. This move had fateful consequences: The Japanese occupation of southern Indochina accelerated the nation and the navy toward a collision with the United States. With a stunning response that neither the army nor the navy had anticipated, in August the United States effectively imposed a total embargo on trade with Japan, including a ban on all oil shipments to that country. This step was soon followed by Britain and the Netherlands. After August 1941 Japan could not import a drop of oil, and thus the navy again had to eat into its precious stocks, so painstakingly amassed.

The navy was now confronted by the sort of situation that a year earlier it had declared would "inevitably" lead to war. Following months of alternating bellicosity and procrastination, the navy now argued the urgency of decision. During an Imperial Liaison Conference in October, which met to discuss the question of whether to open hostilities, Admiral Nagano was adamant: "The Navy is consuming 400 tons of oil an hour. The situation is urgent. We want it decided one way or the other quickly."[27] Thus, in the waning months of 1941, caught in its own logic and in the suddenly shrinking matrices for its strategic planning—time and resources—the Japanese navy plunged down the rapidly steepening slope toward war.

The navy took this course without seriously considering the vital questions that it should have pondered in the summer of 1940: whether a "southward advance" was worth risking an American embargo, whether there were reasonable alternatives to going war over such an embargo, and whether the navy could actually win the sort of war that the United States would surely try to force upon it.[28] The Japanese naval high command, against the better judgment of some of its most competent senior officers, undertook to enter into combat without considering these questions. That it did so can be explained, in part, by the particular configuration of its bureaucratic politics and personalities by the autumn of 1941.

THE TRIUMPH OF THE HAWKS
Decision-Making in the Navy, 1937–41

Although this book will not address the institutional or political history of the Imperial Japanese Navy in depth, it will provide a quick overview of the institutions, processes, and individuals that took the navy to war and were central to the specific strategies to fight it.

As explained, the Navy Ministry was the largest and most important organization of the Japanese navy. By the 1930s, it comprised many bureaus and departments, of which the Naval Affairs Bureau, the Navy Technical Department, and the Naval Aviation Department were the most prominent. In peacetime, certainly, the Navy Ministry was also the most powerful agency of the navy, since the navy minister had charge of all naval forces when the navy was not at war. Moreover, the ministry would represent the navy in the IGHQ (Imperial General Headquarters; see chapter 4) should such a headquarters be established, as occurred during the Sino- and Russo-Japanese wars. During the 1920s, the ministry's dominant position in the navy had been largely satisfactory to the navy's moderate officers—the "administrative group" (Asada Sadao's term)—mainly located within the ministry and generally supportive of a policy of cooperation with the Anglo-American maritime powers under the terms of the naval arms limitations treaties. The ministry's dominance had also been amenable to the government, since the navy minister was technically appointed by the prime minister and thus subject to at least a degree of civilian political influence.

These arrangements had not been to the liking, however, of the antitreaty officers of the so-called fleet faction—the "command group" (again, Asada Sadao's term)—who had been followers of the hard-lining Katō Kanji and Suetsugu Nobumasa and who were mainly found within the Navy General Staff. Members of this group bridled not only at the political viewpoints of their more moderate colleagues in the ministry, but also at the patent disparity in authority between their own general staff and the more powerful army general staff. In the early 1930s, inflamed by several events, of which the ministry's controversial handling of the London Naval Treaty had been the most explosive, officers of this group asserted themselves. In 1932, the vice chief of staff, Adm. Takahashi Sankichi, carried out a revolt against the Navy Ministry to raise the authority of the Navy General Staff. Using the prestige of the newly appointed chief of staff, Fushimi Hiroyasu, a prince of the blood, and the pliability of the navy minister, Ōsumi Mineo, Takahashi and his allies on the general staff forced the ministry, despite the opposition of most of its department and bureau heads, to accept certain humiliating changes. These transferred several ministry functions to the general staff, the most important of which were the command of naval forces during peacetime and the direction of the Navy Division of IGHQ during war.[29] Once they had strengthened the position of their administrative base, the militant officers worked to weaken moderate elements still further. Their efforts culminated in the "Ōsumi purge" of 1933–34, in which Minister Ōsumi, urged on by Katō Kanji, forced most top-ranking moderates in the navy into retirement. Katō had by then been elevated to the Supreme War Council (a largely ceremonial body charged with examining national security issues), but he masterminded the purge behind the scenes.

Over the next few years, officers of the command group came to occupy places in the middle echelon of the Navy General Staff and, to a lesser extent, within the ministry. In these positions they were successful in removing the navy and the nation from the naval treaty system and ending cooperation with the Anglo-American maritime powers. But the command group exerted its greatest influence through a new bureaucratic phenomenon in the navy: the emergence by the mid-1930s of ad hoc, intraservice committees staffed by section chiefs of the ministry and general staff. Supposedly established to promote integration and consensus within the navy for strategic planning at a time of gathering crisis, these committees, stocked with aggressive middle-echelon officers, increasingly took over the direction of navy policy. The two most powerful of these independent groupings were the First Committee, charged with generating grand strategies for the nation and specific navy policies to implement them, and the Second Committee, charged with recommending organizational "reform" of the navy to remove bureaucratic barriers to more belligerent and expansive navy policies. The First Committee began serious consideration of a "southward advance" policy as early as 1936, and the Second Committee started restructuring the ministry's Naval Affairs Bureau to bring it more in line with the bellicose, pro-German stance of the Japanese army.[30]

Although the militant group within the Japanese navy won a victory over the moderates by making the Navy General Staff the navy's representative in the IGHQ, many officers of this group were unenthusiastic about the IGHQ itself as an institution. They feared that, as in the Sino- and Russo-Japanese wars, the army would dominate the nation's high command.[31] Under the exigencies of the China War, the IGHQ was established by imperial order on 20 November 1937. As it turned out, and contrary to the expectations of the navy staff officers, the navy was generally able to hold its own in the IGHQ. The navy asserted an authority nearly equal to the army's and, if it could not always have its own way, exercised a kind of veto over army plans under certain circumstances. This being the case, the IGHQ illustrated the problems of Japanese decision-making at the highest levels. It was composed of two separate wings that acted independently, an army division and a navy division, each headed by its own chief of staff. The two divisions consisted mostly of officers who had a dual function, as members of their particular service and as members of the IGHQ. On the navy side of IGHQ, following the lead of the Navy General Staff, were the navy minister and chiefs of the most important departments and bureaus of the ministry (fig. 13-1).

The most serious defect in the arrangements of the IGHQ was the general absence of an integrative function akin to that of the Joint Chiefs of Staff created in the United States during World War II. The IGHQ had no overall chief of staff, or any other holder of ultimate authority. It lacked even the concrete representation of unified command. Each of its two principal divisions conducted its business at separate sites (the ministry building, in the case of the navy). Thus, when the two services reached an impasse, as occasionally happened, no individual or group could act as arbiter. The closest the IGHQ came to functioning like a true national command were those occasions when the two staffs met to exchange important information, to discuss major operational plans involving both services, or to provide "liaison" with the government. This last function manifested itself in the *Dai*

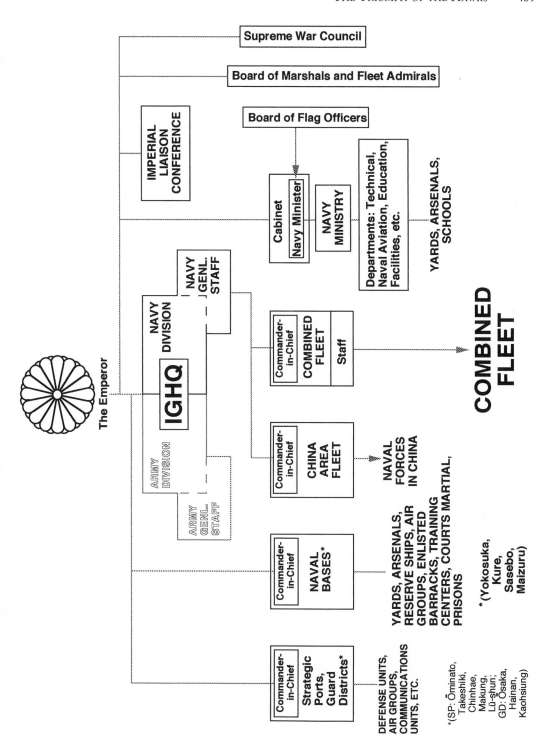

Fig. 13-1. Organization of IJN high command, 1941.

Hon'ei-seifu renraku kaigi (Imperial Liaison Conferences) held periodically, beginning in 1937, to bring together the chiefs of staff and the ministers of the two services with the prime minister and civilian members of the cabinet to thrash out major questions of grand strategy. When held in front of the emperor (at the palace), decisions at the conferences were considered to have automatic imperial approval, making them virtually irreversible. But even these conclaves at the highest level sometimes failed to bring about agreement between the two services, and interservice differences in such cases were simply papered over.[32]

In the view of Nomura Minoru, these arrangements showed the antiquated character of the Japanese command system. Nomura asserts that modern warfare requires that the conduct of military operations be coordinated with foreign policy, political developments, and economic realities, whereas Japanese military concerns were often considered in isolation.[33] Quite apart from the impotence of the civilian government, this lack of coordination resulted from the fragmented nature of the Japanese high command. Within the high command, the Navy General Staff in particular tended to make decisions without reference to other elements in the bureaucracy. For example, Tōjō Hideki, serving as prime minister and also army minister at the start of the Pacific War, did not learn the details of the navy's Pearl Harbor attack until after the Japanese surrender. Similarly, the navy minister was not informed of the plans for the Midway operation until after they were drafted. Even the Imperial Liaison Conference was a flawed mechanism for coordination, since not all its participants were briefed on critical strategic operations .[34]

Thus, by 1940, the Japanese navy had intensified its tendency to operate as a group of semi-independent satrapies, of which the general staff was only the most powerful. In the last two years before the outbreak of the Pacific War, however, it was the ad-hoc, intraservice committees, standing outside the navy's formal bureaucratic structure and composed of aggressive, supremely confident middle-echelon "hawks," that drove navy policy. They were very much the disciples of Katō Kanji, whose ideas still lingered, in their views on the navy as a vehicle for national expansion. Officers like Rear Adm. Oka Takazumi and Captains Nakahara Yoshimasa, Ishikawa Shingo, and Chūdō Kan'ei were strongly pro-Axis, virulently anti-British and anti-American, and ardently expansionist, favoring the "southward advance" and a rapid buildup of Japan's naval strength. Most important, they were able to exploit established practice in the navy's decision-making structure, as well as the gathering crisis atmosphere in the nation and the navy, to initiate policies that were then often automatically approved by those at the top of the navy's high command.

Opposed to the growing influence of this aggressive middle echelon stood an embattled triumvirate of senior officers: Admirals Yonai Mitsumasa, Yamamoto

Isoroku, and Inoue Shigeyoshi. They were the strategic disciples of the late Adm. Katō Tomosaburō, who supported the naval arms limitation system and saw the navy as a deterrent force, not as the edge for Japanese expansion.

By the 1930s, Yonai was a rarity in the navy, an officer with extensive sea experience, a broad perspective on the international scene, and an understanding that Japan's interests were best served by cooperation, not confrontation, with the Anglo-American maritime powers. During the three years he served as navy minister, from 1937 to 1940, Yonai did his best to keep the navy out of politics and out of war. As prime minister for the first half of 1940, he attempted to avoid the perils of an entangling alliance with Germany and Italy. In the end, his efforts and his cabinet were undone by a coalition of expansionists and pro-German sympathizers in both the army and the navy.[35]

Yamamoto, we have seen, of course, as a persistent critic of the navy's battleship orthodoxy when he was chief of the Naval Aviation Department. As vice navy minister he continued this role, but to it added his staunch support for Yonai's opposition to the extremist tendencies among the middle echelon of the navy, particularly to their attempts to draw Japan closer to Nazi Germany. Yamamoto's moderate policies and frank statements in the Diet concerning them so angered right-wing groups that he received numerous threats to his life and was obliged to seek protection from the police.[36] This may have been one of the reasons that, in August 1939, he was appointed to head the Combined Fleet. Having endeavored for three years without success to prevent the navy and the nation from undertaking policies which he believed would lead to a war which, in all likelihood, Japan could not win, Yamamoto, in his new position as head of the navy's greatest fleet, strove to shorten the odds in any Japan-U.S. naval conflict. To that task, Yamamoto brought a prestige and aura unmatched by any previous commander of the Combined Fleet and thus attained an influence in the navy's strategic decision-making that was the equal of the navy minister and the chief of staff.[37]

Inoue, the third member of the triumvirate, had aversions very similar to Yamamoto's. He disliked the bellicose and pro-German views of the extremist elements in the navy and abhorred the battleship fixation of the Navy General Staff. As chief of the ministry's Naval Affairs Bureau from 1937 to 1939 and as chief of the Naval Aviation Department from 1940 to 1941, he exerted his efforts against both of these tendencies in the navy. For Inoue, the navy was an instrument for national defense, not expansionism, and use of the armed forces was justified only if the nation otherwise faced ruin or annihilation. Thus, he had a profound distrust of any long-term arrangement linking the fate of Japan to the military ambitions of Germany and Italy.[38] Yet, if the Japanese navy was to be dragged into war, either through its foolish connections with those two countries or through the

Yamamoto Isoroku

recklessness of its own leaders, Inoue believed that it should at least be prepared to fight the kind of war that its enemies would force upon it.

Up until the summer of 1940, this trio of the most clear-sighted officers in the navy's high command held the line against the expansionist ideas and the Axis sympathies of the navy "hawks." Then, at midyear, the weakening of Britain, the collapse of France and the Netherlands, and the apparent invincibility of German armies combined to undercut the trio's position. Conversely, these developments raised the influence of the militant middle echelon, which advocated the aggressive policies subsequently authorized by the high command. By the autumn of 1940, the navy had finally agreed to support the Tripartite Pact with Germany and Italy and, most importantly, had set its course southward. Having done so, by the navy's own reckoning, a violent collision with the United States could not be long postponed.

Indeed, the navy's *suishi jumbi* (preparatory mobilization) of mid-1940 (see chapter 10) had significantly advanced the navy's war posture. Accounts of the origins of the Pacific War have usually overlooked the importance of this preparatory mobilization. Conventional wisdom has it that the navy began to put itself on a wartime footing only with the imposition of the American oil embargo in the summer of 1941. But the preparatory mobilization makes it clear that the Japanese navy had set itself on a collision course with the United States a whole year before the embargo, since its activation was a giant step toward taking the navy into full-scale hostilities. For that reason, instructions regarding this early mobilization in 1940 and 1941 were held in the tightest secrecy by the navy. The mobilization was also the subject of the most intense consultation and negotiation with the army and the cabinet. It included a major revision, in favor of the navy, of the standing arrangements for the allocation of strategic materials, as well as the requisition and conversion of merchant ships.

Why the navy chose to activate these plans at this time remains unclear. It is probably no coincidence that the plans were activated just when some of the most energetic of the pro-Axis hawks—Admiral Oka and Captain Ishikawa among them—were promoted to important posts in the Navy Ministry. Undoubtedly, a strategic issue was also involved in these initiatives. At a time of spectacular German victories and great changes on the European continent, the mobilizations apparently were part of a navy determination to undertake an exploitation—with force if necessary—of any extraordinary opportunities for Japan in Asia. Eventually the mobilization took on a self-fulfilling quality and itself contributed to the likelihood of war with the Anglo-American naval powers.

Historians have generally seen the Japanese navy as the less culpable of the two services in taking Japan to war. Immediately after the war, many naval officers insisted that the army took the major initiative. Adm. Ōmae Toshikazu, for example, declared that "the navy had no voice in the formulation of national policies; the army had the most influence." Adm. Toyoda Soemu, former commander of the Combined Fleet and chief of the Navy General Staff, agreed that it was the army "which had great political power."[39] These statements, made soon after the Japanese surrender, were self-serving attempts to absolve the navy of responsibility and have contributed to the myth that the navy was a force for moderation and restraint. But it was the navy that insisted on ending the limitation treaties. These treaties provided Japan with a security vis-à-vis the United States that the navy could not provide by its own efforts. Further, it was the bellicose actions of the navy in Shanghai that had provoked a serious incident in 1932 and had brought about full-scale hostilities with China in 1937. Finally, it was navy ambitions toward Southeast Asia in the mid-1930s that begun to reorient Japanese expansionism toward that part of the world. Although the army should bear its share of responsibility, it was the navy that provided the critical impetus toward war in 1941. The navy had an overriding concern for oil and a fear that U.S. naval building would overtake it. Its long tradition of regarding America as its main enemy made war with it seem both natural and inevitable. In this sense, for the Japanese navy, the decision for war was the supreme and tragic example of a self-fulfilling prophecy.

CONVENTIONAL STRATEGY
The Navy's Annual Operational Plans, 1937–41

Ever since World War I, Japanese thought concerning a naval war with the United States had essentially involved a wait-and-react strategy that evolved in three stages: first, searching operations designed to seek out and annihilate the lesser American naval forces permanently stationed in the western Pacific; second, attrition operations against a westward-moving American main battle force coming to assist in the relief or reconquest of American territories there; and third, a decisive encounter in which the American force would be crushed and the Americans forced to negotiate. Although the broad outlines of this strategic scenario remained intact through the 1920s, both the weaponry and the theater of combat had shifted. What had begun as a defense of Japan's home waters conducted purely by surface forces had, by the 1930s, become a reactive strategy involving submarines and aircraft, as well as the battle line. The strategy would culminate in the decisive encounter, which was to be joined in the western Pacific somewhere east of a line between the Bonin and the Mariana Islands.[40]

By the mid-1930s, certain strategic and technological developments changed the pace and timing of Japanese naval planning for a war against the United States. Up to that time, the conquest of the Philippines and Guam had been planned at the opening of hostilities, even before the departure of the U.S. Pacific Fleet from the American west coast. With the end of the treaty era and the lifting of restrictions on American bases in the western Pacific, the navy could no longer assume that those bases would be unfortified. Therefore, the conquest of the Philippines and Guam might have to be delayed until after the destruction of the American battle force. About 1933, the navy had actually begun to consider that in any future Japan-U.S. crisis, the U.S. fleet might cross the Pacific even before the opening of hostilities.[41]

The advent of the land-based bomber had also changed Japanese naval planning against the American enemy. The appearance of the Martin B-10 bomber in the United States forewarned of a potentially augmented American military presence in the Philippines that could thwart Japanese plans. Assuming an American air strength in the Philippines that was not in fact present until the very eve of the Pacific War,[42] the Japanese navy's annual operation plan for 1937 emphasized the early elimination of enemy air power in those islands. The plan began with the initial seizure of the Batan Islands north of Luzon as an advance air base for strikes against American airfields farther south.[43]

But if the possibility of American land-based bombers in the western Pacific threatened to upset Japanese plans for an early and easy occupation of enemy bases there, the advent of the Mitsubishi G3M medium bomber and the big Kawanishi flying boats, as well as the practical end of the nonfortification restrictions in Japan's mandated islands in Micronesia,[44] extended the Japanese navy's offensive power thousands of miles eastward into the Pacific. By 1936, the navy had begun to consider basing a considerable portion of its land-based air power in Micronesia, and toward the end of that year had dispatched a special surface squadron to the islands to make a careful survey of potential air facilities there.[45] Construction of airfields and seaplane ramps, supposedly for commercial aircraft, had begun as early as 1934. In 1937, construction picked up pace in all the Micronesian island groups, but particularly in the atolls of the Marshalls, whose topography and soils easily accommodated such air facilities. By 1940, air base construction in the islands was being accelerated, so that by the summer of 1941 there were eleven naval air bases in Micronesia, equipped with command centers, communications facilities, and ammunition and fuel dumps.[46] The bases lacked, however, real defenses such as hardened facilities, coast artillery, antiaircraft weapons, and offshore mines. There were several reasons for this. The first was the inadequate level of the navy's civil engineering capability, already mentioned. In particular, had the navy possessed earth-moving equipment, the construction of these air facilities would have been much further along than they were when the war began. More important, still, in the years 1937 to 1941, the Japanese navy could not come to a decision whether to fortify the Marshalls—the outer defenses for the Marianas—or to abandon them in order to concentrate on turning the Marianas into a fortress barrier against a westward American naval offensive. Delaying a decision to defend the Marshalls until the eve of the Pacific War, the navy discovered that it then was too late for adequate defenses to be created in either of the two groups. In early 1944, the navy was still feverishly constructing fortifications in the Marshalls when the American amphibious avalanche crashed over them. Six months later, the Marianas had been swept away as well.[47]

In any event, during the late 1930s, Japanese naval planning conceived of these Micronesian air bases as a sort of tripwire behind which counterattacks could be launched against an approaching American fleet. By 1940, the bases' existence and the advantage that they supposedly gave to the Japanese strategic position in the Pacific caused Japanese naval planners to advance the locus of the great fleet encounter. The planned encounter was now moved from a position east of the Marianas to the waters northwest of the Marshalls. Air units based in the islands were seen as actively participating in both the decisive surface engagement and in the annihilating air battle expected to precede it.[48]

Distance and limited Japanese naval air strength, however, posed significant problems both in using the islands for counteroffensives against an approaching enemy and in defending them against enemy attack. Because the island bases were scattered over a distance roughly equal to the span of the American continent, it would be impossible to coordinate simultaneous attacks from all of them against enemy surface units. Rather, successive attacks from selected bases would have to be launched by medium-sized units or smaller, mostly composed of torpedo planes accompanied by high-level bombers (presumably Mitsubishi G3Ms). As the targets would probably be far from the land bases, attacking Japanese aircraft could probably not expect fighter protection.[49] Although the navy planned to garrison the most strategic islands (with *konkyochitai*, or shore-based base units) and to send out regular air patrols from these, the navy never had enough men, planes, or ships to cover every strategic location. As a consequence, Japanese strategy held that when enemy surface forces were reported as approaching any particular island sector, reinforcements would be rushed to that point from the nearest island bases. In case of an attack on the Marshall Islands, which figured most often in these scenarios, reinforcements were supposedly to come from Truk. But what Japanese naval planners tended to overlook was Truk's location, some 900 miles west of the Marshalls. By the time such reinforcements were mobilized, it would probably be too late to try to relieve the Marshalls, since enemy forces would have already occupied bases in the group.[50] This, of course, is exactly what happened to the Japanese position in the Marshalls in early 1944.

Plans for operations against the Royal Navy in East Asian waters remained far less concrete than those against the U.S. Navy. Nevertheless, such operations were an object of study in a number of tabletop war games conducted at the Naval Staff College in 1937, which ended with the "defeat" of British naval forces in the South China Sea. Moreover, the annual operations plan of 1939 specifically referred to the dispatch of Japanese naval units to Malaya and Singapore. As the plan assumed that the Soviet Union would be one of the four countries simultaneously engaged by Japan, it also envisaged dispatch of lesser naval forces to Vladivostok and northern Sakhalin.[51]

Even though its new bases in Micronesia provided the Japanese navy with an advanced position from which to launch a long-range counterattack against a westward thrust of American naval power, in early 1940, Japanese naval strategy still had not changed in its basic concept for a war with the United States. It was, essentially, still a wait-and-react strategy, one which left the time and place for the decisive encounter up to the U.S. Navy.

In that year, however, several developments provoked a sudden shift away from traditional Japanese naval strategy. The first was the new national objective of securing the strategic resources of Southeast Asia, particularly oil. The second was the new window of opportunity to achieve that goal opened by the Allied reverses in western Europe. The third was the emergence of the concentrated carrier fleet as the most powerful offensive force in the navy. The fourth was the growing disparity in the gross naval strength between the two countries, which began to take on critical importance.

In combination, these developments redirected Japanese strategic priorities away from a defensive stance in the western Pacific. The new policy envisaged offensive operations in Southeast Asia that would be jointly conducted with the Japanese army. It also called for offensive operations to strike at the U.S. Fleet before the Americans could interfere with the actual "southward advance" of Japanese military and naval power.[52]

PLANNING THE NAVY'S PROJECTED ROLE IN THE CONQUEST OF SOUTHEAST ASIA, 1940–41

Although the army, rather than the navy, initiated in 1939 a serious study of offensive operations into Southeast Asia, the navy's 1941 annual operational plan, drawn up in 1940, had generally discussed naval operations against Hong Kong, British North Borneo, Malaya, the Philippines, and the Netherlands East Indies.[53] Because of its ambitions in Southeast Asia, the navy had to consider war with four potential enemies when it drafted the 1941 operational plan (the Netherlands was substituted for France as the fourth potential enemy). But since the navy still considered America as its principal threat, to which it devoted the greatest study and planning, operations into Southeast Asia were simply folded into the navy's plans for operations against the United States, which emphasized opening attacks on the Philippines and American possessions in the western Pacific.[54]

Japan's military movement into Southeast Asia in 1940 was similarly orchestrated by the army, which took the leading role in the occupation of Tonkin late that summer. By 1941, however, the navy had begun to exercise its power in French Indochina as well. In January of that year Operation S (a naval demonstration against the French colony by the Second Expeditionary Fleet, employing heavy cruisers, destroyers, and the navy's land-based air units) gave the navy opportunity to survey potential bases in French Indochina, as well as to gather intelligence concerning Malaya and British North Borneo. Then in July 1941, the FU Operation (the joint occupation of Annam, Cochin China, and Cambodia, involving major Japanese naval units), brought Japanese sea power directly into Southeast Asian waters. The resultant crisis in Japan-U.S. relations galvanized the navy into detailed planning for operations in Southeast Asia.[55]

In their plans in the summer of 1941 for operations in Southeast Asia, the army and navy agreed on the overall strategic objective—the acquisition of strategic materials to prepare for a protracted war—but disagreed on the sequence in which the offensive operations were to be carried out. The army held out for attacking Malaya first, then the Netherlands East Indies, and last of all the Philippines. It based its argument on the premise that operations against Malaya would be difficult in any case and that if they were delayed, the British position on the peninsula would become too strong to dislodge. The navy, on the other hand, insisted that the Philippines be attacked first. It reasoned that if Malaya and the East Indies were attacked it would lead to a conflict with the United States in any event. In a conflict with the United States, bypassing the Philippines would become much more difficult, with incalculable consequences for Japanese strategy. Moreover, as the Philippines stood between Japan and the East Indies, American air power in the islands was in a position to threaten Japanese lines of communication between the two regions. This would endanger not only military transport for the invasion of the Indies, which was, after all the great prize, but also the transportation of its treasure house of materials back to Japan.[56]

Ultimately, the two services compromised their differences by agreeing to open the Southeast Asian offensive with simultaneous attacks on Malaya *and* the Philippines. But beyond these objectives, the theater of operations to be covered was so enormous, the attacks to be undertaken from so many directions, and the forces available so relatively modest, that the operations would have to be carried out in three successive stages. The first would move to secure a strategic perimeter: the seizure of American and British possessions in the western Pacific (Guam, Wake Island, and the Gilberts); the occupation of Thailand; and the conquest of northern Malaya, British territories in Borneo, and the Philippines. From that perimeter Japanese forces would drive into southern Malaya, seize Singapore, invade southern Burma, and occupy the northern islands of the East Indies. With those regions in their possession, the Japanese could then occupy Burma and secure the richest prizes of all, Sumatra and Java.[57]

In the projected conquest of Southeast Asia the navy assigned itself two roles: to provide the support forces for the army convoys that would head toward the various area objectives, as specified in joint army-navy invasion plans, and to provide the major share of the air power to be employed in the opening phase of the campaign. Because of the vast size of the theater of operations—approximately 2,000 miles east and west and over 1,000 miles north and south—as well as the relative economy of surface forces planned for the campaign, the navy high command determined that air power would be the vital element in the destruction of the British, Dutch, and American land, sea, and air forces in Southeast Asia. And because the strike against the U.S. Pacific Fleet in Hawaii would use all but one of the navy's fleet carriers, the navy was obliged to rely on land-based air power for the offensive into Southeast Asia. This last offensive would employ the navy's G3M and G4M bomber groups based in Taiwan and southern French Indochina. In particular, these forces would be directed against enemy air forces—British on the Malayan peninsula and American in the Philippines—which flanked and potentially threatened the projected drive toward the Indies.

Another reason has been suggested for the navy's ultimate decision to rely largely on land-based air power in the opening phase of the conquest of Southeast Asia, despite misgivings within the Navy General Staff. The successful example provided by German air operations in Europe in 1940, particularly those in Norway, may well have provided the strategic model for the thrust into Southeast Asia. The significance for naval warfare of Luftwaffe operations in the Norwegian campaign was certainly noted by many officers in the Japanese navy's high command. Many probably took the operations as a confirmation of their own advocacy of land-based air power, and German successes may well have bolstered the navy's confidence in relying upon this type of air power for its "Southern Operations."[58]

By the late summer of 1941, the various pressures pushing Japan toward war made it obvious that the navy must hasten to test its strategic plans for the coming conflict. In September, a series of secret map exercises of increasing importance and intensity were held in Tokyo. The first to focus on the "Southern Operations" was held early in the month under the auspices of the general staff's Operation Section. These were followed a week later by exercises conducted by the Naval Staff College to study the protection of the sea lanes between Japan and Southeast Asia during the invasion. The third and most important exercises were held at the Naval Staff College, 11–17 September, which brought together the ranking members of the Navy General Staff and the principal staff officers and commanders of the Combined Fleet. The exercises focused on the task of seizing control of Southeast Asia while still maintaining control of the western Pacific. This latter problem centered on preventing a westward thrust by American naval forces moving out of Hawaii. The Eleventh Air Fleet held further map exercises at Kanoya Air Base early in October to familiarize all commanders and staff officers of the fleet with the "Southern Operations" plans. Several weeks later, so that all principal commanders and staff thoroughly understood their responsibilities, a final series of exercises was held aboard Yamamoto's flagship, the *Nagato,* anchored in Murozumi Bay, at the western end of the Inland Sea.[59] By mid-October, the Japanese navy had worked out in detail the plans for its role in the conquest of Southeast Asia and the western Pacific.[60]

Because these detailed plans have been delineated so thoroughly elsewhere,[61] the overall scheme will simply be summarized. Attacks would be launched against advanced British and American positions in Asia and the Pacific—Hong Kong, Guam, Wake, and the Gilberts—to assure that there would be no enemy demonstrations in the Japanese rear. The Twenty-third Air Flotilla of the Eleventh Air Fleet, based on Taiwan, would attack and eliminate American offensive air power on Luzon: the bomber bases at Clark and Nichols fields, and the fighter base at Iba, on the coast west of Clark. Elements of the Third Fleet, including the carrier *Ryūjō,* accompanied by destroyers, would move west from Palau to eliminate whatever American air power existed at Davao on Mindanao. The Second Fleet, departing Makung in the Pescadores, and the Southern Expeditionary Fleet, leaving Hainan, would join together to shepherd convoys steaming toward hydraheaded landings along the Thai and Malayan coasts near the isthmus of Kra. Other elements of the Third Fleet would escort military forces landing in Borneo and the Celebes, while the Twenty-second Air Flotilla, consisting of medium bombers operating from bases in southern Indochina, would patrol the Gulf of Thailand, ready to strike at any enemy ships or aircraft threatening the invasions of Malaya or the Philippines. In essence, the scheme was to clear away the enemy outposts, secure the flanks of the Japanese southward thrust—Malaya and the Philippines—and then, using forces that had completed these tasks, to move through Makassar Strait, to concentrate on the central and weakly protected prizes: Java and Sumatra.[62]

This complicated scenario depended on speed, surprise, accurate assessment of enemy strength and capabilities, and near perfect coordination of not only the various phases of the campaign, but also the navy's air and surface units with army air and ground units participating. Maximum speed and maximum success were especially important in the initial air strikes against the Philippines, in order to prevent the United States from moving in reinforcements, particularly air units. Thus, in addition to the medium bomber units it committed to the air offensive, the navy planned to throw in every land-based Zero fighter it possessed in order to achieve complete control of the air at the outset. Surprise, obviously best maintained by the strictest secrecy, would include extraordinary radio discipline and would be aided by the vastness of the campaign theater and the dispersal of forces that Japanese plans dictated.

As discussed in chapter 11, accurate intelligence about Allied strengths and intentions was a hallmark of Japanese planning for the first few months of the war. Indeed, if there was a defect in Japanese intelligence and intelligence analysis concerning the Allied position in Southeast Asia in the last months before the war, it was an overestimation of Allied air strength in Malaya and the Philippines. This led to greater Japanese caution in the first few days of the conflict than the situation warranted. Once Allied air strength in Southeast Asia had been smashed or brushed aside in the initial air attacks, however, Japanese naval aviation in the "Southern Operation" never lost the initiative and suffered remarkably few losses.

Finally, given the appalling disharmony and antagonism that the two services displayed when Japan was thrown on the defensive in the later stages of the Pacific War, the effective coordination of Japanese naval and military planning for the invasion of Southeast Asia is remarkable. In part, Japan's success in this early conflict may be because, once general agreement on the timing of the campaign had been reached, there were no competing strategies and thus no squabbles over scarce military and naval resources. But it may have been partly because of the anomalous role played by the navy. On the one hand, the campaign was initially to be a maritime endeavor, which meant that when it came to the selection of landing sites the navy could often call the shots.[63] On the other, both services clearly understood from the beginning that this was an operation involving the occupation of territory. Thus the navy's roles in the campaign were to be figuratively, if not literally, subordinate: preparing the way for the army landings through air strikes at enemy ground and air units, and convoying army transports to the landing site.

Despite the meticulous planning that the navy brought to its projected operations in Southeast Asia and despite the generally weak position of enemy land, sea, and air forces in the region, the whole enterprise constituted an enormous gamble—a race against time and the ability of Japan's enemies, particularly the United States, to bring superior sea power quickly to bear if the race was lost. From the beginning, in the navy's view, the greatest threat to Japan's southward thrust lay not in the relatively feeble enemy forces it might confront in Southeast Asia, but in a counterthrust by American naval power from the east, across the Pacific. To ward off a counterthrust and to buy time for the venture in Southeast Asia, the Japanese navy ultimately counted on a radical departure from its traditional strategy against its American enemy.

PLANNING THE THUNDERBOLT
The Idea of an Offensive Strike at the U.S. Fleet

By now it should be clear that as late as the beginning of 1941, the Japanese navy planned to use its traditional defensive strategy to fight the U.S. Pacific Fleet. The 1941 annual operational plan still conceived of the Japanese attacks on the Philippines as the lure that would draw the U.S. Pacific Fleet westward. There the fleet would be met in the Marshalls, reduced in size and strength by air and submarine attacks, and then destroyed in midocean by the main force of the Combined Fleet, which would soon include the enormous ordnance of the *Yamato*-class battleships.

By this time, however, criticisms of the navy's traditional strategy against the United States had been guardedly expressed by a few upper-echelon officers including Yamamoto Isoroku, Ozawa Jisaburō, and Ōnishi Takijirō. Essentially, the men had three criticisms: First, the traditional wait-and-react strategy left the initiative in the hands of the U.S. Navy as to where and when to join battle. Some actually questioned whether the U.S. Pacific Fleet would willingly play into Japanese hands and push blindly across the Pacific like a bloodhound on the trail of its quarry. Perhaps the Americans would never steam directly into the western Pacific at all. Indeed, from what little had been learned about the American "Orange" and "Rainbow" plans, there was every reason to believe that the U.S. Navy was more likely to attempt a slow advance through Micronesia, beginning with the Marshalls. Second, the prime element of offensive sea power was no longer the battle fleet with its plodding speed and the limited range of its big guns, but rather naval aviation, which could project its firepower with great speed and range. For that reason, it was increasingly unlikely that the long-antic-ipated confrontation between the Japanese and American battle lines would take place. Finally, in view of all these assumptions, the true confrontation between the Japanese and American navies would not be a gun duel in deep water, but rather a ferocious struggle over the air bases and other facilities that the Japanese were constructing in Micronesia.[64]

It therefore seemed both unnecessary and unwise for the Japanese navy to sit on its haunches waiting for the enemy to attack. The few navies fortunate enough to have carrier aviation capabilities could now plan a preemptive strike against the enemy deep in his own waters. By 1941, the Japanese navy had that capability, and the only question was where and how to use it. To Yamamoto Isoroku, the most valuable objective of such a strike would be the U.S. Pacific Fleet at any of its anchorages in Hawaii.

The conceptual origins of the preemptive aerial strike against the U.S. Pacific Fleet at Pearl Harbor—when and how it was conceived, how it evolved, and along what lines—are not entirely clear to this day. Yamamoto Isoroku is usually iden-tified as the creator of the concept. Hard evidence suggests, however, that before Yamamoto proposed it early in 1941, the idea had been propounded in varying degrees of detail and similarity to the actual attack.

At least some of these conceptual precedents may have stimulated Admiral Yamamoto's thinking on the subject. At furthest remove are the civilian writings of the 1920s and 1930s—Japanese, American, and British—on the possible course of a Japan-U.S. war in the Pacific. Some of this speculation was informed, some of it merely sensational. But references to a Japanese attack on Hawaii were so generalized and so diverse in assumed conditions and outcomes that their existence demonstrates only that such vague ideas were floating about in public during these decades. They do not appear to provide any consistent scheme that would convincingly suggest their impact on Japanese naval plans.[65] Much the same can be said of extravagant claims about the supposed impact of the writings of the noted British journalist Hector Bywater on the planning for a Pacific war by the Japanese navy in general and by Yamamoto Isoroku in particular.[66]

The Japanese navy may have learned of some of the exercises and maneuvers of the U.S. Navy in the 1920s and 1930s that included simulated attacks on Pearl Harbor as part of their training agenda. Two of these war games are worthy of note: the successful attack on army air bases and facilities at Pearl Harbor thirty minutes before sunrise by 152 aircraft from the carriers *Lexington* and *Saratoga* under command of Adm. Harry Yarnell in February 1932, and a similar attack on army and navy facilities near Pearl Harbor and Lahaina Roads by aircraft from *Saratoga* in March 1938.[67] Naturally, Japanese naval officers were not observers at these exercises, nor were they privy to the classified reports that assessed their results.[68] Of course, the Japanese navy may have gleaned some relevant information from radio intercepts during these exercises, but this must have been of the haziest sort.

Whatever his part in conceiving the Pearl Harbor operation, a Japanese officer like Yamamoto was probably more influenced by studies undertaken by fellow professionals in his own navy than by any other source. The general idea of an attack on Pearl Harbor was apparently circulating around the high command for some years, but it is not clear whether the idea included the use of air power. In any event, nothing seems to have come of it.[69] Nevertheless, by 1941, several existing studies did indeed specifically include the use of aircraft to attack American fleet units at Pearl Harbor.

The first of these studies was a series of tabletop war games included as part of the graduation exercises at the Naval Staff College in the autumn of 1927. In one, a Japanese "Blue" fleet, commanded by Lt. Comdr. Takagi Sōkichi and centered on two carriers, accompanied by destroyers, cruisers, and an advance guard of submarines, simulated an attack on Pearl Harbor and U.S. fleet units there, represented by a "Red" Fleet under the command of Lt. Comdr. Kaku Tomeo. Although all the aircraft of both carriers were thrown into the attack, the game's umpires judged that the damage inflicted on the port facilities and the ships in harbor was minimal and that for its pains, the Blue Fleet had suffered the loss of one of its carriers. In the judgment of the umpires and his fellow staff college students after the conclusion of the game, Takagi had been "rash" in launching the attack. In a subsequent exercise, Commander Kaku simulated a successful attack on

Tokyo by his Red Fleet, centered on two carriers. Despite diligent reconnaissance efforts by Blue, Red was judged to have escaped undamaged.[70]

The idea of an air attack on Hawaii as part of a scheme to lure an American fleet out of harbor also evidently cropped up in a lecture delivered in November 1927 by Lt. Comdr. Kusaka Ryūnosuke to senior naval officers gathered at Kasumigaura Naval Air Base. Delivered as part of a pitch to a group of influential commanders and staff officers for greater resources to be devoted to naval aviation, Kusaka's concept involved using a series of air attacks on Hawaii to provoke the U.S. Battle Fleet to come out from San Diego and, supposedly, to cross the Pacific, where it could be destroyed according to orthodox Japanese strategy.[71]

Perhaps the most prescient and specific discussion of the preemptive strike concept, however, was provided in the study undertaken at the Naval Staff College in November 1936. The results of that research, entitled *Tai-Beikoku sakusen yōhei ni kansuru kenkyū* (A study concerning the deployment of forces against the United States) were apparently the product of collaboration of several instructors at the college, one of whom may have been Commander Kaku. The study's most important point concerning Pearl Harbor was that hostilities with the United States should open with an air attack on Pearl Harbor as well as on the Philippines: "In the event that the enemy's main fleet units, particularly his carriers, are at anchor at Pearl Harbor prior to hostilities, sudden and unexpected attacks should be launched on those forces by carrier aircraft and flying boats, similar attacks being launched simultaneously against the Philippines."[72]

Several other Japanese naval officers had tested, written about, or spoken about the concept by the time it was taken up by Yamamoto Isoroku, commander of the Combined Fleet. It is logical to assume that over time, Yamamoto became conversant with their assessments. But if Yamamoto did not originate the concept of a preemptive carrier strike on the U.S. Pacific Fleet at Pearl Harbor, it took someone in the Japanese naval high command with his position, stature, and heretical outlook to make the argument at the highest levels and then push it through to activation over the strenuous opposition of much of the Navy General Staff.

In the view of the officers serving on Yamamoto's staff while he was commander of the Combined Fleet, it was the results of the fleet's naval air training in 1939–40 that provided the immediate stimulus for the formation of Yamamoto's Pearl Harbor plan.[73] Because of Yamamoto's efforts, the fleet had begun to emphasize air power in its annual training and maneuvers and had commenced training that brought together the various air units of the fleet. Of special interest was a simulated raid by carrier-based torpedo planes against warships in harbor and at anchor. Though there was much disagreement on the results of this particular exercise, Yamamoto evidently was persuaded that such an attack, if coupled with surprise, would be a success.[74] By the end of the maneuvers in the spring of

1940 Yamamoto had realized that the range and firepower of Japanese naval aviation could make possible a telling first blow against the American enemy, even in his home waters.[75]

Probably about this time, too, his ideas may have been furthered by a memorandum from his senior staff officer, Capt. Kuroshima Kameto, on the possible opening moves of a Japan-U.S. war. Though making no reference to Hawaii, Kuroshima proposed a long-range surprise attack by carriers against the enemy's battle force, as well as the deployment of the major portion of the navy's land-based air power on Japan's island bases in Micronesia. These, Kuroshima believed, would be the most likely focus for the war's decisive combat.[76]

In reflecting upon the evolution of the preemptive strike concept, however, it is also important to understand its rationale in Yamamoto's thinking. Abundant evidence suggests, of course, that Yamamoto was fundamentally opposed to a war with the United States and Britain.[77] Yet, as commander of the Combined Fleet, he had a keen sense of responsibility that he must have at hand the most effective means for victory if war came. In Yamamoto's view, the navy's current strategic orthodoxy—the wait-and-react strategy—repeated in the 1941 annual plan, was a recipe for ultimate defeat. Unable to bring the U.S. Navy to battle on Japanese terms, the Combined Fleet would simply be worn down in a long war in which the United States could eventually bring its vastly superior industrial might—and thus overwhelmingly superior naval strength—to bear. But what concrete alternatives were there? Air power suggested a solution, but the Japanese navy had too little of it. This being the case, how best to use air power most effectively? The advance of the U.S. Pacific Fleet from San Diego to Pearl Harbor in May 1940 probably furthered the preemptive strike idea in Yamamoto's thinking. As late as late October of that year, however, he still apparently considered the idea too dangerous. Perhaps the remarkable success of the British torpedo bombing attack on Italian ships at anchor at Taranto convinced him that the potential gain was worth the risk.[78] In any event, sometime in November, judging from his communications to a few trusted colleagues, he concluded that a preemptive aerial attack on the Pacific Fleet at its Pearl Harbor base offered the Japanese navy its best chance in a war against great odds.[79]

On 7 January 1941, Yamamoto committed his ideas to paper in his memorandum to Navy Minister Oikawa Koshirō blandly entitled *Gumbi ni kansuru shiken* (Views on military preparations).[80] Its first major point was that the navy needed to greatly expand its air forces. Second, he noted, while fleet training had been based on the wait-and-react strategy leading up to the classic gun battle, in past war games and maneuvers, the navy never did succeed in winning such an encounter. Usually, the exercises were called off before umpires deemed the navy's strength exhausted. Moreover, Yamamoto argued, the power of aircraft and submarines made it unlikely that the decisive gun battle would ever take place. Hence, the navy needed to give its commanders better training in small-unit tactics for the numerous smaller engagements that would most likely occur.[81]

Most of all, in Yamamoto's view, it was essential to change the navy's basic strategy. As a quantitatively inferior naval power, Japan's best hope lay in a qualitatively superior strategy: a violent and crippling first blow at America's main battle force in the first few hours of the war. Time, distance, and geography dictated that this could best be accomplished by an air attack by several carrier divisions on the U.S. Pacific Fleet at Pearl Harbor.

As Yamamoto saw it, the destruction of the main American battle force at the outset of the war could accomplish two objectives: first, it could break American morale—both that of the public in the continental United States and that of the American armed forces in the western Pacific—and second, it could greatly improve Japan's chances in a prolonged war with the United States. In Yamamoto's view, there were several reasons why the latter objective was essential. To begin with, prevention of the enemy's main offensive force from entering the western Pacific for six months to a year would mean that the operations for the conquest of Southeast Asia by Japanese armed forces, and thus Japan's acquisition of the great resources of the area, could proceed as planned, without interruption. With control of these strategic resources consolidated in its hands, Japan would have far less to fear from the industrial might of the United States during a long war. Secondly, destruction of the U.S. Pacific Fleet would mean that the Japanese home islands themselves would be secure from enemy attack.

To drive home his point, Yamamoto described the consequences of a strategy that allowed the American navy to run loose in the western Pacific after the outbreak of hostilities. The threat to the flank of the Japanese invasion of Southeast Asia could prove disastrous. He noted, too, that the diversion of major Japanese naval forces to thwart a westward-moving American fleet could badly upset the carefully worked-out timetable for the conquest of Southeast Asia. Then there was the question of the damage that an American carrier force could wreak upon the Japanese home islands. Here Yamamoto summoned forth the memory of Japanese public terror at the threat of raids on Japanese coasts by the Vladivostok Squadron during the Russo-Japanese War. He recalled the outrage of Japanese civilians at the inability of the navy to bring that squadron to heel. A reading of Yamamoto's Pearl Harbor proposal makes it clear that he believed public morale in both countries would be extremely vulnerable to assaults from the air, a not uncommon assumption among air-power advocates prior to World War II.

Yamamoto did not downplay the enormous risks involved in the operation. While he had complete confidence in the technical and combat skills of the navy's carrier forces to execute it, the enormous distance involved—far greater than any operation in the navy's history—and the great risks of discovery made it a dangerous proposition. The plans for Tōgō's surprise attack on Russian naval forces at Port Arthur were far less complicated, far less taxing, and far less hazardous, and yet their objectives were met only incompletely. It was why, originally, Yamamoto wished to lead the Pearl Harbor strike force himself.[82]

The evolution of the Pearl Harbor plans from this initial proposal by Yamamoto—the personalities involved, the myriad tactical, logistical, and technical challenges the venture presented, the intense training it required, particularly among the navy's air units, the furious debates the operation provoked among the top brass, and the relation of the progress of preparations to the pace and direction of Japan's diplomatic negotiations with the United States—has been dealt with extensively elsewhere, most comprehensively and authoritatively in Gordon Prange's *At Dawn We Slept*.[83] Because of Prange's exhaustive coverage of the topic, only some of the critical issues raised by Pearl Harbor will be highlighted here.

While Yamamoto, in the early spring of 1941, instructed the Combined Fleet staff to study his plan and, in revising it, to work out its details and solve its difficulties, he himself sought to move the plan into command channels where it could be designated as the subject of priority study by the Navy General Staff. In moving from concept to realization, Yamamoto's plan was greatly advanced with the formation, in April 1941, of the First Air Fleet, the powerful naval and air force that now could be made available to the Hawaii operation. But while the impending strike's technical and tactical problems were being intensively studied and rigorous preliminary training begun during the spring and summer of 1941, major resistance to the plan built up. Opposition arose particularly in the general staff, though both the First Air Fleet commander, Nagumo Chūichi, and the Air Fleet's chief of staff, Kusaka Ryūnosuke, also had major reservations.

Since the beginning of the year, the general staff had been proceeding with its planning for a war with the United States on the basis of the 1941 annual operational plan. This in turn was predicated upon the wait-and-react strategy and governed largely by the priorities of the "southern operations" to secure Southeast Asia and its resources for Japan. In the heated arguments during the summer of 1941 between the general staff and Yamamoto's Combined Fleet staff over the wisdom and propriety of the Hawaii operation, the chief of the staff's Operation Section, Capt. Tomioka Sadatoshi, provided an extensive list of objections to the Hawaii plan. In sum, he argued that the Japanese navy could not afford to wager its carefully built up naval air strength in such a desperately risky venture, particularly in view of the fact that it would be needed in other major operations. More than anything else, Tomioka feared that the diversion of surface and air strength to the Hawaii attack would critically undermine the "southern operations" and hence, the major objectives of the coming war. Even if the navy was willing to undertake such an enormous gamble, in Tomioka's view, the Pearl Harbor strike was not really necessary. Of course, there was the danger that the U.S. Pacific Fleet might try to hit the "southern operations" in the flank, but Tomioka argued that the enemy would far more likely launch an attack on the Marshall Islands. That would be all to the good, since the navy had great confidence that it could intercept the enemy there and launch a smashing counterattack.[84]

The bitter controversy between the general staff and Combined Fleet staff was not resolved during the summer of 1941, even as training and preparations for the Pearl Harbor operation continued. Nor was it resolved during the September map exercises at the staff college or in October aboard the *Nagato,* during which the discussions and exercises relating to the Hawaii operation were held separately and accessible only to those few naval officers who would be involved in carrying it out. Of all the points of contention, the sharpest concerned the number of aircraft carriers to be used in the attack. Yamamoto had originally proposed four; the September map exercises simulated an attack with three, which the umpires judged to have achieved only marginal results. But those on the general staff working out the details for the invasion of Southeast Asia insisted on reserving some carriers for the "southern operations," since the navy's land-based air power, specifically its fighters, did not have the range to reach the necessary targets and return.[85]

Then, in early October, the Navy General Staff was brought around to Yamamoto's idea. There were several reasons for this volte-face, some operational, some bureaucratic.[86] To begin with, the compromise between the army and navy on nearly simultaneous attacks on the Philippines and Malaya eased navy planning considerably. The availability of the splendid new carriers *Shōkaku* and *Zuikaku* in late September permitted two other carriers to be released for the "southern operations" and thus eliminated one of the general staff's key objections to the Yamamoto plan. Finally, Yamamoto had taken care to pass the word quietly to the high command that rejection of the Pearl Harbor plan would result in his resignation. Keenly aware of Yamamoto's popularity and prestige within both the navy and the government and faced with the prospect of disharmony, the general staff gave in. Later in the month, however, a new storm of controversy broke when Yamamoto insisted that the Hawaii operation employ all Japan's fleet carriers then in commission. He based his views on the map exercises aboard the *Nagato,* which used six carriers; the results with six carriers were judged far more impressive than with only four carriers. Opposition from the general staff might have derailed the Pearl Harbor strike once and for all, had it not been for the timely success of tests in the Eleventh Air Fleet, which demonstrated that engine adjustments to the Zero fighters based on Taiwan made them operational for flights to the Philippines and return.[87] Now that the task forces involved in the "southern operations" would be supplied with adequate air cover, the last barrier to the Yamamoto plan came down.

On 5 November, the Combined Fleet's Operations Order No. 1 secretly briefed senior officers on the impending war plans, including the cryptic statement, "To the east, the American fleet will be destroyed...."[88] Vice Admiral Nagumo, commander of the First Air Fleet and overall commander of the Pearl Harbor strike force, received his final instructions six days later. On 22 November the strike force began to assemble in its cold and lonely rendezvous, Hitokappu Bay in the Kurile Islands: six carriers, two battleships, two heavy cruisers, one light cruiser, nine destroyers, three submarines, and eight tankers and supply ships. Four days later, in heavy fog, the advance elements of the strike force, including the carriers, departed Hitokappu and sailed into history.

THE JAPANESE NAVY ON THE EVE OF THE PACIFIC WAR

Thus, for nearly two weeks, 26 November to 7 December, Japanese fleets were silently on the move: eastward across the north Pacific toward Hawaii; southward through the South China Sea toward Thailand, Malaya, British North Borneo, and the Philippines; westward from Palau toward Mindanao; and northward from Truk and the Marianas toward Guam and Wake. Hours before the opening of hostilities, Japanese naval aircraft—fighters as well as attack aircraft—were winging their way to targets in nearly all these areas. In all the history of warfare there had been no operations planned to cover so vast an area in so short a time. Few were as complicated in the interdependence of their various elements, and few depended so critically on surprise, precise timing, and a generous portion of luck.

It is a tribute to Japanese planning, intelligence assessments, operational skill—and luck—that for the most part, these operations were indeed successful, to a degree and with a rapidity that astonished the Japanese themselves. To carry out the lightning strategies just described, Japan had assembled naval forces of great power, ideally suited to the tasks which they were assigned. Furthermore, in the formation of the First Air Fleet, which in its essential elements became the Pearl Harbor Strike Force, the navy had put together a tactical organization of revolutionary capability. In its destruction of the American battle line at Pearl Harbor, Japanese naval aviation changed the course of naval warfare in general and the doctrinal priorities of the U.S. Navy in particular.

Yet for all the bold innovation in doctrinal and organizational concept provided by the First Air Fleet and by the plans for the Hawaii operation, the doctrine and force structure of the Japanese navy at the time of Pearl Harbor—and, for a time, afterward—were still shaped by assumptions held for the past two decades concerning the nature of a war in the Pacific between Japan and the United States. First among these was the belief that Japan should aim for a war of rapid offensives and lightning victories, which at the very least would force the United States to enter into a negotiated peace on Japan's terms. The second assumption was that the function of a navy was to obtain command of the seas, a strategic position essential to the survival and, beyond that, the prosperity of an island nation like Japan. For Japan, this meant command of the western and central Pacific. Third, the mainstream leadership—that is, the Navy General Staff—assumed that control of the seas could only be assured once the enemy's main threat to that control, his battle fleet, was decisively defeated. Fourth, the enemy should be confronted with a battle force that, if not his equal in numbers, was his superior in the firepower and armor of its capital ships, in the training of its officers and men, and in the ability to outrange him through multiple tactics and technologies possessed not only by the battle force but by its supporting elements, specifically including carrier aviation. Fifth, and last, the victory in decisive surface battle achieved by such naval power would guarantee the security of the homeland and enhance the prospects of a negotiated peace by which Japan might acquire the strategic territories and resources deemed essential to the nation's survival and prosperity.

That the Japanese navy remained wedded to these assumptions as late as December 1941 can be seen in both its construction plans and its continuing conviction as to the nature and primacy of the decisive battle. As described in chapter 10, the superbattleship *Yamato* was commissioned within days of the outbreak of the war, the *Musashi* was nearing completion, a sister ship was on the ways (though later completed as a carrier), and still more were planned. Devotion of major resources to battleship construction during World War II was not unique to Japan, of course. The British and American navies did so as well, but with less conviction that the apotheosis of naval combat was the all-decisive encounter between battle lines.

The Japanese navy remained wedded to the concept of defensive strategy and the decisive battle for several reasons. The first was that the Navy General Staff had too long concentrated on its conventional strategy for a Japan-U.S. war to adjust itself completely to the new concept involved in Yamamoto's plan. The second was considerably more substantial. In the autumn of 1941, the high command probably had a reasonably accurate assessment of American naval strength. It knew that the ships and aircraft of the U.S. Pacific Fleet stationed at Hawaii represented only a portion—though a major portion—of the entire strength of the U.S. Navy. In the Atlantic, on the American west coast, and at other duty stations, the United States possessed 9 more battleships, 4 carriers, 29 cruisers, 145 destroyers, and 108 submarines, not to mention the warships in all these categories nearing

Map conference of the Navy General Staff, 1942

completion or on the ways (of which the Japanese navy undoubtedly had a fair estimate). Hence, the Japanese high command was forced to recognize that even if Nagumo's strike force destroyed every single American warship normally stationed at Hawaii, much of the rest of the U.S. Navy would still remain afloat. Indeed, even if the *entire* Pacific Fleet could theoretically be destroyed at anchor, the loss would still amount to less than half the total of the American fleet.

For this reason, although the Japanese navy's plans to open the war, particularly its Pearl Harbor scheme, represented an enormous gamble, the navy was also apparently hedging its bets.[89] That is to say, the Navy General Staff was now prepared to risk the Hawaii operation, calculating that it would achieve the stunning successes that Yamamoto hoped for it: the guarantee of a free Japanese hand in Southeast Asia and such loss of American will as would lead to a negotiated peace. On the other hand, the staff also had to recognize that the United States might continue the war, bringing to bear in an extended conflict not only its remaining ships—operational and building—but also its great industrial capacity. In that case, the Japanese navy would have to rely on its conventional strategy, drawing a reconstituted U.S. Pacific Fleet westward toward the bulk of the navy's battle force, which could counterattack and annihilate the enemy according to the tactical principles so long studied and practiced. The authorization for the preemptive strike on Pearl Harbor did not end the Japanese navy's predilection for its conventional wait-and-react strategy, as exemplified by several statements embedded in a grand strategic plan approved—apparently by chief of the general staff, Adm. Nagano Osami—in the Imperial Liaison Conference of 15 November 1941, *three weeks before the Pearl Harbor attack*. In discussing the various means for Japan to bring the war to a victorious conclusion, the plan asserted that "at the appropriate time, we will endeavor by various means to lure the main fleet of the United States [near Japan] and destroy it," and later, that "emphasis will be placed on enticing the American main fleet to come to the Far East. . . ."[90] Whether Yamamoto ever saw the draft plan is not clear; what is apparent is that the navy believed that a U.S. Pacific Fleet, reconstituted at some point after Pearl Harbor, could pose a threat to the perimeter of Japan's projected conquests and that the navy's conventional strategy would be the best way to defeat it.

RETHINKING THE NAVY'S WAR PREPARATIONS
The Radical Views of Inoue Shigeyoshi

In 1941, however, a force structure that still gave primacy to the battleship and a strategy that relied on luring the enemy into fighting a decisive battle line engagement on sharply disadvantageous terms represented thinking that was at once fanciful and outmoded. One flag officer who had seen this clearly was Vice Adm. Inoue Shigeyoshi, chief of the ministry's Naval Aviation Department and one of the trio of increasingly isolated moderates in the high command discussed earlier in this chapter. In January 1941, about the same time that Admiral Yamamoto was penning his thoughts on a radically different strategy for war with the United States, Inoue had attended the staff-ministry consultations to revise the Circle Five plan. Listening to staff representatives insist on the construction of still more *Yamato*-class battleships, Inoue exploded with exasperation at what he considered the staff's outmoded and unimaginative assumptions in making such a proposal. Attacking the plan as a preparation for past, not future, conflicts, Inoue pointed out that rather than providing a rationale for naval construction based on a careful analysis of the kind of war that Japan would have to wage and the kind of weapons necessary to win it, the plan simply constituted a blind, unthinking response to American building programs. Inoue's outburst stunned his colleagues; so flummoxed were they by his denunciation of their schemes that the meeting broke up without further discussion of the plan or of Inoue's scathing critique of it. Several weeks later Inoue, demonstrating that he was not merely a destructive critic, submitted a lengthy memorandum to the Navy Ministry outlining his own alternative scheme for a naval armament program that would give Japan a greater chance for victory in a war with the United States.[91]

The dry title of Inoue's memorandum, *Shin gumbi keikaku ron* (On modern weapons procurement planning) belied the radical nature of its recommendations, for it comprised not merely a proposed schedule of warship construction, but rather a comprehensive attack on the basic assumptions behind the high command's current construction programs and an urgent call for drastic revision of the navy's priorities.[92]

Inoue began by pointing out several stark facts. To begin with, it was impossible for Japan to bring about the total defeat of the United States, because it was obviously beyond Japan's means to capture America's capital, occupy its vast territory, or destroy all its operational forces. Nor could the United States, because of its two enormous coastlines—one unreachable by Japanese forces—and its essential self-sufficiency in most strategic resources, be brought to its knees by blockade. While there was no way for Japan to bring about the complete collapse of American resistance, conversely, it was technically feasible for the United States to bring about the total ruination of Japan: to defeat all its forces, to blockade its home islands—starving the country of all strategic resources—and to seize its capital and occupy all its territory. What Inoue was arguing, one postwar commentator has written, was that a future Japan-U.S. conflict was effectively a chess game in which the United States could checkmate Japan, but Japan could not do the same to the United States.[93]

Inoue Shigeyoshi

Inoue went on to say that a Japan-U.S. naval war would likely be a protracted conflict, not the lightning war that Japan's naval strategists had long studied. Implied in his argument was the idea that in such a extended struggle, the United States must inevitably bring to bear its tremendous industrial might, which Japan could not hope to match. But Inoue was less interested in underscoring the dire consequences of such a turn of events, which he believed were understood by the naval high command. Rather, he was determined to illuminate the reasons why Japan could not count on a quick decision. First, he pointed out, command of the sea was no longer an absolute matter. Although Japan could "secure" the western Pacific at the outset of the war by capturing all American territories in it, including the Philippines, with the maturation of aircraft and submarine technology, command of the sea was no longer one-dimensional, but three-dimensional. Thus command of the sea probably could no longer be achieved by surface battle alone. Indeed, in Inoue's view, the "decisive" surface battle would probably never take place. The development of aircraft and submarine striking power within the last few years had made it probable that a significant number of capital ships on both sides would be destroyed before they could engage each other.

This being the case, Japan should gain control of the air over the western Pacific as a prerequisite to controlling the sea. Here Inoue argued that even the context of command of the air had changed in recent years. Whereas aircraft carriers had until recently been considered the prime element of naval air power, with the rapid development of land-based bombers and flying boats, these latter types of aircraft had become the most potent air weapons. Thus, in Inoue's view, control of the air could be obtained without any surface units (specifically including carriers) and by aircraft alone. Indeed, it was time to think of control of the air by an air force independent of naval ships!

Given the advent of the long-range submarine, even control of the air would be insufficient to provide total control of the sea. Inoue noted that in the Russo-Japanese and China Wars, the Japanese navy had no experience in fighting an enemy with a powerful submarine force. But in a naval war with the United States, Japan could expect that numerous American submarines, in cooperation with aircraft, would deploy across Japan's vital sea lanes, blockading the home islands and tenaciously destroying its maritime commerce in the western Pacific and along the Asian littoral.[94] In Inoue's opinion, Japan's ability to carry on the war, indeed its very survival, would depend upon its ability to protect its ocean transport from American submarine and air attacks, and the campaign to do so would be one of the most critical of the entire conflict. To have any hope in winning such a struggle, the navy would have to construct many convoy escorts and organize powerful mobile task forces, employing surface, air, and submarine elements.

Returning to his earlier theme, Inoue wrote that a decisive fleet engagement involving battleships would be unlikely unless the U.S. fleet commander was ignorant or foolhardy. The United States would far more likely attempt the strategy of the gradual strangulation of Japan, beginning with the successive seizures of Japanese advanced island bases in Micronesia, the Philippines, Taiwan, and the north Pacific. The struggle to prevent this, as well as to take or retake American bases, would be one of the focal points of the war, one that along with the defense of Japan's sea lanes would determine the fate of the nation. Hence, in Inoue's view, landing operations were far more important than the so-called decisive battle, and Japan should begin now to strengthen its amphibious warfare capabilities by emphasizing construction of suitable ships and the organization of appropriate units to perfect its amphibious assault capabilities for capturing enemy island bases.

With the twenty-twenty hindsight of the armchair strategist in the 1990s, one can cavil at Inoue's diagnosis of and prescriptions for the Japanese navy's doctrinal ills. He was obviously wrong, for example, about land-based aircraft superseding aircraft carriers. Yet, obviously, also with the advantage of hindsight, it is clear that Inoue was far more right about the nature of the coming naval war in the Pacific than he was wrong. Certainly, his critique was a much more accurate assessment of its realities than any of the thinking in the Japanese naval high command up to that point. Ultimately, what marks Inoue as a clairvoyant of sorts is that he saw the war not in tactical, but in strategic terms. No single battle, no single weapon, would determine the outcome, but rather an array of balanced forces operating and cooperating in all three dimensions of naval war—air, surface, and subsurface. Even then, he saw, the struggle would be long and desperate and, for Japan, at great odds.

14

EPILOGUE

Reflections on the Japanese Navy in Triumph and Defeat

The focus of this book has been the evolution of the technology, strategy, and tactics of the Imperial Japanese Navy from its emergence as a modern force in the late nineteenth century up to the opening of the Pacific War. For over three decades of that period—from the end of the Russo-Japanese War up to the Pearl Harbor strike—the Japanese navy planned, trained, and armed itself for combat with a single opponent, the U.S. Navy. In assessing Japanese naval preparations during those years, one should survey, if only briefly, the navy's performance in combat against its American enemy during the Pacific War.

For the first two years of the war, the Japanese navy fought—often with great success—using the tactics and the technologies that it had perfected during the interwar period. From early 1944 on, however, it suffered nothing but calamities in the face of the U.S. buildup of forces and the U.S. Navy's extraordinary technological advances in naval warfare. From that time forward, increasingly, the Japanese navy waged a war of desperation. It largely abandoned prewar tactical and strategic thinking, thus placing the 1944–45 phase of the war outside the scope of this book. Included here is thus a summary of Japanese naval strategy from December 1941 to the end of 1943.[1]

THE JAPANESE NAVY IN THE PACIFIC WAR, 1941–43
A Strategic Overview

In considering the merits of the Pearl Harbor attack one must distinguish between those strategic objectives that the navy held at the time and the strategic consequences of the operation that seem clear to the historian writing more than a half century later. Yamamoto Isoroku, the principal architect of the Pearl Harbor plan, never regarded it as the central operation of the opening of the Pacific War. For Yamamoto, as for the rest of the Japanese high command, the attack on the U.S. Pacific Fleet at Hawaii was a secondary operation whose purpose was to ensure the security of the main Japanese objective: Southeast Asia.

Superficially, the attack can be considered a thorough strategic and resounding tactical success. The battle line of the U.S. Pacific Fleet went to the bottom of Pearl Harbor, the multiple operations to conquer Southeast Asia could proceed without interference, and the U.S. Navy was unable to launch a major trans-Pacific counteroffensive for two years. All this at the cost of just twenty-nine aircraft and five midget submarines.[2] The Japanese had accomplished their primary tactical goal, the destruction of American fleet units. This perspective helps explain why the Japanese failed to plan for, or to carry out, the destruction of certain vital installations ashore at Pearl Harbor, particularly the oil storage tanks and the submarine base. These omissions were viewed as major blunders by American strategists at the time and by historians since.

With twenty-twenty hindsight, however, one can question whether the logic behind the attack was indeed sound. Even had the Hawaii operation not been undertaken and the U.S. Pacific Fleet remained undamaged, the Americans probably could not have prevented or slowed the lightning progress of Japanese operations in Southeast Asia. As Samuel E. Morison pointed out after the war, had Japan restricted its assault on American Pacific territories to an attack on the Philippines, "the Battle Fleet (according to the Rainbow-5 plan) would have gone lumbering across the Pacific, very likely to be sunk in deep water by Japanese bombers based on the Marshall Islands."[3] Without air protection, such as American carriers could theoretically provide, a battleship force entering Southeast Asian waters would have risked disaster, as the sinking of the *Repulse* and the *Prince of Wales* would demonstrate. But the American carrier force in the Pacific was seriously deficient in the opening days of the Pacific War. The fighter group of the *Lexington* was equipped with obsolescent Brewster Buffalo fighters, the *Enterprise* with ancient Douglas Devastator torpedo bombers, and the torpedo squadrons of both carriers were trained in out-of-date tactics. Against the greater numbers, superior aircraft, and combat readiness of the Japanese carrier forces, their prospects could not have been promising.

Finally, although the United States could not mount a major trans-Pacific counteroffensive until 1943, this undoubtedly had little to do with the battle damage suffered by the U.S. Navy and much to do with the time and organization necessary to mobilize American industrial might and logistic capabilities for such a vast undertaking. Many months and much effort were necessary to build up the slender American fleet train and acquire enough landing craft, in particular. All in all, these points would seem to argue that Admiral Yamamoto would have done better if he had scrapped his Pearl Harbor plan and reverted to the Japanese navy's traditional wait-and-react strategy against a westward-moving American fleet. Certainly such a strategy would have avoided the tidal wave of American public anger at the timing and nature of the actual attack.

Against this last objection, a postwar Japanese analysis has put the navy's reasoning this way: As a major military and industrial power Japan needed oil; because of the cutoff of American supplies, the only realistic source of oil was the Netherlands East Indies; to move into the East Indies, Japan had to clear both sides of its invasion route, which meant operations against Malaya and the Philippines; to avoid being strategically flanked by the United States—with whom war was inevitable (once the Philippines was attacked)—the U.S. Pacific Fleet had to be knocked out of the war. Viewed strictly in light of these priorities, the possible outrage in American public opinion simply could not be a vital consideration.[4] This reasoning clearly illuminates, however, the narrow focus of Japanese naval thinking and the failure of the Japanese naval high command to think in grand strategic, not just purely strategic, terms.

In the first five months of the war, except for a brief but destructive foray by Admiral Nagumo's task force into the Indian Ocean in April 1942, the Japanese navy essentially limited itself to the strategic goals set forth in its immediate prewar planning. Shortly after the Pearl Harbor operation, serious thought was given to a joint assault on, and occupation of, Hawaii, but interservice wrangling and the issue of shipping aborted the project. Out of the ashes of those plans, the later Midway operation was born.[5] For its part, the conquest of Southeast Asia, the first phase of the Japanese strategy for the Pacific War, was accomplished with a speed that surprised even the Japanese themselves. During this conquest the Japanese navy brushed aside those weak and isolated Allied naval units that were thrown against them.

After its strategic successes in Southeast Asia, the navy turned, for the balance of 1942, to the second phase of its plans: the elimination or neutralization of those strategic points from which the Allies could launch counteroffensives against the periphery of the Japanese conquests. Here, for the first time, the Japanese navy met with serious reverses, first at the Coral Sea, when Japan was forced to abandon its effort to isolate Australia (though tactically, the battle was a draw). The next reverse came at Midway, when Japan's attempt to occupy the stepping-stone to Hawaii was defeated with disastrous loss. The last setback was the seven-month-long Solomon Islands campaign, in which the navy ultimately lost a campaign of attrition.

In each of these campaigns, Japanese naval operations followed a pattern that significantly undercut the prospects for success: the navy's failure to concentrate its forces at a time when it still held the preponderance of naval superiority in the Pacific. Concentration is one of the enduring principles of war, and the cavalier manner with which it was ignored in Japanese planning early in the Pacific War is surprising. Before the Coral Sea battle, Yamamoto had already divided his forces between those being gathered for the Midway operation and those to be used for the offensive in the southwest Pacific. After the strategic reverse in the Coral Sea, the navy temporarily set aside the southwest Pacific and turned its entire attention to planning the Midway campaign. Those plans were a marvel of complexity, but they once again dispersed Japanese forces over vast stretches of the Pacific when in fact American forces confronting them in the center of that ocean might well have been crushed by an overwhelming concentration of Japanese naval might. Indeed, a principal objective in planning the Midway operation was to draw out the U.S. Pacific Fleet—what the Japanese assumed was left of it— into a battle in which the Americans would be decisively defeated because of their inferior strength. To the operation's great detriment, however, quite apart from the diversion of carriers to the Aleutians, the forces headed toward Midway were divided between Nagumo's carrier force and the main body under Yamamoto far to the rear. The failure to concentrate, though doubtless an operational and tactical failure in large part, contributed significantly to the Japanese defeat.

After Midway, the navy (at the army's request) once more turned its attention to the southwest Pacific to meet the Allied counterthrust in the New Guinea and Solomons area. There, in a campaign centered on the struggle for Guadalcanal, both services lost ground, men, and matériel through piecemeal commitment of their forces. These losses occurred even though the navy, certainly, initially had stronger forces than the Allies in the area and at first inflicted greater damage on the enemy than it suffered itself. In the view of the most authoritative study of the Guadalcanal campaign,[6] there was a brief moment of opportunity for the Japanese in the Solomons between mid-September and mid-October 1942, but Yamamoto Isoroku, through indecision and a failure to concentrate his forces, let victory, and thus the initiative, slip through his grasp. In the campaign that followed, the Japanese navy fought with determination, often besting the enemy in individual naval actions, but eventually losing the campaign through a failure to commit sufficient forces in sufficient time.[7]

The consequent loss of strategic initiative made the Solomons campaign the decisive period of the war. More serious to the Japanese navy than the destruction of aircraft, ships, and men was the gift of time and space that it gave to the Allies. During 1943, with the battle lines in the Pacific at a standstill, the Allies were able to gather and reorganize their forces. More important, America's vast industrial plant and scientific skills began to affect the outcome of combat.

Once halted in their drive to expand Japan's strategic periphery beyond the limits of prewar planning, Japan's military services turned their energies in 1943 to the defense of the perimeters of their earlier conquests. The navy's heavy ships withdrew to safe rear areas, and its garrison forces and land-based air units pushed forward to reinforce the defensive barrier—particularly in Micronesia—that was supposed to absorb and wear down the inevitable Allied counteroffensive. This arrangement of forces was essentially an extension of the "tripwire" strategy that the navy had developed in the latter half of the 1930s.

Yet, Japanese preparations to rush to completion a defensive barrier against an American naval counteroffensive were puny compared to the scale of the force gathering against them. Nineteen forty-three was the year that American industry, science, and organizational abilities truly began to change the fundamental strategic equation in the Pacific. Although Japanese and Allied naval forces were in fundamental numerical balance at the end of 1942, the unprecedented scale of American naval construction in 1943 completely upset this equilibrium by that autumn. In consequence, the United States was able to launch against the overextended Japanese positions a type of sea power so revolutionary, so massively armed and equipped, and so devastating in its impact that the Japanese navy was unprepared to respond at any level—strategic, operational, or tactical. The core element of this sea power was the U.S. naval task force, built around a carrier group that had a combined strength of many hundreds of aircraft, surface ships in close support, and a revolutionary system of mobile supply bases that overcame distance and logistic difficulties. Added to this massive air and surface firepower were the amphibious assault capabilities developed by the U.S. Marine Corps. Together, they comprised an offensive force capable of isolating and overwhelming any island bastion defended by the Japanese navy.

At the end of 1943, this offensive power was turned against Japan's defense zone in the Pacific and, over the next six months, overcame or bypassed its island defenses one after another. With the benefit of hindsight one can say that by November of that year, the Japanese navy had irretrievably lost the war in the Pacific. Not only had Japan's defensive perimeter failed to hold, but the main fleet—so carefully husbanded for the opportunity to fight the long-sought decisive battle—could no longer muster sufficient strength for a counterattack.

For the Japanese navy, the holy grail of the Pacific War had continued to be the great decisive surface battle, a concept to which the navy remained committed long after the possibility of its realization had faded. The Midway campaign had been planned in part with the idea of luring out the U.S. Fleet for just such a decisive encounter. At various times in 1942 the *Yamato* and *Musashi*, anchored at the great fleet base at Truk, waited in vain for an opportunity to sortie with the main body of the Combined Fleet to crush the enemy once and for all. Adm. Koga Mineichi's "Z Plan" in 1943 envisioned such a decisive encounter by the Combined Fleet, but came to naught. As late as the spring of 1944, the A-GŌ Plan called for a decisive battle, originally plotted for the vicinity of the western Caroline Islands, but hurriedly shifted to meet the threat to the Marianas in June. By then, the concept had fundamentally changed, of course; naval air power, both carrier- and land-based, had replaced the battle line. A-GŌ did indeed result in a major engagement, the Battle of the Philippine Sea, but on American terms. By then, Japanese naval air power had become so degraded that American pilots referred to the encounter as "The Great Marianas Turkey Shoot."

The Japanese navy was now faced with a stark choice: whether to try to preserve what remained of the Combined Fleet without confronting the cresting wave of American naval power and, inevitably, to see the United States take one Japanese strategic position after another, or whether to throw the fleet in front of the American advance and risk its annihilation. The Japanese disasters at the Philippine Sea and Leyte Gulf in 1944 were the consequence of a desperate attempt to try the second alternative. Fought without much reference to prewar Japanese planning, these battles lie beyond the concerns of this book.

By late May 1945, most ships of the once mighty Combined Fleet had been sunk and its odd-lot remnants were cowering in the bays and anchorages of the home islands under a rain of American bombs. By then, the Japanese naval historian Itō Masanori tells us, Adm. Ozawa Jisaburō, the last commander of the Combined Fleet, "could do little more than stand and look at the waning moon."[8] By the time that USS *Missouri* dropped anchor in Tokyo Bay, the cost in men and material had been tremendous. At war's end, the navy had lost 334 warships and had only 101 remaining, counting small craft. It had lost 300,386 officers and men, including 2 full admirals, 9 vice admirals, 56 rear admirals, and 259 captains.[9]

THE JAPANESE NAVY IN THE PACIFIC WAR IN RETROSPECT

The Japanese navy's strategic conduct of the Pacific War hinged first on its highest level of strategy, or grand strategy. A grand strategy ideally harnesses all the resources of a nation—military, political, economic, and diplomatic—to achieve national policy objectives. The evidence suggests that from the Russo-Japanese War onward, Japan never had a grand strategy. It possessed instead a set of perceived threats, nebulous ambitions, and a keen ability to exploit a strategic opening. Certainly, the three Imperial Defense Policy statements were a poor guide for the army and the navy and an even worse one for the nation as a whole. Fundamental to this lack of a grand strategy were the absence of an effective central coordinating body for national policy and the ongoing and competing interests and ambitions of the two services.[10] Absent a Japanese grand strategy, it is little wonder that the navy considered strategy more in terms of its own interests than those of the nation.

More specifically, the most fundamental character of Japanese naval strategy in the Pacific War was a disconnection between the war that the navy planned for and the war that the navy initiated. This discrepancy between the planned and the actual war seems evident in several ways. To begin with, as a continent-oriented navy for most of its existence, it was used to thinking of strategy in regional and limited terms. The navy succeeded in the Sino-Japanese and Russo-Japanese Wars against regional foes. These successes had been carefully limited theaters of operations and war aims, and had been consummated by peace settlements achieved after negotiations with their defeated enemies.[11] In plotting the opening moves of the Pacific War, the Japanese naval high command may have *believed* it was planning for a limited conflict—it gave no thought for the conquest of the American homeland, for example—but in fact, the Japanese navy's opening moves fatally undercut the possibility that the war would be so confined. By launching a surprise attack on the U.S. Pacific Fleet, seen by Americans as "infamous," the navy created a political, psychological, and, ultimately, strategic climate in the United States that made an unlimited war—a fight to the finish—inevitable. Had the navy foregone the attack on Hawaii and the Philippines and concentrated entirely on the conquest of Malaya and the Netherlands East Indies, the war might have had a quite different ending, given the isolationist mood of the United States in late 1941.

Second, the naval high command assumed that it could determine the pace as well as the direction of the war. In the navy's immediate prewar thinking, the war would be fought in carefully controlled stages: a series of lightning blows at its outset to cripple the Allies in the western Pacific and thus bring about some general balance between the two sides that would be the basis of a negotiated peace. With American energies and resources stretched to the limit between the Pacific and a confrontation with a seemingly invincible Germany, the Japanese believed that the United States would be only too glad to reach a settlement advantageous to Japan.[12] The reality was apparent three years later when the United States, in cooperation with its allies, mounted the Normandy invasion, the greatest landing operation in history, while at the same time launching a massive amphibious invasion of the Marianas.

This disconnection between the navy's prewar strategic plans and the operational realities of the war itself is attested to by Chihaya Masataka, former naval officer and postwar naval historian. Chihaya has commented on the inability of Japanese naval operations to keep up with the operational pace of the enemy by the latter half of the war. Far from determining the pace of the war after 1942, the Japanese navy became increasingly frustrated by the growing ability of the enemy to move farther, faster, and with greater force, as well as by the navy's inability to prevent the enemy's strategic moves.[13]

Moreover, the Japanese navy failed to think through what was entailed in the second stage of its Pacific War strategy, the effort to hold its defensive perimeter with a ring of advanced bases. This strategy was essentially an extension of the "tripwire" strategy that the navy had developed in the latter half of the 1930s. For all its planning, the navy failed to appreciate the size of the arena. The central and western Pacific and the waters of Southeast Asia were to become the largest theater for sustained and intensive operations in human history. Yet, at the Imperial Liaison Conference of 6 September 1941 Chief of Staff Nagano Osami had spoken grandly of creating an "impregnable position" in Southeast Asia, behind which Japan could exploit the raw materials of its conquests.[14] Nagano could not have given much thought to such a scheme. Japan simply did not have the ships and aircraft to defend that much of the globe, and American submarines would soon prove how easy it would be to break and enter into the Southeast Asian storehouse. Nor did the Japanese navy deal with the difficulty of building a defense line in the central and western Pacific, from which the navy could wear down the Allies until they sought a negotiated peace. Between the spring of 1942 and November 1943 the navy's attention to its Pacific defenses was sporadic and belated, with the fortification and garrisoning of some island bases being rushed forward only weeks before the American amphibious offensive surged over them. More basically, however, the navy's strategy of trying to defend a chain of widely separated island bastions with locally deployed, land-based air units was fundamentally unsound. H. P. Willmott has encapsulated the Japanese problem in this regard: "Japan made a basic strategic mistake in trying to fight a protracted war at great distances from the home islands without having the means to hold front line positions in depth and the strength and means to support those forces it committed."[15]

As noted, as late as mid-1944 the Japanese navy counted on a single great naval victory to turn the war around. To this concept, other elements of sea power—including convoy protection and ASW—were often sacrificed, to the

navy's great detriment. The navy's dogged pursuit of the doctrine of decisive battle not only warped its force structure; ironically, it limited the navy's chances for
victory in several major engagements fought. The navy sometimes withheld powerful elements of the fleet from current operations in the expectation that they
would be used at some critical juncture in the future. A good example is the campaign for the Solomons, the only time during the Pacific War when battleships
fought battleships. The navy's reluctance to risk its superbattleships in such a
"small" venture is understandable, and it is all too easy for the armchair strategist
to criticize Japanese decisions more than fifty years after the event. Still, the abject
demise of both the *Yamato* and the *Musashi* under aerial bombardment without
ever having fired a shell at a worthy target superbly demonstrates the futility of the
decisive battle concept. Moreover, the commitment to the doctrine of decisive battle illuminates the navy's failure to think in alternatives. Whereas strategists in the
prewar U.S. Navy had also planned to win a major encounter at sea, the American purpose was obvious: to prepare the way for the blockade and economic
strangulation of Japan. The Japanese never clearly stated their objective and
apparently did not consider the possibility that the United States might continue
the war even after suffering defeat in the decisive battle.[16]

If the Japanese navy vainly chased the chimera of decisive battle across the
Pacific until late in the war, early on it was forced to confront the reality of attrition. As discussed previously, Japanese strategic plans had for decades envisioned
the gradual attrition of a westward-moving U.S. fleet under the constant attack of
light Japanese forces. Ironically, it was the Japanese navy that underwent attrition
on a grand scale. During the Pacific War, attrition—that is, attacks from submarines, aircraft, or small surface ships other than those in a major engagement—
accounted for nearly half the losses suffered by the navy in surface ships from
destroyer up (table 14-1). Nearly all submarines and smaller vessels were also lost
by attrition. What made this situation disastrous was that by the end of 1943, not
only was the U.S. Navy not suffering loss by attrition (or in major engagements,
for that matter) at the same rate, but the vast American building program had
begun to swamp the Japanese navy quantitatively.

Attrition by submarine and aircraft was, of course, the cause of the wholesale
destruction of the Japanese merchant marine. Here again, the Japanese navy was
slow to adjust to the mounting danger. During the first two years of the Pacific
War, while American submarine operations were still hampered with problems of
torpedoes, cautious submarine commanders, logistics, and maintenance, the
Japanese navy did little to strengthen its capabilities in ASW or commerce protection. A significant number of sinkings (nearly 900,000 tons) by American submarines in 1942 should have given ample warning of the vulnerability of Japanese shipping. But as it was only slightly greater than prewar Japanese estimates

Table 14-1

LOSSES OF PRINCIPAL TYPES OF JAPANESE WARSHIPS DURING THE PACIFIC WAR

Warship type	No. lost in named engagements	No. lost by attrition	No. surrendered at war's end	TOTAL
Battleships*	5	5	1	11
Fleet carriers	13	4	4	21
Light carriers	—	4	—	4
Cruisers	17	23	5	45
Destroyers	32	92	17	141
Submarines	—	132	41	171
TOTAL	67	260	68	393

*Does not include the battleship *Mutsu,* which was lost in an explosion while the ship was anchored in Hiroshima Bay, 1943.

and the amount of tonnage replaced, the number of sinkings caused no great concern in the naval high command. As of late 1943, therefore, there were still too few escorts, too many of those with a maximum speed of between 16.5 and 17.5 knots, and too many only marginally armed with ASW weapons and detection equipment. By the beginning of 1944, when American submarine forces were cruising the western Pacific in great number, equipped with reliable torpedoes, led by aggressive commanders, and pursuing wolf-pack tactics, the situation was too late to reverse. At war's end, Japan had only 1.5 million tons of merchant shipping left from a prewar total of 6.4 million tons, and much of this remainder lay damaged or blockaded in Japanese ports.[17] As explained at great length in Mark Parillo's recent work on the subject, the destruction of the merchant marine seriously degraded nearly every aspect of the navy's ability to remain an effective fighting force, not to mention the crippling effect it had on the ability of the nation as a whole to carry on the war.

If American submarines were hampered by a range of technical, tactical, and logistic difficulties in the first years of the war, their Japanese counterparts were tethered by Japanese submarine doctrine. The conventional view of naval historians is that during the Pacific War, the Japanese submarine force accomplished very little, largely because doctrine held that the force should concentrate on fleet operations rather than on attacks on merchant shipping. Given the nature of the task, attacks on fleet units are inherently riskier and more difficult and thus inherently more limiting in their results. Nevertheless, even in its primary mission, the Japanese submarine fleet failed to turn the course of the naval war: not one single major naval engagement in the Pacific was significantly affected by Japanese submarines. As for the navy's neglect of commerce raiding in the war, the verdict is qualified. As Inoue Shigeyoshi argued, it was impossible for the United States to be strangled economically by a Japanese submarine offensive. Thus the Japanese navy's decision not to attack American coastal shipping may have been sound strategy, given the navy's strategic priorities. Yet, despite the immensity of the Pacific, the failure to attack U.S. troop and supply transports en route to the western Pacific was perhaps a major oversight. Such attacks, pressed home aggressively, would have enormously complicated the Allied counteroffensives in the Pacific during the middle and later stages of the war.

The conventionally negative view of Japanese submarines in the war, it should be noted, rests on an unwarranted comparison of Japanese and German submarine successes. True, the Japanese submarine force sank 170 ships and 1 million tons, no match for the enormous destruction wrought by German U-boats, which sank 2,000 ships and 14.5 million tons. But the Japanese navy employed a mere 187 boats. The Germans sent 1,000 U-boats to sea. Another reason for the low success rate of Japanese submarines was the scarcity of targets in the vastness of the Pacific; by comparison, the Atlantic, with its heavy maritime traffic, presented many more opportunities to the submarine predator.[18]

Moreover, although the effect of the Japanese submarine force in World War II was disproportionately small in relation to its size, it was not an utter failure. Japanese submarines actually scored some major successes during the first critical year of the Pacific War, specifically including hits against the most important category of ships: the aircraft carrier. In 1942, Japanese submarines sank two of the six available U.S. carriers (the *Yorktown* and *Wasp)* and so damaged a third (the *Saratoga)* that she missed three of the four major carrier battles that year. During the Guadalcanal campaign, damage to the *North Carolina* by a Japanese submarine reduced the number of available American fast battleships by a third. These were not marginal losses at the time.[19]

Related to the issue of attrition, of course, was the significant difference, by 1941, in the capabilities of the Japanese and U.S. navies in signals intelligence (see chapter 11). The tremendous coup obtained by American naval intelligence in gaining foreknowledge of Japanese plans for the Midway campaign is well documented. Equally important was the American ability, by late 1943, to learn of countless other operational orders affecting ship and aircraft movements. Some of this American intelligence resulted in spectacular Japanese disasters, such as the

interception and destruction of the aircraft in which Yamamoto Isoroku was riding. Other intelligence was critical to the tracking and elimination of Japanese
fleet units, including a large proportion of the Japanese submarine force.

There were, of course, institutional reasons for the navy's defeat in the Pacific
War. No aspect of the Japanese navy's prosecution of the war was more wasteful
of its energies and resources than the interservice feud endemic to both services
since the late nineteenth century. Their latent distrust toward each other turned to
active hostility as the war situation worsened, and that in turn had a corrosive
influence on the effectiveness of each service and on the ability of the nation as a
whole to conduct the war. To begin with, it inhibited overall strategic planning at
a time when there existed no effective coordinating body for such planning. No
major study had ever been undertaken prior to the war as to how the two services
should cooperate during it; once the war had begun, discussions between the two
services on strategy were limited to specific operations and did not attempt a
broad-range consideration of the conduct of the war as a whole. In their joint policy and planning sessions, each service "negotiated" rather than conferred with
the other and, following such meetings, IGHQ issued "agreements" rather than
operational commands.[20]

Such distrust, naturally, also hindered operations. The only really effective
joint operations between the two services were amphibious, and those generally
came at the beginning of the Pacific War. Among such operations, only three times
were the forces of one service subordinated to those of the other (and all three
times, army units were put under naval command). This is not to argue that the
navy made no effort to support army operations. The navy was critical in transporting and protecting the army's invasion operations in Southeast Asia at the
opening of the war, and the navy's efforts to resupply and later withdraw army
garrisons in the Solomon Islands, at the cost of significant losses of ships and men,
are indicative of the sacrifices the navy made for its sister service. There were as
many occasions, however, when the navy simply left the army to fend for itself.[21]

Equally destructive to Japan's conduct of the war was the tremendous duplication of effort in the development and production of technology. Each service was
reluctant to share its production facilities with the other, and the construction of
submarines by the army and the existence of different wavelengths for IFF (identification friend or foe) devices in army and navy aircraft exemplify such duplication.
Another example illustrates this picture of self-defeating interservice antagonism.
After the war, the former German naval attaché recalled that on a wartime tour of
the Nakajima aircraft plant, he was first taken by naval officers through their
development and manufacturing division. At the conclusion of the tour, his navy
guides walked him to a door that was kept strictly closed. When the door opened,

the naval officers bade him good-bye, and on the other side, army officers took him around their facilities, access to which was forbidden to the navy.[22]

Aside from its inability to operate harmoniously with its sister service under a joint command, the Japanese navy had certain command problems of its own. The naval historian Itō Masanori has noted that on the decisive day of the Leyte campaign there were four Japanese admirals at sea and two ashore, all within a 100-mile radius, but each fighting a separate battle, uncoordinated with the others. Itō has argued that this situation was due to the Combined Fleet commander's being in Tokyo, 2,000 miles away, when he should have been in Davao, or at least Manila.[23] Considering, however, that American ships in the same campaign managed to operate successfully together in the heaviest fighting, it seems more likely that a serious defect in the Japanese naval command structure in the Pacific War was an overcentralization of command. The Commander in Chief, Pacific (CinC-Pac), in contrast to Combined Fleet Headquarters, did not try to fight battles.

If the weak point of the Japanese navy in the Pacific War was its strategy, its strength was tactical. Of course, it makes sense to judge the tactical performance of the Japanese navy only during the first two years of the Pacific War, a period when, one can argue, the Japanese navy frequently showed itself the tactical superior of its American enemy. After that, no matter how well or poorly the navy conducted itself in battle, the overwhelming weight of American sea power made tactics irrelevant in determining the outcome. Much the same can be said about Allied tactics in the first four months of the war, when the Japanese navy confronted substantially inferior Allied naval forces in the waters of the East Indies and Japanese tactics counted far less than Japan's sheer preponderance of force. Nevertheless, in the four surface battles that essentially destroyed the ABDA (Allied) Fleet (Makassar Strait, Badung Strait, Java Sea, and Sunda Strait), Japanese operations were marked by effective cooperation between surface and air units (which became less frequent as the war went on) and by the greatest tactical skill in the Japanese navy: night torpedo operations.

It is in the Guadalcanal campaign, however, that one can best evaluate the tactical performance of the Japanese navy. This campaign was only time during the Pacific War that Japanese and Allied (though mostly American) naval forces were in rough balance for any extended period. In the seven engagements of the campaign (eight, if one divides the night actions off Guadalcanal between the cruiser and the battleship encounters) the Japanese usually were able to exchange blow for blow. Four engagements (Savo Island, Cape Esperance, the battles off Guadalcanal, and Tassafaronga) were night surface engagements, which again demonstrated that the Japanese were far better prepared for night combat than was their American enemy. In these encounters, the decades of intense research and training proved their worth in night torpedo operations. The opening round, at Savo Island, was a near textbook operation and closely followed Japanese night battle doctrine. With stealth, a minimum use of searchlights, and the maximum use of torpedoes—with which Japanese cruisers as well as destroyers were amply armed—the Japanese opened the attack. The result was the most resounding ship-to-ship victory that the navy had scored since Tsushima. In this and the other surface battles in the Solomons that followed, Japanese units not only were led aggressively and handled with skilled professionalism, but also fought in tactically cohesive divisions of two to four ships.[24] With skill and tenacity, Japanese commanders like Tanaka Raizō, Hashimoto Shintarō, and Koyanagi Tomiji managed the resupply runs to Guadalcanal—the "Tokyo Express"—and the final evacuation of Japanese troops from that island, a feat repeated by Kimura Masatomi in his evacuation of the Japanese garrison from Kiska in the Aleutians in July 1943.

Historians have greatly emphasized the Japanese navy's failure to exploit battle opportunities to the utmost (Pearl Harbor, the Java Sea, and Savo Island come to mind) and have offered rather tortured cultural explanations of this failure. There were, however, usually sufficient tactical or doctrinal reasons (from the Japanese point of view) why the Japanese commander on the spot did not press his advantage further.[25] Only at the Battle of the Komandorski Islands (March 1943) did a Japanese commander, Adm. Hosogaya Boshirō, apparently let victory slip through his grasp for want of sufficient will; at least the Japanese naval high command thought so, since they relieved him of command shortly after the battle. If Japanese tactical commanders displayed any continuing defect throughout the war, it was a slowness to react to new situations, a tendency to repeat rather unimaginatively certain operations and tactics.

The tactical successes of the Japanese navy in air and surface actions in the first year of the war were clearly the result not only of the professionalism of commanders on the spot, but also of officers and men across the board: intelligent, superbly trained, physically tough, highly motivated, and obedient unto death. The explanation of the high caliber of Japanese crews would indeed seem to be found in Japanese cultural traditions and social norms, supplemented by training of unprecedented rigor, as discussed in earlier chapters. As Richard Frank has suggested in his authoritative study of the Solomons campaign, at least initially, Japanese warship crews may have simply been more experienced, with more training cycles behind them than had crews on the American warships they faced.[26] Certainly, this was true of Japanese air crews whose experience in the China War made them among the best in the world at the beginning of the Pacific War.

No doubt the Japanese navy's emphasis on *seishin* (spirit) was a significant plus factor in the capabilities of all combat elements in the navy during the war. This spirit led to an overconfidence that contributed to the spectacular Japanese

defeat at Midway. Toward the end of the war, however, when the navy was shattered, *seishin* held its remnants together far longer than would have been possible
in other navies faced with similar ruin.

In any case, quality in training and morale could not make up for quantitative
deficiencies in the navy, exacerbated during the war by combat casualties and combat fatigue. The latter evidently was a significant factor in the ultimate defeat of the
navy's efforts to resupply army garrisons in the Solomons.[27] As the Pacific conflict
wore on and inexperienced officers and men replaced the veterans of earlier battles,
the efficiency of Japanese surface units undoubtedly declined. But in no branch of
the service was the impact of combat casualties more keenly felt than in the naval
air arm and in that arm's fighter units. Here, the Japanese navy paid a terrible price
for its training policies of the prewar years. The hemorrhaging of superbly trained,
combat-wise fighter pilots began at the Coral Sea and Midway, but the really severe
losses took place during the fighting in the Solomons. American air units also sustained heavy casualties, but because of a far more flexible training system, the U.S.
Navy could absorb these greater losses and still continue to function effectively.
The Japanese navy could not. With the ranks of seasoned pilots thinning rapidly,
the navy rushed large numbers of inadequately trained pilots into combat with pre-
dictably disastrous results. By mid-1943, with training times drastically reduced,
Japanese naval fighter units were filled with flyers who were little more than student pilots, this at a time when training time in the U.S. Navy was being sharply
increased. The situation became worse in the second half of the war, and in its last
year, the *kamikaze* tactic using pilots with little or no training was essentially the
only recourse left to the navy. As Colin Gray has pointed out, the diminution of
Japanese naval air power in 1943–44 illustrates how a numerically inferior force
declines at an accelerating rate when subject to such pressure.[28]

The tactical schemes of the interwar decades yielded a wide range of combat
results. There can be little doubt that the navy's single most impressive tactical
innovation in the prewar years was the concentration of carrier air power manifested in the First Air Fleet. While it existed, the First Air Fleet, which gave new
direction to war at sea, was the most powerful formation afloat. One can argue
that its disbandment soon after the Hawaiian operation was a major tactical mistake. In any event, the First Air Fleet represented a concept in naval air power—
the hit-and-run strike force—that was superseded by the task force concept. As
developed by the U.S. Navy, the task force was a multicomponent fleet supplied
by a mobile fleet train and able to provide round-the-clock offensive air operations against a target. In the formation of the First Mobile Fleet in 1944 the Japanese navy attempted a similar organization, but shortages in every required element
of the task force, particularly of experienced air crews, made it a feeble reflection
of the original concept.

Other tactical innovations studied and practiced in the prewar years were employed with reasonable success by the navy during the Pacific War, but under different circumstances. Night torpedo tactics were a case in point. Originally intended to be used in the open sea to reduce the strength of a westward-moving American battle fleet, they nevertheless proved quite effective in the more restricted waters of the southwest Pacific. Other tactical innovations were attempted but found to be quite ineffective. An example is the midget submarine program. The use of this type of submersible culminated in the Hawaiian operation, in which they scored no successes and in which five were lost.[29] Indeed, though used elsewhere in the Pacific Ocean, the Indian Ocean, and Australian waters, the midget submarine's combat results were nil.

Similarly, little came of the navy's plans to use submarine-based reconnaissance aircraft or to employ flying boats for offensive operations, including torpedo attacks and bombing runs (though one such bombing attack on American installations at Kwajalein by flying boats caused significant damage). Some less conventional schemes were never used at all. For all the research and training that the Japanese navy devoted to "underwater shots" by its heavy surface units, "long-distance concealed firing" by its torpedo squadrons, and "submerged firing" by its submarine forces, none ever materialized in battle. The reasons were various: either the sorts of engagements in which they were applicable (such as daylight battleship encounters or long-distance torpedo duels between Japanese and Allied cruiser forces) never took place, or commanders on the spot judged the tactics unworkable.

The merits of "outranging" as a foremost tactical principle of the prewar Japanese navy are hard to judge. Although its apotheosis in a gun duel between *Yamato*-class battleships and a U.S. battle line never took place, the idea, imbedded in the design of a variety of Japanese weapons (the type 93 torpedo), ships (the J submarines), and aircraft (the G3M bomber), was sound enough. In some cases, such as the sinking of the *Prince of Wales* and *Repulse,* "outranging" was an element in Japanese success; in others it was an advantage that eventually proved too costly in terms of the consequent sacrifices in design (the lack of defensive armor and armament in the G3M). Sometimes, the ability to outrange was simply vitiated by ineffective Japanese strategy (such as the navy's submarine doctrine).

Given the ultimate scale of the Allied and, particularly, the American superiority in industrial power and the utter annihilation of the Japanese fleet by the end of World War II, H. P. Willmott's analysis of the Japanese navy in the Pacific seems appropriate. Willmott asserts that Japan was doomed to a defeat in the war that it had initiated and that there was nothing its navy could have done to save itself from annihilation.[30] A different view of Japan's potential to fight the war, however, is that various naval decisions during the interwar period could have improved the odds for the Japanese and prolonged the struggle. If the navy had paid greater attention to the vulnerability of Japan to submarine blockades, it might have created much larger ASW forces. Moreover, the Japanese naval forces would have been more effective had the Japanese navy directed its submarine strategy toward the interdiction of supply and communication routes between the U.S. west coast and advanced bases in the Pacific. Had the navy created a significant reserve of personnel, particularly in aviation, by emphasizing competence rather than excellence, the Japanese might have better addressed their manpower shortages. Additionally, the Japanese could have mobilized their scientific and technological talent to accelerate the development of certain technologies, especially radar. Finally, greater cooperation with its sister service would have facilitated planning, reduced duplication, and sped up operations.

Yet, a balanced view of the Japanese navy's performance in the Pacific War requires, as already stated, a careful consideration of the first two years of the conflict. During this time the navy waged the kind of war it had trained for and prepared to fight. Here, if one concentrates on tactical conduct and outcomes, the record is instructive. Excluding the Japanese attack on Pearl and the annihilation of the Japanese convoy and escort force by U.S. Army Air Force bombers at the Bismarck Sea, and combining the cruiser and battleship actions at Guadalcanal on 12–15 November 1942, there were seventeen named battles between Japanese and American naval forces during the first two years of the war. Four were carrier battles: the Japanese navy lost one (Midway), and three (the Coral Sea, the Eastern Solomons, and Santa Cruz) were draws. The remaining thirteen encounters, however, were ship-to-ship engagements, many of them fought at night. Of these, the Japanese navy won six (Savo Island, Tassafaronga, Rennell Island, Kolambangara, off Horaniu, and Vella Lavella), the U.S. Navy won four (Cape Esperance, Vella Gulf, Empress Augusta Bay, and Cape St. George), and three were draws (the night actions off Guadalcanal; the Komandorskis; Kula Gulf). If one adds the four night surface engagements in east Indian waters, January to March 1942 (Makassar Strait, Badung Strait, Java Sea, and Sunda Strait), in which U.S. warships fought as part of Allied naval forces and which all resulted in Japanese victories, the Japanese tally is even more impressive. Furthermore, this accounting excludes the navy's striking successes against British Commonwealth naval forces scored by Admiral Nagumo's carrier force at Port Darwin, Australia, in February, and in the Indian Ocean in April 1942. The record is proof that, pitted against naval forces also employing tactics and technologies developed in the period between the two world wars, the Japanese navy was indeed a formidable fighting force. It was not until the introduction of revolutionary tactics and technologies and the exertion of preponderant naval power by the U.S. Navy early in 1944 that the tide turned decisively against the Japanese.

Reflections on the Imperial Japanese Navy, 1887–1945

As asserted in the introduction, it is hardly surprising that the development of the Japanese navy reflected the course of the modern nation that created it in the late nineteenth century. Both the navy and the nation were heirs to a feudal tradition that left its indelible stamp on the Japanese character. With speed and general success, however, both assimilated Western techniques and synthesized them with indigenous Japanese values. In the process, the nation and the navy rose to front-rank status by the early twentieth century. Moreover, despite Japan's late arrival on the naval scene, by World War I, it stood preeminent in experience in naval combat. In the forty-eight years between the Battle of Lissa in 1866 and the onset of World War I in 1914, there were only five significant sea battles worldwide. The Japanese navy fought and won three of these encounters and thus gained more combat experience than any other navy. In useful combat experience, the Japanese navy was way ahead by World War I. Of the other great naval powers, only the United States and Russia had any experience with naval combat, and after 1905, the Russian navy never again engaged in a fleet encounter.

After World War I, this picture changed sharply. The four or five significant surface actions of that conflict were fought between the British and German navies exclusively. Both the United States and Japan played lesser naval roles, but the U.S. Navy significantly participated in convoy and ASW operations, whereas the Japanese navy was involved only marginally in air and landing operations at Tsingtao and, to a slight degree, in ASW in the Mediterranean.

Their combat experience between 1894 and 1918 extensively shaped the Japanese view of naval warfare in eventually detrimental ways. The navy's success in the three major surface battles, 1895–1905, in Tsushima above all, contributed to its belief that such battles could be decisive in national conflict, or at least, that they could lead to an advantageous peace. The navy's minimal exposure to submarine and antisubmarine warfare led to a failure to understand the true implications of either of these forms of naval warfare.

At all events, Japan's rise as a modern naval power was in large part due to the Japanese success in acquiring modern technology. Like all aspects of Japan's technological development, the nations's acquisition and application of naval technology in the 1870s was far behind the world's other navies. At the same time, however, unburdened by a mass of obsolescent technology that had occasionally impeded naval development in the West earlier in the century, the Japanese navy was free to acquire the West's latest naval technology rapidly.

This process of acquiring technology proceeded in three phases. The first phase relied almost entirely on Western tutelage: the study of foreign technology (through the formal education of Japanese naval officers, the hiring of foreign technical consultants, and the observation of foreign techniques); the importation of foreign ships, weapons, and equipment for service use; and the study of foreign production processes. The second phase emphasized licensed production (while continuing the study of foreign technology): the acquisition of licenses to produce material based on foreign models; the production of limited quantities for service use; and the development of modest improvements in foreign design. The third phase involved indigenous development (while maintaining the study of foreign technology): the development of indigenous designs based on experience gained in the two earlier phases; the expansion of production facilities for such designs; and the production of resultant matériel in quantity for distribution to the various elements of the navy. Once the navy had reached the third phase of technological development and material acquisition, the processes were much the same as in the United States and Western Europe, albeit with limits implied by a smaller and temporally shorter experience base and a less well developed infrastructure.

The Japanese navy adhered to this procedure in the design and development of various technologies. The first Japanese capital ships were built in foreign yards, and as late as 1910, the battleship *Kongō* was ordered from Vickers-Armstrong. Her sister ships, however, were built in Japanese yards according to essentially the same plans. Several types of Whitehead torpedoes were first purchased, then manufactured, in Japan, processes that provided the basis for indigenous torpedo design and manufacture. The navy obtained Whitehead-Weymouth torpedoes in sample quantities to acquire Whitehead technology in general and specifically the technology involved in the new double-acting, horizontal engine that became standard in Japanese torpedoes. The navy first relied on German optical glass, but eventually supplanted this with the optical instruments developed by Nippon Kōgaku. The navy's radial engine technology owed a design debt to Curtiss-Wright and Pratt and Whitney.

Some technological development in the Japanese navy, of course, did not fit the pattern just described. The development of the midget submarine was largely an indigenous concept, and the oxygen torpedo was a technology attempted and abandoned by both the United States and the British navies. By the 1930s and the time of Japan's deepening isolation, moreover, technologies developed in secret or semisecret by Britain and the United States became unavailable to the Japanese navy. The most obvious example is radar, in which the Japanese navy lagged far behind, partly because Allied security minimized Japanese knowledge until it was too late to catch up. This fact goes a long way to explain why the navy never developed fire control radar or high-resolution surface search radar.

Reflecting on the Japanese navy's policy for technological development and material acquisition, it is fair to ask whether the policy was sound. Could some other policy have been better? When the Japanese navy was established in the late nineteenth century, naval technology was in a state of transition as had not been seen for over five hundred years. To be a significant naval power, therefore, Japan had to catch up, acquire existing foreign material and technology very rapidly. There were really two options besides the one Japan selected: the first was to take only general Western guidance and to try to develop Japanese technology on an entirely independent basis. This would have significantly delayed the development of the Japanese fleet. The other was to rely completely on Western suppliers. This would have jeopardized Japanese independence, a dangerous risk considering the likelihood that the Anglo-American naval powers would have eventually embargoed arms to Japan in any event. Given these considerations, the navy's middle-course acquisition policy was probably not only sound, but roughly optimal.

There were, however, some severe impediments to the Japanese navy's technological acquisition process. Some impediments stemmed from the unavoidable consequence of Japan's physical and historical circumstances, and some were the result of an incomplete understanding of the requirements for the development of complex technological systems.

To begin with, Japan suffered from an inadequate resource base. As discussed earlier in the book, inadequate quantities of certain high-performance metals in Japan, particularly high-strength alloy steel, influenced the development of Japanese aircraft engines toward small, light designs. This, in turn, affected the Japanese navy's ability to match the combat performance of American aircraft in the latter stages of the Pacific War. The lack of sufficient high-performance metals also may have caused the navy's reliance on moderate-pressure and moderate-temperature steam in the navy's warship power plants, which in turn caused the navy's ship propulsion technology to lag behind that of the U.S. Navy.[31]

But the inadequacy of Japan's strategic resources was only one of the inherent impediments to technological development and material acquisition in the navy. The disparate character of the Japanese economic infrastructure was another. This unevenness affected how industrial products were developed, tested, and transported. An example was the condition of the Japanese auto-transport system. Although the Japanese rail system was one of the finest in the world, Japan in the 1930s had few metaled roads to speed the local transportation and distribution of goods and services in peacetime, and men, weapons, equipment, and supplies in wartime. Nothing so dramatizes this problem as the fact that after the prototype of the Mitsubishi Zero was completed at the Mitsubishi plant in Nagoya, it was transported for its flight tests at Kagamigahara airfield in Gifu Prefecture by oxcart.[32]

As noted, despite the great rapidity with which the Japanese navy gained proficiency in assimilating new naval technologies from abroad, it continued to operate from a smaller and temporally shorter base of technological expertise. This lesser technical experience and know-how (as compared to the technical base in Western navies) resulted in much naval technology that was less innovative—warships that were simply larger, faster, and more heavily armed, for example. The Japanese base of technological expertise provided for an initial superiority in certain aspects of naval technology at the outset of the Pacific War, but could not sustain that lead against American technology as the war progressed. Finally, the overwhelming problem for Japan—its being vastly outproduced by the United States in key sectors such as aircraft production—may have been compounded by the Japanese workforce's strong tradition of craftsmanship, which relied more on manual skill than on scientific calculation and mass production. Japanese aircraft were sometimes marvels of the engineering art, but their small numbers were not enough to make a difference.[33]

Although Japan brought to perfection certain older naval technologies—torpedoes, optics, and ordnance, for example—it failed to develop the critical "second-stage" technologies, such as radar, that were so much part of the Allied victory in World War II. The navy apparently did not discover modern systems engineering, the organizational technique of dividing large technological systems into subsystems with well-defined interfaces. That technique enabled U.S. engineers to create incredibly complex technical systems. Without systems engineering, the American development of radar, fire control, and aircraft would have been dramatically slowed. The absence of such a system in the Japanese navy may partially explain why Japan's development of radar was so laggard and so inferior. The existence of a fire-control system that lacked servomechanisms and had separate training for a director, a range finder, and the *sokutekiban* suggests either a total lack of integration or at best a very primitive stage of such integration.

Thus, the story of Japanese naval technology in the Pacific War is the story of how the superior "first-generation" technology at the outset of the war was overtaken, both in quality and quantity, by "second-generation" technology. Examples of the former are numerous. Among the most prominent are Japanese naval optics, the Ōmori method of torpedo fire control, and the type 93 torpedo. All were associated with the Japanese navy's great success in night combat during the first year of the war. Japanese navy's optics were perhaps as good as any in the world; early in the war, when American commanders and crews were insufficiently trained in the use of radar, the more experienced Japanese use of optics made a significant difference in night combat. During several night engagements, including Savo Island, Japanese lookouts using these instruments spotted U.S. ships before their own ships were identified by American radar. The Ōmori method of torpedo fire control was in some ways a more sophisticated system than the U.S. Navy's contemporary Torpedo Data Computer.[34] For its part, the speed, range, and warhead of the type 93 put it in a class by itself during these months.[35] Furthering Japanese naval effectiveness, Japanese cruisers had retained torpedo armament during the prewar decade, whereas American cruisers no longer carried it after the early 1930s. As the majority of surface engagements in the first year of the war were cruiser actions, the Japanese navy went into battle with a pronounced advantage in this regard. Later in the war, as the U.S. Navy gained air superiority and radar became universal on U.S. warships, the opportunities for torpedo attacks declined sharply and the torpedo tubes and reload torpedoes simply took up valuable space on Japanese cruisers and destroyers.[36]

The initial superiority of much of Japanese naval technology was demonstrated by examples from earlier chapters: the *Fubuki*-class destroyers, the Zero fighter, the G3M bomber (surpassed in 1941 in the Pacific only by the B-17), and, perhaps, the superbattleships *Yamato* and *Musashi*. All these represented world-class technologies when designed. In their initial entry into combat, each more than lived up to their designers' expectations (except for the superbattleships that were never tactically deployed as originally intended). Yet, like all technologies, they were bound to be become obsolescent or at least to be superseded by other technologies.

Therein lay the problem for the Japanese navy, as for the Japanese armed services as a whole. Because of the limited Japanese industrial and scientific-technical resource base for technological innovation and because of the increasing pressure on Japanese manufacturing facilities simply to continue production of existing designs to replace combat losses, it was difficult to design, develop, test, and then produce new weapons and equipment. This problem was exemplified by naval aircraft design and development. Until the introduction of the Raiden fighter in 1944, Japanese navy fighter pilots flew the same aircraft as those deployed in December 1941.[37] This stands in marked contrast to the successive introduction of improved fighter plane types, such as the F4U and the F6F, by the U.S. Navy during the war.

Serious as was the influence of technological obsolescence in Japan's naval defeat, however, it was not as critical as the complete failure to develop certain "second-generation" technologies. Three such technologies stand out in this regard: radar, the VT (proximity) fuse, and forward-throwing ASW weapons. Radar, of course, was the single most important technological advantage held by the U.S. Navy in the Pacific War. It stripped the protection of darkness away from Japanese torpedo tactics and made irrelevant the superlative quality of Japanese optics; in combination with the installation of the combat information center (CIC) aboard U.S. warships, radar improved fleet air defense enormously, particularly in vectoring combat air patrols toward inbound Japanese air strikes; and SJ radar aboard American submarines made attacks independent of weather and daylight.[38] The VT fuse required no time setting, but was activated by electrical waves generated by a small radiolike device bouncing off the target's surface. The mechanism enormously enhanced the antiaircraft defense of American warships, specifically improving the 5-inch main ordnance on American destroyers as antiaircraft weapons. Between January 1943, when it was introduced, and the end of the war, the VT fuse was the key element in the destruction of 305 Japanese aircraft by shipboard antiaircraft fire.[39] Compounded with the inexperience of Japanese naval air crews during the same period, the lethality of this American countermeasure shattered the air attack systems described in chapter 9. For their part, forward-thrown ASW weapons, in combination with advanced sonar technology, were decisive in hunting down and destroying the Japanese submarine fleet, submarine by submarine. Whereas side- and stern-dropped depth charges could be fired only well after an ASW vessel lost contact with a submarine, forward-throwing projectiles like "Hedgehog," "Mousetrap," and "Squid" attacks could be carried out while anti-submarine craft still had sonar contact with the submarine target.[40]

There were, as well, a host of other new weapons and systems—amphibious landing craft and attack transports, to name a few—that were influential in Japan's ultimate naval defeat. We nevertheless agree with John Ellis that there was no wonder-weapon, or even set of weapons, that led to the Allied victory in World War II. It was rather the ability of the Allies, particularly the United States, to produce a vast quantity of matériel and to organize ways to transport and deploy it in numbers that simply overwhelmed their enemies.[41] Thus, it was not just that the Zero fighter met its match in the Hellcat or Corsair, it was that the American fighters were deployed in such numbers. Behind this fact lay an American appreciation of scientific and industrial war and how to mobilize and exploit the enormous scientific and economic resources of the nation to wage it. Equally important, the U.S. Navy, despite its own attachment to the conventional concept of the great gunnery battle in the Pacific as late as a year or so before the war, had also given thought to alternative strategies and to the problems of logistics and supply in a transoceanic war. American success in producing an endless stream of war material and then in transporting and distributing it to the forward units of the U.S. Navy provided that navy with a margin for operational and organizational error that might otherwise have proven disastrous.

The Japanese navy had no such margin. In all categories of strategic materials, Japan depended on outside sources, the fundamental reason for embarking on war in the first place. The nation's pool of scientific talent, though excellent in a few fields—physics, medicine, and metallurgy, for example—was not only smaller than that in the United States, but also generally less developed. These differences in national strength constituted a serious disadvantage for the Japanese navy, but were made worse because the nation and the navy had given too little thought to the mobilization of the scientific and industrial assets that were available.

The reason for this neglect was that the navy had fundamentally miscalculated the relationship between its strategy, its force structure, and the nation's industrial-technological base.[42] Counting on surprise, speed, and overwhelming firepower, it had for decades planned a lightning offensive war. To this end, the navy had developed an offensive doctrine that would lead to a single annihilating victory. It had designed and developed warships and aircraft whose modest numbers were supposedly offset by their quality and whose specifications were monopolized by speed, range, and firepower. In its naval and air services it had created a small elite of naval professionals—among the world's best—behind which there was essentially no reserve. Once the impetus of the navy's strategic offensive was halted and the conflict turned to a serious attrition of men and material, not only did the navy have too little of everything, but it found that the technological and human assets it did have were unsuited to attritional warfare. Too late, the navy came to recognize that the sacrifice of protection and durability in the design of its ships and aircraft accelerated its losses of men and material.

In the near seventy-five-year history of the Imperial Japanese Navy, the navy's tactical doctrine reflected the synthesis of both Japanese tradition and Western modernity. In stages similar to those of its technological development and material acquisition, the navy came to understand and then master the principles of Western naval tactics. Early on, foreign experts were brought into the navy and Japanese naval officers sent abroad to speed this process. Subsequently, the navy developed indigenous capabilities to study, test, teach, and improve its tactical doctrine. This process continued unevenly during the navy's history. In its early years, during the transition from sail to steam, the navy demonstrated a solid application of scientific method to the development of its tactics. It worked out concepts ashore and then experimented with them in small boats. A similar application took place some forty years later in the development of naval aviation.

Yet, a gradual atrophy of thought in the Japanese navy is evident. Whereas in the late nineteenth century, the navy had been in the forefront of tactical innovation (witness the study of the T tactic about the same time that it was being worked out in the Royal Navy), by the 1920s a certain rigidity had begun to overtake the navy's tactical doctrine. In the 1930s, this trend had hardened into extreme dogmatism. Hori Teikichi, himself a product of the Naval Staff College and naval bureaucracy, recalled after the war that "this kind of creeping formalism spread until it became a kind of strategic orthodoxy and [the navy] ended up as a smug little society which insisted that all ideas on strategy should conform to this orthodoxy. . . ."[43] Anecdotes abound of the indignation with which instructors at the staff college met criticism of the tactical assumptions in the various exercises at the college and of how staff officers often stacked the rules of naval maneuvers to favor a particular tactical outcome.[44] This inflexibility is also apparent in the staff's failure to develop individuals who thought broadly about wholly new approaches to naval warfare. Far from developing new doctrine, the staff was content merely to develop new technology or new tactics.[45] Equally serious was that existing doctrine sometimes failed to receive practical testing at sea. A case in point was the navy's use of submarines. A dogma by the late 1920s, Japanese submarine doctrine remained untested until the late 1930s, when it was found deficient. It remained unchanged, however, when the navy went to war. The navy took a decidedly narrow approach in the study of naval warfare in these years. In its research on World War I, the Japanese navy confined itself to the study of Jutland and devoted little attention to broader strategic, economic, and logistic matters that marked margins of victory and defeat between the war's participants.

In any event, behind the acquisition and mastery of Western tactical principles lay the weight of the Japanese martial tradition. A number of legacies from that tradition found their way into modern Japanese naval doctrine. The emphasis on secrecy and stealth, the use of surprise attack, and the tradition of battle at night or at dawn all had their antecedents in premodern Japanese military history. More important was the psychological inheritance from Japan's recent feudal past.[46] Deeply ingrained in the navy from its beginning to its end was the Japanese martial emphasis on spirit as equivalent and even superior to matériel. At its best, this ethos provided the navy with the fortitude to undertake training at a level of rigor and risk that would have been unacceptable in most navies, to reinforce the offensive outlook characteristic of most navies, and to hold the navy together when it faced overwhelming odds and inevitable defeat. At its worst, the martial spirit led to an arrogance that ignored or discounted enemy capabilities, to an unfounded confidence that the enemy would act or react as the Japanese expected, and to a blindness to material realities that bordered on the irrational.

Related to this emotional link to the nation's past was the strong tendency to see the outcome of battle as the direct result of the favor or disfavor of divine agency. While military establishments have traditionally had recourse at one time or another to rhetoric concerning divine intervention, it is remarkable how often Japanese naval leaders saw victory or defeat as in the lap of the gods. Tōgō's first order to the Combined Fleet, once hostilities of the Russo-Japanese War had commenced, included the injunction, "Be certain of heaven's aid and accomplish a great victory for our Combined Fleet."[47] In his reply to the emperor's message following his victory at Tsushima, Tōgō asserted, "Victory depended not on human agency, but on divine grace."[48] And in drawing up his plans to take Japan into war with the United States, Yamamoto Isoroku wrote that he could not but rely "exclusively on the Emperor's virtue and God's help."[49] These declarations go beyond mere references to luck; they had their origins in the military and religious culture from which the navy had emerged and were as much part of Japanese naval doctrine as the emphases on the offensive and qualitative superiority.

Indeed, this tendency to include psychological elements in tactical and strategic planning also resulted from a continuing perception among Japanese navy men that in facing their principal enemy, the U.S. Navy, they would be faced by superior numbers. As noted, the need to make up for quantitative inferiority by qualitative superiority—both material and nonmaterial—was the single most important and ongoing element in the formation of Japanese naval doctrine. The belief that quality *could* overcome quantity was *the* essential Japanese naval doctrine and, as such, led directly or indirectly to a spectrum of subdoctrines: "using a few to conquer many," outranging the enemy, the doctrine of night combat, the strategy of attrition, and the decisive battle.

More than anything else, it was this clear fixation with qualitative superiority that influenced Japanese naval technology. Although technology and doctrine obviously have a symbiotic relationship, the question of which drives which has been the subject of heated debate among historians, political scientists, and commentators on national strategy. For the Japanese navy at least, from approximately the decade after the Russo-Japanese War to the outbreak of the Pacific War, doctrine (in this instance, the navy's insistence on qualitative superiority) apparently led technology. Among the earlier mentioned examples, the *Fubuki*-class destroyers, the conversion of several *Kuma*-class light cruisers into torpedo cruisers, the midget submarine, the "A"-class cruisers, the Zero fighter, the G3M bomber, the *Yamato*-class superbattleships, and the command cruiser *Ōyodo* are only the most prominent. The design and development of some of these weapons systems was predicated upon the notion that they would be decisively superior to their enemy counterparts. Others were designed and developed on the assumption that they would play a critical role in the decisive surface engagement in which technological and tactical quality would prevail over the enemy's superior numbers.

The imbalance between doctrine and technology in the Japanese navy between the world wars can also be seen in the extreme demands made by the Navy General Staff for the design specifications for ships and aircraft. As shown, the general staff, in pursuit of a particular tactical objective—superior firepower, range, or maneuverability—often issued specifications for one or more extraordinary capabilities. In doing so, the staff tended to give inadequate attention to balanced design. These demands sometimes resulted in warships with more powerful guns but that were dangerously top-heavy, and aircraft that lacked all but the most minimal pilot protection and damage tolerance for the sake of lightness and attendant maneuverability and range. To the distinguished naval commentator, Fukui Shizuo, this situation went to the heart of a serious problem in the entire Japanese military system. "The greatest shortcoming of our country," wrote Fukui after the war, "has not been its poverty, but the fact that technology has been subordinated to policy. This was true even in the navy, which gave the highest consideration to technicians."[50]

In any event, "quality" is a complex proposition when it comes to naval technology. One way to assess it is to judge how well a system deals with a specific tactical or technological problem, such as an encounter between one battleship and another. But more often it can be judged in terms of how effectively a system confronts all the problems that it might meet. In the latter sense, for example, certain American fleet submarines and fleet destroyers were outstanding in their multipurpose uses. Japanese destroyers, and even more, Japanese submarines, evidently were designed to emphasize some functions at the expense of others and sometimes to be single-purpose designs. At the nub of the design issue in these cases were the respective requirements set down by the U.S. General Board and the Japanese Navy General Staff. The U.S. General Board seems to have tended toward a wiser multipurpose approach to design specifications than did the Japanese Navy General Staff.[51]

Moreover, the navy's confidence that it could best a numerically superior enemy with its own qualitative superiority was a dubious proposition from the outset. In modern history no major conflict has ever been won by technologically superior weapons alone, and in those wars where qualitative superiority has appeared to be the deciding factor, the conflicts have been short and the qualitative assets of the victor have been other than technological: superior military organization, staff work, planning, and political leadership, as well as training and morale.[52] Such assets were held by the Japanese navy in the short wars fought with the Chinese and Russian navies in 1894–95 and 1904–5 and contributed greatly to the Japanese success in both those conflicts. The naval war fought with the United States in 1941–45, however, was different both in scale and in character. To this conflict the United States brought two advantages. One was the significant American superiority in organization, planning, staff work, and leadership. The other was the American capacity to produce adequate quantities of ships, aircraft, weapons, and equipment, even if they were sometimes inferior in quality to those of the Japanese navy. In this latter sense, the American victory in the Pacific seems to confirm the dictum attributed to Lenin: "Quantity has a quality all its own."

Finally, among the three elements of sea power studied in this book—technology, tactics, and strategy— it was in this last element that the Japanese displayed the weakest understanding. In the navy's earliest decades, its strategic rationale was clear enough: For an island nation, Japan's existence depended on control of the surrounding seas. Thus the basic strategic requirements were to secure and maintain control of the western Pacific adjacent to the Japanese homeland. By this means, the navy would prevent the entry of any enemy force into Japanese home waters, and thus keep Japan free from invasion.[53] These requirements presented the Japanese navy with a straightforward strategy, a solid justification for the navy's independence from the army, and an understandable rationale for its initial armaments programs. The strategic posture of the navy was purely defensive and had scant concern for the projection of Japan's national power abroad. The navy thus understood "command of the sea" to be regional and therefore limited in scope.

Japanese imperial expansion on the Asian continent in the last decade of the nineteenth century served to complicate this limited, defensive approach to sea power. Once Japan had committed itself to the maintenance of military forces in Korea, the principal role of the navy inevitably became the support of the army's presence on the peninsula through defense of the maritime links to Korea. Nevertheless, in the Sino-Japanese and Russo-Japanese Wars, Japan skillfully exploited its command of the sea. In both wars, Japan had carefully calculated the odds and had fought for limited, near-at-home objectives. In both conflicts, Japan fought against one enemy at a time, in each case a land power whose navy, once defeated, could not replace its losses. Japan's successes had provided the nation and the navy with confidence in the conduct of this type of regionally limited war.

Yet, the navy's new role as a support of the army's land operations, largely dictated by the army's continent-oriented strategy, conflicted with the navy's demand for equal status with the army. In the decades to come, that gap grew with the army's expanding presence on the continent and the navy's increasing demands not just for equality, but for superiority to the army in place and preferment. Faced with this contradiction, the Japanese navy was obliged to find a new strategic rationale. Satō Tetsutarō's *On the History of Imperial Defense* was an attempt to supply that rationale, the projection of national power upon the high seas, a strategic objective that he based upon Alfred Thayer Mahan's theory of sea power. As shown, however, Satō's concept merely deepened the contradictions of Japanese naval strategy. Whereas the projection of naval power by the great Western maritime nations related to the possession of distant overseas territories and was therefore expressed by Mahan in global terms, Japan was a regional power and, moreover, essentially a land power whose imperial territories were close at hand. Lacking territories in the Pacific or in any other ocean, a strategy based upon the projection of naval power upon the "high seas" was meaningless when Satō drafted his magnum opus.

Not much more meaningful were Satō's early references to Japanese interest in the "South Seas." By this he meant South China and Southeast Asia, most of which was already spoken for by Western imperialism, either through direct political control or through indirect economic hegemony. Yet, lacking any tangible strategic interest like that of the army on the continent, the navy began to voice an interest in Southeast Asia in the first decades of the twentieth century, despite the fact that Japan's core interests were continental and closer to home. By the 1930s, of course, the changing technological environment of navies, particularly the shift from coal to oil, caused the Japanese navy to perceive concrete strategic interests in Southeast Asia. The pursuit of those interests at the outset of the 1940s led eventually to war with the Anglo-American naval powers. All of Japan's leaders, including those at the head of the Imperial Japanese Navy, assumed that Japan could once more wage a "limited" war, far from the centers of enemy power, to obtain "regional" objectives—now expanded to comprise all of Southeast Asia—as it had against China and Russia. It is a commentary on a collective failure in strategic vision that the Japanese leadership could not see that the circumstances were vastly different from those earlier conflicts. In 1941, Japan set itself against the world's two strongest maritime and industrial powers that, once recovered from the shock of the initial Japanese offensives, summoned their great resources, overcame the vast distances of the Pacific, and, breaking through Japan's outer defenses, carried the war to the Japanese homeland.[54]

Undoubtedly, however, the most serious strategic failing of the Japanese navy was to mistake tactics for strategy and strategy for the conduct of war. The navy's over-arching concern was for decisive battle—the one great surface engagement on which would ride the fate of Japan and its enemy. It was a concept premised on the ideas of Mahan, apparently validated by Japan's victories at the Yalu and at Tsushima, and supposedly confirmed by the Battle of Jutland. Fortunately for Japan, the navy's two early tactical victories of 1894 and 1905 were made possible by considered strategies. In the Pacific War, strategy was not given reasonable consideration, and the navy's early tactical victories were soon undone by disastrous strategic miscalculations. As one recent analysis of twentieth-century warfare has observed: "Mistakes in operations and tactics can be corrected, but political and strategic mistakes live forever."[55] Of no institution has this been truer than the Imperial Japanese Navy from 1941 to 1943.

From all this, the inescapable conclusion is that the Japanese navy, despite its decades of "preparation" for war with the United States, failed to appreciate the nature of such a conflict. More fundamentally, it can be charged that the Japanese navy neither understood nor prepared for *war* at all. Rather, it believed in and prepared for *battle*. For a generation, the orthodoxy of the general staff, the determinant of the navy's force structure, the guiding principle of tactical doctrine, and the ultimate test of technological design and development had been the single, annihilating surface victory, fought essentially on the navy's terms and intended to force the enemy to his knees. In the process, the navy's fixation on battle had created a fighting force that was both one-dimensional and brittle. Superbly armed and trained by 1941 to launch the thunderbolt strike and ready to risk all in furious combat, the Japanese navy was ill prepared to sustain the effort or injuries of extended war.

Moreover, as others have pointed out, the idea of "decisive" battle was a concept based on the ideas of Mahan. It was an idea that no longer had much validity by the twentieth century, if it ever had (see chapter 4). By then national destinies were measured by the strength or weakness of sinews of national power beyond those purely military: diplomacy, political leadership, trade, economic structure, industrial base, scientific and technological competence, civilian morale, the ability to manipulate public opinion, and the rest of the elements that came to comprise total war. Although Japan as a whole was unable to mobilize these elements in World War II, the Japanese navy had given almost no attention to them at all, even far less than had its sister service. "In an age of total war," Asada Sadao has written, "the Japanese navy conceived the coming conflict in terms of limited war."[56]

This, then, was the Imperial Japanese Navy's ultimate failure to the Japanese nation: the failure to understand and prepare for modern naval war. The furious dedication to training, the obedience unto death, the tactical discipline, and the array of formidable weaponry were perfected for one great naval maneuver that, carried out with clocklike precision, was to insure Japan's triumph over its enemies in less than a week. Though its courage was unrivaled and its tactical skills undoubted, in its focus on battle and in its insistent claim on the nation's resources to prepare for that encounter, the Japanese navy showed how parochial were its interests and how shallow was its grasp of contemporary naval strategy.

*   *   *

Great navies usually leave great naval legacies. This generality does not apply to the Japanese navy, for all its greatness. Bereft of all but a handful of ships at the end of the Pacific War and thereafter formally abolished by decree of the Allied powers occupying Japan, the Imperial Japanese Navy simply ceased to exist, never to be resurrected. In mission, force structure, and ethos, it has had no successor. The postwar Japanese Maritime Self-Defense Force was never intended to project Japanese power abroad. Rather, it has served to complement U.S. naval forces in the western Pacific as part of a bilateral treaty arrangement to preserve the security of Japan. As such, it has no unit larger than a destroyer and no completely independent mission. It calls upon few prewar traditions, has no links to the Japanese imperial house, and, under the present Japanese constitution, is not actually considered a navy at all. Only in the professional competence of its personnel does it bear resemblance to the old imperial navy.

If the Imperial Japanese Navy left to postwar Japan any discernible legacy at all it is in the human technical skills that armed it, served it while it existed, and then survived it decades after it lay wrecked upon the sea bottom. Many who designed and developed the warships, aircraft, and technologies of the old navy put their skills to work in the creation of the super-express trains, the cameras, the mammoth tankers, and the superlative automotive engines that became the wonder of the postwar world.[57] Considering Japan's place in the global economy today, perhaps that is the most important legacy of all.

Appendix

Biographies of Prominent Naval Officers

Akiyama Saneyuki (1868–1918) was born in Ehime Prefecture. His older brother was Akiyama Yoshifuru, who became a prominent general in the Japanese army. Akiyama Saneyuki was graduated from the Naval Academy in 1890 and for the next half-decade served as navigation officer on several warships before becoming a torpedo specialist. He spent the years 1897–99 in the United States, during which time he was able to observe American military and naval operations against Spain in the Caribbean and had the opportunity to absorb a good deal of American strategic and tactical thought, including that of Mahan. Following several months' residence in Britain in the spring of 1900, he was appointed instructor at the Naval Staff College in 1902. Upon its formation, he was made staff officer of the Combined Fleet in 1903, concurrently serving as senior staff officer of the First Fleet. Promoted to the rank of commander during the war, he drafted the orders for the Combined Fleet that were designed to prepare it to meet the Russian fleet, May 1905. Returning to the staff college, he was instructor there, 1905–8. He attained the rank of captain in 1908 and held several ship commands after the war. While serving on the general staff, he returned to the staff college for a third and final stint, 1912–14. Promoted to rear admiral in 1913, he was appointed chief of the Ministry's Naval Affairs Department, 1914, and after a tour of Europe and the United States, briefly commanded a torpedo flotilla. Retiring at the rank of vice admiral in 1917, he died suddenly of appendicitis in early 1918.

Arima Ryōkitsu (1861–1944), an 1886 graduate of the Naval Academy, held both staff and sea assignments during his career. During one of these shipboard assignments in 1902 he visited Port Arthur and familiarized himself with the harbor and its defenses. Following his appointment as operations officer on the staff of the Combined Fleet in 1903, he went on to a series of fleet commands after the Russo-Japanese War, retiring with the rank of admiral in 1919. He became chief priest of the Meiji Shrine in 1931 and was made privy councilor that same year.

Chihaya Masataka (1910–) is a prominent writer on naval and maritime affairs. He graduated from the Naval Academy in 1930 and attended the Naval Staff College during the Pacific War. A gunnery specialist by training, he had numerous shipboard assignments during the prewar decade and served as antiaircraft officer aboard the battleship *Musashi* in 1942, rising to the rank of commander by war's end. After the war, he emerged as a leading commentator on the prewar navy.

Chūdō Kan'ei (1894–1985) finished the Naval Academy in 1916 and was graduated from the staff college in 1929. His career was largely involved with Southeast Asia, and in the early 1930s, along with Ishikawa Shingo and Nakahara Yoshimasa, he was one of those who developed a passionate interest in a "southward" strategy for the navy. He served as naval attaché in Bangkok in 1936, was stationed in French Indochina in 1940, and was naval attaché in Rangoon, 1943. At war's end he was vice chief of staff of the South Area Army.

Dewa Shigetō (1855–1930) entered the Japanese navy in 1872 and held various shipboard assignments in the 1880s followed by ministry assignments in the early 1890s. He had two ship commands prior to the Sino-Japanese War and was flag captain of Itō Yūkō's flagship *Matsushima* at the Battle of the Yalu, September 1894. After several fleet staff and ministry appointments he was made rear admiral and commander of the Standing Fleet in 1900. He served as chief of the Ministry's Naval Affairs Department and was concurrently vice chief of the Navy General Staff, 1902–3. Appointed commander, First Fleet, 1903, and of the Fourth Fleet, 1904, he led the Second Fleet at the Battle of Tsushima in 1905 as vice admiral. He held a succession of high fleet and base commands for the remainder of his career and retired as admiral in 1920.

Egusa Takashige (1910–44) graduated from the Naval Academy in 1929 and in 1933 passed his flight training with honors at Kasumigaura, where he had specialized in dive-bombing. His reputation as a dive-bomber pilot grew, highlighted by a series of devastating raids he led against military installations on the China coast in the early months of the China War. At the start of the Pacific War, he led the dive-bomber group from the carrier *Sōryū* in attacks on Pearl Harbor, Wake Island, Amboina, and Port Darwin. His planes sank two British cruisers and a carrier in the Indian Ocean. He was wounded at Midway and died in an aerial assault on American fleet units off Saipan, 15 June 1944.

Fujimoto Kikuo (1887–1935) was born in Ishikawa Prefecture and entered the naval architecture branch of the Tokyo Imperial Engineering College in 1908, graduating in 1911. For the next six years he served as a naval constructor at the Yokosuka Naval Arsenal and underwent advanced training in naval architecture in Britain, 1917–21. Appointed constructor lieutenant commander in 1919, he served as assistant to Hiraga Yuzuru in the Basic Design Section of the Fourth Division (the Naval Technical Research Institute), Navy Technical

Department, 1921–25, concurrently serving as lecturer at the engineering college, 1921–22. He replaced Hiraga as head of the Basic Design Section in 1925, was promoted to constructor captain in 1927, and served as a member of the Japanese delegation to the Geneva naval conference that same year. Promoted to constructor rear admiral and appointed to head the Navy Technical Research Institute in 1934, he was officially reprimanded for the faulty design of the torpedo boat *Yuzuru* that led to its capsizing. Replaced by Capt. Fukuda Keiji in 1935, he died soon afterward.

Fukuda Keiji (1890–1964) was the second son of Vice Adm. Fukuda Umanosuke, a prominent naval architect of the Meiji period. He was graduated at the naval architecture course in the School of Engineering at Tokyo Imperial University in 1914. His career as a naval constructor was spent almost entirely at the Yokosuka Naval Arsenal and at the Naval Technical Research Institute (the Fourth Division of the Navy Technical Department). Taking over from Fujimoto Kikuo as head of the Basic Design Section of the institute in 1934, Fukuda was responsible for the supervision of plans for the superbattleships *Yamato* and *Musashi*. Promoted to vice admiral in 1940, he was appointed head of the institute in 1941. He ended his career as chief inspector for the Navy Technical Department during the Pacific War.

Fukutome (also Fukudome) **Shigeru** (1891–1971) was graduated from the Naval Academy in 1912 and from the Naval Staff College in 1925. Largely known as a staff officer of great influence and ability, he also held some important commands during the Pacific War. His early assignments included staff positions with the Navy General Staff, Navy Ministry, and Combined Fleet. He was chief of the Operations Section, General Staff, 1935–38. Promoted to rear admiral, 1939, he was chief of staff, Combined Fleet, 1939–41 and 1943–44. Promoted to vice admiral in 1942, he was made commander, Second Air Fleet, which comprised all the land-based air forces in the Philippines and, later, Taiwan. His command was all but annihilated in the air battles over Taiwan and the Sibuyan Sea in October 1944. Fukutome ended the war in command of the remnants of Japanese naval and air forces at Singapore and, as such, signed the surrender documents at Singapore on behalf of the Japanese navy, September 1945. Imprisoned for a while at Singapore for war crimes, upon his release he served as an advisor to the postwar Japanese government on the reorganization of its defense program.

Prince Fushimi Hiroyasu (1875–1946) was a professional naval officer who had been trained at the Naval Academy and had taken both courses at the Naval Staff College, but there is little doubt that his royal lineage was a significant supplement to his relatively modest talents. After five years of study in Germany, 1889–94, and two years in Britain, 1908–10, he held several ship commands. Promoted to rear admiral in 1913 and to admiral in 1922, he was briefly and successively president of the staff college, commander of the Second Fleet, and in charge of Sasebo Naval Base. His appointment to chief of the Navy General Staff in 1932 was largely made to balance the army's appointment of Prince Kan'in to head the Army General Staff. He retired in 1941 with the largely honorary rank of admiral of the fleet. As chief of staff, he was a willing instrument of navy pressure on the government and once even attempted to influence the emperor directly on the navy's behalf (much to Hirohito's irritation). A recent work by one of Japan's most distinguished naval historians has argued that along with Tōgō Heihachirō, it was Fushimi Hiroyasu who stood in the shadows behind Katō

Kanji's efforts to wreck the treaties. He and Tōgō (Fushimi by virtue of exalted position and Tōgō by hallowed reputation) were free to influence policy in this regard without criticism or even public observation.

Genda Minoru (1904–89) graduated from the Naval Academy in 1924 and took his flight training at Kasumigaura in 1928–29. After service with the Yokosuka Naval Air Group and aboard the *Akagi* he was assigned as flight instructor at Yokosuka, 1932–37. During this time, he was promoted to lieutenant commander and led the stunt team, the "Genda Circus." He passed through the Naval Staff College in 1937, where he rankled more conservative and surface-oriented officers with his unorthodox views on air power. He served as a staff officer with a combined air group in China and later as commander of the Yokosuka Naval Air Group. After a stint as assistant naval attaché in London in 1938–40, he was handpicked by Adm. Yamamoto Isoroku as chief air officer of the newly formed First Air Fleet. In that capacity he played a major role in shaping the tactical plans for the attack on Pearl Harbor. He subsequently served in carriers in the Indian Ocean, at Midway, and in the Solomon Islands. Later he saw duty on the Eleventh Air Fleet Staff at Rabaul. Promoted to captain in 1945, he was charged with the air defense of the home islands, where he served until the Japanese surrender. After the war he was in business for some years, held high-ranking positions in the Japanese Air Self-Defense Forces with the rank of general, 1955–62, and was elected to the Diet, where he served from 1962 to 1986.

Hashimoto Shintarō (1892–1945) finished his Naval Academy training in 1913 and was a student at the Naval Staff College, 1925–26. Known principally as a torpedo specialist, he held several destroyer commands in the 1920s and destroyer division commands in the 1930s. Commanding a destroyer force during the fighting in the Solomons in 1942–43, he energetically maintained supply runs to Japanese garrisons in those islands. Promoted to vice admiral in 1944, he was killed in action, May 1945.

Hiraga Yuzuru (1878–1943) was graduated in 1901 from Tokyo University as a naval architect and was commissioned as a lieutenant, junior grade, in the ship constructor branch. Thereafter he was assigned as engineer to the Yokosuka Navy Yard and then to the Kure Navy Yard in 1904, where he became chief engineer. From 1905 to 1909 he studied at the Royal Naval Academy at Greenwich, during which time he had the opportunity to learn a great deal about the design of the *Dreadnought,* the details of which he passed on to his superiors in Tokyo. Upon his return he was promoted to the rank of lieutenant commander and was appointed chief constructor at the Yokosuka Navy Yard during the building of the battleship *Yamashiro* and the battle cruiser *Hiei.* As chief of the Basic Design Section of the navy's Technical Research Department, he was responsible for the design of the *Nagato,* 1916–17. Promoted to captain in 1919, the next year he was appointed chief constructor for the eight-eight fleet plan and designed most of the capital ships intended for that projected fleet. After the plan was canceled by the Washington Naval Treaty of 1922, he was sent to Europe and the United States to gather intelligence and research data on foreign warship design and construction, 1923–24. His cold personality, his stubbornness, and his dogmatic ideas about warship design put him at odds with the Navy General Staff, whose members nicknamed him "Yuzurazu," which means "inflexible." Despite the constant friction with the naval staff over his design of the *Yūbari, Furutaka,* and *Myōkō* cruiser classes, he became head of the Ship

Design Section of the Technical Department in 1925 and was promoted to vice admiral the next year. Continuing friction with the Navy General Staff, however, led him to resign from the navy in 1930. Two years later he joined the faculty of Tokyo University and he became its president in 1938, from which position he conducted a notorious purge of its more liberal faculty members.

Hori Teikichi (1883–1959) was one of the brightest of those moderate officers forced out of the navy by right-wing factionalism in the early 1930s. Graduating from the Naval Academy in 1904, he was twice a student at the Naval Staff College, 1909–10 and 1916–18. Though he had a number of important ship commands during his career, he was principally known for his effectiveness in administrative positions, notably in the ministry's Naval Affairs Bureau, 1929–1931. He achieved vice admiral's rank in 1933, but because of his moderate views, was forced into retirement by the right-wing purge conducted under Minister Ōsumi Mineo. He later held several important executive positions in private business.

Hosogaya Boshirō (1888–1964) graduated from the Naval Academy in 1908 and from the Naval Staff College in 1920. He held several cruiser and battleship commands in the interwar period, rising to the rank of vice admiral by 1939. He was appointed commander of the Fifth Fleet in the northern Pacific in July 1942. Because of his uninspired leadership at the battle of the Komandorski Islands (west of the Aleutians) in March 1943, he was relieved of his command and placed on reserve status. He ended the war as governor of Japan's beleaguered Micronesian territories.

Ijūin Gorō (1852–1921) was a little-known but important navy leader of the Meiji period (1868–1912). As a young samurai from Satsuma, he fought in the battles that put the Meiji emperor on the throne in 1868. He attended the Naval Academy, 1871–74, and studied technical subjects at the Greenwich naval college, 1877–83. He served at sea for a time, but most of his career was spent on the Navy General Staff and as a weapons specialist. Although he received credit for the invention of a new fuse for shells that came to bear his name, it seems that at most he supervised its development. He helped work out the technical details of naval cooperation when the Anglo-Japanese Alliance was concluded in 1902. As vice chief of staff in the Russo-Japanese War, he was the real brains behind Adm. Itō Yūkō, the staff chief. At the end of his career, he was himself chief of the Navy General Staff (1909–14).

Imai Akijirō (1905–) was a proponent of a navy amphibious arm. He graduated from the Naval Academy in 1926. After varied sea duty he attended gunnery school and excelled sufficiently to become a gunnery instructor. He was attached to the Special Naval Landing Force at Shanghai, 1937; after more service in China and study at the Naval Staff College, he submitted an ambitious plan for a naval landing force to the Navy General Staff that, though it attracted attention, was not adopted. He served with various base and landing forces during the war. At the time of the surrender he had reached the rank of commander and was serving as aide-de-camp to the emperor.

Inoue Shigeyoshi (Inoue Seimi, 1889–1975), brother-in-law of Gen. Abe Nobuyuki, graduated from the Naval Academy in 1909 and the Naval Staff College in 1924. His early naval career, which included two years on detached duty in Switzerland, 1918–20, and an assignment as naval attaché in Rome, 1927–28, mixed sea billets with some important staff assignments ashore. By 1935, he had attained flag rank and in 1937 was appointed chief of the Naval Affairs Department in the Navy Ministry. Two years later, he became chief of staff of the China Area Fleet and attained the rank of vice admiral. In his capacity as chief of the Naval Aviation Bureau, to which he had been appointed in 1940, he launched a major attack on shipbuilding plans and the navy's general strategic posture that foresaw the nature of the coming war with the United States. Eased out of his position by the navy brass, he was transferred in August 1941 to command of the Fourth Fleet, with headquarters at Truk. As such, he was in overall command of the forces that took Guam and Wake Islands at the outset of the Pacific War. Subsequently, with his headquarters in Rabaul, he was overall commander for Operation MO, which was designed to take Port Moresby and led to the Japanese reverse at the Coral Sea, May 1942. Relieved of command of the Fourth Fleet in October of that year, he became superintendent of the Naval Academy. Toward the end of the war, he came back into favor and assumed the concurrent positions of navy vice minister, chief of the Navy Technical Bureau, and chief (once again) of the Naval Aviation Bureau. He had attained the rank of admiral by war's end.

Ishikawa Shingo (1894–1964). The experience and insight gained over the years in a series of varied and sensitive assignments provided this officer with unusual influence in shaping naval policy in the decade before the Pacific War. He graduated from the Naval Academy in 1914 and from the Naval Gunnery School in 1921 and attended the Naval Staff College in 1927. Promoted to commander in 1926, he served briefly as gunnery officer aboard the battleship *Fusō* in 1927 and as a battleship division staff officer in 1928. His assignment as a member of the Navy Technical Department, 1929–31, gave him a good grounding in warship design and construction. From 1931 to 1933 he served in the Third Section of the Naval Intelligence Division of the Navy General Staff, where he was one of a small group of naval officers who devoted careful study to the strategic resources of Southeast Asia and Melanesia with a view to their future acquisition by Japan. After several fleet staff assignments and lesser ship commands, during which he was promoted to captain, he became head of the navy's Special Service Agency (its intelligence apparatus abroad) in Japanese-occupied North China. Chief of the Second Section of the Naval Affairs Bureau in the Navy Ministry from November 1940 and a member of the powerful policy-making "First Committee," he was by then one of the navy's most influential middle-echelon officers and, as such, one of its most militant voices in pressing for hostilities against the United States. His participation in actual combat was somewhat less noteworthy. He was appointed vice chief of staff of the Southwest Pacific Area Fleet in June 1942 and was promoted to rear admiral that year. He briefly commanded an air group in 1943, but ended the war in various administrative capacities concerned with munitions and transportation outside the navy.

Itō Yōji (1901–55) was a radar specialist. He graduated from Tokyo University in electrical engineering in 1923 and, unusual for a naval officer of the time, eventually earned a doctorate in that field. He entered the naval service as a constructor in 1924, rising to the rank of constructor captain by the Pacific War. Though he had extensive study in Germany during the interwar years, he spent most of his naval career in the Navy's Technical Research Center.

Itō Yūkō (Itō Sukeyuki, 1843–1914) had seen action as a youth in the Satsuma encounters with the British in the 1860s. He served in several paddle-frigates in the early navy and held eight ship commands, 1871–83. He became rear admiral in 1886, served in the Navy Ministry, and was president of the Naval Staff College, 1889–90. Serving as commander of the Combined Fleet in 1894–95, he led Japan's naval forces against the Peiyang Fleet. He was promoted to the rank of admiral in 1898 and subsequently was the chief of the Navy General Staff, 1895–1905.

Kabayama Sukenori (1837–1922) began his career as a Satsuma samurai, fighting against the British and later the shogunate. After the Restoration he became one of the foremost field commanders in the new Imperial Japanese Army. Following a period as a high-ranking officer in the new national police force, he was persuaded by Saigō Tsugumichi, his Satsuma comrade in arms, to accept a commission in the navy. Without the slightest sea experience, he entered the navy as a rear admiral in 1884. He nevertheless made genuine contributions to the naval service, among them the establishment of the *Gunjibu*, the Military Affairs Department that was a forerunner of the Navy General Staff, and the enactment of several naval expansion plans. He was recalled from retirement to serve as chief the Navy General Staff in the Sino-Japanese War. At this post he made up for his lack of naval experience with his aggressive attitude and inspirational leadership. Following the war he became governor general of Korea. Elevated to the rank of count, he served in several governments as cabinet minister at the end of his career.

Kaku Tomeo (1893–1942) was graduated from the Naval Academy in 1914, from the Naval Air Training School in 1919, and from the Naval Staff College in 1927. Involved in naval aviation from the beginning of his career (except for a cruiser command), he held staff and command assignments at various naval and air bases in the 1920s and 1930s. Given command of the carrier *Hiryū* in September 1941, Kaku went down with his ship at the Battle of Midway.

Kamimura Hikonojō (1849–1916), a Satsuma man, entered the navy in 1871 and spent most of the next twenty years on shipboard assignments. He was captain of the protected cruiser *Akitsushima* during the Sino-Japanese War and fought in the cruiser at the Battle of the Yalu. He reached flag rank in 1899 and was appointed chief of the Naval Affairs Department of the Navy Ministry in 1900, vice chief of staff in 1902, and commander of the Reserve Fleet in 1903. After his service as commander of the Second Fleet in the Russo-Japanese War, he was given command of the Yokosuka Naval Base and was made a baron in 1907. Rising to the rank of admiral in 1910, his last command was the First Fleet, 1909–11.

Katō Kanji (Katō Hiroharu, 1870–1939) was born in Fukui Prefecture, the son of an early Meiji naval officer. After his graduation from the Naval Academy in 1891, he held numerous shipboard assignments, 1893–99, followed by service in Russia, 1899–1902. There, he was one of several Japanese naval officers who gathered extensive intelligence on the Russian navy prior to the Russo-Japanese War. Promoted to lieutenant commander in 1903, he held a number of important bureaucratic and diplomatic assignments over the next ten years, including service as an aide-de-camp to Prince Fushimi during the latter's visit to Britain in 1907, and as naval attaché in London, 1909–11. During this latter assignment, he capitalized on friendships in the Royal Navy to learn of the ordnance plans for the *Lion* class of British battle cruisers. This information led him to recommend the installation of 14-inch guns in the battle cruiser *Kongō*, then under construction in a British yard. Promoted to captain in 1910, he held ship commands over the next several years, including the new battle cruiser *Hiei*. Reaching the rank of rear admiral in 1916, he headed the Naval Gunnery School and then commanded the Fifth Division in 1918. His promotion to vice admiral in 1920 followed his appointment as president of the Naval Staff College the same year. In 1922 he served as naval aide to Katō Tomosaburō at the Washington Naval Conference, where he emerged as an outspoken foe of the arms limitation treaties. He filled the post of vice chief of the Navy General Staff, from 1922 to 1923. He commanded the Combined Fleet for two years after that, achieving the rank of admiral. Katō reached the pinnacle of his influence in 1930 when, as chief of the Navy General Staff, he launched a campaign to block the London Treaty by claiming that it infringed upon his and the emperor's authority. Forced to resign over the crisis, he nevertheless helped engineer the demise of the navy's moderate leadership in the years immediately following. He retired from the navy in 1935.

Katō Tomosaburō (1861–1923), a native of Hiroshima, was graduated from the Naval Academy in 1880 and from the Naval Staff College in 1889. After several shipboard assignments, including duty aboard the cruiser *Yoshino* on its maiden voyage from British yards in 1891, he assumed the first of many increasingly responsible positions in the Naval Affairs Bureau of the Navy Ministry, 1894–1901. These assignments were followed by a stretch of staff duty with the fleet. By the end of the Russo-Japanese War, having reached the rank of rear admiral, he had been chief of staff of, successively, the Standing, the Second, the First, and the Combined Fleets. Serving as vice minister from 1906 to 1909, he was promoted to vice admiral in 1908 and admiral in 1915, three months after his appointment as navy minister. Granted a barony in 1920, his successful coordination of Japanese naval affairs at the Washington Naval Conference, 1921–22, contributed to his selection as prime minister, June–December 1922. Raised to viscount and admiral of the fleet in August 1923, he died that same month. He was undoubtedly the most farsighted leader produced by the navy and was its outstanding statesman.

Kimura Masatomi (1891–1960) was one of the navy's foremost sea commanders in World War II. After his graduation from the Naval Academy in 1913, he spent almost all his career in the interwar years in small warships, principally destroyers. Promoted to rear admiral early in the war, he served as commander of the escort force for a large convoy passing through the Bismarck Sea, which was nearly annihilated by American bombers in March 1943. After recovering from wounds incurred in that encounter, he returned to duty, flawlessly conducting the evacuation of Japanese troops from Kiska in the Aleutians in June 1943. He was in command of one of the last offensive actions of the Japanese navy in World War II, the futile raid on American positions on Mindoro, the Philippines, February 1944.

Kishimoto Kaneharu (Kishimoto Kaneji, 1888–1981) was the navy's most prominent underwater weapons specialist. After graduating from the Naval Academy in 1909, he studied at the Naval Staff College in 1916 and at the Torpedo School in 1917. Specializing in torpedo warfare, he spent most of the 1920s in command of destroyers and destroyer units. His work at Kure on the oxygen torpedo began in 1932 when he was chief of the Second Section of the First Bureau of the Navy Technical Department. As chief of the Torpedo Proving Facility at the Kure Arsenal beginning November 1935, he was also responsible for the development of the navy's secret midget submarine project. He was promoted to rear admiral in

December 1936, and his last important career assignment was chief of the Torpedo Division of the Kure Naval Arsenal, from which position he continued his supervision of the oxygen torpedo and midget submarine projects. He retired from the navy in 1940.

Kondō Nobutake (1886–1953) was graduated from the Naval Academy in 1907 and passed through the Naval Staff College in 1919. During his early career he had numerous sea, staff, and foreign residence assignments. In the 1930s he served as president of the Naval Staff College and chief of staff of the Combined Fleet and vice chief of staff. As commander of the Second Fleet, 1941–43, he helped carry out the invasions of the Philippines, Malaya, and Java, and commanded the main support forces for the attempted invasion of Midway. He held important commands during the battles of the Eastern Solomons, Santa Cruz Islands, and Guadalcanal.

Koyanagi Tomiji (1893–1978) passed through the Naval Academy in 1914 and was graduated from the Naval Staff College in 1926. A torpedo specialist, he served on destroyers and destroyer division staffs during the interwar years. He also taught at various naval schools and held a cruiser and battleship command. After receiving his promotion to rear admiral in November 1942, he was in command of the Second Destroyer Flotilla and, as such, helped evacuate Japanese troops from the Solomons in February 1943. During the Leyte Gulf campaign in which he was wounded, he served as commander of the First Strike Force in the battleship *Yamato*. He finished his naval service as vice admiral.

Kurita Takeo (1889–1977) was a capable and courageous officer who held several major commands during the Pacific War, most notably at Leyte Gulf. He passed through the Naval Academy in 1910 and was graduated from the Naval Staff College in 1917. A torpedo specialist, he spent most of the interwar period aboard destroyers. He was promoted to rear admiral in 1938 and became a vice admiral early in the Pacific War. He held important operational commands at the battles of Midway, the Santa Cruz Islands, and the Philippine Sea. At the Battle off Samar (Leyte Gulf campaign), during which he was commander of the main Japanese force and had his flagship sunk from under him, he made the critical decision to break off the battle in the face of apparently overwhelming odds.

Kuroshima Kameto (1893–1965) was one of the more eccentric navy officers. He was graduated from the Naval Academy in 1916. Following an early career at sea as a gunnery officer, he attended the Naval Staff College and later became renowned as a staff officer and planner. As senior fleet operations officer under Yamamoto Isoroku, he drafted the original plan for the Pearl Harbor attack. He held positions on the Navy General Staff until the end of the war.

Kusaka Ryūnosuke (1892–1971) was graduated from the Naval Academy in 1913, passed through Naval Gunnery School in 1920, and was graduated from the Naval Staff College in 1926. After several shipboard assignments, he was appointed instructor at both the Kasumigaura Naval Air Station and the Naval Staff College. Promoted to commander in 1930, he was assigned to the staff of the First Carrier Division and, four years later, with the rank of captain, worked at the Naval Aviation Department. Then followed various staff assignments at sea and in Tokyo, interspersed with carrier commands. He attained the rank of rear admiral in November 1940, and when the First Air Fleet was reorganized into the Pearl Harbor strike force, he was made its chief of staff. He played a major role in formulating plans for the aerial assault on Hawaii and for the Midway operation. After serving as chief of staff, Southeast Area Fleet, 1943–44, he became chief of staff of the Combined Fleet. He ended the war as vice admiral in command of the Fifth Air Fleet based on Kyūshū.

Mikawa Gun'ichi (1888–1981) inflicted the greatest single defeat sustained by the U.S. Navy. He passed through the Naval Academy in 1910 and was a student at the Naval Staff College in 1916 and 1922–24. A specialist in navigation, he also served extensively overseas, particularly in diplomatic assignments in Paris and Geneva in the 1920s. During the 1930s he held several cruiser and battleship commands. As vice admiral and commander of the Eighth Fleet, he was involved in some of the heaviest fighting in the Solomons campaign of 1942, including the night battle of Savo Island at the beginning of the campaign, during which he delivered a crushing defeat of a largely American force of cruisers and destroyers.

Misu Sōtarō (1855–1921) held a variety of staff and sea assignments in the early part of his career, including several ship commands, a stint as superintendent of the Naval Academy, and service as chief of the Navy Ministry's personnel department. He was appointed commander of the Second Fleet in 1903, and the First Fleet in 1905. At the Battle of Tsushima he commanded the First Division in the *Nisshin*. He went on to become, successively, commander of the Port Arthur naval base and vice chief of the Navy General Staff. Made a baron, he retired in 1913 with the rank of admiral.

Mizuno Hironori (1875–1945) was an important publicist of the Japanese navy. He graduated from the Naval Academy in 1898 and served as commander of a torpedo boat in the Russo-Japanese War. After the war, he was put in charge of the archives of the Navy Ministry and was later attached to the War History Section of the Navy General Staff. Using his experience of the war and his knowledge of the historical record of the war, he produced several books intended to promote public enthusiasm for the navy. His most famous work was *Kono issen* (This one battle), a dramatic and colorful account of the Battle of Tsushima written in 1910.

Murata Shigeharu (1909–42) was one of that later generation of Japanese naval officers who spent nearly all of their tragically short careers in aviation. After graduating from the Naval Academy in 1930, he took his flight training at Kasumigaura in 1933–34. He was among the pilots who carried out the attack on the U.S. gunboat *Panay* in 1937. He held a number of section commands both ashore and on carriers in the late 1930s. Appointed commander of the *Akagi*'s torpedo squadron, he led the torpedo attack at Pearl Harbor and participated in carrier operations in the Bismarck Archipelago, at Port Darwin, and in the Indian Ocean in the winter and spring of 1942. He became commander of the torpedo squadron of the carrier *Shōkaku* in July 1942 and died leading a torpedo attack on the *Hornet* in October of that year.

Nagano Osami (1880–1947) was more of an administrative officer than a sea commander, starting out early in his career on bureaucratic track with a post in the Naval Affairs

Bureau of the navy ministry. Like Yamamoto Isoroku, he had significant experience of the United States. He studied there during the years 1913–15 and was naval attaché in Washington, 1920–23. During his long career, he held only one ship command, that of the light cruiser *Hirado*, in 1919. Yet during the 1930s he represented the navy at arms limitation conferences abroad and came to occupy virtually every important post in the navy. These included vice chief of the Navy General Staff, commander of the Yokosuka Naval Base, navy minister, and commander in chief of the Combined Fleet. He was in semiretirement as a member of the Supreme War Council when named chief of the Navy General Staff in 1941, at which point he was the senior officer in the navy. As staff chief, he did not provide strong leadership, being influenced by hard-lining subordinates and becoming increasingly bellicose as war approached. He opposed Yamamoto's plan for a surprise attack on Pearl Harbor, but reluctantly gave his approval when Yamamoto threatened to resign as commander in chief of the Combined Fleet. He remained chief of the Naval General Staff for most of the war, until February 1944, posting a lackluster record. Put on trial after the war as a Class A war criminal, he died of illness before any verdict was reached.

Nagumo Chūichi (1886–1944) was graduated from the Naval Academy in 1908 and passed through the Naval Staff College in 1920. During his career he held numerous sea commands ranging from gunboats to carrier groups. As a torpedo expert he was a strong advocate of combining sea and air power, though he was never comfortable in command of carriers, as he lacked expertise in aviation. Nevertheless, he was given command of the First Air Fleet in April 1941. In that position, despite his opposition to Yamamoto's plans for the Pearl Harbor operation and the subsequent criticism from some quarters that his refusal to sanction a second strike was overly cautious, he directed Japan's carrier forces during their greatest victories of the Pacific War: the Hawaii operation, the attacks on Rabaul and Port Darwin, and the sweeping away of Allied naval forces from the eastern Indian Ocean in the winter and spring of 1942. With the sinking of his four carriers at Midway, however, he evidently lost whatever aggressiveness he had and was relegated to shore commands in 1942–43. Called back to the front lines in March 1944, he was given command of an essentially paper fleet at Saipan and died by his own hand in the futile defense of that island against American forces that June.

Nakahara Yoshimasa (1892–1944) was graduated from the Naval Academy in 1913 and passed through the Naval Staff College in 1926. He was head of the influential War Guidance Office in the Navy General Staff, 1934–36. After several cruiser commands he became a member of a general staff committee to study the possibilities of a southward advance, while concurrently serving as a member of the newly influential Naval Affairs Bureau of the Navy Ministry. Promoted to rear admiral, he was made head of the Ministry's Personnel Bureau in 1940. Chief of staff of the Southeast Asia Fleet in 1942, he was promoted to vice admiral in 1943 and was killed in action in February 1944.

Nakajima Chikuhei (1884–1949) was graduated from the Navy Engineering Academy in 1907 and was a student in the engineer staff officer course at the Naval Staff College, 1911–12, after which he was sent for training at the Glenn Curtiss Flying School at Hammondsport, New York. He resigned from the navy in 1917 to found his own aircraft company and eventually became a leading aircraft manufacturer in Japan. Elected to the Japanese Diet, he became a powerful political figure and held several ministerial posts in the 1930s.

Niimi Masaichi (Niimi Seiichi, 1887–1993) was graduated from the Naval Academy in 1908. After more than a decade of sea duty he attended the Naval Staff College and gunnery school. It was as an officer on the Navy General Staff in 1922 that he wrote his report on protecting merchant shipping. After teaching at the Naval Staff College, he held three successive cruiser commands. He went on to a series of administrative posts before retiring in 1944.

Nomura Kichisaburō (1877–1964) is principally known to Americans as Japan's ambassador to the United States during the ill-fated talks with Secretary of State Cordell Hull in the months prior to the Japanese attack on Pearl Harbor, but he had numerous American contacts before then. He was graduated from the Naval Academy in 1898. Although he did not attend the Naval Staff College, he was appointed as naval attaché in Washington during World War I. Promoted to captain in 1917, he was a member of the Japanese delegations to the conferences at Versailles and Washington after the war. Attaining the rank of rear admiral in 1922 and vice admiral in 1926, he was vice chief of staff, 1926–28, and was commander of Japanese naval forces in China at the time of the Sino-Japanese hostilities in Shanghai in 1932. Promoted to admiral in 1933, he retired in 1937, but was called to serve as foreign minister in the civilian cabinet in the fall of 1939. He was selected as ambassador to Washington in 1940, largely because of his friendships and solid reputation in the U.S. Navy.

Nomura Minoru (1922–) is a distinguished naval historian of the postwar era. He completed his Naval Academy training in 1942 and saw service aboard the battleship *Musashi* and the carrier *Zuikaku*. He also served on the Navy General Staff and, at the end of the war, at the Naval Academy. In the postwar period he worked for the Demobilization Bureau and as defense counsel to naval officers on trial at the International Military Tribunal for the Far East. He also pursued advanced studies at Keiō University and was awarded the Ph.D. degree. In 1956 he went to work for the Defense Agency, where he became a member of the Military History Department of the Defense Research Institute. There he was a principal figure in the research and writing of the naval volumes of the institute's War History Series, the official history of Japanese military and naval operations, 1937–45. He has been professor of maritime defense studies at the National Defense College and now, semiretired, teaches at a college in Nagoya while continuing to contribute actively to scholarship. He is the author of numerous articles and several important books on the prewar navy and on the Pacific War.

Ogasawara Chōsei (Ogasawara Naganari, Ogasawara Nagayo, 1867–1958), from an old noble family, was a viscount before entering the navy. Graduated from the Naval Academy in 1887, he attended the Naval Staff College in 1891–92. After serving aboard a cruiser in the Sino-Japanese War, he was attached to the Intelligence Section of the Navy General Staff and later held several shipboard assignments. Promoted to the rank of commander in 1904, he spent the next seven years on the Navy General Staff, where he became a leading expert on codes and ciphers and was made responsible for editing the general staff histories of the war. He was best known, however, for his influential image-building of the navy after the war. By the time he reached flag rank in 1914, his colorful and exhaustive writings on the navy had earned him the sobriquet *bunsai teitoku,* the "literary admiral." The bulk of his writing was done after his retirement in 1921, and his stream of books on the Russo-Japanese War, including two biographies of Admiral Tōgō and a book on the battleship *Mikasa,* stimulated public enthusiasm for the navy in the 1920s and 1930s.

Ōi Atsushi (1902–1994) was graduated from the Naval Academy in 1923. After intensive English language study in Japan in 1928–30, he was a special student at the University of Virginia and at Northwestern University, 1930–32. During the 1930s, he served on several fleet staffs and was a member of the British Section of Naval Intelligence, reaching the rank of commander. Promoted to captain during the Pacific War, his most important posting during the war years was his assignment as operations officer with the navy's Maritime Escort Headquarters, from November 1943 to the end of the war. During the American occupation of Japan he worked in the Historical Section of SCAP Headquarters.

Oka Takazumi (1890–1973) passed through the Naval Academy in 1911 and completed his studies at the Naval Staff College in 1923. A submariner by specialization, Oka nevertheless held numerous staff assignments during his career, most importantly in the Naval Affairs Bureau (which he headed, 1940–44) and served briefly as navy vice minister in 1944. He was another ardent advocate of *nanshin* (southward advance) and, prior to the Pacific War, was the principal leader of the pro-Axis element within the navy. After the war, he was imprisoned for a time as a Class A war criminal.

Ōnishi Takijirō (1891–1945) held a number of early assignments to the navy's first air units during World War I. After studying air combat and reconnaissance in Britain in 1918–21, he was attached to the Yokosuka Naval Air Group. In the mid-1920s he was an instructor at Kasumigaura. As the 1930s progressed he held staff and line positions of increasing responsibility in naval aviation, including flight commands ashore and on carriers and staff assignments with the Naval Aviation Department. Promoted to rear admiral in 1939, he was made chief of staff, Eleventh Air Fleet. As such, he had a part in Yamamoto Isoroku's Pearl Harbor attack plan and in the coordination of the devastating air attacks on the Philippines from bases in Taiwan. Attaining the rank of vice admiral in 1943, he held several important administrative positions in Tokyo before being sent to the Philippines in October 1944 to take command of the First Air Fleet, an entirely land-based air command by then. In that capacity, he developed the concept of aerial suicide attacks on American warships and directed the first such attacks. He took up the position of vice chief of the Navy General Staff in May 1945, and on 15 August 1945, after hearing the emperor's surrender broadcast, committed ritual suicide.

Ōsumi Mineo (1876–1941) passed through the Naval Academy in 1897 and was graduated at the top of his class at the Naval Staff College in 1907. He held several ship commands earlier in his career, but it was his administrative positions, including those of aide-de-camp to Admiral Tōgō (1912), private secretary to the navy minister (1914), and chief of the Naval Affairs Bureau (1922), that gave him a feel for political and bureaucratic maneuvering within the navy. Promoted to rear admiral in 1920 and to vice admiral in 1924, he was appointed navy vice minister in 1925–28 and navy minister in 1931–32 and 1933–36. A slavish adherent among the top brass to the views of the "command group" during these years, he attempted to bully the civilian government into accepting his policies. Made a baron in 1935, he was killed in an air crash in southern China in 1941.

Ozawa Jisaburō (1886–1966) was one of the ablest flag officers in the Japanese navy. After graduation from the Naval Academy in 1909 and from the navy's Torpedo School in

1917, he served mostly at sea as commander of, successively, a destroyer flotilla, a cruiser, and a battleship. As a rear admiral he served as chief of staff of the Combined Fleet (1937) and as commander of the First Carrier Division (1940). Later, as a vice admiral, he commanded the Southern Expeditionary Fleet, which supported the Japanese conquest of Malaya and the Netherlands East Indies in the winter of 1941–42. As commander of the First Mobile Fleet and the Third Fleet in 1944 (Japan's principal carrier forces at that time) he was outmatched and outfought by Admiral Spruance's Task Force 58 in the Battle of the Philippine Sea. In command of the decoy force in the Leyte Gulf campaign, his carriers were smashed at the Battle of Cape Engaño in October 1944. He ended the war as commander of the Combined Fleet, which by then existed only as a force on paper.

Saigō Tsugumichi (Saigō Jūdō, 1843–1902) promoted the navy as an administrator and politician in the 1880s and 1890s. He began his career as a humble samurai of the Satsuma domain. Like his famous older brother Saigō Takamori, he was prominent in the politics and the fighting that put the Meiji emperor on the throne in 1868. Subsequently, as a reform-minded official in the Western-oriented new government, he served in a number of important army posts. In 1885, as part of a maneuver to strengthen Satsuma influence in the government and improve the position of the navy, he became navy minister, though he was in fact a general of the army. He served in a series of other cabinet posts concurrently but was able to improve the prestige and budgetary position of the navy significantly in the 1890s. In October 1894 he was granted full admiral's rank in recognition of his services.

Saitō Makoto (1858–1936) was a distinguished naval administrator and statesman. His career began with his graduation from the Naval Academy in 1879. As a junior officer he was posted to Washington, D.C., where he studied U.S. naval administration and became the first naval attaché of the Japanese Legation. After a number of staff and shipboard assignments he became a member of the Navy Ministry's personnel section under Yamamoto Gombei, who became his strong proponent henceforth. During the Sino–Japanese War he was aide-de-camp to the emperor. He subsequently served as executive officer aboard the cruiser *Izumi* and the battleship *Fuji* and as commanding officer of the cruiser *Akitsushima*. Shortly thereafter, in 1898, he became vice minister of the navy under Yamamoto. He himself was navy minister under Yamamoto's continuing guidance, 1906–14. He later held many high government posts, among them that of governor general of Korea (1919–27 and 1929–31). He served as prime minister in 1932–34 and was lord keeper of the privy seal when assassinated by rebel army officers in the uprising of 26 February 1936.

Sakamoto Toshiatsu (1858–1941), the father of advanced education in the Japanese navy and the navy's foremost internationalist, was one of the "three men of talent" *(sanshūsai)* from the illustrious Naval Academy class of 1877. (Yamanouchi Masuji, who distinguished himself as a weapons specialist, and Saitō Makoto, who made his mark in administration, were the other two.) A gunnery specialist, Sakamoto had been sent to France to study gunnery and torpedo technology and tactics in 1884–88. After that he had taught briefly at the newly established Naval Staff College. He then served as second in command on several warships, including the *Yoshino* at the Battle of the Yalu, and later was a member of the Navy General Staff on several occasions. At the staff college he was senior instructor, 1897–99, and was appointed acting president, 1900–1902. He was named president of the college in 1902, the same year he was promoted to flag rank. He served again as president of the college in 1905–8 and ended his career, appropriately enough, as chief of naval education, 1908–12. Made a baron in 1907, he was a member of the House of Peers from 1917 to 1939.

Sasō Sachū (1852–1905) pioneered naval architecture in Japan. He attended the Naval Academy in 1869–71 and studied naval architecture in Britain from 1871 to 1878. Upon his return to Japan he received a commission as an engineering officer. For most of his career, he served in various positions within the Navy Technical Department, where he had a major role in acquiring the warships with which Japan fought the Sino- and Russo-Japanese Wars. In 1897 he became constructor vice admiral and in 1902 was awarded a doctor's degree in engineering. He was posthumously elevated to the peerage.

Satō Tetsutarō (1866–1942), through his writings, was one of the most influential officers in the history of the Japanese navy. The brother-in-law of Adm. Ogasawara Chōsei, he was graduated from the Naval Academy in 1887 and was a student at the Naval Staff College in 1891–92 and 1906–7. Serving aboard the gun vessel *Akagi,* he was slightly wounded at the Battle of the Yalu in 1894. After service in the Ministry's Naval Affairs Bureau, he was sent by Navy Minister Yamamoto Gombei to study naval history and strategy in Britain, 1899–1900. Promoted to the rank of commander in 1902, he held several ship commands, 1902–7, after which he was assigned as instructor at the Naval Staff College, where he served, 1907–8 and 1910–12. It was in this latter position that he completed his master work, *The History of Imperial Defense,* which became the bible of Japanese navalism. During this period he also set forth his ideas on a hypothetical naval standard and a fixed tonnage ratio compared with the U.S. Navy. Promoted to rear admiral in 1912, he served on the general staff in 1913 and 1914–15 and was briefly vice chief of staff in 1915, followed by several years as president of the college. He retired in 1923 at the rank of vice admiral and became a member of the House of Peers in 1934.

Shimamura Hayao (1858–1923) was a member of the First Section, Naval Division, of the general staff in 1886. He served with the British Mediterranean Fleet in 1888–91 and was appointed a staff officer with the Standing Fleet in 1893. Serving as close advisor to Adm. Itō Yūkō, commander of the Standing Fleet during the Sino-Japanese War in 1894–95, he was wounded aboard the cruiser *Matsushima* during Battle of Yalu, 1894. Attached to the Japanese Legation, Rome, he observed the Greco-Turkish War of 1897. He was promoted to commander in 1897 and captain in 1899, when be became chief, Second (war preparations) Division, Navy General Staff, 1899. As captain of the cruiser *Suma,* he led a landing party at Tientsin during the Boxer Rebellion in 1900. He became chief of staff of the Standing Fleet in 1903 and, as commander of the Second Fleet in 1905, took part in Battle of Tsushima with his flag in the cruiser *Iwate.* He served as commandant of the Naval Academy. From 1908, as vice admiral, he was president of the Naval Staff College. Appointed chief of the Navy General Staff in 1914, he was promoted to admiral in 1915.

Suetsugu Nobumasa (1880–1944) graduated from the Naval Academy in 1899 and from the Naval Staff College ("A" course) in 1909. After several early shipboard assignments, he passed through the Gunnery School in 1907 and served as gunnery instructor afloat and at the school. After a tour of duty on the Navy General Staff, 1912–14, he was sent in 1914 as a naval observer to Britain, where he assimilated a wealth of information on the German U-boat campaign against that country. Returning to Japan in 1916, he was assigned to the Operations Section of the Navy General Staff. He was a member of the Japanese delegation to the naval conference at Washington, where he consistently supported the hard-line position. In 1923, as rear admiral, he took charge of the First Submarine Division and in that position worked out the offensive tactics that he perfected when he was commander in chief of the Combined Fleet a decade later. After retirement from the navy as admiral in 1937, he was sought by Prime Minister Konoe Fumimaro as navy minister. Suetsugu was opposed by others in the navy because of his extremist views, however, and was obliged to accept a purely civilian position in the cabinet instead.

Suzuki Kantarō (1856–1948) had a long and distinguished career in the service of his country. A graduate of the Naval Academy in 1887, he made torpedo warfare his specialty early on in his career. He was commander of torpedo flotillas at Yokosuka and Takeshiki on Tsushima and commanded the Third Torpedo Flotilla during the Sino-Japanese War. Several shipboard assignments and service with the Navy Ministry and the Navy General Staff followed after the war. During his study in Germany, 1901–3, he was promoted to commander. In the Russo-Japanese War he commanded the Fourth Destroyer Flotilla at the battles of the Yellow Sea and Tsushima. By then, he was known throughout the navy as a torpedo specialist, having supplemented his combat experience with several written works on the subject. In this capacity he was chosen to study at the Naval Staff College in 1905–8 and served as head of the navy's Torpedo School, 1910–11. After several ship commands, he reached flag rank in 1913 and was given command of the Second Fleet. He was made navy vice minister in 1914, was promoted to admiral in 1923, and was given command of the Combined Fleet in 1924. Chief of the Navy General Staff in 1925, he was placed on the reserved list in 1929. He became a member of the Privy Council in the 1930s and was given a baronetcy in 1936. This prestigious position left him vulnerable to attacks by young military radicals of the time. He was seriously wounded in the Young Officers' Rebellion of 1936. With his leadership of the Privy Council in 1940–44, he entered the ranks of Japan's elder statesmen. Because of his distinguished service to his country he was appointed prime minister in the last months of the Pacific War and thereby presided over the Imperial Liaison Conferences that led to Japan's surrender in August 1945.

Takagi Sōkichi (1893–1979) went on to become the Japanese navy's foremost intellectual. A graduate of the Naval Academy in 1915 and the Naval Staff College in 1927, he spent nearly his entire career as a staff officer, much of it in research positions. As chief of the Research Section of the Navy Ministry, 1937–39 and 1940–42, he expanded his functions to become the navy's chief political antenna, seeking contact with the leading political figures of the time. His sub-rosa opposition to Japan's decision to go to war temporarily derailed his influence in 1942. Promoted to rear admiral in 1943, he was appointed to the Research Department of the general staff in 1944. His opposition to the war, his drafting of an ultra-secret plan for a negotiated peace, and his participation in an abortive plot to assassinate Tōjō Hideki combined to give him a postwar reputation not unlike that of Admiral Canaris in the German navy.

Takahashi Sankichi (1882–1966) was graduated from the Naval Academy in 1901 and from the navy's Gunnery School in 1909, and later in his naval career passed through both courses at the Naval Staff College. Over the next decade, he held various staff assignments, including an assignment in the Navy Ministry, during which time he toured Europe and the United States. His service at sea included an assignment as executive officer of the battleship *Hizen* and command of the battleship *Fusō*. Promoted to rear admiral in 1925, he served as chief of staff of the Combined Fleet in 1926 and was the first commander of the First Carrier Division, 1928–29. Raised to the rank of vice admiral in 1929, he was appointed president of the Naval Staff College that year. As vice chief of the general staff, 1932–33, he was strongly identified with the navy's hard-lining "fleet faction." He was commander of the Combined Fleet, 1934–36, and retired in 1939 with the rank of admiral.

Tanaka Raizō (1892–1969) gained a reputation in the West—largely at the hands of the American historian Samuel Eliot Morison—as one of the Japanese navy's most brilliant and indefatigable officers in the Pacific War. A torpedo specialist, he was graduated from the Naval Academy in 1913. He held several destroyer and destroyer unit commands in the 1930s, and at the outbreak of the war, with the rank of rear admiral, he commanded the Second Destroyer Flotilla. As such, he participated in the invasions of the Philippines and the Netherlands East Indies and in the battles of the Coral Sea and Midway. He won the respect of his American foes for his tenacity and resourcefulness in the attempt to keep open the Japanese supply lines to the Solomons in the latter half of 1942 and for the defeat he inflicted on superior American forces at the Battle of Tassafaronga in November of that year. He was relieved of his command in December, allegedly for his outspoken criticism of the high command for its strategy in the southwest Pacific.

Tōgō Heihachirō (1848–1934) was one of the most famous Japanese naval figures. He was born in Kagoshima and as a youth participated in the conflict between the Satsuma domain and Great Britain in 1863 and later served on a Satsuma warship in the civil war of 1868. After studying naval science in Britain from 1871 to 1878, he was commissioned a lieutenant in the fledgling Japanese navy. For the next decade and a half, he held numerous sea assignments, including several ship commands. He was captain of the cruiser *Naniwa* at the time of the Kowshing Incident and throughout the Sino-Japanese War. After the war, he served successively as president of the Naval Staff College, commander of the Sasebo Naval Base, and commander of the Standing Fleet. He was appointed commander in chief of the Combined Fleet in 1903. Promoted to the rank of admiral in June 1904, he led that fleet in its operations against Russia, 1904–5, and it was under his command that the Combined Fleet intercepted and destroyed the Russian Baltic Fleet at Tsushima in May 1905. After the war he became chief of the Navy General Staff and was made a count. He was accorded the honorific title of fleet admiral in 1913. He was given charge of the education of Prince Hirohito, the later Shōwa emperor, in 1914–24, and although he held no official post during these years, he remained a figure of powerful influence in the navy and in the country as a whole.

Tomioka Sadatoshi (1900–1970) was born in Nagano Prefecture, the eldest son of a navy admiral, and graduated from the Naval Academy in 1917 and the Naval Staff College in 1929. A man of some urbanity, he studied in France early in his career and was the navy's representative at the League of Nations, 1930–32. While his career included significant sea duty, including a destroyer command in the late 1920s and a cruiser command during the Pacific War, he was primarily a staff officer. In that capacity he served in the Operations Section of the Navy General Staff, 1933–34, and was its chief, 1940–43, during which time he drew up the abortive plans for the seizure of Port Moresby and the invasion of Australia. Promoted to rear admiral in 1943, he was appointed chief of the Operations Division of the General Staff in December 1944 and as such represented the staff at the Japanese surrender ceremony on board the battleship *Missouri.*

Torisu Kennosuke (1908–) was a prominent submariner. He was graduated from the Naval Academy in 1930 and, during the ensuing decade, attended both the Torpedo School and the Submarine School. At the end of the decade he served as torpedo officer aboard several submarines. During the war he held a number of submarine commands and was a staff officer of the Sixth Fleet. In the postwar era he has authored several books on the submarine force and the navy in general.

Tsuboi Kōzō (1843–98) studied at Columbia University in 1872–74 and trained with the USS *Colorado,* flagship of the American Far Eastern Squadron. He held five ship commands and as rear admiral became commandant of the Naval Academy in 1890. Appointed president of the Naval Staff College in 1893, he subsequently served as commander of the Standing Fleet, 1894, and then as commander of the Flying Squadron at the Battle of the Yalu, September 1894. Vice admiral and commander of the Standing Fleet in 1896, he ended his career as commander of Yokohama Naval Base in 1897.

Ugaki Matome (1890–1945) was one of the ablest Japanese naval professionals on the eve of the Pacific War. His extensive diary has been a valuable source of information on the wartime navy. After graduation from the Naval Academy in 1912, he passed through the Naval Staff College in 1924. He held several battleship commands in the 1930s and was promoted to rear admiral in 1938. As chief of staff of the Combined Fleet under Adm. Yamamoto Isoroku, he was involved in planning the Pearl Harbor strategy. Promoted to vice admiral in 1942, he was commander of a battleship division under Adm. Kurita Takeo, with his flag in the *Yamato,* February 1944. As such he was involved in the Leyte Gulf campaign. As commander of the Fifth Air Fleet in February 1945, he controlled Japan's remaining naval air forces in Kyūshū at the end of the war. On the day of the emperor's surrender broadcast, he led several planes in an abortive suicide attack on U.S. forces on Okinawa and perished in the action.

Uriu Sotokichi (1858–1937) was one of the early Japanese students at the U.S. Naval Academy, 1875–81. Over the next decade, he held several shipboard and executive assignments and was attached to the Japanese embassy in Paris, 1892–96. After several ship commands, he served on the general staff. He was appointed commander of the Second Fleet in 1903. After the war he held several base commands, was made a baron, and retired with the rank of admiral in 1913. Before his death he was made a member of the House of Peers.

Yamagata Seigo (1891–1945) graduated from the Naval Academy in 1911 and attended the Naval Staff College in 1922–24. Early in his career he became identified with naval aviation, serving in the Naval Aviation Department as well as holding a carrier command during the 1930s. During the time that he was commander of the Fourth Southern Expeditionary Fleet during the Pacific War (1943–45), his plane crashed in China and he committed suicide to avoid capture.

Yamamoto Gombei (Yamamoto Gonnohyōe, 1852–1933) was the architect of modern Japanese naval power. He was born and grew up in the castle town of the Satsuma domain, Kagoshima. As a boy of sixteen, he fought with the Satsuma army in the Restoration war at Toba-Fushimi and in northern Honshū (1868). He was one of the first to be graduated from the new Naval Academy, in 1874, and took a midshipman cruise to San Francisco. Like other navy leaders, he had significant foreign experience. After his cruise he served for over a year on the warships *Vineta* and *Leipzig* of another fledgling navy, the German, circumnavigating the globe and passing both the Cape of Good Hope and Cape Horn. As a junior officer he had duty aboard five different vessels (1878–81). He became second in command of the screw-corvette *Asama,* 1882–85, and occupied the same position on the cruiser *Naniwa* when it was brought to Japan in 1886 after its construction in Britain. His first command, the sloop *Amagi,* followed. In 1887, as aide to Navy Minister Saigō, he undertook extended visits to Europe and the United States. He made the rank of captain in 1889 and subsequently commanded the cruisers *Takao* and *Takachiho.* His career began to take a political direction when he was appointed director of the Navy Ministry's Secretariat in 1891. Because of his administrative skill he was made rear admiral and chief of the Naval Affairs Department of the ministry in 1895. He attained the rank of vice admiral in 1898 and admiral in 1904. He served as navy minister, 1898–1906, and as prime minister, 1913–14 and 1923–24.

Yamamoto Isoroku (1884–1943). Along with Tōgō Heihachirō, Yamamoto is one of the two Japanese naval figures best known in the West, his fame largely resting on his role in planning the Hawaii operation in 1941 and the Midway campaign of 1942. He was born Takano Isoroku, but was adopted in his youth by the Yamamoto family (no relation to Yamamoto Gombei). After graduation from the Naval Academy in 1904, he was just in time to get an assignment on the cruiser *Nisshin,* on which he served at the Battle of the Japan Sea, losing two fingers in that action. After a number of other shipboard assignments he passed through the "B" course at the Naval Staff College in 1911 and the "A" course in 1916. Promoted to lieutenant commander in 1915, he was sent for study in the United States, where he attended Harvard University from 1919 to 1921. He attained the rank of commander in 1919 and was made executive officer of the cruiser *Kitakami* in 1921. During his tour of Europe and America as aide-de-camp to Adm. Ide Kenji, 1923–24, he obtained the rank of captain. After being executive officer of the Kasumigaura Naval Air Station in 1924 and serving as naval attaché in Washington in 1925–28, his next several assignments all dealt with naval aviation: commanding officer of the aircraft carrier *Akagi,* 1928, chief of the Technical Bureau of Naval Aviation Department, 1930–33, and commander of the First Carrier Division, 1933. He had been promoted to rear admiral in 1929 and attained the rank of vice admiral in 1934. Following his responsibilities at the London Naval Conference, he was made chief of the Naval Aviation Department in 1935. Appointed navy vice minister in 1936, he served concurrently as chief of Naval Aviation Department from 1938 to 1939. Following his appointment as commander of the Combined Fleet, he was promoted to admiral. He was commander of the Combined Fleet when he met his death. In April 1943 the naval aircraft in which he was riding was shot down over Bougainville by American fighter planes. He was posthumously promoted to admiral of the fleet.

Yamanouchi Masuji (1860–1919). Along with Sakamoto Toshiatsu and Saitō Makoto, Yamanouchi became known as one of the "three men of talent" *(sanshūsai)* of the Naval

Academy class of 1877. He spent most of his career ashore at the Kure Naval Yard and Arsenal, though he had considerable experience in naval weapons study abroad, particularly in Britain. After returning from Britain in 1895, he helped to establish the Kure Naval Arsenal in 1896 and at the rank of captain, became its commander in 1898. A vice admiral in 1905, he became commander of the entire Kure Naval Base, one of the navy's most important, in 1906. As the navy's foremost ordnance expert, he was credited with inventing a number of naval weapons, the most important being the Yamanouchi gun carriage. Retiring as a baron, he became a member of the House of Peers and later president of Japan Steel, from which position he was dismissed in the wake of the Siemens scandal in 1914.

Yamaya Tanin (1886–1940) was a native of Iwate Prefecture and was graduated from the Naval Academy in 1886. After several shipboard assignments, he studied at the Torpedo School in 1894. He served as instructor at both the Torpedo School and the Gunnery School, but it was during his tenure at the Naval Staff College, 1899–1902, that he made his mark with his outstanding lectures on tactics to students in the "A" course. Promoted to commander in 1899, he was given command of the cruiser *Kasuga* in 1902 and fought in her in the major engagements of the Russo-Japanese War. Serving on the Navy General Staff after the war, he attained flag rank and was appointed president of the college in 1911. He commanded one of the two divisions that seized the German islands of Micronesia at the outset of World War I. He was made vice chief of the Navy General Staff in 1915, was promoted to admiral, and briefly held command of the Combined Fleet after World War I.

Yokoi Toshiyuki (1897–1969) passed through the Naval Academy in 1918 and was a student at the Naval Staff College, 1928–30. After finishing his flight training in 1922, he served as staff officer with various naval air units during the period between the world wars. During the Pacific War he held a carrier command, and when the navy's kamikaze forces were formed in late 1944, he was made commander of the Twenty-fifth Air Flotilla, a suicide attack unit, with the rank of rear admiral. Appointed chief of staff of the Fifth Air Fleet, he participated in the futile defense of Okinawa in the spring of 1945.

Yonai Mitsumasa (1880–1948) was graduated from the Naval Academy in 1901 and passed through the Naval Staff College in 1914. After various shipboard assignments early in his career, he was a language officer in Russia in 1915–17, and in Berlin in 1920–22. More shipboard assignments followed, including several battleship commands. Promoted to rear admiral in 1925 and vice admiral in 1930, he held several fleet and base commands, before being appointed as commander in chief of the Combined Fleet in 1936. He was promoted to full admiral in 1937 and appointed navy minister. No sooner was he placed on the reserve list in January 1940 than he was picked as prime minister, in which office he served for six months until his cabinet was undermined by the army and hard-lining nationalists in 1940. He withdrew from public life until the collapse of the wartime cabinet of Tōjō Hideki in the summer of 1944, when, in cooperation with Gen. Koiso Kuniaki, he formed a cabinet at the emperor's request. He served as navy minister in that cabinet and also in Japan's last wartime cabinet, that of Suzuki Kantarō.

Yoshimatsu Shigetarō (1859–1935) had a long career both at sea and ashore in which he made significant contributions to naval education. He was graduated from the Naval Academy in 1875. As a junior officer, he acquired much experience of the West, visiting the United

States, Britain, and France. From 1888 to 1891 he studied in France and trained aboard French naval vessels. During the Sino-Japanese War, he served as a division officer on the *Yoshino* and afterward served successively as an instructor at the Naval War College, as a staff officer at several different commands ashore and at sea, and as head instructor at the Naval Academy. By the time of the Russo-Japanese War he was a captain; in that conflict, he commanded the *Tokiwa*, experiencing all the major actions. He reached flag rank in 1905 and subsequently served on naval district staffs and commanded fleets. Yoshimatsu ultimately became superintendent of both the Naval Academy and the Naval War College. He ended his active career as commander of the First Fleet in 1915–16.

Notes

ABBREVIATIONS

Abbreviations for works in Japanese derive from their titles; in English, their author(s). The place of publication is Tokyo unless otherwise noted.

CS   Julian S. Corbett and Edmond J. W. Slade. *Maritime Operations in the Russo-Japanese War, 1904–5.* 2 vols. London: Admiralty War Staff, 1914. Reprint, Annapolis, Md.: Naval Institute Press, 1994.

DHKRK   Japan, Bōeichō Bōeikenshūjo Senshishitsu. *Dai Hon'ei Kaigunbu: Rengō Kantai, ichi, kaisen made* [Imperial General Headquarters, Navy Division, Combined Fleet, no. 1, to the opening of the Pacific War]. Senshi Sōsho series. Asagumo Shimbunsha, 1975.

JJM   Hansgeorg Jentschura, Dieter Jung, and Peter Mickel. *Warships of the Imperial Japanese Navy, 1869–1945.* Annapolis, Md.: Naval Institute Press, 1977.

KG1   Japan, Bōeichō Bōeikenshūjo Senshishitsu. *Kaigun gunsembi, ichi, Shōwa jūrokunen Jūichigatsu made* [Naval armaments and war preparations, no. 1, up to November 1941]. Senshi Sōsho series. Asagumo Shimbunsha, 1969.

KG2 Japan, Bōeichō Bōeikenshūjo Senshishitsu. *Kaigun gunsembi, ni, kaisen igo* [Naval armaments and war preparations, no. 2, after the war's start]. Senshi Sōsho series. Asagumo Shimbunsha, 1975.

KH Kaigun Hōjutsushi Kankōkai, ed. *Kaigun hōjutsushi* [A history of naval gunnery]. Kaigun Hōjutsushi Kankōkai, 1975.

KKG Japan, Bōeichō Bōeikenshūjo Senshishitsu. *Kaigun kōkū gaishi* [An historical overview of Japanese naval aviation]. Senshi Sōsho series. Asagumo Shimbunsha, 1976.

KS Kaigun Suiraishi Kankōkai, eds. *Kaigun suiraishi* [A history of mines and torpedoes of the navy]. Shinkōsha, 1971.

NKK Sonokawa Kamerō et al., eds. *Nihon kaigun kōkōtai* [The Japanese naval air force]. Kōdansha, 1970.

NKKS Nihon Kaigun Kōkūshi Hensan Iinkai, eds. *Nihon kaigun kōkūshi* [A history of Japanese naval aviation]. 4 vols. Jiji Tsushinsha, 1969.

NNK Ikeda Kiyoshi. *Nihon no kaigun.* 2 vols. Isseidō, 1967.

NRKK Toyama Saburō. *Nichi-Ro kaisenshi no kenkyū* [A study of the naval combats of the Russo-Japanese War]. 2 vols. Kyōiku Sentaa, 1985.

SZ Nihon Zōsen Gakkai, ed. *Showa zōsenshi* [History of ship building in the Shōwa era]. Hara Shobō, 1977.

WG Anthony J. Watts and Brian G. Gordon. *The Imperial Japanese Navy.* Garden City, N.Y.: Doubleday and Co., 1971.

INTRODUCTION

1. We have expatiated on these matters in our article, "Japan," 213–21.
2. Sumida and Rosenberg, "Machines, Men, Manufacturing, Management, and Money," 25–39.
3. While the wording of these definitions is essentially our own, in shaping them we have been influenced by the following studies: Alger, *Definitions and Doctrine;* U.S. Department of the Air Force, *Basic Aerospace Doctrine;* Tritten, *Naval Perspectives;* and Hughes, *Fleet Tactics.*
4. Springfield, Mass.: Merriam-Webster, 1988.
5. The standard displacement of a submarine was defined in the 1930 London Treaty as "the surface displacement of the vessel complete (exclusive of water in non-watertight structure) fully manned, engined, and equipped ready for sea, including all armament and ammunition, equipment, outfit, provisions for crew, miscellaneous stores, and

implements of every description that are intended to be carried in war, but without fuel, lubricating oil, fresh water, or ballast water of any kind on board."

6. The gross registry ton is not a measure of weight or displacement, but a measure of volume. It is found by taking the watertight volume of the ship in cubic feet and dividing by 100. Tankers and other bulk carriers are often rated by deadweight tons (DWT), which is the total weight of cargo that can be carried safely. For a World War II tanker, one DWT is approximately equal to 0.62 gross registry tons.

1 CREATING A MODERN NAVY
1868–1894

1. Ballard, *The Influence of the Sea,* 11; and Marder, "From Jimmu Tennō to Perry," 2–8.
2. The admiral and naval historian Ogasawara Chōsei was one of the first to argue that Japan's premodern water force tactics contributed to Japan's modern naval doctrine. See his "Chūko suigun no sempō," 727–51. This prolific author published English translations of his works under the name Nagayo Ogasawara, and many Japanese reference works list him as Ogasawara Naganari, but this book will refer to him by the reading most common in Japan that employs the Chinese pronunciation of the characters of his given name (Ogasawara Chōsei).
3. Marder, "From Jimmu Tennō to Perry," 20–25.
4. Specialists in Japanese medieval history warn against trying to trace a single samurai value system back any further than the Tokugawa Period (1600–1868). As we shall explain in later chapters, certain *tactics* had their antecedents in the medieval period in Japanese warfare. But the *ethical and psychological content* of the Japanese martial tradition, often seen as having existed since "ancient times" in Japan, was, in fact, of much more modern origin. It was, in reality, a selective borrowing by the modern Japanese military of samurai values from the Tokugawa Period of the seventeenth and eighteenth centuries, a period in which the samurai knew little of actual warfare. Thus, *bushidō,* as the term came to be used by the twentieth-century Japanese army and navy, had almost nothing to do with medieval Japanese warfare, but was the product of the attempt to instill values useful to the military of a modern nation-state. See Friday, "Bushido or Bull?" 339–49.
5. For a history of this most famous of Japanese naval installations, see Tompkins, *Yokosuka.*
6. Evans, "The Satsuma Faction," 21–25.
7. Ikeda, *Nihon no kaigun* (cited hereafter as *NNK*), 1:55–58.
8. Ibid., 1:119.
9. Evans, "Satsuma Faction," 234–44; and Tsunoda, "Nihon kaigun sandai no rekishi," 95.
10. *NNK,* 1:123; and Toyama, *Nihon kaigun shi,* 54.
11. These points were first raised by John C. Perry in his "Great Britain and the Emergence of Japan," 310; and by Peter Cornwall, "Manning and Training," 223.
12. Cornwall, "The Meiji Navy," 8.
13. Marder, *Old Friends, New Enemies,* 1:285.

14. Evans, "The Recruitment of Japanese Navy Officers," 229–39.
15. Cornwall, "Manning and Training," 217–18 and 222–24; and Cornwall, "The Meiji Navy," 4–6.
16. Evans, "The Satsuma Faction," 42; Perry, "Great Britain and the Emergence of Japan," 309–11; and Shinohara, *Nihon kaigun oyatoi gaijin,* 163–88.
17. Shinohara, *Kaigun sōsetsu shi,* 336–40.
18. Ibid., 348; and Kaigun Yūshūkai, *Kinsei Teikoku Kaigun shiyō,* 115–16 and 126.
19. Shinohara, *Kaigun sōsetsu shi,* 349–50.
20. Perry, "Great Britain and the Emergence of Japan," 311; and Chesneau and Kolesnik, *All the World's Fighting Ships, 1860–1905,* 218.
21. Yamamura, "Success Ill-Gotten?" 114–20; and Broadbridge, "Shipbuilding and the State in Japan," 606.
22. As explained in the introduction, the tonnage for vessels of this period was measured in English "long" tons of "normal" displacement.
23. Perry, "Great Britain and the Imperial Japanese Navy, 1858–1905," 164–65; Watts and Gordon, *The Imperial Japanese Navy* (cited hereafter as WG), 91.
24. On the theories of the Jeune Ecole, see Ropp, *The Development of a Modern Navy,* 159–67.
25. Yoshimatsu, "Teikoku kaigun senjutsu," 36.
26. Perry, "Great Britain and the Imperial Japanese Navy, 1858–1905," 146–47 and 149; Shinohara, *Nihon kaigun oyatoi gaijin,* 188–92; and Fukui, *Nihon no gunkan,* 9.
27. Itani, Lengerer, and Rehm-Takahara, "Sankeikan," 43, 51–52.
28. *NNK,* 1:142; Shinohara, *Kaigun sōsetsu shi,* 381; Friedman, *Battleship Design,* 59–60.
29. Jentschura, Jung, and Mickel, *Warships of the Imperial Japanese Navy* (cited hereafter as JJM), 98.
30. Ibid., 126, and WG, 221–22, both list six torpedo tubes for the *Kotaka,* and she was so designed, but the tubes amidships were dispensed with during construction. Kaigun Suiraishi Kankōkai, *Kaigun suiraishi* (cited hereafter as KS), 409.
31. *KS,* 11–12.
32. Yoshimatsu, 36; and WG, 221–22.
33. Kaigun Yūshūkai, 138–41.
34. Perry, "Great Britain and the Emergence of Japan," 316; Mayuzumi, "Kaigun hōsen-shi kaiko," 57–58. Beginning in 1885, the navy's largest ships were also armed with torpedo tubes, and by 1893 nearly all Japanese warships were so equipped. *KS,* 409.
35. This idea had both popular and naval manifestations. During the 1880s a flood of romantic fiction concerning the Pacific created a fevered excitement among Japanese youth of the mid-Meiji period about potential Japanese expansion into that ocean. This literary vogue culminated in the popular and wildly imaginative adventure-romance, *Ukishiro monogatari* (The story of the floating castle), published in 1890. The early Meiji navy itself evidently indulged in notions of territorial acquisition in the Pacific. Beginning in 1875, the navy inaugurated a series of high-seas voyages to the far shores of the Pacific by its few oceangoing vessels. Primarily training missions for Naval Academy cadets, these voyages were apparently also regarded by the navy brass as reconnaissance missions searching for undeclared territories in the Pacific, though nothing came of them in that regard. Peattie, *Nan'yō,* 7–9.

36. Several developments during the 1880s prompted these perceptions: a fleeting Japanese interest in 1885 in acquiring the Marshall Islands, an aspiration quickly extinguished by German annexation of that group later the same year; the sinking of the British freighter *Normanton* in 1886 off the coast of Wakayama Prefecture, in which all but twenty-three of the Japanese passengers were drowned when they were abandoned by the captain and crew; and the loss of the protected cruiser *Unebi* on her maiden voyage from Le Havre navy yard, the warship disappearing without a trace en route from Singapore to Japan sometime in October 1887. The ship is thought to have capsized because of her unstable design.

37. Japan, Bōeichō Bōeikenshūjo Senshishitsu, *Kaigun gunsembi, ichi* (cited hereafter as *KG1*), 110; *NNK,* 1:100; and Falk, *Togo,* 131–32.

38. Nakamura, in "Tōgō," argues that this retrenchment—the forced retirement of 10 percent of the navy's officers—was less an intended attack on the Satsuma faction than an effort to improve the navy's efficiency by ridding it of elderly and infirm officers. Nevertheless, 25 percent of those purged were Satsuma men, and the storm of protest from Satsuma officers in the spring of 1893 is ample testimony to the effect of the reform in Satsuma ranks. Shinohara, *Kaigun sōsetsu shi,* 364–66, confirms Yamamoto's intent and points out that many men were shifted to sea duty and shore personnel were drastically reduced by almost 20 percent. Chihaya, *Kaigun keieisha,* 56–64, stresses the radical character of the reforms by imagining reactions to any reform of similar magnitude in the navies of today. Four years after his first personnel reform, while chief of the ministry's Naval Affairs Department, Yamamoto carried out a second personnel reduction, popularly known as the "Hectograph Purge," because the names of officers forced to retire were so numerous that instead of writing out the notifications by hand Yamamoto used a prototype of the mimeograph machine to do so. While factionalism in the navy was not ended by Yamamoto's reforms, the bases of clique alignments shifted from regional loyalties to professional ones centered on policy controversies. *NNK,* 1:113–15; Evans, "The Satsuma Faction," 184–91; and Evans, "The Recruitment of Japanese Navy Officers," 239–40.

39. Evans, "The Satsuma Faction," 242–44; Itō Terubumi, "Rikushu-kaishu ronsō," 17.

40. Itō Terubumi, 17–18 and 30–31; Inaba, *Dai Hon'ei,* 91.

41. Tsunoda, "Nihon kaigun sandai no rekishi," 92; Evans, "The Satsuma Faction," 245.

42. Crowl, "Alfred Thayer Mahan," 474; and Asada, *Arufureddo T. Mahan,* 8. See also Dingman, "Japan and Mahan," 49–66.

43. In 1891, the Navy Ministry (until 1930, the office responsible for preparing naval estimates and budgets) requested 58 million yen to be spent over a nine-year period, to acquire eleven capital ships and numerous lesser vessels. The cabinet cut the plans to two capital ships, and the Diet refused funds for even these two (largely because of legislative dissatisfaction over navy inefficiency at the upper echelons, which the Yamamoto reforms eventually dealt with). The Diet finally passed a navy expansion bill of 18 million yen to be spent over a six-year period, 1893–99. But the warships constructed under this bill, including Japan's first battleships, the *Fuji* and *Yashima,* were not completed in time to participate in Japan's war with China, 1894–95. *NNK,* 1:100–108.

44. Ko Hakushaku Yamamoto Kaigun Taishō Denki Hensankai, eds. *Hakushaku Yamamoto Gombei den,* 1:359. We have shortened Yamamoto's actual words, but the thrust of his meaning is identical to the original.

45. In providing this overview of the navy's organization, we should make clear that our description is not intended to be accurate for any particular year, but rather represents the general institutional arrangements for the navy from late Meiji (the mid-1890s) onward.

2 FIRST SUCCESS
THE EVOLUTION OF JAPANESE NAVAL TACTICS AND THE SINO-JAPANESE WAR, 1894–1895

1. Our summary of the technological and tactical uncertainties discussed in this and the next few paragraphs are drawn largely from Potter, *Sea Power*, 328–38; and Hughes, *Fleet Tactics*, 55–75.
2. Bacon, *A Naval Scrap-book*, 240–41.
3. Padfield, *Guns at Sea*, 208.
4. Yoshimatsu, 32.
5. Excluding torpedo boats, the navy comprised a total of eight warships in 1868, nineteen in 1882, twenty-three in 1889, twenty-seven in 1893, and thirty-one in 1894, the year that hostilities with China broke out. Japan, Kaigunshō, Daijin Kambō, ed., *Kaigun gumbi enkaku, Furoku* vol., foldout chart, *Gunkan ruinen ichiran*.
6. Japan, Bōeichō Bōeikenshūjo Senshishitsu, *Dai Hon'ei Kaigunbu: Rengō Kantai, ichi, kaisen made* (cited hereafter as *DHKRK*), , 48–49. The Combined Fleet was organized specifically for the anticipated outbreak of hostilities with China and remained in being throughout the war, 1894–95. It was disbanded at the end of that conflict and was not reorganized until December 1903.
7. In 1879, according to the preface of Shimamura's book, the Naval Affairs Department of the Navy Ministry had produced a rather general summary of naval tactics, but the introduction of new weaponry in the six-year interval made it obvious that a revised study was needed. Shimamura Hayao, *Kaigun senjutsu ippan*, foreword, 1. Among those works from which Shimamura selected portions were Bainbridge Hoff, *Examples, Conclusions, and Maxims of Modern Naval Tactics* (1884); Comdr. H. V. Noel, *The Gun, Ram, and Torpedo: Maneuvers and Tactics of a Naval Battle in the Present Day* (1874); Randolph, *Problems in Naval Tactics* (1879); Lt. G. R. Bethel, *Remarks on the Maneuvers of Two Vessels in Action* (1881); George A. Elliot, *A Treatise on Future Naval Battles and How to Fight Them* (1885); *The Ram, the Prominent Feature of Future Naval Victories* (1884); and Capt. Philip H. Colomb, *The Duel: A Naval War Game* (1878).
8. Shinohara, *Kaigun sōsetsu shi*, 343; and Yoshimatsu, 33.
9. Yoshimatsu, 33–34.
10. Ibid., 32–34.
11. Shinohara, *Kaigun sōsetsu shi*, 343; *KG1*, 137.
12. Shinohara, *Kaigun sōsetsu shi*, 381.
13. *NNK*, 1:140; Toyama, *Nis-Shin, Nichi-Ro, Dai Tōa kaisen shi*, 73.
14. *KS*, 11–12.
15. Ibid., 463, 493–95.

16. Japan, Kaigun Gunreibu, *Suirai teitai undō kyōhan*, 5.

17. *KS*, 6–11; and Milford, "Torpedoes of the Imperial Japanese Navy," 7–8.

18. Satō recalled that as navigation officer aboard the gunboat *Akagi*, he himself had had a good deal of respect for Chinese naval power ever since his observation of Chinese naval maneuvers (apparently during the Chinese naval visit of 1891). Toyama, *Nis-Shin, Nichi-Ro, Dai Tōa kaisen shi*, 74–75.

19. The authors are indebted to Mark A. Campbell and Capt. Yoshida Akihiko, JMSDF, Ret., for information regarding the Chinese vessels.

20. Nomura Minoru, *Kaisenshi ni manabu*, 46–47.

21. Rawlinson, *China's Struggle for Naval Development*, 179.

22. *NNK*, 1:126; Rawlinson, 171.

23. *NNK*, 1:124–26.

24. Itō's tactical instructions quoted in Toyama, *Nis-Shin, Nichi-Ro, Dai Tōa kaisen shi*, 73–74.

25. The battle is usually known in the West as the Battle of the Yalu, whereas Japanese naval historians call it the Battle of the Yellow Sea. John Perry, more accurately, if idiosyncratically, refers to it as the Battle off the Tayang. Unless otherwise noted, our summary of the battle is taken from Shinohara, *Kaigun sōsetsu shi*, 374–90; Perry, "The Battle off the Tayang," 243–59; and Rawlinson, 167–97.

26. Shinohara, *Kaigun sōsetsu shi*, 389.

27. Perry, "Battle off the Tayang," 257; Ballard, 151.

28. Suzuki Kantarō Denki Hensan Iinkai, *Suzuki Kantarō den*, 19–22.

29. Potter, 352; Hughes, *Fleet Tactics*, 61–62; and Rawlinson, 238, n. 78.

30. *KG1*, 112; *NNK*, 1:139–40; and Potter, 352.

31. We speak here of Itō's main units. The slower speed of his lesser vessels—the frigates *Chiyoda* and *Fusō* and the corvette *Hiei*—brought about some confusion in the Japanese battle line and nearly caused serious consequences. Before the battle, Lieutenant Shimamura had advocated leaving them behind, but he was overruled, as Itō felt he needed even the modest firepower that they could contribute. These matters were brought to our attention by Yoshida Akihiko, JMSDF, Ret.

32. *NNK*, 1:140.

33. Ibid., 1:141.

34. Itani, Lengerer, and Rehm-Takahara, "Sankeikan," 51–54. Among post–World War II naval commentators there has been some dissent from the general condemnation of the *Sankeikan* class and their Canet guns. The late Ōmae Toshikazu believed that by mating speed and firepower, the *Sankeikan*-class design was ahead of its time, and Mayuzumi Haruo has contended that the inability of the ships to deliver continuous fire at the Battle of the Yalu was the result of faulty powder charges and not the Canet gun. Mayuzumi is convinced that had the Canets been able to fire effectively, the Chinese battleships would have been sent to the bottom. Ōmae, "Nihon kaigun no heijutsu shisō," part 1, p. 37; and Mayuzumi, "Kaigun hōsenshi kaiko," 54–65.

35. *KS*, 493, 495.

36. Itō Terubumi, 2l–22; Tsunoda Jun, "Nihon kaigun sandai no rekishi," 92; Evans, "The Satsuma Faction," 246– 47.

37. Gotō, "Kaigun nanshin ron," parts 1, 2. For a brief period soon after the pacification of Taiwan, both services were energized by the *nanshin* idea, particularly as it related to southern China. In 1896, Gen. Kodama Gentarō, the second governor general of Taiwan, submitted an elaborate scheme for southward expansion from Taiwan, and four years later, Kodama secretly cooperated with Yamamoto Gombei's abortive plans to establish, by force, a Japanese sphere of influence in Fukien Province, across the straits from Taiwan. Nothing came of either scheme, and the *nanshin* idea soon became an exclusive preoccupation of the navy.

38. *KG1,* 108–9.

3 PREPARING FOR BATTLE
JAPANESE NAVAL TECHNOLOGY AND DOCTRINE, 1895–1904

1. Even while the Sino-Japanese War was in progress, Yamamoto Gombei had clearly seen the possibility of foreign intervention. In a high-level interministerial conference in the spring of 1895 he laid out for the government Japan's maritime vulnerability to blackmail: without any battleships whatsoever, Japan would be inevitably overwhelmed at sea by any coalition of European maritime powers. Ko Hakushaku Yamamoto Kaigun Taishō Denki Hensankai, 1:387.

2. Padfield, *The Battleship Era,* 148–49.

3. Ropp, 216–17.

4. Hodges, *The Big Gun,* 19–28 and 31–32; Padfield, *The Battleship Era,* 148–49.

5. Padfield, *Guns at Sea,* 211.

6. Edwyn Gray, *The Devil's Device,* 155–59 and 244.

7. Ibid., 144–45; Preston, *Destroyers,* 6–14; and Leather, *Warships in Review,* 229–32.

8. Padfield, *The Battleship Era,* 148–49; and Leather, 79–80.

9. Preston, *Cruisers,* 7–17. By the end of the nineteenth century, cruisers were thus classified into three general categories: unprotected cruisers, which possessed no armor whatsoever; protected cruisers, which had only horizontal armored decks to give some protection to the vital parts of the ship and which were ranked according to displacement into first-, second-, and third-class cruisers; and armored cruisers, which had both vertical and horizontal armor and which were often as large and powerful as older battleships. This classification lasted until shortly before World War I, when light cruisers and battle cruisers were introduced as new warship types.

10. Of the 365 million yen in Chinese reparations, 54 percent was marked for military expansion, and of the 54 percent, the navy took by far the largest share, 38 percent. Another 32.6 percent was tagged for transportation costs and a supplemental budget for torpedo boat construction. Yamamura, 127; and Ono, *War and Armament Expenditures of Japan,* 73.

11. The details of the program are in Japan, Kaigunshō, *Yamamoto Gombei to kaigun,* 348–49.

12. Ibid., 353.

13. Ibid., 355–56; and Nomura Minoru, "Suezu unga," 41–42.

14. In 1898, shortly after he became navy minister, Yamamoto attempted to push through a naval expansion plan of still greater dimensions, one even more binding for the future. Proposing an increase in the size of the navy to 350,000 tons, Yamamoto's draft plan asserted that the navy was "the most essential instrument for the defense of the empire" and that for the foreseeable future the navy's minimum strength should comprise one-half the tonnage of the navies of all those powers that maintained fleets and bases in East Asia. In other words, this was to be a navy three times as large as that then possessed by Japan, one larger than those of Germany and the United States combined. Here Yamamoto overreached himself. Not only was such an expansion plan far beyond the nation's capacity to support, but his blatant assertion of the primacy of the navy in the nation's defense was inevitably challenged by objections from the navy's sister service. Evans, "The Satsuma Faction," 255–56.

15. WG, 9.

16. Japan, Kaigunshō, *Yamamoto Gombei to kaigun*, 350.

17. WG, 104–5; and Chesneau and Kolesnik, 122.

18. WG, 5–6. Detailed specifications and histories of the *Fuji* and *Yashima* are provided in Brook, "Armstrong Battleships Built for Japan," 269–70.

19. Chesneau and Kolesnik, 218. Detailed specifications and history of *Mikasa* and her sister ships are provided in Brook, 278–82.

20. WG, 17–22.

21. Ibid., 104–17.

22. Chesneau and Kolesnik, 237; and WG, 227–35.

23. Hayashi, *Nihon gunji gijutsu shi*, 127.

24. *KG1*, 52. Shinohara, *Kaigun sōsetsu shi*, 409, suggests that Comdr. Oda Kiyozō, developer of the mine, may have smuggled out of Britain highly classified information not only on mines but on torpedoes as well.

25. There is some evidence that the navy obtained this explosive through devious means. A sample of Melinite—a French version of picric acid explosive—was brought back from France under questionable circumstances and was developed at a Japanese naval arsenal by an engineer named Shimose Masakazu, to whom the invention of the new explosive was then attributed. Shinohara, *Kaigun sōsetsu shi*, 410; and Hayashi, 138–44.

26. Ropp, 216–17; and Hayashi, 143

27. Perry, "Great Britain and the Imperial Japanese Navy," 207–42.

28. Chesneau and Kolesnik, 217.

29. See table of comparative naval strengths at the end of the chapter. The reckoning above excludes *Chiyoda* as an armored cruiser, because she was old, small, and lightly armed. The Japanese had 90 torpedo boats, but only 58 were of recent construction.

30. Tsutsui, "Nihon kaigunshi," 58–59.

31. Ibid., 56; and Tsutsui, "Shuryokukan hattatsushi," 29–50.

32. The terms of the treaty can be found in Nish, *The Anglo-Japanese Alliance*, 216–18.

33. *NNK*, 1:178; and Nish, *The Anglo-Japanese Alliance*, 251–55.

34. Nish, *The Anglo-Japanese Alliance*, 213–14 and 251.

35. *NNK*, 1:180–81.

36. Nenryō Konwakai, *Nihon kaigun nenryōshi,* 1:11–12.

37. Ibid., 13–14, 53, 63.

38. Ōta, *Danshaku Sakamoto Toshiatsu den,* 61–62; and Sanematsu, *Kaigun daigaku kyōiku,* 117–22.

39. Cornwall, "The Meiji Navy," 146–51. The staff college, however, was not the only route to higher position in the navy. In the late nineteenth century, certainly, class ranking upon graduation from the Naval Academy was just as important in determining the rapidity of promotion and attainment of preferred position. Evans, "The Satsuma Faction," 210–12.

40. Shinohara, *Kaigun sōsetsu shi,* 400–405; and Japan, Kaigun Kyōiku Hombu, *Teikoku kaigun kyōiku shi,* 5: 645–46.

41. Ōta, 64.

42. Sanematsu, *Kaigun daigaku kyōiku,* 122–23.

43. Nakagawa Shigeshi, *Gensui Shimamura Hayao den,* 41.

44. The *Kaisen yōmurei* (Battle Instructions), unlike the "Fighting Instructions" of the British navy in the eighteenth century, were a set of general principles used as the basis of fleet maneuvers and tactics, not regulations that a commander ignored at his peril. Nevertheless, they represented the heart of tactical doctrine within the Japanese navy and were thus among the navy's highest secrets, being kept under lock and key at all times. All told, the instructions were revised five times—in 1910, 1912, 1920, 1928, and 1934. Revision of the instructions was a complicated matter and required final approval by the emperor himself. It is difficult to trace the history of the Battle Instructions, since only the 1901, 1912, and 1934 versions exist today, the rest undoubtedly having been destroyed in the last few days of the Pacific War. Shinohara, *Kaigun sōsetsu shi,* 405; *KG1,* 135–37 and 140–41; Japan, Bōeichō, Tōgō Bakuryō Gakkō, *Kindai Nihon tōgōsen shi gaisetsu,* 307–8; and Evans conversation with Toyama Saburō, October 1985.

45. Unless otherwise noted, the following discussion of Akiyama's place in the development of Japanese naval doctrine is drawn from Peattie, "Akiyama Saneyuki."

46. Shimada Kinji, *Amerika ni okeru Akiyama,* 39–61; and Rivera, "Big Stick and Short Sword," 106–7. As a corrective to the Peattie article on Akiyama cited in n. 45 above, in his article "Akiyama Saneyuki," Rivera has identified the ship from which Akiyama observed the Battle of Santiago. She was an auxiliary ship under contract to the army and not a warship of Sampson's squadron.

47. Shimada Kinji, *Amerika ni okeru Akiyama,* 318–51.

48. Shinohara, *Kaigun sōsetsu shi,* 409–13. The reason is not clear. Undoubtedly, the U.S. Naval War College would have refused, but the Japanese may have lost interest themselves. Shinohara, 413, asserts that Sakamoto, while attending the international peace conference at The Hague, met Mahan and came away unimpressed.

49. Ibid., 436; and Shimada Kinji, "Akiyama Saneyuki no kaigun heigaku," 96–97.

50. What we know of Akiyama's contributions comes largely from transcriptions made of his lectures and later circulated in either mimeograph or printed form. Those that remain today, each representative of one course he taught at the college, are *Kaigun kihon senjutsu* (Elementary naval tactics) (1903 and 1907 editions), *Kaigun ōyō senjutsu* (Applied naval tactics) (1903, 1907, and 1908 editions), and *Kaigun semmu* (Naval logistics) (1903 and 1908 editions). No text of his course on *Kaigun senryaku*

(naval strategy) is known to exist today, and none of the works above has been translated into English.

51. Akiyama's pamphlet was titled *Heigo kaisetsu* (Military terms explained) (n.p.,
1902). See Shimada Kinji, "Akiyama Saneyuki no kaigun heigaku," 97. Akiyama
also worked to abolish English words that had crept into professional Japanese naval
discourse over the years. He insisted, for example, on *kankyō* for "bridge" and *tan-
tei* for "boat" as a contribution to an independent Japanese naval perspective. Akiyama
Saneyuki Kai, *Akiyama Saneyuki,* 169.

52. Kusumi Tadao, "Akiyama Saneyuki to Nihonkai kaisen," 355. Akiyama's quote is
found in Shinohara, "Akiyama heigaku no himitsu," 123.

53. For an explanation of the evolution and content of war-gaming in the U.S. Navy, see
McHugh, "Gaming at the Naval War College."

54. Shimada Kinji, "Akiyama Saneyuki no kaigun heigaku," 98 and 101.

55. Kusumi Tadao, 354; *KG1,* 126 and 129; and Dohi, "Zujō enshū to heiki enshū,"
86–90.

56. Akiyama Saneyuki Kai, 142–44.

57. Well over a decade ago, one of us wrote an article on Akiyama for the U.S. Naval Institute *Proceedings* (Peattie, "Akiyama"), in which he rather uncritically accepted these
claims at face value. Since then, both authors have become somewhat more dubious. In
an article on the relation of Japanese medieval water tactics to the Battle of Tsushima,
Ogasawara claimed, for example, that Tōgō's famous turn to cross the Russian T had
been anticipated centuries before. See his "Nihonkai kaisen to chūko no suigun,"
242–48. While this may indeed be true, the tactic took on meaning only in the late nineteenth century with the advent of the long-range naval cannon mounted in a revolving
turret by which gunfire could be concentrated at the head of an approaching enemy column. Although these ancient works may have provided a degree of inspiration and
national pride for Akiyama, he was too much the contemporary professional to give
them priority in his thinking over tactical concepts based on modern firepower, speed,
and armor. In this respect, Akiyama said of his own tactical precepts, if not Tōgō's, "I
determined the merits of applied tactics by studying the results of various battles, drawing on those of the past and, especially, making suppositions about those that might
occur in the present day." Shinohara Hiroshi, "Akiyama heigaku no himitsu," 127.

58. Kusumi Tadao, 355; and Shinohara, *Kaigun sōsetsu shi,* 436.

59. Akiyama Saneyuki Kai, 144; Koyama, *Kindai Nihon,* 258–59; Shimada Kinji,
"Akiyama Saneyuki no kaigun heigaku," 106; and Yasui, "Yo no mitaru Akiyama
Saneyuki Chūjō," 141–42. In their mixture of spiritual elements with professional
explanations, Akiyama's lectures at the Naval Staff College have much in common
with those delivered at the Army Staff College in the 1920s by Lt. Col. Ishiwara Kanji,
an equally brilliant and unorthodox officer. See Peattie, *Ishiwara Kanji,* 49–83.

60. *NNK,* 1:230–31; and Koyama, *Kindai Nihon,* 363–80.

61. Shinohara, *Kaigun sōsetsu shi,* 424–31. Contemporary naval officers with fleet experience point out that Yamaya's formation would be extremely difficult to achieve
(correspondence with Capt. Wayne Hughes, USN, Ret., and Lt. Comdr. Carlos R.
Rivera, USNR, Ret.). In *A History of Naval Tactical Thought,* 121, Fioravanzo confirms this point by saying that the "arc of circle" was a possible formation but not
actually used in Western navies.

62. Shinohara, *Kaigun sōsetsu shi*, 426–27.

63. Marder, *The Anatomy of British Seapower*, 517.

64. Shinohara, "Akiyama heigaku no himitsu," 128. Some experts argue that Tōgō Hei-hachirō as commander in chief of the Standing Fleet was using the T in maneuvers as early as 1900. See Nomura Minoru, "Tōgō Heihachirō no senjutsugan," 81.

65. Shimada Kinji, "Akiyama Saneyuki no kaigun heigaku," 98–99.

66. Shinohara, "Akiyama heigaku no himitsu," 127.

67. Ibid., 128.

68. Shinohara, *Kaigun sōsetsu shi*, 439; Nomura Minoru, *Kaisenshi ni manabu*, 91–92; and Nomura Minoru, "Tōgō Heihachirō no senjutsugan," 82–85.

69. For an expert discussion of the early development of fire control in the Royal Navy see Sumida, "The Quest for Reach." For associated developments in the U.S. Navy see Friedman, *U.S. Naval Weapons*, 25–30.

70. Moss and Russell, 33–34.

71. This assessment was provided to the authors by Dr. Frederick J. Milford, 29 July 1994.

72. *KG1*, 115–16.

73. The principal English-language biographies of Tōgō are Nagayo Ogasawara (Oga-sawara Chōsei), *Life of Admiral Togo*; Falk, *Togo and the Rise of Japanese Sea Power*; Bodley, *Admiral Togo*; and Blond, *Admiral Togo*. These comprise a hagiog-raphy of sorts; a critical study of Tōgō and his place in history has yet to be written in either English or Japanese.

74. Itō Masanori, *Dai kaigun o omou*, 144.

75. Chihaya, *Kaigun keieisha*, 109–10.

76. Toyama, *Nichi-Ro kaisenshi no kenkyū* (cited hereafter as *NRKK*), 1:230.

77. Shimada Kinji, "Rengō Kantai sambō Akiyama Saneyuki," 43.

78. *NRKK*, 2:526–29; Kamata, "Nihon kaigun denshin shiwa," 68–71. Japanese radio telegraphy may have lagged behind that of the best Western navies but in practice it proved to be superior to that of the Russians, who had good equipment but for vari-ous reasons could not capitalize on it. See Hezlet, *Electronics and Sea Power*, 43–49.

79. Corbett and Slade, *Maritime Operations in the Russo-Japanese War* (cited hereafter as CS), 1:74, 79, 86. The cable to Hakkō, a key naval base in the first days of the war, was working even before the opening Japanese attacks of the Russo-Japanese War. *NRKK*, 2:525–26.

80. Akiyama Saneyuki Kai, 73–74; Sanematsu, *Kaigun daigaku kyōiku*, 165; and Shi-mada Kinji, "Akiyama Saneyuki no kaigun heigaku," 103.

81. The original Japanese text of the Combined Fleet Battle Plan, with diagrams, is in *NRKK*, 1:384–402. An accurate English translation is in CS, 1:474–91.

82. *NRKK*, 1:387.

83. Ibid., 1:388.

84. Ibid., 1:402.

85. Ibid., 1:237.

86. Ibid., 1:237–38. The "Operation Plan" of December 1903 is undated, but it was probably drawn up after the Navy Staff sounded Tōgō out in midmonth.

87. See CS, 1:63–68, for a wide-ranging analysis of Japan's strategy.

88. In these maneuvers, Japan's naval forces were divided into an eastern (Japanese) fleet whose mission was to prevent the junction of the two elements of a western (Russian)

fleet based in the Yellow and Japan Seas. Instructors and students at the staff college were assigned important staff positions in both fleets. Akiyama, for example, served as operations officer for the western fleet; Yamaya Tanin filled the same function for the eastern fleet. Although the results for the Japanese side were judged only partially successful, the navy gained invaluable experience in preparing for the operations that actually took place in the Russo-Japanese War. Shimada Kinji, "Roshiya sensō zen'ya no Nihon kantai," 60.

89. Shinohara, *Kaigun sōsetsu shi,* 444–45.
90. *NRKK,* 1:239.
91. *NRKK,* 1:359.
92. Shimada Kinji, "Rengō Kantai sambō Akiyama Saneyuki," 38–39.
93. For a general discussion of Japanese intelligence operations in Russia before the Russo-Japanese War, see Nish, "Japanese Intelligence."
94. Shinohara, *Kaigun sōsetsu shi,* 443–45; and *NRKK,* 1:207, 211, 215–17.
95. Shimada Kinji, "Rengō Kantai sambō Akiyama Saneyuki," 41.
96. *NRKK,* 1:242–43. The army wanted to start the war in early January but the Navy General Staff insisted on a delay not only to prepare a naval attack but also to insure the safety of two new cruisers en route from Europe, the *Kasuga* and *Nisshin.*
97. Tanaka, "Nihonkai kaisen to Tōgō Heihachirō," 161. The surprise blockship assault was the brainchild of both Akiyama Saneyuki and Commander Arima. Arima had managed to slip into Port Arthur two years before to make observations and now used his knowledge of the base to work out the specific details of the blockship operation. Yasui, 158; Shinohara, "Akiyama heigaku no himitsu," 119; and Evans conversation with Tanaka Hiromi and Kuwada Etsu, October 1985.

The *Kaisen yōmurei* (Battle Instructions) of 1902, which Akiyama had a large part in drafting, contained detailed instructions for sealing off ports by this method that were undoubtedly written with Port Arthur in mind. Akiyama may have learned much from Admiral Sampson's sinking of blockships in the Spanish-American War.
98. Tōgō was correct in his appreciation of the essential passivity of the Russians. The czar's order of 28 January 1904 in effect "surrendered to Japan everything she needed for her opening movement" by ordering that Japanese landings in Korea as far north as Chemulpo be allowed. CS, 1:57–58, 60–61.
99. *NRKK,* 1:359.
100. Ibid., 359–60.
101. CS, 1:82.
102. *NRKK,* 1:361.
103. Shimada Kinji, "Roshia sensō zen'ya no Nihon kantai," 56–57.
104. KS, 12–13.
105. Makarov's idea of increasing the firing range of torpedoes from several hundred meters to 3,000 and reducing the speed to 12 or 13 knots provoked the interest of the Navy General Staff, which sent the idea on to Navy Minister Yamamoto Gombei. Yamamoto sought the advice of Lieutenant Commander Suzuki because of his experience in torpedo warfare. Suzuki roundly condemned the concept, pointing out that if such attacks were carried out during daylight hours, the torpedo's slow speed would allow the enemy target to take evasive action; if carried out at night, the target would be too indistinct to make a hit. Finally, Suzuki argued, firing torpedoes at

such long ranges would "make our brave men seem cowardly." Despite Suzuki's stubborn opposition to the new torpedo firing policy, it became navy doctrine in the years before the Russo-Japanese War. Suzuki, *Jiden*, 27–28. The running time for a torpedo traveling at 12 knots over 2,500 meters is notably a little over 8 minutes, enough time for maneuvering to avoid torpedoes.

106. For example, since each shot fired caused significant wear in gun barrels (the typical gun barrel could fire from one hundred to three hundred rounds), the number of practice shots from 12-inch and 8-inch guns during the Combined Fleet's gunnery practice in the autumn of 1903 was strictly limited. Shimada Kinji, "Rengō kantai sambō Akiyama Saneyuki," 43–44.

4 TRAVAIL AND TRIUMPH
The Japanese Navy and the Russo-Japanese War, 1904–1905

1. This ambitious work of 147 volumes, referred to today by Japanese historians as *Gokuhi Meiji sanjūshichi-hachinen kaisenshi* (The secret history of naval combat, 1904–5), was largely unknown even within the Japanese navy; it came to light only after World War II. We have not personally inspected it, but in drafting this chapter, have relied mainly on the two-volume study by Toyama Saburō, *Nichi-Ro kaisenshi no kenkyū* (cited as *NRKK),* which draws heavily on it. We have also used Julian Corbett's magisterial *Maritime Operations in the Russo-Japanese War, 1904–5* (cited as CS). Written with Edmond J. W. Slade under the aegis of the Intelligence Division of the Admiralty Staff in 1914, it was little known until its recent republication by the Naval Institute Press. Relying not only upon reports of numerous British observers with the Japanese fleet but also upon the secret Japanese history, it is the best naval history of the Russo-Japanese War published in English.

2. CS, 1:54.

3. *NRKK,* 1:326

4. Ibid., 1:327.

5. Ibid., 1:103.

6. CS, 1:99.

7. The earliest attackers, of the First Destroyer Flotilla, reported attacking at close range, 400–800 meters, whereas later attackers reported firing at 1,000–1,200 meters. The ranges were probably incorrectly estimated because of the intensity of the action and difficult conditions of visibility.

8. *NRKK,* 1:446

9. Destroyers were not equipped with wireless sets until the early summer of 1904, when one vessel of each destroyer squadron at Port Arthur was fitted with a set capable of transmissions of up to 20 miles. *NRKK,* 2:529–30.

10. *NRKK,* 1:446; Toyama, *Nis-Shin, Nichi-Ro, Dai Tōa kaisen shi,* 211; and Herbert W. Wilson, *Battleships in Action,* 1:184.

11. *NRKK,* 1:103.

12. Ibid., 1:449.

13. Toyama, "Lessons from the Past," 63–64; and Herbert W. Wilson, 1:187.

14. Shinohara, "Akiyama heigaku no himitsu," 132.

15. Ibid.

16. Until Hirose's death, the Japanese navy had strict prohibitions against publicizing the names of ships or personnel involved in combat operations. According to one recent study, the navy's apotheosis of Hirose was undertaken to divert public attention from the navy's badly bungling the blockship effort. Ogasawara Chōsei, then a commander on the Navy General Staff, led the public relations effort to raise Hirose's reputation to that of *gunshin* (war god). The effort resulted in the erection of a public statue of Hirose and an idealized account of his death (written anonymously by Ogasawara), which was reprinted in schoolbooks for decades to come. Tanaka, "'Gunshin seizō' enshutsu nooto," 226–29.

17. The secret naval history of the war makes it clear that it was indeed Tōgō himself who advocated the repeated and futile attempts to seal the harbor. He was finally persuaded to abandon the operations by Comdr. Takarabe Takeshi (Yamamoto Gombei's son-in-law), who had been sent out by the general staff for that purpose. *NRKK,* 1:103–4.

18. Although the Japanese navy had no occasion to use them in the Sino-Japanese War, mines had been an important part of the Japanese naval arsenal for some decades. The first mines had been brought from Britain aboard the *Fusō* in 1878, and domestic production of mines started in 1882. By 1886, navy arsenals were turning out floating, contact, and electric mines. *KS,* 271.

19. The Russian figure includes the cruiser *Boyarin,* which, though listed as a casualty of the torpedo, was first disabled by a mine (one of her own). A Russian destroyer ordered to torpedo her could not comply. The *Boyarin* sank in a storm after being abandoned. CS, 1:121.

20. The blockship operation of 24 February covered the debarkation of the Twelfth Division at Chemulpo; that of 27 March, General Kuroki's leapfrogging up the Korean coast to land at Chinnampo (Namp'o); that of 3 May, the landing of the Second Army at P'itzuwo. For an extended exposition of this strategy, see CS, 1: chapters 5, 9, 11, and 12.

21. CS, 1:139–40, 143, 158–59.

22. *NRKK,* 1:391.

23. Ibid., 1:609; CS, 1:377.

24. CS, 1:385.

25. Toyama (*NRKK,* 1:650) claims that Tōgō failed to press home his attack partly because the Battle Plan called for attacks by destroyers and torpedo boats at dusk, but had no provision for attacks by the Japanese main force at that time of day. One can fault the plans—presumably Akiyama's—but one also has to wonder why Tōgō did not thrust the plans aside to seize an opportunity while he had it.

26. CS, 1:406, 412. The Combined Fleet staff made a study of the problem and concluded that despite numerous after-action reports of firing within 400–800 meters, the main reason for failure was discharging torpedoes at excessive ranges. An important secondary reason was the lack of coordinated attacks. *NRKK,* 1:658–62. In addition, fatigue and exhaustion after months at sea battling foul weather and straining to keep up the Port Arthur blockade may have contributed to the failure of the captains and crews of the small craft to press home their attacks at closer ranges. *NRKK,* 1:655.

27. Nomura Minoru, "Kamimura Hikonojō no nintai," 124–25.

28. On this occasion, Imperial General Headquarters, fearful that the Vladivostok squadron might take the opportunity to swing around Shikoku and Kyūshū and enter the Yellow Sea, ordered Kamimura to take his fleet to the southern coast of Kyūshū to head the Russians off. Tōgō, Kamimura's direct superior, not knowing of this order and suspecting correctly that the Russian squadron would head back to the Tsugaru Strait and Vladivostok, instructed Kamimura to proceed at full speed to the western entrance to the Tsugaru Strait and wait for the enemy there. Kamimura obeyed the first order, and the Russian squadron slipped back through the strait unchallenged. Nomura Minoru, *Kaisenshi ni manabu,* 73–74.

29. Rollins, 102.

30. Nomura Minoru, *Kaisenshi ni manabu,* 125.

31. At that, between early September and mid-December, the navy lost four warships and 429 officers and men to mines off the Liaotung Peninsula.

32. The secret naval history of the war contains ten letters written by Akiyama to the navy liaison officer on General Nogi's staff, Comdr. Iwamura Danjirō, during the period 27 November–6 December. The first was written the day after the initial assault on 203 Meter Hill failed, the last on the day the hill was captured. These letters are exceptional for their length, their tone of supplication, and their exhaustive explanation of the strategic necessity of taking the hill. Chihaya, who brought them to light in his *Nihon kaigun no senryaku hassō,* 111–21, argues that Akiyama decisively influenced Nogi and the Third Army in their planning for taking Port Arthur. Further, he believes that Akiyama was the ultimate source of the focus on Hill 203. Akiyama had stopped at Toulon on his way home from study in the United States, probably in 1900, and had been deeply impressed by a visit to Fort Napoleon, formerly the fort of Eguillette, which Napoleon had captured and used to break the siege of Toulon by British and Spanish fleets in 1793. See Chihaya, *Nihon kaigun no senryaku hassō,* 119–20, and the same author's *Kaigun keieisha,* 164–70; the letters are reprinted in full in the appendix of *Kaigun keieisha,* 236–55.

33. In March 1905, the Army General Staff asked for the navy's cooperation in an amphibious operation to occupy the island of Sakhalin, as well as assistance in mounting a landward drive from northeastern Korea to take Vladivostok. The navy refused to consider any such operations until the Baltic Fleet had been met and defeated. This reluctance to cooperate with the army continued even after the defeat of the Baltic Fleet in May. The navy refused to assist the army in landings on the northeastern coast of Korea in the last weeks of the war, though it did join in the occupation of Sakhalin. Tsunoda, *Manshū mondai to kokubō hōshin,* 651–53.

34. The crucial nature of the coming test of arms was now clear to all. Gone were the prewar restrictions on the use of ammunition for practice purposes. In a ten-day period during these exercises, for example, one Japanese battleship expended two thousand rounds of all calibers—its entire practice ammunition allotment for one year. Mayuzumi, *Kaigun hōsen shidan,* 231.

35. Toyama, *Nichi-Ro kaisen shinshi,* 230; *NRKK,* 2:184.

36. Tanaka, "Nihonkai kaisen to Tōgō Heihachirō," 174; CS, 2:149, 200–202.

37. Todaka Kazushige, "Nihonkai kaisen," 227. See analysis in CS, 2:242–43.

38. Akiyama Saneyuki Kai, 196–98. On 13 April 1905 a force under Admiral Kamimura laid 750 mines in the approaches to Vladivostok. *NRKK,* 2:181.

39. Todaka, "Nihonkai kaisen ni teiji sempō wa nakatta," 229.

40. *NRKK,* 1:391.

41. Ibid., 2:222.

42. Ibid., 2:224.

43. Ibid., 2:219, 223–29; and CS, 2:243.

44. The novel device consisted of four mines attached to 100 meters of rope. Many such 100-meter segments, along with dummy mines, would be laid in front of the Russian battleships and across their course by a torpedo boat flotilla and by a captured Russian destroyer (to deceive the enemy). Curious as this stratagem might seem, the Russians took Japanese mines very seriously and anticipated their use. CS, 2:210; Todaka, "Nihonkai kaisen," 229–31; Shima, "Kaigun heigakkō kara," 104–5; CS 2:196, 210. For the complete operational plan of the Surprise Attack Force in the Battle Plan revision, see *NRKK,* 2:223–29; and CS, 2:243.

45. Shima, 108.

46. Ibid., 107–9.

47. On 23 May naval headquarters received word that the Russian fleet had inspected the Norwegian freighter *Oscar II,* under charter by Mitsui, on the Pacific side of the Bashi Channel. Japanese authorities did not put much stock in the Norwegian testimony that the Russians were "going through the Korea Strait to Vladivostok," because the presence of the Russians in the Pacific seemed to indicate a wider route.

48. On 25 May a meeting of all commanders and staff officers except Tōgō was held aboard the *Mikasa.* Astoundingly, sealed orders, without his signature, were prepared, directing the fleet's departure for Hokkaidō on the evening of 26 May if the Russians had not been sighted by noon of that day. This decision was telegraphed to the Navy General Staff in Tokyo, where it was met with consternation. A harshly worded response ordered the fleet to stay where it was. This breach of command and the temporary confusion it engendered have never been explained, since the details until 1982 were buried in the secret official naval history of the war. Nomura Minoru, "Nihonkai kaisen chokuzen mippu meirei," 2–13.

49. Tanaka, "Nihonkai kaisen to Tōgō Heihachirō," 177; Nomura Minoru, *Kaisenshi ni manabu,* 97–98.

50. Padfield, in *The Battleship Era,* 138, notes the severe "tumble home" configuration (the inward slope of a ship's sides from the waterline to the deck) of the Russian capital ships, their high and mostly unprotected sides, and their towering superstructures, which made their stability uncertain.

    For a close study of the ships at Tsushima and of the battle itself, see N. J. M. Campbell, "The Battle of Tsu-Shima," 39–49, 127–35, 186–92, 258–65.

51. In late 1903, in anticipation of war with Russia, the navy ordered gray paint schemes for all its ships except for naval auxiliaries and river gunboats. This color was retained after the war, and the painting system standardized in 1907 was essentially unchanged until the middle of the Pacific War. See Wells, "Painting Systems of the Imperial Japanese Navy," 20–35.

52. *NRKK,* 2:530–31.

53. CS, 2:224.

54. Herbert W. Wilson, 1:243–44.

55. See CS, 2:220–27, for a sharp critique of the Japanese screen across the Korea Strait. Several ships were out of place, and a gap in fact existed through which Rozhestvensky almost escaped.

56. *NRKK,* 2:334. See also the Royal Navy's report: United Kingdom, Admiralty, Naval Ordnance Department, *A Study of the Events of the Russian-Japanese War,* 101.

57. Rozhestvensky had redeployed into two columns at about 1240. V. I. Semenov, who was with Rozhestvensky on the *Suvorov,* wrote, "The Japanese light cruisers [Dewa's division] again approached to port, but this time accompanied by torpedo craft and evidently intending to cross our path. Suspecting that the plan of the Japanese was to lay floating mines ahead of us (as they had done on the 28th of July [10 August, the Battle of the Yellow Sea]), the Admiral decided to deploy the 1st Battle Division in line abreast to starboard. . . . There was a confusion with the signals. . . . As a result instead of line abreast the 1st Division was in line ahead, parallel to the line of the 2nd and 3rd Divisions." Semenov is quoted in Westwood, *Witnesses of Tsushima,* 171.

58. Though this signal is associated exclusively with the battle of Tsushima in the popular mind, Tōgō issued it also on 23 June, when the Russians were coming out of Port Arthur *(NRKK,* 1:570), and earlier, at the first daylight attack on Port Arthur, he had sent almost identical messages (CS, 1:102; and *NRKK,* 1:447).

59. Quote from the Japanese navy's secret history in Toyama, *Nichi-Ro kaisen shinshi,* 248.

60. An account from the 1930s of Tōgō as hero of the T is found in Ogasawara Chōsei, "Tōgō gensui no omokage," 124–34. A solid contemporary analysis of Tsushima from this perspective is that of Nomura Minoru, "Tōgō Heihachirō no senjutsugan," 68–97.

61. See, for example, Westwood's *Russia against Japan,* 145–48. Westwood not only gives an intelligent analysis of Tōgō's perceptions but also is valuable in emphasizing the Russian side of the battle. The most provocative account in Japanese of Tōgō's turn is in Todaka, "Nihonkai kaisen ni teiji sempō wa nakatta," 233–34.

62. Here is the account of Comdr. Matsumura Tatsuo, executive officer of the *Mikasa* at Tsushima: "That day was a bit hazy and there was mist everywhere. The fleet went forward, but the location of the enemy was somewhat unclear. Our only choice, however, was to proceed, using as a basis the reports of the patrol ships and nothing else. Without quite realizing it we had approached to within 10,000 meters. This gave rise to an argument on the bridge about whether to fight on opposite or parallel courses. We had gotten so close, and yet preparations for firing were not complete." Matsumura's reminiscences are quoted in Todaka, "Toyama-shi no gimon ni kotaeru," 19.

63. Mayuzumi Haruo, in his *Kaigun hōsen shidan,* 147–49, argues that it would have been difficult for ships moving at any significant speed to have hit a stationary spot such as the turning point for the Japanese column because of the primitive fire control of that time. Moreover, the historian Toyama Saburō, himself a man of much sea experience in wartime, has argued that even if the Russian warships had been able to concentrate their fire, no Japanese ship captain would have been so improvident as to steer into the storm of shell splashes, and each would have maneuvered around the spot, as he would have around a dangerous shoal. (Evans conversation with Toyama, November 1985.)

Participants in the battle, however, did not discount the danger. And Corbett and Slade, writing with the help of British eyewitness reports, say that Tōgō's attack was "as risky as that of Nelson at Trafalgar." They add, however, that "like Nelson, Admiral Togo probably counted with confidence on the ineffectiveness of the enemy's long range fire."

Corbett and Slade also explain why the Japanese were not easy targets. First, all Japanese ships did not stay strictly in line. The *Nisshin* and *Kasuga,* the last two ships in Tōgō's division, cruisers with a different turning radius than the battleships, came around wide. Kamimura's Second Division did not follow Tōgō's track but circled some 1,000 meters farther away from the enemy. His ships profited from Tōgō's fire, which began before he, in the lead ship of his division, had completed the turn, and he took a while to get back in Tōgō's wake. CS, 2:246–47.

Finally, Corbett and Slade note that "where a fleet exposes itself in this way, the keenness of the hostile gunners, and even of the fire control officers, to make the most of the chance while it lasts will tempt them to fire too rapidly and to trust to the large target rather than to careful and accurate laying on individual ships." The Russian fire on the Japanese turn, they point out, was rapid. CS, 2:247.

64. The Japanese fired at three rates: "deliberate," "normal," and "rapid."

65. For a record of all hits on the *Mikasa* at Tsushima, see *NRKK,* 2:353–62.

66. CS, 2:249.

67. Some Japanese histories celebrate Kamimura's maneuver as an intelligent exercise of initiative and an execution of the "L" tactic. An exercise of initiative it certainly was, revealing the divisional independence that Tōgō allowed his commanders. An execution of the "L" tactic it was not, unless any independent maneuver by the Second Division was to be counted as such.

68. *NRKK,* 2:421; see also CS, 2:304.

69. *NRKK,* 2:462; CS, 2:304–305.

70. An immediate postwar casualty was the *Mikasa,* which lay at Sasebo a few weeks after the conclusion of hostilities. The day that Tōgō left her to take a train to Tokyo for a hero's welcome, the flagship mysteriously caught fire. Before the flames could be extinguished, they reached the after magazine, which, upon exploding, killed many of the crew and sent the ship to the bottom of the harbor. The wreck was eventually raised and towed to Yokosuka, where she was retained as a national monument, her hull encased in cement. Refurbished after World War II, the *Mikasa* is a popular tourist attraction today.

71. Nagayo Ogasawara (Ogasawara, Nagayo), 396–97.

72. Japanese text of the Instruction in Toyama, *NRKK,* 2:504; English text, Nagayo Ogasawara (Ogasawara, Nagayo), 400–402.

73. Willmott, *Sea Warfare,* 32.

74. CS, 2:333.

75. It is impossible to know the precise figure because many of the Russian ships sank and therefore could not be examined. From a detailed study of the problem, Frederick J. Milford concludes that "it is unlikely that the Japanese achieved a 10 percent hit rate." Milford, letter to authors, 7 April 1994.

Akiyama Saneyuki was probably close to the truth when he told the American naval attaché in Tokyo two years after the battle that the Japanese got less than 4 percent. He said that the figure of 40 percent, which he had been quoted as claiming, was a gross misrepresentation by the Japanese press. See National Archives, Records of the Chief of Naval Operations, RG 38, Office of Naval Intelligence, Attaché's Reports, "Report of the U.S. Naval Attaché," 7–8. The Combined Fleet's Battle Plan cautioned gunners not to expect more than 1 percent hits at ranges above 3,500 meters. See discussion of the Battle of the Yellow Sea above; *NRKK,* 1:391.

76. The *Mikasa* was the chief target of the Russian fire throughout the battle, but her fighting effectiveness was in no way impaired. Two of Tōgō's cruisers, the *Iwate* and *Asama,* were badly holed on the water line and another, the *Nisshin,* had three of her heavy guns knocked out. Yet all three were still in action at the end of the battle.

77. British observers reported the ratio of AP to HC in Japanese ships at Tsushima variously as 1 to3 and 1 to 4. United Kingdom, Admiralty, Naval Ordnance Department, 111.

78. Ibid., 31.

79. Hayashi, 143–44. Mayuzumi, *Kaigun hōsen shidan,* 117–21, points out that the Japanese navy preferred the thin-skinned, high-explosive *furoshiki* shell (see chapter 3). Officially known as the *tankō ryūdan* (drawn steel common shell), it was the shell most used at Tsushima and indeed in the entire war. Further, even when Japanese gunners fired the *tekkō ryūdan* (AP shell), it generally had the effect of a high-explosive projectile because it usually burst upon impact and did not penetrate the vitals of the enemy ship. Mayuzumi laments this result, which was caused by the highly volatile charge heating under the compression of impact rather than by any defect in the fuse, but concedes, "we cannot say these [such misfires] were without effect." Shards from such a blast were larger and traveled farther than those of the *furoshiki* shell.

    For amplifying remarks on the effect of Shimose, see Westwood, *Witnesses of Tsushima,* 226; and United Kingdom, Admiralty, Naval Ordnance Department, 32, 46.

80. Falk, 392.

81. Toyama, *Nis-Shin, Nichi-Ro, Dai Tōa kaisen shi,* 280.

82. United Kingdom, Admiralty, Naval Ordnance Department, 15–16.

    Further limitations of Japanese fire control might also be mentioned. At the height of battle, when many ships were concentrating on a single target, they had difficulty observing the fall of shot without range clocks to tell them precisely when their own ship's shells would strike. Range clocks were not introduced into the Japanese navy until 1907. See Kaigun Hōjutsushi Kankōkai, *Kaigun Hōjutsushi* (cited hereafter as *KH),* 785. Salvo fire, an essential for correct spotting, proved impossible to carry out during the battle despite Tōgō's instruction to do so (quoted in Shima, 107). British observers concluded that "the Japanese employed, as a general rule, nothing in the nature of salvo fire." United Kingdom, Admiralty, Naval Ordnance Department, 23.

83. For comments by two famous Western naval men on the strategic principles involved in the naval side of the Russo-Japanese War, see Mahan, *Naval Strategy,* 422–25; and Kemp, ed., *The Papers of Sir John Fisher,* 2:337–38.

84. The basic design of the *Dreadnought* had been decided before the lessons of the Russo-Japanese War were in, as Marder notes in *The Anatomy of British Seapower,* 530–32. But the attaché accounts supported Fisher's demand for high-caliber guns and converted the Board of Admiralty to his views.

85. For an overview of these controversies, see Towle, "The Evaluation of the Experience of the Russo-Japanese War," 65–79.

86. *KS*, 496; Edwyn Gray, *The Devil's Device*, 175; and Marder, *The Anatomy of British Seapower*, 525. Gray asserts that there may have been occasions when Japanese torpedo commanders launched their weapons too close to their targets. When torpedo running distances were too short, the safety fans did not spin down enough to prime the warheads, and thus the weapons were still uncocked when they struck the enemy warships.

87. Herbert W. Wilson, 1:264–65; Edwyn Gray, *The Devil's Device*, 172; *KS*, 464; and Willmott, *Sea Warfare*, 43.

88. Kusumi Tadao, 357.

89. *KS*, 464.

90. Ibid., 495.

91. The "1919 type," developed during the war by Ordnance Comdr. Matsushita Shōtai at Yokosuka, ran 10,000 meters at 38 knots and 20,000 meters at 27 knots. *KS*, 18–20.

92. Ibid., 475, 492, 496–97.

93. Todaka, "Nihonkai kaisen," 235–36; and Shima, 104–5.

94. Nomura Minoru, *Kaisenshi ni manabu*, 80.

95. The authors are indebted to H. P. Willmott for his insights into the consequences of Tsushima, some of which are reflected in this paragraph. Wilmott, letter to authors, 22 August 1994.

5   SATŌ TETSUTARŌ
The Contradictions of Japanese Naval Strategy, 1908–1911

1. Tsunoda, "Nihon kaigun sandai no rekishi," 95.

2. Ibid., 149–50; and Itō Terumi, "Satō Tetsutarō no kokubō," 23–24.

3. It is not clear where in Britain or the United States Satō undertook his research. Information on such foreign naval study by individual Japanese naval officers in the Meiji period is usually fragmentary or nonexistent (probably due to the destruction of the relevant information at the end of World War II), unless there exists a prewar "official" biography, usually compiled posthumously by a memorial committee of fellow officers. Since Satō died in 1942, however, when the wartime navy had little time for such sedate activities, no biography of this influential Japanese naval thinker exists.

4. Tanaka, "Satō Tetsutarō," 150–51; and Itō Terumi, 18.

5. Satō, *Teikoku*, 1:144. In arriving at his conclusion, Satō devoted considerable space to relevant historical examples. Scanning past centuries of naval warfare in the West, Satō noted that in eighteen attempted conquests of an island territory by an attacker without control of the sea, not one was successful. Conversely, in seventy cases where a nation possessing command of the sea attacked an island territory and its fortifications, there were only two examples of failure and these two were due to fundamental mistakes and negligence on the part of the attacker. Satō, *Kaibō shi ron*, 23.

6. Satō, *Teikoku*, 1:198–225; and Itō Terumi, 27–29.

7. But it soon became a key strategic asset. In 1908, the joint board endorsed the development of Pearl Harbor as a fleet base, and construction began when a channel for large vessels was dredged several years later. Even before 1898, American naval planners had worried about Japanese designs on Hawaii. Miller, *War Plan Orange*, 44.

8. These problems are discussed in Sprout and Sprout, *Rise of American Naval Power*, 253–54.

9. Cited by Itō Terumi, 35; and Satō, *Kokubō no sakugi*, 69–70.

10. These points were made by Koyama, *Gunji shisō*, 254; and, over forty years ago, in Kiralfy, "Japanese Naval Strategy," 457–84.

11. Satō et al., *Kokubō mondai*, 8–10.

12. In his thought-provoking study of Japanese naval strategy to 1945, Clark Reynolds makes the telling argument (somewhat flawed in its specifics) that Japan never had a national maritime strategy, for the very reason that its national interests were essentially continental and thus ultimately shaped by its military priorities. Reynolds, "Continental Strategy," 65–71.

13. Satō, *Kokubō no sakugi*. Our copy of this pamphlet is marked *gokuhi* (confidential) and shows other signs of being for internal naval circulation only.

14. Satō et al., *Kokubō mondai*, 8–10, 52–59.

15. *KG1*, 119, 123; and Nakamura Yoshihiko's comments in Kaigunshi Kenkyūkai, ed., *Nihon kaigun no hon*, 39.

16. Satō, *Teikoku*, 23–26.

17. Satō, *Kokubō mondai*, appendix titled "Nichi-Ei-Doku-Futsu-Ro-Bei roku kaigun jitsuryoku kyokusenzu" (Diagram of the strengths of the Japanese, English, German, French, Russian, and U. S. navies). Professor John H. Maurer, U. S. Naval War College, asserts that the United States was unlikely to build a fleet as large as that projected by Satō. The Navy's General Board typically asked for forty-eight modern battleships, and it never came close to attaining the resources to reach this force level. Maurer, letter to authors, 13 August 1992.

18. Satō, *Teikoku*, 2:270–310.

19. It is impossible to say whether the 70 percent formula was the brainchild of Satō or Akiyama. Since their research and contact at the staff college during these years was so close, it most likely was a product of their joint research efforts. We have identified it only with Satō because it was initially set forth in print in his *History* in 1908 and then in 1913 in the pamphlet, "A Study of the National Defense Problem" (see n. 15 above). Nomura Minoru, "Tai-Bei-Ei kaisen," 26–27.

20. That is, a 1.5 to 1 superiority for the attacker corresponds to a 0.67 to 1 (67 percent) inferiority for the defender. If the latter ratio is less than 0.67 then the probability favors a victory for the attacker; if it exceeds 0.67 the probability favors a victory for the defender. For Satō and Akiyama the 70 percent ratio (0.70) may have been nothing more than a convenient number slightly larger than 0.67. *DHKRK*, 158–59.

21. Fiske, "American Naval Policy," 17–24, 49–53.

22. Mark A. Campbell, a student of the age of sail, maintains that naval commanders in that era were conscious of the importance of concentrating force, the basic principle underlying the N^2 Law. Campbell, letter to authors, 16 February 1992. On the other hand, John H. Maurer reminds us of the extremely abstract nature of the Lanchester equations, arguing that no naval battle in the ages of sail or steam ever conformed to them. Naval battles, he notes, are too complex and too chaotic to be governed by such predictive theory, just as the 3-to-1 rule about land combat is highly misleading. Weather, training, morale, leadership, fire control systems, and quality of shell are complex variables to model, too complex to be included in the Lanchester

scheme, but they play a large role in determining victory or defeat. Maurer, letter to authors, 13 August 1992. Nevertheless, as a theoretical gauge of tactical effectiveness the N^2 Law was highly influential in naval thinking in the early part of this century in all the major navies. The Lanchester equations and the calculations of two other Western naval writers (J. V. Chase and Ambroise Baudry) that demonstrated the cumulative effects of modern gunfire are set forth in Hughes, *Fleet Tactics,* 35–37, 66–69. For a thorough mathematical discussion of the Lanchester equations see Morse and Kimball, *Methods of Operations Research,* 63ff. For information on the later influence of the equations in the Japanese navy, see Agawa, *Reluctant Admiral,* 31–33.

23. *KG1,* 138–40.
24. Ibid., 127.
25. Ibid.
26. Ibid.
27. Ibid., 129.
28. In contrast, American strategists placed great emphasis on logistics even before World War I. As early as 1908, nearly 60 percent of the U.S. naval construction budget went for large colliers with rigs for high-speed coal transfer. Miller, 91.
29. Ibid.
30. In December 1906, for example, chief of the Intelligence Bureau of the Army General Staff, Capt. Matsuishi Yasuharu, drafted a proposal for the staff urging that fifty divisions be placed on the Asian continent to establish an expanded Japanese presence there. Uchida Kazutomi, in the analytical introduction to Satō, *Teikoku,* 1:2–4.
31. Quoted in *DHKRK,* 101.
32. Tsunoda, "Nihon kaigun sandai no rekishi," 98.
33. The complete Japanese text of the Imperial Defense Policy of 1907, as well as the interservice negotiations leading up to it and the processes by which it was adopted, are provided in *DHKRK,* 107–122.
34. Itō Terumi, 17. No originals of the three basic documents of the 1907 statement exist; they were undoubtedly burned at the end of World War II. Postwar historians came to know of the document only indirectly until the discovery some years ago of Marshal Yamagata's copy in a private collection. *DHKRK,* 123.
35. Takagi, *Shikan,* 17; and Agawa, 194–95.
36. *DHKRK,* 118.
37. Ōmae, "Nihon kaigun no heijutsu shisō," part 1, p. 44, argues that the major engagements of the Russo-Japanese War had demonstrated that a six-six fleet was tactically unbalanced, but that an eight-eight fleet was, at the time, the maximum number of ships for optimum command and control. *KG1,* 121, suggests that Tirpitz's First Navy Bill of 1898 was the original source of the Japanese eight-eight plan. It is likely, however, that the Second Bill of 1900 was the inspiration, as the former merely provided for nineteen battleships and the latter specified squadrons of eight battleships. See Herwig, *"Luxury" Fleet,* 42.
38. Ōmae, "Nihon kaigun no heijutsu shisō," part 1, p. 42. There was no precise correlation between the eight-eight plan and the 70 percent ratio, because, considering rapid changes in technology, the balance of power, and the international situation, only a gross approximation was possible.

39. *DHKRK,* 118.

40. Nish, "Japan and Naval Aspects," 69.

41. Tsunoda, "Nihon kaigun sandai no rekishi," 98–99; and Nomura Minoru, "Sekai kenkan kyōsō," 106–107.

42. *DHKRK,* 225.

43. The navy was obliged to proceed toward its goal by stages, however. The first capital ships that Japan acquired after 1905 were not seen by the navy as contributing to an eight-eight fleet, since they were pre-dreadnoughts and thus obsolete from the moment they were launched. Moreover, although several dreadnought battleships were launched prior to World War I, their construction had not been identified as part of this larger fleet plan. In1917 brighter economic circumstances and the apparent challenge in naval construction from the United States induced the Diet to fund an eight-four fleet, to be completed in 1923, as a first step toward the navy's goal. In 1918, the Diet authorized the money for the construction of an eight-six fleet, and finally, in 1920, funds were made available for the remaining warships that were intended to complete an eight-eight fleet by 1927.

6 TOWARD AN EIGHT-EIGHT FLEET
The Japanese Navy's Plans for Expansion, 1905–1922

1. See, for example, Fairbanks, "The Origins of the *Dreadnought* Revolution," 246–72; Sumida, "Sir John Fisher and the *Dreadnought*"; and Lambert, "Admiral Sir John Fisher," 639–60.

2. For a detailed discussion of these matters, see Padfield, *Guns at Sea,* 202–28.

3. See, for example, Sumida, *In Defence of Naval Supremacy,* 51–61.

4. Preston, *Cruisers,* 20, 40.

5. Preston, *Destroyers,* 14–17.

6. Herwig, *"Luxury" Fleet,* 88.

7. Wragg, *Wings over the Sea,* 9–25; and Melhorn, *Two-Block Fox,* 6–10.

8. Sumida, "The Quest for Reach," 25; and Friedman, *U.S. Naval Weapons,* 29–30.

9. Lacroix, "The Development of the 'A Class' Cruisers," part 2, p. 60, n. 37.

10. In our understanding of these matters we have been guided by Frederick Milford (letters to authors, 1991–95); and Friedman, *Battleship Design,* 85–97.

11. For saturated steam the temperature is uniquely related to steam pressure; superheating, of course, means raising the steam temperature without increasing the pressure.

12. Friedman, *Battleship Design,* 91; and Preston, *Battleships,* 113.

13. Friedman, *Battleship Design,* 93–94.

14. Ibid., 94–95; and Padfield, *The Battleship Era,* 202–3.

15. Preston, *Battleships,* 191, 195; and Hayashi, 130.

16. Hayashi, 36–37. The *Ibuki* had Curtis turbines imported from the United States.

17. Preston, *Battleships,* 196; and WG, 39–40.

18. Fairbanks, 246.

19. Chihaya and Abe, "IJN *Kongō,*" 265–67.

20. Ibid., 267–68; and Hayashi, 130–31.

21. The request was refused on the grounds that the Japanese public, which had paid for these warships, would not wish them to leave Japan's territorial waters. WG, 40–41.
22. Preston, *Battleships,* 199; and WG, 48–49.
23. Preston, *Battleships,* 200; and WG, 52.
24. The Siemens affair arose after revelations of bribery of high-ranking naval officers in charge of the bureaus of procurement and shipbuilding within the Navy Ministry by agents of the German firm of Siemens, which desired to retain a monopoly over Japanese naval contracts for electrical equipment and wireless installations. Graft was also discovered in connection with the ordering of the *Kongō* from Vickers. The scandal brought dishonor to the navy and ultimately caused the collapse in March 1914 of the cabinet headed by Yamamoto Gombei.
25. Sprout and Sprout, 253–54.
26. Potter, 451; and Hughes, *Fleet Tactics,* 81–85.
27. Potter, 475.
28. Wragg, *Wings over the Sea,* 18, 24, 29–34.
29. Polmar, *Aircraft Carriers,* 25–30.
30. For a summary of the navy's occupation of Micronesia in the autumn of 1914 and the controversy within the navy concerning it, see Peattie, *Nan'yō,* 41–44.
31. Halpern, *A Naval History,* 393
32. Nomura Minoru, *Kaisenshi ni manabu,* 138–66.
33. During the war, the navy had sent an observer delegation to Britain made up of officers from selected specialized fields in technology and tactics to study wartime developments in the Royal Navy. Three of these officers were aboard British ships at Jutland: Comdr. Suetsugu Nobumasa in Jellicoe's Grand Fleet aboard HMS *Colossus;* Lt. Comdr. Shimomura Chūsuke aboard the *Queen Mary* in Beattie's Battle Cruiser Fleet; and Lt. Comdr. Imamura Shinjirō aboard a light cruiser in the Grand Fleet. Shimomura went down with the *Queen Mary* when she was blown up. Following the battle, the Japanese delegation sent the Navy General Staff in Tokyo voluminous reports that served as the basis for years of study by the staff and by the staff college. Yoshida Akihiko, letter to authors, 25 June 1993.
34. Fukui, *Nihon no gunkan,* 13.
35. Hiraga, *Hiraga Yuzuru ikō shū,* 31–69.
36. Fukui, *Nihon no gunkan,* 13; *KG1,* 131–32; Preston, *Battleships,* 201; WG, 56–58; and Hiraga, 39–40.
37. For the Japanese navy, Jutland confirmed the value of the battle cruiser's scouting function. This conclusion, after Jutland, that every first-rank naval power must have a scouting division of battle cruisers and fast battleships, is interesting in light of the disastrous performance of British battle cruisers at Jutland, three of which were sunk because of faulty design. *KG1,* 131–32.
38. WG, 64–65.
39. *KG1,* 66–67; and Nomura Minoru, "Sekai kenkan kyōsō," 106–8. Nomura explains that the last "eight" of the eight-eight-eight fleet concept refers to ships, not years, as usually assumed. He points out that the conventional confusion on this point appears to stem from the navy's earlier decision to set the normal life of a capital ship at eight years of frontline service.

40. Hiraga conceived the two basic designs for all these ships, none of which was ever laid down. Only two of the battleships planned were ever given names—the *Kii* and *Owari*. The identification of the remaining warships never went beyond numerical designations, 11 through 16, though the material for these warships was assembled, ready for the keels to be laid down, when the Washington Treaty led to their cancellation. WG, 65–66.

41. Nomura Minoru, "Sekai kenkan kyōsō," 108–9. Dingman's *Power in the Pacific,* 123–27 and 134–35, argues that the eight-eight fleet program that was eventually authorized by the Japanese Diet was "not a radical attempt to create a new order of sea power in the Pacific but a conservative, bureaucratically generated scheme," and demonstrates that a significant portion of the funds actually appropriated after World War I for naval expansion was allocated for categories other than capital ship construction. Despite Dingman's argument, it is clear that the navy's *original* plans for an eight-eight-*eight* fleet would indeed have created a new order of sea power in the Pacific, for it would have provided Japan with the largest battle force in that ocean.

42. Dingman, *Power in the Pacific,* 123, points out that not only was there a marked shift in the categories of warships to be built under the 1920 appropriations (submarines, for example, accounting for 20 percent of the total number of ships planned), but there was also a major shift in the balance between ship construction and shore facilities, the latter consuming nearly 20 per cent of the naval construction budget for 1921.

43. WG, 127–28; and Preston, *Cruisers,* 51, 53, 65–67.

44. WG, 128–36; and Lengerer, Kobler-Edamatsu, and Rehm-Takahara, "Kitakami," 33–34.

45. WG, 242–65.

46. Carpenter and Polmar, *Submarines,* 71–76; and Japan, Bōeichō Bōeikenshūjo Senshishitsu, *Sensuikanshi,* 1–4. Akiyama Saneyuki, in a 1912 revision of his *Basic Naval Tactics,* noted that "the submarine . . . has begun to transform what, up to now, have been the surface tactics of naval warfare, into three-dimensional sub-surface warfare. The submarine will become a formidable weapon in the future, but because its development is still in its infancy it is a bit too early to rank it as battleworthy. Instead, we may properly regard it at present as a mobile subsurface mine. Its capacity and mobility will increase, and we may assume that it will ultimately become a powerful offensive weapon." Cited in *KG1,* 127.

47. The Japanese submarine *No. 6* accidentally sank to the bottom of the bay while on a training mission because the engine's air inlet valve was not closed in time while the submarine was diving. After four hours the air in the submarine was exhausted, and the commander, Lt. Sakuma Tsutomu, and his crew all suffocated. When the submarine was raised, navy rescuers recovered Lieutenant Sakuma's notes on the final hours of the crew. This record, which revealed their stoicism and devotion to duty in the face of death, caused a sensation and served to elevate *No. 6* and its commander to the pantheon of Japanese naval tradition. Kaigun Yūshūkai, 263–64.

48. As early as July 1915, even before Germany's declaration of unrestricted submarine warfare against the Allies, the Japanese naval observer in London, Comdr. Suetsugu Nobumasa, who as rear admiral shaped the navy's basic submarine doctrine during the interwar period, sent a report to Tokyo concerning the disruption by German submarines of the traditional British naval strategy of close blockade. Japan, Bōeichō Bōeikenshūjo Senshishitsu, *Sensuikanshi,* 28.

49. Carpenter and Polmar, 88.

50. For our discussion of Japanese naval aviation we have relied heavily on the most comprehensive study of the subject, the four-volume history compiled and written by a committee of forty-two former Japanese naval air officers: Nihon Kaigun Kōkūshi Hensan Iinkai, ed., *Nihon kaigun kōkūshi* (cited hereafter as *NKKS*).

51. *NKKS*, 1:302–12.

52. Ibid., 334–36. Considering the valuable service of the "blimps" of the U.S. Navy during World War II, there is some irony in the decision of the Japanese navy to discontinue the use of airships. But because the navy either saw the airship in the rather unimaginative role of naval gunfire spotting or exaggerated its use as an offensive weapon, the airship's antisubmarine possibilities, demonstrated so effectively by the Americans in the Atlantic, were overlooked.

53. Japan, Bōeichō Bōeikenshūjo Senshishitsu, *Kaigun kōkū gaishi* (cited hereafter as *KKG*), 1–2. One of the three officers sent to Hammondsport was Lt. Nakajima Chikuhei, the future Japanese aircraft magnate and influential Diet member. Nakajima's training at Hammondsport is recounted in Watanabe, *Kyojin Nakajima*, 83–84.

54. Polmar, 36–37; and *NKKS*, 4:22–65 and 2:469.

55. Sekigawa, *A Pictorial History*, 12–13; and Mikesh and Abe, *Japanese Aircraft*, 269–70.

56. Ohmae and Pineau, "Japanese Naval Aviation," 70; and *NKKS*, 1:193–95.

57. Lacroix, *Japanese Cruisers*, appendix E; and Japan, Tsūshō Sangyōshō, *Kikai kōgyō*, 143.

58. Lacroix, *Japanese Cruisers*, appendix E.

59. Howe, *The Origins of Japanese Trade Supremacy*, 279.

60. Lacroix, *Japanese Cruisers*, appendix E.

61. Ibid.

62. Lacroix, *Japanese Cruisers*, appendix E; and Nihon Zōsen Gakkai, *Shōwa zōsenshi* (cited hereafter as *SZ*), 1:666.

63. Lacroix, *Japanese Cruisers*, appendix E.

64. *KG1*, 685.

65. Ibid., 686–87; and Nenryō Konwakai, 1:17.

66. The navy actually reckoned its petroleum supplies in kiloliters, but for simplicity we will state supplies in tons with the assumption that 1,000 liters of naval fuel of any kind equals 1 ton.

67. *KG1*, 687, 694–95. One of the first Japanese of the time to draw a connection between Southeast Asia and a solution to the navy's fuel problem was Capt. Matsuoka Shizuo (later a renowned ethnologist of Micronesia and Southeast Asia). In 1918, he wrote a small pamphlet, "Petroleum of the Netherlands East Indies," in which he called for a consistent oil policy for the navy and urged importation of oil from the East Indies as an interim measure on the way to Japanese self-sufficiency in oil. Gotō, part 1, p. 4.

68. *KG1*, 693. Up through the mid-1920s most oil thus stored was from Tarakan, while the petroleum from California was put to day-to-day use by the navy. In the latter half of that decade, however, because of the steep rise in Southeast Asian oil prices, the navy halted the purchase of Tarakan oil altogether and shifted to the cheaper California product. Nenryō Konwakai, 1:17–18.

69. By way of comparison, on the eve of the Pacific War the navy estimated that it would consume about 2.8 million tons in the first year of warfare and 2.7 million tons in the second. See table 14–3; and Nomura Minoru, "Dai niji," 106.
70. *KG1,* 687, 690–94; Gotō, part 1, p. 4; and Samuels, *Japanese State Energy Markets,* 229.
71. Nish, *The Anglo-Japanese Alliance,* 353–57.
72. Nish, *Alliance in Decline,* 46–47.
73. *DHKRK,* 139.
74. Nish, *Alliance in Decline,* 64–74.
75. *KG1,* 145–46. In contrast, a decade before Japanese planning for an American war, the U.S. Naval War College speculated about a war with Japan involving a descent on Hawaii, Alaska, and the American west coast by a Japanese fleet. The scenario cropped up in several student papers submitted to the college from 1897 to 1903. Vlahos, "The Naval War College," 24–25.
76. Nomura Minoru, "Kokka," 26–27. For a further discussion of *Suishi jumbi,* see chapter 10.
77. For the definitive discussion of the origins and evolution of the Orange Plan see Miller.
78. *DHKRK,* 132. At this very time and until the 1920s, U.S. Navy planners considered Amami Ōshima and the Ryukyus in general to be strategic objectives. Miller, 155–58.
79. *KG1,* 146; and *DHKRK,* 133–34. In its comments on the exercise, the Operations Division of the Navy General Staff stressed the importance of the occupation of Guam, which would allow the Combined Fleet to sever the American lines of communication and supply and allow timely intelligence of American intentions. The Operations Division even ventured to sketch the possibility of Japanese demonstrations against Alaska, Hawaii, and the American west coast. *DHKRK,* 134–35.
80. By 1919, the major Japanese landing sites had already been selected: San Fernando and the Lingayen Gulf on northwestern Luzon and Lamon and Tayabas Bays on opposite sides of the southern Luzon coasts. *DHKRK,* 168, 175–76.
81. Ibid.
82. Edward S. Miller asserts that the United States, unlike Japan, had worked out a detailed Pacific strategy by World War I. The concept of such a strategy was fully developed by American planners by 1914, along with the general campaign strategies except for the vital middle-phase Pacific crossing. Miller, letter to authors, 2 February 1990.
83. As early as 1921, the Japanese navy began surveying the islands for suitable bases and making plans for rapid militarization of the islands in the event of war. While these initiatives violated the spirit of its international agreements on the nonfortification of its mandate, the initiatives certainly were not specifically forbidden by the agreements. On the often misunderstood question of Japan's militarization of Micronesia, see Peattie, *Nan'yo,* 234, 230–56.
84. Dingman, *Power in the Pacific,* 192; and Asada, "Japanese Admirals," 152–54, 159.
85. Dingman, *Power in the Pacific,* 192; and Asada, "Japanese Admirals," 146–48.
86. Asada, "Japanese Admirals," 152–54, 159.
87. See, for example, Braisted, *The United States Navy in the Pacific;* Buckley, *The United States and the Washington Conference;* and Asada, "Japan and the United States."

88. Technically speaking, cruisers were not mentioned in the Washington Treaty. Ships above 10,000 tons were counted as capital ships. Those at or somewhat below this figure, of course, were in fact cruisers; they could not carry guns larger than 8 inches.

89. Asada, "Japanese Admirals," 151, 155.

90. Nish, "Japan and the Naval Aspects," 74–75. To balance Japan's retention of the *Mutsu,* the United States and Britain were each allowed to finish two more battleships of up to 35,000 tons.

91. *KG1,* 197–98; and Asada, "Japanese Admirals," 159–61.

7   "Using a Few to Conquer Many"
    The Japanese Navy from the Beginning of the Treaty Era to the First London Naval Conference, 1923–1930

1. Our views in this and the following paragraph are based in part on the analysis by Boyd, "Japanese Military Effectiveness," 142–43.

2. *DHKRK,* 197.

3. Asada, "The Japanese Navy," 235.

4. *DHKRK,* 207–10.

5. One such study, drafted in 1920 by Capt. Harry Yarnell, Comdr. W. S. Pye, and Lt. Comdr. H. H. Holloway (all were from the navy's Operation Division) and entitled "Conduct of an Oversea Campaign," analyzed the problems encountered by a "Black Fleet" in undertaking a transoceanic offensive (in either the Pacific or the Atlantic) and the defensive measures necessary to a "White Fleet" in meeting and defeating it. In regard to the latter, the study anticipated much of the planning actually undertaken by the Japanese navy for defense against an American naval expedition into the western Pacific, including its attrition strategy employing destroyers, submarines, and aircraft.

6. *KG1,* 150–51. Edward S. Miller confirms our suspicion that Japanese thinking on these routes closely paralleled American reasoning during the interwar period. The south-central route was briefly considered in 1923 and then definitely adopted by American planners a decade later. Miller, letter to authors, 1 February 1990.

7. Ōmae, "Nihon kaigun no heijutsu shisō," part 1, p. 46. Interestingly, these differences in viewpoint within the Japanese navy seem to mirror the arguments among American naval planners between what Edward S. Miller has termed "the thrusters," those who advocated a quick American movement across the Pacific, and "the cautionaries," those who wished to move step-by-step, building for a final offensive against Japan. Miller, 77–85.

8. Miller, 77–85.

9. *KG1,* 148.

10. Ibid., 148–49, 152–53.

11. Suzuki, 261; and Kaigun Henshū Iinkai, *Kaigun,* 4:222.

12. Contemporary American planners saw the decisive encounter taking place farther to the west, somewhere off the Ryukyus. Miller, 161.

13. *DHKRK,* 201.

14. *KG1,* 153–54, 196–97; and Omae, "Nihon kaigun no heijutsu shisō," part 1, p. 50.

15. *KG1*, 176; Hata, *Taiheiyō*, 234–35; and U.S. Navy, Chief of Naval Operations, *General Tactical Instructions, United States Navy, Fleet Tactical Publication Number 45,* 26–28. According to Edward S. Miller, despite the obsession of the Japanese navy with the problems posed by the American ring formation, no Orange Plan ever mentioned the formation. Miller feels that the ring formation was "more of a dress parade at sea" than a serious tactical formation. Miller, letters to authors, 1 February and 22 August 1990. On the other hand, the ring formation was used in games at the Naval War College at Newport. Mark A. Campbell, letter to authors, 16 February 1992.

16. It is important to recognize, however, as Edward S. Miller has pointed out, that from the American perspective (at least by the early 1930s) it was the United States Navy that was in fact inferior, absolutely so in some types of ships and comparatively so in all types in terms of actual combat availability. Miller, letter to authors, 1 February 1990.

17. See chapter 6, n. 24.

18. *KG1,* 25–32.

19. Marder, *Old Friends, New Enemies,* 1:296; Boyd, "Japanese Military Effectiveness," 136–37; and Asada, "The Japanese Navy," 229.

20. Quoted in Marder, *Old Friends, New Enemies,* 1:296–97.

21. Japan, Bōeichō Bōeikenshūjo Senshishitsu, *Hawai sakusen,* 60. Lacroix, *Japanese Cruisers,* appendix I.

22. Japan, Bōeichō Bōeikenshūjo Senshishitsu, *Hawai sakusen,* 292–93.

23. Yoshida Akihiko, "San! Kuchikukan ga mapputatsu," 20–24; *KG1,* 188–89; and Kaigun Henshū Iinkai, 4:116–23.

24. *KS,* 523.

25. Marder, *Old Friends, New Enemies,* 1:285–87; and Asada, "The Japanese Navy," 226.

26. Roskill, *Naval Policy,* 1:534–35. Sumida, "'The Best Laid Plans,'" 881–900, however, has modified the picture for the Royal Navy, demonstrating that its failure to modernize was due more to fiscal pressures than it was to rearward-looking doctrine.

27. Marder, *Old Friends, New Enemies,* 1:294; and Asada, "The Japanese Navy," 234.

28. The second revision of the Battle Instructions incorporated the observations of those Japanese naval officers who had served with the British navy at sea during the war. These concepts, accepted in broad outline in 1917 and subsequently tested in the annual fleet maneuvers of 1919, were formally adopted in 1920 by the Navy General Staff, which added the principles of pursuit and the use of aircraft in naval combat. The third revision of the instructions in 1928 incorporated the definitive lessons of naval battle in World War I. *KG1,* 138; and Lacroix, "The Development of the 'A Class' Cruisers," part 5, p. 365, n. 79.

29. *KG1,* 130; Roskill, 1:533–34, 2:174–75; and Pelz, *The Race to Pearl Harbor,* 88, 112.

30. Bagnasco, *Submarines,* 24.

31. Andrade, "Submarine Policy," 50–56; and Talbott, "Weapons Development," 53–71.

32. Japan, Bōeichō Bōeikenshūjo Senshishitsu, *Sensuikanshi,* 29–31.

33. In 1940, a branch of the school was established at Ōtake, opposite the southern tip of Miyajima, across Hiroshima Bay from Kure. In November 1942 the Ōtake branch became the main submarine school for the navy. Ibid., 76–78.

34. Ibid., 29–31.
35. Ibid., 31–32; and *KG1*, 153–54. By 1928, the primacy of Suetsugu's ambush strategy had been institutionalized. That year, the third revision of the Battle Instructions laid down the principle that "the primary mission of submarine divisions is to carry out surprise attacks on the enemy's main force based on an appropriate extended disposition [a picket line]." *KS*, 749.
36. The nomenclature of Japanese submarines is difficult. There are two systems, each complex. One is the method of designating types of submarines, such as the KD. The other is the method of naming individual submarines, such as the *I-51*.

    Type designations derive from acronyms of Chinese characters adopted to describe the size and function of the submarines. For example, the *kaidai* designation derives from characters meaning "navy large model"; another important designation, *junsen,* comes from "ocean-cruising submarine."

    Starting in the 1920s the naming of particular submarines used the first three letters of the traditional *kana* syllabary (phonetic signs for writing Japanese syllables), that is, *i, ro,* and *ha,* followed by numbers. The displacement of the submarine, not its function, determined which letter it received. "First-class submarines," those over 1,000 tons, got the "I" designation; "second class," those from 500 to 1,000 tons, the "RO" designation; and "third class," those up to 500 tons, the "HA" designation. Kaigun Yūshūkai, 272–74; and Yamanouchi and Uchida, *Kaigun jiten,* 214.
37. WG, 313–15; Boyd, "Japanese Military Effectiveness," 150; and Boyd, "The Japanese Submarine Force," 27.
38. Friedman, *Submarine,* 41.
39. Ibid.
40. Japan, Bōeichō Bōeikenshūjo Senshishitsu, *Sensuikanshi,* 70–71.
41. Ibid., 64–65, 67–68, 70–71.
42. Ibid., 58; and Rössler, *The U-boat,* 88. The navy also purchased designs from Vulcan (Hamburg) for a large minelaying submarine, the U-117, which became the basis for the Japanese *I-21* through *I-24* (later *I-121* through *I-124)* series. Rössler, 88.
43. National Archives, Records of the Chief of Naval Operations, RG 38, Office of Naval Intelligence, Attaché's Reports, "Personnel of the Submarine Service."
44. JJM, 173; WG, 318–19; Carpenter and Polmar, 91; and Bagnasco, 181–82.
45. The only Japanese naval thinker who apparently gave any real thought to using Japan's growing submarine fleet for surface raiding was the naval writer and critic Ikezaki Chūkō (1891–1949). In a book on Japanese submarines published in 1929 and reprinted in 1932 as part of his *Taiheiyō senryaku ron* (On Pacific strategy), Ikezaki spelled out his ideas on raiding the American west coast and possibly even east coast ports, and on exploiting the vulnerability of American trade routes in the Pacific.
46. This argument was outlined by Alan D. Zimm in a letter to the authors, 4 September 1992.
47. Friedman, *Submarine,* 40; Japan, Bōeichō Bōeikenshūjo Senshishitsu, *Sensuikanshi,* 72; Carpenter and Polmar, 5; and Francillon, *Japanese Aircraft,* 451–52.
48. *KS*, 750; Japan, Bōeichō Bōeikenshūjo Senshishitsu, *Sensuikanshi,* 32–33; Ōmae, "Nihon kaigun no heijutsu shisō," part 1, p. 48; and *KG1*, 153–55.
49. Pelz, 28–29.
50. Kimata, *Nihon suiraisen shi,* 15–18.

51. *KG1*, 210; *SZ*, 1:481–85; and Watts, "The Japanese 'Special' Type," 2–13.

52. As built, they exceeded design displacement. The first vessels of the class had a trial displacement (carrying a specified amount of ammunition and two-thirds capacity of fuel, feedwater, and provisions) of about 2,070 tons (2,100 metric tons). Later models were still heavier. *SZ*, 1:481.

53. The class was not without its problems. As weight was added in later groups of the class, stability became a concern. All ships of the class had to be reconstructed after storm damage in the Fourth Fleet Incident (see chapter 8), which revealed that not only stability but also longitudinal strength of the hull was insufficient. When the ships were reconstructed with strengthened hulls and ballast to improve stability, the final displacement of vessels of this class was well over 2,000 tons. The *Uranami*, for example, had a trial displacement following refurbishing of 2,427 tons (2,465 metric tons). *SZ*, 1:483.

54. *SZ*, 1:481–83.

55. *KG1*, 211, 445. While this may be true, undoubtedly an equally important reason for limiting the number of large destroyers stemmed from the need for greater numbers of cheaper and smaller auxiliary warships. Nevertheless, so impressive was the *Fubuki* class that it purportedly provoked the design and construction of counterpart classes in other navies. In "The British Tribals, 1935," 49 and 56, Lyon asserts that the *Tribal* class of RN destroyers was designed in response to the *Fubuki* class. Also, the French *Fantastique* class, the German Z class, and the U.S. Navy's eight-gun destroyer leaders were all apparently motivated by the Japanese example.

56. Hughes, *Fleet Tactics*, 75–76.

57. This system was first developed in 1926 by Lt. Comdr. Ōmori Sentarō, an instructor at the Torpedo School. The gyroscope made it possible to set any heading for the torpedo, not just that of the torpedo tube from which it was fired. With this in mind, Ōmori recognized that an essential problem in directing torpedo fire of any particular ship was to select the best possible angle of fire for a torpedo for any given course and speed of the target, taking into account the likelihood that the enemy target would change course after the torpedo was fired. To solve this problem, Ōmori divided the possible headings of the target (from 0 to 180 degrees) into quadrants and calculated the probabilities of the enemy's change of course within each quadrant. He then worked out a series of diagrams that provided the standard (correct) firing angle for any given enemy heading, based on calculations of the zone of maximum probability of hits at that target heading. The Japanese navy soon drew up torpedo fire control tables based on Ōmori's work, showing for each angle of bearing to the target's bow the standard firing angle that gave the best chance of a hit. By 1930, this system had been adapted to an actual mechanism, a torpedo fire control director into which could be fed all relevant data on courses, speeds, and statistical probabilities. By linking torpedoes in their tubes directly to the torpedo fire control director, optimum angles of fire could be continuously set on the basis of ever-changing information up to the moment the torpedo was released. To this extent, the Japanese system was much like the contemporary Torpedo Data Computer in the U.S. Navy. The Japanese system had the additional capability of calculating statistical probability that would include evasive action by the target. *KS*, 489–90.

58. Ibid., 499.

59. Ibid., 493–94; and Ōmae, "Nihon kaigun no heijutsu shisō," part 1, p. 50.

60. The development of Japan's heavy cruisers is most expertly examined by the eminent Belgian specialist, Dr. Eric Lacroix, in "The Development of the 'A Class' Cruisers."

61. The cruiser race of the interwar period is treated in Andrade, "Arms Limitation," 179–90.

62. Preston, *Cruisers,* 70.

63. Lacroix, "The Development of the 'A Class' Cruisers," part 1, pp. 344, 348.

64. The *Yūbari's* normal displacement was 3,100 tons.

65. *SZ,* 1:464–66; Preston, *Cruisers,* 72–73; WG, 138; and Lacroix, "The Development of the 'A Class' Cruisers," part 2, pp. 41–42.

66. Lacroix, "The Development of the 'A Class' Cruisers," part 2, p. 54.

67. *SZ,* 1:465. The *Aoba's* trial displacement on completion was 9,645 tons (9,820 metric tons).

68. Mark A. Campbell, letter to authors, 4 March 1992.

69. Fujimoto proved far more susceptible to staff pressure to design ships that were overloaded with weapons and equipment. Hiraga, sent to Europe to gather technical intelligence, was so infuriated by these changes in design that the staff decided to "kick him upstairs" to the less critical position of chief of the Shipbuilding Section of the Navy Technical Research Institute. WG, 140; and Lacroix, "The Development of the 'A Class' Cruisers," part 3, pp. 330–31.

70. The torpedo mounts and the fifth turret, as well as other fittings and equipment insisted upon by the Navy General Staff, appear to have been the major reason why the *Myōkō*-class cruisers were nearly 1,000 tons (10,940 standard tons) heavier than originally planned or allowed under the treaty limits. The trial displacement of the first of this class to be completed, the *Nachi,* was 13,330 tons upon completion as compared to the designer's original target of 11,850 trial tons. Fukui, *Nihon no gunkan,* 31; and *SZ,* 1:467, 786.

71. The following have been especially helpful with regard to Japanese "cheating": Lacroix, "The Development of the 'A Class' Cruisers," part 3, p. 341; Alan D. Zimm, letter to authors, 4 September 1992; and Mark A. Campbell, letter to authors, 4 March 1992.

    Reconstructions of Japanese cruisers after the era of arms limitation invariably increased their size. For example, the *Myōkō,* 10,940 tons upon completion, displaced 13,000 standard tons after its second reconstruction in 1941. Facts such as these added to the popular impression of Japanese duplicity in tonnages, but most of the added weight came after the treaty era.

72. Lacroix, "The Development of the 'A Class' Cruisers," part 4, pp. 67–69; and Skulski, *The Heavy Cruiser Takao.*

73. *SZ,* 1:467–68; and Lacroix, "The Development of the 'A Class' Cruisers," part 4, pp. 42, 67, 69, 73–74.

74. Roskill, 1:502; and Andrade, "Arms Limitation," 179–80.

75. Marc A. Epstein, the most knowledgeable student of the Geneva conference, emphasizes the dilemma of the Japanese delegation at Geneva in "Naval Disarmament and the Japanese: Geneva, 1927," 221–23, 324. On the one hand, in view of severe financial pressures at home, the members were anxious to head off any possibility of a new cruiser construction race; on the other, they were determined to work for a 10 to 10 to 7 adjustment in any settlement on cruisers that might be reached at the conference. Epstein, letter to authors, 25 January 1994.

76. Roskill, 1:505; and *DHKRK,* 219.
77. During the interwar years the Japanese navy used the rather quaint term *hojo* (auxiliary) for all warship categories below those of battleships, battle cruisers, and aircraft carriers.
78. *KG1, 350–55.*
79. Ōmae, "Nihon kaigun no heijutsu shisō," part 1, p. 49. Apparently, the staff's determinations about range, if reported correctly by Ōmae, were mistaken. Data in N. J. M. Campbell, *Naval Weapons,* 185, shows that in the Japanese navy, the 6-inch gun's maximum range was about 27,000 meters, only 2,000 meters less than the 8-inch gun's 29,000 meters, and the 14-inch gun could reach 35,450 meters.
80. Actually, by the London Treaty, American cruiser strength was to be reduced from 23 to 18.
81. *KG1, 368–71.*
82. In English, the London Naval Conference and Treaty of 1930 have been dealt with in O'Connor, *Perilous Equilibrium*; Roskill, 2; and Kobayashi, "The London Naval Treaty, 1930."
83. Kobayashi, 347; and *KG1, 445–46.*
84. Pelz, 2–3. Notably, however, in total tonnage, Japan continued to enjoy an 80 percent ratio compared with the United States for several years after the London Treaty, since the latter made no effort until 1934 to build up to its treaty limits and, even after that, did not catch up and surpass Japan until the end of the decade.

8   "OUTRANGING" THE ENEMY
The Japanese Navy from the First London Naval Conference to the End of the Treaty Era, 1930–1936

1. *KG1,* 219–20, 396–400; and Asada, "The Japanese Navy," 238–39.
2. *SZ,* 1:468–71. No reliable figures are available on the final standard tonnage of the *Mogami*s; it is clear, however, that their trial displacement was about 13,160 tons (13,400 metric tons) when completed, by which time, incidentally, Japan had renounced the naval limitation treaties.
3. Lacroix, "The Development of the 'A Class' Cruisers," part 7, pp. 247–48; WG, 152; Pelz, 31; *KG1,* 144; and Preston, *Cruisers,* 100–101.
4. Andrade, "Arms Limitation," 185–86.
5. Fukui, *Nihon no gunkan,* 53–55; *KG1,* 446; and Yoshida Toshio, "Aitsugu kuchikukan no junan," 96–100. The *Tomozuru* was not the first Japanese warship to have capsized in a storm. In December 1932, the destroyer *Sawarabi* and three sister ships were operating in the Taiwan straits, often called the "sailor's death trap" because of the terrible storms there. The ships were struck by such a tempest on the night of 5 December, and the *Sawarabi* was rolling heavily in high seas when she was lost to sight in the darkness. She was found the next morning drifting upside down and towed to the Japanese naval base at Makung in the Pescadores. One hundred five of her officers and crew, including the captain, perished in the mishap, and sixteen were saved. There is no evidence, however, that this earlier tragedy was due to a faulty design of the ship.

6. Fukui, *Nihon no gunkan,* 61–65; Yoshida Toshio, 100–103; and Kaigun Henshū Iinkai, 9:132–36.

7. Fukui, *Nihon no gunkan,* 66–69.

8. *KG1,* 439–43, 477–78; Fukui, *Nihon no gunkan,* 55–61, 70–71; and Kaigun Henshū Iinkai, 9:136–42.

9. *KG1,* 613, 616; Preston, *Cruisers,* 101; *SZ,* 1:471; and WG, 153–55.

10. *SZ,* 1:471.

11. Since all magazines were placed forward in the ship, such an arrangement also had the advantage of restricting armored protection to a smaller portion of the hull. WG, 155–57, 269–79; and Lacroix, "The Development of the 'A Class' Cruisers," part 7, pp. 249–55. The British *Nelson*-class battleships also had this turret arrangement.

12. Mark A. Campbell, letter to authors, 8 February 1992.

13. Alan D. Zimm, however, would have us qualify our statement about the ability of Japanese cruisers to sustain damage. He notes that Japanese cruisers had considerably more engine and boiler room subdivisions than contemporary Western designs, including centerline bulkheads—an arrangement advantageous for resisting shell fire but a poor feature considering list and stability. Therefore, in his opinion, these cruisers were vulnerable to underwater damage and sensitive to any flooding. Since over 90 percent of all warships capsize before they sink, he believes that such vulnerability was significant. Zimm, letter to authors, 4 September 1992.

14. Lautenschläger, "Technology," 24–25.

15. *KG1,* 609–10; and Lacroix, "The Development of the 'A Class' Cruisers," part 4, p. 74. Many of these improvements were inspired by the appearance of the British battleship *Nelson* in 1927. The *Nelson* incorporated a number of structural improvements derived from the lessons of Jutland, such as the use of armor as an integral part of the ship, and other improvements, such as the location of fire control systems high up in the foremast, which had been developed since Jutland. In 1924, while the *Nelson* was still being built, Hiraga Yuzuru, who was in Britain gathering information about shipbuilding, brought back many details about her that were useful in the modernization of Japan's own battleships. *KG1,* 609; and Parkes, *British Battleships,* 579, 657.

16. *KG1,* 608; and WG, 63.

17. *SZ,* 1:663; and *Conway's All the World's Fighting Ships, 1922–1946,* 38.

18. *SZ,* 1:663

19. Ibid., 663–64.

20. As the Pacific War began, the standard for power plants of Japanese destroyers (from the *Kagerō* class onward) was steam at 426 pounds per square inch and 662°F. The exceptions were the *Amatsukaze* and *Shimakaze,* which used steam of 568 pounds per square inch and 752°F. These systems were experimental, whereas the U.S. Navy produced large number of destroyers using steam at higher pressures and temperatures. For example, the *Fletcher*-class power plants used 615 pounds per square inch and 850°F, representing perhaps a 15 percent difference in efficiency compared to the Japanese plants.

21. For an interesting comparison of naval aviation development during the interwar period, see Hone and Mandeles, "Interwar Innovation," 63–83.

22. *KG1,* 336–37, 401–6, 450; and Ferris, "A British Unofficial Aviation Mission," 417, 421, 434, 437.

23. This organization, the Kaigun Kōkū Hombu, is sometimes translated as "Naval Air Headquarters," but as it had an administrative rather than a command function, we believe that the term we have used is more appropriate.

24. *KG1*, 174–75, 401–2, 420–21, 435, 451; *KKG*, 6–7; and Sekigawa, 28.

25. *KG1*, 141, 158.

26. This word is from the Japanese *autoreenji*, an example of the navy's creative adaptation of English. In English-language naval writing, "to be outranged" means that the enemy's ship has succeeded in getting beyond your range, not that you can hit the enemy at a distance beyond the enemy's range.

27. The Japanese navy's concept of outranging was not originated by the Japanese. In the first decade of the twentieth century, the Royal Navy developed long-range naval gunnery to achieve effective gun ranges beyond that of the torpedo. See Sumida, "The Quest for Reach."

28. *KG1*, 176–77.

29. Except where otherwise noted, the authors were guided in this general discussion of naval gunnery between the wars by Frederick Milford. Milford, letter to authors, 25 July 1994.

30. Friedman, *U.S. Naval Weapons*, 31–35; and Sumida, "'The Best Laid Plans,'" 684–86.

31. Lacroix, *Japanese Cruisers*, appendix H.

32. Ibid.

33. During the Pacific War, American observers noted the tightness of Japanese salvo patterns (200–300 yards across), a characteristic that could have varying consequences. At the Battle of the Komandorskis, 27 March 1943, for example, significant damage wrought by Japanese fire could have been transformed into critical punishment had the Japanese patterns have been more dispersed, and at the battle off Samar, 25 October 1944, the patterns were too small to achieve many hits. Lorelli, *The Battle of the Komandorski Islands*, 180; and Friedman, *U.S. Naval Weapons*, 25.

34. Friedman, *Battleship Design*, 105–7. As an example of the towering scale of these superstructures on certain Japanese capital ships after their reconstruction, the height of the gun director above the waterline on the *Mutsu* was 34.4 meters (113 feet), on the *Kongō* 38.4 meters (126 feet), and on the *Ise* 39.6 meters (130 feet). Nihon Zōsen Gakkai, *Nihon kaigun kantei zumenshū*. From 130 feet above the waterline, the distance to the horizon was about 24,000 meters or 26,000 yards, that is, about the range of the main battery. Although these battleships appeared preposterously top-heavy, the extremely wide beam of a battleship hull, as compared to the slender hull of a cruiser, actually kept these uniquely Japanese upper works from being a problem.

35. This required the creation of deeper spaces beneath the turrets to accommodate the recoil of the guns when they were fired at their maximum elevation. Unlike Western navies, which achieved this by raising the supporting trunnions, the Japanese navy simply deepened the gun pits within the hull at the sacrifice of valuable space. In at least one case (e.g., the *Ise*-class battleships), however, the two after turrets did not have enough space for their gun pits to be deepened. These guns, therefore, could not be given higher elevation. Friedman, *Battleship Design*, 105.

36. *KH*, 44–45, 749.

37. Ibid., 46, 800.

38. *KG1,* 176–77. Genda, *Shinjuwan,* 42, asserts that supra-smokescreen firing was first developed by the U.S. Navy, which devoted considerable training to it. Alan D. Zimm states that in the Naval War College rules, the war gamers assessed a 40 percent penalty to the accuracy of such fire because of imperfect azimuth control. Zimm, letter to authors, 4 September 1992.

39. *KH,* 353.

40. *KG1,* 171–72.

41. Specialists like Alan D. Zimm express skepticism that such a hit ratio could be achieved at this range. He notes that the Naval War College estimated the hit percentage at 22,000 yards (about 20,000 meters) under "standard battle conditions" (that did not include salvo chasing or maneuvering) at about 2–3 percent. The U.S. Navy therefore considered 22,000 yards to be the maximum effective range for heavy-caliber gunfire. Zimm, letter to authors, 4 September 1992. At any rate, by the start of World War II, the Japanese had confidence that their battleship batteries would be very effective at ranges over 32,000 meters (over 17 miles). *KG1,* 177.

42. Sumida, letter to authors, 27 December 1995.

43. *KH,* 46, 797; and Fukui, *Nihon no gunkan,* 23–25. Tests were also conducted on the old battleship *Aki* in the same year with similar results. Her engineering spaces were flooded after an underwater hit, and she capsized. *KH,* 797.

44. *KH,* 329–30.

45. Fukui, *Nihon no gunkan,* 23–24; and *KH,* 329–30, 352.

46. Chihaya Masataka, letter to authors, 29 September 1993.

47. Friedman, *U.S. Battleships,* 303.

48. U.S. Naval Technical Mission to Japan, "Japanese Projectiles. General Types," 1.

49. Friedman, *U.S. Battleships,* 13, 243.

50. Garzke and Dulin, *Battleships,* 464. We are indebted to Mark A. Campbell for drawing our attention to these points.

51. To date, the two most informative studies of the Japanese navy's oxygen torpedo are Itani, Lengerer, and Rehm-Takahara, "Japanese Oxygen Torpedoes"; and Bullen, "The Japanese 'Long Lance' Torpedo."

52. The British battleships *Rodney* and *Nelson* were equipped with 24.5-inch torpedoes using oxygen-enriched air in the interwar period. Very few of them were ever fired, however, and the torpedo tubes were removed from *Nelson* and blanked off in *Rodney* during World War II. The U.S. Navy experimented with enriched air torpedoes from 1929 to at least 1931. Milford, letter to authors, 30 October 1992.

53. Ibid.

54. *KS,* 108–15.

55. Yokota and Harrington, "Kaiten," 55–58.

56. The origins of the name "Long Lance" for this torpedo have long been a puzzle. It sounds as if it had been derived from the Japanese, but in fact it was not, since no Japanese document or publication refers to it as anything other than the type 93. John De Virgilio, a specialist on the ordnance used by the Japanese navy in its attack on American ships at Pearl Harbor, asserts that the late Roger Pineau told him that the name was created by Samuel Eliot Morison. According to Pineau, who worked closely with Morison on the multivolume *History of United States Naval Operations in World War II,* Morison believed that this formidable piece of ordnance deserved a

special name and thus called it the "Long Lance." John De Virgilio, conversation with Peattie, 31 January 1995.

57. Lacroix, "The Development of the 'A Class' Cruisers," part 5, p. 364; and *KS*, 29–30, 93, 108–14.

58. Lacroix, "The Development of the 'A Class' Cruisers," part 5, p. 364. The improved type 93 had a slightly shorter range and a larger warhead.

59. Ibid. The type 94 was eventually discarded as an aerial weapon because of the expensive and elaborate precautions required in arming aircraft with the torpedo. Marder, *Old Friends, New Enemies,* 1:311. The type 95 torpedo was a smaller (21-inch) version of the type 93 oxygen torpedo developed specifically for submarine use and was tested extensively during the 1939–40 exercises. Although it may have malfunctioned on occasion, the navy had enough confidence in the weapon to take it to sea at the opening of the Pacific War. In actual combat, however, the record of its performance belies the awesome reputation that it earned in the West, since it frequently exploded prematurely or deviated from course. In one notable patrol in the Indian Ocean in April 1942, all five of the participating Japanese submarines suffered malfunctions in their type 95 torpedoes. The problems, eventually corrected, involved the extreme sensitivity of the pistol exploder and the configuration of the torpedo head. *KS,* 30; and Kokubō Senshi Kenkyūkai, "Sensuikan-yō sanso gyorai," 116–31. A modification of the type 95, the type 96, was developed. It used enriched air (38 percent oxygen), but was evidently produced in smaller quantities than the type 95.

60. Hara, *Japanese Destroyer Captain,* 38.

61. Some torpedo men balked at this tactic, which depended on stealth and distance for the results. To Rear Adm. Kumaoka Minoru, submariner and torpedo tactician, the new technique contradicted the traditional *nikuhaku-hitchū* spirit of Japanese torpedo men in general and submariners in particular. Japan, Bōeichō Bōeikenshūjo Senshishitsu, *Sensuikanshi,* 66.

62. Hughes, *Fleet Tactics,* 120, notes that in the Solomons, Japanese torpedo barrages sometimes achieved a hitting rate of 20 percent.

63. *KS,* 490; and *KG1,* 191–94, 620. One monograph asserts that the conversion of these ships was purposely delayed to keep their reconstruction as torpedo cruisers secret as long as possible. Lengerer, Kobler-Edamatsu, and Rehm-Takahara, 38.

64. *KS,* 504–7, 526–28.

65. McKearney, "The Naval Solomons Campaign," 53, 87, 92–93, 128.

66. *SZ,* 1:615–17; Fukaya, "Three Japanese Submarine Developments," 863; and Orita and Harrington, *I-Boat Captain,* 21–22.

67. *SZ,* 1:561–62, 821.

68. Alan D. Zimm believes that the limited range and speed of midget submarines, among other things, would have made them useless in the kind of fleet action that the Japanese envisaged. Zimm, letter to authors, 4 September 1992.

69. *NNK,* 2:149; and *WG,* 362–63.

70. In these same years, war-gaming at Newport had convinced American tacticians that close-in night actions were too hazardous and that superior American gunfire during daylight hours promised the best chance for victory in a surface engagement. This was the principal reason for the American failures in night combat during the first year of the Pacific War. McKearney, 133–38.

71. *KG1,* 196; and Ōmae, "Nihon kaigun no heijutsu shisō," part 1, pp. 49–50.

72. The first optical research by the navy began just prior to the war, and by 1913, the Tsukiji Arsenal had produced some optical equipment. After the *Kongō* arrived with Barr and Stroud range finders mounted on her turrets, Japanese naval research on range finders had made real progress, but after the destruction of the arsenal in the 1923 earthquake and fire, the navy had come to rely on domestic private firms for all its optical needs. Indeed, the Japanese optical industry, and particularly Nihon Kōgaku (the predecessor of Nikon Corporation), got its start through navy contracts. Aoki, "Kōgaku heiki," 437–39.

73. Ibid., 440–41. We believe, however, that one can take such lauditory assessments too far. While not doubting for a moment the fine quality of the Japanese navy's optical equipment, we believe that their vaunted "superiority" during the early night engagements of the Pacific War was exaggerated by both the Japanese and their American enemy at the time and in the decades since. It is our impression that optical equipment equal to Japan's had been developed by other major navies and that Japanese equipment *seemed* superior because the Japanese navy had put so much time and effort in the prewar years into *training* with it at night.

74. *KS*, 520; Lacroix, "The Development of the 'A Class' Cruisers," part 5, p. 363, n. 74; and Marder, *Old Friends, New Enemies,* 1:303.

75. Under the terms of the London Treaty of 1930, the fourth ship of the class, the *Hiei,* had been demilitarized (by removing her armor belt, one of her after turrets, some secondary ordnance, and twenty-five of her boilers) and used as a training ship. She was remilitarized to *Kongō* standards, 1936–40, after Japan's abrogation of the naval limitation treaties. *SZ,* 1:461–62; *WG,* 42–46; and Chihaya and Abe, "IJN *Kongō,*" 272.

76. *KG1,* 204

77. Ibid., 196–98, 201–2.

78. Lacroix, "The Development of the 'A Class' Cruisers," part 5, p. 365, n. 80.

79. The scenario described in the two following paragraphs is taken from *KS,* 507–10, unless otherwise noted.

80. *Kaisen yōmurei* (Battle Instructions) of ca. 1934, part II, "Battle," articles 34–41, in Sanematsu, *Kaigun daigaku kyōiku,* 225–26.

81. Notably, however, while these radical priorities may have been held in theory, the obsession of fleet commanders with "big ships, big guns" apparently made the commanders much more cautious in practice. After World War II, former navy captain Arita Yūzō recalled his skepticism at the time about the use of fast battleships in combat. He also remembered the tendency of commanders in fleet exercises to handle these big ships too protectively and maneuver them too cautiously. *KG1,* 204.

82. *KS,* 510.

83. *Kaisen yōmurei* [Battle Instructions] of ca. 1934, part II, "Battle," article 6, in Sanematsu, *Kaigun daigaku kyōiku,* 219.

84. To underscore the assumption of air superiority as a prerequisite to Japanese victory, the daylight battle was sometimes called *Seikūkenka no kantai kessen* (The decisive fleet battle under conditions of air superiority). *KG1,* 169, 186.

85. Our description of the daylight decisive battle is based on *KS,* 492, 502–7; and *KG1,* 186–87. See also Ōmae, "Nihon kaigun no heijutsu shisō," part 1, p. 47; and the *Kaisen yōmurei* [Battle Instructions] of ca. 1934 in Sanematsu, *Kaigun daigaku kyōiku,* 210–41.

86. *KG1,* 169.

87. Ibid., 172–74.

88. Dr. James J. Tritten of the Naval Doctrine Command remarks on the similarity of Japanese tactics to some aspects of the complex *manoeuvre* warfare advocated by the French theorist, Adm. Raoul Castex. Tritten, letter to authors, 22 December 1994. We have found no direct evidence of Japanese use of Castex's prescriptions, but the Suikōsha and Navy Ministry put out a complete Japanese translation of Castex's *Théories Stratégiques* in five volumes between 1933 and 1937.

89. U.S. Navy, Chief of Naval Operations, *General Tactical Instructions. United States Navy. Fleet Tactical Publication Number 142,* 160–63, and diagram no. 29.

90. Agawa, 196–97.

91. Indeed, from the start, the navy's midget submarines experienced serious mechanical difficulties that cast doubt on their practical employment in a fleet battle. *KS,* 797–98. Moreover, many special ships (torpedo cruisers and midget submarine tenders in particular) were still under construction as war approached, and preparations for the conflict made it impossible to test all the various fleet units in a coordinated decisive battle exercise. *KG1,* 187.

92. *KG1,* 155–58.

93. *DHKRK,* 256–57; and *KG1,* 154.

94. *KG1,* 151–52.

95. Ibid., 166–67.

96. *DHKRK,* 263.

97. Japan, Bōeichō Bōeikenshūjo Senshishitsu, *Hawai sakusen,* 38.

98. *KG1,* 165.

99. Ibid., 177; and Garzke and Dulin, 43–44.

100. Pelz, 33–34; and Asada, "The Japanese Navy," 242–43.

101. Pelz, 34, 150; Chihaya, "IJN Yamato," 130; and *SZ,* 1:526. Alan D. Zimm asserts, however, that the U.S. Navy had performed preliminary design studies in 1914 on warships with 16-inch armor plate, mounting 15- to 18-inch guns in five triple mounts, speeds approaching 30 knots, *and* capable of passing through the Panama Canal. Zimm, letter to authors, 4 September 1992. This sounds as improbable to us as Ishikawa's scheme for 40-knot cruisers noted above.

102. An indication of the secrecy with which the decision was made was that the initial request from the General Staff to the Technical Department was made orally by the chief of the staff's Second Bureau. Eventually, when word of the project leaked out, criticism arose from a few quarters concerning the wisdom of building battleships of such size. But as the authorities responsible for their design and construction never formally announced the project, personal opinions and verbal arguments against it went nowhere. Had a formal protest been drafted, it would have simply been shelved. *KG1,* 489; and *NKKS,* 1:122–23.

103. *SZ,* 1:520.

104. As chief of the Basic Design Section of the department, Fujimoto Kikuo had initially been responsible for the project and had drawn up a preliminary plan for the new class. (One study on the design and construction of these superbattleships asserts that his design proposed a warship of 50,000 tons, armed with twelve 20-inch guns, and capable of 30 knots. Lengerer, "The Japanese Super-battleship Strategy," 91–93.) But

after the *Tomozuru*'s capsizing, as we have related, he was dismissed from his position in the summer of 1934 and was succeeded by Capt. Fukuda Keiji, an experienced naval constructor and protégé of Hiraga Yuzuru. Fukuda was, in fact, greatly guided in his work by Hiraga, who was brought in to serve as principal advisor to the project and who substantially altered Fujimoto's plans.

105. As noted, the *Hiei* had been demilitarized under the terms of the London Treaty. Upon Japan's termination of its participation in the treaty system, in 1936, the navy undertook to remilitarize the *Hiei,* deciding, in the process, to use the battleship as a test bed for various advances in warship design and technology. Among these were the installation of a new type of bridge and the centralization of all control positions in the ship's pagoda mast, features that were incorporated into the design of the superbattleship *Yamato.* WG, 56.

106. Except where otherwise noted, the following summary of Japanese attitudes toward the treaty system in the early 1930s and the Japanese position at the London Naval Conference of 1935 is based on Pelz, 41–43, 158–64; and Roskill, 2:284–300, 313–16.

107. See Peattie, "Forecasting a Pacific War," 115–31.

108. Nomura Minoru, *Tennō.*

109. Agawa, 35, asserts that because of personal skepticism concerning the Japanese position, Yamamoto would have liked to reach some compromise with the Anglo-American naval powers, but at the same time he had pledged to follow to the letter the instructions of his government to obtain parity for Japan or to withdraw from the conference.

9   TO STRIKE FROM THE SKY
Japanese Naval Aviation, 1920–1941

1. For the shifting functions of carrier aviation in the interwar period the best overviews are provided by Friedman, *Carrier Air Power;* and Chesneau, *Aircraft Carriers of the World,* 32–37.

2. The best English-language study of the Sempill Mission is Ferris, 416–39.

3. An excellent summary of the development of the Japanese aircraft industry before and during World War II is provided by Samuels, *"Rich Nation, Strong Army,"* 108–29.

4. Sonokawa et al., *Nihon kaigun kōkūtai* (cited hereafter as *NKK),* 2:168.

5. Mikesh and Abe, 61, n. 37.

6. Mikesh and Abe, 124–25, 135–36, 198–99.

7. *KG1,* 54.

8. Ikari Yoshirō, *Kaigun kūgishō,* 1:17–24. In 1939, the name of the air arsenal was changed to Kaigun Kōkū Gijutsushō (Naval Air Technical Arsenal) and in early 1945 to Dai-ichi Gijutsushō (First Technical Arsenal); the common appellation for the arsenal during the Pacific War was the abbreviation Kūgishō. See also Mikesh, "The Rise of Japanese Naval Air Power," 110–11; and Genda, *Kaigun kōkūtai,* 1:103–4.

9. Samuels, *"Rich Nation, Strong Army,"* 116–18.

10. Ibid., 121–26.

11. On the other hand, while acknowledging that the Naval Aviation Department was the focus of much critical thinking about naval air doctrine and technology during these years, Hone and Mandeles, 77–80, maintain that the ongoing failure of the army and navy to cooperate, as well as the inadequate organizational integration of the navy itself, created serious problems in the development of aircraft. The lack of cooperation between the two services in aircraft design also led to a prodigious waste of time and technological resources and, by the end of the Pacific War, resulted in the development of far too many types of aircraft, a situation which limited the overall number of planes that could be produced. Samuels, *"Rich Nation, Strong Army,"* 127–28.

12. Francillon, *Japanese Aircraft of the Pacific War,* 342–43.

13. *NKKS,* 3:412–16; and Francillon, *Japanese Aircraft of the Pacific War,* 342–47.

14. Horikoshi, *Eagles of Mitsubishi,* 3–8, 26–57.

15. *KKG,* 195; *NKKS,* 3:424; Horikoshi, 93–141; Francillon, *Japanese Aircraft of the Pacific War,* 362–77; Thompson, "The Zero," 32; and Spick, *Fighter Pilot Tactics,* 86.

16. *NKKS,* 3:465–66; Francillon, *Japanese Aircraft of the Pacific War,* 411–16; and Francillon, *Imperial Japanese Navy Bombers,* 11–13.

17. Our use of the term "dive bomber" does not exactly conform to the Japanese terminology of the time. This type was officially a *kanjō bakugeki-ki* (carrier bomber aircraft). Mikesh and Abe, 280, assert that this vague designation was applied because the Japanese navy wished to keep secret its progress in the revolutionary tactic of dive bombing.

18. *NKKS,* 3:476–77; and Mikesh and Abe, 171–72. This aircraft was popularly known as *chūkō,* from the unofficial designation for the type, *chūgata kōgeki-ki,* which meant "medium attack plane."

19. Iwaya, *Chūkō,* 1:38–47; Francillon, *Imperial Japanese Navy Bombers,* 41–45; Francillon, *Japanese Aircraft of the Pacific War,* 350–57; and Bueschel, *Mitsubishi A6M1/2,* 2–13.

20. *NKKS,* 3:479–81; Francillon, *Japanese Aircraft of the Pacific War,* 378–87; and Francillon, *Imperial Japanese Navy Bombers,* 49–53.

21. *NKKS,* 3:498, 503–4; and Francillon, *Japanese Aircraft of the Pacific War,* 277–79, 297–300, 358–61, 408–10.

22. *NKKS,* 3:517–18; and Francillon, *Japanese Aircraft of the Pacific War,* 301–7.

23. *NKKS,* 3:519–20; and Francillon, *Japanese Aircraft of the Pacific War,* 307–13.

24. These matters, as they affected all carrier design in the interwar period, are analyzed by Friedman in *Carrier Air Power,* 9–23; and Brown in *Aircraft Carriers,* 2–7.

25. *SZ,* 1:472–73; and Nagamura Kiyoshi, *Zōkan kaisō,* 136.

26. *SZ,* 1:473–79; Chesneau, 159–62; and Lengerer, "Akagi and Kaga," part 1, pp. 127–39.

27. Lengerer, "Akagi and Kaga," part 1, pp. 134, 136–37.

28. *SZ,* 1:479–80; Chesneau, 163; and *WG,* 177–78.

29. *SZ,* 1:480; and Chesneau, 165–66.

30. *SZ,* 1:480–81; and Chesneau, 166.

31. *SZ,* 1:536; Chesneau, 171–72; Fukaya, "The Shokakus," 639; and Dickson, "Fighting Flat-Tops," 16–18.

32. *SZ,* 1:536.

33. *SZ,* 1:537–39, 544–48; and Chesneau, 179–80, 185.

34. *SZ,* 1:490–91, 548–49, 794; Chesneau, 175–76, 179–80; WG, 187–92; Brown, 24–25; and Lengerer and Rehm-Takahara, part 2, pp. 107, 111.

35. Friedman, *Carrier Air Power,* 13–15.

36. Lengerer, "Akagi and Kaga," part 1, p. 130; and Friedman, *Carrier Air Power,* 13–15.

37. Friedman, *Carrier Air Power,* 20.

38. Ibid., 13–15.

39. *NKK,* 67; *KKG,* 65–66; Lundstrom, *The First Team: Pacific Naval Air Combat,* 455; and Hata and Izawa, *Japanese Naval Aces,* 417.

40. Although divisions between pilot officers and pilot NCOs existed in the U.S. Navy as well, the ratio was nearly the complete reverse of the Japanese situation. In the Japanese navy, moreover, the majority of pilots and observers were not commissioned and therefore had few of the privileges of food and accommodations awarded to the small number who were commissioned. This may have been the cause of the substantial sub-rosa bitterness and contempt toward officer aviators. Cook and Cook, *Japan at War,* 139.

41. Hata and Izawa, 417; Lundstrom, *The First Team: Naval Air Combat,* 456; *KKG,* 152; and U.S. Strategic Bombing Survey, Military Analysis Division, *Japanese Air Power,* 34.

42. Sakai, *Samurai!* 10, 13–15.

43. Ibid., 17.

44. While accurate figures for air crews for both sides at the opening of the Pacific War are elusive, we estimate that there were not more than 3,500 operational pilots in the Japanese navy by that time and 8,000 active duty pilots in the U.S. Navy and Marine Corps. In making these assessments we have drawn upon the following sources: *KG2,* 202; *KKG,* 106; and *United States Naval Aviation, 1910–1980,* 461.

45. Marder, *Old Friends, New Enemies,* 315–16.

46. *NKKS,* 1:721–28.

47. *NKK,* 222; and *NKKS,* 1:716–17.

48. *NKK,* 220; and *NKKS,* 1:749–51.

49. With a range of approximately 2,000 meters (2,187 yards), a speed of 42 knots, and an explosive charge of 150 kilograms (330 pounds), the type 91 was superior to the American torpedo employed at the start of the Pacific War, the Mark XIII. *KS,* 23; and U.S. Strategic Bombing Survey, Military Analysis Division, *Japanese Air Weapons,* 55–56.

50. *NKKS,* 1:757–61; and *KS,* 607–8.

51. *KG1,* 175; *NKKS,* 1:116–17, 756; *NKK,* 221; *KKG,* 193; and Genda, *Kaigun kōkūtai shimatsuki,* 1:153.

52. *NKK,* 68; *KG1,* 175

53. *NKK,* 68; *KKG,* 192; *NKKS,* 1:683–85, 690; *KG1,* 175; and Genda, *Kaigun kōkūtai shimatsuki,* 1:151–152.

54. *KKG,* 185–189.

55. *NKKS,* 1:79, 654–655, 660; and Ikari, *Kaigun kūgishō,* 1:103.

56. Genda, *Kaigun kōkūtai shimatsuki,* 1:112–19.

57. *NKKS*, 1:287–88, 294; and *KKGS*, 59.

58. *NKKS*, 1:288–90, 294: and Caidin, *Zero Fighter*, 28–30.

59. Lundstrom, *The First Team: Pacific Naval Air Combat*, 486–89; and *KKGS*, 195.

60. These early victories of the Zero may have contributed to a dangerous overemphasis on the value of fighter aircraft in a primarily offensive role. For example, the insistence of the navy's air officers on using the bulk of the Midway task force fighter aircraft as escorts for bombers against Midway Island, rather than for the maintenance of an adequate combat air patrol over the Japanese carriers, probably contributed to the ultimate Japanese disaster in that campaign. Prange, *Miracle at Midway*, 373.

61. Ōmae, "Nihon kaigun no heijutsu shisō," part 1, p. 47; *NKKS*, 1:114, 203–4; and Genda, "Evolution," 23.

62. This ambiguity was reflected in the failure to revise the Battle Instructions in light of advances in aviation. The navy attempted to deal with the increasingly controversial problem by issuing new guidelines—*Kōkūsen yōmu sōan* (Draft instructions for air combat)—which paid lip service to aviation. But the guidelines were so narrow and vacillating that they only served to erode still further the absolute character of the Battle Instructions. Ōmae, "Nihon kaigun no heijutsu shisō," part 1, p. 51; *KKGS*, 48–49; and *KG1*, 135–36.

63. Genda, *Shinjuwan sakusen*, 42–43; *KG1*, 176–78; and *KS*, 502.

64. *NKKS*, 1:205–6; and Genda, *Shinjuwan sakusen*, 43–46. A staff college study in November of that year proposed to deploy carriers to encircle the enemy. The formation would provide the advantages of dispersal while still enabling individual carriers to concentrate their attacks, which were to be delivered preemptively and from beyond the range of enemy aircraft. *KG1*, 169.

65. Because of the special requirements of the Pearl Harbor operation, a higher proportion of fighter aircraft was embarked on that occasion, but after Pearl Harbor the navy reverted to attack-structured carrier air groups.

66. Beginning in 1931, the navy issued a series of regulations and instructions that spelled out the organization, function, and training of its land-based forces, within which the most important administrative unit was the *kōkūtai* (air group). Each air group, which could number from approximately twenty-four to a hundred or more aircraft, came under the command of the naval district in which its home base was located and was designated either by a number or by the name of that base. Until the very end of the decade most air groups were composed of a mix of aircraft types, with seaplanes predominating initially, but with carrier-type fighters, dive bombers, and torpedo bombers increasing in numbers, along with land-based twin-engined medium bombers. *KKGS*, 151.

67. *NKKS*, 2:30–37; and Ōmae, "Nihon kaigun no heijutsu shisō," part 2, p. 37.

68. Although this was then a strain on Japan's aircraft production facilities, the greatest problem was augmenting air and ground crews. This task was difficult because of the competing demands of the army and the navy's own requirement that fleet carriers and floatplane-carrying battleships and cruisers maintain their full complements of aviation personnel. Ohmae and Pineau, "Japanese Naval Aviation," 75.

69. *NKKS*, 2:51; the air group total is derived from *KG1*, 435.

70. The memorandum itself, *Kōkō kaizō ni kansuru shiken* (A personal opinion concerning aircraft construction), is reproduced in full in *NKKS*, 1:106–7.

71. *NKKS,* 1:101.

72. *NKKS,* 1:113; Agawa, 104–5; Mikesh and Abe, 175; and Bueschel, *Mitsubishi-Nakajima G3M1/2/3,* 4–5.

73. The noted British naval historian Stephen Roskill, for example, has written of the Japanese navy's "freedom from the controversies which so long plagued naval aviation in Britain." Roskill, 1:531.

74. Genda, "Tactical Planning," 46–47.

75. Ko Ōnishi Takijirō Kaigun Chūjō Den Kankōkai, *Ōnishi Takijirō,* 38–40, 50; and *NKKS,* 1:116.

76. *NKKS,* 1:119–120; and Genda, *Kaigun kōkūtai shimatsuki,* 1:137–47.

77. *KKGS,* 48; *NKKS,* 1:123–24; and Agawa, 93.

78. *NKKS,* 1:124–25.

79. Kaigun Henshū Iinkai, 13:70; and *KKGS,* 88.

80. *KKGS,* 194.

81. Kaigun Henshū Iinkai, 13:70; *KKGS,* 89; and Genda, *Shinjuwan sakusen,* 46–47.

82. Kaigun Henshū Iinkai, 13:71; and *KKGS,* 89.

83. Iwaya, 1:41.

84. Of the 150 fighter aces in the Japanese navy listed in Hata and Izawa, one-third achieved their first victories in air combat over China, 1937–41.

85. It can be argued, of course, that the Condor Legion used fighters to protect its bombers over Spain and the Luftwaffe used fighters to protect its bombers over England in 1940, but the distances hardly qualify as long-range, even for that time.

86. Ōmae, "Nihon kaigun no heijutsu shisō," part 1, pp. 51–52; and *KKGS,* 189, 192. While the navy's air groups proved in the China War that they could cooperate effectively with the army in land operations, army air groups were almost completely ineffective in operations at sea, for which they had very little training. When the Pacific War began, this weakness was glaringly revealed and stands in sharp contrast to the reasonably effective long-range, over-water operations of the U.S. Army Air Force in the Pacific. Iwaya, 1:113–14.

87. *KKG,* 88, 142–43; and *NKK,* 221.

88. Prange, *At Dawn We Slept,* 259–60.

89. Prange, *At Dawn We Slept,* 513; and *KKG,* 91.

90. *NKKS,* 1:693–694; Prange, *At Dawn We Slept,* 271; *KKG,* 192; and Commander in Chief, Pacific and Pacific Ocean Areas, Joint Intelligence Center, Pacific Ocean Area, "Know Your Enemy: Japanese Aerial Tactics against Ship Targets," 21.

91. Some, particularly in the Yokosuka Naval Air Group, complained that distant launching violated the *nikuhaku* tradition of the Japanese navy. *KKG,* 194; and *NKKS,* 1:764.

92. *KS,* 621–26; *NKKS,* 1:765–66; Prange, *At Dawn We Slept,* 104–6, 270–71, 320–22; De Virgilio, "Japanese Thunderfish," 61–68; and Genda Minoru's analysis of the Pearl Harbor operation in Goldstein and Dillon, *The Pearl Harbor Papers,* 17–44.

93. *NKKS,* 1:707; *KKG,* 193, 203; and Genda, *Shinjuwan sakusen,* 47–48.

94. *KKG,* 205.

95. Unless otherwise noted, our understanding and analysis of fleet air defense as it existed in December 1941 is drawn directly from *KKG,* 205–6.

96. Even after the advent of radar, its effective coordination with fleet air defense took

time. Moreover, the damage wrought by Japanese kamikaze aircraft late in the Pacific War demonstrated that it was impossible to defeat a determined air attack completely. John Lundstrom, letter to authors, 16 August 1994.

97. Genda, "Evolution," 24.

98. Genda Minoru was long considered the creator of this concept, and Genda himself claimed that he hit upon the idea while in London as assistant naval attaché. As Genda later told it, he solved the problem after sitting in a London movie theater watching a newsreel that showed a concentration of American carriers steaming together in a box formation. But while Genda's claim to the authorship of this important tactical innovation may indeed be valid, it rests entirely on his own account. Genda, "Evolution," 24. We are inclined to believe that like most developments in the navy's operational doctrine, it was probably the result of discussions over time, by a number of leading tacticians of the day, Genda included.

99. Prange, *At Dawn We Slept*, 101–2; and Ozawa Teitoku Den Kankōkai, *Kaisō*, 20–21.

100. Later, that September, with the commissioning of the *Shōkaku* and *Zuikaku*, a fifth carrier division was added, and the Third, comprising the small carriers *Hōshō* and *Ryūjō*, was detached from the First Air Fleet to provide cover for the main battleship force of the Combined Fleet. *KKGS*, 149–50.

101. *KKGS*, 207; and Prange, *At Dawn We Slept*, 101–2, 106.

102. Genda, "Tactical Planning," 48; and Friedman, *Carrier Air Power*, 56.

103. Ōmae, "Nihon kaigun heijutsu shisō," part 2, p. 40.

104. This estimate is based on *United States Naval Aviation, 1910–1980*, 382.

105. *KKG*, 212–13.

106. See Mark A. Campbell, "The Influence of Air Power," 119–45; and Eugene E. Wilson, "The Navy's First Carrier Task Force," 159–69. Eventually, during the Pacific War, the U.S. Navy carried this concept even further with the creation of the carrier "task force." Accompanied as it was by the fleet train, the task force was capable of staying at sea for extended periods and therefore could carry out continuous offensive operations against enemy targets.

10 THE BATTLE OF THE SHIPYARDS
Japanese Naval Construction, 1937–1941

1. Whereas the Japanese navy, since 1922, had built 196 ships totaling 410,000 tons, the United States during the same period had added not quite 198,000 tons distributed over 40 ships. While the United States had sufficient strength in battleships (15 to the Japanese 9, not counting the demilitarized *Hiei*) and in carriers, it was somewhat behind in cruisers and was badly deficient in destroyers and submarines vis-à-vis Japan. Pelz, 77.

2. Potter, 485.

3. Hone, "Spending Patterns," 457.

4. Potter, 485.

5. Love, *History*, 594–95, 606–7.

6. Ibid., 622–23.

7. *KG1*, 595.

8. Ibid., 477.

9. Ibid., 477, 511–12, 530, 596.

10. *SZ*, 1:517; and *KG1*, 776–93.

11. *SZ*, 1:515; and *KG1*, 535, 581.

12. Toyama, "The Outline," 55–67.

13. *KG1*, 581; and Jerome Cohen, *Japan's Economy*, 193, 210. Naturally, part of the reason for the United States' having far more aircraft was hemispheric defense, or the nation's need to defend both its coasts.

14. Ōmae, "Nihon kaigun heijutsu shisō," part 2, p. 39; *KKG*, 86–87; and *KG1*, 601.

15. *KG1*, 596, 601.

16. Ibid., 594–95.

17. Ibid., 597–98.

18. There were, moreover, two supplements to the modified Circle Five: one in October 1942, which addressed the urgent need for transport submarines, and one in the fall of 1943, which called for the construction of more destroyers and convoy escort vessels. *SZ*, 1:518–19.

19. *SZ*, 1:516–18.

20. *KG1*, 846. The great increase in warship construction in the years immediately prior to the Pacific War can be viewed from various perspectives. In 1931 the Japanese navy built 22,500 gross tons of warships; in 1941, it added 225,159 tons. Annual construction levels of 50,000–60,000 tons in 1937–38 were doubled in 1939, and, with the building of the *Yamato* and *Musashi* well under way, by 1940 Japanese shipyards were turning out 100,000 tons of naval construction per year. Ibid., 597; and Jerome Cohen, 194.

21. Yoshida Akihiko says that there were three categories of reserve status for warships. The *daiichi yobikan* (the most active reserve ships) were only downgraded in personnel, operating with half-crews, but were being held in full operational condition. These ships were usually used as training ships for navy service schools for most of the year, but were often made part of the *Akagun kantai* (Red Fleet), the "enemy" force during the annual fleet maneuvers. The *daini yobikan* (second-level reserve ships) were those undergoing conversion or major overhaul and, with only a skeleton crew aboard, were not operational. The *daisan yobikan* (the lowest—third—level of reserve ships) were "mothballed" ships, in today's terminology. That is, the ships were not operational, had no crew aboard, and were entirely maintained by shore personnel. Yoshida, letter to authors, 17 December 1993.

22. The "preparatory fleet mobilization" plans were activated in two overlapping phases. The first started in late 1940; the second, in the summer of 1941. Mobilization centered particularly on the requisition of civilian merchant shipping, some 1,740,000 tons in the first phase and 600,000 tons in the second. The plans also included important changes in fleet organization, including the creation of a new Sixth (submarine) Fleet, a new Eleventh Air Fleet, the reorganization of the First and Third Fleets, the establishment of a Fifth Fleet and a new Southern Expeditionary Fleet. But the major effect of the plans was to authorize a sharp increase in the proportion of strategic materials allocated to the navy. *KG1*, 757–61; *DHKRK*, 509–12, 546–49; and Kaigun Henshū Iinkai, 4:188–94.

23. Jerome Cohen, 251.

24. *SZ,* 1:738.
25. Ibid.
26. Willmott, *The Barrier and the Javelin,* 522.
27. See, for example, McNeill, *The Pursuit of Power;* and Kennedy, *The Rise and Fall of the Great Powers.*
28. The source for the American figures is Tiffany, *The Decline of American Steel,* 27. For the Japanese figures, see U.S. Strategic Bombing Survey, Military Analysis Division, *The Effects of Strategic Bombing,* 112. The disproportion in steel production was increased by Japan's importing of nearly all its iron ore, scrap iron, and coking coal, and worsened by the fact that the last two materials were mainly supplied by the United States.
29. Unless otherwise noted, the data and analysis in the next six paragraphs are drawn largely from an unpublished monograph by Frederick J. Milford, "U.S. and Japanese Destroyer Construction between the Wars," July 1993.
30. The manual was NAVSHIPS 341–5066. It was used for the *Fletcher, Sumner,* and *Gearing* classes, all of which had nearly identical engineering plants of 60,000 horse-power. Frederick J. Milford, letter of 1 November 1993.
31. The Japanese were acutely conscious of the need to speed up construction. When possible, Japan made strenuous efforts to increase production and achieved some success in the construction of smaller vessels. For example, the first of eighteen small transports (1,500 tons standard) built at Kure in 1943 took 135 days to complete, and the last only 75 days. Fukui Shizuo, *Nihon no gunkan,* 198–201.
32. Jerome Cohen, 253.
33. Ibid., 257.
34. Ibid.; and U.S. Strategic Bombing Survey, Military Supplies Division, *Japanese Naval Shipbuilding,* 2.
35. More has been written in English (and probably in Japanese) about the *Yamato*-class battleships than any other ships in the Japanese navy. Lengerer, "The Japanese Super-battleship Strategy" and Chihaya, "IJN Yamato," have already been cited. Matsumoto and Chihaya, "Design and Construction," is authoritative, since as young naval officers Matsumoto and Chihaya were involved in the construction of these ships. Garzke and Dulin, 43–116, provide expert analysis of the structure and engineering of these two ships. Skulski, *The Battleship Yamato,* has detailed drawings of *Yamato,* but minimal text, a good deal of it derived from the Matsumoto and Chihaya article. Yoshimura's *Build the Musashi!* was originally published in Japanese and makes interesting reading, but is somewhat journalistic and marred by occasionally careless translation. A series of articles by Tim Thornton has explored the structural weaknesses in the ships of the class, which led to their destruction: "Air Power"; "The Sinking"; and *"Yamato:* The Achilles Heel." Spurr, *A Glorious Way to Die,* has interesting detail from the American as well as the Japanese side of *Yamato*'s destruction. In a category by itself is the moving and reflective memoir of *Yamato*'s last days by Yoshida Mitsuru, who as a young ensign and assistant radar officer on the ship, survived her catastrophic end. Written soon after the war and eventually hailed as a literary masterpiece, Yoshida's account has been given a superb English translation and introduction by Richard Minear under the title *Requiem for Battleship Yamato.*
36. Garzke and Dulin, 44.

37. *SZ,* 1:526.

38. Matsumoto and Chihaya, 1110–11. The *Yamato*'s keel was laid November 1937, the *Musashi*'s in March 1938. The *Yamato* was launched August 1940, the *Musashi* in November of the same year. The *Yamato* had her service trials in October 1941 and joined the Combined Fleet just after the outbreak of the Pacific War two months later. The *Musashi* had her service trials in June 1942 and joined the fleet that August.

39. Ibid.; Yoshimura, 13–44, 113–16; and Niwata Shōzō, "Senkan Yamato," 134–36. The navy's public position was that the *Yamato* and *Musashi* did not exist. Chihaya Masataka has recalled that when he was secretly posted to the *Musashi* still in dry-dock in 1941, there was simply a blank space next to his name on the yearly list of officer assignments. Chihaya, *Nihon kaigun no ogori shōkōgun,* 45.

40. For some interesting observations on Western ignorance in this regard, see Wark, "In Search," 189–211; and Muir, "Rearming," 473–85.

41. According to Hans Lengerer, the original design of these battleships had called for the 18-inch ordnance to be replaced in five years by 20-inch guns. The thinking behind this arrangement seems to have been based on the confidence that the U.S. Navy had no knowledge of the superbattleships or of the size of their main batteries and that the largest caliber for guns aboard American battleships was 16 inches. Given these facts, the Japanese navy therefore assumed that it could maintain battle line dominance for five years, after which the Americans would probably acquire guns of the same caliber. Lengerer, "The Japanese Super-battleship Strategy," 31, 34–35.

42. Garzke and Dulin, 88, 90.

43. Ibid., 92.

44. Matsumoto and Chihaya, 1105–6.

45. The *Yamato*-class battleships employed three principal types of armor, developed to surpass all previous grades: Vickers hardened (VH) armor, a face-hardened steel used on the main battery turrets and main side belts; molybdenum noncemented (MNC) armor, used in deck plating; and copper-included noncemented (CNC) armor, used in thin deck plates to protect against flying steel splinters. Garzke and Dulin, 96.

46. Matsumoto and Chihaya, 1106–9; Tim Thornton, "*Yamato:* The Achilles Heel," 5; and Garzke and Dulin, 44.

47. Matsumoto and Chihaya, 1109–10. At the time of her destruction, the *Musashi* sank when both sides of her armored box were flooded, along with the watertight compartments of the magazine rooms.

48. In theory, the adoption of diesel machinery would have been more economical in terms of fuel consumption (a critical factor in the restricted use of both the *Yamato* and *Musashi* during the Pacific War). Among the major navies, however, only Germany had developed a truly dependable large diesel engine for use in warships during the years the *Yamato* was being designed and constructed. The Japanese failure in this regard was only too well known in the navy as the result of trouble experienced with the large submarine tenders *Taigei* and *Tsurugizaki.*

49. Garzke and Dulin, 106, 108.

50. Skulski, *The Battleship Yamato,* 7; Garzke and Dulin, 110–11; and *NNK,* 2:103.

51. *NKKS,* 1:126.

52. Richard Minear's introduction in Yoshida Mitsuru, *Requiem.*

53. These service histories are provided in detail in Garzke and Dulin, 54–74.

54. The *Yamato*'s fuel consumption was 7.7 tons per hour at 16 knots ("standard speed"), 14 tons per hour at 19.2 knots ("cruising speed"), and 62.7 tons per hour at 27.68 knots maximum speed during trials in October 1941. *SZ*, 1:689.

55. A detailed explanation of the nature of this defect is provided in Thornton, *"Yamato: The Achilles Heel,"* 5–8.

56. These points are explained in Garzke and Dulin, 113.

57. Thornton, "The Sinking," 33.

58. Garzke and Dulin, 67–72. Those authors point out that American naval analysts learned a great deal from the *Musashi*'s destruction and concluded that the ship could have been finished off more quickly had the attacks concentrated on one side of the ship, maximizing the possibility that she would capsize.

59. The ideas set forth in the next two paragraphs are derived largely from the observations made by Thornton in *"Yamato: The Achilles Heel"* and "Air Power."

60. Thornton, "Air Power," 33. Furthermore, the set of overall compromises selected for the final design of these battleships resulted in a sensible ratio between the three most important elements of a warship, which, in this case, made up 58 percent of the displacement of these ships: 33.9 percent, or 22,895 tons, devoted to armor; 16.9 percent, or 11,661 tons, to weaponry; and 7.7 percent, or 5,300 tons, for machinery. Thornton, *"Yamato: The Achilles Heel,"* 5.

61. Torpedo protection in the *Yamato* class is a complex issue. There is conflicting data concerning design specifications, and the extent of actual damage to the ships by torpedoes and gunfire is impossible to determine. Among the studies that explore this issue are Thornton, *"Yamato: The Achilles Heel"*; the same author's "Air Power"; and Garzke and Dulin, esp. 96–101.

62. Garzke and Dulin, 115.

63. Thornton, "The Sinking," 29–30. Not only did the 9-ounce shell of the 25-millimeter cannon lack the punch to destroy the rugged airframes of American naval aircraft, its sights were also inadequate, its magazines held too few rounds, and the weapon could not be trained or elevated fast enough for high-speed targets. N. J. M. Campbell, *Naval Weapons*, 200.

64. Thorton, "The Sinking," 27. Of course, it is important to remember that by World War II, the essential element of fleet air defense was fighter cover, a protection available to neither of these battleships when they were sunk.

65. Garzke and Dulin, 89. See also the speculative article by Hone and Friedman, *"Iowa* vs. *Yamato,"* 122–23.

66. By the late summer of 1942, in any event, the superbattleship strategy was dead, a victim not so much of the battleship's demise as of the carrier's rise as the prime element of naval power and of Japan's desperate need for more warships of this category after the carrier losses at the battle of Midway. The *Shinano*, the third ship of the *Yamato* class, was finished during the war as Japan's largest carrier, only to be sent to the bottom by an American submarine several weeks after she was commissioned. Work on the fourth ship in the class was halted, even as the *Yamato* was being commissioned in December 1941. As we have mentioned, five more capital ships—three battleships and two battle cruisers—had been projected under the Circle Five construction program. The first battleship would have been a slightly improved version of the *Yamato*. The other two were originally conceived (in 1938–39) as "super-*Yamato*s," ships of

90,000 tons, 19.6-inch main battery guns, and a 30-knot maximum speed. These plans were later scaled back. Although the designs were essentially completed by early 1941, the demand for other warship categories halted the design work and any further consideration of these monsters. Plans for the construction of two battle cruisers, drawn up as a response to the American *Alaska*-class ships, which the Japanese had heard were being constructed, were similarly aborted, victims of more urgent construction needs for the navy and, by the beginning of the Pacific War, of the utter obsolescence of the battle cruiser idea. Garzke and Dulin, 84–87.

67. O'Connell, *Sacred Vessels*.
68. Agawa, 93.
69. *KG1*, 595.
70. *SZ*, 1:549–50. WG, 162–63, seems to be in error in describing this class as being equipped for a role as high-speed scout cruisers for the Combined Fleet.
71. KG1, 215; *SZ*, 1:549; and WG, 161–63.
72. Layman and McLaughlin, *The Hybrid Warship*, 78. The aircraft planned for use with the Ōyodo, the Kawanishi E15K (type 2, "Norm") high-speed reconnaissance seaplane, featured a jettisonable central float, retractable wing floats, contra-rotating propellers, and a top speed of about 300 knots with main float jettisoned. The aircraft is an interesting example of Japanese designers' tendency to attempt the impossible, in this case to produce a reconnaissance floatplane that could outrun the fastest enemy fighters. Francillon, *Japanese Aircraft*, 314–16.
73. *SZ*, 1:550–551; WG, 163–64; and Layman and McLaughlin, 77–79.
74. *KG1*, 596.
75. *SZ*, 1:555; WG, 283; and Whitley, *Destroyers,* 200–201.
76. See Chihaya and Abe, "IJN *Yukikaze*," 221–44.
77. *SZ*, 1:556; Whitley, 203; and WG, 285–86.
78. *SZ*, 1:556–58; Whitley, 204–5; and WG, 288–89.
79. Willmott, *Victory and Supremacy*.
80. Whitley, 187–88, 204.
81. *KG1*, 596.
82. *SZ*, 1:607; Japan, Bōeichō Bōeikenshūjo Senshishitsu, *Sensuikanshi,* 60–61; WG, 331–32; and Carpenter and Polmar, 101.
83. *SZ*, 1:607; Japan, Bōeichō Bōeikenshūjo Senshishitsu, *Sensuikanshi,* 60–61; WG, 332–33; and Carpenter and Polmar, 102.
84. *SZ*, 1:607; Japan, Bōeichō Bōeikenshūjo Senshishitsu, *Sensuikanshi,* 60–61; WG, 335–36; and Carpenter and Polmar, 104. They were *I-16, I-18, I-20, I-22,* and *I-24.*
85. WG, 336, 340; Carpenter and Polmar, 105, 123; and *SZ*, 1:605.
86. Friedman, *Submarine,* 31. For a detailed discussion of the development of the American "fleet boats" see Alden, *The Fleet Submarine.*
87. Designed for service in the China War, the *Fushimi* and *Sumida* were laid down in 1939 (as replacements for two older gunboats of the same name) and completed in 1939 and 1940, respectively. Displacing 304 tons, they were driven by turbine-powered, oil-fired engines that produced 2,200 shaft horsepower and were capable of 17 knots maximum speed. They were armed with one 8-centimeter antiaircraft gun and two 25-millimeter machine guns. *SZ*, 1:564; and Kaigun Henshū Iinkai, 10:253–54.
88. Fock, *Fast Fighting Boats,* 271–72.

11 BEHIND THE FLEET
    Collateral Elements of the Japanese Navy, 1937–1941

1. This and the next two paragraphs are drawn from Potter, 639–44; and Ballantine, *U.S. Naval Logistics*, 1–37.
2. Schneider, *The Navy V-12 Program*, xi and 323–24.
3. Edward S. Miller, letter to authors, 9 October 1994; and Wildenberg, "Chester Nimitz," 52–62.
4. See, for example, Baxter, *Scientists against Time*, 1–25; and Bush, *Modern Arms and Free Men*, 7–8, 205–9.
5. Hinsley, "An Intelligence Revolution," 8.
6. Except where otherwise noted, the next five paragraphs are based on Parillo, *The Japanese Merchant Marine*, 49–83.
7. *KG1,* 420.
8. Parillo, 57–58.
9. By 1939, 40 percent of Japanese freighters and 70 percent of Japanese tankers could do 12 knots or better, as compared to 25 and 20 percent, respectively, for freighters and tankers in the U.S. merchant marine. Ibid., 59.
10. Ibid., 60.
11. Lengerer and Rehm-Takahara, 17.
12. Ibid., 19; and JJM, 249–52.
13. Most tankers that supported Japanese naval operations in the Pacific during World War II were of this type. The older *Shiretoko*-class oilers were simply too slow by then.
14. Parillo, 47–49.
15. For a discussion of the brief commerce-raiding exploits of these two ships, see Layton, "24 Sentai," 54–61.
16. *SZ,* 1:517; and Parillo, 74–78.
17. Parillo, 80–81.
18. Jerome Cohen, 254–55.
19. Chihaya, *Nihon kaigun no senryaku hassō,* 215–17.
20. Wildenberg, 52–62.
21. Kusaka, "*Rengo Kantai,*" 141; Chigusa, "Conquer the Pacific," 177–86; and Prange, *At Dawn We Slept,* 322–23.
22. *KG1,* 818.
23. Ibid.; Chihaya, *Nihon kaigun no senryaku hassō,* 104–5, 218–19; and Chihaya, "An Intimate Look," 322. This last is a translation of an essay by Chihaya shortly after the end of the war examining the causes of the Japanese navy's defeat. That essay forms the core of the book-length study published decades later as *Nihon kaigun no senryaku hassō,* just cited.
24. Agawa, 127.
25. An example of this reliance on human labor was the construction of an airfield on Eten Island in the Truk group, Micronesia, before the war. Leveling one-half of the island for an airstrip took nearly seven years, 1934–1941, largely because the work was undertaken with dynamite, pickax, and shovel.

26. Chihaya, *Nihon kaigun no senryaku hassō,* 220–28; Chihaya, "An Intimate Look," 357–58; *KG2,* 450–51; and U.S. War Department, *Handbook,* 78–80.

27. Chihaya, *Nihon kaigun no senryaku hassō,* 356–59.

28. *KG2,* 212.

29. *KG1,* 682.

30. Prados, *Combined Fleet Decoded,* 71, has suggested some of the points raised here, but we have used the figures in *KG1,* 638–39.

31. *KG1,* 683. To the reader with any knowledge of the U.S. Navy in World War II and the relative effectiveness of the "ninety-day wonders" produced by American officer candidate schools, this attitude may seem preposterous. It reflects, we believe, a significant difference in cultural values between the Japanese emphasis on tradition and experience in the mastery of a particular task or discipline and the American assumption that given the right methods of training, anyone with education and reasonable intelligence can acquire a satisfactory capacity to do a required task. Moreover, in the U.S. Navy in World War II, with very few exceptions, regular navy officers held all ship commands down to the destroyer escort level and even DE commands were held by USNR officers, mostly lieutenant commanders, with substantial service at sea.

32. *KG1,* 652–54, 658, note to table. An example of the navy's shortage of qualified officers was the difficulty of producing Naval Staff College graduates from 1940 to 1943, since the officers enrolled were all called away to duty stations. Coox, "The Effectiveness of the Japanese Military," 78.

33. The navy used this last policy particularly in the submarine service, which from 1943 onward was filled by younger and younger officers. *KG2,* 214.

34. Ibid., 201.

35. Ibid., 213. For the sake of conveying the essential meaning of this quotation, we have taken the liberty of rearranging the sentence order of the original Japanese text.

36. *KG1,* 682.

37. Ibid., 629–30; and *KG2,* 213.

38. Chihaya, *Nihon kaigun no senryaku hassō,* 105–6.

39. In this section we have strictly focused on the naval aspects of Japan's oil situation before the Pacific War. We fully recognize that the navy was only the largest single consumer of petroleum in prewar Japan and that the Japanese oil crisis was therefore far wider and far more complex than the narrower concerns of the Japanese navy outlined here.

40. We will reiterate the conversion used in our discussion of naval fuels. The Japanese navy calculated its fuels in kiloliters (1,000 liters, or 1 cubic meter). For fuel oil, 1,129 liters equals 1 (long) ton; for aviation fuels the number of kiloliters in a ton would be more. Indeed, for different grades of petroleum with different specific densities, the conversion figures will be different. In the interest of simplicity, however, we have decided to assume that 1 ton equals 1,000 liters of naval fuel of any kind. In the following discussion, we caution the reader that no definitive figures on stockpiles, consumption, and so forth, are available because of government secrecy, interservice rivalry, and the wholesale destruction of documents at the end of the Pacific War. We have endeavored to choose the most reliable figures from among many conflicting estimates.

41. Ohmae, "Stockpiling of Liquid Fuel," 4.

42. Ibid., 11–12; and Barnhart, *Japan Prepares for Total War,* 16–147.

43. Because of the ongoing hostility and mistrust between the two armed services, as well as Japan's failure to develop an overall fuel policy in these years, from 1931 to the outbreak of the Pacific War, the navy concealed its stockpiling of oil and construction of storage tanks. The navy variously camouflaged these items within its budget to avoid having to share its resources with the army and to prevent cuts in appropriations. Ohmae, "Stockpiling of Liquid Fuel," 4.

44. The navy was able to stockpile 104,000 tons of aviation gasoline in 1936; 99,000 tons in 1937; 97,000 tons in 1938; 150,000 tons in 1940; and 371,000 tons in 1941. *KKG,* 109.

45. Ibid.

46. Samuels, *Japanese State Energy Markets,* 177; Anderson, *The Standard-Vacuum Oil Company,* 76–77; and Nomura Minoru, "Dai niji," 96–97.

47. Nomura Minoru, "Dai niji," 96.

48. While naval and air operations in the war obviously increased the navy's fuel consumption, increased demands from the civilian sector and private industry exerted greater pressure on the nation's fuel supplies. Expecting that commodity regulations and foreign exchange controls would be imposed by the government, civilian planners made unprecedented claims for fuel appropriations based on their greatly exaggerated estimates of future consumption. *KG1,* 729–30.

49. The actual distribution of fuel within the Combined Fleet was decided by the annual training program for each type of ship: forty-five days for battleships, fifty days for cruisers, and sixty days for destroyers and battleships. Ohmae, "Stockpiling of Liquid Fuel," 9.

50. Ōmae, "Nihon kaigun no heijutsu shisō," part 2, pp. 89–90; and *NKKS,* 2:662.

51. Ohmae, "Stockpiling of Liquid Fuels," 7–8.

52. As early as 1933, an informally organized research group of activist middle-echelon officers within the navy had begun to study the possibility of exploiting the strategic resources of Southeast Asia, particularly oil. The Tai-Nan'yō Hōsaku Kenkyū Iinkai (Policy Study Committee for the South Seas area), or Tai-nanken for short, comprised some twenty-one middle-echelon officers. Its purpose was to explore the economic penetration of Southeast Asia, particularly the Netherlands East Indies, and the transfer of its resources into Japanese hands. Much of the rhetoric of its deliberations, as well as some of its basic conclusions, were later reflected in the ideology and rhetoric of the Greater East Asian Co-Prosperity Sphere. Hatano, "Shōwa kaigun no nanshin ron," 278–79; and Gotō, part 2, pp. 34–35.

53. Nomura Minoru, "Dai niji," 100–101.

54. *KG1,* 722–28; Barnhart, *Japan Prepares for Total War,* 168.

55. Kaijō Rōdō Kyōkai, *Nihon shōsentai,* 226–28.

56. Nenryō Konwakai, 1:657.

57. Ibid.; Nomura Minoru, "Dai niji," 108; and Japan, Bōeichō Bōeikenshūjo Senshishitsu, *Dai Hon'ei Kaigunbu, Rengō Kantai, roku,* 114–15. The declining figures in successive years, of course, reflect losses and supply problems rather than decreased need.

58. During the war, however, even Southeast Asia produced less oil than the navy had

supposed. Prewar calculations by navy planners had estimated that the East Indies would produce 2 million tons in 1942, 6 million by 1943, and 10 million in 1944. By a reliable estimate, however, the region produced only 1.09 million tons in 1942, 2.6 million in 1943, and 1.06 million in 1944. Gotō, part 2, pp. 61–62.

59. Chihaya, *Nihon kaigun no senryaku hassō,* 104. An example of this constant problem was the restriction placed on planning for the A-GŌ Operation of 1944. The plans called for the Combined Fleet to sortie from its Southeast Asian base and defeat the American fleet in the waters off Palau, a scheme undone by the sudden thrust of U.S. forces at the Marianas, much farther to the northeast. When A-GŌ was activated, the fleet did not have enough refined oil to fight as far north as the Marianas and thus had to use near-at-hand Borneo oil, whose composition posed a greater fire hazard and was much harder on ships' boilers. Had the Japanese been able to count on more oil and tankers to carry it, the navy could have devised a less restrictive plan. Nomura Minoru, "Dai niji," 108–9.

60. Nomura Minoru, "Dai niji," 102–4.

61. Chihaya, *Nihon kaigun no senryaku hassō,* 101–2.

62. *NKKS,* 2:634–36.

63. The term "radar" was, of course, an American wartime designation of this technology and was adopted for general use; the Japanese naval term was *dempa tanshingi* (electronic wave search device).

64. *KG1,* 29–30; Matsui, "Nihon no kaigun no dempa tanshingi," 444; and Wilkinson, "Short Survey of Japanese Radar," part 1, pp. 370–71. Wilkinson, an operations analyst for the U.S. Army Air Force in World War II, was sent to Japan at the end of the war to study all phases of Japanese electronics and radar, from research to operations.

65. Matsui, 443, 445; and Friedman, *Naval Radar,* 96–97.

66. Matsui, 445.

67. Nakagawa Yasuzō, *Dokyumento,* 111.

68. Japan, Bōeichō Bōeikenshūjo Senshishitsu, *Kaijō goei sen,* 30; and Matsui, 446.

69. The first air-search set was installed aboard a Japanese warship (the battleship *Ise)* in May 1942. In comparison with American and British sets, succeeding shipboard air-search radars were poorly designed and constructed. The navy could not produce an effective fire-control radar, nor did it ever develop an effective shipboard organization of radar-obtained information—a plotting team and apparatus as materialized in the combat information centers so common in American ships by the end of the war. No Japanese submarines were equipped with actual radar, but some did have the "poor man's radar"—search receivers that provided some indication of range from the comparative strength of signals received. Airborne radar was similarly retarded: the G4M ("Betty") attack bomber, the first Japanese aircraft to be so equipped, had no radar until 1944, and no IFF (Identification Friend or Foe) system was available until the spring of that year. Matsui, 446; and Guerlac, *Radar in World War II,* 921–24.

70. Lt. Comdr. Matsui Muneaki, who dealt with radar development during a tour with the 2nd Naval Arsenal, asserts that it was the Battle of Cape Esperance, 11 October 1942, that convinced the Japanese that the U.S. Navy was using radar-controlled firing at night. According to Matsui, 452, the results of the battle completely reversed the navy's indifference to radar.

71. Ibid., 452–53.

72. LeComte, "Radar and the Air Battles of Midway," 29.

73. Nakagawa Yasuzō, 80.

74. Ibid., 456–57; and Wilkinson, part 1, p. 372.

75. The night action of Kula Gulf, 5–6 July 1943, was one of the few exceptions to this unequal state of affairs. Search radar aboard his flagship gave the Japanese commander at least the initial tactical advantage. Dull, *A Battle History*, 275.

76. The best comprehensive study of Japanese intelligence in general is Barnhart, "Japanese Intelligence," 424–55.

77. Rear Adm. Takeuchi Kaoru, chief of the U.S. section of the information division, recalled after the Pacific War that through most of the war, his section "never attempted to play the part of forecaster. We never attempted to reach conclusions but we passed information on to those whose duty it was to deploy forces. . . . I impressed my subordinates with this procedure." U.S. Strategic Bombing Survey, Military and Naval Intelligence Division, *Japanese Military and Naval Intelligence*, 20.

78. Marder, *Old Friends, New Enemies*, 1:335.

79. U.S. Strategic Bombing Survey, Military and Naval Intelligence Division, *Japanese Military and Naval Intelligence*, 21; and Chapman, "Japanese Intelligence," 155.

80. U.S. Strategic Bombing Survey, Military and Naval Intelligence Division, *Japanese Military and Naval Intelligence*, 1–2, 20.

81. Ibid.

82. Sanematsu, *Jōhō sensō*, 43–44; and Chapman, "Tricycle Recycled," 271–72.

83. U.S. Strategic Bombing Survey, Military and Naval Intelligence Division, *Japanese Military and Naval Intelligence*, 29–31.

84. Drea, "Reading Each Other's Mail," 189.

85. Ibid., 185–90; and Sanematsu, *Jōhō sensō*, 44, 65–67.

86. The most comprehensive treatment of U.S. naval intelligence operations against the Japanese navy before and during the Pacific War is that in Prados.

87. Dorwart, *Conflict of Duty*, 93–94, claims that the gunboat *Panay* was one of the U.S. Navy's most successful spy ships and that when the ship was attacked and sunk by Japanese navy bombers, it was "crammed with intelligence material, including a secret Japanese bombsight, a code book, technical pamphlets, and signal equipment."

88. Zacharias, "The Orange Maneuvers," 12–19.

89. *Gold Star*'s clandestine mission was probably not known to most of her crew. The novelist Richard McKenna, who served aboard her in the 1930s, makes no mention of her intelligence activities in his recollection, "Life Aboard the USS *Gold Star*," in *The Left-Handed Monkey Wrench* (a collection of his shorter writings), 107–40. Detailed reports on the "Gold Star" intercepts can be found in National Archives, Records of the National Security Agency, RG 457, "Various Reports."

90. Chapman, "Japanese Intelligence," 150–51.

91. Ibid., 154; and Drea, "Reading Each Other's Mail," 185–90.

92. Nomura Hisashi, "Jōhōsen," 356–57.

93. Ibid., 357; and Kahn, *The Codebreakers*, 582–83.

94. Dingman, "The Pacific Theater: Comments," 225–26.

95. In the prewar years, the German navy was reluctant to exchange signals intelligence techniques with the Japanese navy because it always viewed such collaboration as

one-sided. Therefore, although the Japanese navy acquired some valuable technical, operational, and strategic intelligence from the Germans in this period, there is little evidence that the Japanese and German naval general staffs exchanged information about interception and decryption techniques. Lietzman and Wenneker, *The Price of Admiralty,* 1:205, n. 14; 215, n. 12; 226, n. 6; and 2:577, n. 10.

96. The high-level U.S. machine cipher was implemented by the Converter M-134-C, otherwise known as SIGABA to the Army Signal Corps and the ECM to the U.S. Navy. This machine was a generation later than the Enigma machine and throughout the war resisted all attempts to break messages enciphered on it. The Allies believed that it was secure enough to use for the transmission of ULTRA intelligence. Postwar research reveal that this faith was not misplaced. Kahn, 510; Lewin, *The American Magic,* 153; and Putney, *ULTRA and the Army Air Forces,* 82–83.

97. In 1930, for example, American cryptanalysts could read about 85 percent of the coded messages used in the Japanese grand maneuvers that year. National Archives, Records of the National Security Agency, RG 457, "Various Reports." That same year the Japanese navy's operations code was replaced by a new version, which remained in place until 1938. Though the U.S. Navy was thus given a serious setback in its effort to read Japanese naval messages, by great effort and the introduction of IBM tabulating machinery, American naval cryptanalysts were able to reconstruct the code by 1936, one of the most remarkable feats in the history of cryptanalysis up to that time. Safford, "A Brief History," 8.

98. Ibid., 9.

99. A list of these is provided in Kahn, 586.

100. Ibid., 586–88.

101. Ibid., 586; and Safford, 9–10.

102. Costello, *Days of Infamy,* 279–301, emphasizes that in the year before the Pacific War, the U.S. Navy had too few cryptanalysts at work to break JN-25-B. He argues that if the Americans could have decrypted the ciphers they had intercepted in the autumn of 1941, they would have learned of the Japanese plans for the assault on Hawaii.

103. Supposedly, this was largely due to the recovery of code books from the submarine *I-124,* the first full-sized submarine sunk in World War II by American and Australian naval forces, off Port Darwin in January of that year. Yoshida Akihiko, letter to authors, 17 December 1993. As of this writing, the import of this recovery is not clear to us. Sanematsu Yuzuru, *Jōhō sensō,* 173–74, claims that the codes recovered from the *I-124* gave away Japanese plans for the MO Operation (the occupation of Port Moresby and Tulagi and the destruction of U.S. naval forces blocking these initiatives). Drea, *MacArthur's Ultra,* 74, asserts that navy divers recovered only the Japanese navy's water transport "S" code books and that the resulting intelligence was used to interdict some Japanese naval convoys.

104. JN-25-B was replaced on 1 June 1942 by JN-25-C9.

105. Parillo, 91.

106. This and the next two paragraphs are drawn from U.S. Strategic Bombing Survey, Military and Naval Intelligence Division, *Japanese Military and Naval Intelligence,* 22–24. While those pages refer specifically to Japanese combat intelligence during the Pacific War, they are obviously also relevant to the years immediately preceding the war.

107. Indeed, Capt. Ōmae Toshikazu, chief of the Planning Section of the Operations Division of the Navy General Staff late in the Pacific War, recalled after the war that he usually discounted by 50 percent the returning air crews' claims of their destruction of enemy ships and aircraft. Ibid., 24.

108. Ibid., 34.

109. Ibid., 46–47.

110. The most stunning intelligence coup was achieved when a German raider seized the British freighter *Automedon* in November 1940 and, as a result, captured secret British Cabinet papers. Turned over to the Japanese Navy General Staff, these papers clearly revealed how weak and overstretched was the British position in Southeast Asia. This information undoubtedly played a major role in shaping Japanese invasion plans for the region. Chapman, "Signals Intelligence Collaboration," 251–56.

111. Barnhart, "Japanese Intelligence," 447; and U.S. Strategic Bombing Survey, Military and Naval Intelligence Division, *Japanese Military and Naval Intelligence,* 21–22. John Prados, who recently chronicled U.S. naval intelligence during the Pacific War, asserts that before the war, American naval attachés, particularly those in Tokyo, kept their superiors surprisingly well informed about Japanese navy ships, personnel, and weapons. The problem, he insists, is that much of this information was dismissed by the brass in Washington. Prados, 32.

12 UNEVEN WEAPONS
Submarine, Antisubmarine, and Amphibious Warfare Capabilities in the Japanese Navy, 1937–1941

1. Unless otherwise noted, our discussion of submarine and ASW strategies and technologies in this and the following three paragraphs are based largely on Hezlet, *The Submarine,* 108–23.

2. Talbott, 57–68; Andrade, "Submarine Policy," 54–55; and Weir, "The Search for American Submarine Strategy," 34–48.

3. Henry, "British Submarine Policy," 80–107.

4. Ibid., 93–95.

5. See, for example, the chapter "Failure to Learn: American Antisubmarine Warfare in 1942" in Cohen and Gooch, *Military Misfortunes,* 59–94.

6. Our discussion of amphibious warfare is largely based on Millett, "Assault from the Sea," 67–143.

7. Among the best works on the subject are the Millett work already cited; Millett's *Semper Fidelis;* Isely and Crowl, *The U.S. Marines;* and Clifford, *Amphibious Warfare Development.*

8. After these tests of crew effectiveness, the navy concluded that submarines operating close to an unalerted enemy base could remain on station for seven days before being relieved and for three days if enemy antisubmarine patrols were frequent. More distant surveillance of an enemy fleet could be maintained for a month, and commerce-raiding operations in enemy waters could be sustained from one to three months. Japan, Bōeichō Bōeikenshūjo Senshishitsu, *Sensuikanshi,* 41. These figures seem conservative in light of the later experiences of submarine forces in World War II, in which crews demonstrated extraordinary stamina under the strains of combat.

9. Japan, Bōeichō Bōeikenshūjo Senshishitsu, *Sensuikanshi,* 40.

10. Ibid., 750.

11. *KS,* 764–65.

12. Japan, Bōeichō Bōeikenshūjo Senshishitsu, *Sensuikanshi,* 39–42.

13. Ibid., 41–42.

14. Sakamoto, *Nihon sensuikan senshi,* 33. Sakamoto, the principal editor of the *Sensuikanshi* of the series by Japan, Bōeichō Bōeikenshūjo Senshishitsu cited above, was himself a submariner during the Pacific War. At the beginning of the conflict he was torpedo officer aboard Submarine *I-1* and, as such, participated in the Hawaii operation. Later, he held three successive submarine commands.

15. U.S. Naval Technical Mission to Japan, "Japanese Submarine Operations," 14–15.

16. Japan, Bōeichō Bōeikenshūjo Senshishitsu, *Sensuikanshi,* 43.

17. Ibid., 46.

18. Ibid., 43.

19. Ibid., 44; and Sakamoto, 34–35. The navy had also experimented with designs for small submarines of high underwater speed and, in 1938, had actually built such a craft. Its short, highly streamlined hull, powerful batteries, and electric motors gave it an exceptional underwater speed of 21 knots, but its low displacement and underpowered diesel engine made the submarine's surface speed too low (a little over 13 knots). Sakamoto, 40; and WG, 330–31.

20. Japan, Bōeichō Bōeikenshūjo Senshishitsu, *Sensuikanshi,* 44–46.

21. Ibid., 50.

22. *KS,* 763.

23. Friedman, *Submarine,* 9.

24. U.S. Naval Technical Mission to Japan, "Japanese Submarine Operations," 9.

25. Alan D. Zimm, letter to authors, 6 December 1993. For these aspects of American submarine training and tactics before the war, see Blair, *Silent Victory,* 66–67, 156.

26. Torisu, "Dai Roku Kantai," 96.

27. For commentary along these lines, see Torisu, "Japanese Submarine Tactics," 442–52.

28. Even in the British navy and merchant marine, the lessons of convoy escort in World War I had to be debated once more at the outset of World War II. For a discussion of this problem, see Winton, *Convoy,* 123–25.

29. Sanematsu, *Kaigun daigaku kyōiku,* 203–204; and Japan, Bōeichō Bōeikenshūjo Senshishitsu, *Kaijō goei sen,* 13–14.

30. Oi, "Why Japan's Antisubmarine Warfare Failed," 388. Asada asserts that the Japanese navy also greatly underestimated the capability of American submarines to conduct an extended blockade, calculating that two weeks would be the limit of their endurance. During the Pacific War, American submarines were often a month or more on patrol. Asada, "The Japanese Navy," 235.

31. Japan, Bōeichō Bōeikenshūjo Senshishitsu, *Kaijō goei sen,* 4–5. The navy would definitely commit to the defense of Japanese maritime traffic passing through the South China Sea only in the case of war with Britain alone. The rationale for this greater geographic commitment in the case of a conflict with a lesser foe was that the navy would have a surplus of naval forces to do the job. Thus, admits the official history, commerce protection was to be based not on the nation's strategic needs, but on the forces available. Ibid., 5–6.

32. Ibid., 9.

33. Ibid., 5–7, 11; and Oi, "Why Japan's Antisubmarine Warfare Failed," 410.

34. Morley, *The Final Confrontation*, 277–78.

35. *Japan, Bōeichō Bōeikenshūjo Senshishitsu, Kaijō goei sen*, 56–57.

36. Ōi, *Kaijō goei sambō*, 5–8; and Morley, *The Final Confrontation*, 278.

37. Oi, "Why Japan's Antisubmarine Warfare Failed," 390; and Japan, Bōeichō Bōeikenshūjo Senshishitsu, *Kaijō goei sen*, 17. This general indifference of the navy high command seems not to have greatly improved during the first year of the Pacific War. After the war, an army officer assigned liaison duties with the Navy General Staff wrote of the feeble efforts to effect a system of convoy escort by the Navy Division of IGHQ. His account underscores the lack of any relevant doctrine or procedures for convoy escort; the absence of any earlier data, documents, or books from which to create such doctrine; and the ridiculously few personnel assigned to sea defense. Of those who were assigned, most were officers who were physically unfit for sea duty. In this officer's view, the army, with more men and material to transport than the navy, was much more concerned about convoy escort than its service rival. Horie, "The Failure of the Japanese Convoy Escort," 1073.

38. Parillo, 65, 67; and Oi, "Why Japan's Antisubmarine Warfare Failed," 390–91.

39. Parillo, 67–68. We should note, of course, that armed escort was supplied by the Combined Fleet for troopship convoys, usually in the form of accompanying destroyers. But at the outset of the war, as there was no convoy system organized for merchant shipping, individual merchant ships were simply encouraged to sail independently.

40. According to Hans Lengerer, the term *kaibōkan* originally meant an overage warship unfit for anything but defensive service. Later, the term came to mean "coast defense ship," but this English-language definition is deceiving since, in the West, it came to mean an armored warship with a few heavy guns and designed strictly for use in coastal waters. The Japanese navy never constructed any ships of this type. Lengerer, "Japanese 'Kaibōkan' Escorts," part 1, p. 124.

41. WG, 375; *SZ*, 1:564; and Lengerer, "Japanese 'Kaibōkan' Escorts," part 1, p. 127.

42. WG, 378–79; Lengerer, "Japanese 'Kaibōkan' Escorts," part 1, pp. 127–28; and Parillo, 96.

43. WG, 476–79; and Parillo, 102–4.

44. Parillo, 110.

45. Japan, Bōeichō Bōeikenshūjo Senshishitsu, *Kaijō goei sen*, 23–25, 28; and U.S. Naval Technical Mission to Japan, "Japanese Sonar and Asdic."

46. Parillo, 108–9.

47. Japan, Bōeichō Bōeikenshūjo Senshishitsu, *Kaijō goei sen*, 562.

48. The army's Fifth, Eleventh, and Twelfth Divisions were designated to undertake amphibious landings, and the shipping engineer regiments attached to these divisions each had a landing craft squadron. Although trained in amphibious operations, such operations were not considered their primary function.

49. Eiji Kusumi (Kusumi, Eiji), "'Rikusentai' (Japanese Marine Corps)," 64.

50. Japan, Bōeichō Bōeikenshūjo Senshishitsu, *Chūgoku hōmen*, 46–47; and Kaigun Henshū Iinkai, 11:127–32.

51. Suekuni, "Senshi ni miru," 34.

52. Ibid., 37–38; and Japan, Bōeichō Bōeikenshūjo Senshishitsu, *Dai Hon'ei Rikugunbu,* 300.

53. Suekuni, 40–41.

54. Millett, "Assault from the Sea," 100–101; and U.S. War Department, *Handbook,* 76. All these units grew in size and firepower during the decade, particularly the Special Naval Landing Force at Shanghai, which quickly acquired a fortresslike headquarters, an infantry garrison of regiment size, light tanks, 155-millimeter howitzers, and an antiaircraft battery.

55. *Shinshū-maru,* laid down in 1933 and completed in 1935, carried tanks on the lower deck and fighter aircraft or dive-bombers in a hangar in the superstructure. These and some thirty-seven landing craft of various sizes were handled by the ship's derricks and heavy crane. The design was so successful that in 1941 the army later commandeered two merchant liners under construction and converted them into similar ships. *SZ,* 1:767–68.

56. Millett, "Assault from the Sea," 94–97

57. Suekuni, 41.

58. Ibid., 42

59. Millett, "Assault from the Sea," 92.

60. This concept was most keenly supported by the Combat Section of the navy's Gunnery School, which sent a memo to the general staff, ministry, and staff college, proposing the creation of a single, permanent amphibious arm for the navy. In 1940, in anticipation of island warfare in the central Pacific, Lt. Comdr. Imai Akijirō, an officer with extensive combat experience in the naval landing forces, sent a memorandum to the general staff. In it, he provided the details of such a proposal: the creation of a force of 40,000–45,000 men, to be assigned to six different defense sectors in Japan's Micronesian territories and able to undertake either offensive or defensive operations. Both proposals were ignored. Kaigun Henshū Iinkai, 12:161–62.

61. Ibid., 174–78. Of these operations, the assault on Timor, 19–20 February 1942, was perhaps the most skillful use of combined arms in seizing an objective. Stewart, "The Japanese Assault on Timor," 202–9.

62. This confidence led to the Japanese navy's apparent willingness to share its knowledge of naval landing operations with the Germans in the late spring of 1940. After the collapse of France that spring and the move of the Japanese embassy from Paris to Vichy, a small Japanese naval group, including certain officers with a specialized knowledge of naval landing operations, remained in Paris in the hope that their expertise might further the German plans for an invasion of Britain. Lietzman and Wenneker, 1:240, n. 8, and 2:579, n. 21.

63. Ibid.; Willmott, *Empires in the Balance,* 153; and Evans, "The Japanese Navy."

64. Kaigun Henshū Iinkai, 12:161–62.

65. Two other amphibious landings, at the Battle of the Points on Bataan, March 1942, and at Milne Bay, New Guinea, August 1942, do not qualify as amphibious assault by the navy as defined here. The first was undertaken by army troops, and the second was an essentially unopposed landing that was subsequently thrown back by the Allies.

13   THE GREAT GAMBLE
      The Japanese Navy Plans for War, 1937–1941

1. Even the English-language works on the Japanese side of the origins of the Pacific War are too numerous to list here, though the following titles represent either the most reliable or the most recent general studies of the subject: Morison, *History;* Feis, *The Road to Pearl Harbor;* Borg and Okamato, *Pearl Harbor as History;* Iriye, *The Origins;* Conroy and Wray, *Pearl Harbor Re-examined;* Willmott, *Empires in the Balance;* Frei, *Japan's Southward Advance;* Ike, *Japan's Decision for War;* Barnhart, *Japan Prepares for Total War;* Spector, *Eagle against the Sun;* and the various volumes edited by Morley: *The China Quagmire; Deterrent Diplomacy; The Fateful Choice; The Final Confrontation;* and *Japan Erupts.*

2. For the navy's views on relations with the Soviet Union in the 1930s, see Chapman, "The Imperial Japanese Navy," 150–206.

3. *DHKRK,* 318.

4. Gotō, part 1, pp. 9–12.

5. In the final policy revision, the navy believed that it had scored a victory of sorts by having the United States listed ahead of Russia as the primary enemy of Japan, but in the negotiations between the two services during the drafting of the revision, it was agreed that the order in which the two principal countries were listed did not necessarily imply the relative importance of either. *DHKRK,* 318.

6. *Gendaishi shiryō,* 8: part 1, pp. 354–55.

7. *Gendaishi shiryō,* 8: part 1, p. 361.

8. Asada, "The Japanese Navy," 244; and Hatano and Asada, "The Japanese Decision to Move South," 383–84.

9. Crowley, *Japan's Quest for Autonomy,* 285–89.

10. *DHKRK,* 370–71.

11. Ibid., 374–75.

12. Japan, Bōeichō Bōeikenshūjo Senshishitsu, *Dai Hon'ei Kaigunbu: Dai Tōa Senso,* 466–78.

13. *DHKRK,* 374–75. In the first map exercises relevant to a Japan-Britain naval war held at the staff college in late 1938 or early 1939, a Japanese Blue Fleet was judged to have decisively defeated a British Red Fleet in the South China Sea. Ibid., 389–90.

14. Ibid.

15. Aizawa, "Kaigun ryōshiki," 179–88.

16. In September 1936, hawks within the Navy General Staff had seized upon an incident of anti-Japanese violence in the Chinese coastal city of Pakhoi as a pretext for the occupation of Hainan. This would have given the navy an advance base in the South China Sea for future operations in Southeast Asia. The crisis blew over when the Nationalist Chinese withdrew their troops and the army blocked navy efforts to exploit the incident. Asada, "The Japanese Navy," 245.

17. Cited in Tsunoda, "The Navy's Role," 242.

18. Ibid., 242–43.

19. Ibid., 243–46; and *DHKRK,* 447–48. It seems that in raising the question of commerce protection in East Asian waters Japanese navy strategists were thinking of surface attacks rather than submarine warfare.

20. Frei, 147; and *Gendaishi shiryō,* 10: part 3, pp. 169–71.

21. Tsunoda, "The Navy's Role," 253–57.

22. Ibid., 258–59.

23. The central element of the pact was the article stating that, if one of the three signatories were attacked by any power not then engaged in the European or China wars, the other two would come to its assistance. Though not specifically stated in the agreement, it is clear that this wording was directed specifically against the United States.

24. Tsunoda, "The Navy's Role," 291.

25. Frei, 149; Barnhart, *Japan Prepares for Total War,* 198–200.

26. Ike, 50–51.

27. Ibid., 186.

28. These points are raised by Asada, "The Japanese Navy," 258; and Tsunoda, "The Navy's Role," 262.

29. Asada, "The Japanese Navy," 230–41; and *DHKRK,* 240, 246.

30. Asada, "The Japanese Navy," 232–33.

31. *DHKRK,* 362–63.

32. Marder, *Old Friends, New Enemies,* 1:90–91. In theory, the Supreme War Council was supposed to mediate differences between the two services if a stalemate arose, but this would have required an assertive chairman for the council. As its chairman was the elderly Prince Kan'in Kotohito, the council displayed no energy at all in mediation. *DHKRK,* 363.

33. Nomura Minoru, "Riku-kaigun," 93.

34. Marder, *Old Friends, New Enemies,* 1:92–93.

35. The politics surrounding Yonai's resistance to the Tripartite Pact with Germany and Italy and the resultant collapse of his government are treated in Marder, *Old Friends, New Enemies,* 1:105–13; and Asada, "The Japanese Navy," 246–49. A slightly revisionist treatment that sees Yonai as more accommodating to army views than usually acknowledged is provided in Krebs, "Admiral Yonai," 79–81.

36. Agawa, 157–67.

37. Prange, *At Dawn We Slept,* 15–16.

38. Inoue Shigeyoshi Denki Kankōkai, *Inoue Shigeyoshi,* 223–29.

39. Both quotations are from Coox, 12.

40. The 1936 annual operational plan, drawn up in 1935, called for the following disposition of forces: The Third Fleet was to be sent to the Philippines to assist in the conquest of those islands and, upon completion of its mission, to be ready to cooperate with the main force of the Combined Fleet in home waters. Elements of the Second Fleet would be dispatched to the northwest Pacific to guard against any American foray from that direction. The Fourth Fleet would take up station in Micronesia to defend important sites in the islands and to attack advance bases the enemy might establish there. Part of the Combined Fleet would be sent to Hawaii and the American west coast, remaining in the area of the enemy main force, reporting on its movements, and, if the opportunity arose, destroying it. Finally, the main force of the Combined Fleet would stay in Japan's home waters, ready to move out and destroy the enemy main force when the opportunity arose. *DHKRK,* 263–66.

41. Ibid., 345–46.

42. In early 1937, the U.S. Army Air Corps in the Philippines had one bombing squadron of obsolete Keystone biplane bombers, replaced that year by twelve Martin B-10s just as the B-10s were being phased out from USAAC squadrons in the United States. Far from being a potent strike force, the entire air strength in the Philippines was both obsolete and pitifully small. We are indebted for this information to Professor Brian Linn, Texas A & M University, currently undertaking a major study of the U.S. Army in the Pacific during the interwar period.

43. *DHKRK,* 345–46.

44. For a discussion of the nonfortification issue in relation to Japan's legal claim over its League of Nations mandate in Micronesia and of Japan's gradual militarization of the islands, see Peattie, *Nan'yō,* 230–56.

45. This squadron, composed of the seaplane tender *Kamoi,* a mine layer, and several destroyers, also stopped at several ports in the Philippines and the Netherlands East Indies. The ostensible purpose of these visits was to make a round of courtesy calls, but in fact the squadron surveyed those Western colonies for sites suitable as future air bases. *DHKRK,* 346–47.

46. Four of these bases were constructed in the Marianas (Pagan, Aslito, Garapan, and Tinian), four in the Carolines (Pelelieu, Arakabesan, Eten, and Ponape), and three in the Marshalls (Wotje, Kwajalein, and Taroa).

47. *KKG,* 110–11; and Chihaya, *Nihon kaigun no senryaku hassō,* 122.

48. *KKG,* 136, 207.

49. Ibid., 203.

50. Ibid., 207–8.

51. *DHKRK,* 389–90, 396, 399–400.

52. In framing the Japanese navy's perspectives in this way we have been influenced by Koda, "A Commander's Dilemma," 69–70.

53. No complete official record of the 1941 annual plan still exists, only a penciled version that came into the hands of Prime Minister Yoshida Shigeru after the war. The text of this version has many deletions and additions, and fifteen pages are missing. Thus, an understanding of the 1941 plan must be drawn from the navy's plan of the previous year and from the army's 1941 operational plan. *DHKRK,* 500–501, 505–6. We have relied in large part on such inferences drawn by the author-compilers of the Senshi Sōsho by Japan, Bōeichō Bōeikenshūjo Senshishitsu, as cited in the relevant notes.

54. *DHKRK,* 551; and Japan, Bōeichō Bōeikenshūjo Senshishitsu, *Hitō-Maree,* 34–36.

55. Japan, Bōeichō Bōeikenshūjo Senshishitsu, *Hitō-Maree,* 20, 23–24, 30–31.

56. Ibid., 36–37.

57. Willmott, *Empires in the Balance,* 73–74.

58. Chapman, "Tricycle Recycled," 275–76, 291–92. In mid-April 1940, Vice Adm. Kondō Nobutake, vice chief of the Navy General Staff, expressed amazement at the successful German landings in Norway in the face of great odds, and several weeks later, Vice Adm. Yamagata Seigo, chief of the General Affairs Section of the Naval Aviation Department, reportedly asserted that "the achievements of the German Air Force in Norway . . . have indicated a turning point in the history of warfare." Ibid., 277.

59. Even though most ships of the Combined Fleet were to be used in the operations in Southeast Asia, Yamamoto showed little direct interest in these matters. Being fully

occupied with planning for the Hawaiian operation, he left them almost entirely in the hands of the commanders who were to head the invasion fleets. Japan, Bōeichō Bōeikenshūjo Senshishitsu, *Hitō-Maree,* 338–40.

60. Ibid., 45–47.

61. In particular, see Prange, *At Dawn We Slept,* 224–25; Willmott, *Empires in the Balance,* 75–78; Willmott, *The Barrier and the Javelin,* 71–80; and Morison, *History,* 164–68.

62. Willmott, *Empires in the Balance,* 75.

63. Planning for the Malaya landings is a case in point. Adm. Ozawa Jisaburō, commander of the escort force that was to shepherd the landings, insisted on Kota Baru as the first and principal landing site, despite the strenuous objections of army commanders involved. Japan, Bōeichō Bōeikenshūjo Senshishitsu, *Hitō-Maree,* 338–40. In planning for the invasion of the Philippines, the navy essentially left the landing sites to the decision of the army, which had been studying the problem for decades and had settled on the best landing sites long before 1941.

64. *NKKS,* 1:264–65.

65. In assessing these writings, moreover, it is important to remember that the U.S. Fleet was not stationed at Pearl Harbor until the late spring of 1940. Thus, much speculation in the interwar decades concerning Pearl Harbor dealt with the possibility of an attack on the port and surrounding facilities, not with strikes against main American fleet units in Hawaii.

66. The subtitle of Honan's *Visions of Infamy: The Untold Story of How Hector C. Bywater Devised the Plans That Led to Pearl Harbor* encapsulates the author's thesis. With insubstantial evidence and shakier logic, Honan attempts to prove that the Japanese navy's plans for the Pacific War were copied largely from Bywater's 1925 novel, *The Great Pacific War: A History of the American-Japanese Campaign of 1931–33.* Among his various arguments, Honan asserts that Yamamoto's plans for the invasion of the Philippines relied almost entirely on Bywater's ideas. In fact, it was the Japanese army, not the Japanese navy (and certainly not Yamamoto), that had been responsible for such plans ever since 1909. But Honan's most dramatic claim is that first and foremost, Bywater's writings started Yamamoto thinking about a surprise air attack on the U.S. Pacific Fleet at Pearl Harbor in 1941. Honan's idée fixe on this proposition is based on a blend of selective evidence, post hoc arguments, and the unspoken implication that Japanese naval professionals could not think through such a plan for themselves. In any event, the notion has not found much support among professional naval historians in the West and, indeed, has been specifically rejected by Nomura Minoru, doyen of naval historians in Japan. (In his introduction, Honan lists Nomura Minoru as one of the Japanese authorities whom he consulted in writing his book.) Nomura, letter to authors, 5 November 1991.

67. For a detailed description of these war games see Reynolds, *Admiral John J. Towers,* 236–39, 276–79.

68. We view with skepticism the frequent claims by American writers that Japanese naval officers visually observed these exercises. Similarly, hearsay evidence (in Reynolds, *Admiral John J. Towers,* 238) that Japanese planning for the Pearl Harbor operation was influenced by these American naval maneuvers is too unsubstantiated to be very credible.

69. If we are to believe Prange, *At Dawn We Slept,* 14–15, the general staff had for some years considered making Pearl Harbor a target for its annual map exercises, but had always dropped it as impractical.

70. Takagi, 13–16.

71. *NKKS,* 1:101–2.

72. Ibid., 261.

73. Japan, Bōeichō Bōeikenshūjo Senshishitsu, *Hawai sakusen,* 60–63.

74. Dull, 8.

75. Early in 1940, as he appreciatively watched the repeated successes of Japanese torpedo bombers carrying out simulated attacks on capital ships under way, Yamamoto supposedly remarked to his chief of staff, Adm. Fukutome Shigeru, "It makes you wonder whether we couldn't launch an air attack on Pearl Harbor." Fukutome, *Shikan,* 79–80, believed that at the time, Yamamoto's remark was probably offhand, since his ideas about the Hawaii operation were still unformed and the U.S. Pacific Fleet had not yet taken up its station at Pearl Harbor.

76. Kuroshima's memoirs date this memorandum in February 1940, though it is possible that it was a year later. Japan, Bōeichō Bōeikenshūjo Senshishitsu, *Hawai sakusen,* 78–79.

77. Ibid., 75–78.

78. Dull, 8, asserts that Yamamoto requested that detailed studies of the Taranto raid be made by Japanese naval attachés in London and Rome.

79. Ibid., 78–81.

80. As Prange, *At Dawn We Slept,* 15–16, has pointed out, Yamamoto's drafting of a major strategic plan and his dispatch of it directly to the navy minister were highly unorthodox departures from accepted practice in the Japanese navy. In the first place, line commanders, even the commander of the Combined Fleet, did not normally propose strategy— that was the responsibility of the Navy General Staff. In the second, any such proposal should have gone to the chief of the general staff, rather than to the navy minister. Yamamoto short-circuited this route because the minister controlled personnel appointments and Yamamoto wished to command the operation he was proposing. That Yamamoto had the confidence to submit his plan in this way is an indication of both his independence and his influence.

81. Japan, Bōeichō Bōeikenshūjo Senshishitsu, *Hawai sakusen,* 82.

82. This and the three preceding paragraphs are based largely on ibid., 84–85.

83. Among other excellent studies of Japanese planning for the Hawaii operation are relevant portions of the Agawa biography of Yamamoto, already cited; Fukudome [Fukutome], "The Hawaii Operation"; Dull, chapter 1; Uchida and Tsunoda, "The Pearl Harbor Attack," 83–88; Barnhart, "Planning the Pearl Harbor Attack," 246–52; Koda, "A Commander's Dilemma," 63–74; and Hata, "Admiral Yamamoto's Surprise Attack," 55–72.

84. Japan, Bōeichō Bōeikenshūjo Senshishitsu, *Hawai sakusen,* 96–99; and Dull, 7.

85. Japan, Bōeichō Bōeikenshūjo Senshishitsu, *Hawai sakusen,* 98.

86. This paragraph is based largely on Barnhart, "Planning the Pearl Harbor Attack," 250–51.

87. Despite the long range of the Zero fighter, the more than 1,000-mile round-trip

between the Philippines and the navy's air bases in southern Taiwan initially posed a for-midable problem. It was solved by extending the Zero's combat radius by reducing engine cruising speed, adjusting the propeller speed, and setting the fuel mixture as lean as possible. Koichi Shimada (Shimada, Koichi), "The Opening Air Offensive," 82.

88. Dull, 10–11.

89. This paragraph is based on information provided in Hata, "Admiral Yamamoto's Surprise Attack," 68–69.

90. The entire document, *Tai-Bei-Ei-Ran-Shō sensō shūmatsu sokushin ni kansuru fukuan* (Draft proposal for hastening the end of a war against the United States, Great Britain, the Netherlands, and Chiang [kai-shek]), is translated in Ike, 247–49.

91. *NKKS,* 1:144–45; Seno, "A Chess Game," 30–31; Inoue Shigeyoshi Denki Kankō-kai, 283–303; Miyano, *Saigo no kaigun taishō,* 162–66; and Shinohara, "Taiheiyō sensō no kensha," 96–103.

92. Our discussion of Inoue's memorandum in the next five paragraphs is based on the original Japanese text provided in its entirety in *NKKS,* 1:133–45 and, to a lesser extent, on an English translation of the document, provided in Seno, 31–34.

93. Seno.

94. Inoue proposed that Japan also deploy its long-range submarines along the American west coast to attack American shipping, but perhaps he was thinking less of blockad-ing the United States, a possibility that he had already discounted, and more of inter-dicting American supply routes to the western Pacific and thus significantly reducing American pressure on Japan.

14 Epilogue
Reflections on the Japanese Navy in Triumph and Defeat

1. Our discussion of the Japanese navy's strategy in the Pacific, 1941–43, has been shaped largely by Rosinski's durable essay, "The Strategy of Japan," written a year after the end of the war.

2. Hata, "Admiral Yamamoto's Surprise Attack," 64–66.

3. Morison, *Strategy and Compromise,* 68.

4. Uchida and Tsunoda, 88. For conventional views on the folly of the Pearl Harbor attack, see Prange, *Pearl Harbor: The Verdict of History,* 554–58, 565–67; and Will-mott, *Empires in the Balance,* 137–41.

5. The navy's plans for the occupation of Hawaii are expertly discussed in Stephan, *Hawaii under the Rising Sun,* 89–121.

6. Frank, *Guadalcanal,* 606.

7. See also McKearney, 13.

8. Masanori Ito (Ito, Masanori), *The End of the Imperial Japanese Navy,* 211. For an overview of the composition and final disposition of the remnants of the Japanese navy at the end of the war, see Lundstrom, foreword to *Japanese Naval Vessels.*

9. Based on Willmott, appendix A in *The Barrier and the Javelin,* 526–30; *KG1,* 638–39; and Japan, Keizai Antei Hombu, Sōsai Kambō, Kikakubu, Chōsaka, *Tai-heiyō sensō,* 52–53.

10. Yokoi Toshiyuki, former flag officer in the Japanese navy, argues that the agreement, "Draft Proposal for Hastening the End of a War against the United States, Great Britain, the Netherlands, and Chiang," approved by the Imperial Liaison Conference of 15 November 1941 (see chapter 13), was the only grand policy statement ever drawn up before the Pacific War began. Yokoi, "Thoughts on Japan's Naval Defeat," 70.

11. Rosinski, 102–4, 119.

12. Ikeda, "Japanese Strategy," 144.

13. Chihaya, *Nihon kaigun no senryaku hassō,* 162–66.

14. Ike, 140. In his remarks on building an "impregnable position," Nagano referred to the "Southwest Pacific," but it is clear that he meant Southeast Asia. Viewed from Japan, what has come to be called Southeast Asia is actually to the southwest. For a scathing critique of the contradiction between Admiral Nagano's belligerent advocacy of war and his failure to think through any consistent strategy to wage it, see Tsunoda Jun's article in Morley, *The Final Confrontation,* 113–4, 268–79.

15. Willmott, *Victory and Supremacy.* Cited with permission of the author.

16. This line of thought was suggested to us by Edward S. Miller, letter to authors, 22 August 1990.

17. Parillo, 203–4.

18. Torisu, "Japanese Submarine Tactics," 440–41.

19. Frank, 250.

20. Parillo, 224–25; and Coox, "The Effectiveness of the Japanese Military," 7.

21. For an example of this selfishness, see Peattie, *Nan'yō,* 294.

22. Krebs, "The Japanese Air Forces," 233.

23. For the first several years of the war, Combined Fleet Headquarters was located at sea, primarily aboard the *Yamato* or *Musashi.* But in the spring of 1944, it was transferred to the cruiser Ōyodo, anchored off Kisarazu in Tokyo Bay. It moved ashore to Hiroshima that summer and in September of that year to a Tokyo suburb, where it remained for the rest of the war. Masanori Ito (Ito, Masanori), *The End of the Imperial Japanese Navy,* 208–10.

24. McKearney, 149–59.

25. See, for example, Marder's explanation that a Japanese cultural emphasis on technique rather than results explains the failure of Adm. Mikawa Gun'ichi to attack the American transports at Guadalcanal after his destruction of the U.S. naval force at Savo Island. Marder, "Bravery Is Not Enough." After the war, however, Mikawa insisted that he was following Japanese battle doctrine, which stressed that the destruction of the enemy fleet automatically brought about command of the sea and that all other considerations were secondary. Ohmae, "The Battle of Savo Island," 242, 244.

26. Frank, 604.

27. Ibid.

28. Ibid.; and Colin S. Gray, *The Leverage of Sea Power,* 255.

29. A recent study of the midget submarines at Pearl Harbor is the thorough but undocumented work by Burlingame, *Advance Force: Pearl Harbor.*

30. Willmott, *Victory and Supremacy.*

31. Frederick J. Milford, letter to authors, 17 September 1993.

32. Horikoshi, 64–65.

33. This last point is made in Howe, *Japanese Trade Supremacy*, 313.

34. Conversation with Comdr. Wayne Thornton, USN, 15 October 1994.

35. Other contemporary torpedo types achieved mixed results. The navy's successes with the airborne type 91 during the first six months of the war so impressed the Luftwaffe that Germany similarly tried to equip the Luftwaffe's 10th Air Corps in the Mediterranean, though it appears that because of the logistic difficulties of distance and Allied interdiction, little came of this initiative. Lietzman and Wenneker, 4:986, n. 16. On the other hand, we have already pointed out (chapter 8, n. 59) that the type 95 torpedo, the submarine version of the type 93, experienced numerous malfunctions.

36. Baker, "Japanese Naval Construction."

37. Dull, 342.

38. Guerlac, 925–34.

39. Baldwin, *The Deadly Fuze*, 233–49.

40. Roscoe, *United States Destroyer Operations*, 55–61.

41. Ellis, *Brute Force*, 495.

42. Coox, "The Effectiveness of the Japanese Military," 19.

43. Agawa, 196–97..

44. A few examples should suffice. Hori Teikichi remembered that during a discussion after a map maneuver simulating a Japan-U.S. war, one of the participants criticized the exercise for its emphasis on operations in the Philippines, since it was possible that an American fleet would threaten the Japanese mainland directly. He was rebuked by a general staff officer for questioning an operational policy already decided by the staff. Ōi Atsushi recalled that in a map exercise at the staff college just before the Pacific War, the results were deliberately manipulated to show that Japan's maritime transport would not be dealt a fatal blow. After the war, Fuchida Mitsuo and Okumiya Masatake recalled that in pre-Midway map exercises aboard the *Yamato* in May 1942, the Combined Fleet chief of staff, Adm. Ugaki Matome, set aside the rulings of the umpires and arbitrarily reduced the damages to Japanese carriers so as to favor the Midway invasion plan. Agawa, 197; Sanematsu, *Kaigun daigaku kyōiku*, 199–201; and Fuchida and Okumiya, *Midway*, 96.

45. This tendency was pointed out to us by Capt. James R. FitzSimonds, USN, letter to authors, 4 November 1994.

46. One must be careful about using the terms "feudal" or "*bushidō*" in relation to the outlook of the modern Japanese army and navy on the conduct of war. Certain *tactics*—surprise attack, attack by night, and the close-in thrust of small groups of men against the heart of the enemy, for example—definitely had their antecedents in the medieval period of Japanese warfare. Varley, *Warriors of Japan*, 53. But the *psychological and ethical content* of the Japanese martial tradition dated back only to the more recent Tokugawa era and was the result of a selective borrowing process designed to promote values of importance to the modern military. See chapter 1, n. 4.

47. *NRKK*, 1:438. Over forty years later, Admiral Toyoda, commander of the Combined Fleet, repeated the first phrase in a signal sent to Adm. Kurita Takeo on 24 October 1944 when he thought Kurita was withdrawing subsequent to an American air attack: "Be certain of heaven's aid and attack with all your forces." Ikeda, *Nihon to kaigun*, 37.

48. Cited in Todaka, "Nihonkai kaisen," 235.

49. Goldstein and Dillon, 114.

50. Fukui, *Nihon no gunkan,* 129.

51. Frederick J. Milford, letter to authors, 26 November 1994.

52. Handel, "Numbers Do Count," 225–26.

53. Japan, Bōeichō Bōeikenshūjo Senshishitsu, *Hondo hōmen,* 1.

54. Rosinsky, 119.

55. Millett and Williamson, "Lessons of War," 85.

56. Asada, "The Japanese Navy," 256.

57. These matters form a central theme of Samuels, *"Rich Nation, Strong Army."*

Sources Cited

For books the place of publication is Tokyo unless otherwise noted. The names of Japanese authors are listed in Japanese order, surname first without a comma, but with commas in English-language publications.

Agawa, Hiroyuki. *The Reluctant Admiral: Yamamoto and the Imperial Navy.* Translated by John Bester. Kōdansha International, 1979.

Aizawa Jun. "Kaigun ryōshiki to nanshin-Hainan-tō shinshutsu mondai o chūshin shite" [The rational faction in the navy and the southward advance, centering on the occupation of Hainan]. In *Dai-niji sekai taisen: hassei to kakudai* [World War II: origins and escalations], edited by Gunji-shi Gakkai. Kinseisha, 1990.

[Akiyama Saneyuki.] *Heigo kaisetsu* [Military terms explained]. N.p., 1902.

Akiyama Saneyuki Kai, ed. *Akiyama Saneyuki.* Akiyama Saneyuki Kai, 1933.

Alden, John D. *The Fleet Submarine in the U.S. Navy: A Design and Construction History.* Annapolis, Md.: Naval Institute Press, 1979.

Alger, John. *Definitions and Doctrine of the Military Art Past and Present.* The West Point Military History Series, ed. Thomas E. Griess. Wayne, N.J.: Avery Publishing Group, 1985.

Anderson, Irvine H., Jr. *The Standard-Vacuum Oil Company and United States East Asian Policy, 1933–1941.* Princeton, N.J.: Princeton University Press, 1975.

Andrade, Ernest, Jr. "Arms Limitation and the Evolution of Weaponry: The Case of the Treaty Cruiser." In *Naval History: The Sixth Symposium of the U.S. Naval Academy,* edited by Daniel Masterson. Wilmington, Del.: Scholarly Resources, 1987.

————. "Submarine Policy in the United States Navy, 1919–1941." *Military Affairs* 35 (April 1971).

Aoki Shōsaburō. "Kōgaku heiki kōgyō no kaiko" [Recollections of optical weapons manufacture]. In *Kaisō Nihon kaigun* [The Japanese navy remembered], edited by Suikōkai. Hara Shobō, 1985.

Asada Sadao. *Arufureddo T. Mahan* [Alfred T. Mahan]. Amerika Koten Bunko series, vol. 8. Kenkyūsha, 1977.

Asada, Sadao. "Japan and the United States, 1915–1925." Ph.D. diss., Yale University, l963.

————. "Japanese Admirals and the Politics of Naval Limitation: Katō Tomosaburō vs. Katō Kanji." In *Naval Warfare in the Twentieth Century,* edited by Gerald Jordan. London: Croom Helm, 1977.

————. "The Japanese Navy and the United States." In *Pearl Harbor as History: Japanese-American Relations, 1931–1941,* edited by Dorothy Borg and Shumpei Okamoto. New York: Columbia University Press, 1973.

Bacon, Reginald Hugh Spencer. *A Naval Scrap-book: First Part, 1877–1900.* London: Hutchinson, [1925].

Bagnasco, Erminio. *Submarines of World War II.* Annapolis, Md.: Naval Institute Press, 1977.

Baker, Arthur Davidson, III. "Japanese Naval Construction, 1915–1945: An Introductory Essay." *Warship International* 24, no. 1 (1987).

Baldwin, Ralph B. *The Deadly Fuze: The Secret Weapon of World War II.* San Rafael, Calif.: Presidio Press, 1986.

Ballantine, Duncan S. *U.S. Naval Logistics in the Second World War.* Princeton, N.J.: Princeton University Press, 1947.

Ballard, G. A. *The Influence of the Sea on the Political History of Japan.* New York: E. P. Dutton, 1921.

Barnhart, Michael. *Japan Prepares for Total War: The Search for Economic Security, 1919–1941.* Ithaca, N.Y.: Cornell University Press, 1987.

————. "Japanese Intelligence before the Second World War: 'Best Case' Analysis." In *Intelligence Assessment before the Two World Wars,* edited by Ernest R. May. Princeton, N.J.: Princeton University Press, 1986.

————. "Planning the Pearl Harbor Attack: A Study in Military Politics." *Aerospace Historian* 29 (Winter/December 1992).

Baxter, James Finney. *Scientists against Time.* Boston: Little, Brown and Company, 1946.

Blair, Clay. *Silent Victory: The U.S. Submarine War against Japan.* Philadelphia: Lippincott, 1975.

Blond, Georges. *Admiral Togo.* Translated by Edmond Hyams. New York: Macmillan, 1960.

Bodley, R.V.C. *Admiral Togo.* London: Jarrolds Publishers, 1935.

Borg, Dorothy, and Shumpei Okamato, eds. *Pearl Harbor as History: Japanese-American Relations, 1931–1941.* New York: Columbia University Press, 1973.

Boyd, Carl. "Japanese Military Effectiveness: The Interwar Period." In *Military Effectiveness.* Vol. 2, *The Interwar Period,* edited by Allan Millet and Williamson Murray. Winchester, Mass.: Unwin and Hyman, 1988.

———. "The Japanese Submarine Force and the Legacy of Strategic and Operational Doctrine Developed between the World Wars." In *Selected Papers from the Citadel Conference on War and Diplomacy*. Charleston, S.C.: Citadel Development Foundation, 1979.

Braisted, William R. *The United States Navy in the Pacific, 1909–1922*. Austin, Tex.: University of Texas Press, 1971.

Broadbridge, Seymour. "Shipbuilding and the State in Japan since the 1850s." *Modern Asian Studies* 11 (1977).

Brook, Peter. "Armstrong Battleships Built for Japan." *Warship International* 22, no. 3 (1985).

Brown, David. *Aircraft Carriers*. New York: Arco Publishing, 1977.

Buckley, Thomas H. *The United States and the Washington Conference, 1921–1922*. Knoxville: University of Tennessee Press, 1970.

Bueschel, Richard M. *Mitsubishi A6M1/2 Zero-sen in Imperial Japanese Naval Air Service, Arco-Aircam Aviation Series. No. 18*. New York: Arco Publishing, 1970.

———. *Mitsubishi-Nakajima G3M1/2/3 and Kusho L3Y1 in Japanese Naval Service, Arco Aircam Aviation Series, No. 35*. Berkshire, U.K.: Osprey Publishing, 1972.

Bullen, John. "The Japanese 'Long Lance' Torpedo and Its Place in Naval History." *Imperial War Museum Review*, no. 3 (1988).

Burlingame, Burl [William G.]. *Advance Force: Pearl Harbor*. Kailua, Hawaii: Pacific Monograph, 1992.

Bush, James Vannevar. *Modern Arms and Free Men*. New York: Simon and Schuster, 1949.

Bywater, Hector. *The Great Pacific War: A History of the American-Japanese Campaign of 1931–33*. 1925. Reprint, Boston: Houghton Mifflin, 1942.

Caidin, Martin. *Zero Fighter*. New York: Ballantine Books, 1969.

Campbell, Mark A. "The Influence of Air Power upon the Evolution of Battle Doctrine in the U.S. Navy, 1922–1941." Master's thesis, University of Massachusetts at Boston, 1992.

Campbell, N. J. M. *Naval Weapons of World War II*. London: Conway Maritime Press, 1985.

———. "The Battle of Tsu-Shima." Parts 1–4. *Warship* 2 (1978): 39–49, 127–135, 186–92, 258–65.

Carpenter, Dorr, and Norman Polmar. *Submarines of the Imperial Japanese Navy*. Annapolis, Md.: Naval Institute Press, 1986.

Chapman, John. "The Imperial Japanese Navy and the North-South Dilemma." In *Barbarossa: The Axis and the Allies,* edited by John Erickson and David Dilks. Edinburgh: Edinburgh University Press, 1994.

———. "Japanese Intelligence, 1918–1945: A Suitable Case for Treatment." In *Intelligence and International Relations, 1900–1945,* edited by Christopher Andrew and Jeremy Noakes. Exeter Studies in History, no. 15. Exeter, England: Exeter University Publications, 1986.

———. "Signals Intelligence Collaboration among the Tripartite Pact States on the Eve of Pearl Harbor." *Japan Forum* 3 (October 1991).

———. "Tricycle Recycled: Collaboration among the Secret Intelligence Services of the Axis States." *Intelligence and National Security* 7 (July 1992).

Chesneau, Roger. *Aircraft Carriers of the World, 1914 to the Present: An Illustrated Encyclopaedia*. London: Arms and Armour Press, 1984.

Chesneau, Roger, and Eugene Kolesnik, eds. *All the World's Fighting Ships, 1860–1905.* New York: Mayflower Books, 1979.

Chigusa, Sadao. "Conquer the Pacific Ocean aboard the Destroyer *Akigumo*: War Diary of the Hawaiian Battle." In *The Pearl Harbor Papers: Inside the Japanese Plans,* edited by Donald M. Goldstein and Katherine V. Dillon. New York: Brassey, 1993.

Chihaya Masataka. *Kaigun keieisha Yamamoto Gombei* [Naval administrator Yamamoto Gombei]. Purejidentosha, 1986.

———. *Nihon kaigun no ogori shōkōgun* [The Japanese navy's syndrome of arrogance]. Purejidentosha, 1990.

———. *Nihon kaigun no senryaku hassō* [Strategic concepts of the Japanese navy]. Purejidentosha, 1982.

Chihaya, Masataka. "IJN *Yamato* and *Musashi*." In *Warships in Profile.* Vol. 3, edited by Antony Preston. Garden City, N.Y.: Doubleday, 1974.

———. "An Intimate Look at the Japanese Navy." In *The Pearl Harbor Papers: Inside the Japanese Plans,* edited by Donald M. Goldstein and Katherine V. Dillon. New York: Brassey, 1993.

Chihaya, Masataka, and Yasuo Abe. "IJN *Kongō,* Battleship, 1912–1944." In *Warships in Profile.* Vol. 1, edited by John Wingate. Windsor, Berkshire, U.K.: Profile Publications, 1971.

———. "IJN *Yukikaze,* Destroyer, 1939–1970." In *Warships in Profile.* Vol. 2, edited by John Wingate. Windsor, Berkshire, U.K.: Profile Publications, 1973.

Clifford, Kenneth. *Amphibious Warfare Development in Britain and America.* Laurens, N.Y.: Edgewood, 1983.

Cohen, Eliot A., and John Gooch. *Military Misfortunes: The Anatomy of Failure in War.* New York: Free Press, 1990.

Cohen, Jerome. *Japan's Economy in War and Reconstruction.* Minneapolis: University of Minnesota Press, 1949.

Commander in Chief, Pacific and Pacific Ocean Areas, Joint Intelligence Center, Pacific Ocean Area, "Know Your Enemy: Japanese Aerial Tactics against Ship Targets," *JICPOA Weekly Intelligence,* 20 October 1944.

Conroy, Hilary, and Harry Wray, eds. *Pearl Harbor Re-examined: Prologue to the Pacific War.* Honolulu: University of Hawaii Press, 1990.

Conway's All the World's Fighting Ships, 1922–1946. Annapolis, Md.: Naval Institute Press, 1984.

Cook, Theodore, and Haruko Cook, eds. *Japan at War: An Oral History.* New York: Free Press, 1992.

Coox, Alvin. "The Effectiveness of the Japanese Military Establishment in the Second World War." In *Military Effectiveness.* Vol. 3, *The Second World War,* edited by Alan R. Millett and Williamson Murray. Boston: Allen and Unwin, 1988.

Corbett, Julian S., and Edmond J. W. Slade. *Maritime Operations in the Russo-Japanese War, 1904–5.* 2 vols. Admiralty War Staff, 1914. Reprint, Annapolis, Md.: Naval Institute Press, 1994. (Abbreviated CS in notes.)

Cornwall, Peter. "Manning and Training in the Japanese Navy in the Nineteenth Century." In *Changing Interpretations and New Sources in Naval History: Papers from the Third United States Naval Academy History Symposium,* edited by Robert William Love, Jr. New York: Garland Publishing, 1980.

————. "The Meiji Navy: Training in an Age of Change." Ph.D. diss., University of Michigan, 1970.

Costello, John. *Days of Infamy.* New York: Pocket Books, 1994.

Crowl, Philip. "Alfred Thayer Mahan: The Naval Historian." In *Makers of Modern Strategy: From Machiavelli to the Nuclear Age,* edited by Peter Paret. Princeton, N.J.: Princeton University Press, 1986.

Crowley, James. *Japan's Quest for Autonomy.* Princeton, N.J.: Princeton University Press, 1966.

De Virgilio, John F. "Japanese Thunderfish." *Naval History* 54 (winter 1991).

Dickson, W. David. "Fighting Flat-Tops: The Shokakus." *Warship International,* no. 1 (1977).

Dingman, Roger. "Japan and Mahan." In *The Influence of History on Mahan: The Proceedings of a Conference Marking the Centenary of Alfred Thayer Mahan's "The Influence of Sea Power upon History, 1660–1783,"* edited by John B. Hattendorf. Naval War College Historical Monograph Series, no. 9. Newport, R.I.: Naval War College Press, 1991.

————. "The Pacific Theater: Comments." In *The Intelligence Revolution: A Historical Perspective,* edited by Walter T. Hitchcock. Proceedings of the Thirteenth Military History Symposium, U.S. Air Force Academy, Colorado Springs, Colo., 12–14 October 1988.

————. *Power in the Pacific: The Origins of Naval Arms Limitation, 1914–1922.* Chicago: University of Chicago Press, 1976.

Dohi Kazuo. "Zujō enshū to heiki enshū no jissai" [The practice of map exercises and war games]. *Rekishi to jimbutsu* (May 1979).

Dorwart, Jeffrey M. *Conflict of Duty: The U.S. Navy's Intelligence Dilemma, 1919–1945.* Annapolis, Md.: Naval Institute Press, 1983.

Drea, Edward. *MacArthur's Ultra: Codebreaking and the War against Japan, 1941–1945.* Lawrence: University of Kansas Press, 1992.

————. "Reading Each Other's Mail: Japanese Communications Intelligence, 1920–1941." *Journal of Military Affairs* 55 (April 1991).

Dull, Paul S. *A Battle History of the Imperial Japanese Navy, 1941–1945.* Annapolis, Md.: Naval Institute Press, 1978.

Ellis, John. *Brute Force: Allied Strategy and Tactics in the Second World War.* New York, Viking Press, 1990.

Epstein, Marc. "Naval Disarmament and the Japanese: Geneva, 1927." Ph.D. diss., State University of New York at Buffalo, 1995.

Evans, David C. "The Japanese Navy in the Invasion of the Philippines." Paper presented at the annual meeting of the American Historical Association, Chicago, Ill., December 1991.

————. "The Recruitment of Japanese Navy Officers in the Meiji Period." In *Changing Interpretations and New Sources in Naval History: Papers from the Third United States Naval Academy History Symposium,* edited by Robert William Love, Jr. New York: Garland Publishing, 1980.

————. "The Satsuma Faction and Professionalism in the Japanese Naval Officer Corps of the Meiji Period, 1868–1912." Ph.D. diss., Stanford University, 1978.

Fahey, James C. *Ships and Aircraft of the U.S. Fleet.* Various editions. (New York: Herald-Nathan, n.p., and Ships and Aircraft, 1939–1945).

Fairbanks, Charles H., Jr. "The Origins of the *Dreadnought* Revolution: A Historiographical Essay." *International History Review* 13 (May 1991).

Falk, Edwin A. *Togo and the Rise of Japanese Sea Power.* New York: Longmans, Green and Company, 1936.

Feis, Herbert. *The Road to Pearl Harbor: The Coming of the War between the United States and Japan.* Princeton, N.J.: Princeton University Press, 1950.

Ferris, John. "A British Unofficial Aviation Mission and Japanese Naval Developments, 1919–1929." *Journal of Strategic Studies* (September 1982).

Fioravanzo, Giuseppe. *A History of Naval Tactical Thought.* Translated by Arthur W. Holst. Annapolis, Md.: Naval Institute Press, 1979.

Fiske, Bradley A. "American Naval Policy." *U.S. Naval Institute Proceedings* 31 (January 1905).

Fock, Harold. *Fast Fighting Boats, 1870–1945: Their Design, Construction, and Use.* Annapolis, Md.: Naval Institute Press, 1973.

Francillon, René J. *Imperial Japanese Navy Bombers of World War II.* Windsor, Berkshire, U.K.: Hilton Lacy, Publishers, 1969.

——. *Japanese Aircraft of the Pacific War.* Annapolis, Md.: Naval Institute Press, 1987.

Frank, Richard B. *Guadalcanal: The Definitive Account of the Landmark Battle.* New York: Random House, 1990.

Frei, Henry. *Japan's Southward Advance and Australia: From the Sixteenth Century to World War II.* Honolulu: University of Hawaii Press, 1991.

Friday, Karl F. "Bushido or Bull? A Medieval Japanese Historian's Perspective on the Imperial Army and the Japanese Warrior Tradition." *History Teacher* 27 (May 1994).

Friedman, Norman. *Battleship Design and Development, 1905–1945.* New York: Mayflower Books, 1978.

——. *Carrier Air Power.* Greenwich, U.K.: Conway Maritime Press, 1981.

——. *Naval Radar.* Greenwich, U.K.: Conway Maritime Press, 1981.

——. *Submarine Design and Development.* Annapolis, Md.: Naval Institute Press, 1984.

——. *U.S. Battleships: An Illustrated Design History.* Annapolis, Md.: Naval Institute Press, 1984.

——. *U.S. Destroyers: An Illustrated Design History.* Annapolis, Md.: Naval Institute Press, 1982.

——. *U.S. Naval Weapons: Every Gun, Missile, Mine, and Torpedo Used by the U.S. Navy from 1883 to the Present Day.* Annapolis, Md.: Naval Institute Press, 1982.

Fuchida, Mitsuo, and Masatake Okumiya. *Midway: The Battle That Doomed Japan.* Annapolis, Md.: Naval Institute Press, 1955.

Fukaya, Hajime, with M. E. Holbrook. "The Shokakus: Pearl Harbor to Leyte Gulf." U.S. Naval Institute *Proceedings* 78 (June 1952).

——. "Three Japanese Submarine Developments." U.S. Naval Institute *Proceedings* 78 (August 1952).

Fukudome [Fukutome], Shigeru. "The Hawaii Operation." In *The Japanese Navy in World War II: In the Words of Former Japanese Naval Officers.* 2nd ed., edited by David C. Evans. Annapolis, Md.: Naval Institute Press, 1986.

Fukui Shizuo. *Nihon no gunkan: waga zōkan gijutsu no hattatsu to kantei no hensen* [Japanese warships: our development of ship construction technology and changes in warships over time]. Shuppan Kyōdōsha, 1959.

Fukutome Shigeru. *Shikan: Shinjuwan kōgeki* [Historical view of the Pearl Harbor attack]. Jiyū Ajiasha, 1955.

Garzke, William H., Jr., and Robert O. Dulin, Jr. *Battleships: Axis and Neutral Battleships in World War II.* Annapolis, Md.: Naval Institute Press, 1985.

Genda Minoru. "Evolution of Aircraft Carrier Tactics of the Imperial Japanese Navy." In *Air Raid: Pearl Harbor!* Edited by Paul Stillwell. Annapolis, Md.: Naval Institute Press, 1981.

———. *Kaigun kōkūtai shimatsuki* [A record of the particulars of the naval air service]. Vol. 1, *Hasshin* [Takeoff]. Bungei Shunjū, 1961. Vol. 2, *Sentō* [Combat]. Bungei Shunjū, 1962.

———. *Shinjuwan sakusen kaikoroku* [Recollections of the Pearl Harbor operation]. Yomiuri Shimbunsha, 1972.

———. "Tactical Planning in the Imperial Japanese Navy." *Naval War College Review* 22 (October 1969).

Gendaishi shiryō [Documents on modern history]. *Nitchū sensō* [The China-Japan war], vols. 8–10, 12–13; *Taiheiyō sensō* [The Pacific war], vols. 34–36, 38–39; *Dai hon'ei* [Imperial General Headquarters], vol. 37. Misuzu Shobō, 1964–75.

Goldstein, Donald M., and Katherine V. Dillon, eds. *The Pearl Harbor Papers: Inside the Japanese Plans.* New York: Brassey, 1993.

Gotō Ken'ichi. "Kaigun nanshin ron to 'Indoneshia mondai'" [The navy's southward advance arguments and the "Indonesian problem"]. Parts 1–2. *Ajia yū* 31 (July 1984); (October 1984).

Gray, Colin S. *The Leverage of Sea Power: The Strategic Advantage of Navies at War.* New York: Free Press, 1992.

Gray, Edwyn. *The Devil's Device: The Story of Robert Whitehead, Inventor of the Torpedo.* London: Seeley, Service, and Company, 1975.

Guerlac, Henry. *Radar in World War II.* Los Angeles, Calif.: Tomash Publishers, 1987.

Halpern, Paul G. *A Naval History of World War I.* Annapolis, Md.: Naval Institute Press, 1994.

Handel, Michael. "Numbers Do Count: The Question of Quality vs. Quantity." *Journal of Strategic Studies* 4 (September 1981).

Hara, Tameichi, with Fred Saito and Roger Pineau. *Japanese Destroyer Captain.* New York: Ballantine Books, 1961.

Hata Ikuhiko. *Taiheiyō kokusai kankei shi: Nichi-Bei oyobi Nichi-Ro kiki no keifu* [A history of international relations in the Pacific: the genealogy of Japan-U.S. and Japan-Russia crises, 1900–1935]. Fukumura Shuppan Kan, 1972.

Hata, Ikuhiko. "Admiral Yamamoto's Surprise Attack and the Japanese Navy's War Strategy." In *From Pearl Harbor to Hiroshima: The Second World War in Asia and the Pacific, 1941–45,* edited by Saki Dockrill. New York: St. Martin's Press, 1994.

Hata, Ikuhiko, and Yasuho Izawa. *Japanese Naval Aces and Fighter Units in World War II.* Translated by Don Gorham. Annapolis, Md.: Naval Institute Press, 1989.

Hatano Sumio. "Shōwa kaigun no nanshin ron" [The southward advance concept of the Shōwa navy]. *Rekishi to jimbutsu* (December 1984.)

Hatano, Sumio, and Sadao Asada . "The Japanese Decision to Move South (1939–1941)." In *Paths to War: New Essays on the Origins of the Second World War,* edited by Robert Boyce and Esmond Robertson. New York: St. Martin's Press, 1989.

Hayashi Katsunari. *Nihon gunji gijutsu shi* [A history of Japanese military technology]. Haruki Shobō, 1972.

Henry, David. "British Submarine Policy, 1918–1939." In *Technical Change and British Naval Policy, 1860–1939,* edited by Bryan Ranft. Kent, U.K.: Hodder and Staughton, 1977.

Herwig, Holger. *"Luxury" Fleet: The Imperial German Navy 1888–1918.* London: George Allen and Unwin, 1980.

Hezlet, Arthur. *Electronics and Sea Power.* New York: Stein and Day, 1975.

———. *The Submarine and Sea Power.* New York: Stein and Day, 1967.

Hinsley, Harry. "An Intelligence Revolution." In *The Intelligence Revolution: A Historical Perspective, Proceedings of the Thirteenth Military History Symposium,* edited by Walter Hitchcock. Washington, D.C.: U.S. Government Printing Office, 1991.

Hiraga Yuzuru. *Hiraga Yuzuru ikō shū* [The collected posthumous works of Hiraga Yuzuru]. Edited by Naitō Shosui. Kyōdō Shuppansha, 1985.

Hodges, Peter. *The Big Gun: Battleship Main Armament, 1860–1945.* London: Conway Maritime Press, 1981.

Honan, William. *Visions of Infamy: The Untold Story of How Hector C. Bywater Devised the Plans That Led to Pearl Harbor.* New York: St. Martin's Press, 1991.

Hone, Thomas C. "Spending Patterns of the United States Navy, 1921–1941." *Armed Forces and Society* 8: 3 (spring 1982).

Hone, Thomas C., and Mark D. Mandeles. "Interwar Innovation in Three Navies: U.S. Navy, Royal Navy, Imperial Japanese Navy." *Naval War College Review* 40 (spring 1987).

Hone, Thomas C., and Norman Friedman. *"Iowa* vs. *Yamato*: The Ultimate Gunnery Duel." U.S. Naval Institute *Proceedings* 109 (July 1983).

Horie, Y. "The Failure of the Japanese Convoy Escort." U.S. Naval Institute *Proceedings* 82 (October 1956).

Horikoshi, Jiro. *Eagles of Mitsubishi: The Story of the Zero Fighter.* Translated by Shojiro Shindo and Harold N. Wantiez. Seattle: University of Washington Press, 1981.

Howe, Christopher. *The Origins of Japanese Trade Supremacy: Development and Technology from 1540 to the Pacific War.* London: Hurst and Company, 1996.

Hughes, Wayne P., Jr. *Fleet Tactics: Theory and Practice.* Annapolis, Md.: Naval Institute Press, 1986.

———. "Naval Tactics and Their Influence on Strategy." *Naval War College Review* 39 (January–February 1986).

Ikari Yoshirō. *Kaigun kūgishō.*[The Naval Air Technical Arsenal]. 2 vols. Kōjinsha, 1985.

Ike, Nobutaka, ed. and trans. *Japan's Decision for War: Records of the 1941 Policy Conferences.* Stanford, Calif.: Stanford University Press, 1967.

Ikeda Kiyoshi. *Nihon no kaigun* [The Japanese navy]. 2 vols. Isseidō, l967. (Abbreviated *NNK* in notes.)

———. *Nihon to kaigun* [Japan and the navy]. Chūkō Shinsho series, no. 632. Chūo Kōronsha, 1981.

Ikeda, Kiyoshi. "Japanese Strategy in the Pacific War, 1941–1945." In *Anglo-Japanese Alienation, 1919–1952: Papers of the Anglo-Japanese Conference on the History of the Second World War,* edited by Ian Nish. Cambridge: Cambridge University Press, 1982.

Ikezaki Chūkō. *Taiheiyō senryaku ron* [On Pacific strategy]. Seishinsha, 1932.

Inaba Masao, ed. *Dai Hon'ei* [Imperial General Headquarters]. Gendaishi Shiryō series, vol. 37. Mizu Shobō, l967.

Inoue Shigeyoshi Denki Kankōkai, ed. *Inoue Shigeyoshi.* Inoue Shigeyoshi Denki Kankōkai, 1982.

Iriye, Akira. *The Origins of the Second World War in Asia and the Pacific.* New York: Longman, 1987.

Isely, Jeter, and Philip Crowl. *The U.S. Marines and Amphibious War.* Princeton, N.J.: Princeton University Press, 1951.

Itani, Jiro; Hans Lengerer; and Tomoko Rehm-Takahara. "Japanese Oxygen Torpedoes and Fire Control Systems." In *Warship 1991,* edited by Robert Gardiner. Greenwich, U.K.: Conway Maritime Press, 1991.

———. "Sankeikan: Japan's Coast Defense Ships of the *Matsushima* Class." In *Warship 1990.* London: Conway Maritime Press, 1990.

Itō Masanori. *Dai kaigun o omou* [Pondering a great navy]. Bungei Shunjūsha, 1956.

Ito, Masanori, with Roger Pineau. *The End of the Imperial Japanese Navy.* Translated by Andrew Y. Kuroda and Roger Pineau. New York: W. W. Norton, 1962.

Itō Terubumi. "Rikushu-kaishu ronsō, senji Dai Hon'ei jōrei o megutte" [The army first–navy first controversy, centering on the regulations for the Imperial General Headquarters in wartime]. *Gunji shigaku* 7 (December 1972).

Itō Terumi. "Satō Tetsutarō no kokubō" [Satō Tetsutarō's national defense]. *Kaikankō no hyōron* 4 (1966).

Iwaya Fumio. *Chūkō: kaigun rikujō kōgekiki taishi* [The medium bomber: a unit history of the navy's land-based attack aircraft]. 2 vols. Shuppan Kyōdōsha, 1956–58.

Japan, Bōeichō Bōeikenshūjo Senshishitsu [later Bōeichō Bōeikenshūjo Senshibu]. *Chūgoku hōmen kaigun sakusen (1): Shōwa jūsannen sangatsu made* [Naval operations in the China theater, no. 1: to March 1938]. Senshi Sōsho series. Asagumo Shimbunsha, 1974.

———. *Dai Hon'ei Kaigunbu, Dai Tōa Sensō kaisen keii* [Imperial General Headquarters, Navy Division: particulars of the opening of the Greater East Asia War]. Senshi Sōsho series. Asagumo Shimbunsha, 1974.

———. *Dai Hon'ei Kaigunbu, Rengō Kantai, ichi, kaisen made* [Imperial General Headquarters, Navy Division, Combined Fleet, no. 1, to the opening of the Pacific War]. Senshi Sōsho series. Asagumo Shimbunsha, 1975. (Abbreviated *DHKRK* in notes.)

———. *Dai Hon'ei Kaigunbu, Rengō Kantai, roku, dai sandan sakusen kōki* [Imperial General Headquarters, Navy Division, Combined Fleet, no. 6, the latter period of third-stage operations]. Senshi Sōsho series. Asagumo Shimbunsha, 1971.

———. *Dai Hon'ei Rikugunbu, ichi, Shōwa jūgonen gogatsu made* [Imperial General Headquarters, Army Division, no. 1, up to May 1940]. Senshi Sōsho series. Asagumo Shimbunsha, 1967.

———. *Hawai sakusen* [The Hawaii operation]. Senshi Sōsho series. Asagumo Shimbunsha, 1967.

———. *Hitō-Maree kaigun shinkō sakusen* [Offensive naval operations in the Philippines and Malaya]. Senshi Sōsho series. Asagumo Shimbunsha, 1969.

———. *Hondo hōmen kaigun sakusen.* [Naval operations in home waters]. Senshi Sōsho series. Asagumo Shimbunsha, 1975.

————. *Kaigun gunsembi, ichi, Shōwa jūrokunen jūichigatsu made* [Naval armaments and war preparations, no. 1, up to November 1941]. Senshi Sōsho series. Asagumo Shimbunsha, 1969. (Abbreviated *KG1* in notes.)

————. *Kaigun gunsembi, ni, kaisen igo* [Naval armaments and war preparations, no. 2, after the war's start]. Senshi Sōsho series. Asagumo Shimbunsha, 1975. (Abbreviated *KG2* in notes).

————. *Kaigun kōkū gaishi* [An historical overview of Japanese naval aviation]. Senshi Sōsho series. Asagumo Shimbunsha, 1976. (Abbreviated *KKG* in notes.)

————. *Kaijō goei sen* [The maritime protection war]. Senshi Sōsho series. Asagumo Shimbunsha, 1971.

————. *Sensuikanshi* [A history of (Japanese) submarines]. Senshi Sōsho series. Asagumo Shimbunsha, 1979.

Japan, Bōeichō, Tōgō Bakuryō Gakkō, ed. *Kindai Nihon tōgōsen shi gaisetsu, sōan* [Draft history of Japanese joint operations in modern times]. Tōgō Bakuryō Gakkō, 1984.

Japan, Kaigun Gunreibu. *Meiji sanjūshichi-hachinen kaisenshi* [The history of naval combat, 1904–5]. 4 vols. Kaigun gunreibu, 1909–10.

————. *Suirai teitai undō kyōhan* [Torpedo squadron operations manual]. Kaigun Gunreibu, 1894.

Japan, Kaigun Kyōiku Hombu. *Teikoku kaigun kyōiku shi* [History of education in the Imperial Japanese Navy]. 7 vols. Kaigunshō, 1911.

Japan, Kaigunshō, ed. *Yamamoto Gombei to kaigun* [Yamamoto Gombei and the navy]. Hara Shobō, 1966.

Japan, Kaigunshō, Daijin Kambō, ed. *Kaigun gumbi enkaku* [History of naval armament]. 1 vol. and *Furoku* [Appendix] vol. Kaigun Daijin Kambō, 1934. Reprint, Gannandō Shoten, 1970.

Japan, Keizai Antei Hombu, Sōsai Kambō, Kikakubu, Chōsaka, ed. *Taiheiyō sensō ni yoru waga kuni no higai sōgō hōkokusho* [Overall report on Japanese losses in the Pacific War]. Keizai Antei Hombu, Sōsai kambō, Kikakubu, Chōsaka, 1949.

Japan, Tsūshō Sangyōshō, ed. *Kikai kōgyō* [The machinery industry]. Shōkō Seisakushi series. Shōkō Seisakushi Kankōkai, 1976.

Jentschura, Hansgeorg; Dieter Jung; and Peter Mickel. *Warships of the Imperial Japanese Navy, 1869–1945*. Annapolis, Md.: Naval Institute Press, 1977. (Abbreviated JJM in notes.)

Kahn, David. *The Codebreakers: The Story of Secret Writing*. New York: Macmillan, 1967.

Kaigun Henshū Iinkai, ed. *Kaigun* [The navy]. 15 vols. Seibun Tosho, 1981.

Kaigun Hōjutsushi Kankōkai, ed. *Kaigun hōjutsushi* [A history of naval gunnery]. Kaigun Hōjutsushi Kankōkai, 1975. (Abbreviated *KH* in notes.)

Kaigunshi Kenkyūkai, ed. *Nihon kaigun no hon: sōkaisetsu* [Books on the Japanese navy: a general commentary]. Jiyū Kokuminsha, 1984.

Kaigun Suiraishi Kankōkai. *Kaigun suiraishi* [History of mines and torpedoes of the navy]. Shinkōsha, 1979. (Abbreviated *KS* in notes.)

Kaigun Yūshūkai, ed. *Kinsei Teikoku Kaigun shiyō* [Basic history of the Imperial Japanese Navy in modern times]. Kaigun Yūshūkai, 1938.

Kaijō Rōdō Kyōkai, ed. *Nihon shōsentai senji sōnan shi* [A history of the wartime disaster of Japan's merchant fleet]. Kaijō Rōdō Kyōkai, 1962.

Kamata Yoshirō. "Nihon kaigun denshin shiwa" [Historical facts about telegraphy in the Japanese navy]. *Kaigun bunko geppō* (September 1981).

Kemp, Edward, ed. *The Papers of Sir John Fisher.* 2 vols. London: The Navy Records Society, 1964.

Kennedy, Paul. *The Rise and Fall of the Great Powers. Economic Change and Military Conflict from 1500 to 2000.* New York: Random House, 1987.

Kimata Jirō. *Nihon suiraisen shi* [History of Japanese torpedo warfare]. Tosho Shuppansha, 1986.

Kiralfy, Alexander. "Japanese Naval Strategy." In *Makers of Modern Strategy: Military Thought from Machiavelli to Hitler,* edited by Edward M. Earle. Princeton, N.J.: Princeton University Press, 1941.

Kobayashi Tatsuo. "The London Naval Treaty, 1930." In *Japan Erupts: The London Naval Conference and the Manchurian Incident, 1928–1932,* edited by James William Morley. Translations from *Taiheiyō sensō e no michi* series (1962–63). New York: Columbia University Press, 1984.

Koda, Yoji. "A Commander's Dilemma: Admiral Yamamoto and the 'Gradual Attrition' Strategy." *Naval War College Review* 46 (autumn 1993).

Ko Hakushaku Yamamoto Kaigun Taishō Denki Hensankai, eds. *Hakushaku Yamamoto Gombei den* [Biography of Count Yamamoto Gombei]. 2 vols. Ko Hakushaku Yamamoto Kaigun Taishō Denki Hensankai, 1938. Reprint, Hara Shobō, 1968.

Kokubō Senshi Kenkyūkai, ed. "Sensuikan-yō sanso gyorai ni tsuite" [Concerning the submarine-carried oxygen torpedo]. *Kokubō* 21 (July 1972).

Ko Ōnishi Takijirō Kaigun Chūjō Den Kankōkai, ed. *Ōnishi Takijirō* [Ōnishi Takijirō]. Ko Ōnishi Takijirō Kaigun Chūjō Den Kankōkai, 1963.

Koyama Hirotake. *Kindai Nihon gunji gaisetsu* [A summary of modern Japanese military affairs]. Itō Shoten, 1944.

———. *Gunji shisō no kenkyū* [Studies in military thought]. Shinsensha, 1970.

Krebs, Gerhard. "Admiral Yonai Mitsumasa as Navy Minister (1937–39): Dove or Hawk?" In *Western Interactions with Japan: Expansion, the Armed Forces, and Readjustment, 1859–1956,* edited by Peter Lowe and Herman Moeshart. Sandgate, Folkstone, Kent, U.K.: Japan Library, 1980.

———. "The Japanese Air Forces." In *The Conduct of the Air War in the Second World War: An International Comparison,* edited by Horst Borg. New York: Berg, 1992.

Kusaka, Ryunosuke. "*Rengo Kantai* (Combined Fleet), Extracts." In *The Pearl Harbor Papers: Inside the Japanese Plans,* edited by Donald M. Goldstein and Katherine V. Dillon. New York: Brassey, 1993.

Kusumi, Eiji. "'Rikusentai' (Japanese Marine Corps)." *Marine Corps Gazette* (September 1989).

Kusumi Tadao. "Akiyama Saneyuki to Nihonkai kaisen" [Akiyama Saneyuki and the Battle of Tsushima]. *Chūō kōron* (August 1965).

Lacroix, Eric. "The Development of the 'A Class' Cruisers in the Imperial Japanese Navy." Parts 1–7. *Warship International* 14, no. 4 (1977); 16, no. 1 (1979); 16, no. 4 (1979); 18, no. 1 (1981); 18, no. 4 (1981); 20, no. 3 (1983); 21, no. 3 (1984).

———. *Japanese Cruisers of the Pacific War.* Edited by Linton Wells II. Annapolis, Md.: Naval Institute Press, forthcoming.

Lambert, Nicholas, "Admiral Sir John Fisher and the Concept of Flotilla Defence, 1904–1909." *Journal of Military History* 59 (October 1995).

Lautenschläger, Karl. "The Dreadnought Revolution Reconsidered." In *Naval History: The Sixth Symposium of the U.S. Naval Academy*, edited by Daniel Masterson. Wilmington, Del.: Scholarly Resources, 1987.

———. "Technology and the Evolution of Naval Warfare." *International Security* 82 (Fall 1983).

Layman, R. D., and Stephen McLaughlin. *The Hybrid Warship: The Amalgamation of Big Guns and Aircraft*. London: Conway Maritime Press, 1991.

Layton, Edwin T. "24 Sentai: Japan's Commerce Raiders." U.S. Naval Institute *Proceedings* 102 (June 1976).

Leather, John. *World Warships in Review, 1860–1906*. London: MacDonald and Company, 1976

LeComte, Malcolm A. "Radar and the Air Battles of Midway." *Naval History* 6: 2 (summer 1992).

Lengerer, Hans. "Akagi and Kaga." Parts 1–3. *Warship: A Quarterly Journal of Warship History*, no. 22 (April 1982); no. 23 (July 1982); no. 24 (October 1982).

———. "Japanese 'Kaibōkan' Escorts." Parts 1–3. *Warship: A Quarterly Journal of Warship History*, no. 30 (April 1984); no. 31 (July 1984); no. 32 (October 1984).

———. "The Japanese Super-battleship Strategy." Parts 1–3. *Warship: A Quarterly Journal of Warship History*, no. 25 (January 1983); no. 26 (April 1983); no. 27 (July 1983).

Lengerer, Hans, Sumie Kobler-Edamatsu, and Tomoko Rehm-Takahara. "Kitakami." *Warship: A Quarterly Journal of Warship History* no. 37 (January 1986).

Lengerer, Hans, and Tomoko Rehm-Takahara. "The Japanese Aircraft Carriers *Junyo* and *Hiyo*." Parts 1–3. *Warship International*, no. 33 (January 1985); no. 34 (April 1985); no. 35 (July 1985).

Lewin, Ronald. *The American Magic*. New York: Farrar Straus Giroux, 1982.

Lietzman, Joachim, and Paul Wenneker. *The Price of Admiralty: The War Diary of the German Naval Attaché in Japan, 1939–1943*. Edited and translated by John Chapman. 4 vols. Ripe, East Sussex, U.K.: Saltire Press, 1982.

Lorelli, John A. *The Battle of the Komandorski Islands, March 1943*. Annapolis, Md.: Naval Institute Press, 1984.

Love, Robert W., Jr. *History of the U.S. Navy, 1775–1941*. Harrisburg, Pa.: Stackpole Books, 1992.

Lundstrom, John B. *The First Team and the Guadalcanal Campaign: Naval Fighter Combat from August to November 1942*. Annapolis, Md.: Naval Institute Press, 1994.

———. *The First Team: Pacific Naval Air Combat from Pearl Harbor to Midway*. Annapolis, Md.: Naval Institute Press, 1984.

———. Foreword to *Japanese Naval Vessels at the End of World War II*, compiled by Shizuo Fukui. Annapolis, Md.: Naval Institute Press, 1991.

Lyon, David. "The British Tribals, 1935." In *Warship Special*. Vol. 2, *Super Destroyers*, edited by Antony Preston. Greenwich, U.K.: Conway Maritime Press, 1978.

Mahan, Alfred Thayer. *Naval Strategy*. Boston: Little, Brown, and Company, 1911.

Marder, Arthur. *The Anatomy of British Seapower: A History of British Naval Policy in the Pre-Dreadnought Era, 1880–1905*. New York: Alfred Knopf, 1940.

———. *Old Friends, New Enemies: The Royal Navy and the Imperial Japanese Navy*. Vol. 1, *Strategic Illusions, 1936–1941;* Vol. 2, *The Pacific War, 1942–1945,* by Arthur Marder, Mark Jacobsen, and John Horsfield. New York: Oxford University Press, 1981–90.

———. "Bravery Is Not Enough: The Rise and Fall of the Imperial Japanese Navy (1941–1945)." Lecture presented at the University of California at Irvine, 7 February 1978.

———. "From Jimmu Tennō to Perry: Sea Power in Early Japanese History." *American Historical Review* 51 (October 1945).

Matsui Muneaki. "Nihon no kaigun no dempa tanshingi" [Japanese navy radar]. In *Kaisō no Nihon kaigun* [The Japanese navy recollected], edited by Suikōkai. Hara Shobō, 1985.

Matsumoto, Kitaro, and Masataka Chihaya. "Design and Construction of the *Yamato* and *Musashi.*" U.S. Naval Institute *Proceedings* 79 (October 1953).

Mayuzumi Haruo. *Kaigun hōsen shidan* [Historical discussions of naval gun battles]. Hara Shobō, 1972.

———. "Kaigun hōsenshi kaiko" [The history of naval gunnery in retrospect]. *Kaigun bunko geppō* (September 1981).

McHugh, Francis. "Gaming at the Naval War College." U.S. Naval Institute *Proceedings* 90 (March 1964).

McKearney, T. J. "The Solomons Naval Campaign: A Paradigm for Surface Warships in Maritime Strategy." Unpublished thesis, Naval Postgraduate School, Monterey, Calif. 1985.

McKenna, Richard. *The Left-Handed Monkey Wrench*. Annapolis, Md.: Naval Institute Press, 1984.

McNeill, William H. *The Pursuit of Power: Technology, Armed Forces and Society Since 1000 A.D.* Chicago: University of Chicago Press, 1983.

Melhorn, Charles. *Two-Block Fox: The Rise of the Aircraft Carrier, 1911–1929*. Annapolis, Md.: Naval Institute Press, 1974.

Mikesh, Robert C. "The Rise of Japanese Naval Air Power." In *Warship, 1991,* edited by Robert Gardiner. Greenwich, U.K.: Conway Maritime Press.

Mikesh, Robert C., and Shorzoe Abe, *Japanese Aircraft, 1910–1941*. Annapolis, Md.: Naval Institute Press, 1990.

Milford, Frederick J. "Torpedoes of the Imperial Japanese Navy: Surface and Submarine Launched Types." Unpublished monograph, 1993.

———. "U.S. and Japanese Destroyer Construction between the Wars." Unpublished monograph, 1993.

Miller, Edward S. *War Plan Orange. The U.S. Strategy to Defeat Japan, 1897–1945*. Annapolis, Md.: Naval Institute Press, 1991.

Millett, Allan R. *Semper Fidelis: The History of the United States Marine Corps*. Revised edition. New York: Free Press, 1991.

———. "Assault from the Sea: The Development of Amphibious Warfare between the Wars: The American, British and Japanese Experiences." In *Innovation in the Interwar Period,* edited by Allan R. Millett and Williamson Murray. Washington, D.C.: Office of Net Assessment, the Pentagon, 1994.

Millett, Allan R., and Williamson Murray. "Lessons of War." *National Interest* 14 (winter 1988–89).

Miyano Tōru. *Saigo no kaigun taishō: Inoue Shigeyoshi* [The last admiral: Inoue Shigeyoshi]. Bungei Shunjūsha 1982.

Morison, Samuel Eliot. *History of United States Naval Operations in World War II.* Vol. 3, *The Rising Sun in the Pacific, 1931–April 1942.* Boston: Little, Brown, and Company, 1950.

———. *Strategy and Compromise.* Boston: Little, Brown, and Company, 1958.

Morley, James William, ed. *The China Quagmire: Japan's Expansion on the Asian Continent, 1933–1941.* Translations from *Taiheiyō sensō e no michi* series (1962–63). New York: Columbia University Press, 1983.

———, ed. *Deterrent Diplomacy: Japan, Germany, and the U.S.S.R., 1935–1941.* Translations from *Taiheiyō sensō e no michi* series (1962–63). New York: Columbia University Press, 1976.

———, ed., *The Fateful Choice: Japan's Advance into Southeast Asia, 1939–1941.* Translations from *Taiheiyō sensō e no michi* series (1962–63). New York: Columbia University Press, 1980.

———, ed. *The Final Confrontation: Japan's Negotiations with the United States, 1941.* Translations from *Taiheiyō sensō e no michi* series (1962–63). New York: Columbia University Press, 1994.

———, ed., *Japan Erupts: The London Naval Conference and the Manchurian Incident, 1928–1932.* Translations from *Taiheiyō sensō e no michi* series (1962–63). New York: Columbia University Press, 1984.

Morse, P. M., and G. E. Kimball. *Methods of Operations Research.* Cambridge, Mass.: M.I.T. Press, 1951.

Moss, Michael, and Iain Russell. *Range and Vision: The First Hundred Years of Barr and Stroud.* Edinburgh: Mainstream Publishing, 1988.

Muir, Malcolm. "Rearming in a Vacuum: United States Navy Intelligence and the Japanese Capital Ship Threat, 1936–1945." *Journal of Military History* 54 (October 1990).

Nagamura Kiyoshi. *Zōkan kaisō* [Recollections of naval construction]. Shuppan Kyōdōsha, 1957.

Nakagawa Shigeshi. *Gensui Shimamura Hayao den* [Biography of Fleet Adm. Shimamura Hayao]. Sōbunkan, 1933.

Nakagawa Yasuzō. *Dokyumento: kaigun gijutsu kenkyūjo, erekutoronikusu ōkoku no senkusha-tachi* [Factual account: The Navy Technical Research Center, pioneer of the electronic kingdom]. Nihon Keizai Shimbunsha, 1987.

Nakamura Yoshihiko. "Tōgō Heihachirō o meguru kaigun habatsu no shujusō" [Various aspects of navy factions as they relate to Tōgō Heihachirō]. In *Tōgō Heihachirō no subete* [Everything about Tōgō Heihachirō], edited by Shin Jimbutsu Ōraisha. Shin Jimbutsu Ōraisha, 1986.

National Archives. Records of the National Security Agency. RG 457. "Various Reports on Japanese Grand Fleet Maneuvers (June–August 1933)." File SRH-223.

———. Records of the Office of the Chief of Naval Operations. RG 38. Office of Naval Intelligence, Attaché's Reports. "Personnel of the Submarine Service, Japanese Navy, Memo for the Director of Naval Intelligence." 4 November 1928. Register No. 11942, E-7-c.

———. Records of the Office of the Chief of Naval Operations. RG 38. Office of Naval Intelligence, Attaché's Reports. "Report of the U.S. Naval Attaché." 23 January 1907. No. 19.

Nenryō Konwakai, ed. *Nihon kaigun nenryōshi* [A history of Japanese navy fuels]. 2 vols. Hara Shobō, 1972.

Nihon Kaigun Kōkūshi Hensan Iinkai, ed. *Nihon kaigun kōkūshi* (A history of Japanese naval aviation). 4 vols. Jiji Tsushinsha, 1969. (Abbreviated *NKKS* in notes.)

Nihon Zōsen Gakkai, ed. *Nihon kaigun kantei zumenshū* [Collection of plans of Japanese warships]. Hara Shobō, 1975.

———, ed. *Shōwa zōsenshi* [History of ship construction in the Showa era]. 2 vols. Hara Shobō, 1977. (Abbreviated *SZ* in notes.)

Nish, Ian. *Alliance in Decline: A Study in Anglo-Japanese Relations, 1908–23*. London: Athlone Press, 1972.

———. *The Anglo-Japanese Alliance: The Diplomacy of Two Island Empires, 1894–1907*. London: Athlone Press, 1966.

———. "Japan and Naval Aspects of the Washington Conference." In *Modern Japan: Aspects of History, Literature and Society,* edited by W. G. Beasley. Berkeley: University of California Press, 1975.

———. "Japanese Intelligence and the Approach of the Russo-Japanese War." In *The Missing Dimension: Governments and Intelligence Communities in the Twentieth Century,* edited by Christopher Andrew and David Dilks. London: Macmillan, 1984.

Nitchū sensō [Japan-China war]. *Gendaishi shiryō* series, vols. 8–10 and 12–13. Misuzu Shobō, 1964–66.

Niwata Shōzō. "Senkan Yamato kenzō hiwa" [Secret history of the construction of the battleship *Yamato*]. *Rekishi to jimbutsu* (May 1978).

Nomura Hisashi. "Jōhōsen de yabureta teikoku kaigun" [The Japanese navy's defeat in the intelligence war]. *Rekishi to jimbutsu* (January 1985).

Nomura Minoru. *Kaisenshi ni manabu* [Learning from the history of naval combat]. Bungei Shunjūsha, 1985.

———. *Rekishi no naka no Nihon kaigun* [The Japanese navy in history]. Hara Shobō, 1980.

———. *Tennō, Fushimi-no-miya to Nihon kaigun* [The emperor, Prince Fushimi, and the Japanese navy]. Bungei Shunjū, 1988.

———. "Dai niji sekai taisen no Nihon no nenryō mondai to kaigun" [The navy and Japan's oil problem in World War II]. In *Rekishi no naka no Nihon kaigun* [The Japanese navy in history]. Hara Shobō, 1980.

———. "Kamimura Hikonojō no nintai" [The fortitude of Kamimura Hikonojō]. *Rekishi to jimbutsu* (May 1980).

———. "Kokka to riku-kaigun nendo sakusen keikaku" [The Japanese state and the annual operational plans of the Japanese army and navy]. *Gunji shigaku* 10 (June 1974).

———. "Nihonkai kaisen chokuzen mippu meirei" [The sealed orders immediately prior to the Battle of Tsushima]. *Gunji shigaku* 18 (June 1982).

———. "Riku-kaigun no chūō kikō to butai" [The central administrative organs and separate combat commands of the army and navy]. *Rekishi to jimbutsu* (July 1978).

———. "Sekai kenkan kyōsō to 'hachi-hachi-hachi kantai'" [The global naval arms race and the "eight-eight-eight fleet"], *Rekishi to jimbutsu* (May 1978).

————. "Suezu unga to Yamamoto Gombei" [The Suez Canal and Yamamoto Gombei]. *Rekishi to jimbutsu* (August 1976).

————. "Tai Bei-Ei kaisen to kaigun no tai-Bei nanawari shisō" [The outbreak of war between Japan and the United States and Great Britain and the idea of a 70 percent ratio vis-à-vis the United States], *Gunji shigaku* 9 (September 1973).

————. "Tōgō Heihachirō no senjutsugan" [Tōgō Heihachirō's tactical eye]. In *Tōgō Heihachirō no subete* [Everything about Tōgō Heihachirō], edited by Shin Jimbutsu Ōraisha. Shin Jimbutsu Ōraisha, 1986.

O'Connell, Robert. *Sacred Vessels: The Cult of the Battleship and the Rise of the U.S. Navy.* Boulder, Colo.: Westview Press, 1991.

O'Connor, Raymond G. *Perilous Equilibrium: The United States and the London Naval Conference of 1930.* Lawrence: University of Kansas Press, 1962.

Ogasawara Chōsei. "Chūko suigun no sempō" [Tactics of the medieval water forces]. *Shigaku zasshi* 17 (1906).

————. "Nihonkai kaisen to chūko no suigun" [The battle of Tsushima and the medieval water forces]. In *Ogasawara Chōsei to sono zuihitsu* [Ogasawara Chōsei and his writings], edited by Hara Kiyoshi. Ogasawara Chōsei Kō Kyūjūgosai Kinen Kankōkai, 1956.

————. "Tōgō gensui no omokage" [The visage of Fleet Admiral Tōgō]. In *Hijōji kokumin zenshū. kaigunhen* [A nation in crisis series, the navy]. Chūō Kōronsha, 1933.

Ogasawara, Nagayo [Chōsei]. *Life of Admiral Togo.* Seito Shorin Press, 1934.

Ōi Atsushi. *Kaijō goei sambō no kaisō: Taiheiyō sensō no senryaku hihan* [Memoirs of a convoy escort staff officer: a critique of Japanese strategy in the Pacific War]. Hara Shobō, 1975.

Oi, Atsushi. "Why Japan's Antisubmarine Warfare Failed." In *The Japanese Navy in World War II: In the Words of Former Japanese Naval Officers.* 2nd ed., edited by David C. Evans. Annapolis, Md.: Naval Institute Press, 1986.

Ohmae [Ōmae], Toshikazu. "The Battle of Savo Island." In *The Japanese Navy in World War II: In the Words of Former Japanese Naval Officers.* 2nd edition, edited by David C. Evans. Annapolis, Md.: Naval Institute Press, 1986.

Ohmae [Ōmae], Toshikazu. "Stockpiling of Liquid Fuel in Japan: A Navy Report." In *War in Asia and the Pacific.* Vol. 5, *The Naval Armament Program and Naval Operations,* pt. 2, edited by Donald S. Detwiler and Charles B. Burdick. New York: Garland Publishing, 1980.

Ohmae [Ōmae], Toshikazu, and Roger Pineau. "Japanese Naval Aviation." U.S. Naval Institute *Proceedings* 98 (December 1972).

Ōmae Toshikazu. "Nihon kaigun no heijutsu shisō no hensen to gumbi oyobi sakusen" [Changes in tactical thought in the Japanese navy in relation to armaments and operations]. Parts 1–4. *Kaigun Bunko geppō,* no. 6 (April 1981), no. 7 (July 1981), no. 8 (September 1981), and no. 9 (December 1981).

Ono, Giichi. *War and Armament Expenditures of Japan.* New York: Oxford University Press, 1922.

Orita, Zenji, with Joseph D. Harrington. *I-Boat Captain.* Canoga Park, Calif.: Major Books, 1976.

Ōta Azan. *Danshaku Sakamoto Toshiatsu den* [The biography of Sakamoto Toshiatsu]. Tōa Kyōkai, 1952.

Ozawa Teitoku Den Kankōkai, ed. *Kaisō no Teitoku Ozawa Jisaburō* [Recollections concerning Admiral Ozawa Jisaburō]. Hara Shobō, 1971.

Padfield, Peter. *The Battleship Era*. London: Rupert Hart-Davis, 1972.

———. *Guns at Sea*. London: Hugh Evelyn, 1973.

Parillo, Mark P. *The Japanese Merchant Marine in World War II*. Annapolis, Md.: Naval Institute Press, 1993.

Parkes, Oscar. *British Battleships: A History of Design, Construction, and Armament*. Revised edition. London: Seeley Service and Company, 1970.

Peattie, Mark R. *Ishiwara Kanji and Japan's Confrontation with the West*. Princeton, N.J.: Princeton University Press, 1975.

———. *Nan'yō: The Rise and Fall of the Japanese in Micronesia, 1885–1945*. Honolulu: University of Hawaii Press, 1987.

———. "Akiyama Saneyuki and the Emergence of Modern Japanese Naval Doctrine." U.S. Naval Institute *Proceedings* 103 (January 1977).

———. "Forecasting a Pacific War, 1913–1933: The Idea of a Conditional Japanese Victory." In *The Ambivalence of Nationalism: Modern Japan between East and West*, edited by James White, Michio Umegaki, and Thomas Havens. Lanham, Md.: University Press of America, 1990.

Peattie, Mark R., and David C. Evans. "Japan." In *Ubi Sumus? The State of Naval and Maritime History*, edited by John B. Hattendorf. Newport, R.I.: Naval War College Press, 1994.

Pelz, Stephen. *The Race to Pearl Harbor: The Failure of the Second London Naval Conference and the Onset of World War II*. Cambridge, Mass.: Harvard University Press, 1974.

Perry, John Curtis. "The Battle off the Tayang, 17 September, 1894." *Mariner's Mirror* 50 (November 1964).

———. "Great Britain and the Imperial Japanese Navy, 1858–1905." Ph.D. diss., Harvard University, 1961.

———. "Great Britain and the Emergence of Japan as a Naval Power." *Monumenta Nipponica* 21 (1966).

Polmar, Norman. *Aircraft Carriers: A Graphic History of Carrier Aviation and Its Influence on World Events*. London: MacDonald, 1969.

Potter, E. B., ed. *Sea Power: A Naval History*. Englewood Cliffs, N.J.: Prentice Hall, 1960.

Prados, John. *The Combined Fleet Decoded: The Secret History of American Intelligence and the Japanese Navy in World War II*. New York: Random House, 1995.

Prange, Gordon W., with Donald Goldstein and Katherine V. Dillon, *At Dawn We Slept: The Untold Story of Pearl Harbor*. New York: McGraw Hill, 1981.

———. *God's Samurai: Lead Pilot at Pearl Harbor*. New York: Brassey, 1990.

———. *Miracle at Midway*. New York: McGraw Hill, 1982.

———. *Pearl Harbor: The Verdict of History*. New York: McGraw Hill, 1986.

Preston, Antony. *Cruisers*. London: Arms and Armor Press, 1980.

———. *Destroyers*. London: Hamlyn Publishing Group, 1977.

———. *Battleships of World War I: An Illustrated Encyclopedia of the Battleships of All Nations, 1914–1918*. New York: Galahad Books, 1972.

Putney, Diane T., ed. *ULTRA and the Army Air Forces in World War II*. Washington, D.C.: U.S. Government Printing Office, 1982.

Rawlinson, John L. *China's Struggle for Naval Development, 1839–1895.* Cambridge, Mass.: Harvard University Press, 1967.

Reynolds, Clark. *Admiral John J. Towers: The Struggle for Naval Air Supremacy.* Annapolis, Md.: Naval Institute Press, 1991.

———. "The Continental Strategy of Imperial Japan." U.S. Naval Institute *Proceedings* 109 (August 1983).

Rivera, Carlos R. "Akiyama Saneyuki: Japan's Premier Naval Strategist, 1897–1907." Unpublished monograph. Ohio State University, May 1993.

———. "Big Stick and Short Sword: The American and Japanese Navies as Hypothetical Enemies." Ph.D. diss., Ohio State University, 1995.

Rössler, Eberhard. *The U-boat. The Evolution and Technical History of German Submarines.* Translated by Harold Erenberg. Annapolis, Md.: Naval Institute Press, 1981.

Rollins, Patrick. "Russian Commerce Raiders in the Red Sea and Indian Ocean, 1904." *Naval War College Review* 47 (summer 1994).

Ropp, Theodore. *The Development of a Modern Navy: French Naval Policy, 1871–1904.* Annapolis, Md.: Naval Institute Press, 1987.

Roscoe, Theodore. *United States Destroyer Operations in World War II.* Annapolis, Md.: Naval Institute Press, 1953.

Rosinski, Herbert. "The Strategy of Japan." In *The Development of Naval Thought: Essays by Herbert Rosinski,* edited by B. Mitchell Simpson III. Newport, R.I.: Naval War College Press, 1977. Originally appeared in *Brassey's Naval Annual,* 1946.

Roskill, Stephen. *Naval Policy between the Wars.* Vol. 1, *The Period of Anglo-American Antagonism, 1919–1929.* London: Collins, 1968; Vol. 2, *The Period of Reluctant Rearmament, 1930–1939.* Annapolis, Md.: Naval Institute Press, 1976.

Safford, Laurence F. "A Brief History of Communications Intelligence in the United States." In *Listening to the Enemy: Key Documents on the Role of Communications Intelligence in the War with Japan,* edited by Ronald H. Spector. Wilmington, Del.: Scholarly Resources, 1988.

Sakai, Saburo, with Martin Caidin and Fred Saito. *Samurai!* New York: Dutton, 1957. Reprint, Bantam Books, 1975.

Sakamoto Kaneyoshi. *Nihon sensuikan senshi* [A combat history of Japanese submarines]. Tosho Shuppansha, 1979.

Samuels, Richard. *Japanese State Energy Markets in Comparative and Historical Perspective.* Ithaca, N.Y.: Cornell University Press, 1987.

———. *"Rich Nation, Strong Army": National Security and the Technological Transformation of Japan.* Ithaca, N.Y.: Cornell University Press, 1994.

Sanematsu Yuzuru. *Jōhō sensō* [The intelligence war]. Tosho Shuppansha, 1975.

———. *Kaigun daigaku kyōiku* [Higher education in the Japanese navy]. Kōjinsha, 1965.

Satō Tetsutarō. *Kaibō shi ron* [On naval defense]. Kaigun Daigakkō, 1907.

———. *Kokubō no sakugi* [A proposal for national defense]. N.p., 1913.

———. *Teikoku kokubō shi ron* [On the history of imperial defense]. Tokyo Insatsu, 1908. Reprint, 2 vols. Hara Shobō, 1979.

Satō Tetsutarō et al. *Kokubō mondai no kenkyū* [A study of the national defense problem]. N.p., 1913.

Schneider, James G. *The Navy V–12 Program: Leadership for a Lifetime.* Boston: Houghton Mifflin, 1987.

Sekigawa, Eiichirō. *A Pictorial History of Japanese Military Aviation.* Translated by C. Uchida and edited by David Mondey. London: Ian Allen, 1974.

Seno, Sadao. "A Chess Game with No Checkmate: Admiral Inoue and the Pacific War." *Naval War College Review* 26 (January–February 1974).

Shima Ikichirō. "Kaigun heigakkō kara Nichi-Ro sensō shūketsu made" [(Akiyama): from the naval academy until the conclusion of the Russo-Japanese War]. In *Akiyama Saneyuki no subete* [Everything about Akiyama Saneyuki], edited by Shin Jimbutsu Ōraisha. Shin Jimbutsu Ōraisha, 1987.

Shimada Kinji. *Amerika ni okeru Akiyama Saneyuki* [Akiyama Saneyuki in America]. Asahi Shimbunsha, 1969.

———. "Akiyama Saneyuki no kaigun heigaku" [The naval science of Akiyama Saneyuki]. *Rekishi to jimbutsu* (August 1976).

———. "Rengō Kantai sambō Akiyama Saneyuki no sakusen keikaku" [The operational plans of Akiyama Saneyuki, staff officer of the Combined Fleet]. *Rekishi to jimbutsu* (April 1977).

———. "Roshiya sensō zen'ya no Nihon kantai" [The Japanese fleet on the eve of the Russo-Japanese war]. *Rekishi to jimbutsu* (May 1980).

Shimada, Koichi. "The Opening Air Offensive against the Philippines." In *The Japanese Navy in World War II: In the Words of Former Japanese Naval Officers.* 2nd ed., edited by David C. Evans. Annapolis, Md.: Naval Institute Press, 1986.

Shimamura Hayao. *Kaigun senjutsu ippan* [General naval tactics]. N.p., 1887.

Shinohara Hiroshi. *Kaigun sōsetsu shi* [History of the navy's establishment]. Riburopōto, 1986.

———. "Akiyama heigaku no himitsu o saguru" [Probing the secrets of Akiyama's military science]. In *Akiyama Saneyuki no subete* [Everything about Akiyama Saneyuki], edited by Shin Jimbutsu Ōraisha. Shin Jimbutsu Ōraisha, 1987.

———. *Nihon kaigun oyatoi gaijin* [Foreigners employed by the Japanese navy]. Chūō Koronsha, 1988.

———. "Taiheiyō sensō no kensha: Inoue Shigeyoshi" [Sage of the Pacific War, Inoue Shigeyoshi]. *Rekishi to jimbutsu* (September 1973).

Skulski, Janusz. *The Battleship Yamato.* Anatomy of the Ship series. Annapolis, Md.: Naval Institute Press, 1988.

———. *The Heavy Cruiser "Takao."* Anatomy of the Ship series. Annapolis, Md.: Naval Institute Press, 1994.

Sonokawa Kamerō et al., eds. *Nihon kaigun kōkutai* [The Japanese naval air force]. Kōdansha,1970. (Abbreviated *NKK* in notes.)

Spector, Ronald. *Eagle against the Sun: The American War with Japan.* New York: Free Press, 1985.

Spick, Mike. *Fighter Pilot Tactics: The Technique of Daylight Air Combat.* Cambridge, England: Patrick Stephens, 1983.

Sprout, Harold, and Margaret Sprout. *Rise of American Naval Power, 1776–1918.* Princeton, N.J.: Princeton University Press, 1946.

Spurr, John. *A Glorious Way to Die: The Kamikaze Mission of the Battleship "Yamato."* New York: Bantam Books, 1981.

Stephan, John. *Hawaii under the Rising Sun: Japan's Plans for Conquest after Pearl Harbor.* Honolulu: University of Hawaii Press, 1984.

Stewart, R. A. "The Japanese Assault on Timor." In *Assault from the Sea: Essays in the History of Amphibious Warfare,* edited by Merrill Bartlett. Annapolis, Md.: Naval Institute Press, 1983.

Suekuni Masao. "Senshi ni miru jōriku sakusen to sono urakata" [Landing operations seen in military history and their background]. In *Kaigun senshi sankō shiryō* [Reference materials in naval combat history], edited by Jieitai Kambu Gakkō Kyōikubu. Jieitai Kambu Gakkō Kyōikubu, 1984.

Suikōkai, ed. *Kaisō no Nihon kaigun* [The Japanese navy recollected]. Hara Shobō, 1985.

Sumida, Jon Tetsuro. "'The Best Laid Plans': The Development of British Battle-Fleet Tactics, 1919–1942." *International History Review* 14 (November 1992).

———. "British Capital Ships and Fire Control in the Dreadnought Era: Sir John Fisher, Arthur Hungerford Pollen, and the Battlecruiser." *Journal of Modern History* 51 (1979).

———. *In Defence of Naval Supremacy.* Boston: Unwin Hyman, 1989.

———. "The Quest for Reach: The Development of Long-Range Gunnery in the Royal Navy, 1901–1912." In *Tooling for War: Military Transformation in the Industrial Age. Proceedings of the Sixteenth Military History Symposium of the United States Air Force Academy,* edited by Stephen Chiabotti. Chicago: Imprint, 1996.

———. "Sir John Fisher and the *Dreadnought:* The Sources of Naval Mythology." *Journal of Modern History* 59 (October 1995).

Sumida, Jon Tetsuro, and David Alan Rosenberg. "Machines, Men, Manufacturing, Management, and Money: The Study of Navies as Complex Organizations and the Transformation of Twentieth Century Naval History." In *Doing Naval History: Essays toward Improvement,* edited by John B. Hattendorf. Newport, R.I.: Naval War College Press, 1995.

Suzuki Kantarō. *Jiden* [Autobiography]. Edited by Suzuki Hajime. Ōgikukai Shuppanbu, 1949. Reprint, Jiji Tsūshinsha, 1968.

Suzuki Kantarō Denki Hensan Iinkai, ed. *Suzuki Kantarō den* [Biography of Suzuki Kantarō]. Suzuki Kantarō Denki Hensan Iinkai, 1960.

Takagi Sōkichi. *Shikan Taiheiyō sensō* [A personal view of the Pacific War]. Bungei Shunjū, 1969.

Talbott, J. E. "Weapons Development, War Planning and Policy: The U.S. Navy and the Submarine, 1917–1941." *Naval War College Review* 37 (May–June 1984).

Tanaka Hiromi. "'Gunshin seizō' enshutsu nooto: 'kakarezaru senshi'; Ogasawara nikki" [Notes on the production, "creating a war god": the "war history that couldn't be written," from Ogasawara Chōsei's diary]. *Shinchō* 4 (May 1985).

———. "Nihonkai kaisen to Tōgō Heihachirō." In *Tōgō Heihachirō no subete* [All about Tōgō Heihachirō], edited by Shin Jimbutsu Ōraisha. Shin Jimbutsu Ōraisha, 1986.

———. "Nis-Shin Nichi-Ro kaisenshi no hensan to Ogasawara Chōsei" [Ogasawara Chōsei and the editing of the naval histories of the Sino- and Russo-Japanese Wars]. Parts 1–3. *Gunji shigaku* 18, no. 3 (December 1982); no. 4 (March 1983); *Bōei Daigaku Kiyō,* no. 17 (September 1983).

———. "Satō Tetsutarō, kaishu rikujū no rironteki kishu" [Satō Tetsutarō, standard bearer of the theory of naval primacy]. *Bessatsu rekishi tokuhon* (summer 1985).

Thompson, Steven L. "The Zero: One Step Beyond. An Object Lesson in the Element of Surprise." *Air and Space Smithsonian* 4, no. 6 (March 1990).

Thornton, Tim. "Air Power: The Sinking of IJN Battleship *Musashi.*" *Warship* 12, no. 1 (1988).

———. "The Sinking of *Yamato.*" *Warship* 13 (1989).

———. "*Yamato:* The Achilles Heel." *Warship* 9, no. 1 (1987).

Tiffany, Paul A. *The Decline of American Steel: How Management, Labor and Government Went Wrong.* New York: Oxford University Press, 1988.

Till, Geoffrey. *Air Power and the Royal Navy, 1914–1945: A Historical Survey.* London: Jane's Publishing Company, 1979.

Todaka Kazushige. "Nihonkai kaisen ni teiji sempō wa nakatta" [There was no "T" at Tsushima]. *Chūō Kōron,* June 1991.

———. "Toyama-shi no gimon ni kotaeru" [Answering Mr. Toyama's questions]. *Suikō* (March 1992).

Tompkins, Tom. *Yokosuka: Base of an Empire.* Novato, Calif.: Presidio Press, 1981.

Torisu Kennosuke. "Dai Roku Kantai" [The Sixth Fleet]. In *Nihon riku-kaigun kaku tatakaeri* [The way the Japanese navy fought], special issue of *Rekishi to jimbutsu* (winter 1986).

Torisu, Kennosuke, assisted by Masataka Chihaya. "Japanese Submarine Tactics and the *Kaiten.*" In *The Japanese Navy in World War II: In the Words of Former Japanese Naval Officers.* 2nd ed., edited by David C. Evans. Annapolis, Md.: Naval Institute Press, 1986.

Towle, Philip. "The Evaluation of the Experience of the Russo-Japanese War." In *Technical Change and British Naval Policy, 1860–1939,* edited by Bryan Ranft. London: Hodder and Haughton, 1977.

Toyama, Saburo. "Lessons from the Past." U.S. Naval Institute *Proceedings* 108 (September 1982).

———. "The Outline of the Armament Expansion of the Imperial Japanese Navy during the Years 1930–1941." *Revue Internationale D'Histoire Militaire,* no. 73 (1991).

Toyama Saburō. *Nichi-Ro kaisenshi no kenkyū* [A study of the naval battles of the Russo-Japanese War]. 2 vols. Kyōiku Sentaa, 1985. (Abbreviated *NRKK* in notes.)

———. *Nichi-Ro kaisen shinshi* [A new history of the Russo-Japanese naval war]. Tokyo Shuppan, 1987.

———. *Nihon kaigun shi* [History of the Japanese navy]. Kyōikusha, 1980.

———. *Nis-Shin, Nichi-Ro, Dai Tōa kaisen shi* [A naval history of the Sino-Japanese, Russo-Japanese, and Greater East Asia wars]. Hara Shobō, 1980.

Tritten, James J. *Naval Perspectives for Military Doctrine Development.* Norfolk, Va.: Naval Doctrine Command, 1994.

Tsunoda Jun. *Manshū mondai to kokubō hōshin* [The Manchurian question and national defense policy]. Hara Shobō, 1967.

———. "Nihon kaigun sandai no rekishi" [Three periods in the history of the Japanese navy]. *Jiyū* 11 (January l969).

Tsunoda, Jun. "The Navy's Role in the Southern Strategy." In *The Fateful Choice: Japan's Advance into Southeast Asia, 1939–1941,* edited by James William Morley. Translations from *Taiheiyō sensō e no michi* series (1962–63). New York: Columbia University Press, 1980.

Tsutsui Mitsuru. "Nihon kaigunshi ni okeru tai-Ro sembi no tokuchō to seika" [The characteristics and consequences of the preparations for war against Russia in Japan's naval history]. *Gunji shigaku* 6 (November 1970).

————. "Shuryokukan hattatsushi yori mitaru Nichi-Ro kaisen" [Naval battles of the Russo-Japanese War from the perspective of the development of capital ships] *Gunji shigaku* 4 (May 1968).

Uchida, Kazutomi, and Jun Tsunoda. "The Pearl Harbor Attack: Admiral Yamamoto's Fundamental Concept, with Reference to Paul S. Dull's *A Battle History of the Imperial Japanese Navy, 1941–1945." Naval War College Review* 31 (Fall 1978).

United Kingdom. Admiralty. Naval Ordnance Department. *A Study of the Events of the Russian-Japanese War from the Point of View of Naval Gunnery.* London: N.p., 1906 [?].

United States Naval Aviation, 1910–1980. 3rd ed. Washington, D.C.: U.S. Government Printing Office, 1981.

U.S. Department of the Air Force. *Basic Aerospace Doctrine of the United States Air Force.* Vol. 2, *Air Force Manual 1-1.* Washington, D.C.: U.S. Government Printing Office, 1992.

U.S. Naval Technical Mission to Japan. "Japanese Projectiles. General Types." Report no. NTJ-L-0-19. Washington, D.C.: Operational Archives, U.S. Naval History Division, 1974.

————. "Japanese Sonar and Asdic." Report E-10. Washington, D.C.: Operational Archives, U.S. Naval History Division, 1974.

————. "Japanese Submarine Operations." Report S-17. Washington, D.C.: Operational Archives, U.S. Naval History Division, 1974.

U.S. Navy, Chief of Naval Operations. *General Tactical Instructions. United States Navy. Fleet Tactical Publication Number 45.* Washington, D.C.: U.S. Government Printing Office, 1925.

————. *General Tactical Instructions. United States Navy. Fleet Tactical Publication Number 142.* Washington, D.C.: U.S. Government Printing Office, 1934.

U.S. Strategic Bombing Survey. Military Analysis Division. *The Effects of Strategic Bombing on Japan's War Economy.* Washington, D.C.: U.S. Government Printing Office, 1946.

————. Military Analysis Division. *Japanese Air Power.* Washington, D.C.: N.p., 1946.

————. Military Analysis Division. *Japanese Air Weapons and Tactics.* Washington, D.C.: N.p., 1947.

————. Military and Naval Intelligence Division. *Japanese Military and Naval Intelligence.* Washington, D.C.: N.p., 1946.

————. Military Supplies Division. *Japanese Naval Shipbuilding.* Washington, D.C.: U.S. Government Printing Office, 1946.

U.S. War Department. *Handbook on Japanese Military Forces, Technical Manual E 30-480.* Washington, D.C.: U.S. Government Printing Office, 1944.

Varley, Paul. *Warriors of Japan as Portrayed in War Tales.* Honolulu: University of Hawaii Press, 1994.

Vlahos, Michael. "The Naval War College and the Origins of War Planning against Japan." *Naval War College Review* 33 (July–August 1980).

Wark, Wesley. "In Search of a Suitable Japan: British Naval Intelligence in the Pacific before the Second World War." *Intelligence and National Security* 1 (May 1986).

Watanabe Kazuhide. *Kyojin Nakajima Chikuhei* [Nakajima Chikuhei, the titan]. Hōbun Shorin, 1955.

Watts, Anthony J. "The Japanese 'Special' Type 1923." In *Warship Special.* Vol. 2, *Super Destroyers,* edited by Antony Preston. Greenwich, U.K.: Conway Maritime Press, 1978.

Watts, Anthony J., and Brian G. Gordon. *The Imperial Japanese Navy.* Garden City, N.Y.: Doubleday and Company, 1971. (Abbreviated WG in notes.)

Weir, Gary. "The Search for American Submarine Strategy and Design, 1916–1936." *Naval War College Review* 44: 1 (winter 1991).

Wells, Linton, II. "Painting Systems of the Imperial Japanese Navy, 1904–1945." *Warship International,* no. 1 (1982).

Westwood, J. N. *Russia against Japan, 1904–05: A New Look at the Russo-Japanese War.* Albany: State University of New York Press, 1986.

———. *Witnesses of Tsushima.* Tokyo: Sophia University Press, 1970.

Whitley, M. J. *Destroyers of World War Two: An International Encyclopedia.* Annapolis, Md.: Naval Institute Press, 1988.

Wildenberg, Thomas H. "Chester Nimitz and the Development of Refueling at Sea." *Naval War College Review* 46 (autumn 1993).

Wilkinson, Roger I. "Short Survey of Japanese Radar." Parts 1–2. *Electrical Engineering* 65, nos. 8–9 (August 1946); no. 10 (October 1946).

Willmott, H. P. *The Barrier and the Javelin: Japanese and Allied Pacific Strategies, February to June 1942.* Annapolis, Md.: Naval Institute Press, 1983.

———. *Empires in the Balance: Japanese and Allied Pacific Strategies to April 1942.* Annapolis, Md.: Naval Institute Press, 1982.

———. *Sea Warfare: Weapons, Tactics, and Strategy.* Strettington, Chichester, U.K.: Anthony Bird, Publictus, 1981.

———. *Victory and Supremacy: From Tulagi to Tarawa: Japanese and Allied Strategies and the Greater East Asia War to November of 1943.* Annapolis, Md.: Naval Institute Press, in press. Citations by permission of author.

Wilson, Eugene E. "The Navy's First Carrier Task Force." U.S. Naval Institute *Proceedings* 76 (January 1950).

Wilson, Herbert W. *Battleships in Action.* 2 vols. London: Sampson, Low and Marston, 1926.

Winton, John. *Convoy: The Defence of Sea Trade, 1890–1990.* London: Michael Joseph, 1983.

Wragg, David. *Wings over the Sea: A History of Naval Aviation.* Newton Abbott, England: David and Charles, 1979.

Yamamura, Kozo. "Success Ill-Gotten? The Role of Meiji Militarism in Japan's Technological Progress." *Journal of Economic History* 38 (March 1977).

Yamanouchi Daizō and Uchida Jōichirō. *Kaigun jiten* [Navy dictionary]. Kōdōkan, 1942. Reprint, Konnichi no Wadaisha, 1985.

Yasui Sōmei. "Yo no mitaru Akiyama Saneyuki Chūjō" [My view of Vice Adm. Akiyama Saneyuki]. *Taiyō* (March 1918).

Yokoi, Toshiyuki. "Thoughts on Japan's Naval Defeat." U.S. Naval Institute *Proceedings* 86 (October 1960).

Yokota, Yutaka, and Joseph D. Harrington. "Kaiten: Japan's Human Torpedoes." U.S. Naval Institute *Proceedings* 88 (January 1962).

Yoshida Akihiko. "San! Kuchikukan ga mapputatsu: Mihogaseki wan no nijū shōtotsu jiko" [Disaster! The sundering of destroyers: the double collisions in Mihogaseki Bay]. *Kansen to anzen* (July 1985).

Yoshida Mitsuru. *Requiem for Battleship "Yamato."* Translation and introduction by Richard Minear. Seattle: University of Washington Press, 1985.

Yoshida Toshio. "Aitsugu kuchikukan no junan: *Tomozuru* to Yon Kantai jiken" [Successive ordeals of Japanese destroyers: the *Tomozuru* and Fourth Fleet incidents]. *Rekishi to jimbutsu,* May 1978.

Yoshimatsu Shigetarō. "Teikoku kaigun senjutsu kenkyū no sōshi to sono hatten keiei" [Initiation of the study of tactics in the Imperial Japanese Navy and the particulars of its development]. *Yūshū* 17 (May 1930).

Yoshimura, Akira. *Build the Musashi!* New York: Kodansha America, 1991.

Zacharias, Ellis. "The Orange Maneuvers and Analysis of Information Obtained." In *Listening to the Enemy: Key Documents on the Role of Communications Intelligence in the War with Japan,* edited by Ronald H. Spector. Wilmington, Del.: Scholarly Resources, 1988.

Index

About the Authors

David C. Evans served in the U.S. Navy as an ensign and a lieutenant (junior grade), USNR. He holds a master's degree in Japanese and a Ph.D. in Asian history from Stanford University. Evans now teaches history at the University of Richmond, where he is professor of history and associate dean of the School of Arts and Sciences. In 1986, Evans edited *The Japanese Navy in World War II: In the Words of Former Japanese Naval Officers,* published by the Naval Institute Press.

Mark R. Peattie served for nine years with the U.S. Information Agency in Japan, receiving intensive Japanese language training in Tokyo. After earning his Ph.D. in modern Japanese history from Princeton University, he taught Japanese history at the Pennsylvania State University, the University of California Los Angeles, and the University of Massachusetts at Boston. For many years, Peattie was a research fellow at the Edwin O. Reischauer Institute of Japanese Studies at Harvard University. He is currently on the senior research staff of the Hoover Institution on War, Revolution, and Peace at Stanford University. Peattie is the author of *Ishiwara Kanji and Japan's Confrontation with the West* and *Nan'yō: The Rise and Fall of the Japanese in Micronesia, 1885–1945.* He co-edited *The Japanese Colonial Empire, 1895–1945* (with Ramon Myers) and *The Japanese Informal Empire in China, 1895–1945* and *Japan's Wartime Empire, 1931–1945* (both with Peter Duus and Ramon Myers).

The **Naval Institute Press** is the book-publishing arm of the U.S. Naval Institute, a private, nonprofit, membership society for sea service professionals and others who share an interest in naval and maritime affairs. Established in 1873 at the U.S. Naval Academy in Annapolis, Maryland, where its offices remain today, the Naval Institute has members worldwide.

Members of the Naval Institute support the education programs of the society and receive the influential monthly magazine *Proceedings* or the colorful bimonthly magazine *Naval History* and discounts on fine nautical prints and on ship and aircraft photos. They also have access to the transcripts of the Institute's Oral History Program and get discounted admission to any of the Institute-sponsored seminars offered around the country.

The Naval Institute's book-publishing program, begun in 1898 with basic guides to naval practices, has broadened its scope to include books of more general interest. Now the Naval Institute Press publishes about seventy titles each year, ranging from how-to books on boating and navigation to battle histories, biographies, ship and aircraft guides, and novels. Institute members receive significant discounts on the more than eight hundred Press books in print.

Full-time students are eligible for special half-price membership rates. Life memberships are also available.

For a free catalog describing Naval Institute Press books currently available, and for further information about joining the U.S. Naval Institute, please write to:

Member Services
U.S. NAVAL INSTITUTE
291 Wood Road
Annapolis, MD 21402-5034
Telephone: (800) 233-8764
Fax: (410) 571-1703
Web address: www.usni.org